Cognitive-Behavioral Interventions in Educational Settings

COGNITIVE-BEHAVIORAL INTERVENTIONS IN EDUCATIONAL SETTINGS

A Handbook for Practice

Edited by
Rosemary B. Mennuti, Arthur Freeman, Ray W. Christner

Routledge
Taylor & Francis Group
New York   London

Published in 2006 by
Routledge
Taylor & Francis Group
270 Madison Avenue
New York, NY 10016

Published in Great Britain by
Routledge
Taylor & Francis Group
2 Park Square
Milton Park, Abingdon
Oxon OX14 4RN

© 2006 by Taylor & Francis Group, LLC
Routledge is an imprint of Taylor & Francis Group

Printed in the United States of America on acid-free paper
10 9 8 7 6 5 4 3

International Standard Book Number-10: 0-415-95039-2 (Hardcover)
International Standard Book Number-13: 978-0-415-95039-8 (Hardcover)
Library of Congress Card Number 2005011993

Library of Congress Cataloging-in-Publication Data

Cognitive-behavioral interventions in educational settings : a handbook for practice / Rosemary B.
  Mennuti, Arthur Freeman, Ray W. Christner, editors.
       p. cm.
  Includes bibliographical references and index.
  ISBN 0-415-95039-2 (hardbound)
  1. School psychology--Handbooks, manuals, etc. 2. Cognitive therapy for children--Handbooks,
manuals, etc. 3. Behavior modification--Handbooks, manuals, etc. I. Mennuti, Rosemary B., 1947-
II. Freeman, Arthur, 1942- III. Christner, Ray W., 1972-

LB1027.55.C63 2005
370.15'28--dc22   2005011993

Taylor & Francis Group
is the Academic Division of Informa plc.

Visit the Taylor & Francis Web site at
http://www.taylorandfrancis.com

and the Routledge Web site at
http://www.routledge-ny.com

I dedicate this book to my children, grandchildren, great grandchild, and to all children everywhere who continue to teach me and warm my heart and soul.

Rosemary B. Mennuti

My colleagues in the Department of Psychology at Philadelphia College of Osteopathic Medicine have been colleagues and friends for these many years. We have created many new and exciting things together. This volume is just one of many such creations. And to my wife, Sharon, who is my love, my support, and my best friend.

Arthur Freeman

I dedicate this book to wife, Andrea, and my daughter, Alyssa, whose love and encouragement enable me to accomplish anything in my view. I also thank the many students, families, colleagues, and educators, who have touched my life and made my career both stimulating and rewarding.

Ray W. Christner

Contents

PART I   *Foundations*

PART II   *Application of CBT Interventions for Specific Issues*

PART III   Application of CBT Interventions
with Systems

PART IV   Summary

Foreword

When Aaron T. Beck, M.D., developed cognitive therapy in the early 1960s as a treatment for adult depression, he did not know that this system of psychotherapy would later be applied so widely, much less to schoolchildren. I believe, however, that every good cognitive therapist is both a counselor *and* a teacher at heart, as cognitive therapy requires teaching individuals how to change their dysfunctional thinking and behavior in the context of a supportive, caring relationship.

There is a natural fit between cognitive behavior therapy and schools, a connection I discovered 30 years ago when I became (in my first career) a teacher of learning disabled children. I think all good teachers instinctively use cognitive behavioral strategies in the classroom (and with parents) without ever having received formal training in this modality. For example, they help students set goals, monitor their behavior, and evaluate progress. They teach them to solve problems and develop interpersonal skills. They provide positive reinforcement to encourage functional behavior and counteract students' negative cognitions about their competence or intelligence. Often, they teach students skills to deal with anxiety or frustration.

This volume, however, goes far beyond these standard strategies to address serious problems that arise in schools every day. Cognitive therapy has a great deal to offer teachers, school counselors, and administrators in dealing with students who suffer from psychological problems and psychiatric disorders. In workshops and school consultations, I have found that school personnel are uniformly appreciative of a commonsense approach that extends many of the things that they do naturally—and that works.

The major section of this book contains chapters for the major difficulties students present in school: anxiety, depression, eating disorders, substance abuse, ADHD, aggression, and developmental disabilities, among others. These chapters present a clear description of the problem, a review of empirical support for CBT treatments in and outside of schools, assessment methods, a CBT conceptualization of the problem, specific interventions, and illustrative case examples. Another section describes the application of CBT interventions in working with parents and families, in behavioral consultation, and in responding to school crises.

Although I left teaching and began to study psychology and cognitive therapy in particular, I always had in the back of my mind that some day I would return to my roots and apply cognitive therapy to education. I have done so to some degree, working with children, consulting on CBT programs in schools, and codeveloping with my father the *Beck Youth Inventories of Emotional and Social Impairment*. I am very pleased, though, that Drs. Mennuti, Christner, and Freeman have taken the lead in this field and edited this excellent book. All three are professors at the Philadelphia College of Osteopathic Medicine in a department founded by Dr. Freeman over a dozen years ago. Dr. Mennuti is the director of the graduate program in School Psychology, in which Dr. Christner is also a faculty member. I hope that their work will inspire graduate programs in school psychology nationwide to initiate a program in or expand their focus on cognitive behavior therapy.

Judith S. Beck, Ph.D.
Director, Beck Institute for Cognitive Therapy and Research
Clinical Associate Professor of Psychology in Psychiatry,
University of Pennsylvania

Acknowledgments

The idea for this book grew out of our common interests in helping children and families. Attempting to address the various issues presented in schools has been challenging, yet our work together as editors has been exhilarating. Our efforts would not have been possible without the help and support of many individuals. Our colleagues, students, and clients who have mentored us and taught us about cognitive-behavioral interventions and school systems are too countless to mention. We lovingly thank all of them and express our deepest gratitude.

To our contributing authors, we are genuinely grateful for all your hard work and willingness to collaborate on this project. Furthermore, to the many graduate students and colleagues who reviewed chapters for this volume, we appreciated your time and insight. We especially thank the following individuals: Jennifer Brown, Kathleen Carpenter, Alicea Davis, Shawn Dolan, Micelle Downs, Leslee Frye, Lucy Hernandez, Ashley Kase, Mary Sharp-Ross, Kimberly Simmerman, Janine Wargo, and Carolyn Zimmer-Levin.

We would further like to extend our gratitude to the outstanding staff at Routledge Publishing, particularly Dr. George Zimmar and Dana Bliss. Their direction, patience, and guidance proved effective in producing a superior reference for students and practitioners working within school settings.

Finally, we owe a particular debt to our clients in schools, including children, parents, teachers, administrators, and finally school districts, many of whom inspired chapters within our book. In all cases, we have deeply disguised them to protect confidentiality and privacy. They have given us the opportunity to share with you our work together.

Rosemary B. Mennuti
Arthur Freeman
Ray W. Christner

About the Editors

Rosemary B. Mennuti, Ed.D., NCSP, is Professor and Director of School Psychology Programs in the Department of Psychology at the Philadelphia College of Osteopathic Medicine. She comes to academia after a long career in public education, where she worked with children and families for over 25 years as a school psychologist. Her research and clinical areas of interest include eating disorders, female adolescent developmental issues, therapist self-disclosure, and training issues.

Arthur Freeman, Ed.D., ABPP, is Professor of Psychology at the University of St. Francis in Fort Wayne, Indiana. Before his move to Indiana, he was Professor and Chair of the Department of Psychology at the Philadelphia College of Osteopathic Medicine (PCOM). He has remained in the position of professor since his move, teaching in both the Clinical and School Psychology Programs. Dr. Freeman received training from Dr. Albert Ellis and Dr. Aaron T. Beck.

Ray W. Christner, Psy.D., NCSP, is Assistant Professor and Director of Educational Specialist Program in the Department of Psychology at the Philadelphia College of Osteopathic Medicine (PCOM). In addition to working at PCOM, Dr. Christner continues to provide services to children, adolescents, families, and schools. He completed his training in cognitive-behavior therapy (CBT) under the direction of Dr. Arthur Freeman. His research interests include CBT, school-based mental health, consultation, and the process of change.

Contributors

Stuart B. Badner, Psy.D., Colonial Intermediate Unit 20, Easton, Pennsylvania, and Department of Psychology, Philadelphia College of Osteopathic Medicine, Philadelphia, Pennsylvania.

Andrea Bloomgarden, Ph.D., Department of Psychology, Philadelphia College of Osteopathic Medicine, Philadelphia, Pennsylvania.

Jill K. Carey-Melton, Ed.S., Moorestown Public Schools Moorestown, New Jersey, and Department of Psychology, Philadelphia College of Osteopathic Medicine, Philadelphia, Pennsylvania.

Victoria B. Damiani, Ed.D., NCSP, Education and School Psychology Department and Center for Rural Gifted Education, Indiana University of Pennsylvania, Indiana, Pennsylvania.

Beth Doll, Ph.D., Department of Educational Psychology, University of Nebraska-Lincoln, Lincoln, Nebraska.

A. Renee Donoghue, Psy.D., CSP, Widener University, Institute for Graduate Clinical Psychology, Chester, Pennsylvania.

Jason M. Duff, MSN, CRNP, BC, Department of Psychology, Philadelphia College of Osteopathic Medicine, Philadelphia, Pennsylvania.

George J. DuPaul, Ph.D., Lehigh University, College of Education, Bethlehem, Pennsylvania.

Lizette Marie Flammer, M.Ed., Lehigh University, College of Education, Bethlehem, Pennsylvania.

Ellen Flannery-Schroeder, Ph.D., ABPP, University of Rhode Island, Kingston, Rhode Island.

Susan G. Forman, Ph.D., Rutgers University, New Brunswick, New Jersey.

Robert D. Friedberg, Ph.D., Penn State College of Medicine, Milton S. Hershey Medical Center, Hershey, Pennsylvania.

Nicole Gabriel, Psy.D., Delaware County Professional Services, Newtown Square, Pennsylvania.

Elizabeth A. Gosch, Ph.D., ABPP, Department of Psychology, Philadelphia College of Osteopathic Medicine, Philadelphia, Pennsylvania.

Daniel H. Ingram, Psy.D., NCSP, Lincoln Intermediate Unit No. 12, New Oxford, Pennsylvania, and Department of Psychology, Philadelphia College of Osteopathic Medicine, Philadelphia, Pennsylvania.

Christopher A. Kearney, Ph.D., Department of Psychology, University of Nevada, Las Vegas, Nevada.

Russell J. Kormann, Ph.D., is the director of Project: Natural Setting Therapeutic Management (NSTM), a community based behavioral support program at Rutgers. The State University that serves individuals with developmental disabilities and severe behavioral challenges. He is both a licensed, clinical psychologist as well as a state certified school psychologist.

Amie Lemos, M.A., Department of Psychology, University of Nevada, Las Vegas, Nevada.

Lori Lennon, M.S., NCSP, Central Bucks School District, Doylestown, Pennsylvania, and Department of Psychology, Philadelphia College of Osteopathic Medicine, Philadelphia, Pennsylvania.

Dawn M. McDonald, M.A., Department of Psychology, Philadelphia College of Osteopathic Medicine, Philadelphia, Pennsylvania.

Terry M. Molony, Ed.S., M.S.W., NCSP, Cherry Hill School District, Cherry Hill, New Jersey, and Department of Psychology, Philadelphia College of Osteopathic Medicine, Philadelphia, Pennsylvania.

Christy A. Mulligan, M.S., West Chester Area School District, West Chester, Pennsylvania, and Department of Psychology, Philadelphia College of Osteopathic Medicine, Philadelphia, Pennsylvania.

Virginia B. Murphy, Psy.D., Milton Hershey School, Hershey, Pennsylvania.

Samuel O. Ortiz, Ph.D., Department of Psychology, St. John's University, Jamaica, New York.

Michael R. Petronko, Ph.D., Rutgers University, Graduate School of Professional Psychology, Piscataway, New Jersey.

David M. Poponi, M.S.W., Ed.S., Department of Psychology, Philadelphia College of Osteopathic Medicine, Philadelphia, Pennsylvania.

Thomas J. Power, Ph.D., The Children's Hospital of Philadelphia, Philadelphia, Pennsylvania.

Maurice F. Prout, Ph.D., ABPP, Widener University, Institute for Graduate Clinical Psychology, Chester, Pennsylvania.

Mark A. Reinecke, Ph.D., ABPP, ACT, Northwestern University, Division of Psychology, Abbott Hall, Suite 1205, Chicago, Illinois.

Laura Sharp, Psy.D., Department of Psychology, Philadelphia College of Osteopathic Medicine, Philadelphia, Pennsylvania.

Jenna Silverman, M.A., Department of Psychology, University of Nevada, Las Vegas, Nevada.

Diane L. Smallwood, Psy.D., NCSP, Department of Psychology, Philadelphia College of Osteopathic Medicine, Philadelphia, Pennsylvania.

Susan M. Swearer, Ph.D., Department of Educational Psychology, University of Nebraska-Lincoln, Lincoln, Nebraska.

Jessica L. Stewart, Psy.D., Lincoln Intermediate Unit No. 12, New Oxford, Pennsylvania.

Rosemary E. Vile Junod, M.Ed., Lehigh University, College of Education, Bethlehem, Pennsylvania.

Erica M. Weiler, Ph.D., NCSP, ABPP, Milton Hershey School, Hershey, Pennsylvania.

Branlyn E. Werba, M.S., The Children's Hospital of Philadelphia, Philadelphia, Pennsylvania.

Aaron R. Wheeler, B.S., Widener University, Institute for Graduate Clinical Psychology, Chester, Pennsylvania.

Barbara Bole Williams, Ph.D., NCSP, Rowan University, Department of Special Education, Glassboro, New Jersey.

Helen W. Wilson, Ph.D., Yale University, Child Study Center, New Haven, Connecticut.

Part I

FOUNDATIONS

An Introduction to a School-Based Cognitive-Behavioral Framework

ROSEMARY B. MENNUTI, RAY W. CHRISTNER & ARTHUR FREEMAN

In recent years, significant advances have occurred in the use of cognitive-behavioral interventions for child and adolescent emotional and behavioral difficulties. Specifically, cognitive-behavior therapy (CBT) has been applied to a number of common clinical problems in youth, including anxiety, attention-deficit/hyperactivity disorder, conduct disorder, depression, eating disorders, and oppositional defiant disorder, to name a few. Additionally, over the past several years, a number of excellent references have been developed for child and adolescent clinicians on the practical and empirical support of using CBT with youth (see Friedberg & McClure, 2002; Kendall, 2000; Reinecke, Dattilio, & Freeman, 2003). However, despite the growth of literature on the use of CBT with young clients, there remain few resources on its use with children in educational or school settings. Given the critical role schools and school staff have in the cognitive, behavioral, emotional, social, and interpersonal development of children and adolescents, it is only fitting that school-based clinicians and school systems begin considering the implementation of CBT intervention services to help children and adolescents in need. With the growing evidence-base supporting the use of cognitive-behavioral interventions with young clients (see Kendall, 2000; Ollendick & King, 2004), CBT or cognitive-behavioral interventions are promising for use within school settings.

RATIONALE FOR SCHOOL-BASED BEHAVIORAL HEALTH SERVICE

The need for school-based behavioral health services is greater than ever, as a child's or adolescent's health and abilities to learn are built on his or her emotional or behavioral well-being. Research has demonstrated that youth with identified emotional or behavioral disturbances in schools often have less academic success and positive social interactions (Anderson, 2001; Coleman & Vaughn, 2000), as well as higher frequencies of truancy, suspensions, tardiness, expulsions, attention-seeking behaviors, and poor peer relationships (Epstein & Cullinan, 1994). Historically, there has been minimal attention given to onset issues related to mental illness, and thus, interventions have generally focused on treating symptoms as they arise. Kessler, Berglund, Demler, Jin, and Walters (2005) noted that "about half of Americans will meet the criteria for a DSM-IV disorder sometime in their lifetime, with first onset usually in childhood or adolescence" (p. 593). This suggests that if these issues are left untreated or treated ineffectively in youth, they can progress to debilitating mental illness that impacts an individual's functioning as an adult. According to the U.S. Department of Health and Human Services (1999; 2001), the nation is facing a public crisis in mental health care for children and adolescents. Given this, we must begin to ask ourselves, "How can we as school-based professionals be meaningfully involved and actively contribute to diminishing the distress that plagues the life of the children and families of our nation, as well as prevent future distress as they develop into adults?"

The provision of school-based psychological services is not a new trend in education, as these services date back to the turn of the 20th century (Fagan, 2000). At that time, all states endorsed compulsory attendance laws, the average number of school days increased, and public school enrollment was on the rise, all of which contributed to an increase in referrals to address academic problems and behavioral concerns and issues complicated by health problems (Fagan). Today's school-based practitioners continue to receive referrals for similar issues; however, the need for comprehensive school-based mental health services has never been greater. Recent reports have suggested that as many as 10% of children and adolescents in the United States alone have a diagnosed mental health disorder (U.S. Department of Health and Human Services, 2000), and approximately 20% of youth in schools have the need for treatment of a specific mental health problem (Hoagwood & Erwin, 1997). Yet, in a given year, researchers estimate that fewer than 1 in 5 children in need receive the treatment they require (U.S. Department of Health and Human Services, 2001). Interestingly, of the children who receive mental health services, about 70 to 80% receive such services within school settings (Burns et al., 1995).

Considering this information as well as the dominant role that education plays in the lives of youth, we believe the schools are a natural entry point for addressing the mental health needs of children and families. As emotional and behavioral problems arise with students, school-based clinicians will be called upon to design and provide effective and efficient interventions for various presenting problems and populations. Although schools are increasing their efforts to meet the challenge of addressing the mental health issues that affect children in the learning process, implementing services requires not only knowledge of the presenting problem but also knowledge of the theoretical orientation used in treatment and service delivery. In essence, school-based professionals must be well trained and prepared with knowledge and skill to offer prevention and treatment services built on evidence-based practices. Despite this need, many educators and school-based clinicians have not been trained to deal with the growing number of vulnerable children in this manner. Thus, it is essential to provide school-based practitioners with the knowledge and skills to deliver services to children in an effective way. Considering the needs of students and the legal dictum for the provision of psychological counseling in schools, we believe cognitive-behavioral interventions represent a promising option for school-based clinicians as a well-founded, effective treatment model to respond to the demands and needs of children and families today.

COGNITIVE-BEHAVIORAL MODEL OF SERVICE DELIVERY

Evidence for Using CBT

Education and mental health professionals have become familiar with the phrase "evidenced-based practice." The common use of this term illustrates the move toward offering services based on sound theoretical principles and interventions supported through empirically based studies. CBT is one such approach in that it has amassed a growing body of evidence over the past 20 years regarding its efficacy and effectiveness when working with children and adolescents. To date, current studies on the use of CBT with children and adolescents have been generally impressive (Reinecke et al., 2003). However, as noted earlier, despite the positive support of CBT in the literature, most current research on CBT with children and adolescents has involved primarily clinical populations and settings rather than addressing the use of CBT in schools.

Although much of this research has occurred in clinical settings, the promise CBT has as an effective treatment to ameliorate a number of childhood difficulties (e.g., depression, anxiety, and disruptive behaviors) should not be ignored (see reviews in Kazdin & Weisz, 1998; Kendall, 2000; Ollendick & King, 2004; Weisz & Jensen, 1999). In addition, there continues to be ongoing research finding potential uses for CBT with children and adolescents that have yet to be termed "evidence-based." Use of CBT with issues such as eating disorders, posttraumatic stress disorder, substance abuse, school-related problems, and health conditions show potential, yet further investigation is warranted. Although there continues to be a dearth of research on treatment for *all* problems facing children and adolescents today, through the use of clear case conceptualization and continual progress monitoring clinicians can modify cognitive-behavioral interventions to meet their individual client's needs. Notwithstanding the evidence supporting the use of CBT with children and adolescents, it is critical that school-based practitioners have an understanding of the fundamental tenets of CBT and its application to youth in general before applying it within their practice.

The CBT Model

The CBT model with children, as with adults, suggests that emotions and accompanying behaviors are the result of the connection between a given situation, the child's belief system (through which he or she interprets given situations), and the child's thoughts about the event (positive and negative). It is important to view this connection as multidirectional rather than linear, which suggests that there is not a cause-and-effect relationship but, instead, a dynamic interactional process between situational, cognitive, affective, and behavioral components. Having awareness of the situational factors (e.g., social aspects) that activate a student's belief system, being able to link the beliefs with the child's cognitive process, and translating these concepts into clear and helpful strategies for the child are essential for effective interventions. CBT focuses on the way in which a child interprets his or her experiences and how these thoughts ultimately influence his or her emotional or behavioral functioning (Friedberg & McClure, 2002; Reinecke et al., 2003). For example, consider Theresa, a 9-year-old girl who presents with significant anxiety before any testing situation at school. Although it is important to understand the context of her anxiety (e.g., when taking tests), knowledge of her physiological reactions (e.g., nausea, sweaty palm, feeling dizzy), automatic thoughts (e.g., "I didn't study enough; I'm gonna fail.") and her beliefs (e.g., "If I don't get an A, I'm a failure.") are more important to developing interventions than just "combating her anxiety."

CBT represents two interacting perspectives (cognitive and behavioral), which are combined to understand the child or adolescent and to develop interventions to address presenting problems. Behavioral components can be viewed in two ways—environmental influences or skill deficits. Clinicians should examine environmental influences and experiences (e.g., teacher or parent interactions, ineffective parenting, past trauma, etc.) to help conceptualize the students problems, and, in some cases, changes to the environment will be the necessary intervention (e.g., positive behavioral support, token economies, etc.). Alternatively, many problems experienced by students are the result of behavioral skill deficits (e.g., poor self-regulation, underdeveloped social skills, etc.). From the cognitive perspective, there are also two factors to consider—cognitive distortions and cognitive deficiencies (Kendall & MacDonald, 1993). Cognitive distortions involve the errors in thinking, which lead the individual to misinterpret or misperceive a situation or event (Freeman, Pretzer, Fleming, & Simon, 2004). A number of experts in CBT have offered examples of cognitive distortions experienced by individuals, though most of these examples are of adult thoughts (see J. Beck, 1995; Burns, 1999). Christner and Stewart-Allen (2004) provided examples of several cognitive distortions commonly seen in school-aged students (see Table 1.1). Children who display cognitive distortions often experience internalized difficulties (e.g., anxiety and depression). The second cognitive factor, called "cognitive deficiency" by Kendall and MacDonald (1993), suggests deficits in a student's cognitive-processing abilities. Thus, students with cognitive deficiencies may have minimal forethought or problem-solving skills, resulting in impulsiveness and attention problems. Keeping in mind the role of various cognitive and behavioral factors, school-based professionals using a CBT framework will assist students by initiating the acquisition of new skills (both cognitive and behavioral), while also offering opportunities to facilitate a change in cognitive processes and thinking.

Table 1.1 Common Cognitive Distortions Encountered in Therapy with Students in Educational Settings

1.	Dichotomous thinking—The student views situation in only two categories rather than on a continuum. The world is either black or white with no shades of gray. For example, "I'm either a good student or a failure."
2.	Overgeneralization—The student sees a current event as being characteristic of life in general, instead of one situation among many. For example, "Because I failed that science test, I'll never graduate or make it in college."
3.	Mind reading—The student believes he or she knows what others are thinking about him or her without any evidence. For example, "I just know that Mr. P. is angry with me."
4.	Emotional reasoning—The student assumes that his or her feelings or emotional reactions reflect the true situation. For example, "I feel like no one likes me, so no one likes me."
5.	Disqualifying the positive—The student discounts positive experiences that conflict with his or her negative views. For example, "I only did well on those quizzes because Mrs. Jones helped me and I got lucky."
6.	Catastrophizing—The student predicts that future situations will be negative and treats them as intolerable catastrophes. For example, "I better not even try the assignment because I might screw it up, and that would be awful."
7.	Personalization—The student assumes that he or she is the cause of negative circumstances. For example, "My teacher didn't smile at me this morning. I must have failed that test and made her unhappy."
8.	Should statements—The student uses *should* or *must* to describe how he or she or others are to behave or act. For example, "I must always get A's, and I shouldn't make mistakes."
9.	Comparing—The student compares his or her performance to others. Oftentimes, the comparison is made to higher performing or older students. For example, "Compared to my older brother, my work looks like a kindergartner did it."
10.	Selective abstraction—The student focuses attention to one detail (usually negative), and ignores other relevant aspects. For example, "My teacher gave me an unsatisfactory on the last assignment, so this means I'm one of his worst students!"
11.	Labeling—The student attaches a global label to describe him- or herself rather than looking at behaviors and actions. For example, "I'm a loser" rather than "Boy, I had a bad game last night."

(Christner & Stewart-Allen, 2004)

CBT in schools

Although many believe that psychological counseling services are difficult to "fit" into the educational culture, the structure and framework of CBT parallels other educational services, making it more easily accepted among educators (Christner & Allen, 2003; Christner, Stewart-Allen, & Mennuti, 2004; Mennuti & Christner, in press). Given CBT's time-limited, present-oriented, and solution-focused approach (Reinecke et al., 2003), it can be easily adapted to an intervention delivery model that encompasses services at differing levels representing greater specificity, complexity, and intensity. In fact, as will be seen throughout this book, school-based clinicians can offer CBT interventions on a continuum from prevention to early identification to direct individual service.

The components and possible service delivery options of CBT are consistent with the educational environment, where both time and resources are often limited. The solution-focused and present-oriented approach of CBT is also appealing in education, as it addresses the student's issues without overly relying on diagnosing a specific pathology. In addition, the structure of CBT, which focuses on psycho-education, skill building, between-session work (aka "homework"), agenda setting, and progress monitoring, is congruent with most activities already existing in school settings. Thus, although these components assist in providing intervention services, they also strengthen the link between psychological counseling and other services provided in schools.

School-based clinicians have access to the combination of teacher interaction, peer influence, and personal performance efforts and outcomes, all of which offer an insight into a student's perceptions and thought processes that many outside clinicians do not have access to (Mennuti & Christner, in press). We view the school setting as a "natural laboratory" for observing interpersonal dynamics and gathering data about the problems facing students, as well as a "safe" and pure setting for students to "experiment" with newly learned skills from counseling sessions. Often, the problems associated with the generalization of skills learned in counseling or therapy services are that the skills are being taught in a setting far removed from the child's daily environment. Goldstein and Goldstein (1998) noted that for interventions to have the greatest effect, they must be implemented in close proximity to the target behavior. Therefore, offering services within schools rather than in outside settings (e.g., outpatient clinics, inpatient units, etc.) has great advantages, especially given the opportunity for immediate generalization following sessions.

ISSUES AFFECTING COGNITIVE-BEHAVIORAL PRACTICE

Developmental Issues

Although a number of professionals not trained in CBT have criticized it as a "paint-by-number" or manualized approach, those with experience in the application of CBT realize that this is not the case. In fact, practitioners using CBT rely on data obtained through assessment and case conceptualization in order to think strategically about the individual and to plan for effective and specific interventions based on the student's age, developmental level, and presenting problems. It is through a clear case conceptualization of the student and his or her problems that the school-based clinician is able to select and utilize precise interventions to address the area most amenable to treatment at the time. In chapter 3, Murphy and Christner offer a thorough review of case conceptualization, with a specific emphasis on understanding school-related cases.

A major component when working with school-aged children is having a comprehensive understanding of the fundamentals of child and adolescent development. Providing psychological counseling or psychotherapy with children and adolescents is more than knowing a list of specific techniques or strategies. Thus, clinicians well grounded in the foundations of development are more likely to implement interventions compatible with the child's functional level and avoid a trial-and-error approach to finding "what works." Because a child must have the capacity to attend to information, comprehend language, use working memory, and express him- or herself verbally to benefit from a number of cognitive-based strategies, it is essential for school-based practitioners to assess and focus on these individual factors when designing specific programs for a student. Practitioners must determine the precise mix of cognitive and behavioral techniques based on the student's need and developmental level. Take, for instance, a student who is limited in both cognitive and language development. This student will require interventions that have a greater percentage of strategies focusing on behavioral components. We are not suggesting that cognitive techniques are inappropriate for use with younger children or those with severe behaviors but, instead, that cognitive interventions will be less directly relied on for those students at a lower developmental level or who display an increased level of behavior (Christner, Allen, & Maus, 2004; Mennuti & Christner, in press). When looking at developmental level, it is important to note that the developmental level is not always consistent with chronological age.

Risk and Resilience

Research within the field of developmental psychopathology regarding risk factors, protective factors, and resiliency factors (Doll & Lyons, 1998) provides useful information for practitioners working with youth. The work of Coie and colleagues (1993) has focused on identifying risk factors associated with the development of psychological problems. Essentially, risk factors are thought to increase the risk that children will be unable as adults to contribute to society, earn a living, and form healthy families. Coie et al. identified seven domains of risk factors: (1) constitutional handicaps, (2) skill development delays, (3) emotional difficulties, (4) family circumstances, (5) interpersonal problems, (6) school problems, and (7) ecological risks. Within each of the domains, a number of generic risk factors exist that may be found individually or in combination to affect a specific child. Of particular concern are risk factors such as poverty, minimal parent education, marital discord or family dysfunction, ineffective parenting, child maltreatment, poor physical health of the child or parents, parent mental illness or inadequacy, and large family size (Doll & Lyons, 1998). Although many of these specific factors are out of our control, they provide information that may help school-based professionals identify students at risk and offer interventions that may serve protective functions.

Inasmuch as children with risk factors are "at-risk," not all children with these risk factors have poor outcomes. Thus, equally if not more important is understanding factors that serve a protective role for children and adolescents and increase their likelihood of being resilient. Coie et al. (1993) indicated these protective factors serve one of the following purposes: (1) to decrease risk directly, (2) to serve as a buffer through interaction with risk factors, (3) to disrupt the chain reaction from risk factors to disorder, or (4) to prevent the initial occurrence of the risk factor. Rutter (1985) identified three broad domains of protective factors including individual characteristics, interaction with the environment, and broader societal influences (e.g., quality schools).

By using one's knowledge of risk factors, protective mechanisms, and resiliency, clinicians can design interventions for students that minimize areas of risk while fostering their strengths and developing a sense of competency. Interventions occurring early in the treatment process may concentrate on skill building (e.g., social skills, problem-solving skills, etc.) through psychoeducation. In doing this, clinicians will help students correct maladaptive practices that serve as risk factors while further promoting protective factors that minimize risk (e.g., strengthening peer relationships, increasing self-monitoring skills, improving parent-child interactions, and increasing school success). In addition to enhancing interventions directed at the child, school-based clinicians have the potential to apply cognitive and behavioral interventions that enhance protective and resiliency factors by making an impact on the family and school environments. Badner and Carey-Melton (chapter 20) and Christner, Stewart, and Lennon (chapter 19) offer suggestions for applying CBT strategies with parents and families. In addition, Williams, Smallwood, and Molony (chapter 21) provide a detailed account of using CBT in consultation within the school system.

Therapeutic Relationship

Another component central to the use of CBT with children and adolescents is the working relationship. Interestingly, those professionals critical of CBT often claim that it is manualized and that it ignores the relevance of the "therapeutic relationship." Those who are trained in CBT are aware that this claim is far from traditional practice. In fact, Aaron T. Beck and his colleagues (1979) have emphasized the need for active interaction between therapist and "patient," and they note that "slighting the therapeutic relationship" (p. 27) is a common error in the therapy process. It is important, and even necessary, for this interaction to be empathetic and empowering in order to allow the client to explore his or her authentic thoughts and feelings in a way that promotes insight and understanding in order to foster positive movement and change.

The relationship when working with children and adolescents is one of connection and collaboration. When the connection is a positive, authentic relationship, it can facilitate the therapy process and enhance the overall outcome. Despite the clinical relevance of the therapeutic relationship in providing service to youth, there continues to be limited research regarding this dynamic. In one meta-analytic review, Shirk and Karver (2003) found support that the therapeutic relationship has a modest, yet consistent, correlation with therapeutic outcome for youth. Although this finding is important to consider, it is imperative to acknowledge that a factor such as "relationship" is difficult to study quantitatively, and that further investigation in this area is needed. Through the use of qualitative studies the concept of the therapeutic relationship and its role, as it is conceived and valued by children, could be understood first and then quantified based on what children need and know, rather than on a preexisting framework of what we think it is that children need. By taking an in-depth look at the phenomenon of the therapeutic relationship with children, we will enhance our understanding of this process, which is crucial to developing effective treatment.

A collaborative, working relationship between a professional and client (child, adolescent, or adult) is not merely "getting along," nor is it a simple interaction or friendship. Instead, a positive healing relationship is a complex dynamic in which a bond exists. This bond promotes a connection and trust between two people, and an emotional availability and presence that facilitates comfort and openness. Once a sense of safety and trust is established, children can risk being open about who they are and what they believe. Thus, the relationship becomes the foundation on which strategies and interventions can develop and thrive. It is the relationship that is helping and growth fostering, and, in turn, encourages change in treatment and in daily functioning. Although collaboration generally suggests an "equal" or 50/50 involvement between the school-based clinician and child, this is not the case in actual treatment. In fact, a school-based clinician will need to meet a specific student at his or her level (based on age, motivation, etc.), while holding a place for dignity and respect (Mennuti & Christner, in press). Initially, until the student matures in the therapy process, the ratio of student to clinician work may be 30/70 or 40/60.

A number of basic approaches are available to help clinicians facilitate an authentic relationship. For instance, frequent and brief summations throughout the session will likely assist in keeping focus and demonstrating involvement within the session while further establishing and maintaining the relationship. These summations convey to the student that the other person is emotionally available and understands what he or she is saying and feeling. It is also useful to acquire feedback that will help clarify information or misunderstandings. Creating an atmosphere of empowerment and freedom to question facilitates sharing and learning together. It also provides an opportunity for conflict to occur and to be openly discussed and resolved. Finally, the permission and expectation to question, examine, and explore is often uncharacteristic of most school-based interactions, yet it lies at the heart of growth and change for children. Although disconnections can and will occur, a discussion of the rupture in the relationship often leads to a better bond and strengthens the existing therapeutic relationship.

Student Motivation

Final factors that school-based practitioners should consider when providing services to children and adolescent include the student's motivation and attitude. These factors not only affect the collaborative relationship but also impact subsequent intervention implementation and outcomes. Take, for instance, a student who is referred for being disruptive within his classroom. Using a directive approach discussing reasons why he should not disrupt classroom instruction will likely be met with opposition and resulting failure. Instead, clinicians who have know-how will use the student's motivation (e.g., "Let's find ways of getting your teacher off your back.") to increase intervention adherence and further promote the partnership with the student.

The idea of readiness or motivation for change is not a new concept in general, although it is one that is novel to most practitioners in an educational setting. In school settings, when a student has a problem, no matter if it is academic or behavioral, we automatically assume that he or she is ready and motivated to make the necessary change. Consequently, we often develop and implement plans that require "action" for success, which oftentimes fail because the student is neither ready nor motivated. To serve children and adolescents better, we advocate for school-based clinicians to begin matching interventions to the child's "stage of change." The work of Prochaska and DiClemente (Prochaska & DiClemente, 1982; Prochaska, DiClemente, & Norcross, 1992) is among the most frequently cited references in the literature regarding this concept. However, although Prochaska and DiClemente's model has been applied to a number of psychological, psychosocial, and medical issues (see Prochaska, Redding, Harlow, Rossi, & Velicer, 1994), no references exist for its use with youth in general or in schools.

A recent revision of this model by Freeman and Dolan (2001) expands the stages of change model to include 10 stages through which individuals pass during the change process. These include (1) Noncontemplation, (2) Anticontemplation, (3) Precontemplation, (4) Contemplation, (5) Action Planning, (6) Action, (7) Prelapse, (8) Laspe, (9) Relapse, and (10) Maintenance. See Freeman and Dolan (2001) for a thorough review of each of these stages. Although stages of change models have not yet been identified for children and youth clients, using the afore-mentioned model to help "meet the student where he or she is" can have great benefit. School-based clinicians can begin using and monitoring the usefulness of stages of change models with regard to school-related problems, but further investigation is needed to establish empirical support.

COGNITIVE-BEHAVIORAL INTERVENTIONS

When using CBT interventions with youth, a number of valuable strategies are available for responding to the various problems of children. In fact, quite a few detailed approaches exist to address specific disorders in children, many of which we highlight in Part II of this book. To obtain specific cognitive and behavioral techniques beyond what we cover in this volume, we direct the reader to the following books: *Clinical Practice of Cognitive Therapy with Children and Adolescents: The Nuts and Bolts* by Friedberg and McClure (2002), *Clinical Applications of Cognitive Therapy, Second Edition,* by Freeman et al. (2004), and *What Works When with Children and Adolescents: A Handbook of Counseling Techniques* by Vernon (2002).

For our purpose, we challenge school-based professionals to think beyond the simple use of these strategies or techniques with individual students. Instead of limiting interventions to only those students "in need," school-based practitioners must look at the provision of interventions and strategies on a continuum that thereby increases positive outcomes for a number of students. This is not to say that we should stop providing individual services to students, but, rather, that beyond tra-ditional "individual counseling," cognitive and behavioral interventions can be offered within a multilevel framework of universal interventions for all students, selected interventions for those students at risk, and targeted interventions for specific behavioral or emotional problems. Figure 1.1 illustrates a multilevel frame-work for applying cognitive-behavioral interventions and indicates the type and

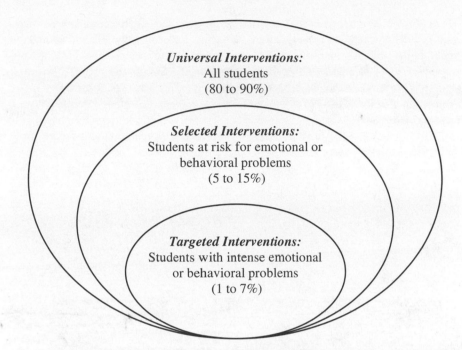

Figure 1.1 Multilevel framework for cognitive-behavioral interventions.

approximate percentage of students who may benefit from interventions at each level.

Universal Interventions

Universal interventions are designed to have an impact on a large number of students within a school setting. The objective of interventions at this level is to increase protective factors and decrease risk in an attempt to prevent the development of emotional, behavioral, or learning problems. Each student receives the same intervention, and commonly, school-based practitioners offer consultation on applying these interventions at a school-wide or class-wide level. Examples of universal interventions include violence prevention, school climate, substance use, school dropout, suicide, and teenage pregnancy prevention programs. Interventions at this level serve a primary prevention purpose, with the goal being to establish a foundation and context from which more costly and individualized interventions are applied. Thus, schools having significant issues of bullying should focus on providing school-wide bullying programs and interventions, rather than targeting individual students involved in specific situations. The need for universal interventions may vary depending on the need of the school. It should be noted that universal interventions are effective for only about 85% of the school population, and, thus, further intervention will be needed for the remainder of the school population (Walker, Ramsey, & Gresham, 2004).

A number of cognitive-behavioral components can be used in universal interventions. For instance, many programs designed for violence prevention focus on social skills, such as anger management, conflict resolution, problem solving, and impulse control. Examples of excellent cognitive-behavioral programs that can be used on a universal basis include *I Can Problem Solve* by Shure (2001), *PATHS* by Kusche and Greenberg (1994), and *Olweus Bullying Prevention Program* by Olweus and Limber (1999).

Selected Interventions

Selected interventions are often thought of as "early intervention" strategies, designed for students who are at a particularly high risk. School-based clinicians may provide these services on an individual basis; however, it is more likely that small-group interventions will be used at this level. The primary goal for selected interventions includes increasing coping skills or protective factors as a means to counter or decrease risk factors. A number of cognitive-behavioral interventions could be used at the selected level. Oftentimes, these interventions target issues such as anger management and impulse control.

School-based practitioners can use their knowledge of CBT principles to design specific programs depending on the needs of the students. For example, at an elementary school with a high rate of school anxiety/refusal at the beginning of the year, the school psychologist and school counselor developed a five-session group that took place over the two weeks preceding the start of the school year. Students selected for the program were identified based on referrals from the previous year's teachers as well as from a screening process developed for incoming kindergarten students. The focus of the group was to teach coping skills such as relaxation and anxiety management, as well as to provide exposure to the school a few days before the students returned. Another example of a selected intervention would be the *Anger Coping Program* developed by Larson and Lochman (2002), which provides a structured protocol for children at risk for anger or aggressive behavior.

Targeted Interventions

Targeted interventions are designed to address students who display the most problematic social, emotional, or behavioral problems. It is not surprising that currently most of the resources for school-based mental health are devoted to students with this level of need. Although there will always be a need to provide services at this level, schools that offer both universal and selected interventions can greatly decrease the need for individual services. In fact, with adequate early intervention and prevention services, only approximately 1% to 7% of students will need extensive and intensive psychological interventions (Walker, Ramsey, & Gresham, 2004). Although oftentimes schools refer these services out to other agencies and professionals, school-based professionals with adequate training and experience can easily offer interventions for these students. Targeted interventions may be offered to students individually or in a small-group format.

When working with individuals at a targeted level, it is necessary to use knowledge of the severity of the student's problems as well as his or her developmental level in order to determine the precise mix of cognitive and behavioral techniques for a given student. As a general rule of thumb, younger and more problematic students will require a greater proportion of behavioral to cognitive interventions. In contrast, more developmentally mature students may be more adept at cognitive techniques, as there is a greater probability that he or she has the capacity to entertain abstract concepts.

Once the school-based clinician has obtained a clear conceptualization of the student's issues, a blend of techniques specific to the student's needs may be chosen. Although most of the literature distinguishes between cognitive and behavioral interventions, professionals must keep in mind that cognitive and behavioral techniques play complimentary roles in intervention. For instance, behavioral strategies, such as relaxation training, can produce both cognitive and behavioral changes. Likewise, cognitive techniques, such as reattribution, can generate parallel results. Although it is beyond the scope of this chapter to describe specific cognitive and behavioral techniques, Table 1.2 offers a list of strategies and techniques for school-based practitioners to explore further.

CHALLENGES TO PROVIDING SCHOOL-BASED SERVICES

Despite the potentially positive effects of providing cognitive-behavioral and school-based mental health programs, there remain a number of challenges and barriers. Given the presence of current educational legislation (e.g., No Child Left Behind), many educators now view the primary purpose of school is for children to receive *academic* instruction. The demands placed on teachers and schools to meet the "standards" and high-stakes testing requirements has ultimately restricted the views of some educators and minimized the focus on student emotional and behavioral needs. Given the high demands placed on teachers and other staff members to meet standards and goals, school-based clinicians must be mindful of the time constraints already facing these individuals. However, knowing the overwhelming and lasting effects that can accompany emotional and behavioral difficulties in children, including academic problems, there is a need for school-based clinicians to educate school

Table 1.2 Common Cognitive and Behavioral Interventions for Youth

Cognitive Interventions	Behavioral Interventions
Examining or Testing the Evidence	Activity Scheduling
Challenging Cognitive Distortions	Behavioral Rehearsal (Role-Playing)
Reattribution	Behavioral Experiments
Decatastrophizing	Contingency Management
Self-Instruction or Self-Talk	Relaxation Training
Problem-Solving Training	Systematic Desensitization
Desensitization Imagery	Social Skills Training
Thought Stopping	Pleasure or Problem Prediction
Refocusing	Self-Monitoring
Evaluating Pros and Cons	Token Economy Systems

systems regarding the necessity to meet the psychosocial needs of children and to enhance positive academic and behavioral outcomes for student success (Mennuti & Christner, in press). To do this appropriately, school-based clinicians must respect the challenges already facing educators, and work collaboratively in the best interest of students. Likewise, for children whose emotional and behavioral issues are significantly interfering with academic functioning, school-based services may assume a prominent role in the child's educational program. One of the most difficult challenges is scheduling weekly appointments with students. To this end, it is essential that various members of the student's educational team coordinate services to provide efficient and effective problem solving.

A further challenge for school-based clinicians is the collaborative relationship between clinician and student. Although a positive relationship is beneficial for therapeutic purposes, in the school environment, there is a greater likelihood for casual interactions with the student to occur (e.g., passing "hellos" in the hallway). Although in some cases this may help facilitate the collaborative relationship with the child, it also may test the school-based clinician's ability to maintain appropriate boundaries. The protection of the child's confidentiality poses an additional conflict when providing school-based mental health services. Other issues including scheduling session times, the referral process itself, and the request for communication (e.g., between referring teachers, parents, and school-based clinicians) may compromise traditional confidentiality standards.

It is imperative that all school-based practitioners providing mental health services consider and address each of the aforementioned issues from the onset of treatment. Having a structure and plan for handling such situations will prevent undue concerns over time. It is important to address each of these concerns with the student and the consenting guardian to avoid confusion or upset as the services progress. Beyond understanding the subtleties of the school system, school-based clinicians must understand the state laws and ethics of their own profession and those of the educational system (Mennuti & Christner, in press).

CONCLUSION

Given the need for short-term, flexible mental health services within the school settings, the CBT model is ideal. The structure and framework of CBT parallels the existing organization of school systems, while allowing for interventions that focus on situation, cognitive, behavioral, affective, and social factors inherent in many difficulties seen in youth. CBT has much promise for enhancing and modifying service delivery in schools, and it has the potential to go beyond providing interventions to individual students. School-based clinicians must use their knowledge of CBT, as well as their understanding of schools and youth in general, to begin looking at a continuum of interventions spanning from universal or school-wide programs to those interventions targeting individual problems of students in need.

Although considerable advancements have occurred with regard to supporting the use of CBT with children and adolescents, a number of areas continue to require attention before full advancements in the use of CBT in schools will occur. Despite the existing evidence base supporting the efficacy and effectiveness of CBT for a variety of child and adolescent problems, further investigation is necessary to obtain a wider knowledge base of problems that can be treated with CBT as well as to expand the use of CBT to a multilevel framework of interventions. Furthermore, notwithstanding the need for school-based mental health programs, there is question regarding the training of school-based clinicians to provide such services. This is a challenge facing university training facilities as well as those organizations providing continuing professional development for school-based practitioners. Finally, using CBT as a means of addressing students' problems will require a paradigm shift for many educators. Most services provided to date in schools, for emotional and behavioral issues, have primarily involved behavioral interventions. The change in service delivery may not only require a shift in thinking regarding the orientation of services but also the need for schools and educators to expand their view toward a continuum of mental health services based on cognitive-behavioral principles.

REFERENCES

Anderson, J. A. (2001). A comparison of the academic progress of students with EDB and students with LD. *Journal of Emotional and Behavioral Disorders, 9*(2), 106–116.

Beck, A. T., Rush, A. J., Shaw, B. F., & Emery, G. (1979). *Cognitive therapy for depression.* New York: Guilford Press.

Beck, J. S. (1995). *Cognitive therapy: Basics and beyond.* New York: Guilford Press.

Burns, B. J., Costello, E. J., Angold, A., Tweed, D., Strangel, D., Farmer, E. M. Z., & Erkanli, A. (1995). Data watch: Children's mental health service use across service sectors. *Health Affairs, 14*(3), 147–159.

Burns, D. D. (1999). *Feeling good: The new mood therapy* (Rev. ed.). New York: Avon.

Christner, R. W., & Allen, J. S. (2003, Spring). Introduction to cognitive-behavioral therapy (CBT) in the schools. *Insight, 23*(3), 12–14.

Christner, R. W., Allen, J. S., & Maus, M. R. (2004, Winter). An overview for selecting CBT techniques in the treatment of youth in schools. *Insight, 24*(2), 8–10.

Christner, R. W., Mennuti, R., & Stewart-Allen, J. (2004, August). School-based Cognitive-Behavior Therapy (CBT). *Pennsylvania Psychologist Quarterly, 64*(8), 22–23.

Christner, R. W., & Stewart-Allen, J. (2004, November). Using cognitive-behavioral interventions for school related problems. Invited presentation at Intermediate Unit No. 1, Coal Center, PA.

Coie, J. D., Watt, J. F., West, S. G., Hawkins, J. D., Asarnow, J. R., Markman, H. J., Ramey, S. L., Shure, M. B., & Long, B. (1993). The science of prevention: A conceptual framework and some direction for a national research program. *American Psychologist, 48,* 1013–1022.

Coleman, M., & Vaughn, S. (2000). Reading interventions for students with emotional/behavioral disorders. *Behavioral Disorders, 25,* 93–105.

Doll, B., & Lyons, M. A. (1998). Risk and resilience: Implications for the delivery of educational and mental health services in the schools. *School Psychology Review, 27,* 348–363.

Epstein, M. H., & Cullinan, D. (1994). Characteristics of children with emotional and behavioral disorders in community-based programs designed to prevent placement in residential facilities. *Journal of Emotional and Behavioral Disorders, 2*(1), 51–58.

Fagan, T. K. (2000). Practicing school psychology: A turn-of-the century perspective. *American Psychologist, 55,* 754–757.

Freeman, A., & Dolan, M. (2001). Revisiting Prochaska and DiClemente's stages of change theory: An expansion and specification to aid in treatment planning and outcome evaluation. *Cognitive and Behavioral Practice, 8,* 224–234.

Freeman, A., Pretzer, J., Fleming, B., & Simon, K. M. (2004). *Clinical applications of cognitive therapy* (2nd ed.). New York: Kluwer Academic/Plenum Publishers.

Friedberg, R. D., & McClure, J. M. (2002). *Clinical practice of cognitive therapy with children and adolescents: The nuts and bolts.* New York: Guilford Press.

Goldstein, S., & Goldstein, M. (1998). *Managing attention deficit hyperactivity disorder in children: A guide for practitioners* (2nd ed.). New York: Wiley.

Hoagwood, K. B., & Erwin, H. D. (1997). Effectiveness of school-based mental health services. *Journal of Child and Family Studies, 6*(4), 435–451.

Kazdin, A. E., & Weisz, J. R. (1998). Identifying and developing empirically supported child and adolescent treatments. *Journal of Consulting and Clinical Psychology, 66,* 19–36.

Kendall, P. C. (Ed.). (2000). *Child and adolescent therapy: Cognitive-behavioral procedures.* New York: Guilford Press.

Kendall, P. C., & MacDonald, J. P. (1993). Cognition in the psychopathology of youth and implications for treatment. In K. S. Dobson & P. C. Kendall (Eds.), *Psychopathology and cognitition* (pp. 387–430). San Diego: Academic Press.

Kessler, R. C., Berglund, P., Demler, O., Jin, R., & Walters, E. E. (2005). Lifetime prevalence and age-of-onset distributions of DSM-IV disorders in the national comorbidity survey. *Archives of General Psychiatry, 62*(6), 593–602.

Kusche, C. A., & Greenberg, M. T. (1994). *The PATHS (Promoting Alternative Thinking Strategies) curriculum.* Seattle, WA: Developmental Research and Programs.

Larson, J., & Lochman, J. E. (2002). *Helping schoolchildren cope with anger: A cognitive-behavioral intervention.* New York: Guilford Press.

Mennuti, R., & Christner, R. W. (in press). School-based cognitive-behavioral therapy (CBT). In A. Freeman (Ed.), *International Encyclopedia of Cognitive Behavior Therapy.* New York: Kluwer.

Ollendick, T. H., & King, N. J. (2004). Empirically supported treatments for children and adolescents: Advances toward evidence-based practice. In P. M. Barrett & T. H. Ollendick (Eds.), *Handbook of interventions that work with children and adolescents: Prevention and treatment* (pp. 3–25). New York: John Wiley & Sons.

Olweus, D., & Limber, S. (1999). *Blueprint for violence prevention: Book nine. Bullying Prevention Program.* Denver, CO: C & M Press.

Prochaska, J. O., & DiClemente, C. C. (1982). Transtheoretical therapy: Toward a more integrative model of change. *Psychotherapy: Theory, Research and Practice,* 276–288.

Prochaska, J. O., DiClemente, C.C., & Norcross, J. C. (1992). In search of how people change: Applications to addictive behaviors. *American Psychologist, 47,* 1102–1114.

Prochaska, J. O., Redding, C. A., Harlow, L. L., Rossi, J. S., & Velicer, W. F. (1994). The transtheoretical modal and HIV prevention: A review. *Health Education Quarterly, 21,* 471–486.

Reinecke, M. A., Dattilio, F. M., & Freeman, A. (Ed.). (2003). *Cognitive therapy with children and adolescents: A casebook for clinical practice* (2nd ed.). New York: The Guilford Press.

Rutter, M. (1985). Resilience in the face of adversity: Protective factors and resistance to psychiatric disorders. *British Journal of Psychiatry, 147,* 598–611.

Shirk, S. R., & Karver, M. (2003). Prediction of treatment outcome from relationship variable in child and adolescent therapy: A meta-analytic review. *Journal of Consulting and Clinical Psychology, 71,* 452–464.

Shure, M. B. (2001). *I can problem solve (ICPS): An interpersonal cognitive problem-solving program.* Champaign, IL: Research Press.

U.S. Department of Health and Human Services. (1999). *Mental health: A report of the Surgeon General.* Rockville, MD: U.S. Department of Health and Human Services, Substance Abuse and Mental Health Administration, Center for Mental Health Services, National Institutes of Health, National Institute of Mental Health.

U.S. Department of Health and Human Services (2000). *Report of the Surgeon General's conference on children's mental health: A national action agenda.* Washington, DC: Author.

U.S. Department of Health and Human Services. (2001). *Mental health: Culture, race, and ethnicity: A supplement to the mental health: A report of the Surgeon General.* Rockville, MD: U.S. Department of Health and Human Services, Substance Abuse and Mental Health Administration, Center for Mental Health Services, National Institutes of Health, National Institute of Mental Health.

Vernon, A. (2002). *What works when with children and adolescents: A handbook of individual counseling techniques.* Champaign, IL: Research Press.

Walker, H. M., Ramsey, E., & Gresham, F. M. (2004). *Antisocial behavior in school: Evidence-based practices* (2nd ed.). Belmont, CA: Thompson Learning/Wadsworth.

Weisz, J. R., & Jensen, P. S. (1999). Efficacy and effectiveness of child and adolescent psychotherapy and pharmacotherapy. *Mental Health Services Research, 1,* 125–157.

2

Multicultural Issues in Working with Children and Families: Responsive Intervention in the Educational Setting

SAMUEL O. ORTIZ

On the whole … we are inadequately prepared to deal with cultural diversity. (Honigmann, 1963, p. 1)

As a graduate student in the early 1980s, I recall a common experience whereby a practicum instructor would suddenly become aware that I was bilingual (and bicultural—but, sadly, this aspect of my background went completely ignored in my training). On finding out that I could speak Spanish fluently, I often heard the same refrain—"Oh, that's great that you'll be able to see Spanish-speaking clients!" Although I appreciated the encouragement, with minor exceptions here and there, such was the extent of the multicultural "training" I received in the clinical psychology program I attended. I relate this story not to find fault with my education, which I believe was exemplary in every respect possible, but, rather, to illustrate the degree to which issues of diversity were and remain poorly understood with respect to psychological service delivery.

Honigmann once noted that inasmuch as "experts who go abroad technically well qualified to cut down infant deaths, improve nutrition, or increase food production are unequipped to understand how the problems with which they must deal are rooted in a foreign way of life" (1963, p. 1), so, too, are the school professionals, technically qualified to identify learning disabilities, modify instructional strategies, and provide therapeutic interventions, largely untrained and unequipped to understand how the problems with which they must deal are defined every bit as much by cultural uniqueness and specificity as they are by science and law. Nowhere perhaps is the need for multicultural training and competency more important than the provision of psychological services and interventions to children and families in the school setting.

As the population of our nation's schools continues to grow more and more diverse each year, the need for systemic reform and a movement toward a "language of critique," not merely a "language of inclusion," is rapidly surpassing a critical level (Giroux, 1985). Likewise, on the individual front, the need for school professionals (psychologists, social workers, specialists, teachers, administrators, etc.) to possess some degree of competency in working with children and families who are culturally and linguistically different from their own will continue to increase proportionately, and will begin to have a greater impact on the psychological services and interventions to be rendered by professionals.

MULTICULTURAL COMPETENCE

The provision of any type of psychological services to a multicultural population in the educational setting is not dependent on a unique or culturally specific set of prescriptions or guidelines as much as it is about developing and applying a set of skills and knowledge that represent a foundation in multicultural competency. That is, successful and effective service delivery is predicated on professionals being competent in dealing with cultural differences, not in the acquisition of a new repertoire of assessment or intervention tools. Much like the instructional idiom, "what's so special about special education," the methods and techniques that form the basis of cognitive-behavioral interventions and that work well with the general population also will work well with diverse children and families *as long as the manner in which they interact with differences in culture is recognized and accommodated.*

The development of multicultural competence, or even monocultural competence for that matter, has not been entirely neglected by the education training system, although it has lagged significantly behind the development of other competencies. Current training standards and guidelines set forth by various accrediting bodies (e.g., APA, NASP, etc.) have long included direct references to multicultural education and training objectives as a means for developing practitioner competence in this area. Unfortunately, the fact that culture is easily misunderstood means that the level and intensity of multicultural education and competency development have varied widely among training institutions. The relative ambiguity and subsequent latitude in interpretation and application of the various training requirements are no doubt responsible for a good portion of the variation across programs and likely result in a broad continuum of competency development, ranging from a simple level of cultural awareness to a sophisticated degree of cultural integration in practice. Regardless of the type of training provided, received, or mastered, it is clear that multicultural competency still has not found its way into routine practice in the schools (Halsell Miranda, 2002; Ortiz & Flanagan, 2002).

As noted previously, it is likely that variability in training and subsequent multicultural competency of graduates rests with the distinction between the issues of consideration of culture versus cultural competency. The former is typically the only one addressed in training and by far the more common issue found in the literature. It implies that the mere acquisition of culture-specific facts and knowledge automatically imbues one with an ability to understand the meaning of any given cultural expression, and is thus enough preparation for professionals working with diverse populations. But this notion makes no more sense than the idea that knowledge of the particular sounds and speech patterns of a foreign language allows one to understand what is being spoken. Granted, it is helpful to know such things, but it is far from sufficient. In contrast, it is the concept of cultural competency that is the better target goal for professionals because it provides the ability to understand the manner in which any given technique, intervention, or skill in their repertoire may interact with any given culture they may encounter. Cultural competency is thus based on the development and acquisition of a set of skills and knowledge regarding the interactive process that occurs between cultural elements that define both the services and interventions to be considered and the population to whom they will be given. Having some facts at hand about a particular culture provides only limited guidance and assistance in working with diverse children and families. It is cultural competence that actually paves the way for successful interventions with multicultural populations.

CULTURALLY COMPETENT INTERVENTION PRACTICES

Overview

It should be apparent to the reader that the focus and purpose of this chapter is slightly different from the others that accompany it in this volume. The basic premise already described is based on the distinction between what interventions to use with multicultural populations and what competencies to have when working with multicultural populations. The former issue is addressed at length in the respective chapters of the book, whereas the latter forms the focus of this chapter and the rest of the narrative.

The following section will outline issues that revolve around the *interaction* between the culture of psychological service delivery and the culture of diverse children and families that have been identified in the school literature (Flanagan & Halsell Miranda, 1995; Halsell Miranda, 2002; Ortiz & Flanagan, 2002). It is the nature of this dynamic relationship that helps practitioners best in their efforts to serve children and families from diverse cultures in an appropriate and ethical manner. The basic issues are divided into three distinct domains and have been largely adapted from the work of Ortiz and Flanagan (2002), who have provided a practical and effective framework for developing multicultural competency in the provision of cognitive-behavioral and other interventions within the educational setting. The focus of each of the three domains to be discussed include: (1) knowledge, (2) communication, and (3) skills.

Knowledge Domain

The Culture of the Family. Without question, practitioners need to look to the family first in their attempts to understand whether any given intervention will be appropriate or useful. There exists no more powerful influence in the total development of the individual than that which is provided by the immediate family environment—a milieu that easily stands as a unique culture unto itself (Frisby, 1998). It is crucial that practitioners develop a knowledge base that includes recognition of the substantial and pervasive influences imparted by the family cultural system. It is the family system that defines what children and families believe in, what they do, how they worship, how they interact with each other, what they expect from the school, how they view treatment and intervention services, and much more. Psychologists and other professionals delivering a variety of cognitive-behavioral intervention services in the schools will need to identify these cultural dynamics in order to select and design the most appropriate techniques in service delivery (Helms & Cook, 1999; Leigh, 1998). It is not surprising that the breadth of the culture of the family is too extensive to be covered in much detail in this chapter. Nevertheless, the provision of intervention services can be guided by an understanding of what constitutes the culture of the family and how family systems function in general.

Tseng and Hsu defined *family* as "the basic sociocultural unit … the nest for the growth of an individual, the resource for social support, and the institution through which culture is transmitted" (1991, p. 1). The family is by no means the only method by which culture is passed down through generations. Yet, it is hard to imagine that any other factor plays a larger role than the family in influencing the growth, development, and well-being of its constituent members (Lewis, Beavers, Gossett, & Phillips, 1976). Families with school-aged children come in contact with the culture of the school immediately on enrollment of one child or another into formal education. Depending on the nature and needs of the family and its members, they also may encounter a wide range of service providers in the schools, including school psychologists and counselors. Perhaps the most common reason why the culture of the family and school may conflict with respect to intervention has to do with identified poor academic progress, particularly if associated with a disability, behavioral problem, or emotional disturbance. Whether the interaction between the family and school culture occurs through formal or informal means, such contact may be construed as positive or negative, largely as a function of the background, experiences, values, and attitudes of the family. Some interactions may be welcomed, whereas others may be seen as threatening, embarrassing, even humiliating (Hanson, 1992). For example, families from many Asian backgrounds, Chinese and Japanese in particular, place considerable value on community, harmony, and "fitting in" (Tseng & Hsu, 1991). To be told that a family member has any type of disability is often viewed as disgraceful and as a weakness that is not well tolerated within the family and its cultural community. Likewise, many families of Hispanic and Latino heritage tend to believe that, once their children enter the school system, the school is wholly responsible for every aspect of their education. In fact, they give so much respect to the school that nothing the school decides is ever questioned, and the families believe that any contact from the school occurs only because a child has misbehaved in some way (Dana, 1993). The respect accorded school professionals by Hispanic families is significant and they would not dare to question or impugn the opinions and decisions made in regard to their children. Unfortunately, this also means that Hispanic families will often see the provision of intervention services as the sole province of the school and may not see themselves as collaborators or partners in the process. Therefore, school-based practitioners need to be aware of such family dynamics in selecting interventions as well as in their implementation. Whether a particular family seems to have a passive/active or negative/positive attitude toward intervention is primarily a function of its cultural values and beliefs. Effective interventions will ensue when the practitioner is able to identify the dynamics of the family and plan accordingly (Dana, 1993).

Consider, for example, that African-American families tend to have regular involvement with extended family members. For practitioners to be effective in their intervention attempts, it will be necessary to take the time to learn more about the relationships that children and families value beyond their immediate family structure (Boyd-Franklin, 1989). Hispanic and Latino families also tend to have kinship relations, such as "padrino" or godfather, which are considered quite formal and are based on religious, not legal or biological, grounds. The extension of the nuclear family in Hispanic and Latino families is an important influence to be considered in psychological service delivery (Padilla, 1980; Ruiz and Padilla, 1979). Apart from those discussed here, there are many more aspects of family cultural systems that are important and relevant to the provision of cognitive-behavioral interventions. Among the most salient to be considered by practitioners would be those related to family structure, kinship, power, and roles (Tseng & Hsu, 1991).

The importance of the culture of the family cannot be overestimated as a fundamental consideration in the provision of an appropriate and individualized approach to service delivery where intervention is tailored to the specific needs of the family, as opposed to being simply expedient or typical. Practitioners must develop an understanding of the various dynamics that comprise family culture and that will affect the selection, implementation, and ultimate effectiveness of any interventions that are considered. Integration of the critical elements of the culture of the family and those of the school will enable professionals in the school setting to respond with an appropriate level of sensitivity when working with children and families from any cultural background they may encounter.

The Culture of the School. Because the provision of intervention services rests upon the interaction between cultures, practitioners need to recognize that the school, or perhaps more specifically the provision of psychological services and interventions within the school setting, constitutes its own unique cultural system. As an employee in an educational setting, it is often too easy to take for granted the various aspects of culture-specific knowledge and practices that are inherent in the system. Consider for a moment the language used in schools that is punctuated by terms such as Individualized Education Program, English as a Second Language, differentiated instruction, balanced literacy, collaborative consultation, functional behavior analysis, and so forth. Those not exposed or familiar with the school system and culture are unlikely to have much of an understanding regarding the meaning of these terms and phrases. Beyond these idiosyncratic aspects, schools represent a type of culture that is largely a reflection of mainstream U.S. ideology and values. The manner in which schools operate and individuals within the system interact with one another is as rule-governed, norm-driven, and value-based as that of any family anywhere. Virtually all behavior, terminology, philosophy, and practices are driven by the larger societal influences in which the culture of the school is embedded. According to Samuda, Kong, Cummins, Pascual-Leone, and Lewis:

> We took for granted, also, the cultural orientation of the [White, Anglo-Saxon Protestant (WASP)] mainstream. The school was, in fact, a reflection of the middle class societal norms and teachers were frequently the purveyors of information couched in terms of a collective mindset that almost totally disregarded any kind of minority sociocultural perspective. (1991; p. vii)

The design and implementation of various cognitive-behavioral interventions must give due consideration to the potential conflicts and dynamics that occur when the values of one culture are introduced into the other. Imagine, for example, that a psychologist believes that a student's problematic behavior requires the use of a behavior modification plan in the home as well as the school. And let us say that the behavior plan calls for the measurement of certain behaviors at one-hour intervals. In terms of the school and psychological culture, one hour means exactly that—one hour. But in the cultural context of the home, an hour may not mean precisely 60 minutes, not because there is an actual difference in the way time is marked, but more because of the way time is viewed. In schools, time is a precious commodity and in psychological interventions, it is imbued with psychometric meaning related to a need for rigor and precision in the sampling process. Thus, when an observation is to be made at 60-minute intervals, it is expected that the observation will be made as close as possible to that interval. Similarly, if a meeting is to be held at 8:00 A.M., it is expected that the meeting will start promptly at 8:00 A.M.

Time is not viewed, however, in the same way by all cultures. In the United States, as in schools and in psychological service delivery, it is often said that "time is money" or "time is running out" or "the clock is running" and it is clear that the passage of time is something to be attended to quite conscientiously lest we "waste any time." Yet, in Hispanic and Latino culture, the word for the passage of time is not *run*, but *walk* or *andar*. That is, time "walks." This difference in word usage underlies a greater cultural value difference in the perception of time, its use, and its meaning. Thus, when a parent of a Hispanic or Latino student fails to make a few observations at the intervals expected or shows up 15 minutes late for an appointment, it is not an indication of indifference to others' schedules or the importance of an intervention but, rather, reflects a personal cultural perspective about time that is simply different than that of the schools or that on which an intervention may be based. This illustration highlights the importance of developing the ability to recognize such events for what they truly are—cultural differences—and not attribute them to other causes or reasons. A practitioner need not know how every culture views time, an impossible task anyway, but only that when issues arise it is most likely a reflection of cultural differences that must first be examined and resolved.

The culture of the schools also needs to be understood by practitioners not just as a culture unto itself but also as a culture that greatly influences the development of the very children who are being "educated" within its walls. Children are not learning just the three "r's" while in school, but are in fact being slowly inculcated with the very values schools hold—values drawn from mainstream U.S. beliefs and practices. These beliefs and practices are often quite political and controversial and subject to the whims of the prevailing societal zeitgeist. Recent attempts, some successful, to dismantle bilingual education in several states (i.e., California, Arizona, Colorado, Texas, and Massachusetts), as well as the contentious debates surrounding the teaching of "creationism" as an alternative scientific explanation or direct replacement for evolution as the origin of life on earth, are excellent examples regarding the manner in which schools mirror prevailing public values, thought, and opinion.

The problem for practitioners in the schools is not that the dominant culture dictates the cultural content of the school, but that children, and families to a lesser extent, are absorbing that content to one degree or another. This process, often called assimilation, may create conflicts for some students, particularly those who are second generation (native-born children of foreign-born parents), because they often are the ones who have to balance the values of the "old world" with those of the new. As children from diverse cultural and ethnic backgrounds are inculcated with such new values, some of which may conflict strongly with the old values of the family, the effects on school performance and family functioning can be broad and far reaching, sometimes with potentially devastating consequences. Consider the following illustration of the nature of the values being imparted in the school setting:

Racism is often characterized, albeit facetiously, as an inherited disease—you get it from your parents. I guess I was lucky; I didn't get it from mine. Like so many other unsuspecting children, I went out and got it from a more authoritative source, school. … I was infected with a far more insidious strain that taught me to hate my *own* people because they were different than what society said they should be … speaking Spanish simply wasn't allowed in school. Bilingual education was but a distant dream, and I was expected to learn English immediately upon entering kindergarten, never mind that my parents could barely speak it.… By second grade, my teacher placed me outside the classroom in a small group where I was teaching other Spanish speaking children how to read in English. I distinctly remember feeling superior to these children aspiring to be as proficient as I was in English.… It wasn't that anyone ever said anything to me overtly, and it wasn't that my parents didn't value their own culture or language. There just always seemed to be a clear, unspoken norm that English was *better* than Spanish and that being white was *better* than being brown. It wasn't based simply on being different; it was a question of value. White culture was superior to all other cultures, including mine. (Ortiz, 1999, p.10, emphasis in original)

Even when the values being absorbed by diverse children in the schools do not have such dramatic and negative effects, problems with interventions can still arise. As the student adopts values from the culture of the school, he or she may be receptive to and more easily understand the reasons for particular interventions that are offered and introduced. Indeed, they may work quite well for the student. However, if the family culture is to be a part of the intervention, problems may arise because the family may not have become as assimilated to mainstream culture as the student, and, therefore, may remain much more reticent to accept or have problems in understanding the need, rationale, or purpose of any given intervention. Either way, the interaction between the culture of the family and the culture of the school represents a frontier that practitioners cannot avoid if their intervention attempts are to prove successful. Practitioners must carefully evaluate and assess the cultural dynamics that are shaping and influencing the development of both the students and families they may encounter in the school setting. Irrespective of the nature of the intervention, its success will be based primarily on the practitioner's success in having identified the crucial dynamics involved in the interaction between the culture of the school and the culture of the individual and his or her family.

Communication Domain

The previous illustration regarding how time is viewed demonstrates that language is essentially inseparable from culture. When practitioners seek to provide services in the schools, it is necessarily negotiated via language. But the language of the school or the practitioner may not be the same or even similar to the language that is a part of the culture of the student or family to be served. A significant dynamic is created in such cases where the effectiveness of communication is influenced by differences that exist in the languages of the school and home. Once again, the provision of appropriate and effective intervention services will be predicated on the practitioner's ability to recognize issues that are related to the linguistic issues pertaining to cultural differences.

It seems obvious that if a service provider speaks the same language as the student or family he or she seeks to serve, the process is significantly facilitated. It has been established that parents feel a greater level of comfort in being able to use their native language with school professionals and that it contributes significantly to the development of rapport between the two parties (Helms & Cook, 1999). Being able to speak and use the student's or family's language is certainly a significant benefit, but it is not necessarily the panacea for ensuring foolproof interventions because languages are not all monolithic to the extent often believed. The Spanish spoken in Spain is not exactly the same as that spoken in Colombia or Mexico or Cuba, although they remain intelligible to each other. The cultural influences on aspects of language such as semantics, usage, grammar, pronunciation, and so forth create dialects, idioms, and regionalisms that are quite culture-specific and may have vastly different implications from one culture to another, despite the fact that all may be described as Spanish-speaking. Moreover, communication is much more than verbal expression. A great deal of communication is mediated via gestural or nonverbal expression as well.

Verbal Dynamics. Cultures vary significantly regarding the balance between verbal and nonverbal communication and how much information is transmitted via each modality or channel (Hall, 1976). Asian, Native American, African-American, Hispanic, and other cultures rely primarily on high-context communication in which a significant amount of meaning in communication is derived from shared experience, history, and implicit messages. Such cultures tend to have less vocabulary because there is little concern about verbal precision, given that meaning extends in great part from the immediate context and usage. Other cultures, such as Anglo-European American, Swiss, German, Scandinavian, and so forth tend to employ a low-context form of communication where meaning is transmitted as precisely, logically, and directly as possible via verbally based exchanges (Dana, 1993). Because schools are a reflection of the dominant culture and values of the greater society, the majority of communication occurring within the school culture tends to be primarily of the low-context variety. When the language and culture of the family does not match that in use by the school or service provider, conflicts and misunderstandings will be inevitable. For example, if a student or his family uses high-context languages, interpersonal verbal interchanges that include specific verbal directions, detailed examples, and extensive elaboration, they may well be perceived as being extremely insensitive and overly mechanistic. Conversely, a practitioner who is comfortable using English, a low-context language, may feel uncomfortable in situations with students or families whose conversational styles involve personal issues, extended silence, obscure phrases, or unfamiliar gesturing. School-based practitioners should attempt to identify the contextual style and communication patterns of the students and families they may be serving so that interventions can be presented accordingly, thereby increasing the likelihood of success (Hanson, Lynch & Wayman, 1990; Lynch, 1992).

The most common way in which differences in verbal dynamics are managed in the schools with children and families is via the use of an interpreter/translator. In many cases, they are invaluable in helping to negotiate successful interactions and bridge the kinds of misunderstandings and conflicts that can arise. Care should be taken, however, to ensure that interpreters/translators are well trained for the specific tasks they will be asked to perform. Providing interpretive services in a general school meeting is not the same as translating intervention recommendations or materials. Moreover, interpreters/translators who are called to meetings on an impromptu basis, particularly if they are employees with duties other than providing such services, may appear unprepared, unprofessional, and often give the impression of a lack of respect. Interpreters/translators also must be selected with caution to ensure that they actually speak the child's or family's native language—not simply a variation of the language. As noted previously, the verbal expressions used by a particular ethnic group (e.g., Puerto Rican or Cuban) can vary considerably from those used by another ethnic group (e.g., Mexican), even though each is using Spanish. Differences in simple vocabulary (*habichuelas* vs. *frijoles*; *espejuelos* vs. *lentes*; *guagua* vs. *autobùs*), the affective component of particular words, use of the formal (i.e., *de usted*) versus the informal (i.e., *de tú*), are all examples of the many dialectical and regional variations that can occur during conversations and affect comfort level and degree of awkwardness.

How an interpreter/translator is used also merits consideration by school-based practitioners. For example, the arrangement of meetings needs to be planned so that the interpreter/translator is in a position to facilitate communication between all participants in the meeting and the parent or child. All too often, the interpreter/translator is placed next to the parent and often limited to simply translating the proceedings for the parent by whispering in his or her ear as events unfold. This is unacceptable practice and prevents the student or parent from participating fully or feeling like he or she is an important part of the meeting. In addition, practitioners cannot assume or expect that an interpreter/translator can or will represent the views of the school or the practitioner. To remain fair and to provide the degree of respect necessary during such interactions, the interpreter/translator can be neither a representative for the school nor an advocate for the parent, and should be trained specifically to interpret and not render any opinions. Practitioners who employ interpreters/ translators may notice that the parent's ability to communicate in their native language with the interpreter/translator often leads to a type of bonding and rapport that generates a sense of trust. Parents often turn to the interpreter/translator for advice and guidance and will tend to rely on his or her judgment because they may believe the interpreter/translator is better informed. This should not be allowed to happen. The role of the interpreter/translator is merely to interpret and facilitate communication between the participants so that it should be clear that it is they who are discussing matter, not the interpreter/translator. The interpreter/translator is rightly a figure in the background, not a central fixture of the meeting.

Nonverbal Dynamics. Unlike verbal dynamics, the potential differences and conflicts that may affect communication from a nonverbal perspective are not as obvious or well known. That is not to say, however, that they merit little attention or have correspondingly less influence on communication. Just as with verbally mediated dialogues, nonverbal exchanges can also have dramatic effects on the interactions between a practitioner and a student or family. One significant example of nonverbal aspects that may affect communication involves eye contact. In Hispanic and Latino cultures, it is considered disrespectful to maintain prolonged eye contact. Deference is shown by lowering the eyes, particularly in interactions where status or power is an issue, such as between student and teacher or child and parent. Extended eye contact is sometimes viewed as an intimate gesture such that in some Asian cultures, eye contact between two strangers is regarded as shameful (Randall-David, 1989; cited in Lynch, 1992).

Practitioners should attempt to recognize the various components of nonverbal communication that can influence the nature of interactions with diverse children and families. Some of the more salient components include specific facial expressions, interpersonal distance (small for Hispanic and Asian cultures, larger for Anglo culture), type of physical contact permitted (e.g., a handshake, hug, slap on the back), gestures that show respect (e.g., bowing in Asian cultures, using titles and calling others by surnames only, no first names, in Hispanic cultures), and the often ritualized methods of greeting and dismissal (Dana, 1993; Lynch, 1992). The meaning and manner of these gestures is also influenced by age, gender, religion, and personal preference, as well as professional status and economic background.

It is wholly unfeasible to expect that practitioners working with diverse children and families need to learn each and every aspect of culturally mediated nonverbal communication. Practitioners should instead focus their efforts on being able to identify actual or potential problems that are reflective of culturally based language differences. Once such conflicts are noted, they can often be readily resolved so that they will not stand as obstacles to effective intervention and service delivery. Recognition and identification of nonverbal issues in communication also necessitate understanding one's own cultural expressions. In the United States, there is a value represented by the tendency in meetings to "get right down to business." This may well be related to the value placed on time but is not a universal norm. Parents from other cultures, for example, those of Hispanic and Latino heritage, are not always comfortable with such rigid and formal opening procedures. They may instead expect that meetings will begin with some polite talk about personal health, family well-being, work, and other such topics not directly related to the purpose of the meeting, before turning attention to the matters that precipitated the meeting. This tends to be the opposite of what happens in schools where issues are kept relatively formal and businesslike, and personal information and issues are kept to a minimum if discussed at all. Even when such an issue is recognized, practitioners may themselves feel uncomfortable or awkward in trying to maneuver through it. Engaging diverse children and families successfully and ensuring the success of planned interventions requires concerted effort on the part of practitioners, including patience, effective listening skills, and a willingness to take the time necessary to establish mutual goals. Practitioners may well feel uncomfortable in making such efforts and might even fail to see the relevancy in providing services or interventions. Parents and their children, however, will undoubtedly show their appreciation, and their receptiveness to intervention attempts will increase correspondingly when deliberate efforts are made to show the proper amount of deference, respect, and cordiality.

Skills Domain

Much as with the knowledge and communication domains, the skill domain in cultural competence is not comprised so much of a set of discrete techniques or collection of facts as it is the ability to recognize when and how cultures differ and conflict. Development of this ability is founded upon cultural self-awareness—recognition of one's own cultural perspective (Helms & Cook, 1999; Leigh, 1998; Lynch, 1992). In the section on knowledge, the culture of the school was discussed and it is the one in which practitioners operate and by which they are influenced. Practitioners, however, must go beyond understanding the impact of school culture on their service delivery or its interaction with the culture of diverse children and families. They must also come to appreciate and understand the impact of their own culture(s) on perceptions of self and others from both within and outside the culture. Successful service delivery in the educational setting relies heavily on the degree to which practitioners have developed personal insight into the values, beliefs, experiences, attitudes, languages, and customs they hold. These are often made known by seeing reflections of the same in others outside the culture. As Shweder (1986) notes, "the best way to get inside yourself is to go outside yourself, and as any good ethnographer knows, if you cannot find yourself in the other, you are not going to find yourself at all" (p. 38).

Self-Awareness. The majority of individuals who reside in the United States are at varying stages of acculturation. That is, they are at different stages in the process of acquiring the culturally mediated information, beliefs, values, and norms established by the dominant culture. Individuals who are foreign-born or who reside in homes in which the native culture is maintained to one degree or another are often characterized as in the process of assimilation, which is similar to acculturation but affected by additional factors, notably the native culture. Those who come to identify with the mainstream values espoused in the United States often identify themselves culturally or ethnically as "American," although the term tends to have its own pejorative and ethnocentric connotations. Nevertheless, there is an identifiable mainstream U.S. culture, which emanated primarily from Western and Anglo-European influences. Many of the cultural markers of the previous cultures remain evident today, for example, the emphasis on individualism, regard for independence, movement toward autonomy, interpersonal competition, mastery, equality, punctuality, materialism, progress, and a future orientation. Mainstream U.S. culture also tends to value and promote general interpersonal interactions that are more informally based as opposed to being formal or rigid. There is also a high regard for individual achievement in most areas of functioning and societal roles as well as an appreciation of very direct and assertive communication styles (Helms & Cook, 1999; Leigh, 1998). Practitioners in the schools will identify with these values to one degree or another and the extent to which they do is critical in understanding how their service delivery and intervention practices are being influenced (Leigh, 1998; Lynch, 1992).

Recognition of culture-specific differences between one's own worldview and that of others is the basis of cultural self-awareness. For example, the current norm regarding school achievement for children in this country is most likely a minimum of a high school education; some might say perhaps even college education has become the standard. Of course, this is a modern value based on industrial and technological innovations, which have necessitated a shift in such beliefs. Not many generations ago, an 8th- or even 6th-grade education was considered quite advanced; yet what parent today would accept their 16-year-old's request to dispense with further education and drop out of high school to enter the workforce straightaway? The reaction is not dissimilar to that which is often encountered in the schools where some Native American and Hispanic-American parents are criticized for having what seems to be a relaxed attitude toward their children's achievement (Huang, 1989; Huang & Gibbs, 1992). Consider that many parents of diverse children in the schools today may have very limited or no education whatsoever. To see their children attend formal public schools for 8 or 10 years straight may represent a kind of blessing and dream that was unimaginable for them and their children when resident in their native country. From one perspective, that much formal schooling does not even represent the minimum expected; from the other perspective, it represents the education of a lifetime. Neither value is better than the other, and practitioners working with diverse families must become aware of these differences and how they influence and interact with the delivery of mental health services and interventions in the school. Other areas where such values may conflict include (1) the mainstream U.S. value on independence and autonomy in young children (compared to emphasis on family unity and cohesiveness found in other cultures); (2) beliefs regarding active promotion of and attainment of developmental milestones (which vary considerably from culture to culture); (3) concerns regarding slight deviations from the norm (differences are either more or less tolerated); and (4) values regarding individual achievement and interpersonal competition (as opposed to cultures that reinforce interpersonal affiliation, cooperation, and reciprocity). Even the most personal beliefs held by practitioners in the schools can come into conflict with those held by children and families in the schools. For example, the dominant philosophy guiding the identification of disabilities in children is rooted in a medical model that ascribes the source of a disability to physiological and other structural physical deficits. Children and families may come from cultures whose notions of disability (if it exists at all) and, more importantly, their treatment and the nature of interventions, may take a purely spiritual form (e.g., some Southeast Asian groups) or include spiritually based practices that are common even in some mainstream religions in the United States (e.g., hands-on healing, immersion in water, anointing with oils, and even snake holding; Chan, 1986; Harry, 1992).

It should be rather evident that approaches to intervention carry their own cultural implications. When those values and beliefs conflict with those held by the children or families who are to be served, the effectiveness of any treatment may be seriously compromised. Only when practitioners are able to engage in honest and genuine efforts at self-appraisal is the mechanism for multicultural competency activated. And it is only when this competency is in place that the delivery of psychological services and interventions has a good chance of succeeding and meeting the needs of culturally and linguistically diverse children and families.

Data Gathering. The collection of data underlies decisions regarding treatment and intervention. Once the relevant information has been amassed, practitioners make judgments regarding what may be the more appropriate and effective forms of treatment or intervention. Because practitioners in the schools must gather data to guide their intervention attempts, they must necessarily understand the cultural implications of any information they might obtain.

Data are not gathered in a vacuum. The very nature of the data collection process represents a core set of values that may affect not only the manner in which information is collected but also what information is collected and how such information is interpreted subsequently. Practitioners are particularly subject to the effects of confirmatory bias (Sandoval, 1998), wherein preconceived notions affect the nature of the data that are gathered as well as how the data are viewed. For example, if a practitioner assumes that the academic difficulties a student is having are caused by some type of emotional problem, then the questions asked in interviews, the scales chosen for evaluation, the observations recorded, and the meaning derived from archival records are all geared toward evaluating the viability of that hypothesis. The traditional culture of assessment and evaluation may not allow or may simply not be able to accommodate cultural factors that are relevant to understanding the student's behavior. Ortiz and Flanagan (2002) have outlined various principles that can assist practitioners in avoiding such errors in practice. These principles include:

1. *Establish rapport and build trust.* Use the knowledge bases regarding displays of respect, and appropriate greeting behavior and exiting behavior. Help the family to feel at ease, respected, and provide the opportunity for the family members to fully participate and contribute to the process of service delivery. Use interpreters/translators as necessary but make sure they are appropriately trained and consult with individuals who are familiar with the culture and languages relevant to the purposes of service delivery.

2. *Identify the presenting problem.* School practitioners should listen carefully to the family's perception of any suspected problem and attempt to

understand it from their perspective. They may feel there is no problem at all. It is also necessary to determine the family's past efforts to resolve the problem and to elicit their present understanding of new intervention strategies and goals. Once these issues have been clarified, the school professional will be in a much better position to negotiate intervention strategies.

3. *Learn the family system.* The structure of the family system must be assessed and determined to the maximum extent possible. Particularly important to evaluate are the areas related to family composition, family members' roles and responsibilities, family's interactional patterns, family's support system, family's childrearing practices, and the family's beliefs about the student's suspected handicapping condition and its source. Knowledge of the relevant aspects of the structure of the family system provides the basis for interventions that are appropriate and individually tailored to the particular needs and resources of the family (p. 354).

SUMMARY

The intent of this chapter was to describe the various cultural dynamics involved in the provision of psychological services and interventions to culturally and linguistically diverse children and families in the educational setting. The rapidly expanding diversity of children and families who come in contact with the schools and services provided by schools has made multicultural competency a necessary reality and no longer a forgotten chapter of study in graduate school. The basic premise expressed throughout the chapter is that practitioners need not have or develop an entirely new repertoire of culture-specific skills or knowledge in order to apply cognitive-behavioral interventions effectively in the schools with diverse populations. On the contrary, it was stated that practitioners should have the ability to recognize when cultural factors, or differences in culture, are operating and affecting treatment and intervention attempts. This is a much more reasonable goal and one that allows practitioners to work with a wide variety of children and families even though they may not be very familiar with their backgrounds and cultures.

Multicultural competency in service delivery was broken down into three major domains: knowledge, communication, and skills. These broad domains were discussed from the perspective of potential cultural conflicts and the dynamic interaction of different cultures. Practitioners were provided with examples that can guide their intervention and treatment attempts and generate a greater likelihood of success when working with diverse populations.

The relative absence and variability of substantive training and supervision in the provision of cognitive-behavioral and other interventions with culturally and linguistically diverse children and families has placed the onus for development of multicultural competency squarely on the shoulders of practitioners already working in the field. Hence, the purpose of this chapter was to provide practitioners with both strategies and information that are readily accessible and that can be used irrespective of the particular intervention that may have been chosen. Nevertheless, the development of multicultural competency is no easy task and requires considerable thought and effort on the part of practitioners in order to hone it into a skill that can be applied routinely into everyday practice. Practitioners need to be flexible, open, and willing to implement new ideas and engage in new behaviors that were not demonstrated or taught in their training programs. Such actions are crucial in enabling service providers in the schools to work effectively and sensitively with culturally different families and, in turn, will enable families to feel more comfortable about their interactions with service providers. Indeed, attempts made by practitioners to communicate and intervene in a culturally respectful and appropriate manner will likely meet with some degree of success if only because it demonstrates sincere efforts to try and understand and appreciate the worldview of the child or family. Ortiz and Flanagan (2002) articulate this point well by stressing that:

> Intervening effectively with students and families will come more from a genuine respect of their native values, beliefs, and attitudes than anything else that might be said or done, especially when their views run counter to beliefs that may be held so dearly. In such cases it must be remembered that school psychologists are not often in positions where they are designing interventions for themselves. Rather, the intervention is for others and they will only be successful in so far as they are culturally relevant to the children and families for whom they are intended. (p. 353)

REFERENCES

Boyd-Franklin, N. (1989). *Black families in therapy: A multisystems approach.* New York: Guilford.

Chan, S. Q. (1986). Parents of exceptional Asian children. In M. K. Kitano & P. C. Chinn (Eds.), *Exceptional Asian children and youth* (pp. 36–53). Reston, VA: Council for Exceptional Children.

Dana, R. H. (1993). *Multicultural assessment perspectives for professional psychology.* Boston: Allyn & Bacon.

Flanagan, D. P., & Halsell Miranda, A. (1995). Best Practices in working with culturally different families. In A. Thomas and J. Grimes (Eds.) *Best practices in school psychology, III* (pp. 1049–1060). Washington DC: National Association of School Psychologists.

Frisby, C. L. (1998). Culture and cultural differences. In J. Sandoval, C. L. Frisby, K. F. Geisinger, J. D. Scheuneman, & J. R. Grenier (Eds.), *Test interpretation and diversity: Achieving equity in assessment* (pp. 51–73). Washington, DC: American Psychological Association.

Giroux, H. (1985). Introduction. In P. Freire (Ed.), *The politics of education.* South Hadley, MA: Bergin & Garvey.

Hall, E. T. (1976). *Beyond culture.* Garden City, NY: Anchor.

Halsell Miranda, A. (2002). Best practices in increasing cross-cultural competence. In A. Thomas & J. Grimes (Eds.), *Best practices in school psychology, IV* (pp. 353–362). Washington, DC: National Association of School Psychologists.

Hanson, M. J. (1992). Ethnic, cultural, and language diversity in intervention settings. In E. W. Lynch & M. J. Hanson (Eds.), *Developing cross-cultural competence* (pp. 3–18). Baltimore: Brookes.

Hanson, M. J., & Lynch, E. W. (1992). Family diversity: Implications for policy and practice. *Topics in Early Childhood Special Education, 12*(3), 283–306.

Hanson, M. J., Lynch, E. W., & Wayman, K. I. (1990). Honoring the cultural diversity of families when gathering data. *Topics in Early Childhood Special Education, 10*(1), 112–131.

Harry, B. (1992). Developing cultural self-awareness: The first step in values clarification for early interventionists. *Topics in Early Childhood Special Education, 12*(3), 333–350.

Helms, J. E., & Cook, D. A. (1999). *Using race and culture in counseling and psychotherapy.* Boston, MA: Allyn & Bacon.

Honigmann, J. J. (1963). *Understanding culture.* New York: Harper & Row.

Huang, L. N. (1989). Southeast Asian refugee children and adolescents. In J. T. Gibbs and L.N. Huang (Eds.), *Children of color: Psychological interventions with minority youth* (pp. 278–321). San Francisco: Jossey-Bass.

Huang, L. N., & Gibbs, J. T. (1992). Partners or adversaries? Home-school collaboration across culture, race, and ethnicity. In S. L. Christenson & J. C. Conoley (Eds.), *Home-school collaboration* (pp. 81–109). Bethesda, MD: National Association of School Psychologists.

Leigh, J. W. (1998). *Communicating for cultural competence.* Boston: Allyn & Bacon.

Lewis, J. M., Beavers, W. R., Gossett, J. T., & Phillips, V. A. (1976). *No single thread: Psychological health in family systems.* New York: Brunner/Mazel.

Lynch, E. W. (1992). Developing cross-cultural competence. In E. W. Lynch & M. J. Hanson (Eds.), *Developing cross-cultural competence* (pp. 35–61). Baltimore: Brookes.

Ortiz, S. O. (1999). You'd never know how racist I was, if you met me on the street. *Journal of Counseling and Development, 77*(1), 9–12.

Ortiz. S. O., & Flanagan, D. P. (2002). Best practices in working with culturally diverse children and families. In A. Thomas & J. Grimes (Eds.), *Best practices in school psychology, IV* (pp. 337–352). Washington, DC: National Association of School Psychologists.

Padilla, A. M. (1980). The role of cultural awareness and ethnic loyalty in acculturation. In A. M. Padilla (Ed.), *Acculturation: Theory, models and some new findings* (pp. 47–84). Boulder, CO: Westview.

Randall-David, E. (1989). *Strategies for working with culturally diverse communities and clients.* Washington, DC: Association for the Care of Children's Health.

Ruiz, R. A., & Padilla, A. M. (1979). Counseling Latinos. In D. R. Atkinson, G. Morten, and D. W. Sue (Eds.), *Counseling American minorities: A cross cultural perspective* (2nd ed., pp. 213–231). Dubuque, IA: Wm. C. Brown.

Samuda, R. J., Kong, S. L., Cummins, J., Pascual-Leone, J., & Lewis, J. (1991). *Assessment and placement of minority students.* New York: C. J. Hogrefe/Intercultural Social Sciences.

Sandoval, J. (1998a). Test interpretation in a diverse future. In J. Sandoval, C. L. Frisby, K. F. Geisinger, J. D. Scheuneman, and J. R. Grenier (Eds.), *Test interpretation and diversity: Achieving equity in assessment* (pp. 387–401). Washington, DC: American Psychological Association.

Shweder, R. A. (1986, September 21). Storytelling among the anthropologists. *New York Times Book Review, 7*(1), 38–39.

Tseng, W. S., & Hsu, J. (1991). *Culture and family: Problems and therapy.* New York: Haworth.

3

A Cognitive-Behavioral Case Conceptualization Approach for Working with Children and Adolescents

VIRGINIA B. MURPHY & RAY W. CHRISTNER

Providing psychological counseling services to children and adolescents is not as simple as knowing and implementing a series of techniques. Although it is important to have an extensive knowledge base of intervention strategies (e.g., your "bag of tricks"), knowing when, for whom, and at what times to apply specific techniques is key to providing services. Through a case conceptualization approach, clinicians have the opportunity to progress from nomothetic information obtained from the literature to idiographic situations within their practice. This process follows a problem-solving approach, which promotes individual and specific intervention planning, while it avoids engaging in "one size fits all" services. A case conceptualization model involves the development of a provisional *description* about an individual's presenting problems and a set of *inferences* about the causes and maintaining factors that helped to establish and perpetuate the presenting problems. This understanding of the individual's specific situation guides in the selection and implementation of strategies and provides a means to monitor the individual's progress.

Although many case formulation approaches exist (e.g., Persons, 1989, 1993; Messer & Wolitzky, 1997; Needleman, 1999), the following case conceptualization model grew out of the frustration that most formulations focus exclusively on adult patients. In our search, we located few case conceptualization models designed for use with children (e.g., Friedberg & McClure, 2002; O'Connor, 2000). Although these conceptualization models contributed to our understanding of the nature of childhood psychological problems, they did not fully capture the various components deemed necessary to formulate an understanding of a child's problems in general and, more specifically, those problems that arise in a school setting. The model presented here incorporates components from several existing case conceptualization approaches, but further addresses contextual and developmental factors that uniquely contribute to the efficient and effective treatment of children and adolescents.

WHY USE A CASE CONCEPTUALIZATION APPROACH?

A case conceptualization is a dynamic and efficient way to capture the multifaceted issues presented by each child or adolescent. From this process flows an individualized intervention or treatment plan that accounts for the child's cognitive, affective, and behavioral functioning, while simultaneously considering cultural and familial context as well as developmental level. An accurate case conceptualization provides the clinician with detailed information about the child's past behavior, explains current behavior, and allows for prediction of future behavior (Needleman, 1999).

Perhaps the most powerful rationale for using a case conceptualization approach can be illustrated with the following example. A 10-year-old Caucasian boy presents to you for psychological counseling because he has seemingly unpredictable, prolonged temper tantrums within the classroom. As a competent professional, you gather extensive background data from parents and teachers, attempt to pin down the antecedents to his outbursts, and begin helping the child identify situational and cognitive triggers to his anger. You offer behavioral strategies to his teacher, and you provide the student with coping statements and relaxation techniques. You soon discover that your interventions are not working. Almost every clinician in the field of child mental health can relate a similar story—despite multiple interventions, the child does not respond, and both the student and the adults who care for him or her experience frustration. A case conceptualization approach provides a clear understanding of the underlying mechanisms that generate and perpetuate the problems and subsequently minimizes the likelihood that a clinician will choose inappropriate interventions or will attempt to "put out fires" by treating individual symptoms as they emerge.

Although empirically based treatment programs exist for a wide variety of childhood disorders (e.g., March & Mulle, 1998; Stark, Sander, Yancy, Bronik, & Hoke, 2000), each youngster is unique; therefore, having an accurate understanding of his or her idiosyncratic cognitive, affective, and behavioral responses is crucial in designing effective interventions. Although using an empirically based or "manualized" treatment program may be perfectly appropriate for some students, it is necessary to base this on each child or adolescent's individual profile and need (Persons, 1989). By using a case conceptualization approach, this individualization can be provided.

Of special consideration when working with children and adolescents is the ways in which developmental level influences case conceptualization and treatment planning. A clear understanding of the child's developmental level across domains is perhaps the most important area for the professional to consider when developing intervention strategies. Assessing developmental level requires a thorough understanding of normal child development, including cognitive, moral, social, and emotional development. The inclusion of developmental level as part of your conceptualization helps to ensure that you will apply interventions that are developmentally appropriate, as well as apt to address the specific set of presenting problems. For example, the 10-year-old boy mentioned earlier may actually be operating as a 5-year-old in terms of his social and emotional development. This knowledge will greatly influence the choice of strategies, the pace of therapy, and the language used during the sessions.

Formulating treatment based on a comprehensive case conceptualization has several benefits beyond the selection of efficient and efficacious interventions. In addition, it provides professionals with information to understand the underlying mechanisms from which an individual's presenting problems stem. Jacqueline B. Persons and colleagues suggest that case conceptualizations provide an "umbrella" under which presenting problems are viewed as stemming from a single underlying mechanism (Persons, 1989; Persons & Tompkins, 1997). This underlying mechanism may be a core belief connected to unlovability, trust, poor self-efficacy, or a multitude of others. In other cases, the underlying mechanism may be an organically based disorder, such as Bipolar Disorder or Schizophrenia. In still other cases, it may be related to the context in which the individual exists, such as in situations of abuse or severe neglect.

With children and adolescents, however, professionals must be aware that it is rare for problems to stem from a single source. Instead, many problems are comprised of multiple, interacting factors, which have an effect on each other (see Figure 3.1). Thus, a child diagnosed as having Attention-Deficit/Hyperactivity Disorder (ADHD) may exhibit a high level of impulsiveness, which is the impetus behind much of his acting out behaviors. However, his behaviors result in a change in his environment, as his teachers and parents more frequently provide reprimands for his misbehavior. This interaction results in a more negative mood, which then exacerbates his behavior outbursts and frustration. Having an understanding of this dynamic allows for the inclusive treatment of all the components, without attempting to treat each factor sequentially. If components of the presenting problem are treated sequentially, the clinician may miss "the big picture" and treat each component in isolation. Inadvertently, this may result in the clinician providing ineffective interventions.

Many mental health professionals practice from a diagnosis-driven model of treatment. Similarly, special education services are offered based on educational classification. A diagnosis or classification simply summarizes a list of symptoms into a single label, yet it does not offer the clinician valuable, idiosyncratic information about the child that can be used to formulate an overall intervention plan. Friedberg and McClure (2002) noted that diagnostic classifications are atheoretical; however, case conceptualizations are derived from the clinician's theoretical framework. Theory-derived (or "top-down") formulations allow the case conceptualization to be grounded in a well-researched, empirically validated theory. In a recent critical analysis of the cognitive case formulation approach (Bieling & Kuyken, 2003), it was noted that many of the elements of cognitive theory have been extensively studied and substantiated. However, further study is required to validate the integrated cognitive components of a case formulation empirically. We are not suggesting that diagnoses have no place within our model. Instead, we suggest that

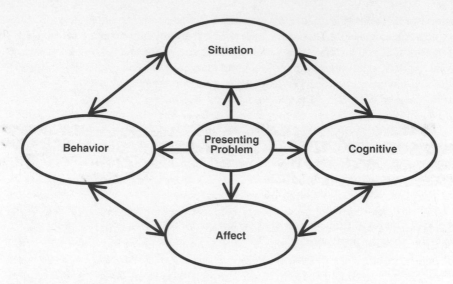

Figure 3.1 Multidirectional interactions.

an accurate diagnosis flows naturally from an accurate case conceptualization.
Diagnoses or classifications are an integral component of a thorough case conceptualization, though they are not a driving force behind case formulation.

The accurate diagnosis of children and adolescents can be a more complex process than with adults. Children's problematic behaviors can be attributed to several diagnostic categories, and children often do not possess the insight or the language skills needed to articulate their problems. For this reason, case conceptualization offers a thorough means to understand the child's problem while developing an individualized program. Returning to the example of the 10-year-old boy described earlier, are his "rage attacks" caused by anger problems (as in Intermittent Explosive Disorder or Oppositional Defiant Disorder), or are they attributable to the fight response (as seen in some children with anxiety disorders)? By contrast, are they best explained by an organically based disorder, such as childhood-onset Bipolar Disorder? Treatment will vary significantly based on the underlying mechanism beneath his rage attacks. A functional behavioral analysis of his explosive outbursts would likely provide valuable information; however, this information alone would not adequately capture the socioemotional, contextual, cognitive, and affective components at work.

A final reason for a case conceptualization approach is that, in many cases, it serves as an intervention tool in itself. A new formulation of the presenting problems can assist the child, or more often his or her family, in viewing the problem in a novel way that allows new avenues for resolution of the problems (Bergner, 1998). In many cases, the sharing of a case conceptualization with a child and his or her family can lead to a moment of insight through which the family can begin to recognize and modify factors that had been maintaining the problem behaviors or emotional states. For example, a case conceptualization was shared with the family of a 10-year-old boy with Obsessive Compulsive Disorder (OCD). In sharing the formulation, the mother came to her own awareness that she was unknowingly contributing to her child's avoidant strategies by insisting that he "just stop thinking" about the focus of his obsessions. She became quite open to altering her approach to her child's symptoms after an accurate case formulation was explained, thus allowing treatment to proceed efficiently and across settings.

EXISTING MODELS OF THE CASE CONCEPTUALIZATION APPROACH

As mentioned earlier, a number of models of case conceptualization currently exist. This section will highlight the major approaches in existence, discuss their contributions to the field of case formulation, and highlight their drawbacks in working with the specific population of children and adolescents in educational settings. There are several commonalities found in most case conceptualization models. Each model explains presenting problems in operationalized terms and allows for the development of hypotheses regarding the cause(s) of the presenting problems. Additionally, all conceptualization models are used as a framework or guide for treatment planning and intervention selection.

J. B. Persons (1989, 1993) developed one of the earliest and most elegant cognitive case formulation models. Her model focuses on two levels: (1) overt symptoms/problems and (2) underlying cognitive mechanisms that serve to establish and maintain the symptoms. A key component of this model is the concentration on core beliefs/schema, which typically comprises the underlying mechanisms responsible for the existence of the presenting problems. This model takes into account the cognitive, affective, and behavioral components of the presenting problems and the origins of the underlying mechanisms, as well as provides guidance regarding the most effective intervention point in therapy, given the case formulation. Person's model is a valuable clinical tool that provides a simple format for recording all components of the conceptualization; however, it was developed based on an adult client population. Its utility with a younger population is somewhat limited, since it does not take into account the developmental and contextual variables, which are so important in child-centered mental health treatment.

J. S. Beck (1995) also developed a case formulation system similar in many aspects to Person's model, but with a clearer focus on the importance of the developmental history of the patient. Her approach integrates developmental experiences, core beliefs, conditional assumptions, and compensatory strategies into a cohesive conceptualization format and, like Person's model, provides a one-page worksheet for outlining all the case formulation steps. Whereas J. S. Beck's model emphasizes the important role of early developmental experiences in maladaptive schema formation, it is clearly a model designed for use with adult populations—the focus is on earlier developmental experiences, rather than a combination of experiences and developmental level.

Like the models developed by Persons and J. S. Beck, Needleman (1999) described an additional case formulation model from a cognitive perspective. His systematized case conceptualization is very similar to the previous models, although an improvement in Needleman's model is his greater focus on the applicability of a case conceptualization approach to many common presenting problems, including depression and several of the anxiety disorders. He also provides a review of the relevant and most currently researched cognitive interventions, and ties them nicely to the case formulation. His work provides a solid approach to cognitive case conceptualization, and readers interested in learning more about the practical aspects of case conceptualization applicability are directed to his work (Needleman, 1999). However, again, his approach is limited in its generalizability to children and adolescents. As is well known, children and adolescents are *qualitatively* different from adults in the ways in which they think, reason, solve problems, engage socially, and behave; therefore, any attempts to make an adult case formulation model "fit" a child's issues would be a grave disservice.

We found two case formulation models developed specifically for use with children and adolescents. One (Friedberg & McClure, 2002) describes a straightforward approach to identifying the interpersonal, cognitive, behavioral, mood, and physiological presenting problems, and emphasizes the role of contextual variables and culture vicissitudes on the development and maintenance of those presenting problems. Developmental history is also a major focus within this model, although there is limitation in the lack of emphasis on developmental level, as compared to chronological age. One of the most valuable aspects of a case conceptualization approach is its ability to inform treatment planning. Although the Friedberg and McClure model is useful in gathering and organizing data, it does not provide a clear rationale for tying case formulation to effective treatment planning and intervention.

The other child-based case formulation model comes from the play therapy literature (O'Connor, 2000), and describes a three-phase case conceptualization approach that heavily emphasizes developmental level in terms of socioemotional, cognitive, and physical functioning. In fact, termination of services is considered only when the child's functioning is as close to being as developmentally and age appropriate as possible, given the child's particular capabilities. This model also takes into account the contextual or familial factors that maintain the problem, the child's responsivity to his or her environment, and the child's misbeliefs (i.e., maladaptive schema) that play a role in the problems. The misbeliefs, however, are not seen as a major causal factor for the problems experienced by the child. Instead, it is the child's emotional and social functioning, viewed through the lens of developmental level, that drives this case formulation model. Again, the link between case formulation and targeted interventions in this model is weak.

COMPONENTS OF CBT CASE CONCEPTUALIZATION MODEL

By taking components from the aforementioned models, we propose a cognitive-behavioral case conceptualization model specifically designed for use with children and adolescents. This model was developed for child and adolescent clinicians in general, but specific emphasis was given to increase its utility for school-based clinicians providing assessment and mental health services. Consistent with other models, our approach views the establishment and maintenance of child and adolescent problems and psychological disorders from a cognitive-behavioral perspective. However, we further emphasize the incorporation of developmental theories and aspects, contextual factors, antecedent behaviors, and impediments to change in developing a thorough case conceptualization and, subsequently, an efficient and effective treatment worksheet (see Figure 3.2).

Problem List

The first step to case formulation is developing an extensive list of the child's or adolescent's difficulties. Clinicians should state the problems in concrete, behavioral terms. With children and adolescents, it is beneficial to list the students' problems across various domains including school, home/family, interpersonal, community, medical, psychological, and legal. There are a number of benefits identified in the literature regarding the usefulness and need for a comprehensive problem list (see Persons & Davidson, 2001; Nezu & Nezu, 1993), many of which we support. First, having a comprehensive list of the child's problems across domains provides information necessary to identify "themes" in the child's behaviors. When clinicians focus solely on one problem area without considering issues in other domains, they may overlook important factors that contribute to understanding the underlying components of the child's problems. Having a list of all the problems from the start will also help minimize the child, parents, or teachers bringing up different issues throughout the treatment sessions. Using the list, the clinician can work with the child, as well as significant adults in the child's life, on examining the sometimes divergent problems and begin identification of the underlying mechanism, which effectively explains the problems on the list. We suggest that problem areas be written using measurable, observable, or functional terms (e.g., "Failing grades in Math, Reading, and Science" rather than "struggling in school"). It is not always easy to solicit a comprehensive problem list, and at times, the list is unclear because of overlap in behaviors. To assist with these issues, in addition to questioning the student and others about problem areas, a number of assessment tools are available that can augment the development of a problem list. Thorough interviews with parents and teachers also help with the development of the problem list.

Assessment Data

Once a general problem list is developed, this list can be clarified or expanded based on the selection of various assessment tools. A thorough assessment provides information about the child that aids in the formulation of a case conceptualization and, ultimately, affects treatment planning and intervention selection. Assessment data can be obtained through various sources including interviews, objective self-report measures, objective parent and teacher checklists, observations, and psychoeducational test data (e.g., cognitive functioning, academic skill assessment, etc.). Each of these is described later in further detail; however, a thorough review of each instrument is beyond the scope of this chapter. In addition to the aforementioned assessment tools, some clinicians use projective measures such as the Rorschach Inkblot Test (Exner, 1993), Thematic Apperception Test (TAT; Murray, 1943), and

Roberts Apperception Test for Children (RATC; McArthur & Roberts, 1982). Although these instruments can have clinical utility in some cases, they are not necessarily useful in school settings for which psychological counseling is being considered. Therefore, further information will not be provided in this chapter.

Interviews. Structured and semistructured interviews are widely used and considered a reliable method for establishing the existence of a diagnosable condition in individuals of all ages. The use of interview tools provides the opportunity to collect standard evaluation data (e.g., diagnostic criteria). Although both structured and semistructured interview procedures offer guidelines for data collection, structured procedures provide less opportunity for flexibility and clinical judgment to explore

---

COGNITIVE-BEHAVIORAL CASE CONCEPTUALIZATION WORKSHEET
FOR CHILDREN AND ADOLESCENTS

Client's Name: _____   Date of Birth: _____

Race: _____   Gender: _____   Age: _____

School/District: _____

PROBLEM LIST

1. _____
2. _____
3. _____
4. _____
5. _____

ASSESSMENT DATA (E.G., COGNITIVE FUNCTIONING, SELF-REPORT, PARENT/TEACHER RATINGS)

_____
_____
_____
_____

DEVELOPMENTAL CONSIDERATIONS

_____
_____
_____

WORKING HYPOTHESIS *(cognitive and/or behavioral)*

_____
_____
_____
_____
_____

ORIGINS OF WORKING HYPOTHESIS

_____
_____
_____
_____

ANTECEDENTS/PRECIPITATING FACTORS

_____
_____
_____

PENN STATE HERSHEY
Milton S. Hershey
Medical Center

August 12, 2014

KATHLEEN PANKIW
2073 FAIRWAY LANE
HARRISBURG, PA 17112–0000

ed for clinical use. Please contact

ksheet for children and

se interviews offer the
a on the student, while
rn, and target behaviors
that specifically address
adolescents (see Hersen

kist for use with children
ld Depression Inventory
nxiety Scale (RCMAS;
Reynolds & Richmond, 1985), the *Youth Self-Report* (YSR, Achenbach, 2001), the

Beck Depression Inventory—II (BDI-II; Beck, 1996), and the *Beck Anxiety Scale* (BAI; Beck, 1992). Some school-based clinicians also use the *Minnesota Multiphasic Personality Inventory—Adolescent* (MMPI-A; Butcher et al., 1992) to assess personality factors with adolescent students. Two self-report measures that are particularly useful in school settings are the *Behavior Assessment System for Children—Second Edition, Self-Report of Personality* (BASC-2; Reynolds & Kamphaus, 2004) and the *Beck Youth Inventories of Social and Emotional Adjustment* (BYI; J. Beck, Beck, & Jolly, 2001).

The *Behavior Assessment System for Children—Second Edition, Self Report of Personality* (BASC-2; Reynolds & Kamphaus, 2004) offers a comprehensive measure of a child or adolescent's perceptions of his or her behaviors including areas of adaptive behaviors and those consistent with DSM-IV-TR criteria. The BASC-2 has forms available for use with students at varying age levels (e.g., 8–11 years, 12–21 years, and 21–25 years). Some of the areas addressed by the BASC-2 include (although this varies with the age of the student) anxiety, attention problems, attitude to school, attitude to teachers, atypicality, depression, hyperactivity, interpersonal relations, locus of control, relations with parents, school maladjustment, self-esteem, self-reliance, sensation seeking, sense of inadequacy, social stress, and somatization. Although the BASC-2, Self-Report of Personality is an excellent initial assessment tool, its limitation is its length, as it can be overwhelming for students to complete on a regular basis. However, it is valuable in the initial session when problem clarification is needed.

Another interesting and recent self-report assessment tool is the *Beck Youth Inventories of Social and Emotional Adjustment* (BYI; J. Beck, Beck, & Jolly, 2001). The BYI consists of five individual scales that can be purchased and administered in a comprehensive format or separately, depending on the clinician's need. The scales were originally normed for students aged 7 though 14 years, though expanded norms ranging from 7 to 18 years of age are expected to be released in 2005 (J.S. Beck, personal communication, June 14, 2005). The scales assess symptoms of depression, anxiety, anger, disruptive behavior, and self-concept. The five scales comprising the BYI are the *Beck Depression Inventory for Youth* (BDI-Y), the *Beck Anxiety Inventory for Youth* (BAI-Y), the *Beck Anger Inventory for Youth* (BANI-Y), the *Beck Disruptive Behavior Inventory for Youth* (BDBI-Y), and the *Beck Self-Concept Inventory for Youth* (BSC-Y). The unique feature of the BYI is that clinicians can administer the combination booklet including all five scales at the initial assessment, and then select specific scales necessary for progress monitoring. Each individual scale only requires 5 to 10 minutes to complete.

Parent and teacher checklists. As with self-report inventories, a number of available scales exist for use with parents and teachers. The two commonly used scales that assess global issues include the *Achenbach Scales* (Achenbach, 2001) and the *Behavior Assessment System for Children–Second Edition* (BASC-2; Reynolds & Kamphaus, 2004).

The Achenbach Scales consist of the *Child Behavior Checklist* (CBCL) and the *Teacher Report Form* (TRF). The scales assess externalizing and internalizing symptoms to common problem areas including aggressive behavior, anxious and depressed symptoms, attention problems, rule-breaking behavior, social problems, somatic complaints, thought problems, and withdrawal. These problem areas are grouped into six DSM-oriented scales to aid in diagnosis. They include affective problems, anxiety problems, somatic problems, attention deficit/hyperactivity problems, oppositional defiant problems, and conduct problems.

The BASC-2 also has both parent and teacher rating scales that assess common clinical and adaptive areas. The clinical scales include areas such as aggression, anxiety, attention problems, atypicality, conduct problems, depression, hyperactivity, learning problems, and withdrawal. The clinical scales can help identify symptoms as well as aid in clarifying clinical diagnosis. The adaptive scales also provide useful information for counseling including functional communication, leadership, social skills, study skills, and adaptability. These areas can assist in treatment planning by identifying deficit areas that need remediation as well as to find students' strengths.

Observations. Observing behaviors in natural settings is a valuable tool when assessing children and adolescents for clinical or psychoeducational reasons. This information adds a personal component to the assessment that serves as a helpful adjunct to interviews, checklists, and other measures. This is the opportunity to see the student's spontaneous behaviors and reactions within the classroom, on the playground, in the cafeteria, at home, or even in a counseling session. The educational setting is a "natural laboratory" for school-based clinicians to observe interpersonal dynamics and to gather data about the problems facing students including antecedents, consequences, and general level of functioning (Mennuti & Christner, in press). Freeman, Pretzer, Fleming, and Simon (2004) described the use of an in vivo interview, in which the clinician accompanies the student into a problem situation, while concurrently interviewing the child regarding thoughts, feelings, and so on. The information gathered during observations and in vivo interviews is rich with clinically useful data.

Psychoeducational evaluations. Although there is little written regarding the use of psychoeducational assessment in CBT, when working with children in general, and more specifically in schools, the data gathered through such assessment procedures can have significant value in the intervention process. Traditional psychological tests, such as intelligence and achievement tests, provide information regarding the student's general cognitive and academic skills level, which can aid in appropriate strategy selection. For instance, when working with a student with a borderline level of intelligence, clinicians will likely rely more heavily on behavioral verses cognitive interventions. Moreover, clinicians working with children having academic problems (e.g., reading, writing, etc.) should minimize use of techniques such as journaling, thought logs, and bibliotherapy. In addition to traditional assessment techniques, other tools such as curriculum-based assessment (CBA) and functional behavior assessment (FBA) can be invaluable tools in this process. Not only does psychoeducational testing provide information useful in treatment selection, but it also rules out other potential contributing factors to the child's difficulties (e.g., specific learning disability, mental retardation, etc.). Frequently, there have been cases in which a student referred for a behavior problem, and after a more thorough assessment, was found to be academically deficient. When the academic deficits were appropriately addressed, there was a noticeable difference in the child's behavioral responses.

Developmental Considerations

Although there are a number of factors that influence and mediate behavior, professionals working with youths must possess an understanding of the fundamental principles of child and adolescent development (Mennuti & Christner, in press). An understanding of developmental issues can help guide case conceptualization as well as treatment planning. Those clinicians grounded in developmental theory will refrain from attempting interventions that are unsuited for the child's functioning level. It is beyond the scope of this chapter to review all theories of development; however, we will highlight several theories that have a direct impact in working with children and adolescents in a counseling setting. For further discussion of child and adolescent development, we suggest the readers consult a general developmental psychology text (e.g., Feldman, 2002; Keenan, 2002).

Understanding cognitive functioning and development is essential when providing therapy to children and adolescents, especially for clinicians working from a CBT perspective (Knell & Ruma, 2003). To benefit from many of the cognitive-based interventions, a child must have the ability to attend to information, comprehend language, use working memory, and verbally express him- or herself (Christner, Allen, & Maus, 2004; Mennuti & Christner, in press; Reinecke, Datillio, & Freeman, 2003). Because of cognitive development factors, young children often have difficulty "describing experiences, labeling emotions, and identifying relationships between thoughts and feelings" (Knell & Ruma, 2003, p. 339). Thus, it is crucial for clinicians to modify cognitive strategies to meet the child's developmental level. It is important to note that developmental level does not always equate to chronological age.

Although it is important to understand the process of development (e.g., language acquisition, motor development, etc.), there are several traditional developmental theories that are essential in understanding the development of children and adolescents for therapeutic purposes. The work of Jean Piaget (1926, 1930) has contributed a great deal of understanding to the cognitive development of children. When working with school-aged children, clinicians may work with children from the preoperational to formal operational stages (see Table 3.1). Children in the preoperational stage (age 2 to 7 years) remain concrete and egocentric in thinking. Knell and Ruma (2003) note that children at this stage may not fully benefit from talk therapy. At the concrete operational stage (age 7 to 12 years), there tends to be a reduction in egocentric tendencies and an increase in the child's capacity to reason. The formal operational stage, which begins around age 12 years for some, is when an individual's thinking and reasoning skills become more logical, and the capacity to handle abstract concepts develops. Although Piaget presents his concept of cognitive development as stages, our experience suggests these stages may be best represented on a continuum. On this continuum, a child's level of functioning is fluid rather than static. That is, a 14-year-old child who demonstrated capabilities consistent with

Table 3.1 Piaget's Stages of Cognitive Development for School-Aged Children and Adolescents

Preoperational Stage (2 to 6 years)	
Animism/fantasy	Egocentrism peaks, then declines
Symbolic play	Perspective taking
Representational thought	Lacks ability to conserve, reverse, generalize
Concrete Operational Stage (7 to 12 years or higher)	
Can reason with help of concrete, tangible objects	Abstract thinking is still a challenge
Can conserve, reverse, etc.	Reasons using the whole or the parts
Formal Operational Stage (12 years and up)	
Idealistic, abstract thinking	Can see the big picture
Can see many angles to problems	Can reason at higher level

formal operational stage at one time may regress and present at a lower level of cognitive functioning, more consistent with a child in the preoperational or concrete operational stages, following a series of stressful events.

Albert Bandura's work in social learning theory (1969, 1997) also presents valuable information when considering development. Social learning theory suggests that learning occurs as a function of observing the behaviors and subsequent consequences experienced by another individual. Bandura indicates that young children need guidance from others as they explore the environment and learn what they can and cannot accomplish. When a student is in a stressful situation, he or she is likely to observe the reactions of others to assist in his or her interpretation of the situation. It is common for children and adolescents to learn their coping strategies from watching adults in their life. Knowledge of the family's coping style provides indispensable information when working with youth. Although social learning helps clinicians explain certain behaviors, it further provides information that can aid in treatment planning. For instance, to help teach and facilitate effective coping skills, a clinician may use the theory of social learning to aid in strategy development.

Another developmental theory often overlooked in psychotherapy (especially CBT) is Erik Erickson's psychosocial theory. Erickon's model involves the development of our interactions and understanding of others, as well as our knowledge and understanding of ourselves as members of society (Erikson, 1963). Erikson suggested that developmental changes occur in eight stages, which represent crises or conflicts that the individual must resolve. Although Erikson's model views psychosocial development in stages that emerge in a fixed pattern, we view Erikson's model to be more fluid, with less emphasis on ages and stages and more focus on conflicts that individuals of all ages must resolve. Ultimately, the resolution of these conflicts affects the individual's perception and way of thinking. Although it is important for individuals to address each conflict, they may not always be resolved in a specific sequence. Additionally, no conflict is ever fully resolved, and individuals may regress to a previously addressed stage when confronted with high levels of stress or conflict. Take, for instance, a 10-year-old student who according to Erikson is addressing the conflict of *industry vs. inferiority.* Although he may be resolving this conflict appropriately and developing a sense of competence, a stressful event such as parental divorce may cause him to regress to a point of dealing with issues of *trust vs. mistrust*. For most children who adequately resolved earlier conflicts, this regression will likely be a temporary setback and they will resolve the conflict once again. However, those children who struggled with the conflict earlier may have increasingly more difficulty at times of regression. The manner in which individuals resolve conflicts helps to formulate their ways of thinking. Figure 3.3 provides information on characteristics of thinking that individuals may develop; however, it should be noted that the individual's way of thinking might take on either a positive or negative tone. For instance, resolution of *trust vs. mistrust* may develop ways of thinking that promote realistic hope for the future, whereas in other cases it may result in thoughts of hopelessness.

The final developmental theory presented here is Maslow's theory of human motivation (1968). Maslow suggested five levels of human needs that individuals need to achieve or satisfy, which he termed *hierarchy of needs*. An individual cannot

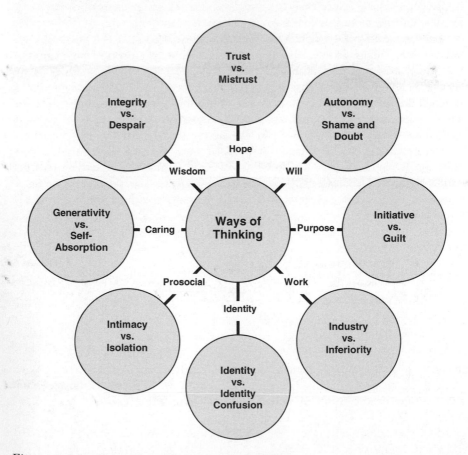

Figure 3.3 Psychosocial conflicts and ways of thinking.

satisfy higher-order needs until he or she first meets his or her lower-order needs. Maslow's hierarchy begins with *physiological needs,* which include food, water, shelter, and clothing. For children and adolescents, this may also involve personal belongings that they value in high regard. This is followed by the need for *safety and security.* Maslow's hierarchy progresses then to *love and belonging,* followed by higher-order needs such as *esteem and meaning* and *self-actualization.* Maslow believed it was necessary for an individual to achieve or satisfy lower-level needs before they can work on higher-order growth needs. However, again, professionals should view this model as fluid, suggesting that although having lower needs met may increase a person's capability of meeting higher-order growth needs, there are many individuals that despite lower-level needs not being met can strive for higher goals. For example, consider counseling a 14-year-old student removed from his home because of physical abuse issues. The uncertainty of his physical safety and security may essentially result in his primary focus being on those issues, whereas his striving to meet other needs such as love and belonging and self-esteem may be present, but have less relevance initially. Thus, at the initial phases of counseling for this student, strategies to help build his support network and to increase his personal sense of safety would likely be the most beneficial starting point for intervention. This is also the case with students whose physiological needs are not being met at home (e.g., eating, sleeping, etc.). The student who is not sleeping because of ongoing parental discord throughout the night will likely be disinterested in interventions targeting her homework completion. These are important factors that clinicians must understand, but they also involve components that clinicians can address when consulting with other school personnel and parents.

As noted earlier, the theories discussed here are not an exhaustive list nor are they thoroughly addressed. It is imperative that professionals working with children and adolescents become familiar with developmental theories and factors to aid in case conceptualization, as well as in intervention design and implementation.

Working Hypothesis

Persons and Davidson (2001) describe the working hypothesis as "the heart of the formulation." Essentially, the working hypothesis is the clinician's application of cognitive-behavior theory to an individual client—that is, moving from nomothetic theory to an idiographic formulation. The working hypothesis offers a means to begin understanding the interacting effects of a child's problems, with the goal being to identify the "core" reason for his or her difficulties. For instance, a student who is feeling anxious in a test-taking situation may not be anxious because of schemata related to "wanting to be perfect." Instead, his anxiety may be the result of stress over not having time to study because of other activities, which results in tests being overly stressful. When working with children and adolescents, there are advantages to viewing the youth's behavior from both cognitive (e.g., J. Beck, 1995) and behavioral (e.g., Haynes & O'Brien, 2000) perspectives.

Origins of Working Hypothesis

Similar to the work of Jacqueline Persons (1989, 1993), we support the need for clinicians to look at historical accounts of situations that highlight how students learned particular schema or behaviors. This section of the case conceptualization may include observational learning or modeling situations, specific examples of skill deficits, or environmental factors. This information can directly flow out of the developmental theories described earlier. Take, for instance, the case of a gifted student who stopped doing her schoolwork. Her schema reflected the belief, "I must be perfect to be loved." In talking with the student and parents, there were a number of examples that highlighted her rewards for "being perfect" (e.g., getting 100% on tests) and the expressed disappointment when she performed below a given expectation (e.g., getting 93%).

Antecedents/Precipitating Factors

In addition to having an understanding of underlying reasons for a child or adolescent to certain thought, feeling, or behavior patterns, it is necessary to have further knowledge of factors and events that "activate" schema and behaviors. The antecedents or precipitating factors serve as "triggers" for the student's behaviors. Antecedents can have a direct effect on a student or they may set the stage for the behavior to occur (Friedberg & McClure, 2002). The antecedents or precipitating events often are listed in the "event" or "situation" section of a thought record or journal.

For an example of the direct relationship between an antecedent and a student's behavior, take the case of Johnny. As Johnny walked down the hall to class, another student accidentally bumped him in the hall. As a result, Johnny felt threatened and reacted aggressively. In contrast, there may be less of a direct relationship, as in the case of Peter. Peter was an aggressive student; however, there was rarely a direct relationship between a situation and his aggressive acts. On further examination, a pattern was noted that his aggression typically occurred on days following an argument with his mother about the morning routine, which "set up" later aggressive acts.

Maintaining Factors/Impediments to Change

When working with children and adolescents, it is imperative that clinicians consider factors that may maintain a student's difficulties or impede the student from making progress. Far too often, school professionals simple look at the lack of progress with a student as the "student's fault." In some circumstances, the student may be failing to take ownership of his or her part in the problem. However, there are a number of factors that professionals should examine. We suggest that clinicians look at four areas when assessing maintaining factors or impediments to change including the following (Christner, 2004):

1. *Individual Factors*—These include characteristics of the student that interfere with his or her progress, such as lack of readiness or motivation to

change, negative thoughts or feelings, or lack of skill development (e.g., problem solving).

2. *Family Factors*—These involve issues experienced at home or related to home-school collaboration, including caregiver cooperation, family's beliefs about education and counseling, collaboration with school, and family stressors and discord (e.g., mental health issues, etc.). Issues related to cultural factors also should be explored in this area.

3. *Systemic Factors*—These include factors of the school environment that interfere with student success, such as ineffective school discipline (e.g., suspensions, etc.), school policies (e.g., zero-tolerance), poor school climate, and safety issues. In addition, situations in which the school does not have proper educational programs or services to meet the child's needs would be in this category.

4. *Teacher/Classroom Factors*—These involve teacher characteristics or actions and classroom procedures that hinder the student's progress, including ineffective behavior management, poor planning, lack of training, and negative thoughts and perceptions (e.g., about the student, his or her job and competence, etc.).

Protective and Resiliency Factors

School-based clinicians also should have awareness of other prominent research in the developmental psychopathology literature including risk, resiliency, and protective factors (Coie et al., 1993; Doll & Lyons, 1998; Rutter, 1985). Coie and others (1993) grouped empirically derived risk factors into seven domains— (1) constitutional handicaps, (2) skills development delays, (3) emotional difficulties, (4) family circumstances, (5) interpersonal problems, (6) school problems, and (7) ecological risks. Similarly, Rutter (1985) identified three broad domains of protective factors including individual characteristics, interaction with the environment, and broader societal influences (e.g., quality schools). Coie et al. (1993) indicated that protective factors work in one of the following ways—(1) directly decreasing risk, (2) serving as a buffer through interaction with risk factors, (3) disrupting the chain reaction from risk factors to disorder, or (4) preventing the initial occurrence of the risk factor.

Clinicians working in schools can use this knowledge of case conceptualization and intervention design. Interventions may initially build social skills and problem-solving skills in order to promote protective factors while minimizing risk factors (e.g., strengthening peer relationships, increasing self-monitoring skills, improving parent-child interactions, and increasing school success). For instance, building social-cognitive skills in angry and aggressive children has been identified as an effective mediator in the reduction of angry or aggressive outbursts (Kazdin & Weisz, 1998).

Diagnostic Impressions/Educational Classification

In educational settings, the idea of diagnosis is rather controversial. Although there are many professionals that support its use, an equal number see diagnosis as a negative "label" that students will carry with them. Although there are some flaws in diagnosis, we believe it is a valuable tool when conceptualizing an individual case and designing interventions. Earlier in this chapter, we discussed the limitations of a diagnosis-driven approach; however, an understanding of the diagnosis can have its value when working with children and adolescents. The primary benefit of diagnosis and classification is to use empirically derived information about a diagnosis as the starting point for your intervention design. If we have a student who meets the criteria for a Generalized Anxiety Disorder, we as clinicians can use evidenced-based treatment protocols as the basis for developing an effective intervention program for the student. Given that randomized trials are developed and based on diagnosis, clinicians can obtain information about empirically supported treatments for the diagnosis and then flexibly apply this information to meet the needs of individual students.

Intervention Plan

Using a comprehensive case conceptualization, clinicians can use this information to guide the development of a treatment or intervention plan. The intervention plan is not part of the case conceptualization per se, but it is naturally developed from the case conceptualization. By using the conceptualization to guide your intervention plan, each student's unique characteristics will be taken into account. For instance, you may have two students being seen for school refusal, but, based on their unique circumstances, their intervention plans may look very different.

As with treatment plans in most settings, intervention plans in schools should include several key points: goals, modality, frequency, level of intervention, level of family involvement, supplemental interventions, and barriers to treatment. The goals are derived from the underlying mechanism, which explains the existence or maintenance of the problems on the problem list. There are typically many ways in which the clinician can approach those goals, and this decision often is dictated by the severity of certain symptoms over others. Like the problem list, the goals should be written in measurable terms. Specific, measurable goals allow the clinician to track treatment progress closely and accurately, which permits a greater accuracy in understanding if the case conceptualization is adequately capturing the nature of the child's problems.

The modality (e.g., cognitive-behavior therapy, behavior therapy, etc.), level of intervention (e.g., individual, group, consultation, etc.), and frequency (e.g., once per week) also should be noted. With most students, it will be necessary to obtain family involvement; however, this will need to be assessed for each student. In addition to prior interventions, clinicians should also document supplemental interventions utilized. These may include things such as a social skills group, tutoring, or special services (e.g., occupational therapy, speech and language therapy, etc.).

The last component that clinicians should address when planning interventions is barriers to treatment. This helps prepare for the obstacles that a student or family may encounter, and develop ways to overcome these barriers from the start. Early awareness of potential difficulties can help both the clinician and student manage them more effectively. When providing interventions at school, there are a number of barriers to be considered including scheduling conflicts, the completion of between-session work, seeing students you are counseling in other settings (e.g., hallway, cafeteria, etc.), and family resistance.

GENERAL CONSIDERATIONS FOR USING A CASE CONCEPTUALIZATION APPROACH IN SCHOOLS

To ensure that clinicians working in schools apply the concepts provided in this chapter in a way that will maximize the potential for effectiveness, we offer a few suggestions. First, clinicians who develop simple, straightforward case conceptualizations are likely to have greater success. It is important to keep in mind that the most parsimonious case conceptualization is usually the most accurate one. A very complex case conceptualization decreases the likelihood that you have uncovered the true underlying mechanism, and it decreases the likelihood that you will put your case formulation to good use in terms of intervention planning. As in the age-old adage of medicine, "if you hear the sound of hooves, think horses, not zebras." Always take into account the most common reasons for childhood psychological and educational problems before considering other reasons. A good solid understanding of the familial, constitutional, educational, and psychological risks factors for children and adolescents will help inform your case conceptualization approach. Doll and Lyons (1998) provide an excellent review.

Second, remember that cognitive-behavioral case formulations are fluid documents based on hypothesis testing (J. S. Beck, 1995). They are not static documents to be completed once and placed in a student's file. Clinicians should revisit them often, judge them for accuracy, and modify them based on the emergence of new data and student progress. Using a model that moves the clinician through a cyclical sequence of assessment, case conceptualization, and intervention planning not only provides a means to select interventions on an individual basis but also offers a method for progress monitoring (see Figure 3.4). This method of progress monitoring

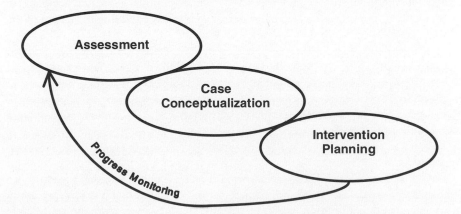

Figure 3.4 Assessment, case conceptualization, and intervention cycle.

is a natural parallel to the existing impetus of progress monitoring in educational areas such as special education services. If a student is not making progress after a period of "stagnation," clinicians should carefully review the case conceptualization with a critical eye and explore the possibility of new hypotheses and intervention goals.

Third, school-based clinicians must be aware of confirmation bias—that is, our natural tendency to hold onto our original formulations, despite existing contradictory evidence. As discussed earlier, a comprehensive problem list can substantially limit confirmation bias, because it includes all issues rather than only those that "fit the theory." Another way to minimize confirmation bias is to engage in peer consultation/supervision and share your case formulations, particularly with your more difficult or complex cases. This may be especially necessary for clinicians who are providing psychological counseling services in schools for the first time in their careers. Colleagues may provide alternate hypotheses regarding the underlying mechanisms, thereby increasing the likelihood that your case conceptualization is accurate and reliable. The results of several investigations suggest that there exists relatively good inter-rater reliability regarding the identification of presenting problems. However, there is relatively poor agreement in the identification of the hypothesized underlying mechanisms, and it appeared that level of training and experience are key factors in reliability (Persons, Mooney, & Padesky, 1995; Eells, Kendjelic, & Lucas, 1998). Thus, in order to increase accuracy and reliability, it is necessary to use a systematized case formulation approach such as the one described here and to engage in regular training, supervision, and consultation regarding your case formulations (see Bieling & Kuyken, 2003, for a critical review of existing research on this subject).

CASE STUDY: "NATALIE"

The following case example highlights the use of the *Cognitive-Behavior Case Conceptualization Worksheet for Children and Adolescents* (see Figure 3.2) with a school-based referral.

Relevant Background Information and Referral Question

Natalie is a 16-year-old biracial girl referred to the school psychologist after repeating the 10th grade. She lived with her father and older sister. Her sister is now attending college. She has a distant, conflictual relationship with her mother, who chose not to raise either child. The contact she has with her mother was described as inconsistent and sporadic. The school requested an assessment and consultation to determine her need for psychological counseling services in school because of emotional and behavioral concerns. Several factors precipitated this request, including Natalie failing 10th grade, being withdrawn, lacking of motivation with regard to her academics, and a recent tendency of isolating herself from both adults and peers. Before her recent academic failure, Natalie was an average to below-average student, often having to attend summer school in order to advance to the next grade level.

Problem List

The following problems were identified through initial interviews with Natalie, her father, and her teachers:

1. Easily distracted in school—"zones out" when the teacher is talking.
2. Is repeating the 10th grade, and has attended summer school every year for the past five years.
3. Takes hours to complete school work, even with close adult supervision.
4. Forgetful, disorganized (i.e., difficulty remembering and getting to extra-curricular activities, appointments, etc.).
5. Constantly feels one step behind classmates, and has fears of disappointing her father with her academic performance.

Assessment

The school psychologist conducted a psychoeducational assessment consisting of administration of the *Woodcock-Johnson Cognitive Assessment* (full battery), *Woodcock-Johnson Achievement Assessment* (full battery), the *Wisconsin Card-Sorting Test,* and the *Integrated Visual and Auditory Continuous Performance Test* (IVA-CPT). In addition, behavior-rating scales, including the *Behavior Assessment System for Children, Second Edition* (BASC-2) and the *Behavior Rating Inventory of Executive Function* (BRIEF) were provided to Natalie, her father, and her teachers for completion.

The findings revealed an average overall cognitive ability but a significant weakness in mathematics fluency and comprehension, as well as chronic problems with attention, focus, self-monitoring, direction of reasoning abilities, and distraction. There were clinically significant elevations on the Depression subscale of the BASC-2 self-report, and follow-up assessment (structured clinical interview) revealed a mild to moderate depression. On further exploration, it was determined that this depressive presentation had been a chronic condition for Natalie since the 8th grade.

Developmental Considerations

Despite her age, Natalie presented as being in the latter stage of Concrete Operations, as she struggled with tasks requiring fluid, abstract reasoning, and means-end thinking. From a socioemotional standpoint, Natalie was resolving the issues of *Identity vs. Identity Confusion,* yet she did not resolve earlier developmental conflicts. This failure to negotiate earlier developmental tasks successfully appeared to be interfering with normal identity formation. When meeting with Natalie, she seemed to be in *Identity Diffusion,* and she resisted taking on age-appropriate responsibilities.

Natalie had unresolved conflicts regarding *Industry vs. Inferiority* that occurred during her elementary school years, when her problems with inattention and distractibility became problematic. Her teachers often overlooked her attention problems, as she always presented as a pleasant and well-behaved child. Her frustration at herself for her forgetfulness, distractibility, and inability to complete assignments at this socioemotional stage led to feelings of inferiority and a chronically low self-concept. In her current socioemotional development, she was beginning to incorporate her feelings of inferiority into her perception of self.

Working Hypothesis

Natalie had schema regarding inadequacy and incompetence, and these schema gave rise to constant beliefs and automatic thoughts such as, "I'm not as smart as the others" and "I can't do this—I'm stupid." These schemas developed from the aforementioned developmental experiences. Depressive features were the result of her negative schema and perception of self. Cognitively, she had great difficulty with abstract thinking and reasoning, and she was essentially a concrete thinker. This difficulty further perpetuates her negative perception of self and feelings of inferiority.

Origins of Working Hypothesis

The presence of persistent attention and distractibility problems, in addition to concomitant limitations in some aspects of executive functioning (e.g., inefficient direct reasoning and poor self-monitoring) were seen as originating factors. Her experiences and failures around these issues further exacerbated her difficulties.

Antecedents

Natalie's failure of 10th grade set the stage for her to seek help for her academic problems. Additionally, however, this situation had a direct impact on increasing her feelings of depression and belief that she was inferior.

Maintaining Factors/Impediments to Change

Individual factors. Natalie's executive dysfunction and chronic attention problems continued to play a role in her academic difficulties as well as her negative thoughts and feelings.

Teacher/classroom factors. Because Natalie was well behaved in the classroom, her teachers overlooked the fact that she was having difficulties. She was not disruptive, so it was difficult for teachers to identify times when she was inattentive. Additionally, Natalie's teachers view her as "a little slow," and place fewer academic demands on her. Given that her cognitive ability was average, a more intensive, remedial approach would have likely been more appropriate.

Family factors. Natalie's older sister enjoyed a great deal of academic success and majored in premedicine at a prestigious university. Natalie's father helped maintain and reinforce her negative self-view by comparing her to her sister, and using this comparison to try to motivate Natalie to succeed academically. Her father's culture highly valued higher education, and he "held up" Natalie's older sister as an example of "how to get ahead in this world."

Protective/Resiliency Factors

Natalie enjoyed a strong bond with her father, and she had the ability and willingness to seek help from others. Her social skills were adequate and her average intellectual ability was an asset.

Diagnostic Impressions/Educational Classifications

Natalie was diagnosed with Attention-Deficit/Hyperactivity Disorder (ADHD), Predominantly Inattentive Type, and Dysthymic Disorder. She further met the criteria for a Mathematics Disorder (educational classification—Specific Learning Disability in Mathematics).

Treatment Plan

Goals. In collaboration with Natalie, the clinician established the following treatment goals based on the above case formulation:

1. Increase Natalie's knowledge of ADHD-I, learning disability, and chronic mood disorder.
2. Increase affective level, as evidenced by brighter affect, decreased fatigue, increased energy level, and increased motivation to complete schoolwork.
3. Increase ability to attend, concentrate, and focus both in the classroom and during homework time.
4. Assist Natalie in talking with her teachers about her attention problems to increase their understanding.

Level of intervention. Based on this formulation, an appropriate level of intervention to start was weekly individual psychological counseling provided at school, for approximately 30 minutes per session.

Level of family involvement. Consultation with Natalie's father was offered on at least a monthly basis.

Supplemental interventions. Natalie was referred for consultation with the school's consulting psychiatrist regarding pharmacological interventions for her attention difficulties. Biweekly consultation was provided with Natalie's teachers. Furthermore, Natalie received Learning Support services to address her learning difficulties.

Barriers to treatment. Her father's resistance to pharmacological interventions for Natalie's attention difficulties was perhaps the greatest treatment obstacle at the outset, as pharmacological treatment has proven efficacy with children diagnosed with ADHD (Barkley, 1998). In an attempt to overcome this obstacle, a major focus of early treatment was to provide sufficient education and support to the father in order for him to make informed decisions regarding options for Natalie's interventions.

CONCLUSION

As noted throughout this chapter and highlighted in the aforementioned case study, case conceptualization is an important tool to assist clinicians in pinpointing causes of presenting problems, even when such problems are seemingly "straightforward." Although many school-based clinicians have the knowledge to identify symptoms of disorders or educational classifications, it is necessary for them to move toward an approach that "guides interventions" and offers an opportunity for frequent progress monitoring. Furthermore, using our case conceptualization model, school-based practitioners will have a device to go beyond problem identification, to identify factors that may inhibit progress toward the goal, to avoid such obstacles, and to enhance the outcomes for students.

REFERENCES

Achenbach, T. M. (2001). *Manual for the ASEBA school-age forms and profiles.* Burlington: University of Vermont.

Bandura, A. (1969). *Principles of behavior modification.* New York: Holt, Rinehart, & Winston.

Bandura, A. (1997). *Self-efficacy: The exercise of control.* New York: Freeman.

Barkley, R. A. (1998). *Attention-deficit hyperactivity disorder: A handbook for diagnosis and treatment* (2nd ed.). New York: Guilford Press.

Beck, A. T. (1992). *Beck Anxiety Scale.* San Antonio, TX: Psychological Corporation.

Beck, A. T. (1996). *Beck Depression Inventory* (2nd ed.). San Antonio, TX: Psychological Corporation.

Beck, J. S. (1995). *Cognitive therapy: Basics and beyond.* New York: Guildford Press.

Beck, J. S., Beck A. T., and Jolly, J. (2001). *Manual for the Beck Youth Inventories of Emotional and Social Adjustment.* San Antonio, TX: The Psychological Corporation.

Bergner, R. M. (1998). Characteristics of optimal case formulation: The linchpin concept. *American Journal of Psychotherapy, 52*(3), 287–300.

Bieling, P. J., & Kuyken, W. (2003). Is cognitive case formulation science or science fiction? *Clinical Psychology: Science and Practice, 10*(1), 52–69.

Butcher, J. N., Williams, C. L., Graham, J. R., Archer, R. P., Tellegen, A., Ben-Porath, J. S., & Kaemmer, B. (1992). *MMPI-A: Manual for administration, scoring, and interpretation.* Minneapolis, MN: University of Minnesota Press.

Christner, R. W. (2004). *The development and validation of the Impediments to Change Scale—Educational Version: A study of children and adolescents with emotional disturbance.* Unpublished doctoral dissertation, Philadelphia College of Osteopathic Medicine, Pennsylvania.

Christner, R. W., Allen, J. S., & Maus, M. R. (2004, Winter). An overview for selecting CBT techniques in the treatment of youth in schools, *Insight, 24*(2), 8–10.

Coie, J. D., Watt, N. F., West, S. G., Hawkins, D., Asarnow, J. R., Markman, H. J., Ramey, S. L., Shure, M. B., & Long, B. (1993). The science of prevention: A conceptual framework and some directions for a national research program. *American Psychologist, 48,* 1013–1022.

Doll, B., & Lyon, M. A. (1998). Risk and resilience: Implications for the delivery of educational and mental health services in schools. *School Psychology Review, 27,* 348–363.

Eells, T. D., Kenjelic, E. M., & Lucas, C. P. (1998). What's in a case formulation? Development and use of a content coding manual. *Journal of Psychotherapy Practice and Research, 7,* 144–153.

Erikson, E. H. (1963). *Childhood and society.* New York: Norton.

Exner, J. E. (1993). *The Rorschach: A comprehensive system: Volume 1: Basic foundations* (3rd ed.). New York: Wiley & Sons.

Feldman, R. S. (2002). *Development across the life span* (3rd ed.). Upper Saddle River, NJ: Prentice Hall.

Freeman, A., Pretzer, J., Fleming, B., & Simon, K. M. (2004). *Clinical applications of cognitive therapy* (2nd ed.). New York: Kluwer Academic/Plenum Publishers.

Friedberg, R. D., & McClure, J. M. (2002). *Clinical practice of cognitive therapy with children and adolescents: The nuts and bolts.* New York: Guilford Press.

Haynes, S. N., & O'Brien, W. H. (2000). *Principles and practice of behavioral assessment.* New York: Kluwer Academic/Plenum Publishers.

Hersen, M., & Turner, S. M. (Eds.). (2003). *Diagnostic interviewing* (3rd ed.). New York: Kluwer Academic/Plenum Publishing.

Kazdin, A. E., & Weisz, J. R. (1998). Identifying and developing empirically supported child and adolescent treatments. *Journal of Consulting and Clinical Psychology, 66,* 19–36.

Keenan, T. (2002). *An introduction to child development.* Thousand Oaks, CA: Sage Publications.

Knell, S. M., & Ruma, C. D. (2003). Play therapy with a sexually abused child. In M. A. Reinecke, F. M. Dattilio, & A. Freeman (Eds.), *Cognitive therapy with children and adolescents: A casebook for clinical practice* (pp. 338–368). New York: Guilford Press.

Kovacs, M. (1992). *Children's Depression Inventory.* North Tonawanda, NY: MultiHealth Systems.

March, J. S., & Mulle, K. (1998). *OCD in children and adolescents: A cognitive-behavioral treatment manual.* New York: Guildford Press.

Maslow, A. H. (1968). *Toward a psychology of being.* Princeton, NJ: Van Nostrand.

McArthur, D.S., & Roberts, G.E. (1982). *Roberts Apperception Test for Children Manual.* Los Angeles: Western Psychological Services.

Mennuti, R., & Christner, R. W. (in press). School-based cognitive-behavioral therapy (CBT). In A. Freeman (Ed.), *International Encyclopedia of Cognitive Behavior Therapy.* New York: Kluwer Academic/Plenum Publishers.

Messer, S. B., & Welitsky, D. L. (1997). The traditional psychoanalytic approach to case formulation. In T. Eells (Ed.), *Handbook of psychotherapy case formulation* (pp. 26–55). New York: Guilford Press.

Murray, H. (1943). *Thematic Apperception Test.* Cambridge, MA: Harvard University Press.

Needleman, L. D. (1999). *Cognitive case conceptualization: A guidebook for practitioners.* Mahwah, NJ: Lawrence Erlbaum Associates, Inc.

Nezu, A. M., & Nezu, C. M. (1993). Identifying and selecting target problems for clinical interventions: A problem-solving model. *Psychological Assessment, 5,* 254–263.

O'Connor, K. J. (2000). *The play therapy primer* (2nd ed.) New York: Wiley and Sons.

Persons, J. B. (1989). *Cognitive therapy in practice: A case formulation approach.* New York: Norton.

Persons, J. B. (1993). Case conceptualization in cognitive behavior therapy. In K. T. Kuelwein & H. Rosen (Eds.), *Cognitive therapy in action: Evolving innovative practice* (pp. 33–53). San Francisco: Jossey-Bass.

Persons, J. B., Mooney, K. A., & Padesky, C. A. (1995). Inter-rater reliability of cognitive behavioral case formulations. *Cognitive Therapy and Research, 19,* 21–34.

Persons, J. B., & Tompkins, M. A. (1997). Cognitive behavioral case formulation. In T. Eells (Ed.), *Handbook of psychotherapy case formulation* (pp. 314–399). New York: Guilford Press.

Persons, J. B., & Davidson, J. (2001). Cognitive-behavioral case conceptualization. In K. S. Dobson (Ed.), *Handbook of cognitive-behavioral therapies* (2nd ed., pp. 86–110). New York: Guilford Press.

Piaget, J. (1926). *The language and thoughts of the child.* London: Routledge & Kegan Paul.

Piaget, J. (1930). *The child's conception of physical causality.* New York: Harcourt-Brace.

Reinecke, M. A., Dattilio, F. M., and Freeman, A. (Eds.). (2003). *Cognitive therapy with children and adolescents: A casebook for clinical practice* (2nd ed.). New York: The Guilford Press.

Reynolds, C. R., & Kamphaus, R. W. (2004). *Behavior Assessment System for Children* (2nd ed.). Circle Pines, MN: American Guidance Service.

Reynolds, C. R., & Richmond, B. O. (1985). *Revised Children's Manifest Anxiety Scale.* Los Angeles: Western Psychological Services.

Rutter, M. (1985). Resilience in the face of adversity: Protective factors and resistance to psychiatric disorders. *British Journal of Psychiatry, 147,* 598–611.

Sattler, J. M. (1998). *Clinical and forensic interviewing of children and families: Guidelines for the mental health, education, pediatric, and child maltreatment fields.* San Diego, CA: Jerome M. Sattler Publishing, Inc.

Stark, K. D., Sander, J. B., Yancy, M. G., Bronik, M. D., & Hoke, J. A. (2000). Treatment of depression in childhood and adolescence, In P. C. Kendall (Ed.), *Child and adolescent therapy: Cognitive-behavioral procedures* (pp. 173–234). New York: Guilford.

Part II

APPLICATION OF CBT INTERVENTIONS FOR SPECIFIC ISSUES

4

School-Based Interventions for Anxiety Disorders

ELIZABETH A. GOSCH &
ELLEN FLANNERY-SCHROEDER

Although anxiety disorders are the most prevalent mental health problem experienced by youth, it is often children with disruptive externalizing problems such as Attention-Deficit/Hyperactivity Disorder (ADHD) that come to the attention of school personnel. Children with anxiety disorders may be overlooked because of difficulty recognizing their internalizing symptoms, unfamiliarity with diagnostic criteria, and misconceptions regarding the negative consequences of these problems. Most school personnel are surprised to learn that approximately 1 in 10 children suffers from an anxiety disorder, with epidemiological studies estimating prevalence rates between 12% to 20% in youth (Achenbach, Howell, McConaughy, & Stanger, 1995; Gurley, Cohen, Pin, & Brook, 1996; Shaffer et al., 1996). Left untreated, these disorders tend to have long-term effects on social and emotional development. Negative consequences associated with anxiety disorders in youth include academic underachievement, underemployment, substance use, lower levels of social support, and high comorbidity with other psychiatric disorders (Velting, Setzer, & Albano, 2004). Moreover, evidence suggests that these disorders demonstrate a chronic course, often persisting into adulthood (Rapee & Barlow, 1993).

Take the example of Chris, an 11-year-old boy who is painfully shy, avoids answering questions in class, never asks his teacher for clarification when confused about assignments, accepts a failing grade rather than risk presenting in class, and does not talk much with other children. Without intervention, his grades will suffer, he will miss out on the mentorship his teacher could provide, and he will be isolated from his peers. Such a child is at risk for failing to achieve important developmental milestones. Research suggests that he is at risk for becoming depressed (Biederman, Faraone, Mick, & Lelon, 1995; Brady & Kendall, 1992) or abusing alcohol and drugs to cope with his anxiety (Compton, Burns, Egger, & Robertson, 2002; Deas-Nesmith,

Brady, & Campbell, 1998). However, if children such as Chris could be identified early in their school years and receive appropriate interventions, this negative trajectory may be avoided. It is the purpose of this chapter to provide information for school personnel to aid them in identifying and intervening with children at risk for anxiety disorders.

UNDERSTANDING ANXIETY DISORDERS

There are eight types of anxiety disorders described in the *Diagnostic and Statistical Manual for Mental Disorders, Fourth Edition, Text Revision* (DSM-IV-TR; American Psychiatric Association, 2000). For the purposes of this chapter, we are limiting our discussion to three of the most common anxiety disorders—generalized anxiety disorder (GAD), social phobia (SP), and separation anxiety disorder (SAD). These disorders tend to cooccur and cognitive-behavioral treatments for these disorders follow similar protocols that are amenable to implementation in the school setting. Other anxiety disorders in youth such as panic disorder, obsessive-compulsive disorder, and posttraumatic stress disorder require unique treatment components (e.g., March, 1995).

The hallmark feature of GAD is at least 6 months of excessive anxiety and worry about a number of events or activities (such as school performance or safety concerns) that the child finds difficult to control (American Psychiatric Association, 2000). These worries are more pervasive, distressing, and of longer duration than typical everyday worries. Often, the worrying occurs without a significant precipitant. Moreover, the worry usually interferes significantly with day-to-day living and is accompanied by physical symptoms such as restlessness, feeling keyed up or on edge, being easily fatigued, difficulty concentrating, mind going blank, irritability, muscle tension, or trouble sleeping.

Social phobia differs from GAD in that the child exhibits marked and persistent fear of specific situations—social or performance situations in which embarrassment may occur (American Psychiatric Association, 2000). When faced with such a situation, these children experience a strong anxiety response that may resemble a panic attack (e.g., experiencing heart pounding, sweating, depersonalization). These children tend to avoid social or performance situations although some may endure them while experiencing intense distress. Adolescents may recognize that their fear is unreasonable, but children may not. The avoidance, fear, or anxious anticipation of these situations interferes significantly with the youth's functioning or causes marked distress. Youth with social phobia may refuse to do presentations in class, write on the board, eat in public, interact with their peers, or talk with teachers because of their anxiety.

Separation anxiety disorder is characterized by at least 4 weeks of excessive anxiety concerning separation from the home or from those to whom the individual is attached (American Psychiatric Association, 2000). This anxiety is beyond that which is expected for the child's developmental level with an onset before 18 years of age and causes significant distress or impairment. Children with this disorder may experience recurrent excessive distress when separation is anticipated or occurs, worry about harm befalling others, or worry that an untoward event will result in separation. They may refuse to go to school or elsewhere. They may demonstrate a fear or reluctance to be alone at home or in other settings and refuse to sleep away from attachment figures. Many of these youth experience repeated nightmares about separation and physical symptoms (e.g., headaches, nausea) when separation occurs or is anticipated.

Numerous clinical trials have demonstrated the efficacy of cognitive-behavioral therapy (CBT) for treating anxiety disorders in children (Dadds, Spence, Olland, Barrett, & Laurens, 1997; Kendall, 1994; Kendall et al., 1997; Short, Barrett, & Fox, 2001; Silverman et al., 1999). The CBT approach tends to be short-term and multifaceted, incorporating a variety of cognitive and behavioral techniques. Although early efforts focused primarily on the child in treatment, more recent studies support incorporating the anxious child's social context, particularly the parents and school, into CBT treatment. A number of treatment manuals that share many common elements have been developed for this population, perhaps best known being the *Coping Cat* program (Kendall, 2000).

EMPIRICAL SUPPORT

Individual and Family Clinic-Based CBT Treatments

Kendall (1994) conducted a randomized clinical trial including 47 anxiety-disordered children randomly assigned to either a cognitive-behavioral treatment or a wait-list control condition. Results indicated that 64% of treated children no longer had their primary anxiety disorder at posttreatment. In addition, improvements were noted on self-report and parent- and teacher-report measures of child behavior. A 1-year follow-up (Kendall, 1994) and a 3-year follow-up (Kendall & Southam-Gerow, 1996) demonstrated maintenance of treatment gains. Kendall and colleagues completed a second randomized clinical trial in which 94 anxiety-disordered children were randomly assigned to a cognitive-behavioral treatment or a wait-list. Seventy-one percent of treated cases no longer had their primary diagnoses at posttreatment (Kendall et al., 1997), and treated children evidenced significantly greater gains on self- and parent-reported ratings of anxiety. Maintenance of treatment gains was evident at 1-year and 7-year follow-ups (Kendall et al., 1997; Kendall, Safford, Flannery-Schroeder, & Webb, 2004). Barrett, Dadds, Rapee, and Ryan (1996), using a modification of Kendall's Coping Cat program for use with Australian youth, added a family management component to the cognitive-behavioral treatment with good effects. Seventy-nine anxiety-disordered children were randomly assigned to one of three conditions: cognitive-behavioral treatment (CBT), cognitive-behavioral treatment plus family management (FAM), and a wait-list control. Approximately 70% of treated children, versus 26% of wait-list children, did not meet criteria for an anxiety disorder at posttreatment. Results suggested that younger children had better outcomes in the CBT versus FAM condition, whereas no differential effects were found between the two active treatments for older children. One-year and 6-year follow-ups demonstrated maintenance of treatment effects (Barrett, et al., 1996;

Barrett, Duffy, Dadds, & Rapee, 2001). Several other researchers also have documented the efficacy of cognitive-behavioral interventions for childhood anxiety (e.g., Silverman, et al., 1999; Spence, Donovan, & Brechman-Toussaint, 2000).

Clinic-Based Group CBT Treatments

Several researchers have adapted Kendall's protocol for use in treating clinic-based groups of anxiety-disordered children (e.g., Barrett, 1998; Flannery-Schroeder & Kendall, 2000; Mendlowitz, et al., 1999; Silverman, et al., 1999). Silverman et al. (1999) and Barrett (1998) compared a cognitive-behavioral treatment to a wait-list control. Results demonstrated that 64% and 75%, respectively, of participants no longer met criteria for their primary anxiety disorder. Self-report measures also demonstrated differential gains for treated versus control conditions, and results were maintained at a 1-year follow-up. Flannery-Schroeder and Kendall (2000) compared individual and group formats to a wait-list control condition. Analyses revealed that 73% of individual and 50% of group (vs. 8% of wait-list) failed to meet diagnostic criteria for their primary anxiety disorder at post-treatment. Self-report measures of adaptive functioning also demonstrated the superiority of the treatment conditions. Treatment gains were maintained at a 3-month follow-up. Similarly, Mendlowitz et al. (1999) found cognitive-behavioral group interventions to reduce symptoms of anxiety and depression in a sample of anxiety-disordered children. The cost and time efficiency combined with the efficacy of group interventions has led several researchers to utilize group formats in school-based interventions for anxiety disorders.

School-Based Group CB Interventions

In a study regarding the effectiveness of a school-based group CB treatment for African-American adolescents with anxiety disorders (Ginsburg & Drake, 2002), 12 adolescents were randomly assigned to either a 10-session group CB treatment involving relaxation, social skills training, cognitive-restructuring, and exposure, or a 10-session attention and support group. Of treatment completers (N = 9; 4 in CBT and 5 in the attention support group), 75% of adolescents in the CBT group and 20% of adolescents in the attention support group no longer received their primary anxiety disorder diagnosis. Additionally, adolescents in the CB treatment demonstrated significant decreases in clinician-rated impairment and self-reported overall anxiety at posttreatment.

In an investigation of the efficacy of CBT with adolescents with social phobia, six adolescents were treated with a 14-session CBT (Masia, Klein, Storch, & Corda, 2001). Treatment components included education regarding the diagnosis of social phobia, cognitive restructuring, social skills training, and exposures. At posttreatment, all six adolescents were classified as treatment responders with moderate to marked improvement in functioning and severity ratings. Three of the six no longer received a diagnosis of social phobia. The adolescents demonstrated significant reductions on a clinician-rated social anxiety scale; however, self-reported social anxiety did not significantly decrease with treatment. Taken together, these studies provide preliminary evidence for the efficacy of school-based group treatment programs for anxious youth.

In recent years, attention has shifted from research on the treatment of mental disorders to research on prevention. Dadds, Holland, Barrett, Laurens, and Spence (1997) conducted a school-based prevention and early intervention study, the Queens-land Early Intervention and Prevention of Anxiety Project, to examine the remediating effects on children at-risk for anxiety disorders. One hundred twenty-eight children identified as "at-risk" for an anxiety disorder(s) were assigned to a CB intervention or monitoring (i.e., control) condition. The 10-session intervention was conducted in a group format using a modification of Kendall's *Coping Cat* anxiety program. Children met weekly in school for 1 to 2 hours in groups of 5–12 children. Immediately following the intervention, both groups demonstrated significant improvements in diagnostic status and on dependent measures; however, at a 6-month follow-up, only the intervention group remained improved. At a 12-month follow-up, results for the two conditions again converged, but significantly greater improvements in the intervention condition were again demonstrated at a 2-year follow-up (Dadds, Holland, Laurens, Mullins, Barrett, & Spence, 1999). Collectively, the research suggests that not only are school-based treatments for anxiety disorders feasible, they appear to show promise of good treatment effects.

ASSESSMENT

Consistent with the empirical orientation of CBT, assessment occurs throughout treatment, providing information required for case conceptualization and treatment planning but also for monitoring change over time. The general approach to assessment incorporates multiple methods (e.g., interviews, report inventories, behavioral observations) and informants (e.g., child, teacher, and parent) to develop an idiographic, developmentally sensitive case conceptualization based on a comprehensive functional assessment. Drawing from Lang's tripartite model (1968), anxiety should be assessed across cognitive, behavioral, and psychological components. Important areas to emphasize include the onset and development of anxiety symptoms as well as the historical and current socialization context (e.g., home and school) within which they developed.

Cognitive and behavioral theories of anxiety indicate that certain types of learning experiences may be important to evaluate. For example, the child's learning history may include conditioning experiences for which extinction trials may be designed. Particular antecedents and consequences may be associated with the child's maladaptive and adaptive responses. It is also important to consider the child's skills in emotional regulation and social interaction as skill deficits may underlie anxiety problems. The child's sense of self-efficacy, probability of threat, dangerousness, and control may be important variables to assess across a variety of situations. If we consider the family as the primary socializing agent, it follows that we must consider parental psychopathology, style, and modeling as well as parental responses to the child's anxiety-related behaviors.

Within the context of these variables, a clear diagnostic picture can serve as a foundation for effective treatment. Structured and semistructured diagnostic interviews such as the *Anxiety Disorders Interview Schedule for DSM-IV, Parent and Child Versions* (ADIS-IV; Silverman & Albano, 1997) permit a thorough assessment of psychiatric disorders. The ADIS-IV provides a structure for assessing symptoms and severity of DSM-IV anxiety, mood, and externalizing disorders. It also includes screening questions related to learning and developmental disorders, substance abuse, eating disorders, psychotic symptoms, and somatoform disorders. Although time limitations may not permit the full administration of the ADIS-IV in school settings, questions from the interview may be incorporated into a general clinical interview to identify anxious symptoms and clarify diagnostic decisions (Velting et al., 2004).

However, diagnosis is only a first step in a meaningful assessment process. The expression of a disorder can vary widely from one youth to the next. For example, one child with school phobia may fear tests and experience performance anxieties, whereas another may experience overwhelming shyness and social concerns, and a third may fear being separated from his or her mother. Moreover, many children meet criteria for more than one anxiety disorder. Some experts believe that an assessment along a continuum of internalizing symptoms may be more helpful for understanding and treating children's difficulties (Achenbach & Edelbrock, 1978). Also, some children may not meet full criteria for an anxiety disorder but still evidence difficulties with anxiety that warrant attention. Report inventories can provide information about broadband as well as specific anxiety symptoms.

Although there are numerous report inventories, we will be limiting our discussion to a few of the most well-known, standardized measures that possess good to excellent psychometric properties (for further review, see Velting et al., 2004). Normative data for these measures enables the clinician to determine whether the child is reporting average or problematic levels of anxiety. Most of these inventories require a second- or third-grade reading level. These measures require only a brief amount of time to complete and score, thus making them highly useful in clinical and school settings. For some anxious children, self-report inventories provide a less threatening means of sharing information about themselves.

A number of inventories assess the global construct of anxiety in children. The *Revised Children's Manifest Anxiety Scale* (RCMAS; Reynolds & Richmond, 1978) and the *State-Trait Anxiety Inventory for Children* (STAIC; Spielberger, 1973) have a long history of use in research as opposed to clinical settings. These measures tend to correlate with other internalizing symptoms (e.g., depression) and have not been useful in predicting whether a child has an anxiety disorder (Velting et al., 2004; March & Albano, 2002; Perrin & Last, 1992). In contrast, the *Multidimensional Scale for Children* (MASC; March, Parker, Sullivan, Stallings, & Connors, 1997) has been found useful in discriminating youth with an anxiety disorder from those with depression or no disorder (Dierker et al., 2001). The MASC also provides information about specific factors of anxiety: physical symptoms (tense/restless and somatic/autonomic subfactors), social anxiety (humiliation/rejection and public performance subfactors), harm avoidance (anxious coping and perfectionism subfactors), and separation/panic anxiety (Velting et al., 2004). The *Screen for Anxiety and Related Emotional Disorders* (SCARED; Birmaher et al., 1997) is a child and parent report inventory that is also useful in assessing symptoms of DSM-IV anxiety disorders and school refusal.

In addition to assessing anxiety as a global construct, it is often helpful to assess specific aspects of anxiety through report inventories. A few measures of note include the *Revised Fear Survey Schedule for Children Child and Parent Versions* (FSSC-R; Ollendick, 1983), the *Social Phobia and Anxiety Inventory for Children* (Beidel, Turner, & Morris, 1995), the *Revised Social Anxiety Scale for Children Child and Parent Versions* (SASC-R; La Greca, Dandes, Wick, Shaw, & Stone, 1988), the *Penn State Worry Questionnaire for Children* (Chorpita, Tracey, Brown, Collica, & Barlow, 1997), and the *Children's Anxiety Sensitivity Index* (Silverman, Fleisig, Rabian, & Peterson, 1991). Of particular interest to school personnel, the *School Refusal Assessment Scale* (SRAS; Kearney & Silverman, 1993) assesses anxiety-related variables that may be involved in motivating and maintaining school refusal behavior (Velting et al., 2004).

Given the critical nature of the teacher's perspective, it is interesting that so few teacher report inventories exist to assess children's anxiety. One useful inventory that assesses child behavior across internalizing and externalizing dimensions is the *Child Behavior Checklist* (CBCL; Achenbach & Edelbrock, 1983), which is a parent-report measure that includes a version for teachers (*Teacher Report Form*, or TRF; Achenbach, 1991). The TRF also includes open-ended questions, which is particularly useful given that teachers have unique opportunities to observe children negotiating academic, personal, and social challenges.

A critical outcome of assessment for children with anxiety disorders is the development of a hierarchy of anxiety provoking situations. Standardized ratings of the child's anxiety and avoidance for each hierarchy item can be compared as the child progresses through treatment as another means of monitoring improvement. It often requires careful evaluation to pinpoint the exact nature of the child's fears and the optimal items to include in a hierarchy. For example, one child we treated had numerous performance concerns. Under careful scrutiny, it became clear that most concerns were related to his perception of his father's reaction to his performance. Thus, it was important to incorporate the father's reaction into this child's hierarchy and treatment.

CBT CONCEPTUALIZATION OF THE PROBLEM

The cognitive-behavioral perspective views anxiety as an adaptive emotional response consisting of physiological, cognitive, and behavioral components. Anxiety can serve as a cue to signal impending danger, alerting a child to engage in adaptive behaviors to avoid stress or negative experiences and triggering the body's "fight or flight" response (Albano & Kendall, 2002). An anxiety response often involves increased arousal of the autonomic nervous system, which may lead to physiological responses such as sweating, increased blood flow to the extremities, headaches, stomachaches, and tightening of muscles. The children's cognitions frequently concern estimations regarding the dangerousness of the threat and their own ability to cope. Behavioral reactions to anxiety differ from child to child but often include attempts to avoid anxiety provoking situations or activities, crying, and expressions of irritability. Although anxiety reactions are often adaptive, some children experience maladaptive levels of anxiety in many situations that are not generally considered dangerous. These children may suffer from an anxiety disorder.

The triple vulnerability model (Barlow, 2000) views anxiety disorders as arising from three vulnerabilities: (a) a general genetic vulnerability, (b) a general psychological vulnerability concerning a sense of impending uncontrollable and unpredictable threat, and (c) a specific psychological vulnerability resulting from early learning experiences that lead a child to experience anxiety in certain situations.

Studies suggest that some individuals are more predisposed to experience increase arousal and anxiety responses to environmental triggers (Manassis, Hudson, Webb, & Albano, 2004). For example, Kagan and his colleagues (Kagan, Reznick, & Gibbons, 1989) have identified a subset of behaviorally inhibited children who demonstrate an increased startle response, greater difficulty being soothed, and greater responsivity to novel stimuli. Family and twin studies also indicate heritability of some types of anxiety disorders (Manassis et al., 2004). Children genetically predisposed to a highly reactive arousal system, frequent negative emotional states, or difficulties understanding social interactions may experience a diminished sense of control over their emotional states, their environment, and their social world.

According to Chorpita and Barlow (1998), a sense of diminished control mediates the relationship between stressful life events and anxiety in early development and moderates this relationship in later development. Children may come to develop a sense of diminished control through experiences with their own predispositions combined with unpredictable, uncontrollable life events. Barlow (2000) hypothesizes that early parenting is one avenue that impacts a child's sense of control. For example, overcontrolled, unpredictable, or unresponsive family environments contribute to a sense of uncontrollability and an external locus of control. Once they have developed a diminished sense of control, children tend to perceive events as uncontrollable, even those events for which the child could exhibit control. Anxious children's cognitions are characterized by overestimations of the dangerousness of situations (e.g., predicting that an interaction with a teacher will frequently lead to being yelled at or humiliated) and underestimations of their ability to cope (e.g., believing that they do not know how to talk with a teacher or cannot handle it if someone is angry with them).

In terms of a specific psychological vulnerability, early socialization experiences (particularly in the family and school environments) contribute to experiencing anxiety in particular areas. As in social learning theory (Bandura, 1977), children may learn specific anxiety responses through modeling or information transmission regarding potential dangers. A child may learn to be anxious by seeing adults experiencing high levels of anxiety, underestimating their own self-efficacy, or delivering excessive warnings about potential harm. Also, children may develop heightened anxiety responses because of particular conditioning experiences that become overgeneralized. For example, a child could have a negative experience presenting in front of the class (e.g., having an anxiety attack, being harshly criticized, or being teased by peers) and then develop a conditioned, generalized anxiety response to social situations. Children also may learn that they can avoid experiencing some anxiety by avoiding situations that evoke anxiety. Mowrer's two-factor theory (1960) posits that their avoidant responses increase in frequency as they are negatively reinforced by decreases in anxiety. Adults in the lives of anxious children also may come to inadvertently reinforce avoidant or dependent behavior.

Following from the tripartite model, treatment could focus on multiple areas depending on the particular vulnerabilities of the child. Primarily, interventions seek to increase a child's sense of control by providing children with opportunities to exercise control over their environment, to engage in mastery experiences, to explore their world with age-appropriate levels of independence, to develop skills, and to develop coping responses (Barlow, 2000). Implementing more adaptive thinking and behavioral patterns is encouraged through teaching skills, modeling, contingency management, and exposure exercises. Interventions could occur individually or in groups within the school setting. Individual or group meetings with parents are often an important component of the treatment. Within the school and family context, treatment interventions encourage consistency, responsive teaching/parenting, adaptive modeling, and the communication of appropriate, adaptive messages regarding potential threats. Most CBT treatments recommend a combination of skill-building exercises and gradual exposure to anxiety-provoking situations to help children increase their sense of self-efficacy and decrease their perception of impending threat.

STRATEGIC AND TECHNICAL INTERVENTIONS

There exists a core set of techniques found in most cognitive-behavioral treatments for anxious youth. Cognitive-behavioral treatments are based on the premise that anxious children may benefit from the internalization and subsequent use of a set of coping skills, as well as repeated and prolonged exposure to the feared objects, situations, or events. Various CB protocols may differ in the number, sequencing, and time devoted to the training of coping skills; however, most treatment packages include instruction in the following four domains: somatic management, cognitive restructuring, problem solving, and contingency management.

Somatic Management

Compared to nonanxious youth, youth with anxiety disorders have less understanding of ways in which they can modify their emotional experiences. In order to best develop skill in modifying one's own anxiety reactions, children must learn to identify their own individualized somatic reactions to anxiety. These individual responses that are unique to each child (e.g., red ears, trembling voice, urge to urinate, nausea, headache) serve as clues for the child to label his or her emotional reaction "anxious." Once labeled, children can learn various cognitive and behavioral strategies to decrease their somatic responses. Relaxation training is a particularly powerful tool that helps children decrease their somatic arousal in a variety of situations.

Cognitive Restructuring

Use of cognitive therapy techniques in the treatment of child anxiety is based on the belief that anxiety stems from irrational or maladaptive thoughts, beliefs, or self-talk. Research has documented that anxious children demonstrate distortions in information processing, memory biases for distressing events, hypersensitivity to threat cues, and a bias toward interpreting ambiguous situations as threatening (Vasey & MacLeod, 2001). Thus, the use of cognitive techniques designed to modify the maladaptive nature of anxious self-talk is compelling.

Various techniques have been developed to assist children with identifying their cognitions in anxiety-provoking situations. Kendall's use of a "thought bubble" is one example (Kendall, 2001). Children are shown various cartoons in which people's thoughts or statements appear in a bubble above their heads. Children are then prompted by the question, "What's in your thought bubble?" Once children are proficient at identifying self-talk, they are then instructed to undergo a rational analysis of the thoughts: Are their predictions likely to happen? Have they happened before? Would it really be so bad if they did happen? Is there another way of looking at the situation? After such an analysis, children can generate coping thoughts to counter their initial anxious thoughts. Younger children may have a more difficult time learning to identify and modify their self-talk. They may rely on coping thoughts based on self-instruction training (Meichenbaum, 1985) as opposed to cognitive restructuring to manage their anxiety reactions.

Problem Solving

Problem-solving methods provide children with training presented by an instructor. The instructor provides either written or verbal strategies intended to help the child control unwanted behavior or initiate coping behavior through the mediation of covert thinking processes. Urbain and Kendall (1980) have emphasized that "Problem solving interventions do, however, place greater emphasis on training at the level of covert thinking processes themselves (e.g., identifying problem issues, generating alternative solutions, evaluating consequences, etc.) in contrast to intervention methods designed to more specifically train discrete behavioral responses to various situations (e.g., relaxation responses, assertive responses, affiliative responses, etc.)" (p. 110). Thus, problem-solving interventions are intended to target the cognitive processes that mediate competence and generalize to various situations.

D'Zurilla and Goldfried (1971) have developed a set of problem-solving skills designed to teach individuals a set of steps to achieve problem resolution, and more recent efforts remain heavily influenced by their work (e.g., Bedell & Lennox, 1997; Nezu & D'Zurilla, 1989; Nezu, Nezu, & Perri, 1989). The approach runs counter to finding solutions to a linear set of singular problems and allows individuals to generalize the technique to other current as well as future problem areas. Bedell and Lennox (1997) have modified the original problem-solving model to include seven steps in the problem-solving process. The seven steps are: (1) recognize the existence of a problem; (2) define the problem in a goal-directed manner in which your own and other's unmet wants are identified; (3) brainstorm problem solutions without evaluation of their possible efficacy; (4) evaluate the potential effectiveness of the alternatives generated; (5) select the best alternative or combination of alternatives; (6) implement the chosen solution; and (7) verify the effectiveness of the chosen solution.

The cognitive-behavioral approach to problem solving requires that the therapist lead the anxious child sequentially through these steps under the guiding principle of collaborative empiricism. Together, the therapist and child generate numerous potential solutions without regard to their potential utility until the alternatives are exhausted. Once the child has identified those alternatives likely to be helpful in the resolution of the problem, he or she has developed an excellent problem-solving strategy.

Contingency Management

One of the fundamental principles of behavior therapy is the emphasis placed on the consequences of behavior. Depending on the aversive or appetitive nature of the consequences, behavior will either decrease or increase as a result. Thus, behavior modification can be achieved through the effective management of contingencies. In efforts to increase brave behavior (i.e., approach rather than avoidant strategies), anxious children are offered opportunities to earn rewards in many CB treatment protocols. Such reward systems are believed to be beneficial in reducing child anxiety by promoting engagement in treatment strategies such as homework, exposure tasks, and self-evaluation procedures. Rewards are used to shape and maintain behavioral improvements but are effective only to the extent that they meet with children's desires and preferences. That is, a reward is only rewarding if it is desired. The successful use of contingency management procedures involves skilled selection of rewards—individualized for each child. Rewards may be material (e.g., small toys, games, sports cards) or social (e.g., playing miniature golf with a parent, seeing a movie with a friend). Often, those rewards at the start of treatment will be material with social rewards being encouraged in the latter half of treatment. In this way, parents will have greater success in the immediate (and less costly) provision of rewards ultimately leading to better maintenance of treatment effects.

Exposure

Following the skill acquisition phase of the treatment, CB therapies use graded exposure tasks (i.e., gradual exposure to feared situations, objects, or events) to practice the use of the newly acquired coping skills. Exposure to feared stimuli involves disconnecting the associative relationship between a behavior and its consequences. This disconnection might involve counterconditioning, a technique that involves an individual confronting a feared situation (directly or imaginally), while engaging in responses that are incompatible with anxiety (e.g., relaxation). Alternatively, extinction involves an individual who is presented with an anxiety-eliciting stimulus and, while making use of cognitive and behavioral strategies (i.e., coping skills), remains in the situation until the anxiety diminishes to a manageable level. It is also changes in underlying cognitive variables (e.g., appraisals, expectancies, self-efficacies) that are believed to be critical to the efficacy of exposure therapy. Exposures may be either in vivo or imaginal and can occur both in and out of the therapeutic environment.

The exposure technique can be conceived of as a gradual shaping process. It involves the use of a hierarchy of anxiety-eliciting objects and events, and also often requires that the therapist address basic component skills first before moving on to more complex situations, events, or interactions. For example, although "meeting a new person" might assume a place on the hierarchy, the component skills (e.g., eye contact) would likely be addressed first. Thus, the exposure process proceeds in a gradual but incremental fashion. The fear hierarchy is created in the spirit of collaborative empiricism in which exposure tasks are conceived of as "experiments." After "experimenting," both the child and therapist will evaluate the "data" (e.g., Subjective Units of Distress scores [SUDs] taken before, during, and after exposures) to evaluate the effectiveness of the exposure procedures. (For further discussion of this issue and a practice-oriented description of the use of exposures in child anxiety treatment, see Kendall, Robin, Hedke, Suveg, Flannery-Schroeder, and Gosch, 2005.)

APPLICATIONS TO THE SCHOOL SETTING

As noted at the start of this chapter, anxiety disorders represent one of the most common forms of psychopathology among children and adolescents. With prevalence estimates reported as high as 21% (Kashani & Orvaschel, 1990) and problematic associated difficulties (e.g., problems in social and peer relations, academic achievement, and future emotional health), prevention and treatment of anxiety disorders is imperative.

School-based cognitive-behavioral interventions for anxiety disorders are compelling for several reasons. First, anxiety is often manifest in the school settings and around issues pertaining to school. It is not uncommon to see anxious children exhibiting perfectionism in homework assignments, test or performance anxiety, school refusal behavior, frequent trips to the school nurse or phone calls home from school, unwillingness to speak up or read aloud in school, difficulty in social interactions, and reluctance to try new things. Many of these behaviors are exclusive to school environments. In CB treatment planning, every effort is made to provide children practice in coping with those situations that elicit anxiety. When this list of anxious situations includes school-related events, experiential strategies should include coping skill practice and exposure within the school setting. Treatment outcome is likely to be enhanced to the degree that this is accomplished. In outpatient or clinic-based treatment, special efforts must be made in order to conduct exposures in school environments. Often, it is the case that therapists use approximations to the school situations (e.g., giving a mock test in a therapy session to a test anxious child, having a socially anxious youngster read aloud in front of the therapist); however, it is likely that these mock trials are not as potent as exposures to "real-world" school events. Thus, school-based interventions are more likely to ensure that skills transfer to the natural environment. This is particularly true for separation and social concerns, which often manifest in school.

Second, school-based interventions are amenable to group or classroom applications, the latter of which can bypass the potential stigmatizing effects of singling out children for special interventions. Coping skills acquisition and practice, the focus of CB treatments, although of particular relevance to anxious children, are likely to benefit nonanxious or mildly (i.e., nonclinically) anxious children as well. Classroom interventions face a captive audience and children are accustomed to learning skills in the school setting. Just as positive health behaviors are taught in traditional health "classes," so might skills for emotional health. Although CB interventions involve standardized application in order to ensure treatment integrity, the interventions are best applied flexibly (for more on the flexible application of CB treatments to childhood anxiety disorders, see Kendall, Chu, Gifford, Hayes, & Nauta, 1998). The ease of classwide application, potential for flexible applications, and provision of a general skill set to benefit all makes school-based interventions for childhood anxiety disorders an attractive approach.

Anxiety-disorder interventions occurring within schools ensure that treatments will have readily available therapeutic features. Schools readily promote multiple system involvements—peers, school, family, community—and attempt to ensure good communication among the many systems impacting schoolchildren. This systems focus is likely to positively impact treatment outcomes. Additionally, it is the case that the readily available resources and situations naturally found within school settings will be excellent fodder for the development of creative and effective exposures. For example, access to peers, school staff, principals, teachers, true-to-life performance activities, and the like provide therapists with ample material to design highly effective exposures that cut to the heart of the child's fears, worries, or phobias. Take the case of a child with significant social anxiety; peer-mediation (e.g., peer-pairing or peer-helping) is likely to be an important therapeutic component that is easy to implement within a school due to the easy access to peers. To the degree that the child's unique sets of anxious behaviors are relearned through in vivo exposure practice, treatment effects will likely be enhanced. In a similar vein, the immediate access to teacher and peer support serve to provide the anxious child with necessary guidance to effectively learn and use the skills taught to combat anxiety.

Proximity to teachers is in and of itself a compelling therapeutic feature for several reasons. Teachers often have important perspectives on children's behaviors. School settings offer teachers unique opportunities to observe children in situations that may be less likely to occur outside of school (e.g., speaking in front of a group of people). It is often the case that teachers can provide critical information about a child's anxieties that is extremely useful in treatment planning. Opportunities for training teachers about the identification and modification of anxious behaviors within the classroom should be promoted to facilitate use of such information. Teachers spend a significant proportion of time with children (approximately six to seven hours a day) and serve as very influential role models. Thus, their familiarity with key concepts in combating child anxiety (promotion of approach behaviors in the face of anxiety-eliciting events, use of positive self-talk) would be of tremendous benefit. With training of teachers as well as other key school personnel, the existing high rates of anxiety disorders may be attenuated by the effective use of proactive rather than reactive strategies. An emphasis on prevention of childhood anxiety disorders should compliment the current emphasis on the successful treatment of these disorders. The following case example illustrates one way in which children's anxiety problems have been successfully treated in the school setting.

CASE EXAMPLE

At the beginning of this chapter, we discussed some of the difficulties experienced by Chris, a dark-haired 11-year-old boy with glasses who was referred to the school psychologist for evaluation to determine if recent academic problems were related to a learning problem or fueled by Chris's anxiety. Although typically not a behavior problem at school, Chris had failed to complete several book reports that were to be accompanied by oral presentations. On several occasions, he had also had "melt-downs" in the classroom when he prematurely gave up on tests or assignments, sometimes crying or trying to leave the classroom. His teacher had tried to talk with him about the problem, but he had little to offer regarding why he was not completing his work. His teacher then talked with his parents, who were surprised to learn about the uncompleted book reports but discussed how Chris's problems with perfection-ism and shyness had interfered in other areas of his life such as playing sports. For example, although Chris has played soccer and enjoyed it, on several occasions in the past year he left the field and refused to play after making small mistakes or during close games. In the current year, he would not play soccer at all, despite his parents' encouragement to do so. They could identify no recent stressors or changes that may have accounted for his difficulties. Given that Chris tended to perform well on other class assignments, they wondered if Chris's long-standing problems with shyness and his tendency to avoid social situations had something to do with his current school problems.

It is important to remember that, at times, children may have an anxiety problem secondary to a learning issue. These children often benefit from interventions that target both the learning and anxiety issues. However, an evaluation of academic achievement and cognitive skills did not reveal cognitive or learning impairments that would account for Chris's difficulties. Along with a general psychosocial inter-view, the school psychologist administered portions of the ADIS with Chris and his parents. She found that Chris met criteria for Social Phobia, Generalized Type (severity rating 6 out of 8) and Generalized Anxiety Disorder (severity rating 5 out of 8). Chris did not report many symptoms but did acknowledge some social anxiety. His parents and his teacher provided the most information about the level of his avoidance. Chris appeared to feel uncomfortable in most types of social situations and avoided talking with people except his family and a few close friends he had known since kindergarten. He managed school by keeping to himself and only talking to the teacher when directly addressed. On the STAIC and the MASC, Chris scored in the clinical range and endorsed many items that he had not discussed in his interview. These measures were administered in the middle and at the end of treat-ment to monitor Chris's progress.

Course of Treatment

To address Chris's school difficulties, he participated in a weekly 18-session, school-based group treatment for children with anxiety problems based on the *Coping Cat* Program developed by Kendall and colleagues. Both group and individual treatment manuals are available from Workbook Publishing. It is important to note that these interventions may be delivered in fewer sessions and can be adapted to the needs of particular children.

Chris's group consisted of three boys who shared similar concerns but also had some unique difficulties. For example, one of the group members (Tom) had fears of separating from his mother that led him to have difficulty attending school, resulting in missed school days, frequent trips to the school nurse, daily calls home, and crying spells in the classroom. The third group member (Freddie) could be described as a "worrier." Freddie's worries involved numerous areas including his performance in school and sports, his parents' finances, his family's health, his own health, and even the health of "Rover," the family pet. Additionally, he exhibited a rigid insistence on punctuality and was overly concerned about looking foolish.

Although educative in nature, the format of the group encouraged participation through questions, games, and humor. Great emphasis was placed on building group cohesion through a variety of exercises (see Flannery-Schroeder & Kendall, 2000) and making the sessions fun. Almost all sessions included time at the end to play games, such as Jenga or Nerf basketball. Children received rewards for completing homework, called *Show That I Can* (STIC) tasks, between sessions to practice new skills and promote generalization of treatment effects. Each treatment session began with a review of these tasks that often served as a means by which the session content could be personalized to the child's current experiences. At various points in the treatment, the therapist arranged meetings with the parents to gather information, update them on their child's progress, and enlist their aid in setting up therapeutic exposures to anxiety-provoking situations at home or school. Teachers also participated by providing information, monitoring in-class exposures, and praising the children for engaging in more adaptive behavior.

The focus of the first session was to build rapport among the group members, introduce them to the program, and encourage their participation. Chris tended to be quiet, responding with one-word answers to most questions. To facilitate group interaction, the boys played a personal facts game, decorated their program workbooks, and made lists of rewards they would like to earn in the program. Chris could only think of two possible rewards, baseball cards and Legos, so the therapist suggested he add to the list over the coming week. Children were encouraged to develop a rich, meaningful reward list that included activities (e.g., renting a movie), social events (e.g., playing a game with Mom), and tangible rewards (e.g., toys).

Sessions 2 through 5 focused on learning about emotions and managing somatic reactions to anxiety. In session 2, the group discussed how different feelings are associated with different physical expressions and these physical expressions can act as clues to identify how someone is feeling. They looked at pictures of kids showing different emotions and took turns guessing what emotion the picture was demonstrating, identifying critical facial and postural clues. They played "feelings charades" and created a "feelings collage." The therapist also introduced the "feelings thermometer," a large picture of a thermometer with ratings from 0 to 8 that identify low to high levels of anxiety. The feelings thermometer helped Chris begin to identify how much anxiety he felt in different situations, giving him a means to notice differences in his levels of anxiety and language for describing his emotional experience to others. Each child then started to write down a personal hierarchy of anxiety-provoking situations including low-, mid-, and high-anxiety-provoking situations. Initially, Chris could only identify a few situations for his hierarchy, but input from teachers and parents led to the identification of numerous anxiety-provoking situations in later sessions.

In session 3, the children discussed how people experience various bodily reactions when feeling anxious. For example, they talked about how a famous basketball player might experience anxiety in his body (e.g., sweaty palms, stomachache) when having to make a free throw in the last second of the game with the score tied. They then talked about their own body's reaction to specific situations and how these reactions can serve as clues to alert the child that he is feeling anxious. Each child took a turn imagining himself in a situation that usually made him anxious to help him identify his bodily reactions. Chris imagined having the teacher call on him in class when he did not know the answer. He reported experiencing tightness in his stomach and "jittery legs." After outlining their bodies on large pieces of butcher paper placed on the floor, the children used markers to illustrate how their body responded to anxiety (e.g., butterflies in the stomach, red lines around the head for a headache, shading in the shoulders for muscle tension).

Session 4 focused on normalizing the experience of anxiety, creating personal anxiety hierarchies, and cohesion building. The children received information about the normal, adaptive nature of anxiety reactions. Chris seemed relieved to hear that 1 out of 10 kids has some difficulties with anxiety and all people experience anxiety in some form as a normal part of life. The therapist provided an example of a situation that made her nervous (speaking in front of other people) and how the steps in the program had helped her cope with this fear. She also talked about the ways the program had helped other children. Chris later stated that he believed the program might help him because the therapist said that the goal was to make anxiety easier to handle, not to make it completely go away, and that other kids had been helped by the program.

In session 5, the group began learning relaxation exercises. The therapist discussed the idea that when someone is feeling anxious and worried it is likely that some parts of his body are tense. If he can relax the tense parts, he will be taking the first step in coping with his anxiety. The children took turns tensing their arms by making fists and noting the differences in the sensations when the arm was relaxed and when it was tense. A volunteer acted like a robot to illustrate tense muscles and another pretended to be a wet noodle to show relaxed muscles. The boys were encouraged to lie down, close their eyes, and do a few progressive relaxation exercises. These exercises involved tensing and releasing different muscle groups to achieve a state of relaxation. See Koeppen (1974) for a young children's relaxation script and Ollendick and Cerny (1981) for an older children's script. Throughout the course of treatment, the boys practiced the exercises by listening to audiotapes of the therapist reading portions of the relaxation script at home. In addition, relaxation was reviewed and practiced in many of the group sessions.

The goal of session 6 was to help the children begin to identify their thoughts (particularly in anxious situations) and to understand that certain types of thoughts may increase their anxiety. We began by showing cartoons with empty thought bubbles and asked the children to identify what they thought the character was thinking. We then linked what the person might feel and do if they had particular thoughts. Alternative thoughts to the same situation were proposed so the children could see that different people may have different thoughts and reactions to the same situation. Through these examples, the children learned that anxiety usually accompanied thoughts related to expecting something bad to happen. This idea led to proposing how one person may feel one way with one type of thought (e.g., expecting something bad to happen) and another way if the same person had a different type of thought (e.g., expecting something good to happen). Different cartoons and scenarios were presented while the children took turns answering questions. Chris was still very quiet in session but would occasionally answer questions and appeared to be listening when others were talking. The therapist then told a story about a mildly anxiety-provoking situation (e.g., a boy drops a book in the hallway) and asked the group to think of a set of thoughts that would help the boy cope (reduce distress) and a set of thoughts that would lead to anxiety (more distress) as well as the behaviors that would likely follow from each set of thoughts. It was proposed that, with some practice, they could learn to change some of their anxious self-talk to coping self-talk to help themselves feel better. They were then introduced to a set of questions to ask themselves to help them begin to change their thinking and a set of "thinking traps" that often "trick" people into feeling anxious.

The group then did a few role-plays in which they began to implement the first 2 steps for coping with anxiety. The therapist had Chris imagine that he was asked a question in class. Chris was directed to follow the first step in coping with anxiety, the "F" step, and ask himself if he was feeling anxious, if his body was sending him any clues (e.g., sweaty palms) that would help him tell that he was anxious. Chris said he felt "jittery" in his stomach and maybe a little anxious. Chris then was asked to engage in step two, the "E" step, and ask himself if he was expecting anything bad to happen. In this case, he thought he would sound stupid, other kids would laugh at him, and everyone would think he was weird. The therapist had Chris fill in a three-column table on a dry-erase board with the situation, his feelings (step one), and his thoughts (step two). Chris identified a few thinking traps characterizing his self-talk. The group then gathering evidence to support and refute Chris's negative expectations. Chris wrote down a few coping thoughts such as, "The kids in this group would not think I was stupid even if I didn't know an answer so maybe the kids in class might not think so," "Even if they laugh at me, they might not think I'm weird because even popular kids get laughed at sometime," "If they laugh at me, it will probably feel bad but only for 20 minutes or so [according to Chris' estimation]; it won't feel bad forever," "Other kids might not really care so much about how I answer the question," and "Just do it."

When engaging in challenging thoughts, it was particularly critical for the therapist to adopt a posture of collaborative empiricism. Sometimes therapists jump in too early to contradict the child's thoughts of potential harm or disastrous social consequences occurring. The child then may give lip service to agreeing with the therapist's challenge but never truly question their negative assumptions and continue to believe them. After all, most of these children have heard parents and teachers tell them how ridiculous or unlikely their fears are and have heard reassurances that the negative events they are predicting will not happen. Although sometimes this information is helpful to the child, they often are more open to questioning their negative assumptions when the therapist takes their concerns seriously and has the child engage in actual data gathering in order to prove or disprove his/her unrealistic thoughts. Also, children rarely just change their way of thinking completely while engaging in cognitive restructuring exercises. Rather, these exercises begin to open the door for change to occur and the children's actual experiences help solidify the adoption of new beliefs.

In session 7, the group focused on learning an approach to problem solving, the third step in their plan for coping with anxiety. The therapist explained that in addition to knowing when you're anxious and changing your self-talk, it is often helpful to take some action or follow a plan to cope with anxiety. The therapist introduced the process of problem solving by proposing a mildly anxiety-provoking situation (e.g., not being able to find your school sneakers when it is time to go to school). The group was instructed to brainstorm as many solutions as possible including silly (e.g., wear my mom's shoes), unhelpful (e.g., throw a temper tantrum), and adaptive ideas (e.g., trace past steps when last wearing the shoes). At first, only one or two solutions were offered but, as the therapist added a few ideas and continued to encourage the children, more and more ideas were proposed. The children were cautioned not to judge the solutions but rather to give any ideas that came into their heads. After a long list of solutions had been developed, the group began to evaluate the solutions—looking at the pros and cons for each. Finally, the group voted and decided which solutions looked the most promising. The therapist then set up a game in which the group drew a card containing an anxiety-provoking situation, read it aloud, and each child wrote as many solutions as he could think of within 1 minute. The children then compared lists, receiving points for solutions that no one else had recorded. Each group member then applied the first 3 steps of their coping plan to an anxiety-provoking situation.

During session 8, the group members focused on the final step in their plan for coping with anxiety, rating and rewarding themselves for trying to cope. First, the group discussed how people tend to do things for which they receive rewards. For example, a dog will learn to shake hands to receive a biscuit, kids may do their chores for an allowance. The children then played a game in which they received a penny candy for each reward they could name, generating an impressive list of activities, toys, and snacks. The therapist pointed out that it can be fun to receive a reward and that people often feel good when they are rewarded or they reward themselves. This point then led to discussing how people often punish and reward themselves, sometimes without even knowing it, by their self-talk. Different positive and negative scenarios were proposed (e.g., a child hits a home run in baseball or the child gets a C on a math test). The children talked about how the characters would feel, what their self-talk might be, and what they would do in each situation. The therapist pointed out that the characters may be less likely to do some things if they punish themselves with negative self-talk (e.g., after saying hello to a class-mate, a boy tells himself that he sounded stupid, so he is less likely to say hello in the future). The therapist offered slight changes to the scenarios to illustrate the importance of rewarding positive effort, not just positive results. The therapist also offered coping models from her own life in which she used reward to help motivate herself and do new things.

Session 9 was devoted to the group reviewing the entire four-step plan for coping with anxiety, the FEAR plan:

Step 1. The "F" Step, "Am I *F*eeling anxious? What does my body tell me?"
Step 2. The "E" Step, "What am I *E*xpecting to happen? What is my self-talk?"
Step 3. The "A" Step, "What *A*ctions and *A*ttitudes can best help me in this situation?"
Step 4. The "R" Step, "What self-*R*atings and *R*ewards do I receive for trying to cope?"

The group practiced the steps by applying the plan to real situations encountered by group members, such as giving a class presentation or taking a test. At the close of the first half of the treatment, the group engaged in a social event (i.e., a pizza party) to further enhance cohesion among group members.

The second half of the treatment consisted of applying the newly acquired skills in a variety of graduated exposures to anxiety-eliciting situations, and group cooperation was very important in this phase of treatment. The anxiety-eliciting situations were tailored to the individual fears of the children as these varied across the group. However, the therapist also strove to address concerns shared by group members by developing group exposures. The practice segments began with imaginal exposures taking place within the group, then progressed to in vivo exposures involving the group as a whole, then to in vivo exposures involving individual group members.

Initial exposures were imaginal in nature and were designed to both target the areas of overlap among the three boys' fears as well as to provide early success experiences, which were incompatible with previous expectations. The latter was accomplished by a very gradual start. Initially, some role-play exposures involved meeting others in the group as if for the first time, imagining traveling to unknown destinations independently, making social and performance blunders, and arriving late to important events (e.g., school, birthday parties).

The next progression in exposures was to move from group imaginal exposures to group in vivo exposures. In this phase, the group members together accomplished superordinate goals. For example, one group in vivo exposure involved a trip to a nearby park to play soccer. Tom, the group member with separation anxiety, was responsible for leading the group to the park with minimal directions, Chris was to make intentional soccer errors during a mock game, and Freddie, the third group member with concerns about punctuality, had to return the soccer ball to the school gym teacher later than requested. Thus, each child's unique anxieties were tapped in a task that could not be accomplished without the cooperation and courageous behaviors of each group member. For some exposures, group members with similar fears were paired to accomplish various tasks. In one exposure, both Chris and Freddie took turns engaging in very silly and potentially embarrassing behaviors to observe others' reactions. Although their expectations were that others would laugh at them, Chris and Freddie were surprised to find that for some observers the silliness was contagious and the onlookers were more apt to join in than to poke fun. Other observers simply ignored the silly group mates.

The last phase of exposures involved each member tackling in vivo exposures independently. For Chris, this meant accomplishing tasks such as making a new friend at school, asking or answering a question in class, purposely making a mistake on a math test, and making numerous speeches with increasing levels of difficulty. Fellow group mates offered creative ideas/support during the preexposure preparation, observed during the exposures, and offered hearty congratulations on their successful completion.

The group concluded by making a videotaped commercial about learning to cope with anxiety. The commercial was developed by the group and was intended to again promote cooperation, problem solving, and group cohesion. In addition, the commercial served to consolidate the information learned throughout the treatment and to reinforce each child's role and participation within the group. Each group member was given a copy of the commercial to take home with them. At the end of treatment, Chris still experienced some symptoms of generalized anxiety and social anxiety but did not meet full criteria for either disorder. His scores on the MASC and the STAIC were in the nonclinical range. He was socializing more with his classmates, talked regularly with his teacher, and was no longer afraid to ask for help when he needed it. He joined a Boy Scout troop and participated when the group went on a camping trip. His parents were particularly pleased that he did not seem to take his errors or mistakes as seriously and could continue to enjoy activities even when not performing perfectly.

SUMMARY

The group treatment case discussed in this chapter serves as just one example of how a cognitive-behavioral approach may be helpful in treating children's anxiety problems in a school context. Shorter treatment protocols using many of the components described in this comprehensive treatment package may be adapted to the school setting for interventions with groups or individuals of diverse ages. Furthermore, great prospects exist for prevention and early intervention in the school setting with youth at-risk for developing anxiety disorders. By providing information regarding the presentation, chronic course, and treatment of anxiety problems in youth, we hope to stimulate greater opportunities for these children to receive preventative and treatment services in schools.

REFERENCES

Achenbach, T. (1991). *Manual for the Teacher's Report Form and 1991 Profile*. Burlington, University of Vermont, Department of Psychiatry.

Achenbach, T. M., & Edelbrock, C. S. (1978). The classification of child psychology: A review and analysis of empirical efforts. *Psychological Bulletin, 85*, 1275–1301.

Achenbach, T. M., & Edelbrock, C. S. (1983). *Manual for the Child Behavior Checklist and Revised Child Behavior Profile*. Burlington: University of Vermont, Associates in Psychiatry.

Achenbach, T. M., Howell, C. T., McConaughy, S. H., & Stanger, C. (1995). Six-year predictors of problems in a national sample of children and youth: I. Cross-informant syndromes. *Journal of the American Academy of Child and Adolescent Psychiatry, 34*, 336–347.

Albano, A. M., & Kendall, P. C. (2002). Cognitive behavioural therapy for children and adolescents with anxiety disorders: clinical research advances. *International Review of Psychiatry, 14*, 129–134.

American Psychiatric Association. (2000). *Diagnostic and statistical manual of mental disorders* (4th ed., text revision). Washington, DC: Author.

Bandura, A. (1977). *Social learning theory*. Englewood Cliffs, NJ: Prentice Hall.

Barlow, D. H. (2000). Unraveling the mysteries of anxiety and its disorders from the perspective of emotion theory. *American Psychologist, 55*(11), 1245–1263.

Barrett, P. M. (1998). Evaluation of cognitive-behavioral group treatments for childhood anxiety disorders. *Journal of Clinical Child Psychology, 27*, 459–468.

Barrett, P. M., Dadds, M. R., Rapee, R. M., & Ryan, S. M. (1996). Family enhancement of cognitive style in anxious and aggressive children. *Journal of Abnormal Child Psychology, 24*, 187–203.

Barrett, P. M., Duffy, A. L., Dadds, M. R., & Rapee, R. M. (2001). Cognitive-behavioral treatment of anxiety disorders in children: Long-term (6-year) follow-up. *Journal of Consulting and Clinical Psychology, 69*, 135–141.

Bedell, J. R., & Lennox, S. S. (1997). *Handbook for communication and problem-solving skills training: A cognitive-behavioral approach*. New York: Wiley.

Beidel, D., Turner, S., & Morris, T. (1995). A new inventory to assess childhood social anxiety and phobia: The Social Phobia and Anxiety Inventory for Children. *Psychological Assessment, 7*, 70–79.

Biederman, J., Faraone, S., Mick, E., & Lelon, E. (1995). Psychiatric comorbidity among referred juveniles with major depression: Fact or artifact? *Journal of the American Academy of Child and Adolescent Psychiatry, 34*, 579–590.

Birmaher, B., Khetarpal, S., Brent, D., Cully, M., Balach, L., Kaufman, J., & McKenzie Neer, S. (1997). The Screen for Child Anxiety Related Emotional Disorder (SCARED): Scale construction and psychometric characteristics. *Journal of the American Academy of Child and Adolescent Psychiatry, 36*, 545–553.

Brady, E., & Kendall, P. C. (1992). Comorbidity of anxiety and depression in children and adolescents. *Psychological Bulletin, 111*, 244–255.

Chorpita, B. F., Tracey, S., Brown, T., Collica, T., & Barlow, D. (1997). Assessment of worry in children and adolescents: An adaptation of the Penn State Worry Questionnaire. *Behavior Research & Therapy, 35*, 569–581.

Compton, S. N., Burns, B. J., Egger, H. L., & Robertson, E. (2002). Review of the evidence base for treatment of childhood psychopathology: Internalizing disorders. *Journal of Consulting and Clinical Psychology, 70*, 1240–1266.

Dadds, M. R., Holland, D. E., Barrett, P. M., Laurens, K. R., & Spence, S. H. (1997). Prevention and early intervention for anxiety disorders: A controlled trial. *Journal of Consulting and Clinical Psychology, 65*, 627–635.

Dadds, M. R., Holland, D. E., Laurens, K. R., Mullins, K. R., Barrett, P. M., & Spence, S. H. (1999). Early intervention and prevention of anxiety disorders in children: Results at 2-year follow-up. *Journal of Consulting and Clinical Psychology, 67*, 145–150.

Dadds, M. R., Spence, S. H., Holland, D. E., Barrett, P. M., & Laurens, K. R. (1997). Prevention and early intervention for anxiety disorders: A controlled trial. *Journal of Consulting and Clinical Psychology, 65*, 627–634.

Deas-Nesmith, D., Brady, K. T., & Campbell, S. (1998). Comorbid substance use and anxiety disorders in adolescents. *Journal of Psychopathology and Behavioral Assessment, 20*, 139–148.

Dierker, L., Albano, A. M., Clarke, G. M., Heimberg, R. G., Kendall, P. C., Merikangas, K. R., et al. (2001). Screening for anxiety and depression in early adolescence. *Journal of the American Academy of Child and Adolescent Psychiatry, 40*, 929–936.

D'Zurilla, T. J., & Goldfried, M. R. (1971). Problem solving and behavior modification. *Journal of Abnormal Psychology, 78*, 107–126.

Flannery-Schroeder, E. C., & Kendall, P. C. (2000). Group and individual cognitive-behavioral treatments for youth with anxiety disorders: A randomized clinical trial. *Cognitive Therapy and Research, 24*, 251–278.

Ginsburg, G. S., & Drake, K. L. (2002). School-based treatment for anxious African-American adolescents: A controlled pilot study. *Journal of the American Academy of Child and Adolescent Psychiatry, 41*, 768–775.

Gurley, D., Cohen, P., Pine, D. S., & Brook, J. (1996). Discriminating anxiety and depression in youth: A role for diagnostic criteria. *Journal of Affective Disorders, 39*, 191–200.

Kagan, J., Reznick, J. S., & Gibbons, J. (1989). Inhibited and uninhibited types of children. *Child Development, 60*, 838–845.

Kashani, J. H., & Orvaschel, H. (1990). A community study of anxiety in children and adolescents. *American Journal of Psychiatry, 147*, 313–318.

Kearney, C., & Silverman, W. (1993). Measuring the function of school refusal behavior: The Social Assessment Scale. *Journal of Clinical Child Psychology, 22*, 85–96.

Kendall, P. C. (1994). Treating anxiety disorders in children: Results of a randomized clinical trial. *Journal of Consulting and Clinical Psychology, 62*, 100–110.

Kendall, P. C. (2000). *Cognitive-behavioral therapy for anxious children: Therapist manual* (2nd ed.). Ardmore, PA: Workbook Publishing.

Kendall, P. C. (2001). Flexibility within fidelity. *Child and Adolescent Psychology Newsletter, 16*(2), 1–5.

Kendall, P.C., Chu, B., Gifford, A., Hayes, C., & Nauta, M. (1998). Breathing life into a manual. *Cognitive and Behavioral Practice, 5*, 177–198.

Kendall, P. C., Flannery-Schroeder, E., Panichelli-Mindel, S. M., Southam-Gerow, M., Henin, A., & Warman, M. (1997). Therapy for youths with anxiety disorders: A second randomized clinical trial. *Journal of Consulting and Clinical Psychology, 65*, 366–380.

Kendall, P. C., Robin, J., Hedtke, K., Suveg, C., Flannery-Schroeder, E., & Gosch, E. (2005). Considering CBT with anxious youth? Think exposures. *Cognitive and Behavioral Practice*, 12, 136–150.

Kendall, P.C., Safford, S., Flannery-Schroeder, E., & Webb, A. (2004). Child anxiety treatment: Outcomes in adolescence and impact on substance use and depression at 7.4 year follow-up. *Journal of Consulting and Clinical Psychology, 72*(2), 276–287.

Kendall, P. C., & Southam-Gerow, M. (1996). Long-term follow-up of a cognitive-behavioral therapy for anxiety-disordered youth. *Journal of Consulting and Clinical Psychology, 64*, 724–730.

Koeppen, A. S. (1974). Relaxation training for children. *Elementary School Guidance and Counseling, 9*, 12–21.

La Greca, A., Dandes, S., Wick, P., Shaw, K., & Stone, W. (1988). Development of the Social Anxiety Scale for Children: Reliability and concurrent validity. *Journal of Clinical Child Psychology, 17*, 84–91.

Lang, P. J. (1968). Fear reduction and fear behavior: Problems in treating a construct. In J. M. Shlien (Ed.), *Research in psychotherapy*. Washington, DC: American Psychological Association.

Manassis, K., Hudson, J. L., Webb, A., & Albano, A. M. (2004). Beyond behavioral inhibition: Etiological factors in childhood anxiety. *Cognitive and Behavioral Practice, 11*, 3–12.

March, J. S. (1995). Cognitive-behavioral psychotherapy for children and adolescents with OCD: a review and recommendations for treatment. *Journal of the American Academy of Child and Adolescent Psychiatry, 34*, 7–14.

March, J. S., & Albano, A. M. (2002). Anxiety disorders in children and adolescents. In D. Stein & E. Hollander (Eds.), *Textbook of anxiety disorders* (pp. 415–427). Washington, DC: American Psychological Association.

March, J.S., Parker, J. D. A., Sullivan, K., Stallings, P., & Connors, K. (1997). The Multidimensional Anxiety Scale for Children (MASC): Factor structure, reliability, and validity. *Journal of American Academy of Child and Adolescent Psychiatry, 36*, 554–565.

Masia, C. L., Klein, R. G., Storch, E. A., & Corda, B. (2001). School-based behavioral treatment for social anxiety disorder in adolescents: Results of a pilot study. *Journal of the American Academy of Child and Adolescent Psychiatry, 40*, 780–786.

Meichenbaum, D. H. (1985). *Stress inoculation training*. New York: Pergamon Press.

Mendlowitz, S. L., Manassis, K., Bradley, S., Scapillato, D., Miezitis, S., & Shaw, B. F. (1999). Cognitive-behavioral group treatments in childhood anxiety disorders: The role of parental involvement. *Journal of the American Academy of Child and Adolescent Psychiatry, 38*, 1223–1229.

Mowrer, O. H. (1960). *Learning theory and behavior*. New York: Wiley.

Nezu, A. M., & D'Zurilla, T. J. (1989). Social problem solving and negative affective conditions. In P. C. Kendall and D. Watson (Eds.), *Anxiety and depression: Distinctive and overlapping features* (pp. 285–315). New York: Academic Press.

Nezu, A. M., Nezu, C. M., & Perri, M. G. (1989). *Problem-solving therapy for depression: Theory, research, and clinical guidelines*. New York: Wiley.

Ollendick, T.H. (1983). Reliability and validity of the Revised Fear Survey Schedule for Children (FSSC-R). *Behaviour Research and Therapy, 21*, 685–692.

Ollendick, T. H., & Cerny, J. A. (1981). *Clinical behavior therapy with children*. New York: Plenum Press.

Perrin, S., & Last, C. G. (1992). Do childhood anxiety measures measure anxiety? *Journal of Abnormal Child Psychology, 20*, 567–578.

Rapee, R. M., & Barlow, D. H. (1993). Generalized anxiety disorder, panic disorder and the phobias. In P. B. Suther & H. E. Adams (Eds.), *Comprehensive handbook of psychopathology* (2nd ed.). New York. Plenum.

Reynolds, C. R., & Richmond, B. O. (1978). What I Think and Feel: A revised measure of children's manifest anxiety. *Journal of Abnormal Psychology, 6*, 271–280.

Shaffer, D., Fisher, P., Dulcan, M. K., Davis, D., Piacentini, J., Schwab-Stone, M., et al. (1996). The NIMH Diagnostic Interview Schedule for Children, Version 2.3. (DISC 2.3): Description, acceptability, prevalence rates, and performance in the MECA study. *Journal of the American Academy of Child and Adolescent Psychiatry, 49*, 865–877.

Short, A. L., Barrett, P. M., & Fox, T. L. (2001). Evaluating the FRIENDS program: A cognitive-behavioral group treatment for anxious children and their parents. *Journal of Clinical Child Psychology, 30*, 525–535.

Silverman, W. K., & Albano, A. M. (1997). *The Anxiety Disorders Interview Schedule for Children (DSM-IV)*. San Antonio, TX: Psychological Corporation.

Silverman, W. K., Fleisig, W., Rabian, B., & Peterson, R. A. (1991). Childhood anxiety sensitivity index. *Journal of Clinical Child Psychology, 20*, 162–168.

Silverman, W. K., Kurtines, W. M., Ginsburg, G. S., Weems, C. F., Lumpkin, P. W., & Carmichael, D. H. (1999). Treating anxiety disorders in children with group cognitive-behavioral therapy: A randomized clinical trial. *Journal of Consulting and Clinical Psychology, 67*, 995–1003.

Silverman, W. K., Kurtines, W. M., Ginsburg, G. S., Weems, C. F., Rabian, B., & Serafini, L. T. (1999). Contingency management, self-control, and education support in the treatment of childhood phobic disorders: A randomized clinical trial. *Journal of Consulting and Clinical Psychology, 67*, 675–687.

Spence, S. H., Donovan, C., & Brechman-Toussaint, M. (2000). The treatment of childhood social phobia: The effectiveness of a social skills training-based, cognitive-behavioural intervention with and without parental involvement. *Journal of Child Psychology and Psychiatry, 41*, 713–726.

Spielberger, C. (1973). *Preliminary manual for the State-Trait Anxiety Inventory for Children ("How I Feel Questionnaire")*. Palo Alto, CA: Consulting Psychologists Press.

Urbain, E. S., & Kendall, P. C. (1980). Review of social-cognitive problem-solving interventions with children. *Psychological Bulletin, 88*, 109–143.

Vasey, M. W., & MacLeod, C. (2001). Information-processing factors in childhood anxiety: A review and developmental perspective. In M. W. Vasey and M. R. Dadds (Eds.), *The developmental psychopathology of anxiety* (pp. 253–277). New York: Oxford University Press.

Velting, O. N., Setzer, N. J., & Albano, A. M. (2004). Update on and advances in assessment and cognitive-behavioral treatment of anxiety disorders in children and adolescents. *Professional Psychology: Research and Practice, 35*(1), 42–54.

5

School Refusal Behavior

CHRISTOPHER A. KEARNEY, AMIE LEMOS &
JENNA SILVERMAN

HISTORICAL BACKGROUND

The advent of child psychology partially resulted from a melding of education and psychology in the early 20th century to address youth with school-related problems. One such problem that has received substantial attention since that time is absenteeism from school. Problematic absenteeism was originally considered a legal problem because attendance was mandatory, and the term *truant* popularly described youth who missed school without proper excuse (Broadwin, 1932). Such truancy was linked to many delinquent behaviors, and the term later became synonymous with surreptitious absenteeism without knowledge of the parents (Berg et al., 1985). Even today, *truancy* is primarily a legal term and one that is part of the diagnostic criteria for conduct disorder (American Psychiatric Association, 2000).

In the 1930s and 1940s, several researchers focused on a particular subtype of youth with traditional truancy, noting that many experienced severe distress and related problems when attending school. Such anxiety-based absenteeism was referred to in different ways, including psychoneurotic truancy, school refusal, school phobia, and separation anxiety. Psychoneurotic truancy referred to youth with problematic absenteeism with internalizing symptoms such as shyness, anxiety, and guilt, as well as attention-seeking behaviors (Partridge, 1939). School refusal referred to youth with anxiety-based absenteeism, a concept analogous to psychoneurotic truancy. School phobia more specifically referred to youth with absenteeism marked by severe separation anxiety and overdependency with mothers (Johnson, Falstein, Szurek, & Svendsen, 1941). Separation anxiety refers to developmentally inappropriate worry about being away from home or primary caregivers and was commonly cited as a main reason for school absenteeism (Estes, Haylett, & Johnson, 1956).

In the 1950s, the concept of school phobia was broadened to resemble previous descriptions of psychoneurotic truancy or school refusal, and various subtypes were introduced. For example, Coolidge and colleagues (1957) proposed neurotic and characterological subtypes that represented youth with (1) panic and sudden onset of absenteeism or (2) depression and paranoia with gradual onset of absenteeism. Related approaches also focused on acute versus chronic distinctions of school phobia (e.g., Kennedy, 1965). Conversely, however, school phobia was redefined in the 1960s as a narrower construct that focused only on youth with a specific fear of some school-related stimulus (Lazarus, Davison, & Polefka, 1965).

More recently, empirical and diagnostic approaches have become more popular methods of organizing youth with problematic absenteeism. Some empirical/statistical approaches involve dividing these youth into those with internalizing or externalizing behavior problems (Young, Brasic, Kisnadwala, & Leven, 1990). Other approaches using factor and related analyses have identified subtypes akin to traditional notions of anxiety-based absenteeism and truancy (e.g., Atkinson, Quarrington, Cyr, & Atkinson, 1989; Berg et al., 1985). Unfortunately, substantial overlap has marked these distinctions. Other researchers have also attempted to differentiate this population diagnostically, but substantial heterogeneity has made these attempts problematic as well (Bernstein & Garfinkel, 1986; Last, Francis, Hersen, Kazdin, & Strauss, 1987; Last & Strauss, 1990).

To coalesce historical terminology regarding this population, the term *school refusal behavior* has been devised to refer to all youth who refuse to attend school or have difficulties remaining in classes for an entire day (Kearney & Silverman, 1996). The term includes youth who miss lengthy periods of school time, those with partial absences (e.g., specific classes or times of the day), those who are tardy to school, those who display severe morning misbehaviors in an attempt to miss school, and those who attend school with great dread and who plead for future nonattendance (Kearney, 2001). This chapter will employ the term *school refusal behavior* to describe this population.

CHARACTERISTICS OF YOUTH WITH SCHOOL REFUSAL BEHAVIOR

In this section, the major characteristics of youth with school refusal behavior are summarized, including prevalence and demographic information, symptomatology and comorbid diagnoses, triggers and short-term and long-term consequences of school refusal behavior, and family dynamics.

Prevalence and Demographic Information

Although nearly impossible to calculate precisely, the estimated prevalence of school refusal behavior is 5–28% of school-aged youth (Kearney, 2001). The behavior is largely present in youth aged 10–13 years, as many initially enter middle or junior high school. However, youth of any age can refuse to attend school and the problem is particularly present among youth entering a new school building for the first time. As such, school refusal behavior tends to be more common during, but is not strictly limited to, the autumn months. School refusal behavior is not highly associated with gender, race, or socioeconomic status. A substantial portion of youth with school refusal behavior miss school for more than two years (42.1%), and most are referred for treatment by school officials (Bernstein, Svingen, & Garfinkel, 1990; Stickney & Miltenberger, 1998).

Symptomatology and Comorbid Diagnoses

As previously mentioned, youth with school refusal behavior show substantial heterogeneity of behavior, with many overlapping symptoms. Common internalizing symptoms include general and social anxiety, fear of school-based stimuli, depression and suicidality, fatigue, worry, somatic complaints, self-consciousness, and separation concerns (Kearney, 2003). Common externalizing symptoms include noncompliance and defiance, aggression, temper tantrums, active avoidance, running away from school or home, refusal to move, and clinging to others (Kearney, 2001). In many cases, these internalizing and externalizing symptoms occur together, meaning that one clinical picture is never wholly representative of this population.

Common fears in this population include academic failure, ridicule or abuse from peers, teachers, tests, reprimands, performances before others, illness, transitions between classes, and separation from home or primary caregivers (Granell de Aldaz, Feldman, Vivas, & Gelfand, 1987; Granell de Aldaz, Vivas, Gelfand, & Feldman, 1984). However, the large majority of youth with school refusal behavior report no specific fears, and few have a specific phobia of school. Common somatic complaints in this population, particularly in those youth with emotional distress, include stomachaches, headaches, abdominal pain, dizziness, nausea and vomiting, sweating, trembling, shortness of breath, and asthma, among others (Bernstein et al., 1997; Stickney & Miltenberger, 1998). Symptoms of depression are also common to youth with school refusal behavior, and often intersect with anxiety symptoms to produce strong negative affectivity (Kearney & Silverman, 1996).

Externalizing symptoms among youth with school refusal behavior are often present as well, and can serve several purposes. Many youth who refuse school, for example, display externalizing behavior problems to force parental acquiescence to their demands to remain home from school, to exaggerate discomfort, to avoid anxiety-provoking situations, to induce suspensions from school, to get attention or tangible rewards from significant others, and/or to hide school refusal behavior from others (Kearney, 2001). School absenteeism has also been linked to fighting with others, vandalism, disruptive behavior, and substance abuse (Berg et al., 1993; Charlton & Blair, 1989; Pritchard, Cotton, & Cox, 1992).

Kearney and Albano (2004) found specific primary diagnoses that were most common to youth with school refusal behavior, including separation anxiety disorder (22.4%), generalized anxiety disorder (10.5%), oppositional defiant disorder (8.4%), major depression (4.9%), specific phobia (4.2%), social anxiety disorder (3.5%), conduct disorder (2.8%), attention-deficithyperactivity disorder (1.4%), and panic disorder (1.4%). However, 32.9% of this sample met criteria for no diagnosis, suggesting that many of these youth either have subclinical problems or refuse school without substantial comorbidity. Others have also found considerable comorbidity with respect to anxiety and depression, although the lack of any cooccurring diagnoses is also common (Bernstein et al., 1997; Bernstein & Garfinkel, 1986; Last et al., 1987; Last & Strauss, 1990).

Triggers of School Refusal Behavior

Researchers have identified some common triggers to school refusal behavior. These often include family transitions and stressors, child or parent illness, changes in school-related phenomena (e.g., classes, teachers), school-based threats or frightening events, separation from parents, extended legitimate absence from school, and starting school for the first time (Smith, 1970; Waldron, Shrier, Stone, & Tobin, 1975). However, many cases of school refusal behavior involve no clear precipitating factors, and an extensive search for them is often fruitless (Kearney, 2001; Timberlake, 1984).

Short-Term and Long-Term Consequences of School Refusal Behavior

If school refusal behavior persists, common short-term effects include declining grades, family conflict, legal troubles, child and parent distress, alienation from peers, and lack of supervision of the child (Kearney, 2001). Long-term follow-up studies generally indicate that about one third of youth with chronic school refusal behavior experience *severe* social/occupational adjustment and psychiatric problems as adults, and another one third experience *some* social/occupational adjustment and psychiatric problems as adults (e.g., Berg & Jackson, 1985; Flakierska, Lindstrom, & Gillberg, 1988; Hibbett & Fogelman, 1990; Hibbett, Fogelman, & Manor, 1990). Early identification and treatment for absenteeism and less severe child and parent psychopathology and family dynamics seem to be good prognostic signs (Kearney, 2001).

Family Dynamics

Many different family dynamics have been associated with school refusal behavior over the past several decades. Kearney and Silverman (1995) identified five main family patterns among youth with school refusal behavior, including healthy, detached, enmeshed, isolated, and conflictive families. Healthy families generally have good communication and problem-solving skills, but the child may be experiencing a circumscribed emotional problem and related difficulties attending school. Detached family members are not particularly involved with one another, which could lead to lack of supervision as well as overpermissiveness. Enmeshed family members, on the other hand, are overinvolved with one another and may be susceptible to separation anxiety or overly restrictive parenting. Isolated family members have little contact with people outside the family, which may impede cooperation with school officials when addressing absenteeism. Finally, conflictive families are marked by verbal and physical aggression and an inability to resolve immediate problems such as school refusal behavior. Of course, families may have multiple elements of these dynamics as well.

ASSESSMENT OF SCHOOL REFUSAL BEHAVIOR

In this section, the major assessment methods used to evaluate youth with school refusal behavior are covered, including interviews, questionnaires, observations and daily logbooks, and other methods.

Interviews

Interviewing youth with school refusal behavior and their family members may be conducted using unstructured or structured formats. Researchers using unstructured interviews have generally focused on the history and nature of a child's school refusal behavior, parental knowledge of absenteeism, comorbid symptomatology, and precipitating factors (e.g., Huffington & Sevitt, 1989). Other relevant information includes demographic characteristics, effects of the child's school refusal behavior on daily family functioning, ongoing life stressors, level of social and academic competence, crisis issues, family member perspectives regarding a child's absenteeism, and relevant cultural variables (Kearney, 2005). Treatment-oriented information is important as well, including reasons for seeking treatment at a particular time, referral source (e.g., family, school, court), obstacles to treatment, and expectations and motivation for treatment.

Structured interviews have been used to diagnose youth with school refusal behavior, the most notable being the *Anxiety Disorders Interview Schedule for Children: DSM-IV: Child and Parent Versions* (ADIS-C: DSM-IV: C/P; Silverman & Albano, 1996). Along with sections that cover various internalizing and externalizing diagnoses, the interview has a section on school refusal behavior that covers history, symptoms, child and parent perspectives, avoided situations, degree of interference, and mediating factors associated with a child's school refusal behavior. The ADIS-C: DSM-IV: C/P has shown good reliability and validity and, though primarily used in research-based settings, is useful for cases referred to general mental health agencies (Silverman, Saavedra, & Pina, 2001; Wood, Piacentini, Bergman, McCracken, & Barrios, 2002).

Although parents and children are often the focus of interviews, school officials should also be queried regarding information important for treatment. Common areas of focus, in addition to those mentioned earlier, should include academic status, makeup work, guidelines and anticipated obstacles for reintegrating a child into school, school rules and alternative educational programs, and past and present attendance patterns (Kearney & Albano, 2000). Guidance counselors, teachers, attendance officers, school psychologists, and specialists are often helpful in this regard.

Questionnaires

Child self-report and parent and teacher questionnaires are also commonly used to assess youth with school refusal behavior, though many of these focus on internalizing symptoms. The most common and relevant child self-report measures for this population include, alphabetically, the *Children's Depression Inventory* (Kovacs, 1992), *Daily Life Stressors Scale* (Kearney, Drabman, & Beasley, 1993), *Fear Survey Schedule for Children-Revised* (Ollendick, 1983), *Multidimensional Anxiety Scale for Children* (March, Sullivan, & Parker, 1999), *Negative Affect Self-Statement Questionnaire* (Ronan, Kendall, & Rowe, 1994), *Revised Children's Manifest Anxiety Scale* (Reynolds & Richmond, 1985), *Screen for Child Anxiety-Related Disorders* (Birmaher et al., 1997), *Social Anxiety Scale for Children-Revised* (and an adolescent version; La Greca & Lopez, 1998; La Greca & Stone, 1993), *Social Phobia and Anxiety Inventory for Children* (Beidel, Turner, & Morris, 1995), *State-Trait Anxiety*

Inventory for Children-Revised (Spielberger, 1973), and *Youth Self-Report Scale* (Achenbach & Rescorla, 2001).

The most relevant parent and teacher measures for this population include, alphabetically, the *Child Behavior Checklist and Teacher's Report Form* (Achenbach & Rescorla, 2001), *Child Symptom Inventory-4* (Sprafkin, Gadow, Salisbury, Schneider, & Loney, 2002), and *Conners Rating Scales for parents and teachers* (Conners, 1997). Researchers often ask parents to complete questionnaires regarding problematic family dynamics as well, with the most common measures including the *Family Environment Scale* (Moos & Moos, 1986), *Family Adaptability and Cohesion Evaluation Scale* (Olson, Portner, & Lavee, 1987), and *Family Assessment Measure* (Skinner, Steinhauer, & Santa-Barbara, 1995).

Child self-report and parent-teacher questionnaires generally focus on the *forms* of misbehavior a child may show. However, the *function* of school refusal behavior can also be reliably assessed using the *School Refusal Assessment Scale-Revised* (SRAS-R; Kearney, 2002). The SRAS-R is a 24-item instrument designed to assess the relative strength of four functional conditions of school refusal behavior (see cognitive-behavioral perspective section below). The measure has both child and parent versions, and six items are devoted to each functional condition. Item means for each functional condition are derived from combined child and parent reports, and treatment can be based on the strongest function. The measure also allows clinicians to examine a profile of secondary functions that may affect a particular case, although this profile should be confirmed via direct observation.

Observations and Daily Logbooks

Observations are often invaluable for confirming hypotheses about the form and function of a particular child's school refusal behavior. Direct observations of behavior in the morning prior to school and during the academic day as a child moves about the school building are especially useful. Unfortunately, direct observations are often difficult for clinicians and educators to do because of the time required to complete them. Therefore, direct observations of a child in the clinic setting can be useful to identify anxious, avoidant, clingy, or resistant child behaviors, as well as relevant parent responses and family dynamics (see Kearney, 2005; Kearney & Albano, 2000). Reports from teachers, school counselors, and other school personnel can also be valuable in visualizing the behavior. In addition, daily logbooks or diaries are helpful for charting daily attendance, problematic misbehaviors, emotional states such as anxiety and depression, and episodes of family conflict.

Other Assessment Methods

In addition to the assessment methods described so far, medical examinations, review of academic and other pertinent records, and formal testing may be used to rule out competing explanations for school refusal behavior and further identify problems that need remediation. Intelligence and achievement tests, for example, may be used to identify learning disorders and academic areas that require further attention.

COGNITIVE-BEHAVIORAL PERSPECTIVE OF SCHOOL REFUSAL BEHAVIOR

As mentioned previously, the symptomatology of youth with school refusal behavior is highly diverse and heterogeneous. As such, taxonomies for classifying and conceptualizing this population based on the forms of behavior have been less than successful (Kearney & Silverman, 1996). An alternative way of classifying youth with school refusal behavior in recent years is a functional model whereby youth are organized according to the reasons why they are missing school or having trouble attending school. This functional model is based on cognitive-behavioral mechanisms; youth are theorized to refuse school for one or more of the following reasons: (1) to avoid school-based stimuli that provoke a general sense of negative affectivity, (2) to escape aversive social and/or evaluative situations, (3) to obtain attention from significant others, or (4) to obtain tangible rewards outside of school.

The initial two functional conditions refer to youth who refuse school for negative reinforcement, or to evade unpleasant school-related circumstances. The latter two functional conditions refer to youth who refuse school for positive reinforcement, or to pursue rewards that are more powerful than school attendance. Of course, youth may also refuse school for a combination of reasons involving negative and positive reinforcement.

Youth who refuse school to avoid school-based stimuli that provoke a general sense of negative affectivity tend to be younger and often cannot identify specific stimuli that trigger their desire to miss school. Instead, these children often report feelings of general dread or nervousness or sadness when attending school, and often have somatic complaints that may or may not be exaggerated. Frequently, these children will attend school under great duress and with pleas aimed toward their parents to miss school in the future. However, many of these children are either tardy to school (e.g., from morning dawdling) or miss school outright. In some cases, specific school-based triggers can be identified, and may surround actual threats. In most cases, however, precipitating factors are not obvious.

Youth who refuse school to escape aversive social or evaluative situations tend to be older and usually can identify specific scenarios or stimuli that help trigger their absenteeism. Common aversive social situations for these youth include initiating and maintaining conversations with peers (including spontaneous small talk), walking in hallways, entering classrooms full of people, being teased or ignored by others, dressing before others, participating in group activities, and playing games with others. Common aversive evaluative situations for these youth include tests, public speaking, writing or eating or dressing before others, performing musically or athletically before others, and answering questions in class. Often these children will skip specific aspects of school such as lunch, physical education and mathematics classes, and examinations. Avoidance of these situations may be obvious but also can be subtle, as when youth hide in the bathroom during lunch or sit near an exit or the back of a room to escape notice.

Youth who refuse school to obtain attention from significant others tend to be younger and generally gear their behavior toward staying home. Although separation anxiety is often a key component, this functional condition is meant to more broadly encompass youth whose misbehavior is designed to maintain parental contact and attention. Many of these children will attend school if a parent stays with them during the course of the day, though others often insist on remaining home or going to work with parents. Even if in school, many of these children will repeatedly request to call their parents during the day, run out of the school building in an attempt to get home, or misbehave so that they are sent home. In addition, these children will often show severe morning misbehaviors in an attempt to remain home. With parental acquiescence, this type of school refusal behavior can be quite chronic.

Youth who refuse school to obtain tangible rewards generally pursue fun activities outside of school during school hours, and usually have little desire to be with their parents or at home. Perhaps most analogous to traditional truancy, these youth miss school to engage in acts such as playing or talking with friends, watching television, sleeping late, riding their bicycle, and participating in delinquent activities. These youth tend to be older and often miss large parts of a school day (e.g., skipping afternoon classes) or fail to attend entirely. Their school refusal behavior may or may not be recognized by their parents, and the function is often associated with highly problematic family dynamics.

Youth may also miss school for a combination of these reasons. For example, a child may initially refuse school to avoid stimuli that provoke negative affectivity. With parental acquiescence, however, the child may discover the many positive amenities of staying home and secondarily refuse school for tangible reinforcement outside of school. Conversely, a youth may have missed school for an extensive period of time for tangible reinforcement and is now anxious about returning to new classes and teachers. Youth who refuse school for multiple reasons are generally more difficult to treat than youth who refuse school for shorter periods of time and for just one reason. However, specific knowledge of a child's functional profile is important with respect to intervention, which is discussed next.

INTERVENTIONS FOR SCHOOL REFUSAL BEHAVIOR

Interventions for youth with school refusal behavior may be generally divided into child-, parent-, and family-based practices. Suggestions for school officials are made later in this chapter.

Child-Based Interventions

Child-based treatment techniques for school refusal behavior often include psychoeducation and self-monitoring, somatic control exercises, cognitive therapy, and exposure-based practices. Each of these is briefly discussed in turn. Psychoeducation refers to teaching children and perhaps family members about the nature of their school refusal behavior and accompanying symptoms of anxiety and depression. An emphasis is often placed on educating children about the forms and functions of their absenteeism as well as the physiological, cognitive, and behavioral aspects of their emotional states. In addition, youth are asked to engage in constant self-monitoring to track patterns of emotional states and treatment progress.

Sequences of symptom components for a child should be identified as well. Some children, for example, awake with somatic complaints and muscle tension (physiological components) that may lead to thoughts of danger or anxiety surrounding school (cognitive components) that may lead to tantrums, avoidance, or refusal to attend (behavioral components). Specific examples from a child's own recent experiences are helpful in this regard (Kearney & Albano, 2000).

For youth with considerable physiological anxiety about attending school, somatic control exercises may be used to reduce arousal and ease reintegration. Muscle relaxation training is commonly employed for these youth, which can take the form of successive tension and release of various muscle groups (Ollendick & Cerny, 1981). Another popular somatic control exercise is breathing retraining, which involves teaching a child to inhale slowly through his or her nose while pushing into the diaphragm to deepen breathing, then exhaling slowly through the mouth (Kearney & Albano, 2000). For younger children, images of a balloon or tire inflating and deflating are often helpful. Youth employing these techniques typically practice them regularly and then apply them to exposure-based practices during stressful situations.

Cognitive therapy is also useful for many adolescents with school refusal behavior, particularly those with irrational thoughts about school attendance, peers, and performances before others. Cognitive therapy for these youth generally involves identifying and labeling distorted thoughts, evaluating these thoughts through self-reflection and questioning, invoking strategies to modify these thoughts toward more realistic ones, and reinforcing oneself for doing so. Common cognitive techniques include having a child examine evidence for and against a specific thought, exploring the true (and usually manageable) consequences of the "worst-case scenario," considering other causes for a negative event, reframing or relabeling a problem more positively or realistically, and conducting behavioral experiments to test the true probability of a negative event, among others (Reinecke, Dattilio, & Freeman, 2003).

Finally, exposure-based practices are often a key treatment component for youth with school refusal behavior. These practices involve gradually reintroducing a child to school via shaping. Often this reintroduction involves certain classes or periods of the school day; for example, a child may attend school for one hour on the first day and add an hour per day thereafter. Exposure-based practices are based on habituation, emotional processing, and enhanced self-efficacy; the child will eventually become more accustomed to his or her surroundings, learn that the surroundings are not dangerous, and feel more in control of his or her surroundings (Kearney, 2005). Exposures are typically linked with many of the other treatment techniques described in this chapter.

Parent-Based Interventions

Parent-based interventions for youth with school refusal behavior often include contingency management, establishment of routines, improving commands, and, in some cases, forced school attendance. Contingency management in this context refers to helping parents establish house rules, especially regarding a child's behavior in the morning before school, as well as rewards and punishments for compliance/attendance and noncompliance/absenteeism, respectively. For young children, a token economy system may be developed, but older children will respond more to praise and other direct reinforcements.

Contingencies in this manner are typically linked with a child's adherence to a morning routine that allows enough time to complete school preparation behaviors. A child should generally be required to arise from bed about 90–120 minutes before the beginning of school, and times should be set for washing, dressing, eating breakfast, brushing teeth, and making final preparations (e.g., filling backpack, putting on jacket). The routine should be flexible to give the child enough leeway for small delays, but strict enough such that failure to meet a required step results in some punishment. Consequences and routines are also linked to modifications in parent commands toward brevity and clarity.

In some cases, forced school attendance may be used. In this procedure, two parents/adults transport a child to school and deposit him or her with school officials, who escort the child to class and maintain good supervision during the course of the day. Forced school attendance should only be used in certain cases, however. In particular, we recommend using the procedure only as a last resort, if the child is missing more school days than not, if the child has no anxiety about attending school, and if parents and school officials cooperate during the procedure (Kearney & Albano, 2000). Ideally, however, the use of consequences in accordance with house rules and routines should be emphasized.

Family-Based Interventions

Family-based interventions for youth with school refusal behavior often include contingency contracting and communication skills training. Contingency contracting in this context involves written parent-child agreements that focus on incentives for attendance or school preparation and disincentives for absenteeism or noncompliance. Contracts are useful ways of enhancing a family's problem-solving process and for reducing conflict, and must be implemented only if all parties agree without coercion. Contracts may be linked to communication skills training whereby family members practice appropriate methods of listening, paraphrasing, and responding to others' statements.

Successful contracts depend on a child's actual attendance at school, of course, so escorting a child to school and from class to class may be necessary to help the youth initially receive contract-mandated rewards. In addition, peer refusal skills training may be implemented to help youth decline peer-based offers to miss school. In this regard, youth can role-play statements or behaviors that allow them to stay in school and yet not lose credibility with their friends (Kearney & Albano, 2000).

Prescriptive Treatment within a Functional Model of School Refusal Behavior

The treatment techniques described here have been utilized within the functional model of school refusal behavior outlined earlier. In particular, treatment packages have been designed and are prescribed for children of various functional conditions. For youth who refuse school to avoid school-based stimuli that provoke general negative affectivity or to escape aversive social and evaluative situations, treatment largely involves child-based psychoeducation, somatic control exercises, cognitive therapy, and exposure-based practices. For youth who refuse school for attention, treatment largely involves parent-based contingency management and related practices. For youth who refuse school for tangible rewards outside of school, treatment largely involves family-based contingency contracting and related skills training.

APPLICATIONS TO THE SCHOOL SETTING

The procedures described so far can be applied in school settings in full or condensed form. For example, school psychologists, guidance counselors, and relevant others could engage in basic anxiety management skills training for youth or make recommendations to parents about consequence strategies. In fact, many of the treatment procedures described so far may be most effective when administered within school-based settings. Doing so, for example, enhances exposure to the school setting, increases supervision of the child, and necessarily involves multiple professionals in treatment (e.g., mental health professionals and school officials). Apart from these formalized treatment procedures, however, frontline school officials may engage in other practices to secure better attendance for a particular youth. Kearney and Bates (in press) covered many of these front-line approaches, and a brief summary is presented here.

One key frontline approach involves supervising a child during the course of the school day. Enhanced supervision should help deter class skipping, excessive behaviors such as telephone calls, and avoidance. Ideally, such supervision would be conducted by a school official, special assistant, or peer "buddy" who monitors the youth throughout the school day. If this is not feasible, then asking teachers to escort a particular child from his or her individual classes to the child's next one may be helpful. Asking teachers to keep a daily journal regarding a child's attendance is also beneficial.

Another key approach is actively removing obstacles to a child's attendance. School officials may, for example, regularly review a child's academic progress and make necessary modifications to class schedules or makeup work. Providing appropriate and tailored academic instruction is also important, as many youth refuse school because their curriculum poorly matches their academic needs. In addition, any conflicts the child may have with teachers or other school officials should be resolved quickly. Along with removing obstacles, providing school-based incentives for attendance is a good idea. This may come in the form of written contracts with the student, increased participation in desired extracurricular activities and social groups, frequent praise, and classroom-based strategies (e.g., token economies) to enhance prosocial behavior.

School-based interventions should also be closely linked to parental behaviors. For example, parents may be asked to contact school officials immediately when a child's absenteeism occurs or is anticipated, restrict a child's activities to academic tasks when illegitimately home from school, commit to a specific attendance goal, and pursue additional psychological treatment as necessary. This is especially important when problems develop in a particular attendance plan, and frequent parent-school official meetings should be scheduled to avert lengthy noncompliance.

Should noncompliance to a particular attendance schedule occur, school officials are encouraged to quickly discover its reasons. Noncompliance often results, for example, following treatment plans that are too ambitious or complicated, the presence of significant treatment obstacles that have not been satisfactorily addressed, lack of supervision of the child, resistance from parents or a child about changes in the status quo, problematic family conflict, and severe psychopathology, among other reasons (Kearney & Bates, 2004). Noncompliance should be addressed on an ongoing basis, and amelioration often depends on frequent, positive contact with family members, incentives for treatment participation, simplification of the treatment plan, providing transportation and other forms of assistance, mobilizing a family's social support network, and coalescing school official meetings with those of social service agencies.

CASE EXAMPLES

Case Example 1

Tyler was a 13-year-old multiracial male who was referred to our clinic for recent episodes of school refusal behavior. Tyler had entered middle school four months earlier and immediately began to experience attendance problems. In particular, he seemed overwhelmed by the presence of many new teachers, classes, diverse peers, and homework assignments. Making matters worse was the fact that several of his neighborhood friends were zoned for another school or had different class schedules than his, which made Tyler feel isolated and depressed.

Tyler was referred for treatment by his school guidance counselor and parents, all of whom were concerned by Tyler's absences and mood changes. The guidance counselor reported that Tyler had amassed 30 full-day and 22 part-day absences in four months. In addition, she said that Tyler often seemed tearful at school and simply wanted to go home. Tyler's parents echoed this report and said that their son had generally been a good student in elementary school but was always sensitive and shy. They reported that Tyler usually waited for his friends to call him to ask him to play, and that his friends were less available since the move to middle school. During a school day at home, Tyler would complete school work or chores assigned by his mother.

The therapist conducted a thorough assessment that consisted of interviews, self-report and parent questionnaires, and logbooks detailing daily emotional states, problematic behaviors (e.g., clinginess, tantrums), and attendance. Assessment data revealed that Tyler met criteria for social anxiety disorder and had some symptoms of depression. In addition, a detailed functional analysis revealed that Tyler primarily refused school to escape aversive social and/or evaluative situations, especially interactions with new peers and performances before others.

The therapist then outlined a treatment plan for Tyler and his parents that involved anxiety management during key social and evaluative situations, as well as gradual reintegration into school. This plan initially consisted of psychoeducation about social anxiety, which was highly applicable to Tyler as he had many physical, cognitive, and behavioral aspects of anxiety. A typical sequence in the morning, for example, involved stomach tightness and nausea that led to worries about looking foolish in school and subsequent behaviors to avoid school. Specific examples from Tyler's experience were utilized in this regard.

Because Tyler was bright, his therapist also introduced cognitive therapy techniques to help modify irrational thoughts in anxiety-provoking situations. A concentration was made on examining evidence for and against thoughts of failure or public humiliation in various situations as well as testing hypotheses about such events. Tyler's social skills needed refinement as well, and he and the therapist spent several sessions practicing these skills. Particular focus was made on peer interactions and oral presentations.

Exposure-based practices comprised the final step of therapy, and Tyler was asked to initially attend those classes he enjoyed most. This early exposure to the school setting was later supplemented by gradual attendance to other classes as well as interactions with others and completion of make-up work involving performances before others. Tyler was also required to join two extracurricular activities to help boost the development of new friendships, and his guidance counselor modified his schedule so that two of his more difficult classes contained friends from elementary school. Over a period of 10 weeks of treatment, Tyler remained somewhat anxious about peer interactions but was attending school full-time.

Case Example 2

Carly was a 16-year-old Caucasian female referred to our clinic for very extensive school refusal behavior. Carly had missed the last several months of school and had a long history of sporadic absences prior to this year. Her school guidance counselor could not provide much information except that Carly was failing all of her classes and seemed likely to drop out of school altogether. Carly's parents were largely frustrated with her behavior and seemed resigned to her dropping out as well. During the initial interview, Carly was cooperative but made clear that she didn't like school and felt it was unnecessary. She pointed out that several of her older friends got jobs without finishing high school, and that she could go the same route.

The therapist conducted an assessment that was similar to Tyler's, although the family members were not cooperative with respect to daily logbooks. Assessment data revealed that Carly did not meet criteria for any mental disorder, although her noncompliance and school absenteeism were obviously problematic. A functional analysis revealed that Carly was largely refusing school for tangible reinforcement outside of school. In particular, Carly enjoyed being with her friends at their homes, often watching television, sleeping, or cruising a nearby shopping mall.

Carly and her parents attended treatment only sporadically, but an attempt was made to engage in contingency contracting to improve school preparation and attendance behaviors. Although both Carly and her parents worked during the sessions to develop a suitable contract, Carly's adherence to it was short-lived. A further attempt to fulfill the contract involved Carly's parents escorting their daughter to school, but this situation eventually proved unworkable.

The therapist then consulted with the guidance counselor about alternative high school programs for which Carly was eligible. Several options were presented to

Carly and her parents, and Carly agreed that a 3-hour late afternoon/early evening program that involved partial credit was most acceptable. This schedule allowed her time with friends and was not so oppressive that she could not handle the work. Her parents agreed to supervise her homework and attendance more carefully, and a contract regarding attendance was developed. Carly successfully attended this program for the duration of the academic year, though the family terminated therapy during the intervening summer.

FINAL COMMENTS

School refusal behavior is a complex, heterogeneous, and prevalent problem that requires thorough assessment, prescriptive treatment, and cooperation among various mental health and education professionals as well as parents and youth. In many cases, a particularly innovative treatment plan will have to be adopted, and may involve targeting various comorbid behaviors and problematic family dynamics. Modified attendance goals (i.e., other than full-time) should also be considered. Mental health and education professionals are also encouraged to keep abreast of rapid developments in assessment and treatment of this population.

REFERENCES

Achenbach, T. M., & Rescorla, L. A. (2001). *Manual for the ASEBA school-age forms & profiles.* Burlington: University of Vermont Research Center for Children, Youth, & Families.

American Psychiatric Association. (2000). *Diagnostic and statistical manual of mental disorders* (4th ed., text revision). Washington, DC: Author.

Atkinson, L., Quarrington, B., Cyr, J. J., & Atkinson, F. V. (1989). Differential classification in school refusal. *British Journal of Psychiatry, 155,* 191–195.

Beidel, D. C., Turner, S. M., & Morris, T. L. (1995). A new inventory to assess childhood social anxiety and phobia: The Social Phobia and Anxiety Inventory for Children. *Psychological Assessment, 7,* 73–79.

Berg, I., Butler, A., Franklin, J., Hayes, H., Lucas, C., & Sims, R. (1993). DSM-III-R disorders, social factors and management of school attendance problems in the normal population. *Journal of Child Psychology and Psychiatry, 34,* 1187–1203.

Berg, I., Casswell, G., Goodwin, A., Hullin, R., McGuire, R., & Tagg, G. (1985). Classification of severe school attendance problems. *Psychological Medicine, 15,* 157–165.

Berg, I., & Jackson, A. (1985). Teenage school refusers grow up: A follow-up study of 168 subjects, ten years on average after inpatient treatment. *British Journal of Psychiatry, 147,* 366–370.

Bernstein, G. A., & Garfinkel, B. D. (1986). School phobia: The overlap of affective and anxiety disorders. *Journal of the American Academy of Child and Adolescent Psychiatry, 25,* 235–241.

Bernstein, G. A., Massie, E. D., Thuras, P. D., Perwien, A. R., Borchardt, C. M., & Crosby, R. D. (1997). Somatic symptoms in anxious-depressed school refusers. *Journal of the American Academy of Child and Adolescent Psychiatry, 36,* 661–668.

Bernstein, G. A., Svingen, P. H., & Garfinkel, B. D. (1990). School phobia: Patterns of family functioning. *Journal of the American Academy of Child and Adolescent Psychiatry, 29,* 24–30.

Birmaher, B., Khetarpal, S., Brent, D., Cully, M., Balach, L., Kaufman, J., & Neer, S. M. (1997). The Screen for Child Anxiety Related Emotional Disorders (SCARED): Scale construction and psychometric characteristics. *Journal of the American Academy of Child and Adolescent Psychiatry, 36,* 545–553.

Broadwin, I. T. (1932). A contribution to the study of truancy. *American Journal of Orthopsychiatry, 2,* 253–259.

Charlton, A., & Blair, V. (1989). Absence from school related to children's and parental smoking habits. *British Medical Journal, 298,* 90–92.

Conners, C. K. (1997). *Conners Rating Scales-Revised.* North Tonawanda, NY: Multi-Health Systems.

Coolidge, J. C., Hahn, P. B., & Peck, A. L. (1957). School phobia: Neurotic crisis or way of life? *American Journal of Orthopsychiatry, 27,* 296–306.

Estes, H. R., Haylett, C. H., & Johnson, A. M. (1956). Separation anxiety. *American Journal of Orthopsychiatry, 26,* 682–695.

Flakierska, N., Lindstrom, M., & Gillberg, C. (1988). School refusal: A 15–20-year follow-up study of 35 Swedish urban children. *British Journal of Psychiatry, 152,* 834–837.

Granell de Aldaz, E., Feldman, L., Vivas, E., & Gelfand, D. M. (1987). Characteristics of Venezuelan school refusers: Toward the development of a high-risk profile. *Journal of Nervous and Mental Disease, 175,* 402–407.

Granell de Aldaz, E., Vivas, E., Gelfand, D. M., & Feldman, L. (1984). Estimating the prevalence of school refusal and school-related fears. *Journal of Nervous and Mental Disease, 172,* 722–729.

Hibbett, A., & Fogelman, K. (1990). Future lives of truants: Family formation and health-related behaviour. *British Journal of Educational Psychology, 60,* 171–179.

Hibbett, A., Fogelman, K., & Manor, O. (1990). Occupational outcomes of truancy. *British Journal of Educational Psychology, 60,* 23–36.

Huffington, C. M., & Sevitt, M. A. (1989). Family interaction in adolescent school phobia. *Journal of Family Therapy, 11,* 353–375.

Johnson, A. M., Falstein, E. I., Szurek, S. A., & Svendsen, M. (1941). School phobia. *American Journal of Orthopsychiatry, 11,* 702–711.

Kearney, C. A. (2001). *School refusal behavior in youth: A functional approach to assessment and treatment.* Washington, DC: American Psychological Association.

Kearney, C. A. (2002). Identifying the function of school refusal behavior: A revision of the School Refusal Assessment Scale. *Journal of Psychopathology and Behavioral Assessment, 24,* 235–245.

Kearney, C. A. (2003). Bridging the gap among professionals who address youth with school absenteeism: Overview and suggestions for consensus. *Professional Psychology: Research and Practice, 34,* 57–65.

Kearney, C. A. (2005). *Social anxiety and social phobia in youth: Characteristics, assessment, and psychological treatment.* New York: Kluwer Academic/Plenum.

Kearney, C. A., & Albano, A. M. (2000). *When children refuse school: A cognitive-behavioral therapy approach/therapist's guide.* San Antonio, TX: The Psychological Corporation.

Kearney, C. A., & Albano, A. M. (2004). The functional profiles of school refusal behavior: Diagnostic aspects. *Behavior Modification, 28,* 147–161.

Kearney, C. A., & Bates, M (in press). Addressing youth with school refusal behavior: Suggestions for front-line professionals. *Children and Schools.*

Kearney, C. A., Drabman, R. S., & Beasley, J. F. (1993). The trials of childhood: The development, reliability, and validity of the Daily Life Stressors Scale. *Journal of Child and Family Studies, 2,* 371–388.

Kearney, C. A., & Silverman, W. K. (1995). Family environment of youngsters with school refusal behavior: A synopsis with implications for assessment and treatment. *American Journal of Family Therapy, 23,* 59–72.

Kearney, C. A., & Silverman, W. K. (1996). The evolution and reconciliation of taxonomic strategies for school refusal behavior. *Clinical Psychology: Science and Practice, 3,* 339–354.

Kennedy, W. A. (1965). School phobia: Rapid treatment of 50 cases. *Journal of Abnormal Psychology, 70,* 285–289.

Kovacs, M. (1992). *Children's Depression Inventory manual.* North Tonawanda, NY: Multi-Health Systems.

La Greca, A. M., & Lopez, N. (1998). Social anxiety among adolescents: Linkages with peer relations and friendships. *Journal of Abnormal Child Psychology, 26,* 83–94.

La Greca, A. M., & Stone, W. L. (1993). Social Anxiety Scale for Children-Revised: Factor structure and concurrent validity. *Journal of Clinical Child Psychology, 22,* 17–27.

Last, C. G., Francis, G., Hersen, M., Kazdin, A. E., & Strauss, C.C. (1987). Separation anxiety and school phobia: A comparison using DSM-III criteria. *American Journal of Psychiatry, 144,* 653–657.

Last, C. G., & Strauss, C. C. (1990). School refusal in anxiety-disordered children and adolescents. *Journal of the American Academy of Child and Adolescent Psychiatry, 29,* 31–35.

Lazarus, A. A., Davison, G. C., & Polefka, D. A. (1965). Classical and operant factors in the treatment of a school phobia. *Journal of Abnormal Psychology, 70,* 225–229.

March, J. S., Sullivan, K., & Parker, J. (1999). Test-retest reliability of the Multidimensional Anxiety Scale for Children. *Journal of Anxiety Disorders, 13,* 349–358.

Moos, R. H., & Moos, B. S. (1986). *Family Environment Scale manual* (2nd. ed.). Palo Alto, CA: Consulting Psychologists Press.

Ollendick, T. H. (1983). Reliability and validity of the Revised Fear Survey Schedule for Children (FSSC-R). *Behaviour Research and Therapy, 21,* 685–692.

Ollendick, T. H., & Cerny, J. A. (1981). *Clinical behavior therapy with children.* New York: Plenum.

Olson, D. H., Portner, J., & Lavee, Y. (1987). Family Adaptability and Cohesion Evaluation Scales (FACES III). In N. Fredman & R. Sherman (Eds.), *Handbook of measurements for marriage and family therapy* (pp. 180–185). New York: Brunner Mazel.

Partridge, J. M. (1939). Truancy. *Journal of Mental Science, 85,* 45–81.

Pritchard, C., Cotton, A., & Cox, M. (1992). Truancy and illegal drug use, and knowledge of HIV infection in 932 14–16-year-old adolescents. *Journal of Adolescence, 15,* 1–17.

Reinecke, M. A., Dattilio, F. M., & Freeman, A. (2003). *Cognitive therapy with children and adolescents: A casebook for clinical practice* (2nd ed.). New York: Guilford.

Reynolds, C. R., & Richmond, B. O. (1985). *Revised Children's Manifest Anxiety Scale manual.* Los Angeles, CA: Western Psychological Services.

Ronan, K. R., Kendall, P. C., & Rowe, M. (1994). Negative affectivity in children: Development and validation of a self-statement questionnaire. *Cognitive Therapy and Research, 18,* 509–528.

Silverman, W. K., & Albano, A. M. (1996). *The Anxiety Disorders Interview Schedule for Children for DSM-IV, child and parent versions.* San Antonio, TX: Psychological Corporation.

Silverman, W. K., Saavedra, L. M., & Pina, A. A. (2001). Test-retest reliability of anxiety symptoms and diagnoses with the Anxiety Disorders Interview Schedule for DSM-IV: Child and Parent Versions. *Journal of the American Academy of Child and Adolescent Psychiatry, 40,* 937–944.

Skinner, H. A., Steinhauer, P. D., & Santa-Barbara, J. (1995). *Family Assessment Measure, Version III (FAM-III).* North Tonawanda, NY: Multi-Health Systems.

Smith, S. L. (1970). School refusal with anxiety: A review of sixty-three cases. *Canadian Psychiatric Association Journal, 15,* 257–264.

Spielberger, C. D. (1973). *Manual for the State-Trait Anxiety Inventory for Children.* Palo Alto, CA: Consulting Psychologists Press.

Sprafkin, J., Gadow, K. D., Salisbury, H., Schneider, J., & Loney, J. (2002). Further evidence of reliability and validity of the Child Symptom Inventory-4: Parent checklist in clinically referred boys. *Journal of Clinical Child and Adolescent Psychology, 31,* 513–524.

Stickney, M. I., & Miltenberger, R. G. (1998). School refusal behavior: Prevalence, characteristics, and the schools' response. *Education and Treatment of Children, 21,* 160–170.

Timberlake, E. M. (1984). Psychosocial functioning of school phobics at follow-up. *Social Work Research and Abstracts, 20,* 13–18.

Waldron, S., Shrier, D. K., Stone, B., & Tobin, F. (1975). School phobia and other childhood neuroses: A systematic study of the children and their families. *American Journal of Psychiatry, 132,* 802–808.

Wood, J. J., Piacentini, J. C., Bergman, L., McCracken, J., & Barrios, V. (2002). Concurrent validity of the anxiety disorders section of the Anxiety Disorders Interview Schedule for DSM-IV: Child and Parent Versions. *Journal of Clinical Child and Adolescent Psychology, 31,* 335–342.

Young, J. G., Brasic, J. R., Kisnadwala, H., & Leven, L. (1990). Strategies for research on school refusal and related nonattendance at school. In C. Chiland & J. G. Young (Eds.), *Why children reject school: Views from seven countries* (pp. 199–223). New Haven, CT: Yale University Press.

6

Understanding and Treating Selective Mutism

CHRISTY A. MULLIGAN &
RAY W. CHRISTNER

Many childhood disorders exist that intrigue mental health and school personnel throughout their professional careers, many of which are rare to see and oftentimes frustrating to treat. Selective Mutism (SM) is one such disorder. Many times, children with SM are not identified until they enter social situations, such as school. This is often the case with these children because the demands to speak outside the home are not placed on them until they enter a school situation, with preschool and elementary school frequently becoming the identifying setting.

The purpose for this chapter on SM is for the professional reader to gain insight and strategies on how to evaluate and treat SM effectively. Although there has been a growth in the literature related to evidenced-based treatments, such as cognitive-behavior therapy (CBT), for a number of childhood problems and disorders, there is relatively little research specific to the evaluation and treatment for SM. Consequently, mental health and school-based service providers (e.g., school psychologists, counselors, social workers, etc.) are often in a quandary as to what treatments work best and how to come to a conclusion for a diagnosis. A common misconception is that children with SM are oppositional or that their behavioral manifestations are the result of an underlying behavioral disorder (e.g., Oppositional Defiant Disorder). This type of thinking is incorrect, as there are no findings suggesting that children with SM present with externalizing or behavioral disorders in the absence of anxiety (Dummit et al., 1996).

WHAT IS SELECTIVE MUTISM?

Toward the end of the 19th century, Kussmaul (1877) described a disorder in which individuals would not speak in certain situations, even though they had the ability to speak. He named this disorder *aphasia voluntaria*, emphasizing what he thought was a voluntary decision not to speak. In 1934, Tramer, when investigating the same symptoms, called the problem *elective mutism* (as cited in Dow, Sonies, Scheib, Moss, & Leonard, 1995), as he believed these children were "electing" not to speak. The new term, *selective mutism*, was adopted in the *Diagnostic and Statistical Manual of Mental Disorders, Fourth Edition* (DSM-IV; American Psychiatric Association, 1994) and has remained in the recent revision of the *Diagnostic and Statistical Manual of Mental Disorders, Fourth Edition, Text Revision* (DSM-IV-TR; American Psychiatric Association, 2000). This new term implies that these children do not speak in "select" situations, which appears to be more consistent with new etiological theories that focus on anxiety issues (Dow et al., 1995). According to the DSM-IV-TR, the essential feature of SM is the persistent failure to speak in specific social situations where speaking is expected, despite speaking in other situations. For instance, it is common that children with SM speak readily at home but say little or nothing when at school or in other social situations.

As with other disorders, the disturbance must interfere with educational or occupational achievement or with social functioning. In the case of SM, this may be seen in social interactions with classmates, as well as a lack of participation in class activities. Although the disturbance must last for at least 1 month, it is not limited to the first month of school. SM should not be diagnosed if the individual's failing to speak is solely because of a lack of knowledge of, or discomfort with, the spoken language required in the social situation. Therefore, children whose lack of speaking is the result of embarrassment related to having a Communication Disorder (e.g., Stuttering, Phonological Disorder, etc.) would not be identified as SM. Additionally, clinicians must rule out the presence of Pervasive Developmental Disorder (PDD), Schizophrenia, or other Psychotic Disorders. Instead of communicating by standard verbalization, children with SM may communicate by gestures, nodding, shaking their head, or pulling and pushing. In some cases, their communication is by means of monosyllabic, short, monotone utterances, or altered voices (American Psychiatric Association, 2000).

LITERATURE REVIEW: SELECTIVE MUTISM

SM is found in less than 1% of individuals and has a tendency to be slightly more common in girls than in boys. The disorder has a variable course, lasting from a few months to a few years (Krysanski, 2003). Extant research supports the theory that social anxiety is etiologically connected to SM, and it should be conceptualized as a type of social phobia (see Black & Uhde, 1995). This reasoning is based on the fact that children with SM manifest many of the same characteristics as children with social anxiety disorders, including social avoidance, distress in social situations, and fear of speaking to strangers (Beidel & Turner, 1998). Diagnostic studies of children with SM (e.g., Black & Uhde, 1995; Dummit et al., 1997) indicate that almost all children with SM also meet the criteria for social phobia, as defined by the DSM-IV. There is also evidence that the age of onset for both SM and social phobia are the same (Dummit et al., 1997). Subsequently, the commonalities between these two disorders, as well as the 90% to 100% comorbidity rate for social phobia among children with SM, have led some researchers and clinicians to suggest that

SM should be conceptualized as a separate disorder, yet a variant of social phobia (Black & Uhde, 1995; Kristensen, 2000). In this case, children with SM are viewed on the "extremely anxious" end of the anxiety spectrum.

However, to date, few studies exist supporting the hypothesis that children with SM score in the "extreme range" on measures of social anxiety. Dummit and colleagues (1997) found that clinician ratings of social anxiety on the *Liebowitz Social Anxiety Scale* (as cited in Dummit et al., 1997) were in the moderate range for children with SM. In other studies, teacher ratings have indicated that although scores of children with SM are higher than the comparison group, their scores are not usually considered in the "clinically significant" range (T score above 70; Bergman et al., 2002). These findings are inconsistent with the conclusion that SM children are "frozen with fear" (Anstendig, 1999). In actuality, it suggests that while children with SM have higher levels of anxiety, there are additional cognitive and behavioral factors that may in fact be involved in and mediate SM.

The behavioral characteristics of children evaluated for SM demonstrate a striking resemblance to the descriptions of "behavioral inhibition" reported in the Harvard Infant Study (Kagan et al., 1988). This study noted that normal children who as infants demonstrated a tendency to withdraw from novel stimuli or strangers, seek a parent, and inhibit play, and vocalizations are "inhibited," versus those who approach and explore and remain talkative in new situations. This inhibited temperamental characteristic appears to be related to other theoretical constructs such as fearfulness, introversion/extroversion, and shyness as personality traits. Additionally, inhibited children have been measured to have higher heart rates, and subsequently, children with consistently high heart rates had the greatest number of specific fears, night terrors, and maternal reports of shyness and fear of school (Ballenger, 1990). Children whose inhibition decreased also showed a drop in heart rate over time.

In a study by Yeganeh, Beidel, Turner, Pina, and Silverman (2003), children diagnosed with social phobia were matched with children diagnosed with both social phobia and SM. Many different measures were used to compare the groups, including self-report measures, parent-report forms, and a behavioral assessment task. This study was one of the first to compare children with SM to children diagnosed with social phobia. Yeganeh and colleagues concluded that although there are some similarities between these two disorders, several differences remain as well. Since all of the children in the study met criteria for a diagnosis of social phobia, it can be determined that all of the children experienced social anxiety. There were contradictory findings regarding whether children with SM had greater social anxiety than those with social phobia alone. Using different measurement strategies, clinicians and blind observers both rated children with SM as significantly more socially anxious than children with social phobia alone. In contrast, there were no differences based on children's self-report of their level of general social anxiety or their specific anxiety during role-play tasks.

Yeganeh and others (2003) derived two plausible explanations for their findings. First, children with SM may have discovered a successful avoidance strategy, which, consequently, helped to reduce their social anxiety. Using this explanation, it is assumed that children with SM lessen their fearfulness by no longer attempting to speak. This form of avoidance successfully decreases their stress to only a moderate level. The second alternate explanation is that adults might overinterpret the child's behavior. That is, adults may presume that a child who does not respond to their caring overtures is "frozen with fear." The children's lack of speech may have resulted in the raters or evaluators inferring a greater level of distress than the children were actually experiencing. Many times, children with SM engage nonverbally and, therefore, are socially appropriate with these types of gestures. If they are socially fearful, this does not appear to transcend into their nonverbal reactions. However, children with social phobia many times will avoid all interactions with other children and adults.

Researchers have found that children with SM often have comorbid symptoms of other disorders, such as speech and language delays, elimination disorders, anxiety disorders, and motor delays. For example, language disorders are quite common in children with SM, as the frequency of language disorders or delays is reported to range between 30 to 65% (Kolvin & Fundudis, 1981; Steinhausen & Juzi, 1996; Wilkens, 1985). In addition, children with SM are susceptible to developing urinary tract infections, as they are inhibited to ask to use the restroom, and, consequently, they will hold their urine all day to avoid using their voice. The prevalence of children with SM who suffer from enuresis varies from 4 to 42% (Black & Uhde, 1995; Dummit et al., 1997; Kolvin & Fundudis, 1981; Steinhausen & Juzi, 1996). Motor delays are also found at a relatively high rate in children with SM, as studies have indicated they are present in as many as 18 to 65% of these children (Steinhausen & Juzi, 1996).

ASSESSMENT OF THE SELECTIVELY MUTE CHILD

Assessing children with SM can be particularly difficult because of their absence of verbal language to communicate. Although language competence is a critical factor for the diagnosis of SM, the effect of language abnormalities on the SM syndrome for the most part has not been addressed (Tancer, 1992). If a child comes from a different country and does not speak the language, this further complicates the diagnostic process. Many children who are not proficient in the majority language stay silent, not because they have SM but because they do not want others to make fun of their pronunciation of words or accent.

Behavior-rating scales are a beneficial tool in assessing the level of anxiety in children. Those scales that are self-report in nature may need to be read to the child with the child being able to use nonverbal responses (e.g., pointing to the answer, holding up fingers corresponding to the number of the answer, etc.). There are several narrow-band scales used to assess anxiety in children including the *Revised Children's Manifest Anxiety Scale* (RCMAS; Reynolds & Richmond, 1985) and the *Beck Anxiety Inventory for Youth* (BAI-Y; Beck, Beck, & Jolly, 2001). Parents and teachers should also complete a behavior-rating scale to assess not only anxiety but also to rule out other comorbid conditions as well. Broad-band scales, such as the *Behavior Assessment System for Children—Second Edition* (BASC-2; Reynolds & Kamphaus, 2004), serve this purpose. Information from parents and teachers allows for assessment across settings. Additionally, a number of structure parent and child interviews exist to assess anxiety and comorbid conditions. Of particular value when working with children with SM are the *Anxiety Disorder Interview Schedules, Child and Parent Versions* (ADIS; Silverman & Albano, 1996). As an adjunct to more traditional assessment instruments, observations within the school (e.g., classroom, playground, and cafeteria) can provide valuable data. In some cases, if the parents have access to a video camera, and are willing to video their child in their natural home environment, data can be obtained in order to assess the child's language skills and to hear if there are any abnormalities in his or her language development.

When assessing the child with standardized assessments, such as an intelligence test, a nonverbal measure will provide the most accurate results. The *Universal Nonverbal Intelligence Test* (UNIT; Bracken & McCallum, 1998) and the *Comprehensive Test of Nonverbal Intelligence* (CTONI; Hammill, Pearson, & Wiederholt, 1996) are both good choices. More conventional verbal-versus-nonverbal batteries are likely to produce falsely low IQ scores. For young children, the *Bracken Basic Concepts Scale* (Bracken, 1998), which correlates fairly well with IQ measures, is another useful tool (Shipon-Blum, 2002). Another option is the use of the Perceptual Reasoning subtests on the *Wechsler Intelligence Scale for Children, Fourth Edition* (WISC-IV; Wechsler, 2003).

It is important to establish a good rapport with all children before any testing situation, and this is especially true when working with a child with SM. Exposing the child with SM to the testing environment multiple times before testing has many benefits during the remainder of the assessment process. If the child becomes visibly anxious during an evaluation, the examiner should cease testing immediately. These visibly anxious symptoms might include hesitancy, difficulty initiating, or shutting down (Shipon-Blum, 2002).

Related service evaluations also serve an important role when working with children with SM. Given the comorbid language and motor conditions, speech and language evaluations can be used to assess auditory processing and receptive language, whereas occupational therapy assessments can determine the child's visual–motor skill development and sensory integration needs.

Finally, it is of extreme importance to obtain a thorough family history, as Black and Uhde (1995) found a high incidence of SM and social phobia within the immediate family. Family background information provides insight to assist in conceptualizing the case, as well as to help identify factors that may influence later treatment outcomes. Family information that is crucial to assess includes past illnesses of the child and within the family, past traumatic events, the onset of SM symptoms, and the history of anxiety or mental health concerns within the family. Obtaining information regarding the physical aspects of the child being evaluated is also necessary. This information can be obtain through the parents, or through the health history documented by the school nurse (e.g., latest physical exam, any medications the child is on, past illnesses or allergies, vision and hearing screenings). Before determining if a child has SM, a medical condition (e.g., such as hearing loss) should be ruled out as a cause for the child not speaking.

CONCEPTUALIZATION OF SELECTIVE MUTISM

Conceptualizing SM from a cognitive-behavior therapy (CBT) framework is often difficult for clinicians, as children with SM do not offer an understanding as to their cognitive process. Additionally, as with all children, cognitions develop throughout childhood into adolescence, and a number of contextual factors (i.e., family, peers, and school) may influence development. As noted by Mennuti and Christner (in press), the specific components of CBT need to be appropriate for the developmental level of the child. Although cognitive strategies can be modified for use with younger children (see Friedberg & McClure, 2002), many of the interventions with younger children tend to involve a greater ratio of hands-on, behavioral interventions and the use of imagery, rather than purely verbal strategies (Drinkwater & Stewart, 2002; Christner, Allen, & Maus, 2003). Behavioral interventions are particularly useful when working with children with SM, given their inhibition to speak outside their immediate family.

Although the research addressing the use of CBT with children diagnosed with SM is scarce, there is a greater volume of literature regarding the effects of CBT with other disorders in general (see Kendall, 2000). Moreover, recent research has supported the efficacy of brief CBT treatment for children and adolescents with a range of anxiety disorders (Zaider & Heimberg, 2003). Extrapolating the findings from studies on other anxiety disorders seen in children, such as social phobia (SP), clinicians can find cognitive and behavioral techniques that may be effective for children with SM.

In conceptualizing SM from a cognitive-behavioral framework, the target objective is to understand SM along an anxiety spectrum. Thus, the focus of treatment is less about "getting the child to talk" and more about acknowledging his or her anxiety and addressing it in an effective manner. Adjunct to reducing the anxiety is the need to further encourage and positively reinforce communication with others. Because the use of cognitive restructuring is more difficult with this population initially, behavioral interventions will likely be more beneficial at the onset of treatment. However, as treatment progresses, the use of cognitive-based interventions will become more prominent.

Although cognitive aspects of CBT are less utilized with children with SM at the outset, cognitive components and strategies are an essential feature in other realms of treatment, particularly when working with the parents. When consulting with parents, it is important that clinicians assess the parents' beliefs and thoughts and use cognitive restructuring to address maladaptive thinking. For instance, it is common for parents of a child with SM to have thoughts such as, "I must make Carly talk at school or the school will think I'm a bad parent." Interestingly, developmental research has identified links between parental and child cognitions (Garber & Robinson, 1997). Parents often experience self-blame, especially when there is a family history of anxiety or a genetic link that may contribute to their children's difficulties. For these reasons, psychoeducational training is invaluable to the parents or caregivers of children with SM. This training can assist parents in their understanding of SM, the evaluation process, the treatment of symptoms, as well as interventions they can use at home.

Those professionals conceptualizing SM from a solely behavioral perspective view it as the product of a long series of negatively reinforced learning patterns (Leonard & Topol, 1993). Alternatively, Pordes (1992) viewed SM as a "learned response in which the refusal to speak is a method of manipulating the environment" (p. 369). Some behavioral researchers have noted that the silent behavior of children with SM serves a particular function, and they have further argued that the environment maintains this way of interacting (Anstendig, 1998). Although this position accounts for some of the behaviors and remains consistent with views of anxiety in general, it would be remiss for clinicians to discount the cognitive components these children experience. However, by conceptualizing cases from a behavioral or "functional" standpoint, clinicians can explain the behaviors to parents and school personnel as adaptive rather than pathological (Powell & Dailey, 1995). No matter what the view of SM, withholding speech usually results in a secondary change in the child, thus maintaining the behavior (Anstendig, 1998). That is, others allow the child to communicate in other ways or stop the demands for speech, which subsequently reinforces the mutism or mute behaviors.

STRATEGIC AND TECHNICAL INTERVENTIONS FOR SELECTIVE MUTISM

Today, the majority of successful interventions for the treatment of SM involve behavioral components, such as reinforcement, stimulus fading, token procedures, shaping procedures, contingency management, self-modeling, or response initiation procedures (Giddan, Ross, Sechler, & Becker, 1997; Kehle, Maduas, Baratta, & Bray, 1998). An advantage to these strategies is that professionals can use all of these interventions across settings, including the home, the school, and the community.

As noted earlier, a child with SM not talking is viewed as a learned response to anxiety. Thus, it is crucial that early interventions with the child exhibiting symptoms of SM focus on teaching coping strategies, in order for the child to learn other ways of coping with his or her anxiety besides not speaking. Shipon-Blum (2002) has noted that the main goals in the treatment of children with SM are to lower anxiety, increase self-esteem, and increase self-confidence in social settings. Again, the emphasis should not be on "making the child speak." Shipon-Blum further notes that as anxiety lowers and confidence increases, the child's verbalizations eventually follow.

Positive reinforcement and desensitization techniques are key behavioral strategies to treat SM. Additionally, removing the emphasis on speaking serves further therapeutic utility (Shipon-Blum, n.d.). With this in mind, clinicians should approach treatment from the point of understanding the child and having the child acknowledge his or her anxiety. One such cognitive-behavioral tool to assess anxiety is a feeling thermometer. The feeling thermometer is widely used to help children identify his or her emotional intensity (Castro-Blanco, 1999; Silverman & Kurtines, 1996). Most children understand the concept of a thermometer and it is a fun, visual way for them to express the strength of what they are feeling. This is ideal for use with children with SM, as they can respond in nonverbal ways. For instance, clinicians can have the child point to the thermometer, or, alternatively, have the thermometer on a sheet of paper that the child can color.

In order to establish a baseline of the child's anxiety, the clinician can have a child rate his or her feelings before having him or her engage in an actual or imagined anxiety-provoking situation. After obtaining a baseline, the clinician can have the child predict his or her anxiety level to a given situation (e.g., standing in front of classmates, being asked a question, etc.). Then, using either imaginal or in vivo experiments with the anxiety-provoking situation, the child can again rate the anxiety using the thermometer. This exercise can serve as a way to test the evidence regarding the child's anxiety. In some instances, the child's actual anxiety is lower than what he or she predicted. In these cases, the child may learn that he or she can approach a task even though he or she anticipated and experienced anxious feelings (Friedberg & McClure, 2002).

Although positive reinforcement is an important component, clinicians should be cautious of introducing it before the child's anxiety lowers, and the child is willing to accept some subtle encouragement. For some children, receiving too much positive reinforcement may be embarrassing, and consequently, this may sabotage the treatment. Slight forms of positive reinforcement may hold a stronger value, such as writing the child a short note, letting him or her keep a sticker book, or a special signal between the professional (e.g., clinician, teacher, etc.) and the child.

Although a number of counseling techniques have the potential to be effective in working with children with SM, clinicians must understand that none of these will prove effective if the pressure for verbalization remains. Thus, as noted earlier, the emphasis of the intervention must be on reducing anxiety, such as providing ways for the child to relax and feel comfortable. Making adaptations to traditional techniques by playing or drawing can provide opportunities for nonverbal outlet.

Cognitive-behavior therapy (CBT) is one approach used to help children with SM. The focus of CBT is on helping the children develop an awareness and acknowledgement of their SM through psychoeducation. Furthermore, one must facilitate children modifying their thoughts and behaviors to help reduce anxieties and worries and increase self-confidence in social settings. CBT interventions should emphasize the child's positive qualities, in addition to addressing areas of need. Although many clinicians may think of CBT techniques as "requiring" verbalization, there are a number of ways to modify these techniques to help children with SM. Knell (1993) has integrated cognitive-behavioral interventions with traditional components of play therapy to derive what she has coined Cognitive-Behavioral Play Therapy. Not only does this approach show promise with younger children, it is ideal when working with a child with SM.

Other important aspects of CBT treatment include parent involvement and peer socialization. Frequently, adjustments may be needed to accommodate the child with SM. Rapee (1997) has noted that parental rearing styles have been associated with anxiety disorders in children. Thus, parent training can be used to help educate parents as well as to assist in providing them skills to help them find creative ways to support and positively reinforce their child's strengths. Token reinforcement systems may work well, and they are frequently used in behavior modification. O'Leary and Drabman (1971) suggested these systems have three basic characteristics: (a) behaviors to be reinforced are clearly stated, (b) procedures are designed for administering reinforcing stimuli when the target behavior occurs, and (c) rules are devised to govern the exchange of tokens for reinforcing objects or events.

Another way to involve parents is by creating exposure opportunities for the SM child. This is a wonderful way to reinforce and process his or her accomplishments by interacting with other children. When using exposure techniques with children, especially those with SM, gradual exposures are the most promising. Clinicians and parents should keep the exposures as realistic as possible (Turk, Heimburg, & Hope, 2001), using in vivo experiences. Parents can be involved in this process by providing opportunities for exposure, while not forcing the child into situations.

An example of a parent-guided exposure would be the case of Janet. Janet had attended four counseling sessions that focused on anxiety reduction techniques (e.g., relaxation training, imaginal exposure, etc.) and social skills training. As a between-session experiment, Janet's parents were to begin a gradual exposure to social situations at home. Her parents were encouraged to start out by inviting one friend to their home for a play date with Janet. Using the home, which is often a comfort zone, for such an experience will likely increase the chance that the child will engage in conversation. It was important to caution Janet's parents that she may not speak during the first play date. However, in Janet's case, she remained quite for the most part, but she began using her voice when playing with dolls by having the dolls speak to each other. By the second play date, Janet began engaging in conversation with her friend and her behavior then began to generalize to other settings, such as school and the community. Not only did this exercise provide an opportunity to expose Janet, it also offered a constructive experience for her to observe positive socialization skills of a peer.

IMPLICATIONS AND APPLICATIONS TO THE SCHOOL SETTING

As many times SM is not seen until the child enters school, school support is essential in treatment. Encouraging the school to address SM as an anxiety disorder will lead to more productive support than that provided by the typical special education and remedial services (Shipon-Blum, 2002). Students with SM may require in-school accommodations, most of which could be offered in a 504 Service Agreement rather than pursuing special education services. In order to address the specific needs of the child, it is important that the school use its resources to conduct a comprehensive evaluation.

There are several suggestions for classroom teachers to employ, which will likely make students with SM feel more comfortable in their educational setting. Teachers should consider making a home visit in order for the child to have an opportunity to feel more comfortable and relaxed with the new teacher on his or her "turf." Additionally, some teachers have agreed to meet the child in the morning before school starts to help lessen anxiety. In fact, in one case, we had a teacher spend the morning having a student with SM teach her the relaxation techniques the child was learning during her counseling sessions. Within the classroom, pairing children with

SM with a "buddy" for breaks, recess, and lunch can serve as a means to increase socialization. In addition, initially the teacher can allow and even facilitate ways the child could respond nonverbally. It is important that teachers understand that children with SM are easily embarrassed; the teacher should avoid drawing attention to the child and minimize eye contact when talking to the child directly. Finally, the teacher should be a point of contact for professionals working with the child outside of school, including physicians, psychologists, or other treating professionals (Shipon-Blum, 2002).

If a child with SM is eligible for special education services, there are several recommendations that should be considered. Shipon-Blum (2002) recommends accommodations such as allowing the child to work in a small group or with a "buddy," encouraging parental involvement in the school, and providing alone time with a friend. Other interventions, including extended time for assignments or tests, taped or written verbal reports, nonverbal communication, preparation for changes in routine, one-on-one time with the teacher, and creative learning environments (e.g., incorporating visual/spatial activities into the curriculum) also should be considered. Related services including speech and language services, occupational therapy, or psychological counseling in schools may be necessary supports for a student with SM.

As progress is being attained, school professionals will often notice improvements in the child's behaviors. Not only will the child with SM verbalize more, but also his or her anxiety will notably subside. Observations of the child smiling more, increasing the frequency of eye contact, having a relaxed body posture, beginning to initiate without effort, and responding more quickly to questions will become more common. The greatest reward for the treatment team of a child with SM is to hear his or her voice communicate to others.

CASE STUDY: TOMMY

Tommy is a 6-year-old only child living with both parents, who are of Russian descent. Tommy was born in the United States; however, his parents were born and raised in Russia and there were a number of cultural considerations. Tommy's parents alternate between speaking Russian and English in the home. They reported that it was important for Tommy to know English because he lives in the United States, although they acknowledged that they wanted Tommy to learn Russian as well.

Tommy was generally a quiet, shy, and somewhat timid child. He would often hide behind his mother or father if someone outside his family spoke to him. Although he spoke at home, he was not a very talkative child. He rarely initiated conversation unless the topic was about his favorite subject, dinosaurs. He especially liked the Tyrannosaurus Rex, which he referred to as "Tyrant lizard king." Tommy was content playing by himself; however, he had a same-age cousin who lived close by and they would play well together.

When Tommy went to preschool, his parents explained to his teacher that he was very shy and did not speak much. His preschool teacher was very nurturing and did not place any speaking demands on him. She was very protective of Tommy, as she felt he was "so fragile." In kindergarten, Tommy's new teacher took a very different approach. She demanded that he speak, and she would punish him for not talking (e.g., no recess, time out, etc.). She would stare at him and remove privileges if he did not answer her questions. Consequently, Tommy's behavior took a drastic change and he began to act out both in school and at home. By a few weeks into the school year, he ceased speaking at school and ignored his teacher's demands. His behavior also became very oppositional, as he would knock over crayons and refuse to pick them up, or he would decline to participate in any structured activities. Tommy went as far as turning his body completely around so he would not face the teacher during story time.

Tommy's parents knew that his education was suffering and they feared it would worsen. Acknowledging their need for help, Tommy's parents sought out assistance through a child psychiatrist, who diagnosed Tommy with SM and Social Phobia. The psychiatrist recommended that Tommy start medication in the form of an SSRI, specifically Prozac. Tommy's parents were very hesitant to place Tommy on any type of medication; however, through consultation with the psychiatrist, they decided to try the medication on a trial basis.

In addition to the medication, Tommy's parents requested psychological counseling services through the school, which the school psychologist provided. These interventions consisted of nine meetings over a 3-week period (30 minutes per session). The school psychologist used CBT strategies with Tommy; however, modifications to the strategies were needed. Tommy initially did not speak during the sessions, although when the school psychologist used puppets to facilitate discussion, Tommy began to speak through the puppets. In this session, Tommy learned relaxation strategies and social skills to help build his confidence. Each session was followed by a "behavioral experiment." For instance, Tommy would have to teach his parents the relaxation training attempted during the session or Tommy would have to go with the school psychologist to another place in the school (e.g., cafeteria, office, etc.) and practice skills such as waving "hello" or making eye contact.

Additionally, behavioral consultation was provided to Tommy's teacher. This began with educating her about SM and helping her understand the connection between his anxiety response and oppositional behaviors. Additionally, a behavior plan was set up within the classroom. The behaviors reinforced began with him facing the teacher when she was reading, cleaning up, and completing activities in the class. The primary goal for the behavioral plan was to set up an environment that was more positive for Tommy. As Tommy progressed, the reinforcement moved to focusing on his nonverbal and eventually verbal responses. With Tommy, however, the reinforcement had to be subtle, such as a thumbs-up sign, giving him 5 minutes to color in a dinosaur coloring book, or a placing a star sticker on his hand.

Tommy's parents noticed a difference in him within 2 weeks. His mood was much happier, and he was verbally expressing himself in ways his parents had never heard before. At school, his teacher no longer tried to make him talk, and, instead, she praised him for all attempts that he made. Tommy showed great improvement, and his oppositional behaviors decreased very quickly when the environment became less threatening. When Tommy began speaking in school, his teacher was impressed by his academic capabilities. Tommy's skills were on or above grade level in all academic subject areas.

Tommy's social skills improved in school as well, as he began making new friends. By the time of his 7th birthday, he invited five friends and his cousin to his birthday party. He remained on medication, which his psychiatrist continued to monitor. The school psychologist also offered continued monitoring. This eventually involved "touching base" with Tommy a few times throughout the school year. The school continued following the behavior support plan, which is provided each year to his teachers, in addition to general information about SM.

CONCLUSION

SM is a rare condition often seen first as children are entering school situations. Many times, educators become frustrated with children presenting SM symptoms, and as a result, these children are seen as oppositional. School-based professionals must have knowledge of the underlying aspects of SM, suggesting this to be a condition that falls along an anxiety disorder spectrum. Although the research on treating children with SM is negligible, current knowledge regarding the use of CBT interventions with anxious children can be used to develop strategies for treatment of SM. It is important that professionals use creativity in modifying these interventions so they do not rely on verbal interactions during treatment.

REFERENCES

American Psychiatric Association. (1994). *Diagnostic and statistical manual of mental disorders* (4th ed.). Washington, DC: Author.

American Psychiatric Association. (2000). *Diagnostic and statistical manual of mental disorders* (4th ed., text revision). Washington, DC: Author.

Anstendig, K. (1998). Selective mutism: A review of treatment literature by modality from 1980–1996. *Psychotherapy, 35,* 381–390.

Anstendig, K. (1999). Is selective mutism an anxiety disorder? Rethinking its DSM-IV classification. *Journal of Anxiety Disorder, 13,* 417–434.

Ballenger, J. (Ed.). (1990). *Neurobiology of Panic Disorder.* New York: Wiley & Liss.

Beck, J. S., Beck A. T., & Jolly, J. (2001). *Manual for the Beck Youth Inventories of Emotional and Social Adjustment.* San Antonio, TX: The Psychological Corporation.

Beidel, D. C., & Turner, S. M. (1998). *Shy children, phobic adults: nature and treatment of social phobia.* Washington, DC: American Psychological Association.

Bergman R. L., Piacentini, J., & McKracken, J. T. (2002). Prevalence and description of selective mutism in a school-based sample. *Journal of American Academy of Child and Adolescent Psychiatry, 41,* 938–946.

Black, B. B., & Uhde, T. W. (1995). Psychiatric characteristics of children with selective mutism: A pilot study. *Journal of the American Academy of Child and Adolescent Psychiatry 34,* 847–855.

Bracken, B. A. (1998). *Bracken Basic Concepts Scale–Revised.* San Antonio, TX: Psychological Corporation.

Bracken, B. A., & McCallum, R. S. (1998). *Universal Nonverbal Intelligence Test (UNIT).* Chicago: Riverside Publishing.

Castro-Blanco, D. (1999, November). STAND-UP: Cognitive-behavioral intervention for high-risk adolescents. Workshop presented at the annual meeting of the Association for Advancement of Behavior Therapy, Toronto, Canada.

Christner, R. W., Allen, J. S., & Maus, M. R. (2004, Winter). An overview for selecting CBT techniques in the treatment of youth in schools, *Insight, 24*(2), 8–10.

Dow, S. P., Sonies, B. C., Scheib, D., Moss, S. E., & Leonard, H. L. (1995). Practical guidelines for the assessment and treatment of selective mutism. *Journal of the American Academy of Child and Adolescent Psychiatry, 34,* 836–845.

Drinkwater, J., & Stewart, A. (2002). Cognitive behaviour therapy for young people. *Current Opinion in Psychiatry, 15,* 377–381.

Dummit, E. S., III, Klein, R. G., Tancer, N. K., Asche, B., Martin, J., & Fairbanks, J. (1997). Systematic assessment of 50 children with selective mutism. *Journal of the American Academy of Child & Adolescent Psychiatry, 36,* 653–660.

Friedberg, R. D., & McClure, J. M. (2002). *Clinical practice of cognitive therapy with children and adolescents: The nuts and bolts.* New York: Guilford Press.

Garber, J., & Robinson, N. S. (1997). Cognitive vulnerability in children at risk for depression. *Cognitive Emotion, 11,* 619–635.

Giddan, J. J, Ross, G. J., Sechler, L. L., & Becker, B. R. (1997). Selective mutism in elementary school: Multidisciplinary interventions. *Language, Speech, and Hearing Services in Schools, 28,* 127–133.

Hammill, D. D., Pearson, N. A, & Wiederholt, J. L. (1996). *Comprehensive Test of Nonverbal Intelligence (C-TONI).* Minnesota: AGS Publishing.

Kagan J., Reznick, J. S., & Snidman, N. (1988). Biological bases of childhood shyness. *Science, 240,* 171–176.

Kehle, T. J., Madaus, M. R., Baratta, V. S., & Bray, M. A. (1998). Augmented self-modeling as a treatment for children with selective mutism. *Journal of Psychology, 36,* 247–260.

Kendall, P. C. (Ed.). (2000). *Child and adolescent therapy: Cognitive-behavioral procedures* (2nd ed.). New York: Guilford Press.

Knell, S. M. (1993). *Cognitive-behavioral play therapy.* New York: Guilford Press.

Kolvin, I., & Fundudis, T. (1981). Elective mute children: Psychological development and background factors. *Journal of Child Psychology and Psychiatry, 22,* 219–232.

Kristensen, H. (2000). Selective mutism and comorbidity with developmental disorder/delay, anxiety disorder, and elimination disorder. *Journal of the American Academy of Child and Adolescent Psychiatry, 39,* 249–256.

Krysanski, V. (2003). A brief review of selective mutism literature. *The Journal of Psychology, 137*(1), 29–40.

Kussmaul, A. (1877). *Die Stoerungen der Sprache (1st ed.)* [Disturbances in linguistic function]. Basel, Switzerland: Benno Schwabe.

Leonard, H. L., & Topol, D. A. (1993). Elective mutism. *Child and Adolescent Psychiatric Clinics of North America, 2*(4), 695–707.

Mennuti, R., & Christner, R. W. (in press). School-based cognitive-behavioral therapy (CBT). In A. Freeman (Ed.), *International Encyclopedia of Cognitive Behavior Therapy.* New York: Kluwer Academic/Plenum Publishers.

O'Leary, K. D., & Drabman, R. (1971). Token reinforcement in the classroom: A review. *Psychological Bulletin, 75,* 379–398.

Pordes, M. D. (1992). Intervention with the selectively mute child. *Psychology in the Schools, 29,* 367–376.

Powell, S., & Dailey, M. (1995). When to intervene in selective mutism: The multimodal treatment of a case of persistent selective mutism. *Psychology in Schools, 32,* 114–123.

Rapee, R. M. (1997). Potential role of childrearing practices in the development of anxiety and depression. *Clinical Psychology Review, 17,* 47–67.

Reynolds, C. R., & Kamphaus, R. W. (2004). *Behavior Assessment System for Children* (2nd ed.). Circle Pines, MN: American Guidance Service.

Reynolds, C. R., & Richmond, B. O. (1985). *Revised Children's Manifest Anxiety Scale.* Los Angeles: Western Psychological Services.

Shipon-Blum, E. (2002). When the words just won't come out: Understanding selective mutism. *Communiqué, 30*(5), 2–4 (Insert).

Shipon-Blum, E. (2002, March). Selective Mutism. Workshop presented at the 22nd annual spring conference for the Association of School Psychologists of Pennsylvania (ASPP), Harrisburg, PA.

Shipon-Blum, E. (n.d.). "When the Words Just Won't Come Out" Understanding Selective Mutism. Retrieved January 6, 2005, from http://www.selectivemutism.org

Silverman, W. K., & Albano, A. M. (1996). T*he Anxiety Disorders Interview Schedule for children for DSM-IV, child and parent versions.* San Antonio, TX: The Psychological Corporation.

Silverman, W. K., & Kurtines, W. M. (1996). *Anxiety and phobic disorders: A pragmatic approach.* New York: Plenum Press.

Steinhausen H. C., & Juzi, C. (1996). Elective mutism: an analysis of 100 cases. *Journal of the American Academy of Adolescent Psychiatry, 28,* 279–281.

Tancer, N. K. (1992). Elective mutism: A review of the literature. In B. B. Lahey & A. E. Kazdin (Eds.), *Advances in clinical psychology* (Vol. 14, pp. 265–288). New York: Plenum.

Turk, C. L., Heimberg, R. G., & Hope, D. A. (2001). Social anxiety disorder. In D. H. Barlow (Ed.), *Clinical handbook of psychological disorders* (3rd ed., pp. 99–136). New York: Guilford Press.

Wechsler, D. (2003). *Wechsler Scale for Children (4th ed.).* San Antonio, TX: Psychological Corporation.

Wilkens, R. (1985). A comparison of elective mutism and emotional disorders in children. *British Journal of Psychiatry, 146,* 198–203.

Yeganeh, R., Beidel, D. C., Turner, S. M., Pina, A. A., & Silverman, W. K. (2003). Clinical distinctions between selective mutism and social phobia: An investigation of childhood psychopathology. *Journal of the American Academy of Child & Adolescent Psychiatry, 42,* 1069–1075.

Zaider, T. I., & Heimberg, R. G. (2003). Non-pharmacologic treatments for social anxiety disorder. *Munksgaard International Publishers Ltd., 108,* 72–84.

7

Understanding Depression in Children and Adolescents: Cognitive-Behavioral Interventions

A. RENEE DONOGHUE, AARON R. WHEELER,
MAURICE F. PROUT, HELEN W. WILSON &
MARK A. REINECKE

Documented as the leading cause of disability among adolescents and adults (World Health Organization), depression typically originates in childhood or adolescence, with early recognition and treatment of symptoms critical to the reduction of later impairment from this disorder (Costello et al., 2002). Adolescents are at the greatest risk for depression, with community prevalence rates ranging from 2.9% to 8%, and as many as 25% of youth meeting criteria for a diagnosis of major depression by late adolescence (Kashani, Reid, & Rosenberg, 1989; Lewinsohn, Hops, Roberts, Seeley, & Andrews, 1993). Although preadolescent children are less likely to be diagnosed with depression, children as young as 4 years of age exhibit symptoms of depression. Children and adolescents who are depressed are at increased risk for continued depression occurring into adolescence and adulthood (Costello et al., 2002; Lewinsohn, Solomon, Seeley, & Zeiss, 2000). Given that depression in youth is linked to impairments in multiple areas (e.g., academic performance, family and peer relationships) as well as with long-term health consequences (e.g., substance abuse and suicide), it is imperative that interventions occur within the school setting.

SYMPTOMS OF MDD AND DYSTHYMIA IN CHILDREN AND ADOLESCENTS

Symptoms of depression among children and adolescents are similar to those presented by adults (Lewinsohn, Pettit, Joiner, & Seeley, 2003), which include depressed or irritable mood, anhedonia (i.e., loss of interest or pleasure in activities), thinking and concentration problems, appetite and weight problems, sleep problems, psychomotor agitation or retardation, fatigue or lack of energy, feelings of worthlessness or excessive guilt, and thoughts of death (American Psychiatric Association, 2000). Some evidence suggests that adolescents are most likely to report depressed mood, sleep disturbance, difficulty with concentration, weight or appetite disturbance, and anhedonia (R. E. Roberts, Lewinsohn, & Seeley, 1995). In addition, children and adolescents who are depressed are likely to present as irritable and angry rather than sad, and such behavior may be mistaken for oppositionality. A diagnosis of major depressive disorder (MDD) requires a period of at least 2 weeks during which an individual has had five or more of the depressive symptoms listed earlier (American Psychiatric Association, 2000). Dysthymic disorder (DD) is a milder, chronic form of depression that requires the presence of depressed or irritable mood for at least a year and two or more additional symptoms. Dysthymia places youth at risk for developing major depression, and many youth are diagnosed with both DD and MDD.

EARLY IDENTIFICATION WITH SUBTHRESHOLD YOUTH

The National Institute of Mental Health Psychosocial Intervention Development Workgroup has advocated for the development of interventions that prevent the onset and recurrence of clinical depression among at-risk individuals (Hollon et al., 2002). Early assessment, monitoring, and intervention of subthreshold depressive symptoms has potential to reduce the progression of clinical depression among youth (Costello et al., 2002; Lewinsohn et al., 2000). Thus, schools provide an ideal setting for evaluating and treating these early subthreshold symptoms. School-based cognitive-behavioral interventions have been shown to reduce the development of depressive disorders among at-risk adolescents (Clarke et al., 1995) and school-aged children (Gillham, Reivich, Jaycox, & Seligman, 1995; Jaycox, Reivich, Gillham, & Seligman, 1994; C. Roberts, Kane, Thomson, Bishop, & Hart, 2003). Although some longitudinal findings call into question the long-term effectiveness of such interventions with preadolescent children (Gillham & Reivich, 1999; C. Roberts et al., 2003), they appear at least to prolong the development of depressive disorders. Furthermore, Gillham and Reivich (1999) noted that early interventions might foster an adaptive attributional style among youth, thus reducing vulnerability to depressive episodes.

EVIDENCE-BASE FOR COGNITIVE-BEHAVIORAL INTERVENTION TO TREAT DEPRESSION IN YOUTH

Use of Individual Cognitive-Behavioral Interventions

A number of studies have examined cognitive-behavior therapy (CBT) treatments of child and adolescent depression, and, generally, they have yielded positive results. For a comprehensive review, see Curry (2001) and Reinecke, Ryan, and Dubois (1998). A meta-analysis conducted by Reinecke et al. (1998) found that CBT is effective in the acute and long-term treatment of depression among adolescents. Although an overall quantitative assessment is not available, studies of CBT with children also tend to provide favorable results (Curry, 2001).

Most studies of the effectiveness of CBT with prepubescent children have been conducted in the school setting. Three studies found that CBT programs were superior to control conditions in reducing depressive symptoms among middle and elementary schoolchildren (Butler, Miezitis, Friedman, & Cole, 1980; Kahn, Kehle, Jenson, & Clarke, 1990; Weisz, Thurber, Sweeney, Proffitt, & LeGagnoux, 1997). Stark, Reynolds, and Kaslow (1987) conducted a small-scale, yet innovative, study of CBT in treating depression among schoolchildren. Twenty-nine elementary schoolchildren, selected because of consistently elevated symptoms of depression, were assigned to one of two 12-session CBT groups, primarily cognitive or primarily behavioral, or to a wait-list control. Posttreatment and 5-week follow-up findings supported significant effectiveness of both treatment conditions over the control group. At 5-weeks follow-up, the primarily cognitive treatment appeared advantageous over the primarily behavioral treatment. In a subsequent study, Stark, Rouse, and Livingston (1991) compared CBT with traditional school counseling. They found that CBT accelerated improvement, but differences were no longer significant at a 7-month follow-up.

Brent and others (1997) compared the effects of CBT, Supportive Behavior Family Therapy, and Nondirective Supportive Therapy on depression in a randomized clinical. Participants included 78 adolescents between the ages of 13 and 18 years, who met criteria for a MDD. CBT demonstrated a more rapid treatment response, a greater overall treatment response, an increase in parental confidence, and a decreased recurrence of depressive symptoms over time.

Use of CBT Group Interventions

A series of randomized controlled outcome studies conducted in Oregon have supported the effectiveness of group CBT for treating adolescent depression in both clinical and school settings. Their intervention, the *Adolescent Coping With Depression Course* (CWD-A), focuses on mood monitoring, social skills, increasing pleasant activities, decreasing anxiety, reducing depressogenic cognitions, improving communication, and conflict resolution (Clarke, Lewinsohn, & Hops, 1990; Lewinsohn, Clarke, Rohde, Hops, & Seeley, 1996). In their first longitudinal outcome study

(Lewinsohn, Clarke, Hops, & Andrews, 1990), 59 depressed adolescents were randomly assigned to a 14-session CBT group, the same CBT group in conjunction with a 7-session parent group, or a wait-list control condition. Youth in both the adolescent-only and parent-and-adolescent CBT groups exhibited greater improvement in depressive symptoms than the control group over a 2-year follow-up period.

Subthreshold Group Interventions

Based on promising results in clinical settings, Clarke and colleagues (1995) adapted the CWD-A program for the school setting and for primary prevention among youth with subclinical levels of depression. One hundred fifty 9th- and 10th-grade adolescents with elevated depressive symptoms, but not diagnosable major depression or dysthymia, were randomly assigned to either a group CBT program or a "usual care" condition. CBT groups were conducted after school by school psychologists and counselors, and they consisted of 15 45-minute sessions over 5 weeks. Over a 1-year follow-up period, youth in the treatment group were less likely to develop depressive disorders than those in the control condition.

Treating CBT with Comorbid Disorders

Several recent studies have examined the effectiveness of CBT in treating depression complicated by comorbid psychiatric symptoms. A study using the CWD-A program (Rohde, Clarke, Lewinsohn, Seeley, & Kaufman, 2001) found that comorbid substance abuse disorders slowed remission of depressive symptoms among adolescents and that disruptive behavior disorders increased recurrence somewhat. Overall, however, comorbid anxiety, disruptive behavioral disorders, and substance abuse had very little impact on treatment effectiveness over a 2-year period. A series of studies in Australia found that a school-based CBT group treatment was effective in reducing depression comorbid with anxiety among children over a 1-year follow-up period (Lowry-Webster, Barrett, & Dadds, 2001; Lowry-Webster, Barrett, & Lock, 2003). Another group of researchers found that CBT implemented in schools reduced depression associated with trauma among Latino elementary and middle school children (Kataoka et al., 2003; Stein et al., 2003).

Overwhelming evidence supports CBT-based group programs as effective treatments for depression among children and adolescents. Moreover, the literature suggests that such treatments are feasible and effective when implemented in school settings, with high school, middle school, and elementary-aged youth. Research with children and adolescents supports CBT as a beneficial treatment in reducing both clinically significant and subthreshold symptoms of depression. Moreover, CBT appears to be effective in reducing symptoms of depression among youth, even in the face of other complicating psychiatric problems.

ASSESSMENT

Assessment of depression in educational settings is a potentially challenging and important task. Proper assessment procedures can identify youth at risk, aid in differential diagnosis, and help in selecting and guiding treatment. Outlined is a comprehensive assessment strategy that will review initial screening to measuring posttreatment gains.

Merrell (2001) provides a model that views assessment as a problem-solving process, which breaks down assessment procedures into four phases: *Phase I:* Identification and Clarification; *Phase II:* Data Collection; *Phase 3:* Analysis; and *Phase IV:* Solution and Evaluation. In Phase I, the assessor addresses any sources of ambiguity surrounding the referral question, such as the identity of the client, the purpose of assessment, and the problems to be assessed. Phase II involves determining what assessment methods are the most appropriate to address the referral questions and then implementing those methods. In Phase III, the clinician reviews the data, determines whether further testing is necessary, decides what additional information is needed, and begins to analyze the findings to answer the referral questions. In the final phase (Phase IV), the clinician uses the collected data to develop a solution and to monitor the solution's effect. By using this basic framework, school-based mental health professionals can establish an assessment decision mind-set, in order to determine the underlying cause of behaviors. For instance, although a problem such as inattention is often viewed as the result of Attention-Deficit/Hyperactivity Disorder (ADHD), a thorough assessment and conceptualization may in fact find another explanation, such as depression, a learning disability, or hearing difficulties.

Moreover, Merrell (2001) delineates a multimethod, multisource, multisetting assessment design that emphasizes a focus on broad-based assessment procedures. By using this design, professionals conducting assessment will collect data from a variety of sources and use a variety of measures. Attending to this level of detail will ensure that the assessment procedures are meaningful and allow for better treatment planning.

The Referral

The first step in identifying depressive disorders is educating your referral sources. Referrals are likely to come from a variety of sources including parents and teachers. To improve the quality of referral questions, school-based mental health professionals should focus on educating teachers and other referral sources in the school as to the nature of internalizing disorders, such as depression. Specifically, information pertaining to the differing symptom presentations, course of illness, and age of onset may draw teachers' attention to problem behaviors and aid in early identification of problems.

The Screening

Once an individual with a potential depressive disorder has been identified, the screening process can begin. The *Beck Depression Inventory-II* (BDI-II; Beck, Steer, & Brown, 1996) consists of 21 items and is intended to assess the severity of depressive symptoms in adolescents and adults ages 13 or older. The BDI-II takes roughly 5 to 10 minutes to complete (Nezu, Ronan, Meadows, & McClure, 2000). Higher scores on the BDI-II are associated with greater depression, with mild depression implicated for scores between 14 and 19, moderate depression for scores ranging from 20 to 28, and severe depression for scores over 28. Recently, Beck, Beck, and Jolly (2001) developed the *Beck Youth Inventories of Emotional and Social Impairment (BYI)* designed for students ages 7 through 14 years. Within the BYI, there are five self-standing scales including the *Beck Depression Inventory for Youth (BDI-Y)*, which consists of 20 statements regarding thoughts, feelings, and behaviors associated with depression. The child responds to each statement (written at a second-grade level) by indicating how true the item is for him or her, based on a 4-point scale. The individual scale takes approximately 5 to 10 minutes to complete. The raw scores are converted into T-scores, with scores from 55 to 59 being mildly elevated, 60 to 69 being moderately elevated, and 70 and above being extremely elevated.

Another useful tool is the *Children's Depression Inventory* (CDI; Kovacs, 1992). The age range for the CDI is from 7 to 17, and it is a downward extension of the BDI, with some of the items being changed to reflect the differences in presentation of depression in children (Nezu et al., 2000). Requiring about 10 to 15 minutes to complete, the CDI provides the assessor with T-scores, with elevations of 65 and above being clinically significant. Lower scores may be considered for screening purposes (Nezu et al., 2000). The BDI-II, BDI-Y, and CDI can be administered in individual or group formats. If literacy is in question, the administrator should have the client read the test instructions aloud for a check. Merrell (2001) also cautions about possible response biases that should be considered with this population, including attempting to appear in a socially desirable manner, compliance, and faking bad. If depression is still a concern, an extensive review of the child's history should be completed and a functional behavioral assessment should be considered, as well as more formal, in-depth assessment procedures.

The Clinical Interview

In terms of conducting the clinical interview with the child, Merrell (2001) recommends using two types of semistructured interviews. The first type is intended to gather information, and the assessor focuses on five psychosocial areas with the child. The interview should include questions about interpersonal functioning, family relationships, peer relationships, school adjustment, and community involvement. In addition, a behavioral interview should be conducted. The goal of the behavioral interview is to obtain information about the child's problem behaviors. The focus is on obtaining information about antecedent and consequent behaviors to the problem behavior. This information may be used in conjunction with a *Functional Behavior Assessment* to add to the degree of specificity of the assessment procedures and establish the groundwork for a behavior plan.

In addition to more informal semistructured interviews, it also may be useful to conduct a more formal assessment. The *Kiddie-Schedule for Affective Disorders and Schizophrenia for School-Age Children-Present and Lifetime Version (K-SADS-PL)* is a semistructured clinical interview that operationalizes the DSM-IV criteria (Nezu et al., 2000). Interviews are conducted with both the parent and the child and typically take about 35 to 45 minutes in school settings. This measure may be used with children ages 6 to 17. Scores are provided for individual disorders as well as global impairment. Only professionals who have received extensive training in diagnosis should administer this tool.

Other Assessment Tools

The *Minnesota Multiphasic Personality Inventory-Adolescent (MMPI-A)* is a broadband measure of personality that can be used with adolescents ages 14 to 18 (Butcher, 2002). The self-report measure requires about an hour to take and may be administered by individuals without formal assessment training. Interpretation may be completed on the computer.

The incorporation of behavior rating scales can add convergence to the battery and provide additional insight. The *Child Behavior Checklist* (CBCL; Achenbach, 2001) and the *Behavior Assessment System for Children—Second Edition* (BASC-2; Reynolds & Kamphaus, 2004) are paper-and-pencil tests that make use of multiple observers, potentially including parents, teachers, and a self-report (Kamphaus & Frick, 2002). The self-report for the *BASC-2* may be used with individuals aged from 8 to 21 and provides information on clinical, school, and personal maladjustment as well as clinical scales. The CBCL's self-report, the *Youth Self-Report (YRP)*, provides measures of internalizing, externalizing, and competence behaviors, and it is intended for use with 11- to 18-year-olds. Teacher and parent rating scales for the two checklists are applicable for children from the ages of 4 to 18.

Taken together, these assessment procedures should lay the groundwork for competent, school-based assessment and treatment interventions. Instruments such as the BDI-II, BDI-Y, or CDI are also still useful as measures of treatment gains once a treatment plan has been initiated. To obtain further details on assessment instruments and strategies, readers are encouraged to review Nezu et al. (2000) and Kamphaus and Frick (2002).

CONCEPTUALIZATION OF DEPRESSION USING VARIOUS COGNITIVE-BEHAVIORAL MODELS

In terms of understanding depression within a cognitive model, the tenants of this model and related models will first be reviewed. Cognitive therapy offers techniques that operate at the level of perception (J. Beck, 1995), as the cognitive model rests on the assumption that one's behaviors and feelings are determined by perception. Feelings about a situation are, therefore, largely based on the interpretation one makes about that experience, and thus emotions are mediated by perception. Perceptions develop in part through automatic thoughts, which are defined as evaluative thoughts unrelated to reason or deliberate thinking. These thoughts are brief, and often individuals are scarcely aware when they occur. More likely individuals are aware of the emotional response that follows these automatic thoughts.

Another primary aspect of cognitive therapy involves beliefs, which begin to form as early as childhood and can involve conceptions about the self, other people, or the world and refer to what is described in the literature as the "cognitive triad." Beck, Rush, Shaw, and Emery (1979) proposed that the content of a depressed individual's cognitions is self-blaming and self-deprecating and here a "negative cognitive triad" exists, which consists of negative thoughts about oneself, the world, and the future.

The most central beliefs that one holds are called core beliefs and are often so engrained that they are not easily articulated. This is especially true among children and adolescents. These core beliefs involve absolutes and definitive rules about the way things "are or must be" (J. Beck, 1995). Core beliefs are rigid, global, and overgeneralized, and they influence the development of intermediate beliefs (e.g., rules, assumptions, attitudes) in which individuals attempt to make sense of the environment. Through these assumptions and attitudes, automatic thoughts are developed, which tend to be specific to the situation and are considered the most surface level of cognition. Beck et al. (1979) believed that the negative thoughts of depressed individuals are integrated into a depressed schema about the world, which serves to distort reality and allows the person to maintain negative thoughts, despite objective evidence of positive experiences in one's life.

The self-schema model of depression elaborates on this notion and posits that the level of depression that one is experiencing "mediates both the content of the self-schema and the efficiency of self-referent processing" (Stark, Best, & Sellstrom, 1989). This model can be viewed as an extension of Beck's cognitive model of depression but recognizes that varying levels of depression will influence the information that one evaluates. In general, the self-schema model of depression predicts that a person's self-schema will guide selective processing, whereby schema-consistent data will be evaluated and nonschematic data will be ignored. In general, the more depressed an individual is, the more this selective processing of data will occur.

A model that accounts for the affective changes involved in depressive episodes is the reformulated learned-helplessness model of depression (Abramson, Seligman, & Teasdale, 1978). This model hypothesizes that affective changes occur because of the expectation that undesirable outcomes will occur regardless of the person's behavior. This theorization implicates cognitions as primary in the development of a "depressive attributional style." This generally refers to a tendency to attribute negative outcomes or events to internal, global, and stable factors and attribute positive outcomes or events to external, specific, and unstable factors. Lewinsohn's behavioral model (1974) accounts for behavioral aspects of depressed individuals. Here, depressive behaviors are related to a reduction in response-contingent positive reinforcement. Essentially, an individual over time does not get reinforcement for adaptive behaviors (extinction) and reinforcement is then received for the lack of production of adaptive behaviors. This low instance of response-contingent positive reinforcement leads to dysphoric mood, fatigue, and somatic complaints that are primary signs of depressive disorders.

CAUSES AND CORRELATES OF DEPRESSION

In the literature, there is an abundance of research on the causes and correlates of depression. The cognitive and behavioral factors that serve to maintain and enhance depressive symptoms have been discussed previously within the review of various models of depression. Other correlates that have been discussed extensively in the literature include academic, familial, and genetic factors related to depression. Understanding academic correlates is essential to implementing treatment programs within the school setting. Students who do not achieve as readily as their peers are at risk for developing a poor academic self-concept, negative self-perceptions and cognitions related to school and to their ability to succeed more globally. Elbaum and Vaughn (2001) proposed that because of the significant role that school experiences play in shaping students' self-perceptions, those students who experience severe difficulties in this setting are considered at-risk for developing poor self-concept. These students are, therefore, likely to then experience the adverse consequences of a poor self-concept, such as a diminished self-image. It is not hard to envision that school plays a prominent role in a student's life experience, and negative feelings about academic identity would therefore significantly reduce a child's sense of self-competence and alter his or her self-perceptions.

Teasing apart the nature versus nurture variables related to familial and genetic factors is widely reviewed within the literature, as both have been shown to influence the development of depressive symptomology (Mash & Barkley, 2003). A basic summary of this literature reveals that depression runs in families, and having just one parent diagnosed with major depression is one of the strongest predictive factors in childhood or adolescent depression. It is also worth noting that maladaptive parenting and ongoing negative interactions between parent and child have been implicated in the development of depression in children and adolescents. These variables speak to the psychosocial factors associated with generational cycles that are maintained within family systems and reveal the importance of understanding the child or adolescent within his or her family context.

COGNITIVE THERAPY IN CONTEXT: APPLICATIONS FOR PROFESSIONALS WORKING WITH STUDENTS

Students diagnosed with depression, or those who have learning difficulties that put them at risk for depressive symptomology, could be understood and treated by applying principles inherent to CBT. There have been studies that have linked depression to lower levels of perceived cognitive competence in students and negative academic self-concept (Asarnow, Carlson, & Gurthrie, 1987). It is possible to predict, based on the literature, that low-achieving students, including those diagnosed with LD, often possess negative core beliefs about themselves in relation to academic endeavors (e.g., "I'm stupid"), which develop into assumptions, expectations, and attitudes about school (e.g., "I'm going to fail," "Even if I try hard, no good will come of it"). These in turn may generate negative images and automatic thoughts in academic situations. When students who hold these beliefs encounter academic situations, they then form negative emotional connotations to academic events that persist long after the events have occurred. Based on this model (J. Beck, 1995), it is not difficult to understand that the underpinnings to negative academic self-concepts can develop through negative associations, assumptions, and beliefs about oneself and school. Attribution errors are a consistent finding in both learning-disabled students and depressed individuals, and therefore, cognitive interventions can be instrumental in terms of altering inaccurate self-perceptions (Abramson, Seligman, Teasdale, 1978; Chapman, 1988).

A cognitively oriented therapist would assist students with negative academic self-perceptions and beliefs by beginning to help the students become aware of automatic thoughts and gradually uncover the core beliefs related to school that the students hold. This process would directly address issues of academic self-concept formation and would work to alter inaccurate self-perceptions. This would be accomplished through an increase in awareness of the beliefs that the student holds related to failure or negative attitudes regarding school performance. This occurs as a student begins to recognize the core beliefs that hinder success, and, subsequently, a change in behavior and emotion can occur. Essentially, by altering self-perceptions, a change in the emotional correlates (i.e., low self-esteem, depressive symptomology) related to negative self-perceptions will follow.

GROUP AND INDIVIDUAL INTERVENTIONS FOR DEPRESSED CHILDREN AND ADOLESCENTS

Group Interventions

Adolescent Coping with Depression Course (CWD-A). The *Adolescent Coping with Depression Course (CWD-A),* as previously stated, has been shown to decrease depressive symptoms significantly (Lewinsohn et al., 1990; Clarke, Rohde, Lewinsohn, Hops, & Seeley, 1999). The CWD-A is a group treatment intended for use with adolescents ages 14 to 18. Treatment occurs in two-hour sessions, twice a week for 8 weeks. The CWD-A is a very structured group intervention that makes use of a treatment manual with scripts, student workbooks, and a brief workbook for parents. Sessions include direct instruction, modeling, individual assignments, and homework, and generally focus on developing skills to better cope with or prevent depression.

CWD-A sessions progress through a series of skills. Therapist treatment manuals and student workbooks can be obtained from Clarke, Lewinsohn, and Hops's Web site (http://www.kpchr.org/public/acwd/acwd.html) free of charge. This is the only way to acquire these treatment manuals, which are essential for the implementation of this treatment package. The CWD-A uses script and details a number of specific strategies during each session. The CWD-A may be adapted for individual use as well. When used with individuals, treatment exercises that would have been undertaken in the group are instead role-played with the therapist. Sessions generally begin with review of homework assignments, and then, skills are taught and practiced. Each session concludes with the assignment of homework and a brief quiz to review skills.

The introductory session focuses on depression and social learning. For this session, participants complete a mood questionnaire, go over class guidelines, become familiar with one another, provide education on the cognitive-behavioral model, introduce a mood diary, and give homework. Homework consists of completing a portion of the student workbook, as well as filling out the mood diary. A short quiz is administered at the end and reviewed to reinforce learning. The diary involves the students' rating how they feel on a likert-type scale ranging from 1 to 7, with 1 being the worst that they have ever felt and 7 being the best that they have ever felt.

Self-observation and change are the focus of session 2. Homework is reviewed at the beginning of the session. Next, the students engage in a conversation-starting activity. Students are then taught "baselining" and how to keep a tally of specific behaviors. An activity is implemented to practice establishing a baseline for pleasant activities. Homework is then assigned where the student is asked to "baseline" some of their pleasant activities, as well as to continue his or her mood diaries. A quiz is then given to review skills.

For session 3, the emphasis is on reducing tension. An activity on meeting new people is introduced and practiced. In addition, psychoeducation is provided on tension and a tension reduction exercise. This exercise is a modified form of progressive muscle relaxation, also known as the Jacobson Relaxation technique. A question-and-answer period is followed by the assignment of this session's homework and a quiz.

In session 4, Learning How to Change, the students develop some of their previous skills in baselining. The participants are taught how to chart their information that they kept track of while baselining. Next, they learn about setting goals for pleasant activities. Finally, they learn how to contract for behavior and establish rewards.

Changing your thinking is the focus of session 5, in which students are taught skills in how to make a plan work and developing conversation skills. A "Controlling Your Thinking" activity is initiated that connects the cognitive component of depression to the skills that they have been developing thus far.

Session 6, The Power of Positive Thinking, continues the work on cognition. Activities are completed on increasing positive thoughts and identifying negative ones. Students learn how to use "positive counterthoughts" to combat negative thinking. This session concludes with establishing a reward contract for combating negative thoughts.

In session 7, the participants learn about "disputing irrational thinking." Work is done to identify irrational beliefs. Next, students are shown how negative externalized beliefs may be leading to personal beliefs. The C-A-B model (*A*ctivating event, defining the *B*elief, and noticing the *C*onsequences) is then presented to conceptualize how events can impact beliefs and lead to consequences. Other strategies are then considered for dealing with activating events.

Session 8, Relaxation, begins with a practice of the C-A-B method learned in the previous session. The students then engage in an activity designed to improve "friendly skills." A few of these skills are things like making eye contact and staying positive. The Benson Relaxation Technique is taught to the students, which involves concentrating on a single word and repeating it to one's self in a quiet area. The students focus on their breathing, saying the word, and relaxing.

Session 9 is the first of two sessions on communication. First, techniques are taught to stop negative thoughts. Education is presented on communication, and a two-part listening exercise is then initiated with an ultimate emphasis on active listening. More education is the presented on providing understanding as opposed to judgmental responses.

In the second communication session, session 10, work focuses on stating feelings. The first half of the session involves appropriately stating positive feelings and self-disclosure. Stating positive feelings focuses on connecting an activating event with a feeling state. The latter half of the session focuses on properly making negative feeling statements. The emphasis here is on identifying the activating events, understanding the beliefs associated with those events, and then the feeling consequences and how to communicate them properly.

Session 11 begins the first of four parts on negotiation and problem solving. Assertive imagery is taught first, where the client is to envision how a scenario would play out if the client were to disclose some feeling to another. Next, a rationale is provided for problem solving and negotiation. Some basic rules for settling disagreements are presented, as well as how to define problems. As in previous sessions, there is a practice at the end involving the skills learned.

Session 12, the second to focus on negotiation and problem solving, begins by teaching brainstorming strategies and methods of choosing a solution. Skills in contracting are taught, such as how to implement a contract and how to follow through. For the latter portion of the session, the students are given time to practice their problem-solving strategies.

Session 13 provides additional tutelage in problem solving and negotiation. Students are guided through problem solving, and then they are instructed on how to problem solve with their parents. Session 14, the final part of the negotiation and problem-solving curriculum, begins with an extensive review of how problem solving with their parents went. In addition, extensive time is allotted for practicing problem-solving skills.

Session 15 focuses on Life Goals. Students are encouraged to develop a life plan and significant time is dedicated to identifying and planning for roadblocks to their life goals. Session 16, the final session, involves prevention, planning, and ending. A mood questionnaire is administered and there is discussion on maintaining treatment gains and emergency planning. Finally, there is a discussion of early recognition of difficulties and a summary of the course.

The ACTION program. The ACTION program, developed by Stark and Kendall in 1996, is another cognitive-behavioral group intervention (Merrell, 2001). The ACTION program is designed for use with younger children (possibly as young as 9) through adolescents. Treatment occurs over 30 1-hour sessions and involves teaching relaxation skills, social skills, and problem solving, as well as identifying cognitions, behaviors, and affect. A student workbook is also used in this treatment as is a therapist manual, but sessions are not scripted. In addition, therapists work more individually with specific students during group meetings.

The ACTION treatment package also has a schedule for sessions. They will be discussed briefly as a means of understanding the overview goals and techniques that are outlined as essential to this treatment program. Session 1 involves *intro-ductions* to the group and *the establishment of appropriate expectations* for the group. During sessions 2–8, *affective education* is a primary treatment goal. Affective education requires group members to identify emotions, label emotions, notice cues related to emotions (both internal and external cues), linking emotions to thoughts and behaviors, and learning skills to cope with unpleasant emotions. Within each of these sessions, other techniques are introduced in conjunction with affective education. In session 2, *a within-group incentive system* is developed and group members are introduced to the concept of *self-monitoring of pleasant emotions.* Session 3 involves the introduction of *the active coping orientation* and the continuation of self-monitoring of pleasant emotions. During session 4, a continuation of previous techniques such as the coping orientation and self-monitoring of pleasant emotions occurs along with the introduction of *pleasant events scheduling.* In session 5, the *introduction of problem solving* occurs within the group and self-monitoring of pleasant emotions continues to be a focus of the group session. During session 6, pleasant events scheduling and self-monitoring pleasant emotions is practiced and then *a problem-solving game* is played. Session 7 involves these same techniques excluding self-monitoring of pleasant events. Within session 8, the group members learn to *apply problem-solving skills* to their experiences with mood disturbance.

In session 9, the group members again are asked to apply problem-solving skills to mood disturbance and are also involved in a *missing solution activity* that allows them to apply their skills. With session 10 comes the *introduction of relaxation* techniques. During session 11, group members are asked to *apply problem-solving skills to interpersonal situations.* Also during this session, pleasant events scheduling is again utilized and the concept of *using relaxation as a coping strategy* is discussed. The group members continue applying problem-solving skills to interpersonal situations and the examination of relaxation as a coping strategy in session 12, with added focus on *self-evaluation of solution implementation.* Session 13 focuses on *the spontaneous use of problem-solving* as well as relaxation techniques, whereas session 14 involves the *introduction of cognitive restructuring* and the *identification of depressogenic thoughts.* Session 15 includes the *practice of catching* (identifying) *negative thoughts* and the *continuation of cognitive restructuring.* During session 16, the group members improve their understanding of cognitive restructuring by continuing to practice catching negative thoughts, *finding evidence to support these thoughts* and then *discussing what to do when a negative thought is true.* Sessions 17 and 18 focus on *the generation of alternative interpretations* of these thoughts is conducted, and specifically in Session 18, *the group identifies negative expectations* that they possess and the *introduction of the What If technique* is incorporated into the group structure. The "What If" technique carries into session 19, and during session 20, *a review of cognitive restructuring* is conducted. Also during session 20, *the introduction to assertiveness training* occurs and the *group practices generating and rehearsing coping statements.*

During session 21, the group focuses on the concept of *positive assertiveness* and continues generating coping statements. Assertiveness training and the generation of coping statements continue into session 22. Within session 23, the group identifies personal standards and areas in need of personal improvement. Also during this session *the introduction to self-evaluation training occurs. The establishment of goals and subgoals for self-improvement* occurs during session 24. Sessions 25 to 28 *focus on self-evaluation training* and strive to work towards the goal of self-improvement. The closing of the group occurs during sessions 29 and 30 and involves the acknowledgment of *termination issues* and *programming for generalization* (where skills and gains in the group can be applied more globally).

Individual Interventions

Individual CBT has been shown through meta-analyses across a variety of studies to be an efficacious treatment for depression in children and adolescents (Reinecke et al., 1998; Lewinsohn & Clarke, 1999). Reinecke et al. (1998) defined CBT as "interventions that seek to promote emotional and behavioral change by teaching children to change thoughts and thought processes in an overt, active and problem-oriented manner" (p. 27). Thus, cognitive-behavioral treatment approaches that possess these characteristics may be considered as effective therapies for the treatment for child and adolescent depression.

Vostanis and Harrington (1994) offered a brief overview of an individual cognitive-behavioral treatment package (as cited in Feehan & Vostanis, 1996). This intervention package addresses affect, attributions, and social skills. The treatment consists of nine 1-hour long session with children ages 8 to 16 years old.

Sessions 1 and 2 focus on emotional recognition. The aim of the first session is mainly to define and describe emotions. The first homework assignment is to record feelings, as well as events and thoughts in a diary. The focus of the second session is similar to the first but the child is asked to find causality among his or her emotions, events, and feelings. The emphasis in session 3 is on self-reinforcement. During this session the child is able to engage in a reward for desired behavior.

Sessions 4 and 5 focus on social problem solving. In session 4, the child is asked to reconsider social situations in which he or she had difficulties and brain-storm alternate solutions. The emphasis in session 5 is on refining social problem solving skills and using role-play techniques.

Sessions 6 and 7 involve cognitive restructuring. The child is taught self-monitoring and asked to provide evidence concerning negative thoughts and attributions in session 6. Negative attributions are then challenged early in session 7. Causes and consequences of the child's behavior are discerned. Session 8 entails a treatment plan review, where links are drawn between skills and goals of treatment. In session 9, the final session, the child is encouraged to use treatment gains and further therapy arrangements are made if necessary.

SUMMARY

Depression is a potentially debilitating disorder found in children and adolescents, which has the potential to impact all aspects of functioning and has ramifications later in life. Youth with depression need interventions that will target the cognitions and behaviors that serve to maintain this disorder. A review of Merrill (2001) was conducted as a means of understanding the essential components to the assessment process when a diagnosis of depression is considered when working with this population. Children and adolescents demonstrate emotional problems different than their adult counterparts and, therefore, will need interventions designed to treat the difficulties associated with depression in a manner that is consistent with their experiences. The basic framework of CBT has demonstrated efficacy in treating depression in adults, and with some modifications, CBT also has been successful in treating depressive symptoms in children and adolescents. Individual and group interventions involve techniques aimed at changing depressive thinking (e.g., problem solving, self-monitoring training) and behaviors (e.g., coping skill enhancement, covert modeling) that will serve to change negative emotional correlates. As children and adolescents spend a large amount of time in the school setting, school-based interventions are a practical and effective choice to treat students who have depressive symptomology.

In this chapter, an overview of the CWD-A and the ACTION group therapies were discussed as a tool for understanding the general format of a cognitive-behavioral group for depressed youths. A brief example of an individual format was provided to see how various cognitive-behavioral techniques would be incorporated into treatment with depressed children and adolescents. Both the individual and the group therapies incorporate a combination of cognitive restructuring techniques to alter distorted thinking and behavioral techniques for the purpose of bringing about symptom reduction and increasing skills related to coping with depressive symptomology.

REFERENCES

Abramson, L. Y., Seligman, M. E. P., & Teasdale, J. (1978). Learned helplessness in humans: Critique and reformulation. *Journal of Abnormal Psychology, 87,* 49–74.

Achenbach, T. M. (2001). *Manual for the ASEBA school-age forms and profiles.* Burlington: University of Vermont.

American Psychiatric Association (2000). *Diagnostic and statistical manual of mental disorders* (4th ed.-text revision). Washington, DC: Author.

Asarnow, J. R., Carlson, G. A., & Guthrie, D. (1987). Coping strategies, self-perceptions, hopelessness, and perceived family environments in depressed and suicidal children. *Journal of Consulting and Clinical Psychology, 55,* 361–366.

Beck, A. T., Rush, A. G., Shaw, B. F., & Emery, G. (1979). *Cognitive therapy of depression.* New York: Guilford Press.

Beck, A. T., Steer, R. A., & Brown, G. K. (1996). *Manual for the BDI-II.* San Antonio, TX: The Psychological Corporation.

Beck, J. S. (1995). *Cognitive Therapy.* New York: Guilford Press.

Beck, J. S., Beck A. T., and Jolly, J. (2001). *Manual for the Beck Youth Inventories of Emotional and Social Adjustment.* San Antonio, TX: The Psychological Corporation.

Butcher, J. N. (2002). *Clinical personality assessment practical approaches* (2nd ed.). New York: Oxford University Press.

Butler, L., Miezitis, S., Friedman, R., & Cole, E. (1980). The effect of two school-based intervention programs on depressive symptoms in preadolescents. *Journal of American Educational Research, 17,* 111–119.

Chapman, J. W. (1988). Cognitive motivational characteristics and academic achievement of learning disabled children: A longitudinal study. *Journal of Educational Psychology, 80,* 357–365.

Clarke, G. N., Hawkins, W., Murphy, M., Sheeber, L. B., Lewinsohn, P. M., & Seeley, J. R. (1995). Targeted prevention of unipolar depressive disorders in an at-risk sample of high-school adolescents: A randomized trial of a group cognitive intervention. *Journal of the American Academy of Child and Adolescent Psychiatry, 34,* 312–321.

Clarke, G. N., Lewinsohn, P. M., & Hops, H. (1990). *Instructor's manual for the adolescent coping with depression course.* Eugene, OR: Castalia Press.

Clarke, G. N., Rohde, P., Lewinsohn, P. M., Hops, H., & Seeley, J. R. (1999). Cognitive-behavioral treatment of adolescent depression: Efficacy of acute group treatment and booster sessions. *Journal of the American Academy of Child and Adolescent Psychiatry, 38,* 272–279.

Costello, E. J., Pine, D. S., Hammen, C., March, J. S., Plotsky, P. M., Weissman, M. M., et al. (2002). Development and Natural History of Mood Disorders. *Biological Psychiatry, 52,* 529–542.

Curry, J. (2001). Specific psychotherapies for childhood and adolescent depression. *Biological Psychiatry, 49,* 1091–1100.

Elbaum, B., & Vaughn, S. (2001). School-based interventions to enhance the self-concept of students with learning disabilities: A meta-analysis. *The Elementary School Journal, 101,* 303–331.

Feehan, C. J., & Vostanis, P. (1996). Cognitive-behavioural therapy for depressed children: Children's and therapists' impressions. *Behavioural and Cognitive Psychotherapy, 24,* 171–183.

Gillham, J. E., & Reivich, K. J. (1999). Prevention of depressive symptoms in schoolchildren: A research update. *Psychological Science, 10,* 461–462.

Gillham, J. E., Reivich, K. J., Jaycox, L. H., & Seligman, M. E. (1995). Prevention of depressive symptoms in schoolchildren: Two-year follow-up. *Psychological Science, 6,* 343–351.

Hollon, S. D., Munoz, R. F., Barlow, D. H., Beardslee, W. R., Bell, C. B., Bernal, G., et al. (2002). Psychosocial intervention development for the prevention and treatment of depression: Promoting Innovation and increasing access. *Biological Psychiatry, 52,* 610–630.

Jaycox, L. H., Reivich, K. J., Gillham, J., & Seligman, M. E. (1994). Prevention of depressive symptoms in school children. *Behaviour Research and Therapy, 32,* 801–816.

Kahn, J. S., Kehle, T. J., Jenson, W. R., & Clark, E. (1990). Comparison of cognitive-behavioral, relaxation, and self-modeling interventions for depression among middle-school students. *School Psychology Review, 19,* 196–211.

Kamphaus, R. W., & Frick, P. J. (2002). *Clinical assessment of child and adolescent personality and behavior* (2nd ed.). MA: Allyn & Bacon.

Kashani, J. H., Reid, J. C., & Rosenberg, T. K. (1989). Levels of hopelessness in children and adolescents: A developmental perspective. *Journal of Consulting and Clinical Psychology, 57,* 496–499.

Kataoka, S. H., Stein, B. D., Jaycox, L. H., Wong, M., Escudero, P., Tu, W. (2003). A school-based mental health program for traumatized Latino immigrant children. *Journal of the American Academy of Child and Adolescent Psychiatry, 42,* 311–318.

Kovacs, M. (1992). *Children's Depression Inventory manual.* North Tonawanda, NY: Multi-Health Systems.

Lewinsohn, P. M. (1974). A behavioral approach to depression. In R. M. Friedman & M. M. Katz (Eds.), *The psychology of depression: Contemporary theory and research* (pp. 157–185). New York: Wiley.

Lewinsohn, P. M., & Clarke, G. N. (1999). Psychosocial treatments for adolescent depression. *Clinical Psychology Review, 19,* 329–342.

Lewinsohn, P. M., Clarke, G. N., Hops, H., & Andrews, J. (1990). Cognitive-behavioral group treatment of depression in adolescents. *Behavior Therapy, 21*, 285–401.

Lewinsohn, P. M., Clarke, G. N., Rohde, P., Hops, H., & Seeley, J. R. (1996). A course in coping: a cognitive-behavioral approach to the treatment of adolescent depression. In E. D. Hibbs & P. S. Jensen (Eds.), *Psychosocial Treatments for Child and Adolescent Disorders: Empirically Based Strategies for Clinical Practice* (pp. 109–135). Washington, DC: American Psychological Association.

Lewinsohn, P. M., Hops, H., Roberts, R. E., Seeley, J. R., & Andrews, J. A. (1993). Adolescent psychopathology: I. Prevalence and incidence of depression and other DSM-III-R related disorders in high school students. *Journal of Abnormal Psychology, 102*, 133–144.

Lewinsohn, P. M., Pettit, J. W., Joiner, T. E., & Seeley, J. R. (2003). The symptomatic expression of major depressive disorder in adolescents and young adults. *Journal of Abnormal Psychology, 112*, 244–252.

Lewinsohn, P. M., Solomon, A., Seeley, J. R., & Zeiss, A. (2000). Clinical implications of "subthreshold" depressive symptoms. *Journal of Abnormal Psychology, 109*, 345–351.

Lowry-Webster, H. M., Barrett, P. M., & Dadds, M. R. (2001). A universal prevention trial of anxiety and depressive symptomotology in childhood: Preliminary data from an Australian study.

Lowry-Webster, H. M., Barrett, P. M., & Lock, S. (2003). A universal prevention trial of anxiety symptomology during childhood: Results at 1-year follow-up. *Behavior Change, 20*, 25–43.

Mash, E. J., & Barkley, R. B. (2003). *Child psychopathology* (2nd ed.). New York: Guilford Press.

Merrell, K. W. (2001). *Helping students overcome depression and anxiety: A practical guide.* New York: Guilford Press.

Nezu, A. M., Ronan, G. F., Meadows, E. A., & McClure, K. S, (2000), *Practitioner's guide to empirically based measures of depression.* New York: Kluwer Academic/Plenum Publishers.

Reinecke, M. A., Ryan, N. E., & Dubois, D. L. (1998). Cognitive-behavioral therapy of depression and depressive symptoms during adolescence: A review and meta-analysis. *Journal of the American Academy of Child and Adolescent Psychiatry, 37*, 26–34.

Reynolds, C. R., & Kamphaus, R. W. (2004). *Behavior Assessment System for Children* (2nd ed.). Circle Pines, MN: American Guidance Service.

Roberts, C., Kane, R., Thomson, H., Bishop, B., & Hart, B. (2003). The prevention of depressive symptoms in rural school children: A randomized controlled trial. *Journal of Consulting and Clinical Psychology, 71*, 622–628.

Roberts, R. E., Lewinsohn, P. M., & Seeley, J. R. (1995). Symptoms of DSM-III-R major depression in adolescence: Evidence from an epidemiological survey. *Journal of the American Academy of Child and Adolescent Psychiatry, 34*, 1608–1617.

Rohde, P., Clarke, G. N., Lewinsohn, P. M., Seeley, J. R., & Kaufman, N. K. (2001). Impact of comorbidity on a cognitive-behavioral group treatment for adolescent depression. *Journal of the American Academy of Child and Adolescent Psychiatry, 40*, 795–802.

Stark, K. D., Best, L. R., & Sellstrom, E. A. (1989). A cognitive-behavioral approach to the treatment of childhood depression. In J. N. Hughes & R. J. Hall (Eds.) *Cognitive-behavioral psychology in the schools: A comprehensive handbook* (pp. 389–433). New York: Guilford Press.

Stark, K. D., Reynolds, W. M., & Kaslow, N. J. (1987). A comparison of the relative efficacy of self-control therapy and a behavioral problem-solving therapy for depression in children. *Journal of Abnormal Child Psychology, 15*, 91–113.

Stark, K. D., Rouse, L., & Livingston, R. (1991). Treatment of depression during childhood and adolescence: Cognitive-behavioral procedures for the individual and the family. In P. C. Kendall (Ed.), *Child and Adolescent Therapy* (pp. 165–206). New York: Guillford Press.

Stein, B. D., Jaycox, L. H., Kataoka, S. H., Wong, M., Tu, W., Elliott, M. N., et al. (2003). A mental health intervention for schoolchildren exposed to violence: A randomized clinical controlled trial. *Journal of the American Medical Association, 290,* 603–611.

Weisz, J. R., Thurber, C. A., Sweeney, L., Proffitt, V. D., & LeGagnoux, G. L. (1997). Brief treatment of mild to moderate child depression using primary and secondary control enhancement training. *Journal of Consulting and Clinical Psychology, 65,* 703–707.

8

Attention-Deficit/Hyperactivity Disorder

GEORGE J. DuPAUL,
ROSEMARY E. VILE JUNOD &
LIZETTE MARIE FLAMMER

Attention-Deficit/Hyperactivity Disorder (ADHD) is a disruptive behavior disorder that describes individuals who engage in developmentally inappropriate levels of inattention, impulsivity, or overactivity (American Psychiatric Association, 2000). Approximately 3 to 7% of school-aged children in the United States can be diagnosed with this disorder, representing approximately one child in every classroom (American Psychiatric Association, 2000; Barkley, in press; DuPaul & Stoner, 2003). Boys outnumber girls with this disorder at approximately a 2:1 to 6:1 ratio (Barkley, in press). Typically, ADHD is a chronic disorder that extends into adulthood for the majority of affected individuals (Barkley, Fischer, Smallish, & Fletcher, 2002).

The diagnostic criteria for ADHD stipulate that children must exhibit frequent symptoms of inattention (e.g., distractibility, difficulty completing assigned tasks), hyperactivity/impulsivity (e.g., interrupting others, fidgeting), or both over an extended time period (i.e., at least 6 months; American Psychiatric Association, 2000). Furthermore, these symptoms must be associated with academic, social, or occupational impairment across two or more settings. Typically, some impairing symptoms are present by age 7 years. There are three ADHD subtypes including Predominantly Inattentive (i.e., only inattention symptoms are present), Predominantly Hyperactive-Impulsive (i.e., only hyperactive-impulsive symptoms are present), and Combined (i.e., both symptom clusters are present).

ADHD rarely occurs in isolation and is typically associated with other behavior, emotion, or learning disorders (Barkley, in press). The most common comorbid conditions are the other disruptive behavior disorders, Oppositional-Defiant Disorder (ODD) and Conduct Disorder (CD; American Psychiatric Association, 2000).

In fact, more than 50% of children with ADHD, especially boys, will have either ODD or CD (Barkley, in press). The combination of ADHD and another disruptive behavior disorder is highly predictive of aggressive, delinquent, and antisocial outcomes in adolescence and adulthood (Barkley et al., 2002; Weiss & Hechtman, 1993). Approximately 30% of children with ADHD also will have a specific learning disability in reading, math, or other subject areas (DuPaul & Stoner, 2003). Of course, the combination of ADHD and LD is a strong predictor of poor academic performance and underachievement. Finally, children with ADHD may be at higher than average risk for emotion disorders such as anxiety disorders and depression (Barkley, in press). Girls with ADHD may be at even higher risk for internalizing disorders than are boys with this disorder (Biederman et al., 2002).

Whether ADHD occurs alone or is exhibited along with comorbid disorders, children with this disorder exhibit many significant problems in school settings. Of greatest concern is the high rate of disruptive behavior that children with ADHD exhibit on a consistent basis in classrooms (Abikoff et al., 2002; Barkley, in press; DuPaul & Stoner, 2003; Vile Junod et al., 2005). For example, Vile Junod and colleagues (2005) found that elementary school-aged children with ADHD engaged in 2.5 to 3 times more off-task motor (e.g., leaving assigned seat), off-task verbal (e.g., talking without permission), and off-task passive (e.g., looking away from assigned activity) behavior than their non-ADHD classmates. This level of off-task behavior can disrupt the learning of children with ADHD and their classmates.

One of the greatest risks associated with ADHD is academic underachievement (Barkley, in press; DuPaul & Stoner, 2003). In fact, one study found that 90% of children with this disorder experience academic difficulties of one form or another (Cantwell & Baker, 1991). Children with ADHD obtain report card grades and achievement test scores that are in the low average to below average range and their performance is significantly below their classmates, with groups differing by as much as 1.5 to 2 standard deviations (DuPaul et al., 2004). Unfortunately, academic difficulties may be experienced across school years wherein students with this disorder are at higher than average risk for grade retention and dropping out of school (Mannuzza, Gittelman-Klein, Bessler, Malloy, & LaPadula, 1993).

Children with ADHD also frequently experience difficulties making and keeping friends (Barkley, in press). Because of their impulsive, aggressive behavior, children with this disorder may be rejected by their non-ADHD peers and have less than average opportunities to build prosocial skills. Over time, children with ADHD and related behavior disorders may befriend each other, thereby increasing the potential for developing more serious, antisocial, and deviant behavior (Patterson, Reid, & Dishion, 1992).

The purpose of this chapter is to provide an overview of cognitive-behavioral treatments (CBT) that might be helpful for children and adolescents with ADHD. Given the myriad of difficulties that children with this disorder experience, it is unlikely that a single intervention or treatment, even a powerful one such as stimulant medication, will sufficiently improve all areas of functioning. Thus, we discuss cognitive-behavioral interventions in the context of other treatments with documented success in this population. First, the recent literature examining CBT effects for children with ADHD is reviewed. Second, specific assessment techniques that can be used to make diagnostic decisions and evaluate interventions are discussed. Next, a conceptualization of ADHD from a cognitive-behavioral perspective is provided as a context for development of interventions. Fourth, strategic interventions for application in school settings are described. Finally, two case examples are presented to demonstrate how these interventions can be individualized to meet specific needs.

LITERATURE REVIEW

Cognitive-behavioral approaches have generated considerable clinical and empirical attention over the past decade (Carr, 2000; Friedberg & McClure, 2002; Graham, 1998; Hibbs & Jensen, 1996; Kendall, 2000) as a result of their increased potential for achieving durable behavioral change. One of the fundamental assumptions on which cognitive-behavioral interventions are based is the belief that cognitions influence emotions and behavior. Children and adolescents are believed to respond to cognitive representations of events, rather than or in addition to the events themselves. In light of this belief, cognitive change is a prerequisite for behavioral and emotional improvement. For the purpose of this chapter, cognitive-behavioral approaches were conceptualized as falling into one of two categories: cognitive-behavior therapy or self-management.

Cognitive-Behavior Therapy

Cognitive-behavior therapy is a psychological treatment intended to change maladaptive thoughts or cognitions and behaviors (Graham, 1998; Kendall, 2000). Research completed over the past 20 years on the effectiveness of cognitive-behavior therapy in addressing behavioral and emotional difficulties among youth has been limited but, for the most part, positive. Controlled outcome studies suggest that cognitive-behavior therapy is superior to placebo and no-treatment conditions for treating depression (Curry & Reinecke, 2003), obsessive compulsive disorder (Pediatric OCD Treatment Study Team, 2004), eating disorders (Bowers, Evans, & Andersen, 1997), posttraumatic stress disorder (Phillips, 2000), and social phobia (Spence, Donovan, & Brechman-Toussaint, 2000). The effect sizes obtained in these studies are comparable to those observed in outcome research with adults, and gains are often maintained over time (Reinecke, Ryan, & DuBois, 1998; Weisz & Weiss, 1993).

Despite the promising results evidenced in some areas of the literature, empirical support for the use of cognitive-behavior therapy for children and adolescents with ADHD is lacking (Abikoff, 1985; Braswell & Bloomquist, 1991; Kendall & Braswell, 1993). Cognitive-behavior therapy is often conducted away from the situation in which the problem behavior occurs. To be optimally effective, intervention strategies must be implemented in close proximity to the target behavior (Goldstein & Goldstein, 1998). Interventions further removed in time and place from the behavior of interest are likely to be less effective, particularly for ADHD symptoms (i.e., inattention, impulsivity, and overactivity).

Self-instruction, which also falls under the umbrella of cognitive-behavior therapy, offers a viable option that is intended to be implemented within the same time and context of the problem behavior. Self-instruction refers to the internalization of self-statements in order to develop self-control over one's own behavior (De La Paz, 1999). Training in self-instruction involves teaching children specific verbalizations to direct their own behavior.

Self-instruction training has been used effectively to increase academic behaviors such as on-task and independent completion of assigned tasks (De La Paz, 1999), increase accuracy with which work is completed (Miller & Brewster, 1992), and decrease disruptive behavior (De La Paz, 1999); however, self-instruction training has not always resulted in positive effects. When applied to problems posed by students with ADHD, research on self-instruction procedures has been characterized by equivocal results and poor generalization. In fact, researchers have speculated that variables other than self-instructions (e.g., reinforcement for memorization of instructions, reinforcement for accuracy of completion) may actually be responsible for the positive results obtained with this procedure (Abikoff, 1985; Kendall & Braswell, 1993; Pfiffner & Barkley, 1990).

Despite the potential promise of self-instruction and related cognitive-behavior therapy, extant data do not support these as efficacious approaches for treating ADHD. It has been suggested that without behavioral components, such as reinforcement, the use of self-instruction procedures and cognitive-behavior therapy for children with ADHD cannot be advocated (Ervin, Bankert, & DuPaul, 1996; Hinshaw, 2000).

Self-Management Interventions

Recent emphasis has been placed on developing interventions designed to teach students specific skills of independence and self-reliance. One promising approach to enhancing independence and self-reliance in students with academic and behavioral difficulties is self-management interventions. Self-management interventions generally involve strategies related to changing or maintaining one's own behavior (Shapiro & Cole, 1994). Students are taught to use strategies that will increase appropriate academic and social behaviors or decrease inappropriate classroom behaviors. In addition, by teaching portable coping strategies that will transfer across behaviors and situations, self-management interventions have the potential for producing durable and generalizable behavioral gains (Shapiro & Cole, 1994).

Self-management generally refers to actions designed to change or maintain one's own behavior. Interventions in the classroom involve teaching a child to engage in various behaviors, such as self-monitoring, self-evaluation, and self-reinforcement. Self-monitoring is the act of systematically observing or recording one's own behavior in an effort to increase the student's awareness of his or her own behavior and ability to function independently. Self-evaluation and self-reinforcement involve a comparison of one's self-observed behavior against an established, desirable standard and, then, consequent self-delivery of a reward for meeting one's goal.

Interventions for teaching students to manage their own behavior in the class-room have burgeoned over the past three decades. Self-management interventions have been shown to effectively remediate a variety of academic and nonacademic problems exhibited by students of all ages and disability categories. Self-management interventions have been useful in diverse areas such as increasing homework completion in general and special education students across elementary and middle schools (Carrington, Lehrer, & Wittenstrom, 1997; McDougall, 1998), increasing on-task behavior in students with learning disabilities as well as those with ADHD (Hoff & DuPaul, 1998), decreasing disruptive behavior in children with hyperactivity (Davies & Witte, 2000; Hoff & DuPaul, 1998), and improving academic performance in the areas of reading comprehension and math problem-solving among students with learning disabilities (McDougall & Brady, 1998; Miller & Brewster, 1992; Miranda, Villaescusa, & Vidal-Abarca, 1997).

Self-management interventions encompass a heterogeneous group of procedures, which have been used with children of all ages to remediate a wide variety of academic and behavioral problems. All of these strategies offer an alternative to traditional teacher-managed behavior modification approaches. With a focus on skill building, each of these self-management strategies attempts in some way to teach students to be more independent, self-reliant, and responsible for their own behavior.

ASSESSMENT TOOLS AND TECHNIQUES

Reliable and valid assessment of ADHD symptoms requires the use of multiple methods and sources to determine the extent to which symptoms are exhibited relative to developmental expectations (Barkley, in press). Assessment methods include diagnostic interviews with parents, teachers, or children; observations of behavior; rating scales completed by teachers and parents; measures related to possible deficit areas (e.g., academic achievement); and self-report ratings. In order for a child to be diagnosed with ADHD, assessment data must indicate that the child exhibits sufficient ADHD symptoms at a frequency that is well beyond expectations for the child's age and gender. Furthermore, symptoms must be present in at least two settings, for at least 6 months, and should be associated with impairment in social or academic functioning (American Psychiatric Association, 2000). As is the case with any psychiatric diagnosis, clinicians must consider and rule out alternative hypotheses (e.g., other disorders or environmental conditions) that could better account for the symptoms. Finally, the assessment of ADHD does not end with diagnosis; rather, data continue to be collected to document treatment effects and to aid in tailoring intervention (DuPaul & Stoner, 2003).

In this section, we provide information on school-based assessment of ADHD using direct observations, behavior ratings, outcome measures, and self-report ratings. More comprehensive discussion of the diagnostic assessment of ADHD is available elsewhere (Anastopoulos & Shelton, 2001; Barkley, in press; DuPaul & Stoner, 2003).

Direct Observation

One of the best methods to determine the frequency of ADHD-related behavior (e.g., off-task) and the context in which the behavior occurs is to directly observe student behavior in classroom and playground settings. Observations typically are conducted on multiple occasions by a single observer (i.e., to obtain a consistent estimate of behavior frequency) who attempts to collect data in an unobtrusive and objective manner. Observation sessions can be of any length; however, these typically range from 10 to 30 minutes. Coding systems have been devised to collect data on ADHD symptoms and disruptive behavior (in the classroom) as well as social interactions (on the playground).

Classroom. A number of behavior observation coding systems have been developed for use in determining the frequencies of various ADHD-related behaviors during classroom task periods (see, for review, Barkley, in press; Platzman et al., 1992). These include the *ADHD Behavior Coding System* (Barkley, Fischer, Newby, & Breen, 1988), the *Hyperactive Behavior Code* (Jacob, O'Leary, & Rosenblad, 1978), the *Classroom Observation Code* (Abikoff, Gittelman-Klein, & Klein, 1977), the *Behavior Observation of Students in Schools* (BOSS; Shapiro, 2003), and the *ADHD School Observation Code* (ADHD SOC; Gadow, Sprafkin, & Nolan, 1996). Each of these systems requires observers to classify behaviors into a variety of categories (e.g., Off-task, Fidgets) using interval recording procedures. Because normative data based on large, representative samples are lacking for these observation codes, the behavior of the referred student should be compared to one or two classmates who have been identified as "typical" or "average" by the classroom teacher. In this fashion, each child would be evaluated relative to a classroom-based standard of behavior.

Platzman and colleagues (1992) reviewed the various observational methods that have been developed for the assessment of ADHD. Importantly, they concluded that observations conducted in the classroom provided data that were better at discriminating children with ADHD from controls than were observations conducted in clinic analog settings. This finding supports the need for educators and school personnel to be involved in ADHD evaluations. Also, three categories of behavior were found to consistently discriminate between ADHD and non-ADHD samples—off-task behavior, excessive gross motor activity, and negative vocalizations (e.g., talking without permission). Thus, observation systems that include these behavioral categories are most likely to provide sensitive diagnostic data.

In addition to coding the child's behavior during task situations, it is sometimes helpful to collect supplemental observation data. For instance, teacher behaviors (e.g., prompts, reprimands, feedback) could be coded as possible antecedent and/or consequent events for child behavior (Whalen, Henker, & Dotemoto, 1981). Such data are critical to determining the function of the challenging behavior and, therefore, are important for treatment planning purposes.

Playground. Observations of children's social interactions may be an important assessment component, particularly if social relationship difficulties are identified as concerns by teachers and parents. Typically, observation systems include categories for both prosocial and negative (e.g., aggressive) behavior. One example of an observation system that has been found useful for collecting data regarding social behaviors in lunchroom and playground settings is the ADHD SOC (Gadow et al., 1996). Generally, children with ADHD exhibit higher than average frequencies of aggressive and negative behaviors (Barkley, in press). Alternatively, in most cases, their rates of positive social behavior are not substantially different from their normal counterparts (Stormont, 2001). Results of these types of observations can be used not only to document the type and severity of social relationship difficulties but also to target specific behaviors for intervention.

Behavior Rating Scales

To be considered clinically significant, ADHD symptoms must be exhibited more frequently than typical children of the same age and gender as the identified child (American Psychiatric Association, 2000). Behavior rating scales are the best available way to determine the developmental deviance of ADHD-related behaviors because normative data typically are available for these measures. Ratings should be completed by parents and teachers in order to assess the cross-situational consistency of ADHD symptoms as well as to gauge the degree to which respondents agree on the nature and severity of child difficulties.

Parent. One or both parents should complete several questionnaires to determine the developmental deviance of the child's ADHD-related behaviors as well as to establish the pervasiveness of problem behaviors across settings. Several general or broadband behavior rating scales with adequate normative data and sound psychometric properties (for review, see Anastopoulos & Shelton, 2001; Barkley, in press) can achieve this purpose, including the *Child Behavior Checklist* (CBCL; Achenbach, 2001a), *Behavior Assessment System for Children—Second Edition* (BASC-2; Reynolds & Kamphaus, 2004), and *Conners Parent Rating Scale* (CPRS; Conners, 1997). Broadband measures facilitate differential diagnosis as competing hypotheses (e.g., presence of other disorders) for the exhibition of ADHD symptoms can be explored.

In addition to a broadband rating scale, the parent(s) should complete two narrowband questionnaires containing items more specific to ADHD-related behaviors: *The ADHD Rating Scale-IV* (DuPaul, Power, Anastopoulos, & Reid, 1998) and the *Home Situations Questionnaire* (HSQ; Barkley, 1990). The *ADHD Rating Scale-IV* provides information regarding the frequency of occurrence of each of the 18 symptoms of this disorder in the home setting. Scores on the Inattention and Hyperactive-Impulsive factors can be compared to normative data to determine the developmental deviance of ADHD symptomatology. Parental responses on the HSQ allow determination of the number of home settings in which behavior problems are exhibited by the child. In addition, the severity of behavior problems within each situation is rated on a 1 (mild) to 9 (severe) Likert scale. The revised version of the HSQ (HSQ-R; DuPaul & Barkley, 1992) provides more specific information regarding the pervasiveness of attention problems across home situations.

It may also be helpful for parents to complete the *Impairment Rating Scale* (IRS; Fabiano et al., 1999) to determine the degree to which a child's ADHD symptoms impair functioning. The IRS contains seven items related to various areas of functioning (e.g., relationships with siblings) that could be affected by ADHD symptoms.

Teacher. As is the case with parent ratings, there are many well-standardized, broadband teacher rating scales available. The three most prominent of these questionnaires are the *Teacher Report Form* (TRF; Achenbach, 2001b), the *Behavior Assessment System for Children—Second Edition* (BASC-2 ; Reynolds & Kamphaus, 2004), and the *Conners Teacher Rating Scale* (Conners, 1997). As mentioned above, these broadband measures have many advantages including a wide coverage of possible problem areas, and extensive standardization samples facilitating normative comparisons by gender and age.

In conjunction with one of these broadband rating scales, inclusion of two or more additional measures should be considered. First, a narrowband measure of ADHD symptoms, such as the *ADHD Rating Scale-IV* (DuPaul et al., 1998), should be used to determine the specific frequency of ADHD-related behaviors from the teacher's perspective. Second, the *School Situations Questionnaire* (SSQ; Barkley, 1990) or the *School Situations Questionnaire-Revised* (SSQ-R; DuPaul & Barkley, 1992) should be completed. The SSQ and SSQ-R provide information regarding the pervasiveness across situations and severity level of conduct and attention problems, respectively.

In most cases, children referred for a diagnostic evaluation of ADHD also are reported to evidence social relationship and academic performance difficulties. Thus, teacher perceptions of student functioning in these areas may need to be assessed as well. There are a number of psychometrically sound, social skills questionnaires that are available including *The Social Skills Rating System* (Gresham & Elliott, 1990) and the *Walker-McConnell Scale of Social Competence and School Adjustment* (Walker & McConnell, 1988). Teacher ratings of academic achievement difficulties can be obtained through use of the *Academic Performance Rating Scale* (DuPaul, Rapport, & Perriello, 1991) or the *Academic Competency Evaluation Scale* (DiPerna & Elliott, 2000). Ratings on one of the latter questionnaires may indicate the need for further assessment of academic skills deficits. Finally, a teacher version of the *Impairment Rating Scale* (IRS; Fabiano et al., 1999) is available to determine teacher perceptions of the degree to which ADHD symptoms impair functioning. The IRS contains six items related to potential areas of impairment of school functioning.

Measures Related to Treatment Outcome

The treatment of ADHD is not only directed toward reduction of symptoms but also toward enhancement of functioning, particularly in the academic and social domains. For this reason, academic and social functioning should be assessed directly both prior to (i.e., baseline) and following intervention. For example, curriculum-based measurement (CBM) can be used to document treatment effects on reading and math achievement (Shapiro, 2003). Teacher ratings of academic performance (APRS or

ACES) also can be helpful in monitoring treatment response in this area. As mentioned earlier, social functioning can be assessed using teacher ratings (SSRS) and direct observations (ADHD-SOC). In some cases, peer ratings or sociometric data can be collected to evaluate treatment-related changes in this domain.

Self-Report Measures

In most cases, children with ADHD do not provide reliable and valid data regarding the extent of their symptoms as well as their academic and social difficulties (Anastopoulos & Shelton, 2001). In fact, some studies suggest that children with this disorder tend to overestimate their performance in areas identified as problematic by their parents and teachers (Hoza et al., 2004). Nevertheless, it is important to include self-report ratings when assessing adolescents with ADHD for several reasons. First, adolescent self-report of ADHD symptoms has been found to correlate highly with parental report (Gittelman et al., 1985), although this is equivocal across studies (see Barkley et al., 2002). Second, regardless of the relationship between self-report and other measures, the former may provide critical information (e.g., presence of depressive symptoms) not available from other sources. Moreover, adolescents are likely to agree more fully with the results of evaluations in which their opinions were given greater attention, and hence, may be more willing to participate with treatment recommendations (Barkley, in press). For these same reasons, self-report and consumer satisfaction data should be obtained from the student during the treatment evaluation stage on an ongoing basis.

COGNITIVE-BEHAVIORAL CONCEPTUALIZATION OF ADHD

The search for an explanation of the core deficits underlying ADHD has been a topic of debate since the conception of the disorder. Proposed underlying mechanisms have emphasized hyperactivity (Chess, 1960), the inability to sustain attention, and poor impulse control (Douglas, 1972), which was later extended to include an overarching impairment in self-regulation (Douglas, 1983), defective motivational processes (Glow & Glow, 1979), deficient stimulus control, diminished sensitivity to reinforcement, and deficient rule-governed behavior (Barkley, 1981, 1989; Haenlein & Caul, 1987). The most recent conceptualization of ADHD has emphasized impairment in delayed responding (i.e., behavioral inhibition) as the central component of the disorder. Barkley's (1997) theory holds that ADHD is a disorder of behavioral inhibition wherein impaired delayed responding to the environment compromises the development of four critical executive functions (i.e., working memory; self-regulation of affect, motivation, and arousal; internalization of speech; and behavioral analysis/synthesis). Impairment in these four executive abilities is associated with deficits in motor control, problems with fluency and syntax, as evidenced by the lack of inhibition of task-irrelevant responses, insensitivity to response feedback, inability to execute goal-directed responses or responses that are novel or involve complexity, and impairment in the ability to re-engage in a task after having been disrupted. In light of the extant literature on ADHD (for a review, see Barkley, 1997) and professional intuition, Barkley's theory makes sense; however, further empirical scrutiny is necessary to unveil its full value and applicability.

Despite the need for more research, the implications of this conceptualization of ADHD are clear. It appears that the core issues and symptoms related to ADHD are not the result of skill deficits, but rather deficits in the performance of appropriate behavioral responses (DuPaul & Stoner, 2003). Specifically, it appears that individuals with ADHD experience an inability to use or sustain the use of an existing, appropriate behavioral repertoire in conjunction with the environmental cues regarding necessary responses in particular settings. Individuals with ADHD appear to experience a relative insensitivity to social consequences of behavior. Instead, behavioral responses are influenced by the environmental antecedents and contingencies of the moment rather than governed by societal norms and the connection between one's present behavioral responses and future consequences of those responses (DuPaul & Stoner, 2003).

Consistent with the current conceptualization of ADHD as an impairment in the cognitive processes that regulate behavioral responding, cognitive-behavioral theory identifies the cognitive and behavioral factors associated with the disorder that impact the individual's ability to regulate and delay his or her behavioral responses. The cognitive factors identified by cognitive behaviorists include difficulties with sustained attention, impulsive cognitive tempo, deficits in impersonal and interpersonal problem solving, deficits in means-end thinking, information-processing errors caused by misattribution of intent or selective attention and recall of environmental information, and deficits in mediation of behavior, affect, and cognition (Anastopoulous & Gerrard, 2003; Braswell & Bloomquist, 1991; Yeschin, 2000). In addition to these cognitive factors, a cognitive-behavioral conceptualization of ADHD also posits behavioral factors that may impair functioning. The behavioral factors include off-task behaviors, noncompliance, deficits in the application and performance of social skills, aggressive behavior, and antisocial behavior (Anastopoulous & Gerrard, 2003; Braswell & Bloomquist, 1991; Yeschin, 2000).

From a cognitive-behavioral perspective, it is the interaction among these cognitive and behavioral factors that contributes to the primary symptoms that have become the hallmark of ADHD (i.e., above-average rates of inattention or heightened rates of hyperactivity and impulsivity). The severity of the difficulties in behavioral regulation associated with ADHD is a direct result of a mismatch between the interindividual characteristics and the structure of environment in which the individual is expected to function. The difficulties experienced by individuals with ADHD are pervasive across multiple domains (e.g., academics, social relationships, behavior at home, school, and community) and, thus, present a need for a comprehensive treatment program that addresses both the cognitive and behavioral difficulties experienced by students with ADHD and promotes generalization of the resulting behavioral change. Cognitive-behavioral interventions have been proposed as a mechanism through which both cognitive and behavioral skill performance deficits associated with ADHD may be addressed within a framework that contains a built-in focus on generalization of behavioral change across multiple domains.

STRATEGIC AND TECHNICAL INTERVENTIONS

Cognitive Based

A cognitive-based approach to intervention focuses on examining the thought processes that precede behavioral responses (Shapiro, DuPaul, & Bradley-Klug, 1998). Children with ADHD usually display impairment in a variety of areas, including peer relationships, aggression, academic functioning, and organization. It is hypothesized that many of these problems are directly related to the hallmark ADHD symptoms of inattention, hyperactivity, and impulsivity. Current literature has begun to suggest these symptoms result from an underlying difficulty of behavioral inhibition (Barkley, 1998; Hinshaw, 2000). Therefore, implementing interventions that seek to alter the development and content of cognitions related to behavioral responses has intuitive appeal. Specific interventions include self-instruction, social problem solving, attribution retraining, and stress inoculation. A description of each of the aforementioned interventions will be provided in the sections that follow; however, there is limited empirical support for the direct application of many of the purely cognitive-based interventions without modifications or combined with other interventions to address the problems experienced by youth with ADHD.

Self-instruction. The main focus of self-instruction is to train an individual to make self statements when confronted with a problem situation in an attempt to encourage and strengthen self-control skills (Meichenbaum & Goodman, 1971). Children with ADHD frequently have immediate reactions to environmental events and act on those responses without thinking through the situation. Self-instruction is an attempt to remediate this deficiency and bolster these self-control skills. This method addresses key problematic areas including impulse control, means-end thinking, problem solving, and sustained attention (Braswell & Bloomquist, 1991). Self-instruction involves a five-step process of talking oneself through four problem-solving stages: problem definition, problem approach, focusing attention, selecting an answer, and evaluation (Nolan & Carr, 2000). Further details of each of these stages will be discussed in the following section.

The ultimate goal of self-instruction is for the individual to internalize problem-solving steps, which will in turn guide behavior. To accomplish this, the following phases are utilized: (a) the instructor verbally models self statements, (b) the child performs this same task with guidance from the instructor, (c) the child then performs the task while instructing him- or herself out loud, (d) the child whispers the instruction to him- or herself while completing the task, and (d) the child privately speaks to self while performing the task (Ervin, Bankert, & DuPaul, 1996). As previously mentioned, although this approach has intuitive appeal, the extant literature is devoid of empirical support for self-instruction in isolation for children with ADHD (Barkley, in press).

Social problem solving. This cognitive intervention is also highly attractive for use with this population due to the match between the function of the strategy and the nature of the disorder. As indicated earlier, social problem solving is closely tied to self-instruction. This skill set pertains to the purposeful planning and organization of thoughts and behaviors to solve problems (Braswell & Bloomquist, 1991). The first step in this process is to recognize that a problem exists. During the problem definition stage, the child learns to comprehend the signal that indicates a problem is present. Perhaps one of the most difficult components to this stage is training the child to realize when it is appropriate to engage in the problem-solving process (i.e., accurately recognizing that a problem exists). Following this stage, the child must generate solutions. It is important that a child does not censure ideas but, rather, is encouraged to think of as many alternatives as possible.

After a list of options has been generated, the child is instructed to engage in consequential thinking. Teaching the child to think ahead and weigh the options is the key component to consequential thinking. Here, the emotional and behavioral implications of the possible solutions on self and others are evaluated. Because an option may be appealing and the immediate consequences of the action are favorable, this still may not be the most viable solution as other factors (e.g., long-term consequences) need to be considered.

The fourth stage in the problem-solving process is to identify obstacles. It is necessary that a child realizes that the plans may not always unfold as anticipated; therefore, obstacle identification and backup plans are required. After completing these four steps, the final stage is execution. Some cognitive-behavior therapists also recommend evaluating the action and its consequences as a sixth stage of problem solving (Braswell & Bloomquist, 1991). Because children with ADHD frequently do not take the time to think through their problems because of poor impulse control (Ervin et al., 1996), it is suggested the problem-solving process could be beneficial, but, unfortunately, as with self-instruction, empirical support for this intervention is lacking (Barkley, in press).

Attribution retraining. Another common problem among children with ADHD is the development of hostility bias. They have a difficult time understanding the thoughts, feelings, and perceptions of other individuals (Braswell & Bloomquist, 1991) and frequently misinterpret the intentions of others (e.g., attribute hostile intent to peer actions that are not aggressive). The goal of attribution retraining is to have children identify these misconceptions and retrain them to think "accurately." In order to accomplish this goal, children are first instructed to try and step outside of themselves to look at a situation objectively, or are presented with a generic case example that they can conceptualize without getting personal. They are then instructed about the importance of realizing how other people feel and can be affected by their actions. Children can enhance these skills through perspective-taking role-play activities, in which the intention is to have the children understand that actions have an impact on others and to think objectively about situations. In attribution retraining, the child learns to more accurately attribute the intentions of the behavior of other individuals (Braswell & Bloomquist, 1991). Again, there is no empirical data to support the efficacy of this intervention for children with ADHD.

Stress inoculation. The stress inoculation approach also incorporates a variety of methods addressed in the aforementioned interventions. There are four main components to the process as identified by Novaco (1978). These stages include recognizing feelings of anger and frustration, interpreting situations accurately when this occurs, coping effectively with this anger, and successfully solving the problem. As is apparent, the stress inoculation process is an incorporation of self-instruction, social problem solving, and attribution retraining, although even when these components are combined, it is not a highly effective strategy for children with ADHD.

Cognitive-Behavioral Based

Although it appears the purely cognitive-based approaches to intervention are not successful with this population, adding a behavioral component to cognitive strategies does hold more promise. Frequently, a contingency component can be added to treatment in order to increase motivation and possibly enhance effect for children with ADHD. The specific cognitive-behavioral methods that will be detailed in this section are self-management, self-evaluation, self-reinforcement, and correspondence training.

Self-management. Once again, the impulsive nature of this population leads to the consideration on self-management techniques. Because children with ADHD lack inhibitory skills, as well as an awareness of their actions, self-management could increase a child's awareness of his or her behavior. Self-management interventions aim to train students to evaluate their actions in light of the teacher's perception (Shapiro et al., 1998). In doing this, the child develops an active awareness of the targeted behavior that may impact self-regulation of the child (Ervin et al., 1996). Self-management teaches children to monitor, record, analyze, and reinforce their own behavior (Davies & Witte, 2000). For example, teachers begin by rating children's target behaviors (e.g., on a scale of 1 [poor] to 5 [excellent]) and then sharing this score with the children (Rhode, Morgan, & Young, 1982). After children are familiar with this process, they are asked to rate their own behavior. This recording step teaches children to be aware of their actions without being dependent on teacher perception. Next, students and teachers match their ratings. If the child's and teacher's scores match, the child is able to obtain a reward, but if they do not, the child cannot earn reinforcement. This allows for teacher feedback and serves as a system of checks and balances so children do not misrepresent their behavior. Because children are responsible for being aware of their behavior and for providing accurate ratings, children are in complete control of attaining reinforcers. This is the basic methodology of this approach, but many variations can be made based on the severity of the behavior and age of the child. Self-management has proven effective in a variety of settings, as well as targeting a myriad of behavioral and academic goals (Hinshaw, 2000).

Self-reinforcement. This intervention strategy is also a variant of self-management, but it is specifically aimed at the reinforcement component. As is evident from its name, self-reinforcement provides the opportunity for children to reward themselves based on their behavior. Self-reinforcement is typically not used on its own but, rather, in conjunction with self-evaluation or as a part of self-management (Shapiro & Cole,

1994). Essentially, rather than another individual providing the reward for a child, the child selects and awards the reinforcer, once the latter has been earned. Hinshaw, Henker, and Whalen (1984) found that this type of reinforcement was more successful and salient than externally administered rewards, both in reducing negative actions and increasing positive prosocial behavior.

Correspondence training. This method focuses on improving the correspondence between what an individual verbalizes about his or her behavior and what a child actually does (Paniagua, 1992). The correspondence reporting can be in either sequence (i.e., "do-report" or "report-do"). The main focus is on increasing the match between verbalizations and actions. In the do-report model, the youngster is taught to accurately report about past behavior and is rewarded for the truthful correspondence between these two components. The report-do method is different only in that a child verbalizes about what his or her actions will be and then carries this action out in the future. Once again, the child is rewarded for accuracy in the correspondence. The empirical support for correspondence training has been limited to case studies in clinic based populations; however, it has been shown to be successful among children with ADHD (Ervin, Bankert, & DuPaul, 1996).

IMPLICATIONS AND APPLICATIONS TO THE SCHOOL SETTING

Children spend a large majority of their day in school; therefore, it is of utmost importance that the efficacy of CBT procedures in classroom settings be considered. Oftentimes, the skills acquired by the aforementioned strategies takes place outside the school; therefore, bringing the skills to school provides a new challenge. School consultation is one method that can be utilized to accomplish this goal. It is important that school personnel receive the training and encouragement to assist the child to use the newly acquired skills in the school environment (Braswell & Bloomquist, 1991). The skills themselves are not setting specific, but children, especially those with ADHD, are not likely to automatically transfer their new knowledge to a different setting without some support. School consultation could provide the opportunity to establish this support.

Not only is it important that children are encouraged to generalize skills across settings, application to different content areas is also important to support, for example, using self-instruction and problem-solving approaches in unique situations. A child may be confident and familiar in applying these skills when confronted with a problem situation with a friend, but this confidence may dissipate when attempted with others (e.g., strangers). A variety of situations should be posed and practice should be provided for each. It is also important that these ideas are reinforced for the child on a regular basis, so that the individual does not "forget" these skills are in his or her repertoire.

School personnel that should take part in adapting procedures to the school setting include teachers, counselors, school psychologists, and social workers (Braswell & Bloomquist, 1991). It is also important to realize that whereas many of these procedures have been examined outside the school setting and brought to schools after the skills have been acquired, in many situations, it is also appropriate for these procedures to be taught in schools. Some strategies are easier to implement than others (e.g., self-management is easier for a teacher to train a child in than correspondence training) and may be more amenable for school settings

Some interventions (e.g., social problem solving) are most appropriately delivered by a school counselor or psychologist in a group setting. Using this method, a relative expert in the field would implement the intervention and the group provides the opportunity for practice. However, these interventions also can be administered on a classwide basis. This would take more training on the part of the teacher but could be appropriate especially for skills such as self-evaluation and self-reinforcement. These interventions are easily applicable and can be implemented with fairly little effort in most school settings. Unfortunately, extant data on this approach do not support its efficacy on a wide scale (Bloomquist, August, & Ostrander, 1991). In fact, the only CBT techniques to have any empirical support are those that involve self-monitoring and self-evaluation, and, even then, these data have been obtained with relatively small samples (Barkley, in press).

CASE 1: KEVIN—STORY MAPPING WITH PROMPT CARD TO IMPROVE READING COMPREHENSION

Background

Kevin was a 9-year-old male diagnosed with ADHD–Combined Subtype who was enrolled in a general education 4th-grade classroom. Teacher referral information indicated that Kevin was performing below grade level in reading comprehension and demonstrated little motivation to perform during reading instruction. Information gathered during a teacher interview indicated that Kevin's performance on assessments of reading comprehension was variable. Specifically, at times, he demonstrated difficulty independently identifying the main idea of a story, sequencing the parts of a story, and drawing inferences from stories; however, at other times he accurately completed assigned comprehension exercises.

Initial Assessment

Curriculum-based assessment in the area of reading indicated that Kevin was reading at a 4th-grade level with 96% accuracy at a rate of 85 words correct per minute, which was indicative of instructional-level reading performance. When presented with comprehension questions immediately following the completion of a 4th-grade passage, Kevin completed the task with 60% accuracy. In addition, standardized achievement testing utilizing the *Woodcock-Johnson Tests of Achievement—Third Edition* (Woodcock, McGrew, & Mather, 2001) indicated that Kevin received a standard score of 90 on the Reading Comprehension Composite, placing him at the 48th percentile in comparison to other males his age who participated in the normative sample.

Behavioral observations conducted during reading instruction indicated that Kevin displayed significantly low rates of on-task behavior (8%) and high rates of off-task behavior (75%), which was mostly passive in nature, such as staring at the papers on his desk or looking away from his assigned task.

Intervention

In light of Kevin's age and grade, as well as limited teacher resources for teacher-mediated intervention implementation, a self-mediated intervention was chosen to address the difficulties that Kevin was experiencing with reading comprehension. Specifically, a story map procedure (Gardill & Jitendra, 1999) was utilized in conjunction with a prompt card that was to be completed independently by Kevin when reading a story.

The story mapping intervention was implemented two times per week during regularly scheduled reading instruction. The story maps provided Kevin with a visual organization and prompt to identify the setting, problem, goal, action, and outcome of each story read in class. A prompt card was created and laminated that prompted Kevin to stop after each paragraph and ask the following questions: Who are the main characters? Where did the story take place? What events occurred? What was the problem? and What was the solution? As he discovered the answers to each of the questions on the prompt card, Kevin was prompted to complete the corresponding portion of the story map. Following completion of the story and map, Kevin completed a computer-generated test of reading comprehension.

Results

Progress monitoring data were collected weekly via the computer-generated reading comprehension exercise, which corresponded to each assigned story. Data indicated that Kevin's average comprehension score for 4th-grade materials was 96%. His weekly scores ranged from 70% to 100% with a majority of his scores falling at 100%. The slope of his weekly comprehension scores indicated a continually increasing trend with Kevin achieving and maintaining 100% accuracy after the fifth week of the intervention.

Teacher ratings of progress toward the established goal indicated that Kevin progressed from "never" (0) demonstrating reading comprehension at or above 80% to "often" (2) performing comprehension tasks with 80% accuracy or better over the course of three months. Standardized achievement testing indicated that Kevin received a standard score of 110 on the Reading Comprehension Composite, placing him at the 60th percentile in comparison to other students his age.

In addition to the academic gains evidenced by the results mentioned here, behavioral observations conducted during reading instruction indicated that the intervention influenced behavioral gains as a secondary outcome. Specifically, Kevin demonstrated increased rates of on-task behavior (68%) and decreased rates of off-task behavior (30%) in comparison to the behavioral information gathered before implementation of the self-mediated intervention.

CASE 2: KYRA—SELF-MANAGEMENT INTERVENTION TO INCREASE WORK COMPLETION

Background

Kyra was a 6-year-old female diagnosed with ADHD–Inattentive Subtype who was placed in a general education 1st-grade classroom. Information gathered during an interview with Kyra's primary teacher indicated that Kyra was experiencing difficulty completing her classroom assignments during math instruction. The general education classroom in which Kyra was placed contained students at multiple instructional levels in math skills, so her teacher utilized small-group formats with centers as an instructional strategy. While the teacher led a small group in math instruction, the other students were asked to complete a group of worksheets that contained practice items from the previous lessons. Kyra would often spend center time staring away from her assigned task and would rarely complete even one worksheet.

Initial Assessment

Curriculum-based assessment procedures were utilized to determine the grade level at which math instruction should occur for Kyra to ensure that the work she was being asked to complete was appropriate for her skill level. This assessment indicated that Kyra was performing at a 1st-grade level at a rate of 12 digits correct per minute with 90% accuracy. Kyra's performance indicated that she possessed the skills necessary to complete basic addition and subtraction facts as well as some basic word problems with minimal assistance from an adult. An informal review of the worksheets that had previously been given to Kyra revealed that the worksheets did indeed contain problems for which she demonstrated the necessary skills.

Direct observations of Kyra's classroom behavior during math instruction indicated low rates of academic engagement (35%) and high rates of off-task behavior that was passive in nature (65%). In addition, functional behavioral assessment procedures (O'Neill, Horner, Albin, Storey, & Sprague, 1997) were utilized to determine the antecedents and consequences that might be maintaining Kyra's consistent failure to complete assigned tasks during math. No consistent patterns were revealed; however, no apparent reward system was in place for successful completion of assigned materials.

Intervention

A self-management procedure was developed and implemented by Kyra's classroom teacher to foster increased independent functioning during center time. Students were typically assigned five worksheets during center time (one per center) to be completed during the course of a 50-minute period. A pie was constructed and divided into five slices. The pie crust and individual slices were laminated. A piece of Velcro was placed on each of the five divided spaces on the crust as well as on the underside of each slice.

Kyra was trained over three school days to use the pie chart. It was explained that each pie slice represented one worksheet for each math period. When Kyra completed an entire worksheet, she was instructed to attach one slice to the pie crust. At the end of each math class, Kyra was to take her pie to the classroom teacher and decide whether she had met her goal set at the beginning of the class period. If she had met her goal, she could choose a prize from the treasure chest that the teacher used as part of her classroom management program.

Kyra would assist the teacher in establishing her goal each day. During the first week, her goal was set at one worksheet. The goal would gradually increase by one worksheet each week until her goal was set at five. The pie was then to be faded and the rewards were to be provided less frequently until the reinforcement schedule was such that Kyra needed to complete all five worksheets on all five school days in order to choose a prize from the treasure chest.

Results

Progress monitoring data indicated that the self-management intervention was highly effective in increasing work completion for this 1st-grade female with ADHD. Specifically, Kyra successfully met her goal of one worksheet per class period on the first three days of implementation. On the fourth day, her goal was increased to two worksheets and again, she successfully completed two worksheets per day across four days. Kyra's work completion behavior continued to increase as the goal increased and fading of the intervention and reward began after four weeks. A slight decline in work completion was noted on the first day that a reward was not received for successful attainment of her goal; however, her performance returned to its previous rate as time progressed. By the seventh week of implementation, Kyra was consistently completing five worksheets per math class with 95–100% accuracy.

SUMMARY

ADHD is a disorder of self-control that involves developmentally inappropriate levels of inattention, impulsivity, and overactivity. Children and adolescents with this disorder frequently have serious academic and social difficulties that require long-term treatment. The only major intervention modalities that have strong empirical support are psychotropic medication (chiefly, central nervous stimulants such as methylphenidate) and contingency management (i.e., behavior modification; Barkley, in press; MTA Cooperative Group, 1999). CBT strategies appear to have promise in addressing the core deficits underlying this disorder; however, empirical support for CBT is lacking, particularly for cognitive-based techniques such as social problem solving. Several controlled case studies and small sample investigations provide more positive support for use of self-management, especially self-monitoring and self-evaluation (e.g., Hinshaw et al., 1984; Hoff & DuPaul, 1998). Clearly, CBT strategies that employ self-management components require further investigation, especially in the context of a multimodal treatment package.

REFERENCES

Abikoff, H. (1985). Efficacy of cognitive training interventions in hyperactive children: A critical review. *Clinical Psychology Review, 5,* 479–512.

Abikoff, H., Gittelman-Klein, R., & Klein, D. (1977). Validation of a classroom observation code for hyperactive children. *Journal of Consulting and Clinical Psychology, 45,* 772–783.

Abikoff, H. B., Jensen, P. S., Arnold, L. E., Hoza, B., Hechtman, L., Pollack, S., Martin, D., Alvir, J., March, J. S., Hinshaw, S., Vitiello, B., Newcorn, J., Greiner, A., Cantwell, D. P., Conners, C. K., Elliott, G., Greenhill, L. L., Kraemer, H., Pelham, W. E., Severe, J. B., Swanson, J. M., Wells, K., & Wigal, T. (2002). Observed classroom behavior of children with ADHD: Relationship to gender and comorbidity. *Journal of Abnormal Child Psychopathology, 30,* 349–360.

Achenbach, T. M. (2001a). *Achenbach System of Empirically Based Assessment: Child Behavior Checklist.* Burlington: University of Vermont, Department of Psychiatry.

Achenbach, T. M. (2001b). *Achenbach System of Empirically Based Assessment: Teacher Report Form.* Burlington: University of Vermont, Department of Psychiatry.

American Psychiatric Association (2000). *Diagnostic and statistical manual of mental disorders (4th ed., text revision).* Washington, DC: Author.

Anastopoulous, A. D., & Gerrard, L. M. (2003). Facilitating understanding and management of attention-deficit/hyperactivity disorder. In M. A. Reinecke, F. M. Dattilio, & A. Freeman (Eds.), *Cognitive therapy with children and adolescents: A casebook for clinical practice* (2nd ed.). New York: Guilford Press.

Anastopoulos, A. D., & Shelton, T. L. (2001). *Assessing attention-deficit/hyperactivity disorder.* New York: Kluwer Academic/Plenum.

Barkley, R. A. (1981). *Hyperactive children: A handbook for diagnosis and treatment.* New York: Guilford Press.

Barkley, R. A. (1989). Attention-deficit hyperactivity disorder. In E. J. Mash & R. A. Barkley (Eds.), *Treatment of childhood disorders* (pp. 39–72). New York: Guilford Press.

Barkley, R. A. (1990). *Attention Deficit-Hyperactivity Disorder: A handbook for diagnosis and treatment.* New York: Guilford Press.

Barkley, R. A. (1997). *ADHD and the nature of self-control.* New York: Guilford Press.

Barkley, R. A. (1998). Attention-deficit/hyperactivity disorder. In E. J. Mash & R. A. Barkley (Eds.), *Treatment of childhood disorders* (2nd ed., pp. 55–110). New York: Guilford Press.

Barkley, R. A. (Ed.). (in press). *Attention deficit hyperactivity disorder: A handbook for diagnosis and treatment* (3rd ed.). New York: Guilford Press.

Barkley, R. A., Fischer, M., Newby, R., & Breen, M. (1988). Development of a multi-method clinical protocol for assessing stimulant drug responses in ADHD children. *Journal of Clinical Child Psychology, 17,* 14–24.

Barkley, R. A., Fischer, M., Smallish, L., & Fletcher, K. (2002). The persistence of attention-deficit/hyperactivity disorder into young adulthood as a function of reporting source and definition of disorder. *Journal of Abnormal Psychology, 111,* 279–289.

Biederman, J., Mick, E., Faraone, S. V., Braaten, E., Doyle, A., Spencer, T., Wilens, T. E., Frazier, E., & Johnson, M. A. (2002). Influence of gender on attention deficit hyperactivity disorder in children referred to a psychiatric clinic. *American Journal of Psychiatry, 159,* 36–42.

Bloomquist, M. L., August, G. J., & Ostrander, R. (1991). Effects of a school-based cognitive-behavioral intervention for ADHD children. *Journal of Abnormal Child Psychology, 19,* 591–605.

Bowers, W. A., Evans, K. K., & Andersen, A. E. (1997). Inpatient treatment of eating disorders: A cognitive milieu. *Cognitive and Behavioral Practice, 4,* 291–323.

Braswell, L., & Bloomquist, M. L. (1991). *Cognitive-behavioral therapy with ADHD children: Child, family, and school interventions.* New York: Guilford Press.

Cantwell, D. P., & Baker, L. (1991). Association between attention deficit-hyperactivity disorder and learning disorders. *Journal of Learning Disabilities, 24,* 88–95.

Carr, A. (Ed.). (2000). *What works with children and adolescents? A critical review of psychological interventions with children, adolescents, and their families.* London: Routledge.

Carrington, P., Lehrer, P. M., & Wittenstrom, K. (1997). A children's self-monitoring system for reducing homework-related problems: Parent efficacy ratings. *Child and Family Behavior Therapy, 19,* 1–22.

Chess, S. (1960). Diagnosis and treatment of the hyperactive child. *New York State Journal of Medicine, 60,* 2379–2385.

Conners, C. K. (1997). *Conners' Rating Scales-Revised; technical manual.* Toronto: Multi-Health Systems.

Curry, J. F., & Reinecke, M. A. (2003). Modular therapy for adolescents with major depression. In M. A. Reinecke, F. M. Dattilio, & A. Freeman (Eds.), *Cognitive therapy with children and adolescents: A casebook for clinical practice* (2nd ed.). New York: Guilford Press.

Davies, S., & Witte, R. (2000). Self-management and peer-monitoring within a group contingency to decrease uncontrolled verbalizations of children with attention-deficit/hyperactivity disorder. *Psychology in the Schools, 37,* 135–147.

De La Paz, S. (1999). Self-regulated strategy instruction in regular education settings: Improving outcomes for students with and without learning disabilities. *Learning Disabilities Research and Practice, 14,* 92–106.

DiPerna, J. C., & Elliott, S. N. (2000). *Academic Competence Evaluation Scale.* San Antonio, TX: Psychological Corporation.

Douglas, V. I. (1972). Stop, look, and listen: The problem of sustained attention and poor impulse control in hyperactive and normal children. *Canadian Journal of Behavioural Science, 4,* 259–282.

Douglas, V. I. (1983). Attentional and cognitive problems. In M. Rutter (Ed.), *Developmental neuropsychiatry* (pp. 280–328). New York: Guilford Press.

DuPaul, G. J., & Barkley, R. A. (1992). Situational variability of attention problems: Psychometric properties of the revised home and school situations questionnaires. *Journal of Clinical Child Psychology, 21,*178–188.

DuPaul, G. J., & Stoner, G. (2003). *ADHD in the schools: Assessment and intervention strategies* (2nd ed.). New York: Guilford Press.

DuPaul, G. J., Power, T. J., Anastopoulos, A. D., & Reid, R. (1998). *AD/HD Rating Scale-IV: Checklist, norms, and clinical interpretation.* New York: Guilford.

DuPaul, G. J., Rapport, M. D., & Perriello, L. M. (1991). Teacher ratings of academic skills: The development of the Academic Performance Rating Scale. *School Psychology Review, 20,* 284–300.

DuPaul, G. J., Volpe, R. J., Jitendra, A. K., Lutz, J. G., Lorah, K. S., & Gruber, R. (2004). Elementary school students with AD/HD: Predictors of academic achievement. *Journal of School Psychology, 42,* 285–301.

Ervin, R. A., Bankert, C. L., & DuPaul, G. J. (1996). Treatment of attention-deficit/hyperactivity disorder. In M. A. Reinecke, F. M. Dattilio, & A. Freeman (Eds.), *Cognitive therapy with children and adolescents* (pp. 38–61). New York: Guilford Press.

Fabiano, G. A., Pelham, W. E., Gnagy, E. M., Kipp, H., Lahey, B. B., Burrows-MacLean, L., Chronis, A. M., Onyango, A. N., & Morrisey, S. (1999, November). *The reliability and validity of the children's impairment rating scale: A practical measure of impairment in children with ADHD.* Poster presented at the annual meeting of the Association for the Advancement of Behavior Therapy, Toronto, Ontario.

Friedberg, R., & McClure, J. (2002). *Clinical practice and cognitive therapy with children and adolescents: The nuts and bolts.* New York: Guilford Press.

Gadow, K. D., Sprafkin, J., & Nolan, E. E. (1996). *ADHD School Observation Code.* Stony Brook, NY: Checkmate Plus.

Gardill, M. C., & Jitendra, A. K. (1999). Advanced story map instruction: Effects on the reading comprehension of students with learning disabilities. *The Journal of Special Education, 28,* 2–17.

Gittelman, R., Mannuzza, S., Shenker, R., & Bonagura, N. (1985). Hyperactive boys almost grown up. *Archives of General Psychiatry, 42,* 937–947.

Glow, P. H., & Glow, R. A. (1979). Hyperkinetic impulse disorder: A development defect of motivation. *Genetic Psychology Monographs, 100,* 159–231.

Goldstein, S., & Goldstein, M. (1998). *Managing attention deficit hyperactivity disorder in children: A guide for practitioners* (2nd ed.). New York: Wiley.

Graham, P. (Ed). 1998. *Cognitive-behavior therapy for children and families.* Cambridge: Cambridge University Press.

Gresham, F. M., & Elliott, S. N. (1990). *Social skills rating system.* Circle Pines, MN: American Guidance Service.

Haenlein, M., & Caul, W. F. (1987). Attention deficit disorder with hyperactivity: A specific hypothesis of reward dysfunction. *Journal of the American Academy of Child and Adolescent Psychiatry, 26,* 356–362.

Hibbs, E., & Jensen, P. (Eds). 1996. *Psychosocial treatments for child and adolescent disorders: Empirically based strategies for clinical practice.* Washington, DC: American Psychological Association.

Hinshaw, S. P. (2000). Attention-deficit/hyperactivity disorder: The search for viable treatments. In P. C. Kendall (Ed.), *Child and adolescent therapy: Cognitive-behavioral procedures* (2nd ed., pp. 88–128). New York: Guilford Press.

Hinshaw, S. P., Henker, B., & Whalen, C. K. (1984). Self-control in hyperactive boys in anger-inducing situations: Effects of cognitive-behavioral training and of methylphenidate. *Journal of Abnormal Child Psychology, 12,* 55–77.

Hoff, K. E., & DuPaul, G. J. (1998). Reducing disruptive behavior in general education classrooms: The use of self-management strategies. *School Psychology Review, 27,* 290–303.

Hoza, B., Gerdes, A. C., Hinshaw, S. P., Arnold, E. L., Pelham, W. E. Jr., Molina, B. S. G., Abikoff, H. B., Epstein, J. N., Greenhill, L. L., Hechtman, L., Odbert, C., Swanson, J. M., & Wigal, T. (2004). Self-perceptions of competence in children with ADHD and comparison children. *Journal of Consulting and Clinical Psychology, 72,* 382–391.

Jacob, R. G., O'Leary, K. D., & Rosenblad, C. (1978). Formal and informal classroom settings: Effects on hyperactivity. *Journal of Abnormal Child Psychology, 6,* 47–59.

Kendall, P. C. (Ed.). 2000. *Child and adolescent therapy: Cognitive-behavioral procedures* (2nd ed.). New York: Guilford Press.

Kendall, P. C., & Braswell, L. (1993). *Cognitive-behavioral therapy for impulsive children* (2nd ed.). New York: Guilford Press.

Mannuzza, S., Gittelman-Klein, R., Bessler, A., Malloy, P., & LaPadula, M. (1993). Adult outcome of hyperactive boys: Educational achievement, occupational rank, and psychiatric status. *Archives of General Psychiatry, 50,* 565–576.

McDougall, D. (1998). Research on self-management techniques used by students with disabilities in general education classrooms. *Exceptional Children, 64,* 151–166.

McDougall, D., & Brady, M. P. (1998). Initiating and fading self-management interventions to increase math fluency in general education classrooms. *Remedial and Special Education, 19,* 310–320.

Meichenbaum, D. H., & Goodman, J. (1971). Training impulsive children to talk to themselves: A means of developing self-control. *Journal of Abnormal Psychology, 77,* 115–126.

Miller, G. E., & Brewster, M. E. (1992). Developing self-sufficient learners in reading and mathematics through self-instructional training. In M. Pressley, K. R. Harris, & J. T. Guthrie (Eds.), *Promoting academic competence and literacy in school* (pp. 169–222). New York: Academic Press.

Miranda, A., Villaescusa, M. I., & Vidal-Abarca, E. (1997). Is attribution retraining necessary? Use of self-regulation procedures for enhancing the reading comprehension strategies of children with learning disabilities. *Journal of Learning Disabilities, 30,* 503–512.

MTA Cooperative Group. (1999). A 14-month randomized clinical trial of treatment strategies for attention-deficit/hyperactivity disorder. *Archives of General Psychiatry, 56,* 1073–1086.

Nolan, M., & Carr, A. (2000). Attention deficit hyperactivity disorder. In A. Carr (Ed.), *What works with children and adolescents: A critical review of psychological interventions with children, adolescents and their families* (pp. 65–101). London: Routledge.

Novaco, R. W. (1979). The cognitive regulation of anger and stress. In P. C. Kendall & S. D. Hoillon (Ed.), *Cognitive-behavioral interventions: Theory, research, and procedures* (pp. 241–285). New York: Academic Press.

O'Neill, R. E., Horner, R. H., Albin, R. W., Storey, K., & Sprague, J. R. (1997). *Functional analysis of problem behavior: A practical assessment guide* (2nd ed.). Pacific Grove, CA: Brookes/Cole.

Paniagua, F. A. (1992). Verbal-nonverbal correspondence training with ADHD children. *Behavior Modification, 16,* 226–252.

Patterson, G. R., Reid, J. B., & Dishion, T. J. (1992). *Antisocial boys.* Eugene, OR: Castalia.

Pediatric OCD Treatment Study Team. (2004). Cognitive-behavior therapy, sertraline, and their combination for children and adolescents with obsessive-compulsive disorder. *Journal of the American Medical Association, 292,* 1969–1976.

Pfiffner, L. J., & Barkley, R. A. (1990). Educational placements and classroom management. In R. A. Barkley (Ed.), *Attention-deficit hyperactivity disorder: A handbook for diagnosis and treatment* (pp. 498–539). New York: Guilford Press.

Phillips, T. (2000). Cognitive-behavioral therapy for post-traumatic stress disorder in children and adolescents. In K. N. Dwivedi (Ed.), *Post-traumatic stress disorder in children and adolescents* (pp. 147–162). London: Englands, Ltd.

Platzman, K. A., Stoy, M. R., Brown, R. T., Coles, C. D., Smith, I. E., & Falek, A. (1992). Review of observational methods in attention deficit hyperactivity disorder (ADHD): Implications for diagnosis. *School Psychology Quarterly, 7,* 155–177.

Reinecke, M. A., Ryan, N., & DuBois, D. (1998). Cognitive-behavioral therapy of depression and depressive symptoms during adolescence: A review and meta-analysis. *Journal of the American Academy of Child and Adolescent Psychiatry, 37,* 26–34.

Reynolds, C. R., & Kamphaus, R. W. (2004). *Behavior Assessment System for Children* (2nd ed.). Circle Pines, MN: American Guidance Service.

Rhode, G., Morgan, D. P., & Young, K. R. (1982). Generalization and maintenance of treatment gains of behaviorally handicapped students from resource rooms to regular classrooms using self-evaluation procedures. *Journal of Applied Behavior Analysis, 16,* 171–188.

Shapiro, E. S. (2003). *Academic skills problems: Direct assessment and intervention* (3rd ed.). New York: Guilford Press.

Shapiro, E. S., & Cole, C. L. (1994). *Behavior change in the classroom: Self-management interventions.* New York: Guilford Press.

Shapiro, E. S., DuPaul, G. J., & Bradley-Klug, K. L. (1998). Self-management as a strategy to improve the classroom behavior adolescents with ADHD. *Journal of Learning Disabilities, 31,* 545–555.

Spence, S. H., Donovan, C., & Brechman-Toussaint, M. (2000). The treatment of childhood social phobia: The effectiveness of a social skills training-based, cognitive-behavioral intervention, with and without parental involvement. *Journal of Child Psychology and Psychiatry, 41,* 713–726.

Stormont, M. (2001). Social outcomes of children with AD/HD: Contributing factors and implications for practice. *Psychology in the Schools, 38,* 521–531.

Vile Junod, R. E., DuPaul, G. J., Jitendra, A. K., Volpe, R. J., & Cleary, K. (2005). *Classroom observations of students with and without ADHD: Differences across academic subjects and types of engagement.* Manuscript submitted for publication.

Walker, H. M., & McConnell, S. R. (1988). *Walker-McConnell Scale of Social Competence and School Adjustment.* Austin, TX: Pro-Ed, Inc.

Watson, T. S., & Steege, M. W. (2003). *Conducting school-based functional behavioral assessments: A practitioner's guide.* New York: Guilford Press.

Weiss, G., & Hechtman, L. (1993). *Hyperactive children grown up* (2nd ed.). New York: Guilford Press.

Weisz, J., & Weiss, B. (1993). *Effects of psychotherapy with children and adolescents.* Newbury Park, CA: Sage.

Whalen, C. K., Henker, B., & Dotemoto, S. (1981). Teacher response to methylphenidate (Ritalin) versus placebo status of hyperactive boys in the classroom. *Child Development, 52,* 1005–1014.

Woodcock, R. W., McGrew, K. S., & Mather, N. (2001). *Woodcock-Johnson III Tests of Achievement.* Itaska, IL: Riverside Publishing.

Yeschin, N. J. (2000). A new understanding of attention deficit disorder: Alternate concepts and interventions. *Child and Adolescent Social Work Journal, 17,* 227–245.

9

A Cognitive-Behavioral Approach with Underachieving Gifted Youth

Underachievement is a complex phenomenon with multiple causes and definitions. Because the term implies failure to meet expectations, questions arise regarding the source of the expectations and whether they are appropriate (Delisle, 1992; Reis & McCoach, 2000). Uncertainty regarding what constitutes potential and how it should be measured is also a factor (Davis & Rimm, 2004). This is especially true for children and adolescents for whom real-world accomplishments are rarely an element in identification of giftedness. For this chapter, the underachiever is defined as a student whose actual academic performance in school is problematic in spite of an identification of intellectual or academic giftedness. Although procedures for the identification vary widely, this is the definition most common in literature about gifted underachievers (Bulter-Por, 1987; Reis & McCoach, 2000).

Although the exact number of gifted underachievers is uncertain, the 1983 Nation at Risk report suggested that over half of gifted children do not demonstrate achievement in keeping with their ability (National Commission on Excellence in Education). Other authors have put the estimate at 50%, especially for gifted males (McCall, Evahn, & Kratzer, 1992). *National Excellence: A Case for Developing America's Talent* (Ross, 1993) highlighted significant problems with our national practices in helping gifted students achieve to their potential. Underachievement is a common topic in books on gifted education (Colangelo & Davis, 2003; Davis & Rimm, 2004; Delisle, 1992; Genshaft, Bireley, & Hollinger, 1995), and the issue was identified as an important target area by a National Research Center on the Gifted and Talented needs assessment (Renzulli, Reid, & Gubbins, 1992). In a 1997 study of the types of counseling issues most important for gifted youth, underachievement earned a mean rating 4.38 with 1 being definitely omit and 5 definitely include. Responders included parents, gifted education coordinators, community counselors, and professors in counseling-related fields (Moon, Kelly, & Feldhusen, 1997).

Underachievement carries personal and societal costs. Gifted students who have poor grades are more likely to be absent and tardy (Peterson & Colangelo, 1996), to drop out of school (Renzulli & Park, 2000), and to set limited goals (McCoach & Siegle, 2003a). Once a pattern of underachievement is established, it is likely to continue and to worsen as students proceed from middle to high school (Dowdall & Colangelo, 1982; Lupart & Pyryt, 1996; McCall, Evahn, & Kratzer, 1992). In a longitudinal study of post–high school development for 14 gifted underachievers, Peterson (2002) found 9 lacked a clear career focus after 4 years. Underachievement is also associated with fear of failure, perfectionism, and various emotional difficulties, although whether these factors are causative or resultant is difficult to determine (Mandel & Marcus, 1988; Rimm, 1995).

FACTORS RELATED TO UNDERACHIEVEMENT IN GIFTED STUDENTS

Why would a student who is intellectually or academically gifted not perform well in school? Researchers are virtually unanimous in their conclusion that there are many possible reasons and that gifted underachievers are a very heterogeneous group (Dowdall & Colangelo, 1982; McCall, Evahn, & Kratzer, 1992; McCoach & Siegle, 2003a). One factor in what is erroneously labeled underachievement could be inappropriate expectations. It should not be assumed that because a student earns a high score on a test of intellectual ability the student is capable of advanced work in all academic areas. This is rarely the case. Inappropriate or incomplete assessment may be another cause of unrealistic expectations when learning disabilities or emotional problems that hinder achievement are overlooked (Mendaglio, 1993). Females and those from multicultural groups or certain geographical locations may underachieve due to peer or societal pressure (Schultz, 2002). Other factors to emerge from the literature are demographics, school environment, family factors, and characteristics of the student.

Demographics

Underachievement in capable students crosses ethnic and socioeconomic lines (Colangelo, Kerr, Christensen, & Maxey, 1993). Although, in general, it is more prevalent in lower socioeconomic status (SES) groups and those whose parents have less education, upper SES groups and those with more highly educated parents are well represented among gifted underachievers. Underachievement is more prevalent among males (McCall, Evahn, & Kratzer, 1992), and there is evidence that males significantly outnumber females among gifted underachievers (Colangelo, Kerr, Christensen, & Maxey, 1993; McCoach & Siegle, 2003a; Peterson & Colangelo, 1996).

School Environment

Inadequate educational programming is commonly mentioned in the gifted education literature as a cause of underachievement (Davis & Rimm, 2004; Colangelo & Davis,

2003). Programs that fail to challenge students create negative feelings about school and permit the development of poor study habits. Students who go through elementary school without having to study develop the false impression that they can learn without effort. This perception is further enhanced by the failure of schools to group capable students together at least some of the time. Thus, the gifted student begins to see him- or herself as brighter than everyone else and as someone who does not have to try hard in order to do well. Peer pressure and an anti-intellectual climate at school are more likely to be factors when gifted students do not spend time together (Moon & Hall, 1998; Moon, Swift, & Shallenberger, 2002) and this may be especially true in multicultural populations (Reis & McCoach, 2000). Programs that ignore the child's interests lose opportunities to engage the student in school and to create an impression of relevance in the student's mind (Butler-Por, 1987).

Family Factors

Family characteristics have been associated with inadequate academic performance among gifted students, especially disorganization, conflict, and modeling of underachievement. Negative attributions in the family regarding learning, school, or work can be contributing factors (Bulter-Por, 1987). Regarding family conflict, that between father and son has been most often mentioned, although daughters can be affected (Moon & Hall, 1998). Underachievement also may be the child's way of expressing feelings of aggression or retaliation against the parent (Baker, Bridger, & Evans, 1998; Reis & McCoach, 2000). In a longitudinal study, Peterson found that family stress was present for all of the gifted underachievers, and that resolution of conflict with parents was associated with later personal and academic progress (2002). Parents also may take too much responsibility, preventing the child from experiencing the reward or consequences of academic success or failure (Zuccone & Amerikaner, 1986).

Characteristics of the Gifted Underachiever

Characteristics within the student have been given the most attention in research studies. Factors that have emerged most frequently are a lack of motivation, negative feelings about school, poor study skills, inaccurate beliefs about self and the educational environment, fear of success or failure, poor concentration, and inadequate work completion (Bulter-Por, 1987; McCoach & Siegle, 2003a; Rimm, 1995). Studies also show inadequate ability to self-regulate or engage in disciplined behavior related to academics (McCoach & Siegle, 2003a). Zimmerman (1994) noted that achieving students successfully use self-regulation strategies such as goal setting, planning, organizing, record keeping, and self-consequences. They pace their studying and are fairly good judges of their own performance.

In their work to develop an instrument to assist with identification of gifted underachievers, McCoach and Siegle (2003b) found level of motivation/self-regulation to be the most significant predictor of membership in the underachievement group. In a study of gifted underachievers 8 to 12 years old, Renzulli, Baum, and Hebert (1995) cited what they termed "emotional issues," including need for attention, perfectionism, and depression, to be the primary contributing factors. Poor self-regulation, learning disabilities, and an inappropriate curriculum were second, with self-regulation being a common problem across the group.

INTERVENTIONS AND THEIR OUTCOMES

Although hypotheses about the causes of underachievement abound, studies of specific intervention techniques (especially with gifted learners) are few. Those that could be considered well researched are fewer still. Evaluation of interventions is often based on impressions and anecdotal reports and studies include few subjects. Most researchers conclude that underachievement among gifted students is a challenging problem with few easy answers. However, some clear trends have emerged. With regard to school programming, challenging curriculum using real-world applications, self-directed learning, utilization of the student's strengths and interests, and involvement of a caring, but not controlling, adult have been consistently recommended (Emerick, 1992; Renzulli, Baum, & Hebert, 1995). Contact with a gifted peer group is considered to be of primary importance by researchers and experts in the field (Davis & Rimm, 2004; Moon, Swift, & Shallenberger, 2002; Renzulli, Baum, & Hebert, 1995).

Some note that counseling has not been particularly successful in alleviating underachievement among gifted students (Butler-Por, 1987; Reis & McCoach, 2000). Yet, others suggest it has promise if objectives are clear and the methodology carefully considered (Dowdall & Colangelo, 1987). Interventions involving families, in addition to an appropriate academic program, appear to have more promise (Zuccone & Amerikaner, 1986) and interventions that include school, family, and the individual child are likely to be most effective (Baker, Bridger, & Evans, 1998). In the search for a methodology with clear objectives, a reasonable connection can be made between common characteristics of the gifted underachiever (e.g., weaknesses in organization, problem solving, goal setting) and the most successful cognitive-behavioral interventions related to academic performance such as self-monitoring (sometimes called self-regulation), modeling, self-talk/relaxation, goal setting, and self-reward (Butler-Por, 1987; Durlak, Fuhrman, & Lampman, 1991; Renzulli, Baum, & Hebert, 1995; Zimmerman, 1994). Although studies that utilize these types of interventions with gifted underachievers do exist, few of the researchers claim a theoretical base in cognitive behaviorism.

COGNITIVE-BEHAVIORAL THERAPY, UNDERACHIEVEMENT, AND GIFTEDNESS

Relevance of Cognitive-Behavioral Therapy

Cognitive-behavioral therapy (CBT) is based on the premise that what we think affects how we feel and what we do; and, that how and what we think is subject to change through intervention techniques such as modeling, reasoning, practice, and reinforcement. Reinecke, Dattilio, and Freeman (2003) define cognition in this context as "an organized set of beliefs, attitudes, memories and expectations" (p. 3).

The topic of gifted underachievement is quite appropriate for a book about cognitive-behavioral interventions in schools because a connection between performance, motivation, and the thoughts and feelings of gifted students is well established in the gifted literature, in general (Robinson, 2002), and in the literature on underachieving gifted especially (McCoach & Seigle, 2003a). Logic would suggest that gifted students would be good candidates for interventions related to thoughts, reason, and education and there is evidence that cognitive-behavioral treatments are more effective with children at more advanced levels of cognitive functioning (Durlak, Furhrman, & Lampman, 1991). In a review of the literature related to the resilience of gifted children, Bland and Sowa (1994) noted, "cognitive appraisal may be a key mechanism used by gifted children as they develop resilience" (p. 78). The authors refer to the gifted child's ability to use mental capacity to evaluate, cope, and adjust to stressful life experiences. With regard to underachieving gifted students specifically, they add, "These children can be taught how to effectively evaluate a situation and use an appropriate coping skill ... teachers can model ... task commitment, setting goals, and adaptability" (p. 79). They recommend that the decisions underachieving gifted students make about control, academic commitment, and challenge be carefully evaluated. For achieving gifted students, habits of resilience may come naturally. For those underachieving, they may have to be taught.

The use of imagery, role-play, problem solving, and self-monitoring, all important aspects of CBT, are in keeping with the techniques often suggested for use with gifted learners (Butler-Por, 1987; Krissman, 1989; Reis & McCoach, 2002). Several researchers have noted that the most successful interventions with gifted underachievers include adjustment of cognitions as they relate to academic behavior and goal setting. In a study of 26 gifted underachievers and 30 gifted achievers, grades 4–8, Baker, Bridger, and Evans (1998) concluded the underachievers could benefit from "instruction in study skills," from "behavioral and cognitive strategies to improve self-management and control," and from "interventions to improve coping skills" (p. 12). Because most gifted learners are less likely to be suffering from academic skill deficits than problems with productivity, these strategies make sense.

Cognitive Aspects of Underachievement in Gifted Students

A student's view of giftedness in general and his or her own giftedness in particular has been found to be closely associated with academic performance and motivation. Those who believe that identification of giftedness is elitist, unfair, or a social detriment are more likely to underachieve. This has been found to be especially true of certain multicultural groups and adolescent females (Ries & McCoach, 2000). There is also evidence to suggest that gifted students who underachieve have negative feelings about school, and that those feelings continue to become even more negative over time, and that, for females, attitudes are likely to decline in middle school (Lupart & Pyryt, 1996).

Several researchers have concluded that underachieving gifted students have weak academic self-concepts (although some dispute this), low academic and vocational goals, and a belief that external factors influence their lives (Butler-Por, 1987; McCall, Evahn, & Kratzer, 1992). They tend to attribute success to ability or luck rather than effort (Laffoon, Jenkins-Friedman, & Tollefson, 1989; Rimm, 1995). However, the clearest distinction between achieving and nonachieving gifted students has emerged in the areas of effort, planning, and self-monitoring (McCoach & Siegle, 2001, 2003a). The goal orientation of underachieving gifted students has been described as "faulty and unrealistic" (McCall, Evahn, & Kratzer, 1992).

Thoughts, feelings, and behaviors of family members also have been found to correlate with underachievement in gifted students. Some families of underachievers model negative thoughts and feelings about education (McCall, Evahn, & Kratzer, 1992). In their study of underachievers (not just gifted) 13 years after high school, McCall, Evahn, and Kratzer noted that those whose families valued education were more likely to have caught up to the achievers in the group. Parents also may have unrealistic expectations for their gifted children or feel overwhelmed by the responsibility of raising a highly capable child (Moon & Hall, 1998).

Clinical experience also shows that parental disagreement regarding beliefs about giftedness in general, giftedness in their child, and ways of alleviating the underachievement play an important role. Attributions regarding the child's weak performance are also important. Parents have more difficulty in addressing the problem if one believes it to be a result of an undiagnosed disability in the child and the other attributes it to laziness. They will not agree on an approach if they have differing views of the issues involved and these differences can lead to paralysis in problem solving. Parental attitudes toward their own potential for success in countering the child's underachievement can also be a factor. For example, parents in one family, who were both active professionals, believed they could not help their child if attending to his schoolwork each night was a requirement. They believed their lifestyle simply did not permit it.

COGNITIVE-BEHAVIORAL INTERVENTIONS

Assessment

The first step in the selection of an intervention for gifted underachievers is to determine the factors related to the underachievement and to delineate specific needs as well as strengths. Assessment plays a broad role in ruling out the presence of learning disabilities or misidentification and in pinpointing specific academic strengths and weaknesses. Specificity with regard to current levels of performance, not just in the classroom but also on individual tests of achievement, is essential to the development of realistic expectations for the student. Standardized tests, as well as curriculum-based assessments, should be done. Traditional academic and intellectual strengths, as well as those most visible outside of school, should be included. Extensive involvement in charitable work or hobbies, for example, should not be overlooked. Assessment also must include a review of the student's academic program to determine whether it is a match with the student's needs and strengths and to assess its quality with regard to best practices in gifted education. A full description of these practices is beyond the scope of this chapter. However, an evaluation of the student and not of the educational program would be irresponsible (see Davis & Rimm, 2004, and VanTassel-Baska, 2003, for components of model programs and curricula). Feedback to the student on his or her academic test results, as well as a forthright discussion of classroom performance, is important in light of evidence that some underachievers have very unrealistic views of their own academic behavior (Holland, 1998).

A full assessment will include the social/emotional arena as well. Because there are multiple factors related to underachievement, it is unwise to assume, for example, that academic self-concept is low or that family conflicts exist. With regard to assessment of thoughts and feelings, many of the traditional clinical techniques appropriate for use with other populations can be used with underachieving gifted students and their families. These include in-depth interviews, rating scales, and self-recording techniques such as journaling or affective response forms. Reports that allow for recording of thoughts and feelings while in the target situation should be part of the assessment. For example, although the student's general feelings and thoughts about homework are important, recording of thoughts and feelings when actually getting ready to do homework is essential if improved homework completion is the target behavior. Evaluation of the presence of anxiety and depression should be part of a thorough evaluation of underachievement. Ratings of self-concept should include a breakdown into various areas such as academic, social, and physical. Assessments of family relationships can be done by self-report forms such as the *Parenting Stress Index* (Abidin, 1995) or the *Family Environment Scale* (Moos & Moos, 1994), and a family interview.

One assessment tool that relates specifically to academic beliefs and attitudes of gifted learners is the *School Attitude Assessment Survey-Revised* (SAAS-R). McCoach and Siegle (2003a, 2003b) describe the SAAS-R as a 35-item instrument designed to measure adolescent students' attitudes toward school, teachers, and goals as well as motivation and ability to self-regulate (organizational skills, learning strategies, and persistence). The instrument seems promising. However, at this writing, it is still unpublished. In general, case conceptualization as described by Friedberg and McClure (2002) including a review of physiological, mood, behavioral, cognitive, and interpersonal factors, with greater or less emphasis as circumstances require, is appropriate.

Rafoth's (1999) *Metacognitive Interview* is an excellent tool for assessing metacognitive skills and strategies. The section on monitoring and self-awareness is especially relevant. Her book, *Inspiring Independent Learning*, suggests interventions directly related to the assessment results.

Another assessment approach is to use an academic assignment as a diagnostic opportunity. Sometimes problematic issues are best pinpointed during the process of carrying out a project. In a study focusing on the issue of productivity in underachievers, teachers noted time and materials management or concentration obstacles for the student as they emerged, and addressed them at the time (Baum, Renzulli, & Hebert, 2004).

Techniques

Which of the CBT techniques are most relevant to work with gifted underachievers? This will certainly depend on the nature of the underachievement as suggested by assessment. Several of the techniques that might be considered are described here.

Modeling. Modeling is important to the learning process. With regard to under-achievement, parental modeling of attitudes and behaviors toward education and educational institutions are the most obvious arenas where modeling is likely to be influential. Less obvious is its impact on perfectionism. Some parents will honestly affirm that they do not pressure their inappropriately perfectionistic son or daughter to get As, nor are they critical. In the clinical experience of this writer, that is very often quite true. These same parents may, however, badger themselves for less than stellar performance at work or on projects at home. They do not condone, but they do model, inappropriate perfectionism. (*Inappropriate perfectionism* is the term used here because perfectionism is not always problematic depending on the context.) Parents, as well as teachers, can model constructive reactions to failure by using self-talk aloud that suggests finding reasons for less than perfect performance, brainstorming possible changes, and then moving on.

As an intervention, modeling can be used in academic settings to assist with inattentiveness and disorganization. Children who fail to attend to signs and steps when doing math problems, for example, can be given cards with steps that start with, "What does this problem tell me to do—add, subtract?" "I will start with the right side." "Did I check my work?" Kendall and Braswell (1985) recommend that the modeling adult say the steps aloud, carry out the behavior, then say the steps quietly, then silently, each time self-rewarding by saying "I did a good job." Children then go through the steps aloud, quietly, etc., as well. This same procedure can apply to any academic behavior.

Goal setting. Specific goal setting is important to gifted students who may have mental pictures of their products that far outpace their ability. It is common, for example, for elementary gifted students to be frustrated when their motor ability to write a report makes it difficult for them to include all of the ideas they initially had. Walking students through a project, asking how they plan to accomplish one part or another, can help them be more realistic. Incorporating periodic checks of their progress in learning or completing an assignment helps in modifying goals, if necessary.

Broader goal setting, including college and career planning and exploration, should not be neglected in intervention programs for underachieving gifted students. They frequently see little relevance to the real world in their academic programs. Mentors can help in this exploration and in making connections between self-management skills and lifelong learning and career advancement (Hebert & Olenchack, 2000).

Organizational skills. For students who have grandiose plans for a project but never get around to actually tackling it, Krissman (1989) suggests breaking tasks down into smaller units with time frames set for each. Other important organization skills include outlines of project plans with timelines and specific lists of what will be accomplished and how. Because gifted students may have less common ways of thinking, it is important for them to have a role in the development of the organizational plan. A notebook organized in chronological order of classes attended each day may make sense to the counselor. However, the student might prefer organization based on which teachers are most likely to check the notebook. Pro-cedures for note taking, determining which books should be brought home, and placement of materials to be taken from home to school may all require some form of instruction and planning. For young children, adults may cue the behavior or check that it is done. However, the plan itself should come from, and be thoroughly understood by, the student.

Metacognitive and study skills. Achieving gifted students often show highly effi-cient and unique learning and memory skills. They may see patterns that facilitate recall or make associations that allow for effective use of information. As the earlier literature review suggests, underachieving gifted students may have to be taught these strategies. For example, they may simply reread material rather than engaging the material in preparation for a test. They may try to remember a large amount of material rather than utilize mnemonic strategies.

Self-regulation/self-monitoring. Zantall (1989) describes self-monitoring as process in which the student is taught to assess whether or not he or she is exhibiting a behavior. Steps listed in the process include, (1) defining the target behavior, (2) teaching the child how to record the behavior, (3) modeling the recording, and (4) having the child repeat instructions for the process. Many studies suggest that underachieving gifted students lack the ability to assess and regulate their own performance, whether predicting their grade on a test or judging how well they are progressing on an assignment.

The use of rubrics to evaluate performance can be helpful to students learning to monitor their academic behavior (Damiani, 2004). Rubrics are the criteria by which a product will be judged and can be provided by the teacher, developed by the student, or done collaboratively. Rubrics also can be generic. That is, a student might develop general criteria for use with all assignments including factors such as "followed teacher directions," "planned ahead," or "turned assignment in on time." In the beginning, the student must formally rate each area. Eventually, the process becomes part of the student's self-talk before turning in any assignment. Rubrics provide realistic, unemotional evaluation systems for students. If rubrics are used initially with the guidance of a counselor, sweeping, inappropriate evaluative self-talk (e.g., "The teacher is going to hate it," or "Mine is going to be the worst one in the class"), which may lead to paralyzing perfectionism, can be checked. Learning or project contracts can help students by identifying materials to be used and setting realistic timelines and quality standards (Krissman, 1989).

Self-monitoring is also important when stress or depression plays a role in underachievement. Students may rate their levels of feeling first for a base rate of incidence and then after the use of an intervention such as positive self-talk or relaxation. An important aspect of self-monitoring is that it brings the student's attention to the target behavior.

Positive self-talk/relaxation. Self-talk can relate to the messages we give ourselves to explain an occurrence or to the instructions we give ourselves to carry out a behavior. For example, a student may explain a poor grade by attributing it to the teacher's dislike for him or her. That thought may be followed by another that says, "Teachers never like me" or "all my teachers have always disliked me." Such self-talk can easily lead to anger, frustration, depression, or giving up. Forsterling (1990) suggests the counselor offer unemotional, cognitive explanations along with reasonable evidence. Reasonable evidence might include instances in which effort has led to a better grade or noting that other students also did poorly. This should be coupled with problem solving on how things might be done differently in the future.

Researchers have noted a connection between the negative explanation we give ourselves for academic failure, especially if it relates to a long-term characteristic or circumstance (e.g., "I am not really gifted, girls can't do math"), and reduced effort to combat failure in the future (Peterson, 1990). Some interesting studies have been done on the impact of unearned praise from teachers and the fostering of self-attributions among students (e.g., "She must not believe I am that smart if she thinks this is good work"; Graham, 1990). So, those interacting with gifted children should guard against the use of unwarranted praise.

Self-instruction is a form of self-talk used to remind the learner how to proceed and what to emphasize in carrying out a task. It consists of strategies and steps to follow (Bradley-Klug & Shapiro, 2003). Friedberg and McClure (2002) say the goal of self-instruction is to "construct new covert speech patterns that prompt more adaptive behaviors" (p. 137).

Even if negative emotions are not a causative factor in a gifted student's under-achievement, inadequate school performance over a long period of time is likely to result in unpleasant associations with schoolwork including frustration, anger, and anxiety. The introduction of goal setting, positive self-talk, and organization skills is unlikely to be successful when strong negative emotional reactions are present. Therefore, relaxation training is a good place to start with the gifted underachiever. Assessment should pinpoint places and times to utilize relaxation. Gifted students are often excellent candidates for this intervention because they have an intellectual understanding of the concept, are capable of remembering the steps after just a few trials, and can create detailed and unique images of peace and tranquility. One highly gifted student made his own relaxation tape with a description of a rain forest. No counselor could have described it better.

Self-reward and pleasant event scheduling. In addition to the obvious goal of increasing the incidence of the target academic behavior, self-reward draws the student's attention to the behavior. It puts control into the hands of underachieving students who often attribute outcomes to outside forces. For students who tend to be perfectionistic and to ruminate on negative aspects of their performance, a reward provides closure to the academic event. As with any behavior change intervention, reinforcers must be realistic, timely, and appropriate. Self-reward and pleasant event scheduling are especially appropriate for gifted children whose ideas of a positive event or reward may be quite different from the general population. When they choose the reward or event themselves, the reinforcing effect is more likely.

With families. CBT interventions also can be helpful to families of gifted under-achievers. The attribution the family gives to the child's underachievement is often central in their choices of ways to address the problem. Parents who attribute poor academic performance to a lack of true giftedness in the child or to a learning disability are likely to focus on different solutions than those who see the issue as laziness or coddling.

Like the students themselves, parents need to set goals, monitor their behavior, and reward themselves for successful change. Education, problem solving, and goal setting are tasks families must undertake (Moon & Hall, 1998). Especially helpful are the generation of alternatives for problem solving and the evaluation of each.

IMPLICATIONS AND APPLICATIONS IN A SCHOOL SETTING

Because the effects of underachievement are cumulative and worsen during and after middle school, intervention should take place as soon as a pattern emerges. An appropriate academic program is essential to alleviation of underachievement for gifted learners and counseling interventions should be in addition to, not instead of, adequate educational programming. The two can go hand in hand, as CBT enhances the student's ability to benefit from instruction through goal setting, self-monitoring, metacognitive, and study skills.

Dubois, Felner, Lockerd, Parra, and Lopez (2003) describe a model for child mental health that includes cognitive, behavioral, emotional, and motivational components. In spite of their high intellect, an important factor in resilience, gifted underachievers often have weaknesses in several of these areas. An effective counseling program will involve students, schools, and families in problem solution and monitoring of progress.

CASE EXAMPLES

Case One: Eric S

The school psychologist saw 9-year-old Eric S at the end of his first semester of 4th grade. He had been identified as gifted by his school district in 2nd grade, but he always had problems with work completion. The problem worsened during his fourth school year with the onset of longer-range assignments such as book reports and science projects. Homework time had always been trying, with Eric either failing to remember he had homework or misplacing the work done. Currently, Mother reports that Eric hates to write and gets very poor grades on written assignments. Grades on tests are good enough, but overall grades are lowered by failure to complete assignments or not following directions on what is done. School personnel have met with Mr. and Mrs. S about dropping Eric from the gifted program. Mrs. S tried asking Eric about homework every night and reviewing it. That worked for the shorter assignments, but for longer range ones, Eric forgets they are due until the last minute and then will spend hours without making any progress.

On an individual test of intellectual ability, Eric scored just into the very superior range. The examiner considered the overall score to be an underestimate because Eric rarely earned points for speed, performing all timed tests in a deliberate and methodical manner and going back to double-check his work. An individual standardized assessment of academic achievement showed Eric to be in the superior range in reading and high average range in math. Performance on the written language task was in the low average range, mostly because he wrote little. A curriculum-based measure yielded similar results in reading and math. A review of language arts work samples showed incomplete and skimpy work. Eric's teacher reported that, in class, he completes math and reading, but not writing assignments.

Behavior rating scales done by Eric's mother indicated a history of anxiety-related symptoms since kindergarten, including headaches and stomachaches. Eric also had a history of sleep problems, which, according to self-reports, he still experiences especially if he has long-range assignments or projects due. Self-ratings indicated adequate self-esteem in all areas but supported Mother's reports of anxiety symptoms. Socially, his behavior is appropriate with participation in some sports and several friends in school and in his neighborhood.

In an interview with the clinician, Eric described himself as lazy and as someone who could do better if he tried. When asked about the classification as gifted, he said the school might have been wrong since he was so young when they tested him. He denied having any problems with long-range assignments and said his writing was fine, but he did not like to do it. He said he felt "jumpy" when he had projects such as a book report or science project due and kept thinking he should do it but could not make himself get started.

In a meeting between Mr. and Mrs. S and the clinician, Mr. S said Eric was lazy and that Mrs. S was in part the cause because she was babying him by checking his homework and always looking for what the "problem" might be. He said he had not done much work in school either and he had turned out fine. Both parents believed they had a good relationship with Eric with Mrs. S making the exception of school-related issues between her and Eric. The relationship with Dad, both agreed, was unaffected by the school problem.

A plan for Eric. The first part of this intervention was to give Eric and his parents a realistic picture of his strengths and needs. The most important points to be made with Eric were:

1. that he was indeed gifted by the definition given in his state
2. that his reading and math skills were strong
3. that he was deliberate with his work and probably would not work well under timed pressure
4. that he probably could do better in writing with some help
5. that it was unlikely that he was lazy, as lazy people do not usually feel pressure to get their work done and Eric did feel that pressure

With Mr. and Mrs. S, it was important to share all of the above information but to help them also see the importance of modeling the attitude that Eric's academic problems were important and worth addressing, and that Eric himself could be the main player in solving them. They had to agree on a course of action both would support and participate in, which they did.

A disconnect existed between Eric's description of himself as lazy and someone who could do better if he tried and the symptoms of anxiety both he and his mother said he showed. To learn more about Eric's thoughts and feelings when faced with homework and writing assignments, an in vivo self-report system was designed. This was done by asking Eric to brainstorm some words to describe what he felt like sitting in front of a writing assignment he knew was due in a few minutes at school, or for homework. He was then asked to do the same thing for how it felt to be thinking about a science project that was due. He came up with words such as "nervous," "pressure," and "no ideas" for the writing assignment. For the science project, he said, "too complicated," "too hard," "too much work," and "hard to figure out what to do."

These words or phrases were used to make brief rating scales representing more or less of the feelings and thoughts Eric had described. He completed them when faced with writing or long-range assignments during a 2-week period. In order to model the importance Dad placed on Eric's improved work completion, Dad was the one to remind Eric to do the scales. A log or journal was avoided because it would have involved writing, which Eric did not like to do. Eric's self-reports in vivo did indeed show that these experiences were stressful for him. This points out the importance of having students do in vivo reporting. Although none of Eric's ratings on the scale of self-esteem, and only some of his descriptions of himself, showed anxiety related to his work, it was clearly revealed in his in vivo self-reports.

Because discomfort was associated with writing and long-range assignments for Eric, that needed to be addressed first. Until the anxiety was reduced, it was going to function as a punisher for attempts to think about and do assignments.

During the next several sessions, Eric was taught relaxation and imagery techniques. He designed his own peaceful imaginary place and described it on tape in his own voice. The tape was associated with muscle relaxation and was to be used whenever Eric had trouble going to sleep. After using the tape for several weeks at home, he began to practice using the imagery and muscle relaxation briefly in trying circumstances away from home, when faced with a writing assignment in class, for example.

Rafoth's *Metacognitive Interview* was carried out with Eric and he was given techniques for addressing his areas of weakness. For his next long-range assignment, Eric and the clinician developed a plan breaking the process into small pieces to be carried out over several weeks. Each time Eric completed a piece, he stayed up an extra half hour to watch TV or listen to his favorite music, self-rewards his parents had agreed to.

Before beginning homework, Eric responded to a brief list of questions to help him plan his evening. What assignments do I have? Am I supposed to do anything for my long-range assignment tonight? How long will I work? How will I reward myself if I work that long? Did I follow the steps for doing my writing assignments? His steps for doing writing assignments were to tape his ideas for what to write on a tape recorder, play them back to himself when writing on a word processor, and then read over to edit what he had written. With the help of Eric's teacher, rubrics were developed for all long-range and writing assignments, and Eric used them to evaluate his work before turning it in. Self-talk included telling himself that he worked a little slowly but did know how to do an assignment and telling himself he had done a good job when the rubric had been addressed.

Several school modifications were necessary. Because Eric had demonstrated mastery in grade-level material in math and reading, he was offered advanced material with less repetition. Instead of being dropped from the gifted program, Eric needed close attention and monitoring. High-interest projects that included presentation modes utilized in the real world, such as PowerPoint and lecture, in addition to writing, were added to his program. A counselor followed Eric and helped him monitor his progress.

Case Two: Maxwell G

Maxwell is a 14-year-old student. His guidance counselor referred him to the school psychologist at the end of the second semester of 9th grade. Maxwell was identified as gifted in 3rd grade. In a meeting before assessment, Mr. and Mrs. G reported that Maxwell had rarely spent any time studying or doing homework but had always had As and Bs. His gifted education program, a pull-out system, had always consisted of a variety of interesting activities that Maxwell seemed to enjoy. However, on entrance to junior high, his grades started to slip mostly because of incomplete homework or lost assignments. Maxwell was usually able to pull the grade up with test performance at the end of the semester. However, this year things were different. Maxwell was in advanced math and sciences classes and had failed both. The parents also reported that Maxwell spent a good deal of his free time participating in Civil War reenactments. He researched the characters carefully and never seemed to tire of playing one more role. When asked for his view of Maxwell's school situation, Mr. G said a way had to be found for Maxwell to improve his work in math and science as there was no point to being identified gifted if one did not excel in those areas. He had always expected his son to go into medicine or research and thought Maxwell would like to do so.

A review of Maxwell's school record showed that he had always had his weakest grades in math and science. Standardized tests from elementary school also showed this to be his weakest area, usually on grade level but sometimes lower.

In sessions with the school psychologist, Maxwell said he did not like math and science much but knew he was good at it. He said he could bring his grades up if he tried and that he just did not study enough. He said, as his father had, that smart people should be good in math and science. When asked about his career plans, he said he would probably be a doctor.

Rating scales given to parents and to Maxwell did not reveal any social/emotional or behavior problems. Maxwell's ratings on self-esteem were high in all areas. A vocational interest inventory, however, yielded high ratings in social science and low ratings in math and hard sciences. A curriculum-based measure in math showed significant gaps, especially when the district's advanced curriculum was utilized in the assessment.

A plan for Maxwell. This is a situation in which the school, the parents, and the student made the erroneous assumption that giftedness meant ability to tackle advanced placement in any academic area. Maxwell's true strengths and needs were not known to him or his parents. When accurate and specific information was provided, the parents and the school agreed that he would be better placed in a grade-level math class. Maxwell still believed he could have tackled the more advanced material, but he was relieved to have less academic pressure. Except for enforcing a set place and time for homework and consequences if terms were not met, the Gs were asked not to discuss schoolwork with Maxwell. This was done to ensure that he took responsibility for his academic performance and so that he might begin to think about his own goals and interests without parental influence.

The vocational assessment was used as a beginning point for discussion of what Maxwell was really interested in. He spent a great deal of time talking about history. He decided to join the school's history club. However, this took even more time away from his schoolwork. Adding up the number of hours he spent on history and subtracting them from the time available in his day, Maxwell began to see he would have to better organize his time if he wanted to keep up with his interest and not earn failing grades. He was asked to keep two different records over a 2-week period. The first was to be a list of exactly what he did when studying for a test or doing homework. For example, did he read, write, and take notes? How long did he work? Second, he was to keep a record of his thoughts and feelings right before and right after doing homework. One column said "thoughts." One column said "feelings," and the third consisted of just a + or – sign for positive or negative thought or feeling. The results of these ratings were pretty surprising to Maxwell. First, they showed that when he was to be "studying," all he listed was reading. Further questioning and the *Metacognitive Interview* revealed that he really had no study skills, such as mnemonic strategies, finding the main idea, or association with prior knowledge. When preparing for a long-term project, he read materials he had found but did not plan ahead or have any concept of how long it might take him to complete the work. Thoughts and feelings showed devaluing labels for what he enjoyed and was good at, and threatening ones for the things he found difficult. For example, thoughts when faced with math were, "I have to be good at this," "This is important," and "Smart people do well at this, why can't I?" In the social sciences, his comments included, "This is easy" and "This is fun."

Maxwell's assumptions about giftedness and the value of social science had to be questioned. He was asked for his evidence that one was easy whereas the other was hard and especially that gifted people should be scientists. The importance of exploration of vocational options was discussed and a method devised for Maxwell to do this. Specific study skills and self-monitoring techniques were taught such as the development of timelines and a study schedule. Maxwell got an electronic scheduling system and made a weekly schedule, making sure to include a certain number of hours for homework so he could spend more time with the history club and reenactment. Being able to tell his father that he may consider options other than medicine for a career, and disagreeing with him about the merits of social science, were issues that will likely have to be tackled in the future. It was expected that improved school performance would help set the stage and give Maxwell confidence for eventually engaging in that communication.

CONCLUSION

Causes of underachievement are varied and include school environment, family factors, and characteristics of the learner. A full assessment of the student's resources and needs is the first step toward an effective intervention. Counseling and behavioral methods are not a substitute for an appropriate academic program.

Evidence regarding the effectiveness of specific interventions in alleviating underachievement is sparse. However, research suggests that students will benefit most from adjustment of cognitions related to academic behavior and goal setting, instruction on study skills, and strategies to improve self-management. Cognitive-behavioral interventions can also be helpful to families of gifted children who are underperforming. Underachievement carries significant personal and societal implications. Effects are cumulative and often worsen during and after middle school. Therefore, the issue should be addressed early on and response to intervention should be carefully monitored. For students prone to underachieve, appropriate skills might have to be reinforced or reintroduced periodically throughout their time in school.

REFERENCES

Abidin, R. R. (1995). *Parenting Stress Index manual.* Odessa, FL: Psychological Assessment Resources.

Baker, J. A., Bridger, R., & Evans, K. (1998). Models of underachievement among gifted preadolescents: The role of personal, family, and school factors. *Gifted Child Quarterly, 42*(1), 5–15.

Baum, S. M., Renzulli, J. S., & Hebert, T. P. (2004). Reversing underachievement: Creative productivity as a systematic intervention. In S. M. Moon (Ed.), *Social emotional issues, underachievement and counseling of gifted and talented students* (pp. 133–156). Thousand Oaks, CA: Corwin Press.

Bland, L. C., & Sowa, C. J. (1994). A overview of resilience in gifted children. *Roeper Review, 17*(2), 77–81 [Electronic version].

Bradley-Klug, K. L., & Shapiro, E. (2003). Treatment of academic skills problems. In M. A. Reinecke, F. M. Dattilio, & A. Freeman, (Eds.), *Cognitive therapy with children and adolescents* (pp. 281–303). New York: Guilford.

Butler-Por, N. (1987). *Underachievers in school: Issues and intervention.* New York: Wiley.

Colangelo, N., & Davis, G. (Eds.). (2003). *Handbook of gifted education.* Boston: Allyn & Bacon.

Colangelo, N., Kerr, B., Christensen, P., & Maxey, J. (1993). A comparison of gifted under-achievers and gifted high achievers. *Gifted Child Quarterly, 37*(4), 155–160.

Damiani, V. B. (2004) Portfolio assessment in the classroom. In A. S. Canter, L. Z. Paige, M. D. Roth, I. Romero, & S. A. Carroll (Eds.), *Helping children at home and at school II: Handouts for families and educators* (pp. S3–129–131). Bethesda, MD: National Association of School Psychologists.

Davis, G. A., & Rimm, S. B. (2004). *Education of the gifted and talented.* Boston: Allyn & Bacon.

Delisle, J. R. (1992). *Guiding the social and emotional development of gifted youth.* White Plains, NY: Longman.

Dowdall, C. B., & Colangelo, N. (1982). Underachieving gifted students: Review and implications. *Gifted Child Quarterly, 26*(4), 179–184.

Dubois, D. L., Felner, R. D., Lockerd, E. M., Parra, G. R., & Lopez, C. (2003). The quadri-partite model revisited. In M. A. Reinecke, F. M. Dattilio, & A. Freeman, (Eds.), *Cognitive therapy with children and adolescents* (pp. 402–433). New York: Guilford.

Durlak, J. A., Fuhrman, T., & Lampman, C. (1991). Effectiveness of cognitive-behavior therapy for maladapting children: A metanalysis. *Psychological Bulletin, 110*(2), 204–214.

Emerick, L. J. (1992). Academic underachievement among the gifted: Student's perceptions of factors that reverse the pattern. *Gifted Child Quarterly, 36*(3), 140–146.

Forsterling, F. (1990). Attributional therapies. In S. Graham & V. S. Folkes (Eds.), *Attribution theory: Attributions to achievement, mental health, and interpersonal conflict* (pp. 123–139). Hillsdale, NJ: Lawrence Erlbaum.

Friedberg, R. D., & McClure, J. M. (2002). *Clinical practice of cognitive therapy with children and adolescents: The nuts and bolts.* New York: Guilford.

Genshaft, J. L., Bireley, M., & Hollinger, C. L. (1995). *Serving gifted and talented students.* Austen, TX: Pro-ed.

Graham, S. (1990). Communicating low ability in the classroom: Bad things good teachers sometimes do. In S. Graham & V. S. Folkes (Eds.), *Attribution theory: Attributions to achievement, mental health, and interpersonal conflict* (pp. 17–36). Hillsdale, NJ: Lawrence Erlbaum.

Hebert, T. P., & Olenchak, F. R. (2000). Mentors for gifted underachieving males: Developing potential and realizing promise. In S. M. Moon (Ed.), *Social emotional issues, under-achievement and counseling of gifted and talented students* (pp. 157–179). Thousand Oaks, CA: Corwin Press.

Holland, V. (1998). Underachieving boys: Problems and solutions. *Support for Learning, 13*(4), 174–178.

Kendall, P. C., & Braswell, L. (1985). *Cognitive therapy for impulsive children.* New York: Guilford.

Krissman, A. S. (1989). Gifted underachievers. *Roeper Review, 11*(3), 160–162.

Laffoon, K. S., Jenkins-Friedman, R., & Tollefson, N. (1989). Causal attributions of under-achieving gifted and non-gifted students. *Journal for the Education of the Gifted, 13*(1), 4–21.

Lupart, J. L., & Pyryt, M. C. (1996). "Hidden gifted" students: Underachiever prevalence and profile. *Journal for Education of the Gifted, 20*(1), 36–53.

Mandel, H. P., & Marcus, S. I. (1988). *The psychology of underachievement.* New York: John Wiley.

McCall, R. B., Evahn, C., & Kratzer, L. (1992). *High school underachievers.* Newbury Park, CA: Sage.

McCoach, D. B., & Siegle, D. (2001). A comparison of high achievers' and low achievers' attitudes, perceptions, and motivations. *Academic Exchange Quarterly, 5,* 71–76.

McCoach, D. B., & Siegle, D. (2003a). Factors that differentiate underachieving gifted students from high-achieving gifted students. *Gifted Child Quarterly, 47*(2), 144–154.

McCoach, D. B. & Siegle, D. (2003b). The School Attitude Assessment Survey-Revised: A new instrument to identify academically able students who underachieve. *Educational and Psychological Measurement, 63*(3), 414–429.

Mendaglio, S. (1993). Counseling gifted learning disabled: Individual and group counseling techniques. In L.K. Silverman (Ed.), *Counseling the gifted & talented* (pp. 131–149). Denver: Love.

Moon, S., & Hall, A. S. (1998). Family therapy with intellectually and creatively gifted children. *Journal of Marital and Family Therapy, 24*(1), 59–80.

Moon, S. M., Kelly, K. R., & Feldhusen, J. (1997). Specialized counseling services for gifted youth and their families: A needs assessment. In S. M. Moon (Ed.), *Social/emotional issues, underachievement, and counseling of gifted and talented students* (pp. 229–248). Thousand Oaks, CA: Corwin.

Moon, S. M., Swift, M., & Shallenberger, A. (2002). Perceptions of a self-contained class for fourth- and fifth-grade students with high to extreme levels of intellectual giftedness. *Gifted Child Quarterly, 46*(1), 64–79.

Moos, R. H., & Moos, B. S. (1994). *Family Environment Scale manual.* Palo Alto: Consulting Psychologists Press.

National Commission on Excellence in Education (1983). *A nation at risk: The imperative for educational reform.* Washington, DC: U.S. Government Printing Office.

Peterson, C. (1990). Explanatory style in the classroom and on the playing field. In S. Graham & V. S. Folkes (Eds.), *Attribution theory: Attributions to achievement, mental health, and interpersonal conflict* (pp. 54–66). Hillsdale, NJ: Lawrence Erlbaum.

Peterson, J. S. (2002). A longitudinal study of post-high-school development in gifted individuals at risk for poor educational outcomes. *The Journal of Secondary Gifted Education, XIV*(1), 6–18.

Peterson, J. S., & Colangelo, N. (1996). Gifted achievers and underachievers: A comparison of patterns found in school files. *Journal of Counseling and Development, 74,* 399–407.

Rafoth, M. A. (1999). *Inspiring independent learning: Successful classroom strategies.* Washington, DC: National Education Association.

Reinecke, M. A., Dattilio, F. M., & Freeman, A. (2003). What makes for an effective treatment? In M. A. Reinecke, F. M. Dattilio, & A. Freeman (Eds.), *Cognitive therapy with children and adolescents* (pp. 1–18). New York: Guilford.

Reis, S. M., & McCoach, D. B. (2000). The underachievement of gifted students: What do we know and where do we go? *Gifted Child Quarterly, 44*(3), 152–170.

Reis, S. M., & McCoach, D. B. (2002). Underachievement in gifted and talented students with special needs. *Exceptionality, 10*(2), 113–125.

Renzulli, J. S., Baum, S. M., & Hebert, T. P. (1995). Reversing underachievement: Creative productivity as a systemic intervention. *Gifted Child Quarterly, 34*(4), 224–235.

Renzulli, J. S., & Park, S. (2000). Gifted dropouts: The who and the why. *Gifted Child Quarterly, 44*(4), 261–271.

Renzulli, J. S., Reid, B. D., & Gubbins, E. J. (1992). *Setting an agenda: Research priorities for the gifted and talented through the year 2000.* [Electronic version] Storrs, CT: National Research Center on the Gifted and Talented.

Rimm, S. (1995). *Why bright kids get poor grades and what you can do about it.* New York: Crown Publishers.

Robinson, N. M. (2002). Individual differences in gifted students' attributions for academic performances. In M. Neihart, S. M. Reis, N. M. Robinson, & S. Moon (Eds.), *The social and emotional development of gifted children: What do we know?* (pp.61–69). Washington, DC: Prufrock.

Ross, P. O. (1993). *National excellence: A case for developing America's talent.* Washington, DC: Office of Educational Research and Improvement.

Schultz, R. A. (2002). Illuminating realities: A phenomenological view from two underachieving gifted learners [Electronic Version]. *Roeper Review, 24*(4), 203–213.

VanTassel-Baska, J. (2003). *Curriculum planning and instructional design for gifted learners.* Denver: Love.

Zantall, S. S. (1989). Self-control training with hyperactive and impulsive children. In J. N. Hughes & R. J. Hall (Eds.), *Cognitive behavioral psychology in the schools* (pp. 305–346). New York: Guilford.

Zimmerman, B. (1994). Dimensions of academic self-regulation: A conceptual framework for education. In D. H. Schunk & B. J. Zimmerman (Eds.), *Self-regulation of learning and performance: Issues and educational applications* (pp. 3–21). Mahwah, NJ: Lawrence Erlbaum.

Zuccone, C. F., & Amerikaner, M. (1986). Counseling gifted underachievers: A family systems approach. *Journal of Counseling and Development, 64,* 590–592.

10

Cognitive-Behavioral Interventions for Participants in Bullying and Coercion

BETH DOLL & SUSAN M. SWEARER

Peer aggression is an all-too-common occurrence in children's daily lives. The nature and frequency of children's peer conflicts shift and change across the developmental stages, such that participation in physical aggression is quite common among toddlers, and participation in verbal and relational aggression becomes quite common in adolescence. In this rough-and-tumble world of children's peer interactions, the ability to cope with and respond effectively to aggressive overtures is a critical adaptive skill (Pellegrini, 2002; Cairns & Cairns, 2000). In some instances, however, the form and intensity of peer aggression make it unlikely that children can respond effectively and unreasonable to expect them to do so. This chapter will describe one form of peer aggression—bullying—that is never adaptive and is often quite damaging to the children who bully and those who are bullied. Bullying will be described as a cognitive-behavioral phenomenon that is part of the broader framework of childhood aggression and that occurs within a social-ecological context.

WHAT IS BULLYING?

Bullying is an extreme form of peer aggression in which one or more students repeatedly and deliberately harms and intimidates one or more vulnerable peers, and gains status or power by doing so (Olweus, 1993b; Pellegrini & Bartini, 2001; Slee, 1995; Smith & Boulton, 1990). Recent definitions of bullying have been broadened to include relational aggression, such as telling lies or engaging in other acts to ruin a peer's reputation, and verbal aggression, such as teasing, taunting, and name calling, as well as physical aggression, such as hitting, shoving, or chasing

(Crick, Bigbee, & Howes, 1996; Olweus, 1994). Like other forms of peer aggression, bullying can be overt, as when bullies make no attempt to hide their identity from their victims, or covert, as when bullies shield their identity from the victims and other onlookers.

A key factor that distinguishes bullying from less malicious forms of peer aggression is the intention of the bully. By definition, bullying always includes an intention to cause harm or, translated into the simpler language of young children, bullies engage in these behaviors "to be mean." Naive adults might wonder at this distinction, assuming that all peer aggression rises out of hostile intentions. However, extended investigations of peer relations have established that children are aggressive toward their peers for many different reasons. Most commonly, children engage in repeated acts of mock aggression during typical play with their friends—verbally teasing or insulting each other; physically hitting, shoving, kicking or knocking each other down; and pretending to walk away or ignore one another (Pellegrini, 1993; Humphreys & Smith, 1984). Outside observers are not always able to discriminate between this mock aggression and actual peer conflict because the difference lies with the children's intentions and perceptions rather than the actual aggressive acts (Walker & Severson, 1992). Researchers have coined the terms *rough and tumble play* and *jostling* to refer to this pretend aggression, and have clearly established that its intention is to have fun together. Still, jostling can dissolve into actual conflict when children misperceive the intention of an aggressing child, and think that they are the target of a legitimate attack (Doll, Song, & Siemers, 2004).

In other cases, children may aggress against each other to defend themselves, their friends, or their possessions. Termed instrumental aggression, these acts occur when physical or verbal aggression appears necessary to acquire or maintain possession of a needed object (e.g., a playground ball, swing, or territory) or to stop another's aggression toward the children or their friends (Crick, 2000). Still, instrumental aggression is not always justified when judged by an uninvolved outsider. Children may overreact to each other if they misjudge the risk of losing a needed object, or overestimate the danger or intention of the aggressing peer.

Even aggressive acts intended to harm other children are not always bullying. Children may lash out at each other in retaliation for a perceived injury that they suffered at the hand of a peer. Retaliatory aggression is often impulsive and prompted by unchecked emotional reactions in the heat of a moment. In contrast, bullying involves repeated and calculated acts that are intended to harm the victims, who may not have committed any act to deserve the ire of the bullies.

Bullying is also distinctive because it is an exercise of dominance—an attempt to display power and to compel victims to concede power (Pellegrini, 2002b). In this sense, bullying is a special case of social coercion, in which one person coerces another into behaving or acting in a particular way. Because of its unique relevance to bullying, this chapter will draw on Patterson's (1982) cycle of coercion to describe the social dynamics that underlie incidents of bullying. Still, although it is possible for there to be single, isolated incidents of coercion, the term *bullying* will only apply when these occur repeatedly over time and reflect an intention to cause harm as well as coerce.

In summary, bullying is distinguished as much by the intention of the bullying child and the perceptions of the bullied child as by the nature of the aggressive acts. Indeed, it is often the case that the pain inflicted on victims is a psychic pain caused by the bullies' words or by loss of face, rather than a physical pain. Consequently, cognitive-behavioral models are uniquely suited to bullying interventions because these directly address the covert cognitions of children involved in bullying as well as the overt acts of aggression.

HOW PERVASIVE IS THE PROBLEM OF BULLYING?

Conservative estimates are that between 10% and 20% of school-aged children will encounter bullying at some point during their school careers (Batsche & Knoff, 1994; Perry, Kusel, & Perry, 1988). That is, bullying is sufficiently prevalent to be considered a normal, albeit dysfunctional, child behavior. Moreover, children cannot be cleanly categorized into bullies, victims, onlookers, or nonparticipants in bullying. Instead, one out of six bullies reports that they also have been victims, whereas one out of four victims reports that they also have bullied (Olweus, 1993b). This and other research clearly establishes that bullying does not emerge solely out of the individual characteristics of children but is also a product of the social environment within which they interact with peers (Swearer & Doll, 2001). Consequently, this chapter is written from the premise that bullying is a social-ecological phenomenon that reflects the social environments within which peer interactions occur. In addition to addressing the behaviors of children who bully and those who are victims, the cognitive-behavioral interventions described in this chapter will also target the peer onlookers, teachers, uninvolved children, and families who form the social ecology as well as the bullies and victims.

One final proviso: Aggression, coercion, and bullying can occur at any age, including in adult workplaces or communities. Although the developmental nature of bullying suggests that these behaviors transcend age, this chapter will be confined to bullying and coercion that occur among children and adolescents, and the developmental changes that can confuse observers of bullying and complicate attempts to intervene.

WHO PARTICIPATES IN BULLYING AND COERCION?

Bullying children and bullied children are the immediate, direct participants in peer bullying incidents. Bullying children's repeated acts of cruelty and intimidation toward peers are attributable, in part, to their predisposition to be impulsive, lack empathy, and dominate (Olweus, 1997a, 1997b). Still, it is disingenuous to refer to children who bully as "bullies," as many of the same children will bully their peers in some situations while being bullied by other peers in other situations (Olweus, 1993, 1994.) Consequently, it is necessary to look outside the child for a portion of the explanation underlying bullying incidents. In particular, children are more likely to bully if adult supervision is minimal and the likelihood of being caught or disciplined is slight (Kasen, Berenson, Cohen, & Johnson, 2004); if the bullied child appears to be weaker and less powerful than themselves, and unlikely to retaliate effectively (Hodges & Perry, 1999; Hazler, Miller, Carney, & Green, 2001); if onlooking peers act to encourage or assist with the bullying act when they observe it (Olweus & Linber, 1999); or if no one steps in to defend or assist the bullied child (Salmivalli, 2001).

Children who are bullied typically are, or appear to be, unable to defend themselves against aggression. This is possibly because of physical weakness or clumsiness, limited intellectual aptitude, ineffective verbal skills, or a lack of protective support from peers or the classroom teacher (Hazler et al., 2001; Hodges & Perry, 1999; Pellegrini, Bartini, & Brooks, 1999). However, if effectively removed from the social environment where they were bullied, many children are able to establish normal, nonbullied roles within the new peer group. Victims never deserve the bullying, but they may perpetuate it by keeping the incidents a secret from supervising adults, either because they fear retaliation or because they do not expect adults are able or willing to stop the bullying (Pepler, Craig, Ziegler, & Charach, 1994). A key factor that contributes to children being bullied is their friendships within the peer group: Children who have several friends and whose friends are willing to stand up and defend them in the face of peer coercion are unlikely to become frequent victims of bullying (Salmivalli, 2001; Schwartz, McFayden, Dodge, Pettit, & Bates, 1999).

Importantly, both bullying and bullied children report substantial psychological distress. Bullying children report a general unhappiness with school (Forero, McLellan, Rissel, & Barman, 1999), significantly higher rates of depression and suicidal ideation (Kaltiala-Heino, Rimpela, Mortunen, Rimpela, & Rantanen, 1999; Swearer, Song, Cary, Eagle, & Mickelson, 2001), and feelings of ineffectiveness and interpersonal distress (Kumpulainen et al., 1998). Children who are bullied report high levels of anxiety (Craig, 1998; Swearer et al., 2001) and diminished levels of peer acceptance (Olweus, 1993; Pellegrini, Bartini, & Brooks, 1999). Cognitive-behavioral interventions have been demonstrated to be effective in addressing both anxiety and depressive disorders (Kendall, 1992; Stark et al., 1996), further strengthening the rationale for using cognitive-behavioral models of intervention to stop or prevent peer bullying.

Onlookers are children who witness the bullying and do not act to prevent it. Social-ecological research has identified onlookers as key participants in bullying incidents. In some instances, onlookers will reinforce the bullying behavior with laudatory comments to the bullying child, by conceding prestige or privilege to him or her, or by joining in the bullying behavior (Oliver, Hoover, & Hazler, 1994; Olweus, 1993a; Pellegrini et al., 1999). Even if they do not join in or actively encourage the bullying, their silence becomes tacit permission for the bullying child to continue the coercion. Conversely, onlooking peers can actively discourage bullying by coming to the defense of the victim, interrupting the bullying, or reassuring and reaffirming the victim (Salmivalli, 2001). In many respects, the onlooking students have more influence over the bullying behavior than victims do, and, in some cases, more influence than the students who are bullying. Thus, the social cognitive framework underlying onlooking behaviors are key to bully prevention and intervention.

Key participants in peer bullying are the supervising adults who are vested with the responsibility of enforcing behavioral rules. Because most bullying occurs between classmates, much of the research has appropriately investigated the role of teachers who supervise peer behavior at school (Hanish, Kochenderfer-Ladd, Fabes, Martin, & Denning, 2004; Salmivalli, Lagerspetz, Bjorkqvist, Osterman, & Kaukiainen, 1996). There is substantial evidence that teachers are prone to minimize bullying when they observe it, believing that the aggressive acts were normal child-hood horseplay or that they were harmless (Stephenson & Smith, 1989). Perhaps as a result, teachers have been repeatedly shown to underrespond to bullying when it does occur, and to be ineffective when they do respond (Boulton & Underwood, 1992; Craig, Henderson, & Murphy, 2000; Craig & Pepler, 1997; Craig, Pepler, & Atlas, 2000, Olweus, 1991). Most important, teachers generally do not realize that they have overlooked so many incidents of bullying, and so are unaware of their ineffectiveness (Pepler et al., 1994).

Parents rarely witness bullying incidents themselves, and so rely on the second-hand reports of their children, other children, or teachers for their understanding of what has occurred. Still, there is substantial evidence that parental values and parenting practices hold great influence over the occurrence of bullying. In this respect, parents represent "shadow participants" in bullying incidents, rarely present but frequently shaping the occurrence through messages that they conveyed to their children in advance of the event and after it has occurred. For example, harsh and rejecting parents increase the risk that their child will behave in coercive, aggressive ways toward their peers (Olweus, 1993b, 1997a). Parents who model frequent physical aggression in the home, and particularly those who use physically aggressive discipline with their children, are more likely to have children who bully (Loeber & Dishion, 1984). Indeed, there is longitudinal evidence that participation in bullying is transmitted across generations when parents who bullied others during their own childhood encourage, prompt, or permit their children to bully (Farrington, 1993; Eron & Huesmann, 1990). Conversely, other evidence suggests that children who are bullied tend to have parents who are overly supportive and predispose them to acquiesce in the face of bullying (Baldry & Farrington, 2000). When bullying is prevalent within a school, some parents may insist that teachers intervene to stop bullying when their child is the victim, whereas other parents resent teachers' interventions if their child is bullying. Consequently, Olweus and Limber (1999) have emphasized the importance of parental participation in bullying prevention programs both to increase parental awareness of bullying and to engage families in confronting bullying when it occurs and protecting children who are bullied. Parent components of bullying interventions act to create a common voice among families so that schools are supported in taking planned and thoughtful actions to confront bullying.

A SOCIAL-COGNITIVE MODEL OF PEER BULLYING

This chapter's cognitive-behavioral model of peer bullying builds on Patterson's (1982) model of social coercion. Unprovoked, a bullying child aggresses against the victim, making either an explicit demand ("Give me the swing") or an implicit one ("Move out of my way"). Each time the victim resists, the bullying child escalates the aggression, talking louder, pushing harder, or saying meaner taunts. Left uninterrupted, the bullied child eventually concedes, and the concession acts to reinforce the bullying child's aggression and increases the likelihood that the aggression will recur. Moreover, if the concession stops the bullying, "conceding" is reinforced for the victims who learn that their humiliation and pain is lessened by giving in quickly.

Still, this cycle of coercion occurs within a larger social-ecological framework: The bullying child's aggression is also reinforced by the increased prestige and respect it garners from onlooking peers (Pellegrini et al., 1999; Rodkin, 2004), and by the sense of power and triumph that occurs. Alternatively, the bullying child's aggression could be punished by the disciplinary intervention of a supervising adult, or by the taunts and assaults of friends coming to the defense of the victim. Any resistance on the part of the bullied child could be punished by the taunts and assaults of onlooking peers, or could be reinforced by reassuring comments or active defense of supportive peer friends.

The influence of settings and contexts is also critical. The bullying child's aggression is more likely to occur in situations in which there are no apparent supervisors or friends to come to the defense of the victim. Similarly, the onlookers are more likely to encourage or tacitly permit bullying in situations where they are quite certain that the bullying will be uninterrupted and unobserved. Even more broadly, the bullying child's aggression is more likely to occur if the child's parents tacitly accept or encourage the use of peer aggression, and have modeled coercive interactions for the child at home.

The social-cognitive perceptions of all participants in bullying are as critical to this model as are the aggressive behaviors, because the perceptions of participants serve to perpetuate and escalate bullying incidents (Swearer & Cary, 2003). Within a social cognitive framework, the cognitive distortions of children when they are bullying include magnification (e.g., "It's only in fun"), emotional reasoning (e.g., "Kids who act so nerdy deserve to be picked on"), personalization (e.g., "He's got to learn not to snitch on me"), or minimization (e.g., "Everybody gets picked on; she has to learn to take it"). Some distortions of onlooking children who encourage bullying are similar to those of bullying children, including emotional reasoning (e.g., "Kids like that bring it on themselves") and minimization (e.g., "It's only teasing; it's not that big a deal"). In addition, the common distortions of onlooking children may reflect a sense of powerlessness, including overgeneralization (e.g., "I'll be next if I step in") or selective abstraction (e.g., "I can't stop it" or "They won't do what I say"). Shifting these cognitive distortions is a key component of redirecting the onlookers' behavior so that they confront and discourage bullying. Finally, the distortions of children who are bullied reflect their lack of power, including all-or-nothing thinking (e.g., "Bullying is never going to stop"), minimization (e.g., "It's not that bad—I can tough it out"), and magnification ("This is awful; I would rather die").

Adults, too, engage in cognitive self-statements that distort their response to bullying incidents. For example, the cognitive distortions of teachers who fail to interrupt bullying include minimizations (e.g., "Fourth graders act like this; it's not that bad"), emotional reasoning (e.g., "She's got to learn to handle herself with other kids"), and personalizing (e.g., "She brings it on herself; the kids don't like her whining"). Parents of children who bully may convince themselves that their children's behavior is justified (e.g., "If he hit her, she probably did something to deserve it" or "Other kids pick on him all the time, and nobody steps in to stop it") or is normal childhood play (e.g., "Everyone gets teased when they're a kid; that kid has to learn to take it").

Applying a traditional cognitive-behavioral model of change, interventions to interrupt this coercive cycle of bullying must target the cognitive distortions that precede or accompany bullying behaviors, in addition to the aggressive acts. In particular, cognitive restructuring must be an integral component of treatment strategies to reduce bullying so that dysfunctional cognitions are reduced in frequency while functional cognitions take their place. Students, teachers, and parents need to examine their beliefs and cognitions about bullying and then work toward modifying negative beliefs and distorted cognitions about the instrumentality of bullying behaviors. These cognitive distortions can perpetuate the cycle of bullying, especially if the participants and onlookers are not confronted and do change their beliefs about the role of bullying.

ASSESSMENT OF BULLYING AND COERCION

Demands that schools take action to stop peer bullying are equally likely to be made when specific bullying incidents have come to the notice of school or community leaders, or when local or national media stories have heightened concerns about bullying. In either event, it is critically important that the assessment describe the nature and frequency of peer bullying incidents as these are perceived by the children who participate in them; capture the children's social-cognitive perceptions of bullying incidents that occurred; describe the consequences of bullying as these were experienced by children in the peer group; and identify the setting events within the school and community that facilitate bullying behaviors. A multiple-method, multiple-informant approach in assessing bullying is the best approach (Espelage & Swearer, 2003). Given the central importance of children's perceptions within the coercive cycle of bullying, much of important information will be drawn from children's reports and descriptions.

Child Surveys

Children are the most knowledgeable informants about bullying that is occurring within their peer group. They are more likely than supervising adults to be present when bullying incidents occur, and they are more intimately aware of the cognitive behaviors (attitudes, beliefs, thoughts) that cooccur with the overt bullying behaviors. Specific information that is needed to prepare for bullying interventions includes child descriptions of (1) whether they have bullied other children or been bullied by other children within the recent past; (2) the likely times and places when bullying occurs in their class or school; (3) whether their classmates are likely to stick up for them if someone tries to bully them; (4) how likely it is that a teacher or other adult will intervene in the event that someone tries to bully them; and (5) whether the teachers' attempts to stop bullying are usually successful or unsuccessful.

The most efficient and effective way to gather this information is to collect systematic written surveys from all children in the class or school, and examples of bullying surveys are common throughout the literature (Espelage, Bosworth, & Simon, 2001; Olweus, 1989; Rigby & Slee, 1999; Solberg & Olweus, 2003; Swearer & Cary, 2003). The most widely used survey worldwide is the *Olweus Bully/Victim Questionnaire* (Olweus, 1989) and this survey has been used to estimate prevalence rates of school bullying (Solberg & Olweus, 2003). Surveys query students directly about how often they engaged in bullying behaviors or were bullied over a specified time period, the locations where bullying occurs, who participated in bullying, how school personnel responded, and attitudes toward bullying. Most bullying surveys are anonymous, but when children write their names on the surveys, extraordinary measures should be taken to ensure their confidentiality so that their comments do not become the basis for future coercion or retaliation.

An alternative to the use of longer surveys to assess bullying is the use of self-report scales. Self-report scales are typically shorter in length (Espelage, Holt, & Henkel, 2003) and also query students about their behavior during a specified time period (e.g., past 30 days; Reynolds, 2003). Scales typically do not include a definition of bullying and instead ask respondents to rate specific behaviors that are reflective of bullying or of being bullied. Whether a school chooses to use survey methodology or self-report scales largely depends on the specific questions that the school has.

A special challenge posed by asking children about bullying is that they cannot always differentiate between bullying and other intentionally mean aggressive behaviors. In middle schools, it is usually sufficient to provide children with a clear definition of bullying, explain how bullying differs from other forms of peer aggression, and briefly discuss a few examples of "bullying" and "not bullying" (Olweus, 1989; Swearer & Doll, 2001). In elementary schools, an alternative strategy is to read one or two storybooks about bullying to the class, and link the bullying survey back to the story (i.e., Who in the class has had someone pick on them over and over and over again, like Marylou? Have you ever been like Lynell and picked on someone else over and over and over again? Do those things ever happen in this class? And so on …). Even then, it is important to recognize that children's descriptions of bullying incidents may be confounded with reports of other types of peer conflicts, leading to an overestimation in the prevalence of bullying within a peer group.

Whenever assessments rely on children's reports, questions are raised about the reliability of their information. This is especially important in bullying assessments, where there may be little or no confirmatory information, because many of the incidents that children describe occur outside the notice of adults. The reliability of child reports is heightened when their perceptions are aggregated across all children within a classroom or school. In fact, children's aggregated descriptions of peers' social adjustment have been repeatedly found to be consistent, stable over time, and highly predictive of important life outcomes such as completing school or serving successfully in the military (Barclay, 1992; Gresham, 1986). Children's reports are also more reliable when the questions are clear and unambiguous and phrased in language that is developmentally appropriate. Using a common response format throughout the survey (e.g., Yes, Sometimes, No) makes it easier for children to describe their perceptions accurately. Finally, children are more likely to answer honestly and carefully if they are told in advance, why the information is being gathered, what will be done with it, how their privacy will be protected, and whether they will find out the results.

Peer Reports

It is not necessary to know the identities of specific children who are bullying or being bullied in order to intervene effectively. In fact, if there is not a culture of confidentiality around the assessment of bullying, children are less likely to be honest in their appraisal of the problem. Because bullying incidents emerge out of the larger peer context, it can be counterproductive to focus intervention efforts only on those children who are presently involved when the participants in bullying can shift and change across time. There will be cases, however, when schools will be interested in identifying the specific children who are bullying and being bullied. In this case, the best assessment strategy to use is sociometric nomination, in which children are asked to list classmates who frequently bully or are bullied (Boulton, 1997). Using these lists, children who receive a disproportionately large number of nominations for either role can be selected for focused intervention. Still, sociometric assessment's requirement that children evaluate their classmates can be controversial in school districts (Bierman & McCauley, 1987; Cook & Iverson, 1993; Crick & Ladd, 1989). Despite convincing evidence to the contrary, critics worry that sociometric nominations can cause children to view certain peers more negatively and completing nominations violates school norms prohibiting derogatory comments about classmates (Bell-Dolan, Foster, & Sikora, 1989; Deno, Mirkin, Robinson, & Evans, 1980). In this event, self-nominations have also been used to identify participants in bullying.

Adult Informants

Data also may be collected from parents and school staff about their perceptions of school bullying. The advantage of assessing adult perceptions and beliefs about bullying is that adults hold decision-making power and directly influence the school milieu. Additionally, data collected from parents and school staff can be compared with student data. Often these comparisons across informants provide useful information that can be targeted for prevention and intervention efforts. This multi-modal approach to the assessment of bullying makes intuitive sense given a social-ecological conceptualization of the phenomenon. Bullying affects the individual, the peer group, the school, the family, the community, and society at large. Given the pervasive impact of bullying, it stands to reason that the most effective assessment will be multi-informant and multimodal.

COGNITIVE-BEHAVIORAL INTERVENTIONS FOR BULLYING

For most of the problems discussed in this book, cognitive-behavioral interventions can be delivered alternatively in home, school, or community settings. However, interventions to interrupt and confront peer bullying are almost always centered within school settings because bullying is a disturbance in peer interactions, and schools offer the largest, naturally occurring peer group. Still, effective bullying interventions incorporate home and community components, because bullying activities can occur outside of school grounds even when the dynamics of bullying are supported by the school-centered peer group. Consequently, the intervention programs discussed here are comprehensive bullying programs that address bullying behaviors and the cognitions underlying these in school settings, while integrating home and community into the intervention.

The Olweus Bullying Prevention Program (Olweus & Limber,1999) confronts peer bullying by strengthening the supervision of children who bully; implementing consistent, nonhostile discipline for children who bully; decreasing social isolation among children who are targeted; and enlisting student and adult bystanders in confronting bullying when it occurs. Implementation begins with the distribution of the *Olweus BullyVictim Questionnaire* to determine the nature, prevalence, and locations of bullying at a school. Simultaneously, the school forms a Bullying Prevention Coordinating Committee to examine the survey data and to coordinate the program. Survey data almost always refutes widely held adult beliefs by demonstrating that bullying is a significant problem in the school. Given this new understanding, the coordinating committee defines schoolwide rules against bullying, and establishes a coordinated system of supervising students to interrupt bullying on school grounds. All members of the school staff, including nonteaching staff, are then trained to enforce the rules and confront bullying. More important, the training is supported with periodic staff discussion groups that challenge prevailing cognitions that minimize and enable bullying (e.g., "Kids are like this") and replace them with more accurate cognitions that support assertive actions to prevent bullying (e.g., "Bullying must be stopped" and "No child should be treated this way"). Similar meetings are held with parents to actively engage their cooperation with bullying prevention efforts by reinforcing accurate understandings of bullying (e.g., "Bullying cannot be allowed in my child's school"). Finally, classroom interventions include reinforcing school-wide rules against bullying and encouraging prosocial norms and behavior. Regular classroom meetings with students increase their knowledge about bullying and encourage empathy, reframing student cognitions about bullying (e.g., "Bullying is a big deal" and "I can stop bullying when I see it"). The end result is that children who bully receive consistent, nonhostile correction and victims of bullying are provided with protection and support from multiple sources within the school—their teachers, peers, and families.

The Olweus Bullying Prevention Program has been identified as a "Blueprint for Violence Prevention" by the Center for the Study and Prevention of Violence and as an Exemplary Program by the Center for Substance Abuse Prevention. In a quasi-experimental study of 2,500 children in Bergen, Norway, the *Olweus Bullying*

Prevention Program resulted in 50–70% reductions of bullying and victimization and increases in school satisfaction (Olweus, 1993b, 1994). A second study replicated the program with 6,388 4th through 6th graders in South Carolina and found reductions in self-reported bullying of approximately 25% (Melton et al., 1998).

Bully Busters (Horne, Bartolomucci, & Newman-Carlson, 2003) is a classroom-administered intervention program that addresses bullying from kindergarten to middle school. Two program manuals (K–5 and 6–8) help teachers and students recognize the antecedents, behaviors, and consequences in the bullying cycle. More important, the program guides students to replace negative thoughts about bullies (e.g., "You are a nerd") with positive alternatives, to plan ways to stop bullying when they see it, and to differentiate between harassment situations that they can handle themselves and those that they cannot (e.g., "I need this much help from others"). Other cognitive-behavioral components of *Bully Busters* include anger management, conflict resolution, affective education, empathy training, cognitive retraining, social skills training, and problem-solving skills training. Activities for students are interspersed with chapters for classroom teachers that describe bullying dynamics and prompt them toward more accurate and effective self-statements about bullying intervention. *Bully Busters'* strengths are that it addresses the social ecology in which bullying behaviors occur and the manuals are well written, easy to use, and easy to implement (Horne, Orpinas, Newman-Carlson, & Bartolomucci, 2004).

Given the individualized nature of the *Bully Busters* program, and the fact that it is relatively new, there are fewer outcome studies documenting its effectiveness. In one elementary school, after *Bully Busters* was implemented, there was a 40% reduction in mean scores for aggression and a 19% reduction in mean scores for victimization among kindergarten through 2nd-grade students and a 23% reduction in mean scores for victimization among students in 3rd through 5th grades (Orpinas, Horne & Staniszewski, 2003). In another study, *Bully Busters* was found to be an effective intervention for increasing teachers' knowledge and use of bullying intervention techniques and for reducing the amount of bullying in classrooms (Newman-Carlson & Horne, 2004).

Intervention with identified bullies or bullied children presents a particular challenge because any actions taken must protect the bullied student without prompting bullies to retaliate and further punish the victim. To prevent retaliation, Maines and Robinson's (1998) *No Blame Approach to Bully Prevention* works to induce empathy for the victim on the part of the onlookers and the bully. Once a bullying interaction has been identified in a classroom, the adult meets first with the bullied child to describe fully the bullying problem, who is involved, and the impact that the bullying has had on the child's daily life. Next, the bullied child communicates a story about the bullying through a written note, picture, or film. Then, and without the victim being present, adults meet with a small group of peers including the identified bullies and onlookers to discuss the bullying. They read the victim's note, talk about the tragic impact of the bullying on the victim's life, and ask the group to identify what they will do to stop the bullying. *No Blame* meetings are especially potent in replacing onlookers' distorted cognitions (e.g., "It's not that big a deal") with more accurate ones and in enlisting the peer group as allies of the bullied student. Moreover, the work that they undertake to present their story to classmates similarly helps bullied children reframe their cognitive self-statements (e.g., "Bullying is never going to stop") to be more accurate and more empowering. *'No Blame'* meetings are sufficient to stop the bullying in 60% of all cases, by sensitizing the surrounding peer group to the serious harm that they are doing (Maines & Robinson, 1998).

IMPLICATIONS AND APPLICATIONS TO THE SCHOOL SETTING

Left uninterrupted, peer bullying presents a significant problem for children in most North American schools. Consequently, most schools will benefit from school-wide intervention that targets all participants in bullying—onlooking peers, supervising adults, parents, and the children who bully or are bullied. A major focus must be on confronting and correcting the cognitive distortions that act to enable and maintain bullying, and replacing these with a systemwide understanding that peer bullying is destructive and cannot be tolerated. The three programs described here have some evidence of effectiveness in interrupting and reframing the bullying climate of a school and, ultimately, of reducing the prevalence of bullying among children. In every case, however, these manualized programs must be adjusted to the unique social ecology that has emerged in each school. As a result, it will be critically important to monitor the prevalence of bullying within each building and in response to the interventions that are implemented.

TWO CASE EXAMPLES

Individual Example

A 4th grader in an orthodox Hebrew day school, Avi was the target of constant bullying on the bus ride home each afternoon. Three older students would hide his books, tear his homework, "accidentally" spit on him, and, on one occasion, had thrown his hat and gloves out the window of the bus. It was this last incident that prompted Avi's parents to meet with the principal and demand that the mistreatment be stopped. The principal's first impulse was to suspend the older boys, but Avi protested loudly, insisting that the discipline would only make his situation worse. Then, the school counselor conducted a broad assessment of the conditions that were fostering the bullying and subsequently used the *No Blame Approach* (Maines & Robinson, 1998) to reshape the peer group's understanding of the bullying and stop its escalation.

Conversations with other children who rode the bus confirmed that Avi's victimization was severe and daily, and that three 6th-grade boys were the bullies. Once the children arrived at school, supervision was close and constant and there was little opportunity for the bullying to continue in the cafeteria, classrooms, or playground. Asked why they didn't come to Avi's defense, the children explained that he became very angry and lashed out at everyone on the bus, and they were afraid of being hurt themselves, either by the older boys or by Avi. Sometimes, they said,

Avi seemed to deserve his fate. He often tattled on the 6th graders to the Rabbi, the school's religious leader, and then they were kept in from recess or lost other privileges as a result. It was hard to feel sympathetic for Avi. Frequent onlooker coverants were "Avi brings it on himself" and "There's nothing we can do to stop it."

Avi was a reluctant participant in the counselor's plans. He told her that there was not much either of them could do to stop the bullying and that he expected it to continue until he left the school at the end of 8th grade. He had no clear explanation for why the 6th graders were assaulting him, except that they had a lot of fun at his expense. He begged her not to make it worse. Avi blamed the bullying for the fact that he had few other friends in school because "I'm a dangerous kid to be friends with" and reported that he spent most of recess playing alone. The best plan, he explained, was to not quite finish his work during the morning, so that he could stay inside during the lunch recess to finish it up. Avi's cognitive behaviors that shaped his response to the bullying were, "This is never going to stop," "No one's on my side," and "I can't do anything about it."

A few teachers at the day school had heard that Avi was picked on but were unaware of the extent of the bullying. Avi's own teacher described him as very bright but socially awkward student who often offended other children with his comments and was difficult to get to know. She was unaware that he was bullied by older students, and initially suggested that he had exaggerated the problem. Her dominant cognition was, "Avi has to learn to get along with the other kids." Finally, an important participant in Avi's bullying was the Rabbi, whose disciplinary actions angered the older boys and led them to feel justified in paying Avi back. He was unaware that payback was happening whenever he took action against the bullying students.

Following the *No Blame Approach*, the counselor first helped Avi write a letter to his classmates, describing how he felt and what he was thinking when the bullying was occurring. This was hard for Avi, because he had focused his attention on the injustices committed by the older boys and on retaliating against them in numerous small ways, tattling and picking at them when he could. In writing his letter, Avi had to think, instead, about how he was feeling and what he was thinking. This prompted him to reexamine the logic underlying some of his hopelessness: Was there really nothing that he could do to stop the bullying? Were none of the other students sympathetic to him? With the counselor's assistance, Avi made a plan to substitute useful cognitions for his maladaptive ones: When the older boys began to pick on him, he would look around the bus to see if anyone looked sympathetic, and would move to sit next to them. When he started to think that no one was on his side, he would substitute, "Other kids hate bullying, too." In addition, Avi made a list of things he might do to interrupt the bullying: (1) keeping all of his papers and loose objects zipped inside his backpack; (2) sitting in the front seat of the bus, next to the driver; (3) stop reporting the three boys to the Rabbi, so they wouldn't have an excuse to retaliate; and (4) acting friendly to other students on the bus, so he could be part of a group.

Next, the counselor met with a group of 10 students, including the bullying students and several bystanders. She explained that Avi had a problem with the bullies, and, using his letter, described his desperation and his sense of hopelessness.

In a matter-of-fact way, she said that she was not interested in blaming anyone for the bullying but she knew that the group could make it stop. On a chart tablet, she helped the group list their ideas for helping that included sitting next to Avi, helping him get his things back, or telling the 6th graders to stop. The group's discussion challenged their cognitive explanations for Avi's bullying, substituting "We are responsible for helping Avi" and "Avi doesn't deserve to be treated like this."

Finally, the counselor and Rabbi met together with the school's teachers to create a bully prevention plan. After reliving some of their own experiences with bullying when they were children, the teachers came to understand that victims were rarely to blame for being picked on. Instead, they wrote a school rule prohibiting bullying and made plans to teach a unit on bullying in each classroom. At the end of the units, they would announce their intention to stop bullying whenever they were told about it. In essence, the teacher meeting changed their cognitive response to bullying to "Bullying is never okay" and "Teachers are responsible for stopping bullying."

School Example

Staff at a mid-sized middle school realized that there were a number of students who were experiencing problems with bullying. Students would come to the counseling office and complain about being bullied. The counseling staff noted that the students who were consistently bullied would state, "There's nothing anyone can do" and "If I say anything the bullying will just get worse." The administrative staff responded by placing the bullies in in-school suspension or suspending them. The bullies would state, "I don't care, go ahead and suspend me." The counseling staff also responded to the needs of bullied students by holding support groups for these students. However, over time, the school personnel collectively realized that these interventions were ineffective.

The school decided to address bullying by participating in a 5-year longitudinal research project in partnership with a local university. Surveys describing the prevalence and nature of bullying in the school were collected every spring, and the researchers provided yearly feedback to the school. After the first year's survey, the school staff seemed disinterested in the feedback, making comments such as, "Isn't bullying just a normal part of growing up?" and "If I have to do one more program, forget it!" After the second year's survey, the staff seemed a bit more interested and invested. By the third year, school staff had become very involved in bullying prevention.

The survey data held important surprises for the school. It became apparent that the earlier support groups for victims also had included bully-victims because this school had a high proportion of students who both bullied others and were bullied themselves. Moreover, a subset of bullies had very high depression ratings. There was a discrepancy between students and teachers in terms of their knowledge about bullying in the school. Finally, the school discovered that bullying occurred most frequently in the hallways. These findings then prompted several changes in school policies and practices. Children who bullied were screened out of group treatment. Then, bullying children were no longer automatically suspended but, instead, were referred for individual therapy to address any underlying emotional distress. Hallway monitors were added to limit opportunities for bullying during class breaks. Finally, twice-yearly classroom presentations confronted teachers and students with the myths and distortions about bullying, and provided more accurate and useful information about ways to interrupt bullying when it occurred. The subsequent 2 years showed a reduction in bullying and office referrals. Additionally, the staff became energized about the issue and this level of enthusiasm affected both the students and the parents. The school became a place where bullying was not tolerated and when it did occur, interventions were data-based and compassionate.

SUMMARY

The accumulated research on peer bullying has established that bullying is a prevalent and destructive childhood social behavior. Intervening to stop bullying is complicated by popular beliefs that locate responsibility for coping with bullying on the shoulders of the children who are bullied. In contrast, careful examinations of bullying dynamics show that victims are the least powerful participants in peer bullying interactions, and that responsibility for interrupting and confronting bullying children must lie with supervising adults and onlooking peers. Teachers, classmates, friends, and family can be powerful allies in schoolwide efforts to reduce bullying, once they are convinced that bullying is a problem, recognize the actions they can take to interrupt it, and understand the importance of their participation. That is why identifying, confronting, and correcting the cognitive distortions that enable peer bullying is an essential component of any antibullying intervention. In particular, schoolwide cognitive-behavioral interventions are especially well suited for addressing school bullying because these address the prevalent cognitive distortions that perpetuate bullying in addition to altering the immediate contingencies that reward or discourage bullying behaviors. Their impact will be magnified when these interventions incorporate regular schoolwide assessment to track changes in the prevalence of bullying and identify unique conditions in the school's social ecology to promote or discourage bullying. Over time, and with careful and deliberate efforts, schools can become bully-free zones.

REFERENCES

Baldry, A. C., & Farrington, D. P. (2000). Bullies and delinquents: Personal characteristics and parental styles. *Journal of Community and Applied Social Psychology, 10,* 17–31.

Barclay, J. R. (1992). Sociometry, temperament and school psychology. In T. R. Kratochwill, S. N. Elliott, & M. Gettinger (Eds.), *Advances in School Psychology, Vol. VIII.* Hillsdale, NJ: Lawrence Erlbaum Associates.

Batsche, G. M., & Knoff, H. M. (1994). Bullies and their victims: Understanding a pervasive problem in the schools. *School Psychology Review, 23,* 165–174.

Bell-Dolan, D. J., Foster, S. L., & Sikora, D. M. (1989). Effects of sociometric testing on children's behavior and loneliness in school. *Developmental Psychology, 25,* 306–311.

Bierman, K. L., & McCauley, E. (1987). Children's descriptions of their peer interactions: Useful information for clinical child assessment. *Journal of Clinical Child Psychology, 16,* 9–18.

Boulton, M. J. (1997). Teachers' views on bullying: Definitions, attitudes, and ability to cope. *British Journal of Educational Psychology, 67,* 223–233.

Boulton, M. J., & Underwood, K. (1992). Bully/victim problems among middle school children. *British Journal of Educational Psychology, 62,* 73–87.

Cairns, R. B., & Cairns, B. D. (2000). The natural history and developmental functions of aggression. In A. J. Sameroff, M. Lewis, & S. M. Miller, (Eds.), *Handbook of Developmental Psychopathology* (2nd Edition). New York: Kluwer Academic/Plenum Publishers.

Cook, G. R., & Iverson, A. M. (1993, April). *An investigation of parental non-consent in sociometric research.* A paper presented at the annual convention of the National Association of School Psychologists, Washington, DC.

Craig, W. M. (1998). The relationship among bullying, victimization, depression, anxiety and aggression in elementary school children. *Personality and Individual Differences, 24,* 123–130.

Craig, W. M., Henderson, K., & Murphy, J. G. (2000). Prospective teachers' attitudes toward bullying and victimization. *School Psychology International, 21,* 5–21.

Craig, W., & Pepler, D. J. (1997). Observations of bullying and victimization on the schoolyard. *Canadian Journal of School Psychology, 2,* 41–60.

Craig, W., Pepler, D., & Atlas, R. (2000). Observations of bullying in the playground and in the classroom. *School Psychology International, 21,* 22–36.

Crick, N. R. (2000). Forms of aggression. In W. Craig (Ed.), *Childhood social development: The essential readings.* Oxford: Blackwell Publishers.

Crick, N. R., Bigbee, M. A., & Howes, C. (1996). Gender differences in children's normative beliefs about aggression: How do I hurt thee? Let me count the ways. *Child Development, 67,* 1003–1014.

Crick, N. R., & Ladd, G. W. (1989). Nominator attrition: Does it affect the accuracy of children's sociometric classifications? *Merrill-Palmer Quarterly, 35,* 197–207.

Deno, S. L., Mirkin, P. K., Robinson, S., & Evans, P. (1980). *Relationships among classroom observations of social adjustment and sociometric ratings scales* (Research report #24). University of Minnesota: Institute for Research on Learning Disabilities.

Doll, B., Song, S., & Siemers, E. (2004). Classroom ecologies that support or discourage bullying. In D. Espelage and S. Swearer (Eds.), *A social-ecological perspective on bullying prevention and intervention in American schools* (pp. 161–184). Mahwah, NJ: Lawrence Erlbaum Associates.

Eron, L. D., & Huesmann, R. L. (1990). The stability of aggressive behavior—even onto the third generation. In M. Lewis & S. M. Miller (Eds.), *Handbook of developmental psychopathology* (pp. 147–156). New York: Plenum.

Espelage, D. L, Bosworth, K., & Simon, T. R. (2001). Short-term stability and prospective correlates of bullying in middle-school students: An examination of potential demographic, psychosocial and environmental influences. *Violence & Victims, 16,* 411–426.

Espelage, D. L., Holt, M. K., & Henkel, R. R. (2003). Examination of peer group contextual effects on aggressive behavior during early adolescence. *Child Development, 74,* 205–220.

Espelage, D. L., & Swearer, S. M. (2003). Research on school bullying and victimization: What have we learned and where do we go from here? *School Psychology Review, 32,* 365–383.

Farrington, D. P. (1993). Understanding and preventing bullying. In M. Tonry & N. Morris (Eds.), *Crime and Justice, Vol. 17.* Chicago: University of Chicago Press.

Forero, R., McLellan, L., Rissel, C., & Barman, A. (1999). Bullying behaviour and psychological health among school students in New South Wales, Australia: Cross-sectional survey. *British Medical Journal, 319,* 344–348.

Gresham, F. M. (1986). Conceptual issues in the assessment of social competence in children. In P. S. Strain, M. J. Guralnick, & H. M. Walker (Eds.), *Children's social behavior: Development, assessment and modification.* New York: Academic Press.

Hanish, L. D., Kochenderfer-Ladd, B., Fabes, R. A., Martin, C. L., & Denning, D. (2004). Bullying among young children: The influence of peers and teachers. In D. Espelage & S. Swearer (Eds.), *Bullying in American schools: A social-ecological perspective on prevention and intervention* (pp. 141–159). Mahwah, NJ: Lawrence Erlbaum Associates.

Hazler, R. J., Miller, D. L., Carney, J. V., & Green, S. (2001). Adult recognition of school bullying situations. *Educational Research, 43,* 133–146.

Hodges, E. V. E., & Perry, D. G. (1999). Personal and interpersonal antecedents and consequences of victimization by peers. *Journal of Personality and Social Psychology, 76,* 677–685.

Horne, A. M., Bartolomucci, C. L., & Newman-Carlson, D. (2003). *Bully busters: A teacher's manual for helping bullies, victims and bystanders* (*Grades* K–5). Champaign, IL: Research Press.

Horne, A. M., Orpinas, P., Newman-Carlson, D., & Bartolomucci, C. L. (2004). Elementary school bully busters program: Understanding why children bully and what to do about it. In D. Espelage & S. Swearer (Eds.), *Bullying in American schools: A social-ecological perspective on prevention and intervention* (pp. 297–325). Mahwah, NJ: Lawrence Erlbaum Associates.

Humphreys, A., & Smith, P. K. (1984). Rough and tumble in preschool and playground. In P. K. Smith (Ed.), *Play in animals and humans* (pp. 241–270). London: Basil Blackwell.

Kaltiala-Heino, R., Rimpela, M., Martunen, M., Rimpela, A., & Rantanen, P. (1999). Bullying, depression, and suicidal ideation in Finnish adolescents: School survey. *British Medical Journal, 319,* 348–351.

Kasen, S., Berenson, K., Cohen, P., & Johnson, J. G. (2004). The effects of school climate on changes in aggressive and other behaviors related to bullying. In D. Espelage & S. Swearer (Eds.), *Bullying in American schools: A social-ecological perspective on prevention and intervention* (pp. 187–210). Mahwah, NJ: Lawrence Erlbaum Associates.

Kendall, P. C. (1992). *Coping cat workbook.* Ardmore, PA: Workbook Publishing.

Kendall, P. C. (1994). Treating anxiety disorders in children: Results of a randomized clinical trial. *Journal of Consulting and Clinical Psychology, 62,* 100–110.

Kumpulainen, K., Rasanen, E., Entonen, I., Almqvist, F., Kresanov, K., Linna, S., Moilanen, I., Piha, J., Puura, K., & Tamminen, T. (1998). Bullying and psychiatric symptoms among elementary school-age children. *Child Abuse & Neglect, 22,* 705–717.

Loeber, R., & Dishion, T. J. (1984). Boys who fight at home and school: Family conditions influencing cross-setting consistency. *Journal of Consulting and Clinical Psychology, 52,* 759–768.

Maines, B., & Robinson, G. (1998). The no blame approach to bullying. In D. Shorrocks-Taylor (Ed.), *Directions in educational psychology* (pp. 281–295). London: Whurr.

Melton, G. B., Limber, S. P., Cunningham, P., Osgood, D. W., Chambers, J., Flerx, V., Henggeler, S., & Nation, M. (1998). *Violence Among Rural Youth.* Final Report. Washington, DC: U.S. Department of Justice, Office of Justice Programs, Office of Juvenile Justice and Delinquency Prevention.

Newman-Carlson, D., & Horne, A. M. (2004). Bully Busters: A psychoeducational intervention for reducing bullying behavior in middle school students. *Journal of Counseling & Development, 82,* 259–267.

Oliver, R., Hoover, J. H., & Hazler, R. (1994). The perceived roles of bullying in small-town Midwestern schools. *Journal of Counseling and Development, 72,* 416–420.

Olweus, D. (1989). *The Olweus Bully/Victim Questionnaire* [Mimeo]. HEMIL-senteret, Univesitetet I Bergen, Norway.

Olweus, D. (1991). Bully/victim problems among school children: Basic facts and effects of a school based intervention program. In I. Rubin & D. Pepler (Eds.), *The Development and Treatment of Childhood Aggression.* Hillsdale, NJ: Erlbaum.

Olweus, D. (1993a). Bullies on the playground: The role of victimization. In C. H. Hart (Ed.), *Children on playgrounds: Research perspectives and applications* (pp. 85–128). Albany: State University of New York.

Olweus, D. (1993b). *Bullying at school: What we know and what we can do.* Cambridge: Blackwell.

Olweus, D. (1994). Annotation: bullying at school: Basic facts and effects of a school-based intervention program. *Journal of Child Psychology and Psychiatry, 35,* 1171–1190.

Olweus, D. (1997a). Bully/victim problems in school: Knowledge base and an effective intervention program. *The Irish Journal of Psychology, 18,* 170–190.

Olweus, D. (1997b). Tackling peer victimization with a school-based intervention program. In D. P. Fry & K. Bjorkqvist (Eds.), *Cultural variation in conflict resolution: Alternatives to violence* (pp. 215–234). Mahway, NJ: Lawrence Erlbaum Associates.

Olweus, D., & Limber, S. (1999). The Bullying Prevention Program. In D.S. Elliott (Ed.), *Blueprints for violence prevention.* Boulder: Regents of the University of Colorado.

Orpinas, P., Horne, A. M., & Staniszewski, D. (2003). School bullying: Changing the problem by changing the school. *School Psychology Review, 32,* 431–444.

Patterson, G. R. (1982). *Coercive family process.* Eugene, OR: Castalia.

Pellegrini, A. D. (1993). Elementary-school children's rough and tumble play and social competence. *Developmental Psychology, 24,* 802–806.

Pellegrini, A. D. (2002a). Affiliative and aggressive dimensions of dominance and possible functions during early adolescence. *Aggression and Violent Behavior, 7,* 21–31.

Pellegrini, A. D. (2002b). Bullying and victimization in middle school: A dominance relations perspective. *Educational Psychologist, 37,* 151–163.

Pellegrini, A. D., & Bartini, M. (2001). Dominance in early adolescent boys: Affiliative and aggressive dimensions and possible functions. *Merrill-Palmer Quarterly, 47,* 142–163.

Pellegrini, A. D., Bartini, M., & Brooks, F. (1999). School bullies, victims and aggressive victims: Factors relations to group affiliation and victimization in early adolescence. *Journal of Educational Psychology, 91,* 216–224.

Pepler, D. J., Craig, W. M., Ziegler, S., & Charach, A. (1994). An evaluation of an anti-bullying intervention in Toronto schools. *Canadian Journal of Community Mental Health, 13,* 95–110.

Perry, D. G., Kusel, S. J., & Perry, L. C. (1988). Victims of peer aggression. *Developmental Psychology, 24,* 807–814.

Reynolds, W. M. (2003). *Reynolds Bully Victimization Scales for Schools manual.* San Antonio, TX: The Psychological Corporation.

Rigby, K., & Slee, P. (1999). Suicidal ideation among adolescent school children, involvement in bully-victim problems, and perceived social support. *Suicide & Life-Threatening Behavior, 29*(2), 119–130.

Rodkin, P. C. (2004). Peer ecologies of aggression and bullying. In D. Espelage and S. Swearer (Eds.), *Bullying in American schools: A social-ecological perspective on prevention and intervention* (pp. 87–106). Mahwah, NJ: Lawrence Erlbaum Associates.

Salmivalli, C. (2001). Peer-led intervention campaign against school bullying: Who considered it useful, who benefited? *Educational Research, 43,* 263–278.

Salmivalli, C., Lagerspetz, K., Bjorkqvist, K., Osterman, K., & Kaukiainen, A. (1996). Bullying as a group process: Participant roles and their relations to social status within the group. *Aggressive Behavior, 22,* 1–15.

Schwartz, D., McFayden-Ketchum, S., Dodge, K., Pettit, G. S., & Bates, J. E. (1999). Early behavior problems as a predictor of later peer group victimization. Moderators and mediators in the pathways of social risk. *Journal of Abnormal Child Psychology, 27,* 191–201.

Slee, P. T. (1995). Peer victimization and its relationship to depression among Australian primary school students. *Personality and Individual Differences, 18,* 57–62.

Smith, P. K., & Boulton, M. (1990). Rough and tumble play, aggression and dominance: perception and behavior in children's encounters. *Human Development, 33,* 271–282.

Solberg, M. E., & Olweus, D. (2003). Prevalence estimation of school bullying with the Olweus Bully/Victim questionnaire. *Aggressive Behavior, 29,* 239–268.

Stark, K. D., Kendall, P. C., McCarthy, M., Stafford, M., Barron, R., & Thomeer, M. (1996). *ACTION: A workbook for overcoming depression.* Ardmore, PA: Workbook Publishing.

Stephenson, P., & Smith, D. (1989). Bullying in the junior school. In D. P. Tattum & D. A. Lane (Eds.), *Bullying in schools.* Stoke on Trent: Trentham.

Swearer, S. M., & Cary, P. T. (2003). Perceptions and attitudes toward bullying in middle school youth: A developmental examination across the bully/victim continuum. *Journal of Applied School Psychology, 19,* 63–79.

Swearer, S. M., & Doll, B. (2001). Bullying in schools: An ecological framework. *Journal of Emotional Abuse, 2,* 7–23.

Swearer, S. M., Song, S. Y., Cary, P. T., Eagle, J. W., & Mickelson, W. T. (2001). Psychosocial correlates in bullying and victimization: The relationship between depression, anxiety, and bully/victim status. *Journal of Emotional Abuse, 2,* 95–121.

Walker, H. M., & Severson, H. (1992). *Systematic screening for behavior disorders.* Longmont, CO: Sopris Press.

11

Working with Angry and Aggressive Youth

RAY W. CHRISTNER, ROBERT D. FRIEDBERG & LAURA SHARP

Over the past decade, the world has become accustomed to seeing scenes of youth aggression and violence in the mainstream media such as the murder of a school principal, an intruder attacking a classroom, hostages held inside a school, or the massacre at Columbine High School. Events such as these have challenged our beliefs that children are safe at school. However, despite the powerful media coverage of violence in schools today, these events are actually rare. In fact, reports from the National School Safety Center (2001) show a decline in school homicide of 63% over the past 19 years.

Although schools generally remain safe from large-scale acts of violence, a more common and serious concern that schools face is handling students who present with extreme anger, disruptive behaviors, and concurrent aggression on a regular basis. We are not attempting to minimize the seriousness of homicides that occur within schools, but, instead, we are highlighting the seriousness of the ongoing anger and aggression in youth that is not often revealed to the public. Kaufman and colleagues (2000), in a report published by the U.S. Departments of Education and Justice, suggested that approximately 15% of high school students reported being involved in a physical altercation on school grounds within the past 30 days. Situations of verbal harassment, beatings on the school bus, disrespect to teachers, fights in the hallways, and so on, are more prominent and disturbing to the educational environment.

Notwithstanding the documentation of aggressive behavior found in the literature for many years, there has been an absence of clearly effective treatments for these severe behaviors (Kazdin, 1987). Recently, however, literature regarding evidence-based explanations and treatments for aggressive and antisocial behaviors has become more prevalent (see Larson & Lochman, 2002; Lochman, Whidby, & FitzGerald, 2000; Walker, Ramsey, & Gresham, 2004). In this chapter, we review current explanations for aggressive behaviors in youth, with the primary focus being on social cognitive theory, in order to assist school-based clinicians to formulate case conceptualizations for individual students. From this foundation, we will further discuss cognitive-behavioral assessment and intervention techniques, with specific focus on those easily applied in educational settings.

TYPES OF AGGRESSIVE BEHAVIORS

For the most part, researchers have viewed aggression as hostile, injurious, or destructive behavior directed at another person (Kendrick, Neuburg, & Cialdini, 1999). Although aggression is thought of as intentional behavior aimed at hurting others (Baron & Richardson, 1994), in early childhood years, mild to moderate levels of aggressive or oppositional behaviors are common (e.g., a 3-year-old who hits another child for taking away his toy). However, the majority of children develop the necessary self-regulation skills to control impulsive behaviors and emotions appropriately, as they progress through early elementary school years (Larson & Lochman, 2002). Yet, there are others who do not.

Although many people believe that children and adolescents who display aggressive behavior have a diagnosed mental health condition, many do not, and, instead, their aggressive behaviors are in response to environmental stressors or life events. For instance, a 10-year-old student who had minimal behavioral difficulties at school, on finding out his parents were separating, began displaying aggressive and disruptive behaviors with peers and adults. His behaviors are not the result of a diagnosable condition, but instead, involve adjustment to a specific situation. By contrast, those children and adolescents who continually exhibit high levels of anger and aggression may in fact have a diagnosable disorder, with the most common disorders including Conduct Disorder (CD), Oppositional Defiant Disorder (ODD), and Intermittent Explosive Disorder. Likewise, many youth have comorbid conditions such as Attention-Deficit/Hyperactivity Disorder (ADHD), Learning Disorders, speech and language problems, Anxiety Disorders, and Mood Disorders (Bloomquist, 1996; Kendall, 2000).

Regardless of the diagnostic label, before treating youth displaying disruptive or aggressive behaviors, it is essential to understand the underlying framework for such behaviors. In an early attempt to conceptualize aggression, Dollard, Doob, Miller, Mowrer, and Sears (1939) noted that aggressive acts arose out of negative emotion and they are designed to injure the person or object of aggression, which they termed *hostile aggression*. Kendrick and others (1999) described this as *emotional aggression*, and noted that the hurtful behaviors stem from angry feelings. An example of this may be the child who has his books knocked out of his hands accidentally at school, and as a result becomes angry and emotional, eventually lashing out at the other student. It is important to note, however, that not all aggression is hostile or emotionally based. In fact, some aggressive behaviors, referred to as *instrumental aggression*, are not designed to hurt another person. Instead, they are used to gain an external reward or accomplish some other goal (Larson & Lochman, 2002; Kendrick et al., 1999). An example of this would be the "schoolyard bully" who takes another child's lunch money. This child does not intend to injure his victim out of anger; he just wants the lunch money.

Dodge (1991) proposed an alternate theory of aggression in children and youth consisting of two additional types of aggression—*reactive aggression* and *proactive aggression*. Although Dodge cautioned that all aggressive behaviors have aspects that are both reactive and proactive, he distinguished between the two. *Reactive aggression* is an aggressive act that is emotionally driven, whereas *proactive aggression* involves an aggressive act that is instrumentally driven. Those students who are reactively aggressive tend to be easily provoked into angry and aggressive behavior, and consequently, their peers generally reject them. Dodge noted that reactive students are often hypervigilent for aggressive cues in their environments and frequently they misinterpret the intentions of others as being hostile. In contrast, students who are proactively aggressive are inclined to be bullies, and they display little emotion when behaving aggressively. Although these students also have peer difficulties, they oftentimes also show leadership qualities (Dodge).

Additionally, Crick and Grotpeter (1995) identified *relational aggression*, which involves "behaviors that are intended to significantly damage another's friendships or feelings of inclusion by the peer group" (p. 711). They noted that these children try to replace the lack of friendships with others by spreading gossip or rumors about them. Relationally aggressive children tend to engage in the same hostile attributional biases as those children who are physically aggressive and highly reactive to relationship distress.

THE NEED FOR EFFECTIVE INTERVENTIONS IN SCHOOLS

The need for effective interventions for children and the families of children with high levels of anger and aggression is evident. Prolonged and stable aggression is associated with the increased occurrence of substance abuse, delinquency, psychopathology, teenage pregnancy, academic failure, and escalating violent and antisocial behavior (Parker & Asher, 1987). For this reason, there is a need for emphasis on understanding aggression and developing effective intervention plans for dealing with aggression in the school setting.

Unfortunately, many of the current strategies employed in school settings lack effectiveness. With the increase in attention given to handling and preventing large-scale incidents of school violence, many schools have taken a "get tough" attitude, often consisting of "zero tolerance" toward aggressive behaviors. Although these types of "policy-based" programs may make parents and school staff feel something is being done, in reality, these programs do little to change behavior of children who have the tendency to be aggressive. Additionally, the effectiveness of these programs is further undermined when small offenses become part of the "zero tolerance" net (e.g., child being reprimanded for violating the school's weapons policy by bringing nail clippers to school).

In addition, one of the more common methods for handling aggressive students in schools involves punishment, such as reprimands and suspension. Punishment often sends an inappropriate message to aggressive children, in that it sets the example that the person with the "power" is in control. Given that aggressive youth are already striving for increased control and power, this may further reinforce their belief that control over others brings them power in situations. Of greater concern, however, is the fact that punishment does nothing to change behavior over time. In order for lasting changes to occur, students who are aggressive must learn through the modeling, teaching, and reinforcing of prosocial skills (Goldstein, Glick, & Gibbs, 1998).

In working within school settings, other commonly used techniques offered by school personnel are based on catharsis. These techniques are thought to help the student "get their aggression out" by using such methods as punching a pillow or using a stress ball. Interestingly, although many practitioners believe such methods reduce aggression, research exists that shows that the use of catharsis actually increases the levels of aggression in individuals using these methods (Goldstein et al., 1998).

REVIEW OF EFFECTIVE INTERVENTIONS PROGRAMS FOR SCHOOLS

Although a number of the popular approaches to handle aggressive behaviors in school are ineffective, there are a number of approaches that have been shown to effect change in children displaying aggressive behavior. We will focus on three primary programs grounded in cognitive-behavioral theory, including the Anger Coping Program, Social Problem Solving, and Parent Training Programs.

Anger Coping Program

Anger control training is a cognitive-behavioral treatment used with children and adolescents who have difficulty managing anger or aggressive behaviors. This training includes a set of procedures designed to restructure the individual's cognitive processes and develop self-control. This is accomplished by helping children change their appraisal of potential trigger events and by prompting them to use coping strategies, such as positive self-talk, self-instructions to relax and slow down before responding, and problem-solving strategies (Kazdin, 1994).

One such anger control-training program that has empirical support after rigorous evaluations of its use for school-aged children is the *Anger Coping Program* by Larson and Lochman (2002). This involves a group intervention for children ages 8 to 12 years who are experiencing anger and aggression problems. The program incorporates group activities for children with support from and education for parents and teachers. The *Anger Coping Program* has shown to have positive effects on children's aggressive behavior at home and at school (Larson & Lochman, 2002; Lochman, Burch, Curry, & Lamprom, 1984; Lochman, Coie, Underwood, & Terry, 1993). The program has also been shown to have positive effects on the social competency and social-cognitive skills of children who have participated in the program (Larson & Lochman, 2002). Controlled clinical research has demonstrated that this program reduces teacher-directed and parent-directed aggression, improves on-task behavior in the classroom, enhances participants' ability to be verbally assertive, and increases participants' social competency and academic achievement. The *Anger Control Program* also has been shown to produce a reduction in children's substance abuse (Larson & Lochman).

The program's effects on participants' social-cognitive processes have been maintained through a 3-year follow-up and its effects on behavior problems have been maintained through at least 1 year after completing the program. At a 3-year follow-up of boys who were involved in the group, it was found that the boys who were in the group showed lower levels of substance use, higher levels of self-esteem, and better social problem solving than boys who did not participate in the group (Lochman, 1992).

Social Problem Solving

Problem-solving skills training is another cognitively based technique shown to have success in reducing aggressive and antisocial behavior among children. Cognitive processes such as perceptions, self-statements, attributions, and problem-solving skills are central to behavior problems (Kazdin, 1994). This training involves the development of skills to address deficiencies and distortions in how the child perceives and approaches a social situation. Although there are many variations of problem-solving skills training, Kazdin (1994) identified characteristics that are shared among programs. The common characteristics include (1) emphasis on the process of how children approach situations rather than focusing on outcomes of situations; (2) children are taught to engage in step-by-step approaches to solve interpersonal problems; (3) treatment utilizes structured tasks involving games, academic activities, and stories; and (4) therapists play an active role in treatment by modeling, providing cues to prompt the use of skills, role-playing, and delivering feedback.

Social Problem Solving (SPS) is a type of problem-solving skills training that has been successful with children who display angry and aggressive behaviors. According to SPS theory, children display aggressive behaviors because they lack interpersonal cognitive problem-solving skills, such as brainstorming solutions, predicting the consequences, and linking causes to effects in interpersonal interactions. Without these skills, children are more likely to have social encounters that are frustrating to them, which may lead to misbehavior or aggression (Shure & Spivack, 1988). Shure and Spivack's *I Can Problem Solve* program is an example of a program designed to teach students how to generate possible solutions and how to consider the consequences of their actions. Through *SPS* programs, children also learn to use self-talk to consider how the other child might feel, what might happen next, and what else the children could do. Children who understand that behavior has causes and consequences, that people have feelings, and that there is more than one way to solve problems tend to have fewer behavior problems than those who merely react to the problem (Shure, 1994). Shure further noted that if children learn to solve typical everyday problems, they are less likely to become impulsive, insensitive, withdrawn, aggressive, or antisocial.

Parent Training Programs

Parent training programs are another effective way to treat dysfunctional angry or aggressive behavior in children and adolescents. In fact, parent training programs are one of the most widely used therapeutic interventions for families and children (Serketich & Dumas, 1996), with the most frequent application being with parents of disruptive and conduct disorder children and adolescents (Kazdin, 1994). Through parent training, parents meet with a clinician to learn behavior techniques used to alter the negative or dysfunctional behaviors that are the basis for the clinical referral (Kazdin).

Although there are many different parent-training models, Kazdin (1994) cited several common characteristics that exist among them. First, the intervention is conducted primarily with the parents, who then directly implement the procedures in the home. It is common for little or no direct intervention to occur between the clinician and the child. Second, the parents are trained to identify, define, and observe behaviors in new ways. Looking at specific behaviors of interest is essential for the delivery of consequences for evaluating if the program is achieving the desired goals. Third, intervention sessions cover social learning principles and procedures that are associated with them, including positive reinforcement (e.g., the use of social praise, tokens, or points for prosocial behavior), mild punishment (e.g., use of time-out from reinforcement, loss of privileges), negotiation, and contingency contracting. Parent training programs also use session time for parents to see how techniques are implemented, to practice using techniques, and to review the behavior change programs in the home.

Research has shown that parent-training programs are effective. Seretich and Dumas (1996), in a meta-analytic study, found that children whose parents participated in behavioral-based parenting training were better adjusted after the session than 80% of children whose parents did not participate. The effects of the parent training generalized fairly well to the children's classroom behaviors and the parents' personal adjustment. Parent training has also been found to have a positive effect on the behaviors of the children's siblings and measures of pathology, especially depression (Kazdin, 1996).

A popular parent-training program is Barkley's (1997) *Defiant Children* program, in which issues such as understanding why children behave inappropriately and how to increase compliance, chose disciplinary methods, improve school behavior, and increase positive interactions with children are addressed. Barkley identifies four main goals for his program. First, it is important to improve parental management skills and competence in dealing with child behavior problems. Next, parents must increase their knowledge of the causes of inappropriate childhood behavior and the concepts underlying the social learning of the behavior. This program specifically seeks to improve child compliance through the use of commands, directives, and rules provided by the parents. The final goal is for parents to increase family harmony by improving parental positive attention; providing clear guidelines, rules, and instruction; giving discipline in a timely and fair manner; and relying on principle-guided parenting behavior.

COGNITIVE-BEHAVIORAL CONCEPTUALIZATION OF ANGER AND AGGRESSION

Cognitive Distortions and Deficiencies

Kendall and his colleagues have indicated that children who display angry and aggressive behavior tend to display both cognitive distortions and cognitive deficiencies (Kendall & MacDonald, 1993). Cognitive distortions are information-processing errors that affect an individual's ability to gather information and assimilate that information into his or her existing repertoire (J. S. Beck, 1995). Thus, students transform incoming information to fit their preexisting notions. For example, a child who has been teased by peers is more likely to see a neutral situation of two children whispering as their talking about him or her. Because her existing schema is that children talk badly about her, she has gathered information from the situation that is easy to assimilate with his or her preexisting schema and has ignored other information in the situation or other explanations for the behavior of the other students. We find it helpful to consider distortions as dynamic thought processes that interact with the environment to shape thought content.

There are a number of cognitive distortions in which angry or aggressive children and adolescents may engage. A common cognitive error involves *dichotomous* or *all-or-nothing thinking*, in which there are no shades of gray in the student's absolutistic world. For instance, others are viewed as friends or foes, bastards or buddies, prey or predators. Another error involves hostile attributional bias and misinterpretation of unfairness, which is a type of *mental filtering*. With aggressive youth, negative attention is often drawn to any possibility of intentional slight, injustice, threat, or provocation. Because these students are using mental filters, their focus is on the negative or potentially aggressive aspects of the situation. Thus, these students jump to conclusions without thorough contemplation of all of the aspects of the situation. An example of this mental filtering would be Madeline, a 10-year-old student, who noticed another child using her pencil. Maladaptive mental filtering lead her to perceive the situation as a purposeful attempt to take her possession and hurt her rather than viewing it as the other child accidentally taking her pencil.

Emotional reasoning is another highly prevalent cognitive distortion seen in angry and aggressive children. With emotional reasoning, individuals base their thoughts and actions exclusively or predominantly on their emotional state (J. S. Beck, 1995). Consequently, they act impulsively and without much cognitive mediation. Essentially, youngsters are led astray by strong emotions (e.g., "If I am this angry, I must have been treated unjustly."). Finally, aggressive and angry children commonly have highly developed personal codes, imperatives, and rules, which take the shape of *rigidified should statements* (e.g., "No one should tell me what to do." "Parents should always give me what I want." "A good friend should obey and defer to me." "I should never let anyone get over on me."). These distorted personal views have a moralistic flavor to them, and when these personal rules are broken, youngsters become enraged and seek to punish transgressors.

As opposed to cognitive distortions, *cognitive deficiencies* refer to an individual's lack of the necessary skills or abilities in given situations (Kendall & MacDonald, 1993). Basically, in situations where the child must respond, he or she does not possess the skills needed (e.g., problem-solving skills, verbal skills) to handle situation. Take for example that case of C. J., a 9-year-old student. When a peer angers him, he is quick to push or hit the other student. His difficulties are not necessarily because of cognitive distortions, but, instead, reflect his hasty problem-solving style, so the focus was on teaching him problem-solving skills and self-monitoring rather than restructuring his thoughts. When a child has difficulty with problem solving such as trouble generating alternative solutions, deciding which solution is most appropriate in the situation, and actually implementing appropriate solutions, the clinician must use this information to tailor interventions in a way best suited to meet the child's needs (Kendall et al., 1992).

Social Learning Theory

Social Learning Theory (SLT), based on the work of Bandura (1973), provides valuable information in conceptualizing anger and aggression. Essentially, Bandura noted that individuals cognitively reflect on their behavior, create new behaviors, consider the consequences of past behaviors, and draw conclusions just by watching the behavior of others. Thus, children and adolescents can learn to use anger and aggression to cope with various situations just by observing, imitating, experiencing (both directly and indirectly), and rehearsing the angry and aggressive behaviors of others (Bandura, 1973).

Larson and Lochman (2002) indicated three main ways that individuals socially learn aggressive behaviors, which include (1) observational learning of live or media-based aggressive models, (2) direct experience of being rewarded for aggressive behavior, and (3) self-regulatory processes. With observational learning, individuals learn new behaviors through observing the behavior of others and how they are rewarded or punished for their actions. Behaviors that elicit favorable responses are kept in an individual's behavioral repertoire and those that are ineffective are discarded (Bandura 1973, 1983). Individuals also learn aggression through direct experiences, such as corporal punishment or physical abuse in the home, in which the child sees aggression used to control another person's behavior, to be powerful, to deal with stress and frustration, or to get one's needs met in other ways. Finally, SLT also stresses that self-regulatory processes affect aggressive behavior. Through self-regulation, children have the ability to select behaviors based on the consequences that they anticipate. Also, through self-monitoring, children can manage their behavior by examining consequences from their environment and internal consequences such as self-reward and self-punishment (Bandura, 1973).

Information Processing

Understanding the way in which children and adolescents process information is of further value in conceptualizing anger and aggression. Social Information Processing (SIP) emphasizes how individuals process information, store it in the short- and long-term memory, and make decisions based on the limits of information they can process (Goetz, Hall, & Fetsco, 1989). Commonly, SIP involves the use of six sequential cognitive operations in solving social problems. Children and adolescents who exhibit cognitive distortions or cognitive deficiencies in these cognitive operations tend to display maladaptive behaviors such as aggression.

The first operation is the *encoding*. Here an individual attempts to gather sensory information about an event. Those who are socially competent are often able to select the relevant cues from the environment and attend to them (Dodge, 1986). In contrast, those who are aggressive may primarily attend to only hostile cues, while minimizing attention on nonhostile cues (Larson & Lochman, 2002). Next is the *representation and interpretation phase*, in which the individual gives meaning to the encoded information and integrates it into his or her memory (Dodge, 1991). It is in this phase that cognitive distortions can alter an individual's perception of an event. Take for instance, Jonathan, a 12-year-old aggressive student. When walking through the hall, a classmate bumps into him. Although there was no intent, Jonathan scans the environment for aggressive cues and interprets the nonaggressive events as a "personal attack." Most students in Jonathan's situation would have noticed the awkward smile of the other student as apologetic, whereas Jonathan viewed the smile as the other student's way to show she is superior to him or happy that she knocked into him.

According to SIP, after interpreting the information, the individual moves on to *goal selection*, in which the individual selects a behavioral or affective outcome for the social situation (Crick & Dodge, 1994). Using the aforementioned situation, a nonaggressive student may choose a goal of making the other person feel better and getting on with his day. An aggressive student, by contrast, is likely to choose a defensive or aggressive goal.

The individual then moves on to the *response access or construction* step, where he or she must recall or generate possible responses to meet the desired goal. Those children who have a tendency to be aggressive often access or generate responses with an aggressive tone, such as cursing, yelling, pushing, or hitting. The fifth step involves the individual making a decision regarding which of the generated responses to choose, which is called the *response decision process*. Once he or she chooses a desired response, then he or she moves to the *behavior enactment process*, which involves acting out the chosen response (Dodge, 1985). In the *behavior enactment process*, the individual must have the skills necessary to carry out the actions. Often, even if the aggressive child chooses a nonaggressive response, he or she does not have the skills (i.e., verbal, social) to carry those actions out (Larson & Lochman, 2002). With our hallway example, if Jonathan chooses to respond by telling the other person to be more careful in the future, his statement may come across in a threatening manner because he does not have the necessary verbal and social skills to address the person in a neutral or helpful way.

Coercive Family Process

Although aggressive youth often are identified by their families as problematic, the children often reflect the dysfunction, conflict, and maladaptive processes within the family (Kazdin, 1994). Oftentimes, parents lack the skills to manage the child's inappropriate behavior effectively and they inadvertently end up reinforcing the child's coercive behaviors through a coercive family process (Larson & Lochman, 2002). Commonly, parents and children attempt to use negative behavior to control one another. As parents use commands, yelling, blaming, and criticism to try to control the child's behavior, the child in turn uses tantrums, yelling, blaming, and stubbornness in an effort to control the parent (Bloomquist, 1996). This conflict is usually resolved with either the parent or the child giving in, which reinforces both of them. One example would involve the parent giving a command, the child acting in a negative way, and the parent withdrawing the command. For instance, 5-year-old Olivia dropped her fork to the floor, and her mother directed her to pick up the fork. Olivia in turn responds by dropping to the floor, crying and screaming. Her mother then responds by picking up the fork, thus reinforcing Olivia's behavior. Another example would involve the parent giving a command, the child acting in a negative way, the parent acting in a more negative way, and the child complying. Using the example of Olivia, here her mother tells her to pick up the fork, and again Olivia drops to the floor and begins to cry and scream. In turn, her mother yells and smacks Olivia, resulting in Olivia complying and picking up the fork. Using these unhealthy approaches to resolve sets the stage for future problems.

COGNITIVE-BEHAVIORAL INTERVENTIONS

A number of cognitive and behavioral interventions are available for use when working with angry or aggressive students. However, before discussing specific techniques, it is important to note that effective cognitive-behavioral treatment of anger and aggression problems requires both *skill acquisition* as well as *skill application.* Simply put, children must be able to "show that they can" (Kendall et al., 1992). Most aggressive youngsters can easily acquire a basic understanding of anger management and problem-solving skills, but the pivotal process involves helping them apply these tools in a given situation. Thus, clinicians will need to be creative in finding ways to assist students in applying these techniques in the "heat of the moment." Several authors have described games and activities that are useful to achieve this within a counseling situation (see Feindler & Guttman, 1994; Kendall, 1988).

The programs listed earlier in this chapter (e.g., *Anger Coping Program*) provide a number of specific interventions for use with children and adolescents displaying aggressive behavior. However, a number of other strategies exist that are beneficial for working with angry and aggressive students. Although this chapter is not intended to provide a comprehensive review of all cognitive and behavioral strategies used with angry and aggressive students, we offer several examples here.

Self-Monitoring

Monitoring oneself through recording problematic situations, thoughts, feelings, and behaviors are pivotal skills to teach angry and aggressive children. Bloomquist and Schnell (2002) noted that "enabling children to increase their self-awareness and self-evaluation is the goal of self-monitoring and self-evaluation training" (p. 135). Typically, children with disruptive behaviors and externalizing problems are not good self-observers. Therefore, clinicians are well advised to obtain self-monitoring data from multiple sources (e.g., parents, teachers, other caregivers), including the youngster, and to offer the child an easy, engaging, and meaningful way to track his or her thoughts, feelings, and behaviors.

Behavior logs are standard fare for noting aggressive children's problems. *Hassle logs* (Feindler & Ecton, 1986; Feindler & Guttman, 1994) are diaries that capture situational, behavioral, and emotional components, which were used originally in residential and other institutional settings. We have found that they are equally well suited for use in school settings as well. Teachers, aides, counselors, and emotional support workers can provide assistance in completing the logs. Through identifying "hassles," the child can start to become aware of the emotional triggers to his or her aggressive or angry outbursts. Other useful scaling devices for self-monitoring include thermometers and rulers. Friedberg and McClure (2002) suggested using an *anger gage* or *speedometer* to help youngsters track feelings and behaviors. A danger or overload warning could be placed at the higher speeds, with the goal being for the child to keep his or her "speed" (i.e., frustration, anger, aggressive feelings) out of the danger zone. The speedometer metaphor is useful for many children, and clinicians can talk to the student about what happens if a car is driven constantly at high speeds (e.g., the engine burns out, use up a lot of gas, more likely to lose control, etc.). Moreover, this lays the foundation for intervention for "slowing down" the anger or "using their brakes" to control the speed.

Social Skills Training

Social skills training is another set of cognitive-behavioral techniques that have been shown to be helpful in teaching children and adolescents to control anger and aggression. Social skills training focuses on developing interpersonal competencies that reduce aggression and isolation, as well promote adaptive interpersonal relationships (Speigler & Guevremont, 1998). Typically, social skills training involves *skill acquisition,* in which students are taught the skills, and *skill application*, in which students practice what they learned (Beidel & Turner, 1998; Kazdin, 1994).

There are a number of creative social skills training methods and programs available. One such method, developed by Bloomquist and Schnell (2002), suggests that clinicians use games such as a problem-solving charades exercise. Additionally, they mentioned Guevremont's (1990) idea of a talk show format when one character is the "host" and another child is "guest." The host interviews the guest about triggers to anger, short- and long-term ways to cope with anger, and past and potential consequences to those coping strategies. Bloomquist and Schnell further recommended the "probe" challenges found in the *Peer Coping Skills Program* (Prinz, Blechman, & Dumas, 1994). This exercise teaches students a variety of verbal and nonverbal communication skills through a hierarchically tapered set of challenges (e.g., "Find out something that made your partner angry this week."). Popular books, movies, and television shows can be very useful media in teaching social skills (Cartledge, 1996). Several media options offer the advantage of providing culturally responsive models. For instance, *Positive Adolescents Choices Training* (PACT; Hammond & Yung, 1991) is a social skills training program that is especially sensitive to racial, ethnic, and cultural issues. With PACT, teens learn how to give positive feedback and negative feedback, accept negative criticism, resist peer pressure, solve problems, and negotiate conflicts.

Problem-Solving Training

Teaching problem solving is a fundamental strategy in working with disruptive children (Barkley, Edwards, & Robin, 1999; Kazdin, 1996; D'Zurilla, 1986). In general, aggressive and angry children learn to identify or name the problem, brainstorm to generate multiple alternatives, evaluate the consequences of each alternative, decide which option is best, and experiment with their choice. After students have completed the process, they then engage in self-reward. Kazdin (1996, p. 383) offers five useful self-instructions to promote effective problem-solving:

1. What am I supposed to do?
2. I have to look at all my possibilities.
3. I had better concentrate and focus in.
4. I need to make a choice.
5. I did a good job or I made a mistake.

Determining the advantages and disadvantages of a particular option is another problem-solving opportunity. By listing the pros and cons of a specific action, youngsters can gain valuable perspectives. Friedberg, Mason, and Fidaleo (1992) designed a useful worksheet, called *Looking at Both Sides Now,* which is used to help youngsters consider the advantages and disadvantages of specific courses of action.

Time Projection

Lazarus (1984) designed time projection as a self-management task to decrease impulsive behavior and emotional reasoning. Many aggressive and conduct-disordered children engage in *crash and burn* decision making. They impressionistically rush to judgment, disregarding situational subtleties and unforeseen consequences or disadvantages, which result in inappropriate reactions and behavior. In using time projection, the clinician asks youngsters to reflect on how they will feel and what they will do differently in 6 hours, 1 day, 1 month, 6 months, 1 year, and 5 years. It is quite improbable that students will feel and act the same way in 1 hour as they will in 5 years. Clinicians should make sure the children write down (or the professional writes for them if writing is a frustration for the student) their responses so they will clearly see that feelings change over time. In this way, the children learn that making decisions with long-standing consequences based on transient emotional states is unproductive.

Self-Instruction and Stress Inoculation

Self-instruction aims to interrupt and modify children's stream of dysfunctional thoughts. By focusing on changing a child's inner dialogue, it works like a dam to slow the youngsters current of maladaptive self-talk. Meichenbaum (1985) initially suggested developing self-statements to help clients prepare for a stressor, encounter it, and then self-reward themselves for proper coping. For example, if a child needs to work in a group with a child he does not get along with, self-statements such as, "I can smile and be polite," "I can ignore," and "I did a great job" may help the child better cope with the stressful situation.

Vernon (2002) offers a very creative self-instructional exercise, called *Don't Pop Your Top*, which helps angry youngsters manage their angry feelings. The exercise requires a glass jar with a screw-on lid, 20 strips of red paper, and a pencil. The exercise begins with the child writing down negative cognitions, such as unmet demands, perceptions of unfairness, frustrations, and beliefs about everything having to go his or her way on the strips of paper. The strips of paper are then placed in the jar, and the clinician explains that building up these personal imperatives make the "top pop." Next, the strips are tested, and Vernon suggests the clinician asks three questions: "Does everything have to be fair?"; "Can I stand it if it isn't?"; and "Can I always get what I want?" (p. 158). Once a belief is evaluated, it is eliminated from the jar.

Surf the Angry Sea (Friedberg, Friedberg, & Friedberg, 2001) is a self-instructional exercise for elementary school children. This procedure makes use of the metaphor likening anger to ocean tides. When children get overwhelmed with angry feelings, it is just like a wave crashing over their heads and flooding them with angry feelings. The trick is to surf the waves, keep your balance, and ride out the angry feelings.

Like all other cognitive-behavioral methods, self-instructional methods are best applied in the context of negative emotional arousal. Lochman, Barry, and Pardini (2003) offer several inventive methods for children to practice their self-instructional skills. For instance, they have children try to memorize ten playing cards in 5 seconds as a way to induce frustration and then practice coping thoughts. Lochman et al. also recommend building domino towers over a certain height as a way to create frustration. Certainly, playing a tower game such as *Jenga* could also be helpful ways to facilitate the application of these skills in frustrating situations.

Reattribution

Most children attempt to search for explanations, and, as previously discussed, aggressive children make mistakenly see deliberate and malevolent attributions for often accidental and benign situations. Reattribution techniques help youngsters look for another explanation for distressing situations (Bloomquist & Schnell, 2002).

A priming technique can often pave the way for more sophisticated reattribution techniques (Riskind, 1991). One useful priming technique is *Accidental versus On Purpose* (Friedberg & McClure, 2002), in which children are presented with 10 situations (e.g., a classmate does not say hello or someone cuts ahead of you in line) and instructed to circle whether they think it happened on purpose or by accident. Next, they list five ways to tell if someone is doing something on purpose or by accident. Last, they conclude by determining what is important about deciding whether someone is doing something on purpose or by accident.

Formal reattribution starts with the fundamental question, "What is another way of looking at ___" (J. S. Beck, 1995). More specifically, a child who attributes deliberate intent to accidental circumstances could be coached to construct alternative explanations. Consider Hector, who became angry when Erik "put his notebook on my desk." Hector reported intense anger (8 out of 10 on a feelings thermometer), and described his thought as, "He's trying to get over on me; seeing if I will let him get away with it." In this instance, the clinician may want to use a *Responsibility Pie* (Friedberg & McClure, 2002; Seligman, Reivich, Jaycox, & Gillham, 1995), which would begin by asking the child: "What other things besides Erik testing you could explain his notebook being on your desk?" Each alternative is listed and then a percentage is allocated to each potential cause. The hostile attribution is rated last. Each percentage represents a slice of the pie, and, once the entire pie has been completed, the youngster is asked to develop a conclusion.

Bloomquist and Schnell (2002) summarize several interesting additional methods for attributional retraining. Social dilemmas (e.g., tripping over a misplaced backpack) could be role-played, and the children could then be asked to search for explanation. Moreover, children can have to collect "data" supporting their explanation. Citing Braswell and Bloomquist (1991), Bloomquist and Schnell also recommended the *Kids Court* exercise. In this intriguing method, provocative situations are role-played, children act as both the prosecution and defense attorneys, and other children serve as the jury. Children learn how to evaluate the rationale for hostile attributions and weigh the data for alternative nonhostile explanations.

Cognitive Restructuring

Cognitive restructuring methods involve rational analysis and disputation, and, generally, they are best indicated later in treatment with more emotionally mature children. Cognitive restructuring emphasizes changing both the content and process of a youngster's thinking. Guided discovery and Socratic dialogues with students promote cognitive restructuring, and tests of evidence are standard restructuring tools (J. S. Beck, 1995). There are several workbook exercises to help clinicians construct a test of evidence (Friedberg, Mason, & Fidaleo, 1992; Friedberg et al., 2001). In general, children's beliefs are listed as hypotheses on the top of a piece of paper (e.g., "Jason is trying to make me look bad in front of the class.") with two columns labeled "facts/clues that make me totally believe this" and "facts/clues that make me doubt this." The clinician and student then place the facts in each column. Once the columns are completed, the clinician checks to see if there are any thoughts or feelings on the list, and if so, they are removed from the column because the lists are strictly fact-based. Finally, the clinician and youngster draft a conclusion based on an analysis of both columns.

Angry youngsters' *all or none beliefs* may benefit from cognitive restructuring techniques by using a continuum technique (J. S. Beck, 1995; Padesky, 1994). In order to scaffold a continuum, the youth's all or none label (e.g., "My mother's a controlling bitch!") is placed on each end of a line (e.g., at one end, 100% controlling bitch and at the other end, 0% controlling bitch). Criteria that define each pole are operationalized (e.g., "What does someone who is a 100% controlling bitch do/not do? What does someone who is a completely noncontrolling bitch do/not do?"). Then, people are placed on the continuum according to how closely they fit the absolute criteria. Together, the clinician and child use the data to produce a conclusion that makes sense.

Parent Training

Guiding parents toward reasonable goals is an important part of parent training. Therapists should explain the graduated nature of enduring behavior change. It is highly unlikely things will turn around dramatically in a week. Additionally, many parents hold the expectation that their child should always obey on the first request. We generally tell parents that it is reasonable to expect compliance after a second or third reminder. There are a number of parent training programs available for purchase. Two programs we have found very useful are *Defiant Children* (Barkley, 1997) and *Defiant Teens* (Barkley, Edwards, & Robin, 1999). Each of these provide a step-by-step approach to parent training focusing on improving management of behaviors, as well as positive communication and attention.

CONCLUSION

The incidents of angry and aggressive behaviors in schools continue to be of concern in today's society. Although the media has focused on high-profile events such as school shootings, of equal concern are students who display extreme anger and frequently aggressive acts such as fighting, bullying, disrupting class time, and engaging in socially inappropriate behaviors. It is incumbent on schools to develop programs to address these issues. For many students, schoolwide or group efforts would be sufficient. These efforts include programs such as *Anger Coping Program* and *Social Problem Solving*. However, other students may require more intense, individualized interventions combining a variety of cognitive and behavioral strategies to improve skills deficiencies and restructure maladaptive thinking. Parent training programs further serve as an important adjunct to work with students. Overall, school professionals can use cognitive-behavioral strategies to design effective intervention programs to serve students who display anger and aggressive behaviors.

REFERENCES

Bandura, A. (1973). *Aggression: A social learning analysis.* Englewood Cliffs, NJ: Prentice Hall.

Bandura, A. (1983). Psychological mechanisms of aggression. In R. G. Geen & E. I. Donnerstein (Eds.), *Aggression: Theoretical and empirical reviews* (Vol. 1, pp. 1–40). San Diego, CA: Academic Press.

Barkley, R. A. (1997). *Defiant children: A clinician's manual for assessment and parent training.* New York: Guilford Press.

Barkley, R. A., Edwards, G. H., & Robin, A. L. (1999). *Defiant teens: A clinician's manual for assessment and family intervention.* New York: Guilford.

Baron, R. A., & Richardson, D. R. (1994). *Human aggression* (2nd ed.). New York: Plenum.

Beck, J. S. (1995). *Cognitive therapy: Basics and beyond.* New York: Guilford Press.

Beidel, D. C., & Turner, S. M. (1998). *Shy children, phobic adults.* Washington, DC: APA.

Bloomquist, M. L. (1996). *Skills training for children with behavior disorders: A parent and therapist guidebook.* New York: Guilford.

Bloomquist, M. L., & Schnell, S. V. (2002). *Helping children with aggression and conduct problems: Best practices for intervention.* New York: Guilford.

Cartledge, G. C. (1996). *Cultural diversity and social skills training: Understanding ethnic and gender differences.* Champaign, IL: Research Press.

Crick, N. R., & Dodge, K. A. (1994). A review and reformulation of social information-processing mechanisms in children's social adjustment. *Psychological Bulletin, 115,* 74–101.

Crick, N. R., & Grotpeter, J. K. (1995). Relational aggression, gender, and social-psychological adjustment. *Child Development, 66,* 710–722.

Dodge, K. A. (1986). A social information-processing model of social competence in children. In M. Perlmutter (Ed.), *Cognitive perspectives on children's social and behavioral development: The Minnesota symposium on child psychology* (Vol. 18, pp. 77–125). Hillsdale, NJ: Erlbaum.

Dodge, K. A. (1991). The structure and function of reactive and proactive aggression. In D. J. Pepler & K. H. Rubin (Eds.), *Development and treatment of childhood aggression* (pp. 201–218). Hillsdale, NJ: Erlbaum.

Dodge, K. D. (1985). The cognitive regulation of anger and stress. In P. C. Kendall & S. D. Hollon (Eds.), *Cognitive-behavioral interventions: Theory, research, and procedures* (pp. 241–285). New York: Academic Press.

Dollard, J., Doob, L. W., Miller, N. E., Mowrer, O. H., & Sears, R. R. (1939). *Frustration and aggression.* New Haven, CT: Yale University Press.

D'Zurilla, T. J. (1986). *Problem-solving therapy: A social competence approach to clinical intervention.* New York: Springer.

Feindler, E. L., & Ecton, R. B. (1986). *Adolescent anger control.* New York: Pergamon.

Feindler, E. L., & Guttman, J. (1994). Cognitive-behavioral anger control training. In C. W. LeCroy (Ed.), *Handbook of child and adolescent treatment manuals* (pp. 170–199). New York: Lexington Books.

Friedberg, R. D., Friedberg, B. A., & Friedberg, R. J. (2001). *Therapeutic exercises for children: Guided self-discovery through cognitive-behavioral techniques.* Sarasota, FL: Professional Resource Press.

Friedberg, R. D., Mason, C., & Fidaleo, R. A. (1992). *Switching channels: A cognitive-behavioral work journal for adolescents.* Sarasota, FL: Psychological Assessment Resources.

Friedberg, R. D., & McClure, J. M. (2002). *Clinical practice of cognitive therapy with children and adolescents: The nuts and bolts.* New York: Guilford.

Goetz, E. T., Hall, R. J., & Fetsco, T. G. (1989). Information processing and cognitive assessment I: Background and overview. In J. N. Hughes & R. J. Hall (Eds.), *Cognitive-behavioral psychology in the schools: A comprehensive handbook* (pp. 87–115). New York: Guilford Press.

Goldstein, A. P., Glick, B., & Gibbs, J. C. (1998). *Aggression replacement training: A comprehensive intervention for aggressive youth* (Rev. ed.). Champaign, IL: Research Press.

Guevremont, D. C. (1990). Social skills and peer relationship training. In R. A. Barkley (Ed.), *Attention-deficit/hyperactivity disorder: A handbook for diagnosis and treatment* (pp. 540–572). New York: Guilford.

Hammond, W. R., & Yung, B. R. (1991). Preventing violence in at-risk African-American youth. *Journal of Health Care for the Poor and Underserved, 2,* 359–373.

Kaufman, P., Chen, X., Choy, S., Ruddy, S. A., Miller, A. K., Fleury, J. K., Chandler, K. A., Rand, M. R., Klaus, P., & Planty, M. G. (2000). *Indicators of school crime and safety, 2000* (NCES 2001–017). Washington, DC: U.S. Department of Education and Justice.

Kazdin, A. E. (1987). Treatment of antisocial behavior in children: Current status and future directions. *Psychological Bulletin, 102,* 187–203.

Kazdin, A. E. (1994). Psychotherapy for children and adolescents. In A. E. Bergin & S. L. Garfield (Eds.), *Handbook of psychotherapy and behavior change* (pp. 543–594). New York: Wiley.

Kazdin, A. E. (1996). Problem solving and parent management in treating aggressive and antisocial behavior. In E. S. Hibbs & P. S. Jensen (Eds.). *Psychosocial treatments for child and adolescent disorders: Empirically based strategies for clinical practice* (pp. 377–408). Washington, DC: American Psychological Association.

Kendall, P. C. (Ed.). (2000). *Child and adolescent therapy: Cognitive-behavioral procedures.* New York: Guilford Press.

Kendall, P. C., & MacDonald, J. P. (1993). Cognition in the psychopathology of youth and implications for treatment. In K. S. Dobson & P. C. Kendall (Eds.), *Psychopathology and cognition* (pp. 387–430). San Diego: Academic Press.

Kendall, P. C. (1988). *The stop and think workbook.* Philadelphia, PA: Temple University Press.

Kendall, P. C., Chansky, T. E., Kane, M. T., Kim, R. S., Kortlander, E., Ronan, K. R., & Siqueland, L. (1992). *Anxiety disorders in youth: Cognitive behavioral interventions in youth: Cognitive behavioral interventions.* Boston, MA: Allyn & Bacon.

Kenrick, D. T., Neuberg, S. L., & Cialdini, R. B. (1999). *Social Psychology: Unraveling the Mystery.* New York: Allyn & Bacon.

Larson, J., & Lochman, J. E. (2002). *Helping schoolchildren cope with anger: A cognitive-behavioral intervention.* New York, NY: Guilford Press.

Lazarus, A. A. (1984). *In the minds' eye: The power of imagery for personal enrichment.* New York: Guilford Press.

Lochman, J. E. (1992). Cognitive-behavioral intervention with aggressive boys: Three-year follow-up and preventative effects. *Journal of Consulting and Clinical Psychology, 60,* 426–432.

Lochman, J. E., Barry, T. D., & Pardini, D. P. (2003). Anger control training for aggressive youth. In A. E. Kazdin & J. R. Weisz (Eds.), *Evidence-based psychotherapies for children and adolescents* (pp. 263–281). New York: Guilford.

Lochman, J. E., Burch, P. P., Curry, J. F., & Lampron, L. B. (1984). Treatment and generalization effects of cognitive-behavioral and goal setting interventions with aggressive boys. *Journal of Consulting and Clinical Psychology, 52,* 915–916.

Lochman, J. E., Coie, J. D., Underwood, M., & Terry, R. (1993). Effectiveness of a social relations interventions program for aggressive and nonaggressive rejected children. *Journal Consulting and Clinical Psychology, 61,* 1053–1058.

Lochman, J. E., Whidby, J. M., & Fitzgerald, D. P. (2000). Cognitive-behavioral assessment and treatment with aggressive children. In P. C. Kendall (Ed.), *Child and adolescent therapy: Cognitive-behavioral procedures* (2nd ed., pp. 31–87). New York: Guilford Press.

Meichenbaum, D. H. (1985). *Stress inoculation training.* New York: Pergamon.

National School Safety Center. (2001). School-associated violent deaths report [Online]. Retrieved November 10, 2004, from http://www.nsscl.org

Padesky, C. A. (1994). Schema change processes in cognitive therapy. *Clinical Psychology and Psychotherapy, 1,* 267–278.

Parker, J. G., & Asher, S. R. (1987). Peer relations and later personal adjustment: Are low-accepted children at risk? *Psychological Bulletin, 102,* 357–389.

Prinz, R. J., Blechman, E. A., & Dumas, J. E. (1994). An evaluation of peer coping skills training for childhood aggression. *Journal of Clinical Child Psychology, 23,* 193–203.

Riskind, J. H. (1991). A set of cognitive priming interventions for cognitive therapy homework exercises. *The Behavior Therapist, 14,* 43.

Seligman, M. E. P., Reivich, K., Jaycox, L., & Gillham, J. (1995). *The optimistic child.* Boston: Houghton & Mifflin.

Serketich, W. J., & Dumas, J. E. (1996). The effectiveness of behavioral parent training to modify antisocial behavior in children: A meta-analysis. *Behavior Therapy, 27,* 171–186.

Shure, M. B. (1994). *Raising a thinking child.* New York: Pocket Books.

Shure, M. B., & Spivack, G. (1988). Interpersonal Cognitive Problem Solving. In R. H. Price, E. L. Cowen, R. P. Lorion, & J. Ramos-McKay (Eds.), *14 Ounces of Prevention: A casebook for practitioners* (pp. 69–82). Washington, DC: American Psychological Association.

Spiegler, M. D., & Guevremont, D. C. (1998). *Contemporary behavior therapy* (3rd ed.). Pacific Grove, CA: Brooks/Cole.

Vernon, A. (2002). *What works when with children and adolescents: A handbook of individual counseling techniques.* Champaign, IL: Research Press.

Walker, H. M., Ramsey, E., & Gresham, F. M. (2004). *Antisocial behavior in school: Evidence-based practices* (2nd ed.). Belmont, CA: Thompson Learning/Wadsworth Publishing.

12

Personality Disorders among Children and Adolescents: Are Euphemistic Labels Hindering Time-Sensitive Interventions?

ARTHUR FREEMAN & JASON M. DUFF

Suzie is a 13-year-old female who was referred for a school evaluation by her middle school teachers. Her mother came to the school meetings unwillingly and initially refused an evaluation. Rather than alienate and anger the mother further, it was decided to allow them to get an "outside" evaluation by a clinician of their choosing if they disagreed with the comprehensive findings of the school. The impetus and demand behind the present evaluation was that Suzie would receive homebound instruction until she had a psychological evaluation since her behavior had become a threat to others. Suzie's mother voiced her belief that the evaluation demand was "just so much bull—t," and just meant to "hassle" her and her daughter; however, she agreed to an evaluation.

By Suzie's report, she had witnessed her parent's extensive domestic discord. Both her mother and her father were known drug abusers. Her father was currently incarcerated. He had no contact with Suzie or her mother.

The staff at her school reported periods of "intense emotional outbursts." For example, in the beginning of the year, the teachers observed Suzie being extremely warm and open to the newest student in the class, Jessica. She quickly approached Jessica and began referring to her as her new best friend. A few days later when Suzie observed Jessica talking to some of the other girls in the class she began to yell at her, "I hate you. I never want to talk to you again."

It has been rumored that Suzie has been sexually active with more than one of the high school boys in the neighborhood. She had admitted smoking marijuana and drinking beer with this same group of boys. She had been picked up on more than one occasion for curfew violations. The most recent episode prompting a request for an evaluation involved Suzie's math teacher announcing that she would be going out on maternity leave. Suzie became very emotional and began acting erratically. "Everybody is always leaving me," she lamented. She described feelings of hatefulness for everyone, especially her mother and father, but then went on to say that she felt extremely alone and voiced interest in killing herself. Her mother was contacted to come in and pick her up so that she could be taken to a hospital emergency department for what was clearly a crisis situation. However, her mother took her immediately home and told her, "You had better knock off your shit because I am not going back down to that damn school." The school's response was that Suzie would remain on homebound instruction until she was thoroughly evaluated. The list of diagnoses that Suzie had thus far been given by a therapist she had previously seen includes:

Axis I: Adjustment Disorder, with mixed disturbance of emotions and conduct, 309.4
            R/O Bipolar Disorder; most recent episode manic without psychotic features, 296.43
            Cannabis abuse
            ETOH abuse
            R/O ADHD
Axis II: Deferred
Axis III: None
Axis IV: School/learning problems; problems with primary support; discord with teachers and classmates; legal involvement
Axis V: GAF = 35

Subsequent to the evaluation, the mother did not follow up on any of the school or clinical recommendations. Suzie refused to go to school. Her mother moved out of the city and Suzie was placed in a number of foster placements, and finally in a children's shelter.

Suzanne was a 28-year-old, twice-divorced mother of three who had recently lost her job. She was on the verge of being displaced from her apartment because of constant fighting with her neighbors and landlord. She was brought into the emergency room by Mark, her boyfriend of 6 months. He appeared infuriated and verbally expressed his anger, "This is ridiculous. This is the third time this month. I am done with you." On hearing this proclamation, Suzanne became even more hysterical then she had been entering the hospital. Suzanne had been at the crisis center many times before, mostly for her unpredictable and impetuous behavior with subsequent suicidal gestures and threats. She had seen four different therapists over the past 15 months. There were brief psychiatric contacts with many more clinicians over the past decade. Over the course of 15 years she had been on 20 different medications for issues such as depression, anxiety, "mood swings," impulsiveness,

ADHD, bipolar disorder, and sleep disturbance. She was 45 pounds overweight because of the adverse effects of the various mood stabilizers, antipsychotics, and antidepressants that she had been taking.

Suzanne was known for her intense, erratic, and dramatic changes in behavior and mood. As a child, she was often referred to as moody or emotional. Her "episodes," as her family called them, usually occurred in response to a real, imagined, or threatened abandonment and symptoms were transient, often with Suzanne returning to her previous behavior. However, as an adult the moody and emotional "episodes" had been occurring more frequently and tended to last anywhere from a few minutes to a few hours. Over the years, she had developed a relationship pattern in which she would become increasingly more demanding and clinging to her partners until she eventually would alienate herself from them. Suzanne would use the threat of self-harm whenever a partner would attempt to terminate their relationship. This irrational ultimatum would often lead to the significant other giving in and thus maintaining the relationship. Her actions during one perceived breakup (her boyfriend was leaving town on business) resulted in her overdosing on prescription pills and being taken to the emergency room once again. For Suzanne, a "relationship" could be initiated when she perceived someone as being nice to her. For example, a man who was her neighbor saw her struggling with a torn shopping bag and helped her carry her groceries. Suzanne saw his act of kindness as the beginning of a relationship. When he saw her afterward and did not act in a "relationship" manner, she was hurt and depressed.

Suzanne had demonstrated impulsive, self-damaging behaviors that included excessive spending and careless sexual flings and has been dealing with substance dependence issues for years. She was presently receiving SSI and spent her time at home sleeping and eating.

Axis I: Major Depressive Disorder, severe, recurrent without psychotic features 296.33
            Polysubstance Dependence 304.80
Axis II: Borderline Personality Disorder 301.83
Axis III: Obesity
Axis IV: Unemployed; twice divorced; discord with neighbors/landlord; insufficient welfare support; h/o incarceration with charges pending for marijuana possession
Axis V: GAF = 30

Jimmy, aged 14, was the academic star of his class, just as he had been since kindergarten. He started school having been taught to read by his mother, a school-teacher now working at home with her four children. His father was an attorney. He was the youngest of the children, with a sister who was 2 years older and two brothers 3 and 5 years older. His eldest brother was a second-year student at Harvard with an interest in law school. His second eldest brother was a freshman at the Johns Hopkins University in the school of engineering. His sister was a senior in high school, having been skipped ahead 1 year. She had expressed interest in pursuing a medical career.

Jimmy was overweight, had few friends, choosing instead to focus all of his energies on schoolwork. His academic success was lauded by the school and reinforced by his parents. On the rare occasion when Jimmy came home with an examination paper with less than a perfect grade, he was made to miss television and to "study harder." Over the years, he was known to cry in class when he had a less-than-perfect paper. He was picked on by other children because he was "teacher's pet." Metaphorically, Jimmy was the child who reminded the teacher at 2:55 on Friday afternoon that the teacher had failed to assign homework for the weekend, thereby earning himself significant teasing after school. Because Jimmy was crying in class after a particularly horrible experience, he got two questions wrong on an eight-question quiz and received a grade of 75%. He tried arguing for the correctness of his responses without avail. His counselor requested that his parents meet with her. Both parents came to the meeting. Jimmy's father dealt with the meeting as if he were taking a deposition. He was critical of the school, demanded that Jimmy be allowed to retake the test, and critical of the teacher. When the counselor pointed out Jimmy's weight, lack of friends, poor social skills, and his being the victim of teasing, his father just kept asking, "How is he doing in school?" No referral was ever made for evaluation.

Jimmy went on to Harvard, where he obtained a 3.96 grade point average. This was followed by law school at the University of Pennsylvania, where he served on the law review. He did not date throughout college and law school, focusing his energies during the latter experience on obtaining a good clerkship. This was followed by joining a prestigious law firm in Philadelphia specializing in contract law.

James is a 42-year-old father of two. He is married and has a son aged 8 years and a daughter aged 7 years. He has been married to Carol for 10 years. He is being seen with his wife for couples' therapy. The referral was at her demand, as she threatened she would leave him and take the children unless James altered his behavior. Her complaint was that he was demanding and even threatening when things were not done perfectly. The precipitating moment came during a dinner for his parents on the parents' 50th wedding anniversary. Carol spent a week cleaning the house so that it would be perfect. She prepared special dishes for the occasion. During the dinner, James noticed that one of the home-baked diner rolls was burned. He threw the roll across the room and shouted at Carol that she "could not do anything right." Carol also reported that he would quiz the children at the dinner table on issues of history, current events, and general knowledge. He was verbally aggressive and punitive with the children when they made a mistake. When she asked him not to respond in an aggressive manner, James responded that it was his job to train the children's minds. James seems mystified by her reaction. He is, he states, raising his children as he and his siblings had been raised.

By now, the reader has surmised that Suzie and Suzanne are the same person just as are Jimmy and James two versions of the same person. During the 15 years that euphemistic labels and nomenclature were applied, Suzie's unstable pattern of interpersonal relationships, self-doubt, poor self-image, unstable affect and marked impulsivity or Jimmy's obsessive-compulsive, self-punitive, and demanding style have been allowed to become more powerfully reinforced and ingrained in their pattern. Because they were not properly diagnosed at an early age they both went many unnecessary years with erroneous or partial treatment for issues that might have been treated successfully.

Kernberg, Weiner, and Bardenstein (2000), Bleiberg (2001), and Freeman and Rigby (2003) have raised the question: Are children who manifest certain traits displaying what may be precursors to later personality disorders, or can they be diagnosed as having a personality disorder during childhood or adolescence? Clinicians have responded in a number of ways. The responses range from the affirmative to the negative with a host of ethical, "legal," and conceptual issues evoked for support. The goal of this chapter will be to revisit that question and present arguments for and against the diagnosing of children and adolescents as having personality disorders. We will view the issue through the lens of the cognitive-behavioral model and examine what techniques would be useful for children and adolescents.

Since its inception in 1952, the *Diagnostic and Statistical Manual of Mental Disorders* (*DSM*) has classified people's problems according to diagnostic categories and offered brief descriptive statements. Only since the third edition (*DSM-III*, 1980) has the *DSM* provided explicit criteria for each of these categories. The process, recognized as a top-down paradigm, begins with concepts of disorders proposed by committees who then choose the characteristic criteria for defining each disorder, ideally based on the empirical support for the nosology. Throughout the six editions of *DSM*, categories have changed. Some were added, whereas others were dropped or moved to research positions. Therefore, we must recognize that the specific set of disorders that are currently described in *DSM-IV-TR* (2000) is not etched in stone. They are merely the current set of definitions and should be viewed as the language of the day.

The *DSM-III* introduced the concept of the multiaxial system so that diagnosis could reflect more than a primary clinical syndrome. The major reason that *DSM-III* established multiaxial diagnosis was to underscore the distinction between mental and personality disorders or traits. The subsequent editions, *DSM-III-R* (1987), *DSM-IV* (1990), and *DSM–IV-TR* (2000), have continued with the multiaxial system of diagnosis (Maxmen & Ward, 1995). Another one of the most relevant changes in *DSM-III* came when the theoretical model changed from a primarily psychodynamic model to a more behaviorally based model.

Individuals with personality disorders are frequently encountered in each and every jurisdiction of mental health services. If you ask most clinicians, they will most probably respond that individuals diagnosed with Personality Disorders are the most challenging on their caseload to treat. A number of reasons exist for this statement to be maintained. As Freeman and Jackson (1998) state, "The diagnosis of personality disorder is evocative and viewed frequently as prognostically negative, indicative of potential treatment difficulty, predictive of storminess both within and outside of the therapy, having a potential for acting out, offering possibilities for displays of behavior that may lead to danger to self and others, or, at its worst, all of the above" (p. 319).

The authors put forth the notion that personality disorders can and should be recognized, diagnosed, and treated accordingly in children and adolescents. In Suzie's case, we might speculate that if a personality disorder had been diagnosed earlier, the far more serious diagnosis might have brought action that was more intensive on her behalf. Why should she have to wait several years to finally "earn" the diagnosis for this extremely debilitating yet treatable disorder? One might make the point that if it walks like a duck, looks like a duck, and quacks like a duck, it is most probably a duck and should be treated as such.

ARGUMENTS AGAINST DIAGNOSING PERSONALITY DISORDERS IN CHILDREN AND ADOLESCENTS

One argument could be that Suzie should not carry the diagnosis of a personality disorder until she has reached early adulthood (whenever that is). The maturation into adulthood at the age of 18 is a Western tenet that may not apply in many other cultures or in some subgroups of Western culture. The right to vote, bear arms, and carry the diagnosis of a personality disorder should not be mandated by an arbitrary and culturally implied entry point for adulthood.

Whereas most clinicians generally agree that personality pathology originates in childhood and adolescence, and most adults with personality disorders readily identify childhood and adolescent manifestations of the disorder, it seems almost surprising that there is a question regarding early diagnosis. Any time there is the possibility to address a mental health disorder as early as possible, clinicians should take advantage of it with the utmost priority, as you would expect with any medical condition.

Another argument against diagnosing personality disorders in childhood is that children's bodies and personalities are rapidly developing and in a constant state of flux (Bleiberg, 2001; Freeman & Rigby, 2003). An inaccurate view of the individual is obtained by using a single snapshot to diagnose such a serious mental health disorder. Our response is that any time a clinician sits down to assess an individual they will perceive a glimpse or a small portion of the overall picture. Based on the evaluation data, school reports, reports of parents and other caretakers, and reports of friends and siblings, the original snapshot is enhanced in an almost digital manner. Now much finer details are obvious when before there was a broad and sweeping view. To avoid assumptions and unnecessary generalizations, it is vital for the clinician to obtain as much information as possible and gain valid corroboration. The clinician can observe or receive reports of how the child or adolescent is interacting within his or her current environment. Assumptions may be made about how an individual functions across the variety of context in which he or she lives, works, and attends school, but ultimately a comprehensive history is necessary to complete the picture. The fact is that behaviors will most likely change across different contexts and overall patterns of behavior will be modified. We further respond to this criticism by implying that all diagnoses are conditional, and they can and should be revised once the clinician obtains more information and develops larger and clearer conceptualization.

For those who point to the "illegality" of diagnosing children and adolescents with a personality disorder, we would recommend reading more than the criteria sets. Alone, these imply that the problem is manifested "beginning by early adulthood." This statement does not say that it begins *in* early adulthood but, rather, *by* early adulthood, thereby implying that symptoms begin earlier. In point of fact,

DSM-IV-TR (2000) states, "Personality disorders may be applied to children or adolescents in those relatively unusual instances in which the individual's particular maladaptive personality traits appear to be pervasive, persistent, and unlikely to be limited to a particular developmental stage or an episode of an Axis I disorder. It should be recognized that the traits of a Personality Disorder that appear in childhood often, not persist into adult life. To diagnose a Personality Disorder in an individual under age 18 years, the features must have been present for at least one year. The one exception to this is Antisocial Personality Disorder, which cannot be diagnosed in individuals under age 18 years. Although, by definition, a Personality Disorder requires an onset no later than early adulthood, individuals may not come to clinical attention until relatively late in life" (p. 687).

The inherent problem with Personality Disorders is that they often become "carry-over" diagnoses. This leads to another popular argument against diagnosing Personality Disorders in youth. The belief is that teachers, clinicians, and all those involved in the care of the youth will simply give up on them after they receive such a "terminal diagnosis." The argument states, "How can you label a child like that. Don't you know that diagnosis is going to stick with him or her for the rest of his or her life?" We readily admit that this is a possible scenario; however, we believe no more so than with any other diagnosis. In fact, it may be far less pejorative than Bipolar Disorder for which the individual will need to maintain a pharmacological regimen for a lifetime. The stabilization of symptoms such as impulsiveness, depression, and poor anger control will be beneficial and, in some cases, necessary for treatment to even begin. However, without recognition of the individual's core beliefs and attitudes and pathology, stabilization and maintenance are all that may be gained.

Freeman and Rigby (2003) express concern over the possibility of acceptance of the reality of personality disorders in children and adolescents carry with it the potential for malpractice. Care must be taken to avoid inappropriate diagnosis applied to socially and culturally different groups. Behavior must deviate markedly from the expectations of the individual's culture. The *DSM-IV-TR* (2000) clearly states, "Judgments about personality functioning must take into account the individual's ethnic, cultural, and social background. Personality disorders should not be confused with problems following immigration or with the expression of habits, customs, or religious and political values professed by the individual's culture of origin. Especially when evaluating someone from a different background, it is useful to obtain additional information from informants who are familiar with the patient's cultural background" (p. 687).

ASSESSMENT

Any child or adolescent who warrants a possible Axis II diagnosis must receive a comprehensive assessment. The clinician must evaluate the child's behaviors, affect, and cognition across a variety of situations, as well as obtain a thorough family and developmental history. Every attempt should be made to contact current and previous teachers, family, and primary care providers. This aids in the assessment of the chronicity and pervasiveness of the current issues (Freeman & Rigby, 2003). Personality traits are enduring patterns of perceiving, relating to, and thinking about the environment and oneself that are exhibited in a wide range of social and personal contexts. Three questions present themselves: (1) At what point does the mental health community intervene to modify behavior? (2) At what point do we determine that the situation is more chronic than acute? and (3) At what point do we consider a pattern of behavior to be maladaptive? According to *DSM-IV-TR* (2000), only when personality traits are inflexible and maladaptive, as well as cause significant functional impairment or subjective distress, do they constitute Personality Disorders. This enduring pattern is inflexible and pervasive across a broad range of personal and social situations and leads to clinically significant distress or impairment in social, occupational, or other important areas of functioning. Personality disorders are characterized by an enduring pattern of inner experience and behavior that deviate markedly from the expectations of the individual's culture. They are manifested in at least two of the following areas: cognition, affectivity, interpersonal functioning, or impulse control.

Based on Freeman and Rigby (2003), we would pose the following assessment questions:

- Does the reported and/or observed behavior have a normal developmental explanation? For example, a dependent 3-year-old is normal. The same dependence is a 15-year-old is a basis for concern.
- Does the behavior change over time or setting? Is it cyclical, variable, and unpredictable, or is it constant, consistent, and predictable? By definition, personality disorders are pervasive and persistent and will not likely show great variability.
- Could the behavior be the result of discrepancies between the child's chronological age and his or her cognitive, emotional, social, and/or behavioral ages? Again, the issue of developmental stages must be assessed.
- Does the child function similarly in different environments? For example, does the behavior relate to the child's placement at home or in school?
- Is the behavior culturally related? Are the observed behaviors, such as difficulty in making and maintaining eye contact, culturally based?
- Who has made the referral, and why was it made at this point? Is it that the child is disturbed or disturbing to others, and why?
- Is there agreement between parents, or between parent(s) and teacher(s), on the cause, need, and purpose of the referral? The issue of pervasiveness must be assessed.
- What are the expectations being made of the clinician in responding to the referral? For example, how does the child's behavior compare or contrast with the behavior of other children in the family or socioeconomic and sociocultural setting? For example, how does the child's behavior compare or contrast with the behavior of other children at that age or in that social group?
- What is the history of the child's behavior in terms of length of existence, duration when stimulated, and ability of the child to control, contain, or withdraw from the behavior? History and context will illuminate the picture.

- Does the child see the behavior as something that he or she is interested in modifying? The egosyntonic nature of the behavior is emblematic of personality disorders. In fact, with a successful and highly driven child, his or her obsessive style may be rewarded by both the school and the parents.
- What are the differing views of the child's behavior? Are the clinician's sources of data reliable? For example, what is the parent report of the child's behavior at home? How does the child relate to siblings, neighborhood friends, clubs, sports, organizations, church activities, adult relatives, pets, and self-care?
- Has there been recurrent physical, emotional, sexual, or verbal abuse? The parental view of discipline versus child abuse is a key element to be considered.
- Within societal norms, is the parental behavior inappropriately sexual or seductive? Is incest suspected?
- What is the parent's view of privacy for the child? How are boundaries established and maintained in the family? Are the parents inappropriately, unreasonably, or unjustifiably interfering with the child's relationships with other children?
- Within societal norms, are the parents inappropriately involved with the child's personal hygiene beyond the child's necessity?
- What is the impetus for the current referral? Are the caregivers' intentions altruistic or are they attempting to obtain disability, social security, custody, or some other accommodation? If so, is it a reasonable request?
- When assessing the current behaviors, it is necessary to determine what function those same behaviors have served in the past. The twin questions of the value and the purpose of the behavior must be explored.
- How has the family reacted to this point? Are they embarrassed? Has psychological intervention been expected? Is it welcome? Is this part of the family norm? Are other family members also receiving psychological services?
- In adolescents, the history of dating and relationships should be explored.
- When assessing the constancy and consistency of the behavior, has it been determined if there were any recent, unsettling events: Moving? New school? Death of a family member or friend? Any recent family illnesses? A timeline may even be beneficial to assess for the compounding of multiple, back-to-back events.
- How is the child or adolescent's perception of him or herself different from his or her ideal self or the person that others would like him or her to be? For example, the obsessive-compulsive adolescent may feel constant pressure from the real or perceived influence of others to be perfect as evidenced by the core belief of "I must not err."
- Whom does the child consider a support or a stable figure in his or her life?
- The essential question here is: Who might the clinician be able to count on as a potential therapeutic ally?

CONCEPTUALIZATION

Cognitive therapy is founded on the assumption that behavior is adaptive and there exists an interaction among an individual's thought, feelings, and behaviors (Dobson & Dozois, 2001; Freeman & Reinecke, 1995; Reinecke, Dattilio, & Freeman, 2003). The prominent feature of cognitive behavior therapy with youth understands the development of the individual's cognitive and perceptual processes that accompany his or her behavioral repertoire.

Beck, Freeman, Davis, and associates (2004) assert that assessment of personality disorders requires a working knowledge of both the general definition of a personality disorder and disorder specific criteria. Clinicians run the risk of becoming too focused on the content of personality structure and may overlook or not fully appreciate the general criteria for personality disorder.

Cognitive-behavior therapy (CBT) is based on the idea that the way in which you interpret situations has a very strong impact on how you feel about and behave in response to those situations. CBT is both interactive and problem-focused (Kuehlwein, 2002). Freeman et al. (1990, 2004) cite Beck, Rush, Shaw, and Emery (1979) when describing the approach known as "collaborative empiricism." Simply stated, this is the idea of working together to test the client's thoughts, beliefs, and assumptions, assess the belief, then challenge or restructure the belief. For this collaboration to occur effectively, the clinician and the client must mutually agree on goals of treatment. Whether or not a child or adolescent is capable of developing this skill is, at best, questionable. Operating as they do at more concrete and even preoperational levels of cognitive processing, they may need interventions that are far more concrete/behavioral than cognitive/affective.

After the initial evaluation and conceptualization, the agreed-on goals must be discussed with the parent(s) and possibly the child, and then prioritized. The time and effort put into establishing these goals cannot be overlooked, as most students with personality disorders will present in what Freeman and Dolan called the anti-contemplative stage of change (see Freeman & Dolan, 2001, for a complete review of the Revised Stages of Change). They are not, at this point, available for contemplation or even precontemplation. To move them forward into precontemplation where they will at least consider a change is critical. This is what we can refer to as building an intervention (Freeman & Dolan, 2001). The readiness for change must be assessed with both the child and within the child's family or support system. With most individuals, it is generally good practice to encourage as much collaboration as possible.

DEVELOPMENTAL ISSUES

CBT staples such as collaborative empiricism, rational disputation, Dysfunctional Thought Records (DTRs), Socratic questioning, and the use of homework, considered by some to be the backbone of CBT, may serve an older adolescent or young adult better than they would a child or early adolescent. The focus of CBT with adults is on misattributions, impaired or limited problem solving, cognitive distortions, negative automatic thoughts, maladaptive schemas, and misperceptions. These interventions may prove to be difficult for young children who may present with limitations in describing their experiences, labeling emotions, and identifying relationships between their thoughts and feelings (Knell & Ruma, 2003). The two options that we are faced with from a cognitive-behavioral context are (1) simplify our interventions or (2) assist the child or adolescent in developing the skills necessary to benefit from such techniques. There are two necessary factors to initiate change: (1) possessing the skills to make change and (2) possessing the motivation to change. As with all forms of therapy, the patient must be invested (at least interested) or find value in treatment to even allow change to develop. This applies to both the child and to the family/support system. For example, for both Suzie and Jimmy, their family support systems were resistant to change.

TREATMENT

Given the erroneous belief that personality disorders are exclusively diagnosed in adults, it would seem equally erroneous to assume CBT only provides adult interventions. As we will discuss later, the treatment of children and adolescents with CBT has been very promising. CBT with children and adolescents requires more than simply modifying techniques that were developed for use with adults. Presenting these techniques in an unmodified form will be of little benefit to children, for they lack social, linguistic, and cognitive sophistication (Reinecke et al., 2003).

The main treatment orientation for personality disorders up until relatively recently has continued to be psychodynamic. In fact, some conditions, such as the concept of Borderline, Narcissistic, or Histrionic (Hysterical) Personality disorders, are mainly the result of psychodynamic thinking.

The CBT treatment must focus on two elements. The first set of treatment issues must focus on concrete concepts, such as misinterpretation of information, reality testing, adaptive responses along a continuum, rather than attempt to emphasize on the child gaining insight into his or her problems. The second goal is to increase the broad range of skills, such as basic problem-solving skills. The overall goal is to improve on and add to the child's current repertoire of coping skills. The CBT clinician conceptualizes the problems as the manner in which individuals react to their environment in terms of their unique perception of it. The cognitive model theorizes the existence of structured schemas, which are actively constructed over the course of development and can be conceptualized as a template that guides perception, processing, recollection, interpretation, and analysis of incoming information. Schemas assist in selecting and organizing incoming experiences, translating them into habitual emotional and behavioral strategies. It is when these schemas become dysfunctional or distorted that they give rise to maladaptive patterns of reacting to the environment around them. These maladaptive strategies have the potential of becoming habituated and reinforced, leading to repetitive and pervasive impairments in interpersonal, social, occupation, or school functioning. Beck, Freeman, Davis, and associates (2004) recognize the presence of both overdeveloped and underdeveloped cognitive assumptions. An example of this is the individual with Paranoid Personality Disorder who in completely benign situations automatically galvanizes their overdeveloped, extensively generalized and flawed cognitive expectancies of being hurt or taken advantage of by others (Millon & Davis, 1996).

Beck and colleagues (2004, p. 21) developed a model of specific schemas for the various personality disorders. They posit that it is possible to demonstrate a typical cognitive and behavioral style that is associated with each of the personality disorders. The awareness of these basic beliefs and attitudes, otherwise known as core beliefs, aid in conceptualization and will guide treatment strategies.

The crux of the clinician's responsibility is to identify what schemas are driving the child's cognitions, affects, and behaviors (Freeman, 1983; Freeman & Leaf, 1989; Freeman, Pretzer, Fleming, & Simon, 1990, 2004; Freeman & Rigby, 2003). Beck and colleagues (Beck, Rush, Shaw, & Emery, 1979; Beck, Freeman et al., 1990; Beck et al., 2004) posited the notion that dysfunctional beliefs could be readily brought into conscious awareness. The theory is that these core assumptions about the self, world, and future "seem" unconscious because of the same nonpatholgical mechanisms by which other habits of thinking and behaviors have become automatic and out-of-awareness (Young, 2002).

Kendall and Choudhury (2003) reported that the early efforts to apply CBT to problems in youth focused on the external childhood problems that bothered adults. It was only after CBT for the disruptive behavior disorders had substantiated valid results did attention turn to the internalizing disorders. Only recently has the diagnosis of personality disorders in youth been even considered (Bleiberg, 2001; Freeman & Rigby, 2003; Kernberg, Weiner, & Bardenstein, 2000). Over the past 10 to 15 years, CBT with children and adolescents has rapidly developed. Reinecke and colleagues (2003), speaking on the research of the last 20 years with youth, recognized the dearth of empirically supported results as compared to the volumes supporting adult interventions. However, they go on to comment on the effectiveness and promise of the cognitive-behavioral treatments for behavioral and emotional difficulties among youth. CBT remains one of the most widely researched approaches for treating psychological problems in youth (Henin, Warman, & Kendall, 2002). Nonetheless, it is recognized that there is a paucity of research into the effectiveness of CBT techniques when treating personality disorders. However, it must be noted that there is adequate empirical support to continue with such clinical interventions. Personality disorders may be present in as many as 50% of clients seen in outpatient settings, and, therefore, Beck and colleagues (2004) present the argument that it would hardly be feasible to discontinue theoretical and clinical work until more empirical research has been completed.

One extremely difficult aspect of working with youth clients with personality disorders is the fact that they are remarkably astute at defeating efforts to help them. What is so readily referred to as maladaptive behavior has, at some point, served to ensure their emotional survival. The patterns that eventually lead to a diagnosis of personality disorder were once important and purposeful in their development. These patterns and maladaptive strategies that personality disordered children and adolescents utilize are at risk of becoming increasingly ingrained as they develop and grow.

An absence of delineated boundaries between normality and illness begins to develop. As a result, part of the inherent difficulty lies in the fact that many of the dysfunctional beliefs have become a part of the overall cognitive organization. An organization that would surely suffer without the considerable time and effortful precision that is necessary to determine which parts of the overall structure are in need of attention. The individual's poor insight and the perception of his or her symptoms as being typical make personality disorders more challenging to conceptualize than the more characteristic, episodic mental health disorders.

A destabilizing event, such as the loss of a primary caregiver, may be enough to exacerbate an otherwise adequate level of functioning. The means with which they attempt to ensure this emotional survival are incredibly stressful and painful, not only for themselves but for their families as well. Treatment is often unsuccessful as clinicians themselves often show difficulty managing the emotional reactions elicited by these clients (Bleiberg, 2001; Freeman & Rigby, 2003).

Reinecke et al. (2003) cite the work of Mahoney and Nezworski (1985), which suggested that rationally based models of psychotherapy are insensitive to developmental issues and the tasks faced by children and adolescents. Issues that, thus far, have been rarely assessed in the literature include their unspoken and often assumed beliefs about the reliability of relationships, personal security, and the stability of family.

It is essential to note that the child cannot be treated without the involvement of the home and the school systems, both separately and as a team. Freeman (2003) writes about one of the worst therapy failures in his clinical practice involving a 15-year-old boy. The problem in the therapy was that Freeman, despite his years of experience, did not recognize and accept the power and influence of the adolescent's mother. She quickly sabotaged therapy and withdrew her son from therapy when she believed her power would be limited. There must be a team approach that includes the parents, teachers, school counselor, individual or family clinicians, family physician, psychiatrist, and school psychologist. Ideally, we would recommend that the school psychologist be the case manager. The school psychologist has the knowledge, background, and status to coordinate the information that needs to be collected. In addition, the school psychologist has the ability to develop treatment protocols that can be implemented in the classroom. In the real world, this may not be possible inasmuch as the school psychologist may be focused on assessment. It is nevertheless essential that someone on the team serves a coordinating function or the child may fall between the many broad cracks in the system. The need for a high level of the child and parent involvement must be clearly established from the beginning of treatment. The familial aspects of the personality disorder cannot be overlooked or trivialized. Individuals with personality disorders, especially those diagnosed as antisocial and borderline personality, generally have a poor sense of boundaries, so it is vital to present the expected behavior and goals clearly and explicitly to all involved parties.

In structuring a CBT session, it must be determined what change abilities the child and his or her support system possess, as well as what the value of change is for that system. It is likely that these individuals (parent, child, and family system) have most likely presented for services because someone else found their behavior to be unsettling. They may at times be influenced by the impetus of avoiding punitive interventions. Therefore, it is essential early on to use the self-interest that drives their motivation for the benefit of therapy. By avoiding direct confrontation and using the technique of guided discovery, it is possible to identify the ways in which impulsive actions, inappropriate expressions of anger, failure to anticipate the consequences of actions, and so forth block the client from attaining his or her desired goals (Freeman et al., 2004).

Therapeutic Formats

There are a number of formats for counseling or psychotherapy session involving a variety of combinations and permutations. We cannot recommend one format over the other. The format will be a function of the clinical goals, the individual's availability, and the need for the therapy at that time. It will shift in the course of the therapy.

1. The child or adolescent can be seen alone. We do not recommend this. Without family involvement, whatever is done in the session can easily be undone in the car on the way home.
2. The child and parents can be seen together. This allows the parent(s) to be directly involved in the sessions. It also allows the clinician to engage the parents as therapeutic allies in the treatment. Furthermore, it allows the clinician to model specific behavioral interventions. Finally, there is a diagnostic function in observing the child/adolescent and his or her parent(s) interacting.
3. The parent(s) and child can be seen for alternate sessions or even split sessions. This allows the parent to have "alone" time with the clinician to deal with personal issues but also to be part of the psychoeducational work that will be necessary. It also has the advantage of limiting the time the clinician is with the child. It must be stressed that to have a child in a therapy session for the traditional 45 or 50 minutes is likely unreasonable. It would be of far greater value to have the child or adolescent in the session for 20 minutes and the balance of the time with the parent(s) alone or with the child and parent together.
4. The parent(s) can be seen without any major involvement of the child. Taking our cue from Freud's treatment of "Little Hans" (Freud, 1955), the parent(s) need to be the vehicle for change. If the parent(s) can build the child-rearing skills, parenting options, and a reduction of frustration, it will have a salutary effect on the child.

The Therapeutic Alliance

Personality disordered individuals tends to have significant difficulty establishing or maintaining an effective therapeutic relationship. If the driving force into treatment is not a judicial ultimatum, it is most likely the presence of an interpersonal problem, which is often very common among individuals with characterological disorders. This is why the therapeutic alliance is such a potent vehicle for modification of a person's core beliefs (Young, 2002).

The clinician must constantly monitor his or her own responses (countertransference) to the child, the parent(s), the family, the situation, or to school policies and personnel caused by the ease of becoming frustrated and annoyed. The clinician must be careful not to display fear, anger, or disgust without openly acknowledging his or her feelings to him- or herself. These individuals are watchful of any indication that these feelings may be present. An example of this is the clinician who because of a personal issue, picking her sick child up at school, had to reschedule an appointment. The individual's interpretation was that the clinician's actions were a response of disgust and repulsion. Unfortunately, the clinician was unaware of the individual's reaction and went many more weeks before the individual revealed the basis of their impaired relationship and declining therapeutic progress. It is important to address such issues promptly so as to avoid any misinterpretation. Self-disclosure must be used judiciously. Here again, knowing too much about the clinician can be interpreted as friendship, and it may in fact be frightening for many individuals. In addition, some youth with personality disorders or their parents may thrive on intimidation, avoidance, coercion, distrust, and self-doubt. For example, the father of a child diagnosed as conduct-disordered made an apparently casual reference to knowing where the clinician lived and having driven past the clinician's home. All of this requires the presence of a clinician who does not appear weak or vulnerable. Appropriate behavior must consistently be presented so as not to enforce or encourage the idea that it is acceptable to live "outside the rules." This holds especially true with borderline and antisocial personality disordered youth. The establishment and maintenance of structure allows the individual to be more collaborative, which ultimately strengthens the therapeutic alliance that is essential to change (Freeman et al., 1990, 2004; Beck, Freeman, Davis, & Associates, 2004).

Practitioners of CBT aim to teach clients how to notice, catch, monitor, and interrupt the cognitive-behavioral chains and to produce more adaptive coping responses. In addition, cognitive behavior clinicians encourage clients to identify high-risk situations that they may encounter and explore ways to prepare, handle, and deal with failures should they occur. Clients are encouraged to make self-attributions when they generate change and receive positive results (Meichenbaum, 2000).

FUTURE CONSIDERATIONS

"Cognitive therapy with children, as is work with adults, is founded upon the assumption that behavior is adaptive, and that there is an interaction between the individual's thoughts, feelings, and behaviors" (Reinecke, Dattilio, & Freeman, 1996, p. 2.). Cognitive-behavioral treatments are of benefit to children because they can be modified and tailored to meet the specific needs of the child. Therapeutic interventions focus on concrete concepts such as misinterpretation of information, reality testing, adaptive responses along a continuum, and basic problem-solving skills, rather than emphasizing insight. Everyday problems at school or home are addressed with the goal of developing a wider and better repertoire of coping skills. Using this basic framework, various cognitive-behavioral interventions can be utilized such as time management skills training, assertiveness training, problem-solving training, relaxation training, social skills training, self-management training, behavior analysis skill training, activity scheduling, self-monitoring, and developing adaptive self-talk.

There is the need to develop protocols and research on each of the personality disorders in children and adolescents. We must develop new and more effective diagnostic tools, and sharpen our experience with existing tools. We have to evaluate "best practices" for treatment. What works best, with whom, in what time frame, and under what circumstances? We will have to be able to evaluate what are the idealistic goals for treatment. We will have to be ready to pay the price in staff time, clinician effort, and economic cost to treat these children.

Choosing to ignore the reality of personality disorders among children and adolescents, to downplay the problem, or to search for euphemistic terms all denigrate the severity and impact of these disorders on the present and future life experience. The sooner that we can accept the reality of personality disorders in children and adolescents, the sooner clinicians will focus their efforts on appropriate assessment, conceptualization, diagnosis, and treatment. Finally, to recognize the reality of personality disorders, ideally, can relieve the suffering of these children.

REFERENCES

American Psychiatric Association. (2000). *Diagnostic and statistical manual of mental disorders* (4th ed., text revision). Washington, DC: Author.

Beck, A. T., Freeman, A., & Associates (1990). *Cognitive therapy of personality disorders.* New York: Guilford Press.

Beck, A. T., Freeman, A., Davis, D. D., & Associates. (2004). *Cognitive therapy of personality disorders* (2nd ed.). New York: Guilford Press.

Beck, A. T., Rush, A. J., Shaw, B. F., & Emery, G. (1979). *Cognitive therapy of depression.* New York: Guilford Press.

Bleiberg, E. (2001). *Treating personality disorders in children and adolescents: A relational approach.* New York: Guilford Press.

Dobson, K., & Dozois, D. (2001). Historical and philosophical bases of the cognitive-behavioral therapies. In K. Dobson (Ed.), *Handbook of cognitive behavioral therapies* (2nd ed., pp. 3–39). New York: Guilford Press.

Freeman, A. (1983). Cognitive therapy: An overview. In A. Freeman (Ed.), *Cognitive therapy with couples and groups* (p. 1–10). New York: Plenum Press.

Freeman, A. (2003). We're not as smart as we think we are. In J. A. Kottler & J. Carlson (Eds.), *Bad therapy: Master therapists share their worst failures* (pp. 123–130). New York: Brunner-Routledge.

Freeman, A., & Dolan, M. (2001). Revisiting Prochaska and DiClemente's stages of change theory: An expansion and specification to aid in treatment planning and outcome evaluation. *Cognitive Behavioral Practice, 8,* 224–234.

Freeman, A., & Leaf, R. (1989). Cognitive therapy of personality disorders. In A. Freeman, K. M. Simon, L. Beutler, & H. Arkowitz (Eds.), *Comprehensive handbook of cognitive therapy* (pp. 403–434). New York: Plenum Press.

Freeman, A., & Jackson, J. T. (1998). Cognitive behavioural treatment of personality disorders. In N. Tarrier, A. Wells, & G. Haddock (Eds.), *Treating complex cases: The cognitive behavioural approach* (pp. 319–339). Chichester: John Wiley & Sons.

Freeman, A., Pretzer, J., Fleming, B., & Simon, K. (1990). *Clinical applications of cognitive therapy.* New York: Kluwer Academic/Plenum Publishers.

Freeman, A., Pretzer, J., Fleming, B., & Simon, K. (2004). *Clinical applications of cognitive therapy.* (2nd ed.). New York: Kluwer Academic/Plenum Publishers.

Freeman, A., & Reinecke, M. (1995). Cognitive therapy. In A. Gurman & S. Messer (Eds.), *Essential psychotherapies: Theory and practice* (pp. 182–225). New York: Guilford Press.

Freeman, A., & Rigby, A. (2003). Personality disorders among children and adolescents: Is it an unlikely diagnosis? In M. A. Reinecke, F. M. Dattilio, & A. Freeman (Eds.), *Cognitive therapy with children and adolescents: A casebook for clinical practice* (2nd ed.). New York: Guilford Press.

Freud, S. (1955). The case of Little Hans. *The Standard Edition (Volume 10), Translated by James Strachey.* London: The Hogarth Press.

Henin, A., Warman, M., & Kendall, P. C. (2002). Cognitive behavioural therapy with children and adolescents. In G. Simos (Ed.), *Cognitive Behaviour Therapy: A Guide for the Practising Clinician* (pp. 275–313). London: Brunner-Routledge.

Kendall, P. C., & Choudhury, M. S. (2003). Children and adolescents in cognitive-behavioral therapy: Some past efforts and current advances, and the challenges in our future. *Cognitive Therapy and Research, 27,* (1), 89–104.

Kernberg, P., Weiner, A. S., & Bardenstein, K. K. (2000). *Personality disorders in childhood and adolescence.* Northvale, NJ: Aronson.

Knell, S. M., & Ruma, C. D. (2003). Play therapy with a sexually abused child. In M. A. Reinecke, F. M. Dattilio, & A. Freeman (Eds.), *Cognitive therapy with children and adolescents: A casebook for clinical practice* (2nd ed. pp. 338–368). New York: Guilford Press.

Kuehlwein, K. (2002). Cognitive treatment of depression. In G. Simos (Ed.), *Cognitive Behaviour Therapy: A Guide for the Practising Clinician* (pp. 3–48). London: Brunner-Routledge.

Mahoney, M., & Nezworski, M. (1985). Cognitive-behavioral approaches to children's problems. *Journal of Abnormal Psychology, 13*(3), 467–476.

Maxmen, J. S., & Ward, N. (1995). *Essential psychopathology and its treatment* (2nd ed., pp. 1–18). New York: W. W. Norton & Company.

Meichenbaum, D. (2000). Cognitive-behavioral therapy in historical perspective. In B. Bongar & L. E. Beutler (Eds.), *Comprehensive textbook of psychotherapy: theory and practice* (pp. 140–154). New York: Oxford University Press.

Millon, T., Davis, R. D., & Contributing Associates (1996). *Disorders of personality: DSM and beyond* (2nd ed.). New York: John Wiley & Sons, Inc.

Reinecke, M. A., Dattilio, F. M., & Freeman, A. (Eds.). (1995). *Cognitive therapy with children and adolescents: A casebook for clinical practice.* New York: Guilford Press.

Reinecke, M. A., Dattilio, F. M., & Freeman, A. (2003). What makes for an effective treatment? In M. Reinecke, F. M. Datillio, & A. Freeman (Eds.), *Cognitive Therapy with Children and Adolescents* (pp. 1–18). New York: Guilford Press.

Young, J. E. (2002). Schema-focused therapy for personality disorders. In G. Simos (Ed.), *Cognitive behaviour therapy: A guide for the practising clinician* (pp. 215–218). London: Brunner-Routledge.

13

Cognitive Behavioral Interventions for Individuals with Developmental Disabilities in School Settings

MICHAEL R. PETRONKO & RUSSELL J. KORMANN

In 1975, Congress enacted a public law (PL 94–142) that provided federal funding to states to support programs that provide thorough and efficient education for all students, regardless of handicapping condition (including Development Disabilities [DD]), in regular public schools. The intent of this law, originally entitled the *Education of All Handicapped Students Act* and now called the *Individuals with Disabilities Education Act* (IDEA), was to challenge schools to design individualized programs that would facilitate the educational process in spite of the handicap. This milestone legislation resulted from the tireless efforts of countless advocacy groups, the delineation of which goes far beyond the scope of this chapter. Suffice it to say that the intent of this legislation was to provide more than access alone, but more important, as Turnbull, Turnball, Shank, and Smith (2004) indicate, "benefit" from the educational process. Obviously, without this legislation this chapter would not exist. However, because of this legislation, and, more important, because of its emphasis on accessibility and individualized benefit, iatrogenic effects have been produced that uniquely challenge applications of cognitive-behavioral treatments (CBT) for individuals with developmental disabilities in school settings.

Before 1975, people with developmental disabilities did not attend public schools. Indeed, many were institutionalized in large congregate-care facilities that often called themselves schools: The Vineland Training School (NJ) and The Woods

School (PA) are but two examples. Many regular school students along with the retinue of professional and lay people in the community never met a person with a developmental disability. As such, how could it be expected that the public education community, including parents (of both classified and nonclassified students), other students, bus companies, school boards, teachers, taxpayers, police, the medical community, child study teams, and so on, would be equally supportive of inclusion? If not, one must query the overt/covert effects of lack of support as they impact on utilizing CBT in these environments. This is especially true with regard to who are the potential consumers (clients) of CBT interventions, who are the referral sources, who are the active and ancillary therapists, what kind of resources are available to support programming, and so on. Remember, legislation was required to provide for inclusion of a group of individuals who not long ago were professionally categorized as educable, trainable, or neither educable nor trainable. Vestiges of these labels linger today in the form of attributional biases and prejudice.

Perhaps this example might provide a context. Recently when walking down the hall of a middle school, an 8th grader was observed yelling out loud to another, "You retard." This statement has become commonplace to describe a wastebasket of thoughts, beliefs, or behaviors, which are viewed to be "nonmainstream" by members of the presumed "in-group." We might add that this derogatory term was also heard at a social gathering attended by teachers to describe the same ideas. Given this state of affairs, how then can we expect the principles of mainstreaming or inclusion, in which people with diverse intellectual abilities are mandated to commune in the same school, to be implemented—more important, embraced? The history of developmental disabilities is replete with overt and covert forms of bias, segregation, and disregard. Remember that in the same hall in which the besmirched comment could be heard walk students who have cognitive deficits. They know what the statement means and to whom it implies. Does this connote inclusion? Who indeed might be expected to make a referral for a student with a developmental disability who demonstrates signs of depression? Would the same difficulty be experienced for a student without a disability? Therefore, what does this say about the daunting task of considering CBT interventions in the schools? This chapter will focus on these iatrogenic effects, and propose remedies with which to promote effective interventions.

LITERATURE REVIEW

To say that there is a paucity of published research on the use of CBT with people with developmental disabilities in general, no less in the schools in particular, is an understatement. In order for research to be conducted with any population, one must first acknowledge that a group or person in that group presents with symptoms that CBT has been designed to treat. This has not been the case with developmental disabilities. For example, mental health professionals have long been aware of the concept of "dual diagnosis" in the general population as it applies to the comorbidity of mental illness and substance abuse, but the application of the concept to persons with developmental disabilities and comorbid psychiatric disorders only dates back to the mid-20th century. It still remains largely unrecognized by the mental health community. The anonymity of this population of "dually diagnosed" is of more striking significance when compared to the high prevalence of mental health problems in individuals with developmental disabilities as compared with nondisabled individuals. According to the *Diagnostic and Statistical Manual of Mental Disorders, 4th Edition, Text Revision (DSM-IV-TR*; American Psychiatric Association, 2000), psychiatric disorders are at least three to four times more prevalent among people with mental retardation than among the general population. Such a high prevalence statistic is not surprising on consideration of the physical, psychological, and social vulnerabilities of persons with developmental disabilities (Martinez & Petronko, 2003). Many individuals with mental health challenges concomitant with their developmental disability are now facing new tensions as they assimilate to life in the community whereas the national deinstitutionalization movement continues to press forward (Petronko & DiDomenico, in press). The behavioral manifestations of these comorbid conditions as they impact on a school environment unaccustomed to tolerating deviance or disruption poses a constant threat to the various freedoms of life in the community for people with dual diagnosis. The sheer volume of litigations pitting parent against school board attests to the need for professional attention and the propagation of evidence-based treatments circa CBT in the schools. Once a professional enlightenment occurs in which behavioral excess in this population can be viewed as expressions of stress instead of an archaic understanding of the condition of developmental disability, real change can occur. Most recently, there have been concerted efforts to shed many of the myths regarding the oxymoron implied when discussing cognitive therapies with those suffering cognitive deficits (Petronko & DiDomenico, in press; Nezu, Nezu, & Gill-Weiss, 1992).

One explanation for the professional community not considering an emotional disorder to be concomitant with a developmental disability was posited by Reiss (Reiss, Levitan, & Szyszko, 1982) and is called diagnostic overshadowing. Diagnostic overshadowing proposes that psychiatric symptoms are not independently identified as mental health problems but are instead attributed to the condition of mental retardation. The premise of this bias is, if you have the diagnosis of Mental Retardation, you are immune from experiencing other mental health conditions such as depression or the full array of anxiety disorders. The phenomenon of diagnostic overshadowing logically infers a "treatment overshadowing" bias (Spengler, Strohmer, & Prout, 1990); for instance, if a psychiatric disorder has not been acknowledged, mental health treatment is not likely to be recommended. Even when a mental health issue has been accurately identified, there is a prevailing attitude that people with MR/DD cannot benefit from CBT because they do not have the verbal or cognitive skills necessary to participate. Given that most therapists rely predominantly on verbal, intellectually based approaches, this belief creates another conjecture that psychiatric symptoms are not independently identified as mental health problems, but are instead attributed to the condition of mental retardation. As we consider what to do about this truly unacceptable condition, we need to recognize that it is not the individual with the disability alone who needs to be the focus of attention, but, rather, other key people who also need to be brought into the CBT process.

SCHOOL-BASED ASSESSMENT AND TREATMENT ISSUES

As has been stated, the provision of psychological services to students with developmental disabilities and behavioral challenge (i.e., dual diagnosis) in the classroom poses a number of rather significant problems. The most pressing of which seems to be the question addressed earlier in this chapter, namely "Who is the Client?" If one looks at most referrals made to school Child Study Teams (CST), the answer to this question appears obvious. The student is clearly the person that generates the referral, his or her behavior is the primary (if not only) reason that CST members are concerned, and the rationale for intervention is almost always centered on how the school's clinical service team can improve the child's behavior so that he or she can be maintained in the current classroom setting. Moreover, a glance at the Individuals with Disability Education Act (IDEA) makes it very clear to all school districts as to their charge when attempting to serve a student with a disability and any psychological or behavioral challenge: (1) provide *all* students, regardless of disability with a free and appropriate education (FAPE), (2) provide an appropriate evaluation, (3) provide an individualized education program (IEP), (4) in the Least Restrictive Environment (LRE), (5) ensure parent and student participation in the process, and (6) provide adequate procedural safeguards to guarantee all of the above (IDEA: Congress, 2002; Desktop Reference, 2001). Specifically, IDEA states:

> The CST must address through a behavioral intervention plan (BIP) any need for *positive behavioral strategies and supports* (614(d)3(B)(i)). In response to disciplinary action by school personnel, the IEP team must, within 10 days, meet to develop a *functional behavioral assessment* to collect information. This information should be used for developing or reviewing and revising an existing behavioral intervention plan to address such behaviors (615(k)(1)(B)). In addition, *states are required to address the in-service needs of personnel* (including professionals and paraprofessionals who provide special education, general education, related services, or early intervention services) *as they relate to developing and implementing positive intervention strategies* (653(c)(3)(D)(vi)). (IDEA, 1997)

The goal is clearly to assist the student in maintaining an inclusive placement in the LRE. The reality of such a charge, however, involves addressing a problem that is oftentimes disruptive to not only the referred student's academic performance but also very often his or her classroom peers. The literature is mixed regarding the impact on academic progress for students with and without disabilities in traditional versus inclusive classrooms (Cole, Waldron, & Majd, 2004; Daniel & King, 1997; Kauffman, 1995). It is quite common for nondisabled peers' ability to completely profit from their own educational experience to be compromised when a student with a severe behavioral disorder (i.e., aggression, tantrums) is introduced into an inclusive setting without effective clinical support (Wallace, Doney, Mintz-Resudek, & Tarbox, 2004; Shanker, 1994–1995; Vaughn & Schumm, 1995). As we begin to consider clinical intervention, the question of "point of entry" seems to be critical in attempting to identify "the client."

The point of entry for CBT in the public schools can be described as "primary," as the referred student is the recipient of the vast majority of the psychological intervention. Effective treatment requires adequate cognitive skills in order for the patient to understand the connection between faulty cognitions (irrational beliefs, automatic thoughts, and attributional biases) and problematic behavior. Treatment is often designed to not only challenge these faulty cognitions through psychoeducation but also to develop a therapeutic behavioral treatment plan that causes the patient to experience the altered result when their belief systems are challenged through shifts in behavioral outcome (i.e., exposure and response prevention; Mahoney, 1974). The utility of a CBT approach with dually diagnosed individuals has been discussed at length elsewhere (Petronko & DiDomenico, in press; Prout & Nowak-Drabik, 2003) as has its applicability to the population of individuals with developmental disabilities affected by psychological conditions that they can identify as stressors. The problem with consistent and successful application of CBT with the DD population, however, seems to center on issues of cognitive integrity, motivation, and the ability to follow through with treatment recommendations. Many students with severe behavioral or psychological challenges made known to CSTs present clinicians with an additional problem: Most are managed by a variety of school personnel including classroom teachers, assistants and aides, all of whom play an integral role in the execution of their IEP. So when one thinks about the development of a treatment plan to address a CST referral, one must not only consider "what is to be done" but also who will be "the recipient" of the service.

CBT CONCEPTUALIZATION OF THE PROBLEM

Kormann and Petronko (2002) and Luiselli, Wolongevicz, Egan, Amirault, Sciaraffa and Treml (1999) addressed the myriad of treatment models that have been available to persons with dual diagnoses in both community and academic settings. Issues such as how "the problem" is conceptualized, behavioral competence of staff, irrational beliefs, burnout, and motivation are but a few of the factors that have played an integral role in the development of treatment plans for students with dual diagnoses. In much of the literature reviewed, however, one theme seemed to be rather clear: In order to develop a treatment plan that will meet IDEA and LRE specifications and that has some likelihood for maintenance over time, a natural setting model must be employed.

The natural setting model indicates that an inherent open-mindedness is essential in addressing not only where to look for information with regard to assessment but also where to look for intervention possibilities. As we will learn in the next section, Natural Setting Therapeutic Management (NSTM) has developed a four-factor assessment schema with which to provide as broad an array of information, devoid of as few preconceptions or biases as possible, in which to construct a robust intervention. It is presumed that the CBT intervention will address more than the individual person with the disability. Thus, it is not uncommon to focus on the school staff's attributional biases via in-service training, as we work with the medical team to consider depression and anxiety to play a role in understanding behavior (delay the urge to automatically prescribe), as the parents are trained, and finally as other students who may have been intolerant are addressed along with the school system to increase their acceptance of diversity. In order to accomplish this, it is essential to have an empirically driven method available with which to address the complex assessment and intervention task at hand. A multifactor assessment program as practiced in NSTM (Petronko, 1987) based on a problem solving/clinical decision-making process (Nezu & Nezu, 1989) will provide CBT treatments that will cover the key factors involved with the development and maintenance of the referred behavior and consequently maximize successful outcome. The four key factors represented in this model include the student, the behavior manager, the environment, and the system.

STRATEGIC AND TECHNICAL INTERVENTIONS IN SCHOOL SETTINGS: THE NSTM MODEL

Currently based at Rutgers, The State University of New Jersey, Project Natural Setting Therapeutic Management (NSTM) was originally conceived (Petronko, Anesko, Nezu, & Poss, 1988) as an alternative to institutional services for people with dual diagnosis residing in the community. The project is a behavioral consultation and training program designed to enrich the therapeutic capacity of a referred person's natural environment by increasing the behavioral competency of the caretakers in that setting (Petronko, Harris, & Kormann, 1994; Petronko & Nezu, 1982).

The focus of the NSTM service is on helping indigenous staff members improve their ability to carry out behavioral strategies that are developed by clinical staff. Classroom personnel (i.e., teachers, aides) are viewed as the primary agents of change, who must be able to not only understand the behavioral techniques presented in training sessions but also to successfully implement them. Behavioral knowledge has not been shown to correlate highly with programmatic change, so it is imperative that a measure of process be used that is consistent with the expected outcome (Nezu, 1987). It does not appear to be sufficient for staff members to be able to understand and define behavior management or CBT concepts. It does appear critical that they be able to execute behavioral techniques in a situation that closely resembles one with which they struggle daily. To that end, role-playing, modeling, and in-vivo coaching are used extensively in combination with traditional, didactic training in the development of behavioral expertise. The use of role-play has been demonstrated to be a highly effective method for both assessing behavioral competence, and also for teaching behavioral skills (Jahr, 1998; Nezu, 1987).

The NSTM team, therefore, is responsible for training the academic staff in behavioral assessment and applied behavior analytic techniques, practicing them in an analog setting, fine tuning each skill via videotaped review, and piloting them through in-vivo instruction with the referred person. Progress through the training sequence is guided by the behavioral mastery of each skill and relies entirely on the acumen of the classroom staff member. It is clear, however, that other factors affect the academic team's ability to acquire and become competent with training material. Issues such as burnout, stress, staff morale, availability of material resources, and a myriad of administrative variables can have significant impact on a staff member's ability to benefit from a training service (Wallace et al., 2004; Moore, Edwards, Sterling-Turner, Riley, Dubard, & McGeorge, 2002; Jahr, 1998).

IMPLICATIONS AND APPLICATIONS TO SCHOOL SETTINGS

The goal of the NSTM model is to transform the classroom setting into a therapeutic milieu that can support behavioral change. Petronko (1987) developed such a model, which encompasses four factors: (1) the student with a dual diagnosis; (2) the staff members responsible for implementing program components, designated as the behavior managers; (3) the environment, including classmates, building variables, classroom schedules and routines, and other aspects that define the classroom environment of the student served; and (4) the larger system within which the first three factors are embedded. The larger system is seen as a combination of building, district, and perhaps legal variables that impact on a school's ability to provide adequate services to its students with dual diagnoses. Figure 13.1 presents this model graphically.

This multifactor approach does not assume that the student with the disability has the problem per se, but, rather, that the referred behavior is likely to be complex and reflect dysfunction in one or more of the above four areas (Gresham, McIntyre, Olson-Tinker, Dolstra, McLaughlin, & Van, 2004). Therefore, the NSTM four-factor model yields intervention strategies that address not only the short-term goal of remediating the presenting problem but also the more important long-range purpose of maintaining change over time. The acquisition of management skills by staff members (i.e., behavior managers) is central to the success of the consultation approach, which is accomplished through the mastery of social problem solving (Iwata, Wallace, Lindberg, & Conners, 2000; Horner & Carr, 1997; Nezu & Nezu, 1989, 1991; Petronko & Nezu, 1982). That is, the goal of intervention is to achieve lasting change by transferring ownership of the entire therapeutic process to those who are directly affected by it, the originally referred student, and those who are responsible for his or her behavioral well being.

Project NSTM attempts to affect this transfer of ownership in two important ways. First, it emphasizes training staff members, in the strategies necessary for them to assume the primary responsibility for implementing and subsequently maintaining habilitative programs. It is necessary for these support persons to believe that they are truly the behavior managers, can be effective in this role, and therefore must be the ones who carry out any treatment regimen. This represents a large conceptual leap for many staff members. Most have historically enlisted the aid of professionals (CST members, school psychologists) and simply followed their orders or recommendations. Project NSTM alters the role of classroom staff from virtual bystanders into primary and active service providers, a position that they have unwittingly held, albeit without training, for months or years. An attributional change seems required and often takes time in session to accomplish. Without that change, classroom staff may wait for the clinician to ascertain the problem and decide what is to be done, rather than actively participating in plan development. Second, and

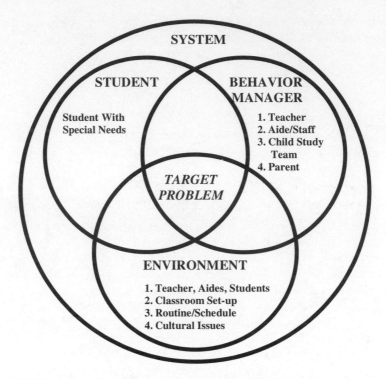

SYSTEM = the global climate in which the other three factors exist,
i.e., Federal (i.e., IDEA), State (Educational Codes & Budgets),
Teaching & Treatment Philosophies (i.e., Discrete Trials)

PROJECT NTSM
RUTGERS UNIVERSITY
797 HOES LANE WEST
PISCATAWAY, NJ 08854-8022

Figure 13.1 Four factor assessment from project NTSM, Rutgers University.

perhaps more significantly, it requires that the site for training and intervention be in the natural environment of the referred student, as this is the most clinically relevant setting and the one most likely to allow maintenance of change after formal termination of an intervention. Therefore, all of the work is completed in the student's classroom(s) with all teachers involved in his or her programming. This may include related services staff (i.e., Speech, Physical Therapy, Occupational Therapy, Physical Education, Art, and Music) and, in the case of older students, a rather large number of both regular education and special education teachers.

The goal of treatment ownership seems inextricably tied to motivation. Project NSTM consultants ask staff who are often overwhelmed, undersupported, and perhaps "burned out" to do more at the very time when their availability of emotional and physical resources may be at its lowest. Project NSTM has found great success in providing staff with an increased sense of self-efficacy by recognizing them as the most important therapists in the change process and by recognizing that the classroom environment must be utilized if a natural setting based treatment plan is to be put into place. It is this process that allows teachers and aides to become treatment professionals and thereby naturally accept ownership over the intervention process.

CASE STUDIES

Each case study to be presented will address the four factors: student, behavior manager, environment, and system, as they reflect assessment and intervention challenges with proposed remedies.

Case Study One

Student. Steven is a 12-year-old male currently receiving educational programming in a regular education 5th-grade classroom. He was referred for an assessment of behaviors that impact on his ability to be successful both academically and socially. These behaviors include noncompliance with teacher requests or programmatic requirements (i.e., schedule transitions), problems with anger control, as well as other disruptive behaviors that require staff feedback. Steven has been diagnosed with Asperger Syndrome (AS) and reportedly struggles with a variety of social-skills deficits that may be related to both this diagnosis and his current behavioral presentation. Specifically, Steven's attention is variable, often fluctuating between active involvement in an activity with which he is interested and engagement in a variety of "off task," disruptive, and "silly" behaviors when the activity is of little value to him. In the past, these behaviors have been even more serious, including aggression directed at both persons and property. These behaviors can draw a significant amount of attention to him from staff and peers alike, forcing him to tolerate interpersonal feedback that may be positive (i.e., other students laughing at/with him) or negative (i.e., staff reprimand and redirection). In either case, Steven is forced to utilize socialization skills that may not be as developed as his same-aged peers, causing anxiety, frustration, and, at times, displays of anger. Steven participates in the regular education 5th-grade curriculum throughout the academic day with the support of a one-to-one teaching assistant and also participates in several scheduled ancillary support services such as occupational therapy, speech therapy, and resource room.

Behavior Managers. Steven receives academic support from a classroom teacher and a one-to-one educational assistant, both of whom have worked with special needs students within the 5th grade for several years. The classroom teacher presents as a highly motivated and cooperative woman who is dedicated to helping Steven reach his potential this year as well as preparing him for the transition to middle school in the fall. Both the teacher and the aide recognized the need for behavioral intervention and possess significant background in Applied Behavior Analysis (ABA). They did not appear to be overly affected by Steven's behavior and could tolerate his episodes without undue emotional reactivity. At the time of referral, the classroom staff had been operating an individualized behavioral system with Steven for some time that was based on a modified token system that rewarded him for academic, behavioral, and socialization performance, and penalized him for infractions ranging from "failing to accept consequences" to "handling classroom property with force." Rewards were delivered via "points" tallied on a token sheet that could be exchanged at the end of either the academic day or week for a variety of reinforcers. Steven also had access to a room within the elementary school in which he could "vent" his anger and frustration when necessary. This "safe room" was located on the first floor and was filled with pillows that Steven could punch, throw, and so on under the supervision of his aide. Staff reported that Steven would use this room almost daily and that the duration of his "stays" was typically 25 to 30 minutes.

In general, Steven's intervention was vague in terms of behavioral specificity and presented with too many behavioral targets and an overemphasis on penalizing negative behavior, which affected the consistency and success of its execution. Steven, however, seemed to understand that there was a connection between behaviors on the chart and the delivery of rewards, although this connection was not specific enough. The safe room portion of Steven's program was equally unclear both in the criterion for implementation as well as in the procedure to be followed once Steven arrived. It clearly represented a target for consultation focus.

Environment. Steven receives ancillary academic support from a one-to-one classroom assistant throughout his day who has made a rather concerted effort to provide the minimal amount of personalized support needed for Steven to be successful. To that end, the aide spends as much time as he can "floating" about the room, assisting any students who may need support. As he does this, he attempts to be continuously aware of Steven and his engagement with the classroom activity, returning to help him whenever necessary. This allows Steven to benefit from one-to-one support when it is required but not to be saddled with the stigma of having an aide that constantly sits next to or behind him at all times. Staff report and classroom observation seemed to indicate that the aide has successfully forged a helping relationship with Steven that meets these aforementioned goals. It is important to note that the aide will not remain with Steven next year as he graduates to the middle school. Effective and early planning for this transition will be critical to Steven's success as he moves to a new environment.

The classroom environment is designed to maximize the social interaction of its students. It is comprised of six sets of desk "clusters" that include four desks in each. Steven's desk "cluster" is located in the middle of the classroom and is surrounded by the other five. It allows him to have easy perceptual access to all aspects of the room and permits his aide the ability to "pass by" with great frequency as he moves about the room. It also, however, positions Steven in a location that could potentially maximize distraction by its central location. During observations, Steven appeared to be an accepted member of the classroom, interacting with other students intermittently and participating in class activities with some effort. He also appeared to occasionally "tune out" information being presented to the class through playing with his materials, picking at labels on shelves, looking around the room or in his desk, or fidgeting at his seat. He also would intermittently reengage in the classroom activity and it was at these times that he showed the ability to complete most of the academic activities to which he was exposed. This tendency to "float" in and out of the educational experience was described by the teacher as common for Steven and indicative of the endemic challenge associated with his behavioral repertoire.

System. The current behavioral referral resulted from a rather adversarial relationship between Steven's parents and the local school district. Debate regarding not only the current school's ability to serve Steven, but also the ability of the middle school to which he would be transferring in the next academic year, was in question as the case progressed. The threat of litigation through the Due Process procedure stimulated the initiation of this referral, albeit late in the academic year (March), and caused the consultation to take on a dual purpose. Staff and administration at Steven's current program were the immediate recipients of behavior consultation services and clearly functioned as the trainees and "implementers" of the current intervention. Staff and administration at the middle school quickly became critical participants in the consultation process as the issue of "behavioral preparedness" of Steven's new staff became as important as was the behavioral competence of his elementary school staff for which the intervention was currently being developed.

Clinical Contact. Weekly training sessions were held with Steven's elementary school staff to complete a multifactor behavioral assessment and significantly revise his current behavioral intervention based on the functional behavioral assessment (FBA) data collected. Intervention addressed antecedent and consequent conditions that were affecting Steven's behavior and resulted in a rather significant increase in his behavioral performance along with a reduction in disruptive behaviors. The utilization of his "safe room" dropped to less than one time per week and the duration of his stay there decreased to less than 10 minutes per visit.

Transition services with the middle school personnel took the form of three meetings with administration and all academic personnel to be involved in Steven's program at the middle school. Presentations on AS, the behavioral intervention successfully utilized at the elementary school, and important transition procedures relevant for a student with AS were completed. Two transition meetings with Steven and his former staff were completed at his new school to review differences between the two buildings, to review new procedures for the "anger management" room (guidance office) and to familiarize him with the new surroundings. Two transition visits were held with Steven, his mother, the middle school principal, and his new academic staff, during which he had the opportunity to "walk his schedule," pick out his locker, and meet all of his teachers (including his new one-to-one assistant). Steven embarked on his new academic experience utilizing an updated form of his behavioral intervention 2 days later and, to date, has earned all of his behavioral goals without use of his "safe room."

Clinical Case Study Two

Person. William is a 20-year-old African-American male student with cerebral palsy and severe mental retardation referred to Project NSTM for severe self-injury (SIB).

William's SIB takes the form of striking the top and sides of his head with open hands approximately 300 to 400 times per day. His SIB has caused him to lose his sight through bilateral retinal detachment, which has been evaluated as inoperable because of the ongoing nature of his behavior. William is nonverbal and possessed no obvious form of communication at intake. His mother reported that his adaptive daily living skills are extremely limited and that he requires hand over hand or total support to complete them. He has been suspended from three school programs (both in-district and out-of-district special needs programs) in the past 3 years because of the severity of his behavior and now spends the majority of his day sleeping, lying in bed, or sitting on a chair in the hallway listening to sounds and intermittently engaging in SIB. His mother reported that William had significantly more skills and much less behavioral difficulties several years before the current referral. These skills included being able to make his own breakfast, feeding, dressing and toileting himself independently, and attending a school program for an entire day.

Behavior manager. His mother, a 56-year-old woman, married to a custodian at a local college, functions as the head of the household and the primary caretaker for her children. She is responsible for the communication with all state service personnel and the coordination of all services as well as the management of all the family's needs. William's father presented as solely involved in the financial support of the family and was uninvolved in behavioral services. Mother reported that she placed few demands on William for fear that they would stimulate a behavioral episode. She has worked at a developmental center in the past and therefore has significant experience with the population and some exposure to behavior management techniques.

Environment. William lives in a single-family home in an urban section of northern New Jersey with his natural parents and two sisters, one of whom has been diagnosed with mild mental retardation. Two other siblings live in homes directly adjacent to and behind William's and one of his uncles living next door is diagnosed with undifferentiated schizophrenia and chronic health concerns. As noted, William's behavior has eliminated day program options and has severely limited his daily routine.

System. William was receiving minimal support services from the State Division of Developmental Disabilities at intake. His mother had been unaware of the range of services available to her son regarding any of his disabilities nor skilled in obtaining necessary referral information. William's school district was providing home instruction and was extremely pessimistic about their ability to find an out of district program that could adequately serve him given the behavioral profile that he presented. It seemed as if they were waiting for William to "age out" of academic services, thus ending their programmatic and financial responsibility. Finally, William's mother was not very efficient in managing the administrative system and had lost any hope of finding academic or prevocational programming for her son.

Clinical contact. Project services focused not only on assessing and treating William's behavior but also assisting his classroom staff in becoming more successful interacting with the professional community (i.e., the behavioral consultant). It was clear that William required a host of clinical services ranging from ongoing medical and psychiatric support to assistance with his visual impairment and communication deficits. A functional behavioral assessment revealed that the SIB served two main functions. The first was to obtain reliable and immediate interpersonal contact. This took the form of staff responding immediately to the demonstration of the SIB with a high concentration of verbal and physical interaction. Second, it allowed William a viable method of communication, as staff would present him with a variety of options during the aforementioned interaction, ultimately identifying something that he desired. Behavioral training involved providing William with an alternate way of communicating his needs, expressing "yes" and "no," and obtaining high levels of positive interpersonal contact. Services identified and obtained during assessment ranged from consults with the local commission for the blind (travel training and the development of basic signs), the department of education (augmentative communication devices), the state division of developmental disabilities (physical and occupational therapy and the procurement of adaptive equipment), and a local psychiatrist (diagnosis and treatment for bipolar disorder). A differential reinforcement of incompatible behavior (DRI) intervention was developed utilizing his teacher as the behavior manager. Extensive role-plays, in-vivo trials, and didactic education provided staff with both the competence and confidence to be able to successfully carry out a behavioral intervention. William's behavior has decreased to approximately 20 to 25 instances of SIB per day and his staff reports an ongoing sense of efficacy and control over William's behavioral excesses. Finally, contact was made with providers of vocational programming to identify a behavioral criterion and transition plan for William that would provide support for all involved. After 2 years of behavioral service, William was gradually transitioned into a community-based vocational program, where he currently functions without major behavioral incident.

SUMMARY AND CONCLUSION

School-based clinical support for students with developmental disabilities and accompanying emotional or behavioral disorders presents the field with a unique set of questions and challenges. Issues of type of service, "point of entry," and transfer of ownership are but a few of the concerns commonly noted in both the psychological and special education literature. An overriding factor in service delivery systems is the federal mandates made by IDEA that all students receive a free and appropriate education in the least restrictive environment. Cognitive-behavior therapy (CBT) has long been considered the "cutting edge" technology for a variety of behavioral and psychological disorders. Although CBT has typically been presented as a primary service to treatment recipients (the patient), this chapter presented an alternate model in which tenets of CBT can be utilized with the primary behavior managers (academic and related services staff) who work with referred students every day. The emphasis of this model, encapsulated by the Project NSTM program, is to improve behavioral competence of indigenous personnel, improve staff's sense of self efficacy, and thus address issues of morale and burnout and ultimately encourage a "transfer of ownership" of behavioral programming from clinical personnel (i.e., the behavioral consultant) to the classroom staff. As the emphasis on educational inclusion increases, it is clear that students being served in regular education settings will present increasingly diverse clinical profiles. The burden, therefore, has fallen on the traditional service delivery system to provide academic staff members with the skills necessary to become competent behavior managers. Nationally and internationally, many programs have recognized the need for training protocols that view these caregivers as the true agents of behavioral change and treat them as such rather than relying solely on professionals to provide treatment on a conventional or private practice basis. Project NSTM represents such a model that marries the concepts of providing service in the setting in which the referred student receives programming while effectively addressing the complex constellation of treatment roadblocks that challenge behavioral service providers in academic settings.

REFERENCES

American Psychiatric Association. (2000). *Diagnostic and statistical manual of mental disorders* (4th ed.). Washington, DC: Author.

Cole, C. M., Waldron, N., & Majd, M. (2004). Academic progress of students across inclusive traditional settings. *Mental retardation, 42*(2), 136–144.

Daniel, L., & King, D. (1997). Impact of inclusion education on academic achievement, student behavior, and self esteem and parental attitudes. *Journal of Educational Research, 91*(2), 67–80.

Desktop reference for special education. (2001). Desktop Reference. http://www.oreilly.com

Gresham, F. M., McIntyre, L. L., Olson-Tinker, H., Dolstra, A., McLaughlin, V., & Van, M. (2004). Relevance of functional behavioral assessment research for school-based interventions and positive behavioral support. *Research in Developmental Disabilities, 25,* 19–37.

Horner, R. H., & Carr, E. G. (1997). Behavioral support for students with severe disabilities: Functional assessment and comprehensive intervention. *Journal of Special Education, 31,* 84–104.

IDEA: Congress to reauthorize education bill in 2002. (2002). *Advocate, 1,* 11.

Iwata, B. A., Wallace, M. D., Kahng, S., Lindberg, J. S., Roscoe, E. M., & Conners, J. (2000). Skill acquisition in the implementation of functional analysis methodology. *Journal of Applied Behavior Analysis, 33,* 181–194.

Jahr, E. (1998). Current issues in staff training. *Research in Developmental Disabilities, 19,* 73–87.

Kauffman, J. M. (1995). Inclusion of all students with emotional or behavioral disorders: Let's think again. *Phi Delta Kappan, 76,* 542–546.

Kormann, R. J., & Petronko, M. R. (2002). Community-based behavioral, therapeutic training programs. In J. A. Mulick & C. S. Holburn (Eds.), *Dual Diagnosis Program Models.* Schenectady, NY: National Association on Dual Diagnosis.

Luiselli, J. K., Wolongevicz, J., Egan, P., Amirault, D., Sciaraffa, N., & Treml, T. (1999). The family support program: Description of a preventive, community-based behavioral intervention for children with pervasive developmental disorders. *Child and Family Behavior Therapy, 21*(1), 1–19.

Mahoney, M. J. (1974). *Cognition and behavior modification.* Cambridge, MA: Ballinger Publishing Company.

Martinez, K., & Petronko, M. R. (2003, November). *Stress and stress vulnerability: A review of generic stress literature with a developmentally disabled population toward integration and synchrony.* Poster presented at the 37th Annual Convention of the American Association for the Advancement of Behavior Therapy. Boston, MA.

Moore, J. W., Edwards, R. P., Sterling-Turner, H. E., Riley, J., DuBard, M., & McGeorge, A. (2002). Teacher acquisition of functional analysis methodology. *Journal of Applied Behavior Analysis, 35,* 73–77.

Nezu, A. M., & Nezu, C. M. (1989). (Eds.) *Clinical decision making in behavior therapy: A problem solving perspective.* Champaign, IL: Research Press.

Nezu, A. M., & Nezu, C. M. (1991). Problem solving skills training. In V. E. Caballo (Ed.), *Handbook of behavior modification and behavior therapy techniques.* Madrid: Siglio Veintiuno de Espana Editores, S.A.

Nezu, C. M. (1987). *Development of the behavioral role play activities test (BRAT): An empirically based observational measurement of behavioral child management skills.* Unpublished doctoral dissertation, Fairleigh Dickinson University, New Jersey.

Nezu, C. M, Nezu, A. M., & Gill-Weiss, M. J. (1992). *Psychopathology in persons with mental retardation: Clinical guidelines for assessment and treatment.* Champaign, IL: Research Press.

Petronko, M. R. (1987, April). *Natural Setting Therapeutic Management (NSTM), who is the client?* Invited workshop presented at the 8th Annual National Conference of the Young Adult Institute, New York.

Petronko, M. R., Anesko, K. M. Nezu, A., & Pos, A. (1988). Natural setting therapeutic management (NSTM): Training in the natural environment. In J. M., Levy, P. H. Levy & B. Nivin (Eds.), *Strengthening families* (pp.185–193). New York, NY: Young Adult Institute Press.

Petronko, M. R., & DiDomenico, D. M (In press). Cognitive-behavior therapy with dually diagnosed individuals. In Freeman, A. (Eds.), *Encyclopedia of cognitive behavior therapy.* Boston, MA: Kluwer.

Petronko, M. R., Harris, S. L., & Kormann, R. J. (1994). Community-based training approaches for people with mental retardation and mental illness. *Journal of Consulting and Clinical Psychology, 62,* 49–54.

Petronko, M. R., & Nezu, A. M. (1982, November). *Natural setting therapeutic management for the severely developmentally disabled.* Workshop presented at the 16th Annual Convention of the Association for Advancement of Behavior Therapy, Los Angeles, CA.

Prout, H. T., & Nowak-Drabik, K. M. (2003). Psychotherapy with persons who have mental retardation: An evaluation of effectiveness. *American Journal on Mental Retardation, 108,* 82–93.

Reiss, S., Levitan, G. W., & Szyszko, J. (1982). Emotional disturbance and mental retardation: Diagnostic overshadowing. *American Journal of Mental Deficiency, 86,* 567–574.

Shanker, A. (1994–95). Full inclusion is neither free nor appropriate. *Educational Leadership,* 18–21.

Spengler, P. M., Strohmer, D. C., & Prout, H. R. (1990). Testing the robustness of the diagnostic overshadowing bias. *American Journal on Mental Retardation, 95,* 204–214.

Turnbull, R., Turnbull, A., Shank, M., & Smith, S. (2004). *Exceptional Lives: Special Education in Today's Schools* (4th ed.) New York: Pearson Publishers.

Vaughn, S., & Scumm, J. (1995). Responsible inclusion for students with learning disabilities. *Journal of Learning Disabilities, 28,* 264–270.

Wallace, M. D., Doney, J. K., Mintz-Rudek, C. M., & Tarbox, R. S. F. (2004). Training educators to implement functional analyses. *Journal of Applied Behavior Analysis, 37*(1), 89–92.

14

Cognitive-Behavioral Interventions with Autism Spectrum Disorder

DANIEL H. INGRAM

Autism Spectrum Disorder (ASD) is complex, as each individual with an ASD presents unique sets of characteristics that are truly distinctive to his or her own being. Children and adolescents with ASD often experience dysfunction and discord in their family unit, in their school life, as well as within their own personal world. However, despite the unique nature of ASD, school-based clinicians having a strong knowledge base regarding the nature of ASDs, as well as a combination of the scientific principles of Applied Behavior Analysis (ABA) and the clinical framework of Cognitive Behavior Therapy (CBT), are likely to contribute to effective interventions and treatment in the schools and in home settings.

Traditionally, CBT theory is thought of as a direct or straight line connection between a specific situation or event, the core beliefs of a person through which the situation is perceived and interpreted, the immediate or automatic thoughts that mediate or modulate a specific response, and the resulting behavior or emotional reaction that results when filtered through his or her core belief system. However, when working with children and adolescents, a multidirectional pattern more likely exists (Mennuti & Christner, in press). This is often more apparent and relevant when working with children having an ASD, as there are often misunderstood cognitive factors including beliefs and automatic thoughts. Clinicians must consider that the beliefs and thoughts of these children have been shaped by the "autism experience." In turn, a multidirectional response pattern exists, in which the behavior outcomes may or may not be logically connected to the precipitating event or situation. Thus, when using CBT principles with children having ASD, it is "the prism of autism" and the inherent illogical distortions and skill deficits that both magnify the problems and challenge the clinician. It is only by fully understanding the many ways ASD is expressed that professionals can fully appreciate and help provide effective interventions to assist these children. To understand the thought patterns, the emotional responses, and, ultimately, the presenting behavior of children with ASD, it is incumbent upon the clinician to attempt to understand the autistic mind. Although CBT is thought of as a brief treatment modality, it is without question that professionals working with student with ASD will require additional time, as well as greater patience and commitment.

The purpose of this chapter is to explore the mind-set and behaviors often displayed in the schools by children with ASD. Additionally, this chapter will offer a description of how to combine the principles of CBT and ABA to develop effective interventions to address the special needs of these children within the school setting.

UNDERSTANDING ASD

Leo Kanner, psychiatrist, first described autism in 1943, as he published a series of descriptions about children seen in his clinic who exhibited a number of atypical behaviors, all of whom exhibited a lack of interest in the people around them (Kanner, 1943). These children further demonstrated peculiar interactions and reaction to the world around them. The common thread found in all of the children was their self-absorption and inability to take the perspective of others.

Today, ASD is viewed as a developmental disorder that affects all aspects of how a person views his or her world and learns from his or her experiences. Those with ASD generally lack the desire or need for contact with others, and the attention to and approval of others are not important to them. However, it is important to stress that both social contact and lack of desire for reciprocal social interaction are not an absolute lack of desire for affiliation, but a relative one. That is, individuals can, and often do, seek out contact with others, display affection, and establish reciprocal social interactions, but the terms and topics of these contacts are general. Depending on the specific definition of ASD used, approximately 650 to 1,000 out of 10,000 children are born with ASD (American Psychiatric Association, 2000). Boys are four to five times more often identified than girls to meet the criteria for ASD, and Asperger's Disorder (which falls along the ASD continuum) may affect boys up to 10 times as often as girls (American Psychiatric Association). It is generally reported that 75%–80% of children with ASD also have comorbid mental retardation (American Psychiatric Association, 2000); however, there are also children with ASD who are mentally gifted or high functioning as well. In fact, the majority of those children who are not mentally disabled have normal to high levels of nonverbal abilities, though they exhibit a significant impairment in verbal capacity (i.e., language). Despite most research suggesting genetic links to ASD (Siegel, 1996), there are other documented risk factors associated with pregnancy and delivery that are suspect (Siegel, 1996). Notwithstanding the increased knowledge about ASD, the current state of science has yet to establish a consistent and proven cause.

Because so much variability exists in the manifestation of characteristics of ASD, it is imperative that professionals making such a diagnosis use standard diagnostic criteria, as set forth in the *Diagnostic and Statistical Manual, Fourth Edition, Text Revision* (*DSM-IV-TR*; American Psychiatric Association, 2000). According to the American Psychiatric Association, there are 12 diagnostic criteria grouped into three primary areas: (1) a qualitative impairment in social interaction, (2) a qualitative impairment in communication, and (3) a pattern of restricted repetitive and stereotyped behavior, interests, and activities. Within each of these groups, four specific criteria describe functional sets of symptoms that an individual with ASD may display. For a person to receive a diagnosis of ASD, he or she must meet 6 out of the 12 possible criteria. Of the criteria, at least two must reflect difficulties in social development, two must indicate communication issues, and at least one must suggest restricted stereotypical behaviors.

Social development and the disregard of reciprocal social interaction are the most pervasive and debilitating aspects of ASD. In those with ASD, both the level of interest in others and the levels of attachment to others are not always absent, yet the quality of the attachments is very different. Clinicians are likely to see this more in children who are higher on the ASD spectrum, such as those with Asperger's syndrome or higher functioning Autism. Although the children may have interest in others, their interest tends to be self-serving. In these situations, they rarely consider the interests, feelings, or reactions of another person. They further tend to be aloof, isolated, or "in their own world." Although individuals with higher functioning ASD often are willing to relate to others, they are persistently unsure of how to initiate or maintain reciprocal social interactions (Siegel, 1996).

Another feature of ASD that makes interventions and treatment endeavors difficult is the concept of "theory of mind." In essence, theory of mind is the belief that others have a mind capable of thinking or believing something different from themselves. Because of this difficulty, those with ASD struggle to comprehend the thoughts and behaviors of others, particularly as they relate to their own behavior. This results in difficulty interpreting the verbal and nonverbal intentions of others. Furthermore, the absence of theory of mind also makes self-introspection difficult, especially relative to examining their thoughts or ideas as they relates to their own behaviors. In other words, individuals with ASD live in a dichotomous, black and white, here and now world, to which they respond to in a predictably rigid and ritualistic way. Their manner of living is extremely rule-governed, and they are most comfortable when in a conventional, rule-based world based on their perceptions and needs. Inasmuch as this rigid and inflexible rule-based paradigm serves as a comfort or self-protection, it also further alienates, isolates, and frustrates individuals with ASD. Keeping this in mind, clinicians must use treatment interventions that follow a predictable, rule-based, and specific plan.

ASSESSMENT OF AUTISM SPECTRUM DISORDER

Assessment of children with ASD requires an experienced examiner who has full knowledge of the disorder, including the qualitative impairments in reciprocal social interaction and communication, as well as the pattern of stereotypical ritualistic behaviors. In addition to the traditional diagnostic criteria set, clinicians must further assess domains that also influence how ASD is presented within the individual child (e.g., cognitive, language, etc.). Given the complexity and variability of behaviors across settings, a complete and comprehensive assessment requires data collection across multiple domains and environments. In order to ensure a comprehensive and useful evaluation, it is imperative for the data to be collected using an interdisciplinary approach. Depending on the child's needs, professionals essential in offering a thorough evaluation of ASD include school psychologists, speech-language therapists, occupational therapists, teachers, and parents. All evaluations for ASD should assess the core domains of social competence, communication (e.g., verbal, nonverbal, and pragmatics), behavior variability, and environmental influences (Shriver, Allen, & Matthews, 1999).

Observation, either formal or informal, is a key tool used by the professional assessing an individual for ASD. Observations serve to provide clarity to behavior variability, which is often the most striking difference reported by parents, educators, and specialists. Both direct observations of the child (e.g., in the classroom, lunch, recess) and indirect observations (e.g., by parent and teacher reports) are accepted methods of gathering information. A particularly interesting technique used in a comprehensive assessment of ASD is a structured playground observation. A functional observation checklist for use on the playground has been developed to provide a systematic format to conduct observations during play periods (Troxell & Ingram, 2000). The ability to observe children's play in a naturalistic setting unimpeded by adult facilitation or restrictive rules provides an uncontaminated assessment of the social schemas typical of children's interactions.

Other direct observation assessment instruments include the *Mayes Observation Checklist for Young Children* (Mayes & Calhoun, 1999) and the *Autism Diagnostic Observation Schedule* (Lord, Rutter, & LeCoteur, 1994). In addition, verbal structured interviews with parents, teachers, and the child should be completed as part of a comprehensive assessment.

INTERVENTIONS WITH ASD

There are a number of reported interventions with children and adolescents with ASD. For the purpose of this chapter, two primary interventions will be covered: Applied Behavior Analysis (ABA) and Cognitive-Behavior Therapy (CBT). There is considerable literature and documentation of the use of ABA in treating individuals with ASD (see Maurice, Green, & Luce, 1996). Although ABA can be an effective stand-alone intervention with this population, some students with ASD, especially those who are higher functioning, have the potential to benefit from the additional use of CBT as a treatment modality. However, it must be noted that, to date, there is no specific research demonstrating its potential with these children. Further research is both needed and warranted in this area.

Principles of Applied Behavior Analysis

Traditionally, ABA has been concerned with the improvement and understanding of human behavior. By definition:

> Applied Behavior Analysis is the science involving the breakdown of skills into small, discrete tasks taught in a highly structured and hierarchical manner. Central to the

successful application of this method is the art of differential reinforcement. (Maurice, Green, & Luce, 1996, p. 8)

This definition specifies six essential aspects of ABA. First, ABA is deeply rooted as a scientific practice. As such, the attitude and methodology of science guides the practice and implementation of ABA. Second, behavior change procedures are described in a systematic, technological manner. This avoids clinician's attempting to interpret behaviors, and instead relies on straightforward descriptive wording. Third, all procedures must be conceptually derived from the basic principles of behavior analysis. Fourth, the focus of ABA interventions is to change socially significant behavior. Finally, the fifth and sixth aspects specify that the improvement and understanding of behavior be embedded with the experimentation (Maurice, Green, & Luce, 1996). ABA seeks to make meaningful improvements in people's lives and to systematically analyze the behavioral factors responsible for that improvement.

From an ABA view, ASD is a syndrome of behavioral deficits and excesses with a biological basis, which are amenable to change through carefully constructed interactions with the physical and social environment. By using ABA techniques, clinicians assist the individual in eliminating those deficits and excesses by providing multiple opportunities for the learner to develop and practice skills that are more useful and acceptable in a variety of social situations and environments (Green, 1996). ABA interventions begin with a comprehensive assessment of current skills and needs, which the clinician identifies through systematic and detailed observation of the child in a variety of situations. When observing the child, the clinician records his or her actions (e.g., what he or she does) and inhibitions (e.g., what he or she does not do), as well as the antecedents (e.g., what occurred before the behavior) and reinforcements or consequence (e.g., what occurred after the behavior). Based on this systematic and detailed observation, the clinician selects specific behaviors upon which to focus. The behaviors selected are known as "target behaviors." Target behaviors are specific and are manipulated or altered based on the A-B-C principle of intervention (Antecedent-Behavioral Response-Consequence). Each A-B-C cycle constitutes a learning trial (Green, 1996). Authentic ABA programming uses all intervention techniques to accomplish the task of skill generalization (Sundberg & Partington, 1998).

Applied Behavior Analysis and Autism

It is quite apparent that people with ASD present a unique set of behaviors even when compared to others with disabilities. They present a wide array of combinations of social interactions, communication skills, sensory needs, and behavior difficulties. When combined with the wide range of intellectual abilities, splinter skills, and unique personalities and abilities, ASD is a very difficult disorder to provide therapeutic interventions. Those with ASD often have untapped potential, which can improve the quality of their life as well as the countless contributions they may make to society in general. The uniqueness of ASD and the myriad of ways in which persons with ASD manifest their disability have proven to be fertile ground for the advancement of countless interventions and treatment strategies (Olley & Getentag, 1999). There seems to be no shortage of interventions and in some cases promised "recovery" that is continually being promoted to parents and professionals. Unfortunately, for desperate parents and uninformed professionals, several of these so-called interventions (e.g., facilitated communication, colored lenses, etc.) have demonstrated to have little worth (Simpson & Myles, 1995). At the same time, several well-established treatments for children with ASD exist (Heflin & Simpson, 1998a). When used appropriately and consistently, a number of programs demonstrate positive outcomes for individuals and their families (see Heflin & Simpson, 1998b). When working with ASD, two key factors must be considered in order to enable these children to make significant progress. First, children with ASD should be identified as early as possible, as early identification also leads to early intervention. Second, when offering interventions to children and families, clinicians should concentrate on using evidenced-based strategies. Essentially, this involves clinicians knowing the literature and modifying techniques to fit each student based on a thorough assessment and case conceptualization.

Among the best-known and most researched interventions are those based on ABA (Anderson & Romanczyk, 1999). When considered objectively, overwhelming scientific evidence exists to support the use of behaviorally based principles in the treatment of individuals with ASD. To practitioners in the field, ABA has the potential for a wide array of applications. Although many see ABA as a stand-alone intervention, it can be used in conjunction with other evidence-based methods, which together have the potential to produce significant benefits for individuals with ASD.

ABA relies on the specific and accurate determination of antecedent variables and consequences and the interaction between them, and then uses this information to plan desired learning and behavior change programs in a systematic fashion (Alberto & Troutman, 1999). Professionals who use ABA for individuals with ASD specifically examine and target socially appropriate behaviors and responses that alter the manner in which they interact within society. As noted earlier, this inability to "fit in" to society is the greatest impediment to success for individuals with ASD. Using detailed environmental analysis and manipulation of Establishing Operations (EO), or sometimes referred to as Motivating Operations (MO), meaningful changes often occur in the behavioral repertoire of the individual with ASD. The concept of EO or MO is particularly significant in developing a plan for those with ASD. MO refers to an event or thought that alters the reinforcement of a particular stimulus (Wilder & Carr, 1998). The ability to determine and manipulate the MO of an ASD individual is very important in evoking the desired meaningful change in social behaviors. Essentially, MOs are thoughts or needs that occur before a behavior that affects a response or makes a certain response more likely to occur. In basic terms, motivation is concerned with the wants, needs, and desires of a person. In behavioral terms that which is wanted or needed would then function as reinforcement if the individual seeking it could attain it. Thus, the determination of the MO provides insight into the needs and desires of a person, and in turn, allows for the manipulation of the behavioral response in order to have that need met. However, as previously discussed, because individuals with ASD lack theory of mind, this interferes with their ability to know their own mind or think about what they are thinking. This would then interfere with their ability to know their own mind relative to their inappropriate social behavior. This lack of ability for self-introspection creates a roadblock in determining the motivating operations that drive both their typical and atypical behaviors. It is only through careful and systematic observation of behavioral responses, a thorough working knowledge of the individual, and an established relationship that it may be possible to determine the MO of individuals with autism.

An additional difficulty in children with autism spectrum disorder is that MOs are often transient, and, thus, capturing or contriving a MO can be quite challenging. Capturing a MO involves capitalizing on it as it occurs naturally in the environment, whereas contriving a MO involves manipulating some object or event in the daily routine of the individual (Sundberg, 1993). This can be difficult as the clinician or observer must be able to discriminate whether the response is because of the availability of reinforcement or the effectiveness of reinforcement (Michael, 1982). MOs play an important role in many clinical interventions. The failure to recognize the role of the MO in controlling human behavior could also result in an incomplete behavioral assessment. MOs likely play a significant role across areas of ABA application (e.g., behavioral medicine, behavior gerontology, correction behavior analysis, business and industry; Sundberg, 1993). Therefore, it seems appropriate that the common three-term contingency—**S**timulus-**R**esponse-**C**onsequence—should be expanded to a four-term contingency—**M**otivating **O**peration-**S**timulus-**R**esponse-**C**onsequence (Sundberg).

Cognitive-Behavior Therapy with ASD

Another modality of treatment that should be considered with working with ASD is Cognitive-Behavior Therapy (CBT). However, there is far less documentation regarding its use and effectiveness with this population. Nonetheless, a number of the tenets of CBT could be useful when working with students diagnosed with ASD.

The term "cognitive therapy" was first used by Dr. Aaron T. Beck in the early 1960s at the University of Pennsylvania to describe a structured, short-term, present-oriented psychotherapy for depression, which was directed toward solving current problems and modifying dysfunctional thinking and behavior (Beck, 1995). The general premise of cognitive therapy is that distorted or dysfunctional thinking that alters mood and behaviors is a common thread that permeates all mental disturbances. Other major theorists such as Albert Ellis, Donald Meichenbaum, and Arnold Lazarus have developed forms of psychotherapy, all under the umbrella of CBT. Although many variants of and variations to CBT exist, they are all unified by the theoretical proposition that problems arise as a direct result of faulty patterns of thinking and behavior. Secondary to these faulty patterns, individuals have a tendency to misinterpret situations in ways that undermine their ability to cope (Enright, 1997). Because of this difficulty with coping, the individuals develop abnormal behavior patterns that exacerbate and operationalize their problems. Using Beck's original model of depression, clinicians can characterize the thinking patterns and behaviors of individuals with ASD. This includes the notion that negative thinking has its origins in attitudes and assumptions arising from experiences early in life. These assumptions can be positive and motivating in some cases, but they can also be held too rigidly making them highly resistant to change (Enright, 1997). This is consistent with the clinical definition of ASD, as these individuals tend to be rigid in their thinking and establish rituals and stereotypical behaviors that maintain their faulty atypical beliefs and ideas.

The treatment paradigm for CBT involves working on cognitive and behavioral components that cause or maintain the individual's problems. Cognitive interventions provide specific challenges when working with ASD, as these individuals have difficulty with theory of mind and self-introspection of their own thoughts and ideas. However, the behavior components and interventions hold greater promise when using CBT as a therapeutic intervention for ASD. CBT is more appropriate for individuals higher on the ASD spectrum, such as those diagnosed with Asperger's Disorder. Higher-functioning students with ASD have well-developed verbal skills and increased awareness of being different and needing to "fit in," which provides a motivational factor not available to those with severe ASD or comorbid intellectual deficits.

Although there has been very little work done with regard to the use of CBT with ASD, a working model can be derived by using treatment programs focusing on comorbid symptoms from other disorders. For instance, children with ASD often have similar symptoms and behavioral characteristics consistent with Generalized Anxiety Disorder (GAD), Social Phobia, and Obsessive-Compulsive Disorder (OCD). Thus, clinicians can modify and use treatment protocols developed for these populations with ASD.

The individual with ASD is a composite of the above disorders in his or her thoughts, needs, and behavioral responses. One can operationally define ASD as a disorder that is based on excessive fears and worries while avoiding social situations that force them to operate outside of their comfort zone. Thus, individuals with ASD often manage their lives by establishing ritualistic behaviors, rigid rules by which they abide, and atypical/asocial behavior responses that facilitate escape from those things that are difficult or unpleasant for them. Given the similarities in symptoms, it logically follows that similar strategies and interventions used for GAD, Social Phobia, and OCD may very well be effective in treating individuals with ASD, particularly those who are high functioning.

Cognitive Behavior Therapy–Applied Behavior Analysis–Autism

Although ABA and CBT are presented here as individual treatment modalities, by combining these two orientations for treatment, clinicians may find further utility and effectiveness in treating children with ASD. This enables change to occur in not only behavioral characteristics but also in the cognitive elements that maintain behaviors over time and that often serve as impediments to generalization of behavioral change.

The processing and behavioral responses of children with high-functioning ASD generally present a distorted perception of the world. They misperceive demands or events in the environment, which causes pervasive stress and often agitation. If the individual takes the precipitating situation to an extreme, and escape or avoidance is not provided, the individual is likely to resort to bizarre, repetitive, stereotypical, and perseverative thoughts and actions. This is often the classic picture people have when they hear the word autism. Those with ASD may exhibit rocking, complex motor acts (e.g., finger flicking), repetitive verbal response patterns, or aggressive agitated behavior that can be self-directed (e.g., self-injurious behavior) or directed toward others. The difficulty for the clinicians, teachers, and parents is the inability of the child with ASD to cognitively formulate the cause of his or her distress and then verbalize these thoughts and ideas. An additional factor that may further exacerbate this difficulty is the maladaptive input the individual with ASD receives from his or her senses. Sensory hyperreactivity or hyporeactivity is a basic problem that most children with ASD exhibit. Many individuals with ASD display difficulties in the regulation of their reaction by reacting either too much or too little to things that are seen, heard, touched, and that move (Siegel, 1996).

ASD, in its primary form, is considered a communication disorder. This does not imply that individuals with ASD cannot verbalize, albeit they often have difficulty relative to comprehending, interpreting, and responding to both verbal and nonverbal communication. Consequently, these communication deficits in their internal language system are dysfunctional and not available as a strategy when faced with a distressing situation; therefore, motoric actions are usually observed.

Given the uniqueness of and variability in individuals with ASD, as well as other complicating factors, formal CBT methods have not typically been major forms of treatment for ASD (Lord, 1996). However, given the behavioral emphasis in CBT, many of the tenets and interventions are similar to ABA principles that are successful in treating children with ASD. Both CBT and ABA rely on the principles of behavioral assessment and behavior observation to develop target goals that are then treated with behavior response strategies. The use of the basic A-B-C paradigm (Antecedent-Behavior-Consequence) is consistent between CBT and ABA. The addition of the concept of MO may be the "missing link" in tying the cognitive aspect of CBT to the pure behavioral view of ABA. Of course, as mentioned earlier, establishing the MO, can be very challenging because of the numerous sensory, behavioral, and environmental variables that disrupt the thoughts and actions of individuals with ASD. Nevertheless, if it is possible to establish the MO, it may add to the clinician's ability to devise a behavioral intervention or to choose strategies that shape the individual's response. For example, a behavior that often seems like an irrational act may make perfect sense when one understands the meaning (or motivation) to the person who is exhibiting the behavior. Thus, a child with ASD may stick his or her head under a cube type chair during opening circle time in school, yet she still answers all of the questions asked by the teacher. This atypical behavior may be driven (MO) by the hypersensitivity to the auditory and visual stimuli typically present during an opening circle activity in a classroom setting. Thus, what appears to be bizarre and perhaps irrational behavior is simply self-treatment in an autistic child. Using systematic desensitization, successive approximations, backward chaining, and relaxation interventions (e.g., deep pressure), the child may ultimately be able to become an active part of the opening circle activity. By understanding and determining the MO before the antecedent behavior, the choice of strategies is likely to be more effective and more specific to the target goal. In one sense, the ability to understand and possibly discuss with high-functioning individuals with ASD the MO would be synonymous to determining and discussing automatic thoughts and cognitive distortions with typical children. The formula of MO-A-B-C (Motivating Operation-Antecedent Behavior-Behavior-Consequence) may be one that connects ABA to CBT when working with individuals with ASD.

In the previous example, the specific behavior exhibited by the child should be conceptualized in terms of the context in which it occurs and the role the atypical behavior serves in regulating and adapting the environment to the needs of the child. The implication for treatment is that when individuals with ASD engage in unusual behaviors, these may be attempts at communicating intentions, which they otherwise do not know how to express (Schopler & Reichler, 1971). Although these behaviors are not easy to change, they are amenable if individuals with ASD develop alternative ways of communicating or if the clinician addresses the situation that maintains the atypical behavior.

An additional complication in treating ASD is that the primary deficit in high functioning ASD has to do with differences in specific aspects of thinking such as metarepresentation and "theory of mind" (Baron-Cohen, Leslie, & Frith, 1985). These theories focus on the question of whether or not children with ASD have the ability to understand and perceive that others have thoughts different from their own. This is the basis of ASD's self-focus and what appears to be egocentric behavior. It also has been suggested that ASD reflects a specific deficit in metarepresentation, that is, the ability to think about thinking or about other forms of representation (Leslie, 1987). It then makes sense that a child with ASD who does not understand that not everyone thinks like he or she thinks or are interested in his or her interests has a disadvantage when involved in social interactions that demand social reciprocity. If such deficits represent the essence of ASD, then the use of "standard" cognitive techniques requiring self-evaluation and reflection may be problematic (Stark, 1990). It is therefore incumbent on clinicians and interventionists working with ASD children to have a thorough working knowledge of ASD and its complexities. In addition, an extensive working knowledge of the principles of ABA and CBT, as well as the interventions and strategies aligned with these systems, is essential. It should be noted that some researchers question the appropriateness of cognitive treatment for children under 12 or 13 years of age, a developmental language level reached by very few adolescents with ASD (Lord, 1996). However, recently there has been increased literature supporting the use of CBT with younger children (see Friedberg & McClure, 2002; Knell, 1993).

IMPLICATIONS TO SCHOOL

As with all children, those with ASD spend a large part of their waking hours in school or involved in school-related activities. In light of this, they receive much of their therapeutic support and behavioral programming in school or in programs under the guidance of educational professionals. Of greater significance is the tremendous amount of both social demands and opportunities that exist in the school setting. Thus, the social deficits that a child with ASD manifests secondary to his or her disorder are generally evident and displayed throughout the school day. The behavioral and social-emotional manifestations of ASD often create barriers for acceptance and participation within the school setting. Consequently, school-based professionals (e.g., school psychologists, guidance counselors, etc.) must be prepared to assist the educational team in addressing and treating the social deficits displayed. A reality today is that schools and school professionals are frequently confronted with "figuring out what to do" with difficulties that students, including students with ASD, experience in their day-to-day participation in school and school-related activities (Christner & Allen, 2003).

Children with developmental disabilities often present a more complex picture, have more comprehensive needs, and create greater behavior challenges to school personnel than do students in the general population. For this reason, it is imperative that children with ASD receive psychological counseling or interventions in school to assist them in dealing with the here-and-now social demands and social issues that confront them on a daily basis. Schools today are a microcosm of society to include societal ills and challenges. As children with ASD leave the educational arena, they must be prepared to face the myriad of choices, decisions, and outcomes that will be expected of them if they are to become contributing members and active participants in their homes and communities. Taking these issues and demands into account, it is essential to provide therapeutic support and guidance in conjunction with educational programs of children with ASD. The school setting serves as a natural laboratory to assist students in improving on their areas of difficulty (Christner & Allen, 2003; Mennuti & Christner, in press). Thus, the use of an integrative approach, linking CBT to ABA, represents a promising option for professionals who support children with ASD within the school setting. The key to the use of CBT in the schools with children diagnosed with ASD is finding school personnel who have a strong knowledge base in ASD, as well as a firm grasp of the principles of ABA and the tenets of CBT. Those who possess these skills can provide a valuable service to educators, parents, and the children themselves within the educational program and the school environment.

CASE EXAMPLE

John is a 12-year-old Caucasian boy with high-functioning ASD. He entered psychological counseling services at school at the request of his parents who are struggling to manage John in the home and at school. The school-based team supported the inclusion of these interventions as part of John's educational program.

John presented ongoing challenges over the course of his life secondary to his ASD. His most recent eccentricity and aversion both stressed his family and teachers and stymied his progress. John developed a very strong aversion to meat in any form and all other references to meat or meat products (e.g., saying the word *meat*, seeing pictures of meat, smelling meat, watching others eat meat, seeing a food pyramid in the school cafeteria). His aversion to meat was so great that it caused ongoing dysfunction in John's life at home and in school. His parents requested the assistance of the school in helping John to overcome his aversion to meat and to restore a sense of normalcy to the family. For instance, John did not eat a meal with his family for many years due to his meat aversion. His mother stated, "We would just like a family meal," or "We would love to have an occasional meal at a restaurant as a family." The school-based clinician was familiar with John and his family from numerous previous encounters over several years.

The best way to characterize John was as "a study in contrasts." He was a very high-functioning, verbal young man who functioned in the moderate range of ASD. John had a unique ability in the areas of mathematics, physics, and chemistry. At the age of 4, John announced to his family that he was not able to understand positive and negative integers. He was obsessed with numbers and his parents would take him to a local university physics fair, held annually. At 8 years of age, John was able to solve the physics problems that were on the blackboard as challenges to the undergraduate physics students. He had a clear and concise understanding of chemistry and chemical reactions. John loved statistics and would often bring a college-level chemistry or statistics book with him to use as recreational reading as well as a calming technique. His bedtime ritual included reading time before turning his lights out, in which John's choice was his chemistry books. In contrast to this extraordinary gift for mathematics and natural sciences, John was still a little boy in many other ways. For example, at 10 years of age, he still believed in Santa Claus and the Easter Bunny. As can be seen, there was a childlike innocence that surrounded his genius. John had numerous sensory eccentricities and obsessions that inhibited him from operating in the world in a typical way, far too many than could be accounted for. His aversion to clothing and shoes in particular was a long and arduous struggle for his parents, which has continued to this day. John struggled with other dislikes, such as flushing toilets, collars on his shirts, the "S" sound, clothing made of any material other than cotton, coats, crying babies, bare feet, bald-headed men, cleaning himself after using the toilet, and hair washing to name just a few. He also obsessed over ceiling fans and had an extensive photograph album of ceiling fans. Despite these other behaviors, his current aversion to meat and meat products was creating most of this dysfunction at home, in school, and in all public places.

During the first session with John, he was quiet and wary of why he was there and what we would be working on this time. He set his boundaries from the beginning, as he stated what he would and would not do for and with the clinician. The clinician referred to this as John "marking his territory" and establishing or negotiating territorial boundaries. This was a typical routine at the beginning of many counseling sessions with John. Although he knew the clinician from previous meetings, he was somewhat negative and guarded during the first session.

The first session was spent creating a therapeutic alliance and generally discussing his aversion to meat. Because John was reactive to any use of the word *meat*, he suggested we use the term "edible animal byproducts" instead. The clinician did not agree with John on his term, and continued to use the word *meat* conversationally. The references to meat caused a distinct and persistent behavioral response in John, which he referred to as "squiring." This involved John saying, in a very loud voice, "*SQUIRE*" each time the clinician used the word *meat* conversationally. In discussing the "squiring" procedure with John, it was noticeable that this was his way of canceling the clinician's reference to meat. It was also loud, obnoxious, intrusive, and conversationally offensive to the listener, which was an attempt for secondary gain—to get the clinician to stop.

In attempting to develop a treatment plan and treatment goals, it was apparent that John was not interested in changing his stand on meat and was quite negative to any suggestions or goals suggested, thereby placing John in the anticontemplative stage of readiness to change. John had no need to change his stance about meat; it was a deeply ingrained internal belief that was based on his love of several cows at a farm he had visited weekly over the last several years. His belief system and cognitive distortion was that any reference to meat was synonymous with killing or destroying the animals he loved and that brought him comfort and acceptance. Thus, John's automatic thoughts and negative reactions consistently and immediately emerged at even the sound of the word *meat*.

In John's mind, there was no reason to change his behavioral response. Any attempt to even discuss the possibility was met with agitation, aversion, and, when necessary, aggressive escape tactics. There was no apparent motivation for John to move from his staunch, but perfectly logical to him, stance against any reference to meat.

In the subsequent sessions, the clinician and John explored his love of math and physics, as well as what that meant to John in the future. He had been using his vast knowledge of physics and math to build intricate models of farm equipment with his Lego's and other toy-based building materials. His knowledge of engineering, gears, gear ratios, and so on was growing, and John spent much of his free time designing equipment. This interest led to a discussion of what John would like to do in the future on leaving high school. To the clinician's delight, John's intent was on becoming an engineer and designing farm equipment. In fact, John had a serious and standing offer from a German based firm that designs and builds farm machinery to join their firm once he obtained his engineering degree. John was very excited, in a matter-of-fact nonemotional manner, about this future possibility. Although having and maintaining long-term "dreams" and goals is quite unusual in individuals with ASD, John certainly was exhibiting long-term, goal-directed desires that were obviously very important to him.

At this point, the clinician and John developed a plan and strategy that linked the principles of ABA to CBT in order to solve the meat crisis. The dream of becoming an engineer was very strong and John could be quite introspective (in a concrete way) about his desire to be an engineer. This internal desire became the motivating operation (MO) on which the treatment plan was developed. The gradual implementation to references of meat (verbal) without "squiring," iconic representations of meat, and finally the presence of actual meat (sandwiches) were the discriminative stimuli (DS) used by the clinician in helping John systematically move towards his final goal. The move toward his goal was completed through the use of CBT strategies, including systematic desensitization, in-vivo experimentation, gradual exposure to feared situations both real and imagined, target setting, activity scheduling, role-playing, behavioral rehearsal, therapist modeled coping behaviors, relaxation therapy, and reinforcement and reward. Of the strategies, relaxation training was not successful with John. The other techniques and strategies, however, assisted in providing support to John in his journey to entering and accepting the presence of meat in his world.

The intervention period with John occurred over a period of approximately 6 to 8 months. The changing factor in getting John "hooked" to making a change in his behaviors was the use of the MO of becoming an engineer. This became the central theme or primary goal of the treatment plan. The first step in the process was to link engineering and meat in John's mind in a practical and logical way that negated his cognitive distortions and negative automatic thoughts. By helping John cognitively conceptualize that his future engineer colleagues would likely discuss engineering plans and projects at lunch and are likely to eat meat at these sessions, John was able to accept and try some initial target goals. John was able to conceptualize cognitively that for him to be a "real engineer" and to be part of the engineering community he would inevitably be exposed to meat. This eventually made sense to John, as it was explored with him over several months, and target goals were added as the treatment plan moved forward.

The treatment plan consisted of gradual exposure in the therapy room to references to meat (verbally), then the presence of pictures (photographs of raw meat), trips to the supermarket to walk through the meat aisles, and finally the therapist eating meat sandwiches in the therapy room during the sessions. The eating exercises started with chicken sandwiches because it was white meat and not tied to cattle, and then moved to red meat such as beef sandwiches. Homework assignments were given to John and his family to increase his presence at the dinner table with them, where they were eventually able to eat meat in John's presence. This was very difficult and only partially successful because of John's verbal agitation within the home setting. The culminating goal was for John to invite the clinician to his home for a picnic that featured steak. John remained at the table with the clinician and his family while engaging in appropriate social conversations and interactions. The final target goal was successfully completed with a wonderful steak (rare) dinner and a delightful social experience with John and his family.

CONCLUSION

ASD is a complex disorder and individuals with ASD are truly "unique" in their own way. This disorder can, and often does, create dysfunction and discord in the family unit, school life, and within the inner world of the child. The short-term nature of CBT makes it a very helpful intervention technique for use in the school setting. Even though CBT is designed as a short-term therapeutic option, there is no question that additional time, patience, and commitment by the clinician will be necessary when working with high functioning individuals with ASD and their families. By understanding the nature of ASD and by combining the scientific principles of ABA and CBT, treatment is possible and can successfully address the needs of students with ASD in a school setting.

REFERENCES

Alberto, P., & Troutman, A. C. (1999). *Applied behavior analysis for teachers (5th ed.)*. Saddle River, NJ: Merrill.

American Psychiatric Association. (2000). *Diagnostic and statistical manual for mental disorders* (4th ed., text revision). Washington, DC: Author.

Anderson, S. R., & Romanczyk, G. (1999). Early interventions for young children with autism: Continuum-based behavioral models. *Journal of the Association for Persons with Severe Handicaps, 24,* 162–173.

Baron-Cohen, S., Leslie, A. M. & Frith, U. (1985). Does the autistic child have a "theory of mind"? *Cognition, 21,* 37–46.

Beck, J. (1995). *Cognitive therapy: Basics and beyond.* New York: Guilford Press.

Christner, R. W., & Allen, J. S. (2003, Spring). Introduction to cognitive-behavioral therapy in the schools. *Insight, 23(3),* 12–14.

Enright, S. J. (1997). Cognitive behaviour therapy. *British Medical Journal, 314,*1811.

Friedberg, R. D., & McClure, J. M. (2002). *Clinical practice of cognitive behavior therapy with children and adolescents: The nuts and bolts.* New York: Guilford Press.

Green, G. (1996). Early behavioral interventions for autism: What does research tell us? In. C. Maurice, G. Green, & S. Luce (Eds.). *Behavioral Interventions for Young Children: A manual for parents and professionals,* 29–44. Austin, TX: PRO-ED.

Heflin, L. S., & Simpson, R. L. (1998a). Interventions for children and youth with autism: Prudent choices in a world of exaggerated claims and empty promises. Part I: Interventions and treatment option review. *Focus on Autism and Other Developmental Disabilities, 13,*194–211.

Heflin, L. S., & Simpson, R. L (1998b). Interventions for children and youth with autism: Prudent choices in a world of exaggerated claims and empty promises. Part II: Legal/policy analysis and recommendations for selecting interventions and treatments. *Focus, 13,* 212–220.

Kanner, L. (1943). Autistic disturbances of affective contact. *Nervous Child, 2,* 217–253.

Knell, D. M. (1993). *Cognitive-behavior play therapy.* Northvale, NJ: Jason Aronson.

Leslie, A. M. (1987). Pretense and representation: The origin of "theory of mind." *Psychology Review, 94,* 412–426.

Lord, C. (1996). Treatment of a high functioning adolescent with autism: A cognitive-behavioral approach. In M. A. Reinecke, F. Dattilio, & A. Freeman (Eds.), *Cognitive therapy with children and adolescents.*(pp. 394–404). New York: Guilford Press.

Lord, C., Rutter, M., & LeCoteur, A. (1994). *Autism Diagnostic Observation Schedule (ADOS).* Los Angeles, CA: Western Psychological Services.

Maurice, C., Green, G., & Luce, S. C. (1996). *Behavior interventions for young children with autism.* Austin, TX: PRO-ED.

Mayes, S. D., & Calhoun, S. L. (1999). Symptoms of autism in young children and correspondence with the DSM. *Infants and Young Children, 12,* 90–97.

Mennuti, R., & Christner, R. W. (in press). School-based cognitive-behavioral therapy (CBT). In A. Freeman (Ed.), *International encyclopedia of Cognitive Behavior Therapy.* New York: Kluwer.

Michael, J. (1982). Distinguishing between discriminative and motivational functions of stimuli. *Journal of the Experimental Analysis of Behavior, 49,* 213–227.

Olley, J. G., & Gutentag, S. S. (1999). Autism: Historical overview definitions and characteristics. In D. B. Zager (Ed.), *Autism: Identification, education and treatment* (pp. 3–22). Mahwah, NJ: Erlbaum.

Schopler, E., & Reichler, R. J. (1971). Developmental therapy by parents with their own autistic child. In M. Rutter (Ed.), *Infantile autism: Concepts, characteristics and treatment* (pp. 206–227). London: Churchill.

Shriver, M. D., Allen, K. D., & Matthews, J. R. (1999) Assessment and treatment of children with autism in the schools. *School Psychology Review, 28(4),* 535–537.

Siegel, B. (1996). *The world of the autistic child: Understanding and treating the disorder.* New York: Oxford University Press.

Simpson, I. L., & Myles, B. S. (1995). Facilitated communication in children and youth with disabilities: An enigma in search of a perspective. *Focus on Autism and Other Developmental Disabilities, 16(2),* 68.

Stark, R. (1990). *Childhood depression: School-based interventions.* New York: Guilford Press.

Sundberg, M. L., & Partington, J. W. (1998). *Teaching language for children with Autism or other developmental disabilities.* Pleasant Hill, CA: Behavior Analysts, Inc.

Sundberg, M. L. (1993). The application of establishing operations. *The Behavior Analyst, 16,* 211–214.

Troxell, L. B., & Ingram, D. H. (2000). *Functional playground observation checklist.* Unpublished assessment instrument.

Wilder, D. A., & Carr, J. E. (1998). Recent advances in the modification of establishing operations to reduce aberrant behavior. *Behavioral Interventions, 13,* 43–59.

15

Female Adolescents with Eating Disorders: A Cognitive-Behavioral Approach

ROSEMARY B. MENNUTI, ANDREA BLOOMGARDEN & NICOLE GABRIEL

Eating disorders have become increasingly prevalent among children and adolescents in contemporary society (Graber, Brooks-Gunn, Paikoff, & Warren, 1994). In fact, eating disorders are becoming a very concerning health epidemic in female adolescents in most Western countries (Grave, 2003; Lewinson, Hops, & Roberts, 1993). These disorders cause many health and psychological hazards to the lives of their victims. If serious enough, they can even cause death (Grave, 2003; Kohn & Golden, 2001).

Research has indicated that eating disorders (e.g., Anorexia Nervosa, Bulimia Nervosa, and Eating Disorder, NOS) tend to develop in late childhood and continue throughout late adolescence and into adulthood (Lask & Bryant-Waugh, 2000). Thus, the emergence of eating disorders and negative eating patterns is a concern that many female adolescents will experience within their adolescent and school-aged years (Grave, 2003). Currently, it is estimated that 1 to 3 in every 500 girls (nearly 2.5 million girls) presents or will exhibit restrictive or bingeing and purging behaviors between the ages of 12 and 19 (Graber et al., 1994). Furthermore, recent studies claim that 5 to 15% of school-aged and high school–aged females experience some symptoms, if not all the criteria for a diagnosable eating disorder (Graber et al., 1994). It is important to note that although the focus of this chapter is primarily on female adolescents with eating disorders, there also has been an increase of male adolescents who report symptoms of disordered eating patterns (Striegel-Moore & Smolak, 2002).

These statistics reveal a disturbing trend among young adolescents. It is imperative to recognize and understand the seriousness of these statistics in order to begin developing programs to detect, treat, and prevent eating disorders, and, thus, help decrease this growing negative trend. Consequently, it has been suggested that because many school personnel have consistent interactions with a large number of students, they can play an integral part in the prevention and early detection of adolescents who manifest symptoms of eating disorders or disordered eating (Boes, Ng, & Davison, 2004; Massey-Stokes, 2000). These individuals are inherently placed in an ideal position to begin to identify and institute early prevention measures to aid students with negative eating patterns (Massey-Stokes, 2000). It is intended that through early detection and prevention, school mental health professionals, nurses, and teachers will be able to identify issues surrounding negative eating and be able to provide a proactive approach to decrease this epidemic and promote healthy development (Boes et al., 2004; Grave, 2003).

ADOLESCENT FEMALES AND EATING DISORDERS

The developmental stage of adolescence presents many stressors and challenges for young individuals. Some of these challenges include coping with the psychological and physical changes of puberty, transitioning toward independence and autonomy, developing relationships with friends, and achieving an integrated self-identity (Graber et al., 1994; Massey-Stokes, 2000). Many of these conflicts can jeopardize both their health and well-being. Because the period of adolescence is a time of rapid emotional, physical, social, and psychological maturation, successful transitions are critical to their overall health and quality of life (Massey-Stokes, 2000).

Female adolescents are often in a flux of change, thus making them vulnerable to the many influences around them (Graber et al., 1994). At times, the pressures of life become too much for them to handle and they feel completely out of control (Attie & Brooks-Gunn, 1989). They strive to make good decisions and increase sense of self, but sometimes their choices lead them in a different direction. This alternate pathway can lead them to develop negative coping patterns, which inevitably contribute to disconnection in relationship, silence of inner voice, and poor self-esteem (Surrey, 1991; Brown & Gilligan, 1992). These negative characteristics can potentially pave the path for the development of an eating disorder (Kohn & Golden, 2001; Massey-Stokes, 2000; Mishne, 1986). Generally, eating disorders are classified under Anorexia Nervosa, Bulimia Nervosa, and Eating Disorder, NOS (Grave, 2003). According to Fairburn and Walsh (2002), an eating disorder can be defined as "a persistent disturbance of eating behavior or behavior intended to control weight, which significantly impairs physical health or psychological functioning. This disturbance should not be secondary to any recognized general medical disorder or any psychiatric disorder" (p.171).

Specifically, the diagnostic criteria for anorexia nervosa include "a refusal to maintain body weight at or above a minimally normal weight for age and height, an intense fear of gaining weight or becoming fat, a disturbance in the way which one's body weight or shape is experienced, and finally, amenorrhea" (American

Psychiatric Association, 2003, p. 589). The diagnostic characteristics for bulimia nervosa include "recurrent episodes of binge eating. An episode of binge eating can either be eating, in a discrete period of time, an amount of food that is definitely larger that most people would consume during a similar period of time or a sense of lack of control over eating during an episode, recurrent inappropriate compensatory behavior in order to prevent weight gain such as self-induced vomiting, or misuse of laxatives, diuretics, enemas, or other medications; fasting; or excessive exercise, the binge eating and inappropriate compensatory behaviors both occur on average, at least twice a week for 3 months, self-evaluation is unduly influenced by body shape and weight, and the disturbance does not occur exclusively during episodes of Anorexia Nervosa" (American Psychiatric Association, 2003, p. 594).

Finally, the diagnostic criteria for Eating Disorder, NOS, includes "all other atypical eating disorders that do not meet the criteria for any specified Eating Disorder" (American Psychiatric Association, 2003, pp. 594–595). Pipher (1994) indicates that eating disorders or patterns of negative eating emerge as a coping mechanism for female adolescents to express their internal emotions in an effort to maintain a sense of control. When female adolescents lose their inner voice, and their awareness of personal needs, the outcome becomes an exerted effort to respond to external expectations. The symptoms of an eating disorder become a true projection of what the female adolescent is feeling about herself and her environment (Surrey, 1991). According to Steiner-Adair (1991), when adolescents feel that they have lost their ability to verbally express their thoughts, feelings and opinions, their bodies become the external self that speaks, metaphorically, through behavior. The adolescent's self-worth is evidenced in her attempts to communicate through her illness (Steiner-Adair, 1991).

Often times, this strategy takes on a life of its own, and the mechanism becomes a preoccupation for adolescents to control their weight, life, and world. Pleasure is often replaced by negative feelings of anger, despair, and guilt. Their restricting or bingeing/purging behavior becomes a secretive habit, one that is followed by guilt and sadness (Pipher, 1994). On the outside, the adolescent presents as a sociable individual who wants desperately to please others and be accepted by peers and family. On the inside, female adolescents with eating disorders feel empty, out of control, unable to speak their true feelings, and poor about their sense of self. They become a slave to their eating disorders and, consequently, lose their voice and true identity (Pipher, 1994; Steiner-Adair, 1991).

Female adolescents with eating disorders also encompass many developmental, psychological, cultural, and behavioral characteristics within their disorder. Developmentally, adolescents experience many physical and psychosocial changes during the adolescent years. These include physical pubertal changes (e.g., increase in body fat) and social emotional changes (e.g., transitioning between childhood and adulthood, loosening connections to parents, and becoming more independent and autonomous), as well as the development of a stable and cohesive personality identity (Attie & Brooks-Dunn, 1989; Graber et al., 1994). According to researchers, the increase of body fat at pubertal transformation is one of the most significant changes that may contribute to negative eating behaviors and to adolescent desire to be thin (Attie & Brooks-Dunn, 1989).

Within the psychological realm, many of adolescents' perceptions, beliefs, and attitudes are distorted (Attie & Brooks-Dunn, 1989; Mishne, 1986). One of the major distortions is body image, including shape and weight. This distortion is geared by the desire to be thin, loss of weight, and the fear of being fat (Hsu, 1996; Lask & Bryant-Waugh, 2000). Eventually, these distortions become a means to mood regulation. Adolescents find calmness and security not only in food, but also in the act of purging. This act becomes very addictive not only for the control, but also to achieve a sense of solace and to provide a means of expressing their anger and guilt. In time, this is the very behavior that cannot be controlled and results in feelings of extreme distress and helplessness (Costin, 1996). Episodes can be precipitated by many different factors such as anxiety, tension, or boredom. Rarely is hunger the catalyst for the restricting and bingeing/purging patterns (Brownell & Fairburn, 1995).

Within the cultural realm, society contributes significantly to the development of adolescents' cognitive distortions. This is because of the emphasis on being thin. In Western culture, being thin and physically fit has come to symbolize attractiveness, competence, control, and success (Fallon, Katzman, & Wooley, 1994; Mishne, 1996). In addition, there has been an increasing trend of a thin beauty ideal. Society attributes self-worth to an individual's level of attractiveness and molding potential to fit a particular standard. The standards set by society are unrealistic for many adolescents to achieve. As a result, they attempt to take control of the situation themselves. It is because of this unrealistic standard set by society that adolescents strive to be thin, no matter how great the cost may be to their own health and bodies (Attie & Brooks-Dunn, 1989).

METHODS OF ASSESSMENT

As Pipher (1994) points out, at any give time, 50% of all American women are on some kind of diet. By the age of 5, children have internalized cultural norms about body size teaching them to hate and fear fat kids and fat people (Frontline, 1998). Thus, the natural inclination for children to love and be curious about their own bodies, and all bodies, is short-circuited as they integrate denigrating cultural judgments into their own developing body image. By adolescence, the issues surrounding changes in one's body, peer pressure, and cultural norms contribute to the fact that eating disorders are among the most common psychiatric problem that affects young women (Kreipe & Birndorf, 2000). How do school personnel begin to identify and assess for disordered eating patterns, distorted body image, excessive exercising, or full-blown eating disorders? A good interview is often the most powerful means to assist in identification. Standardized and informal assessment measures also can be used to help screen for eating disorders, develop strategies, and measure treatment progress.

Interviews

Assessing for the presence and severity of an eating disorder requires of the interviewer both the knowledge of which questions to ask, and the ability to truly embody a nonjudgmental collaborative stance with the student. When beginning a session with a student who has been referred as potentially having an eating disorder, it is important to use all of the skills that one has acquired for building rapport. These may include such things as asking the student about her perceptions of what is happening in her life in general, in her family, with her friendships, and in the school setting. Because eating disorder symptoms may mirror an adolescent's emotional struggles, or serve as a metaphor for her relational experiences, it is crucial to understand the adolescent in context, viewing the symptoms as a language for expressing her feelings. That context can be as broad as how she views herself in relation to societal expectations of what girls and young women are supposed to be, or as specific as noticing particular themes of interpersonal conflict in family relationships. The eating disorder symptoms are not a separate, invading entity that have landed unwittingly upon this girl. Instead, they may either be an expression of, or a solution to, some form of suffering for which she does not yet have the language to express. In sum, the interview style should be interactive and dynamic, respecting the adolescent as the expert of her own experience.

In the beginning, it is helpful to ask the student what her understanding is of why she is here for this meeting. After hearing what she knows and expects of the meeting, the interviewer can collaboratively create an agenda for the session by explaining what his or her understanding is of the reason for the meeting, and what concerns will be covered in this one session. Although the interviewer wants to leave the appointment with a sense of how severe and imminently dangerous the eating disordered symptoms that are present may be, he or she also wants to confirm that the student feels respected, empowered, and not shamed by this personal sharing about her eating and body image. Thus, whereas at minimum the interviewer needs to know how dangerous the situation is, it is essential to pace questions and provide time for in-depth answers. Additionally, hearing the student articulate her perspective about eating, body image, and other aspects of her life are as important as getting details about what she is doing.

Initially, open-ended statements and questions such as, "Tell me about yourself," "Who do you hang out with," and "What do you do when you are not in school," are helpful for opening a dialogue with the student about who she is, what her life is like, and how she is feeling about herself. After some discussion has ensued, questions about how she feels about herself in relation to her body and eating can follow more naturally. Knowing how she feels about the topic of body and eating helps the interviewer to be sensitive to possible feelings of shame, fear, being overwhelmed about the symptoms, and even about sharing them at the interview. Discussion of the details of an eating disorder is a very personal disclosure, requiring much courage on the student's part, and often requires a tangible sense that the interviewer is not judging her for engaging in these behaviors. Although it has been stated that eating-disordered clients are typically poor historians about their symptoms, some of the distortions may be because the symptoms can be very embarrassing to admit, particularly in a culture that alternately derides people for "overeating" and lauds extreme degrees of food restriction as "strength." Thus, food and body image are sensitive subjects, and a student who feels either judged or objectified could find it easier to lie or inaccurately report these behaviors.

Gentle but direct questions about the eating disorder symptoms are usually needed to elicit the information to determine a diagnosis. One nonjudgmental way to begin is to ask the student to describe a typical day with regard to her eating—What does she normally eat, when, and how? If the answer is vague or very general, such as "I eat breakfast at 6, lunch at 12, and dinner with my family," then the interviewer must ask very specific questions. For example, "What do you normally eat for breakfast?" "Who are you with?" "How long does it usually take to eat?" "Where do you usually eat it?" "Do you enjoy it?" and "How do you feel after you eat it?" Specific questions help the student understand the level of detail the interviewer is looking for. These should be posed out of a natural curiosity to enhance the interviewer's understanding of the student's relationship with food, behaviorally and intrapsychicly.

The interviewer needs to know exactly what behaviors the student engages in. These include purposefully restricting caloric intake, compensatory behaviors such as vomiting, use of Ipecac, use of laxatives, diuretics and overexercising, bingeing on large amounts of food, perceived bingeing, and eating often but never eating specific meals. To put these behaviors in context, asking the student about her family's eating norms, particular family members who may have eating issues, or cultural and ethnic views about food, body, and women's roles can reveal pertinent information. The whole pattern of how someone eats, including what time of day, how much, types of foods typically eaten (e.g., carbohydrates, protein, fats, desserts), how the student feels about her eating (e.g., out of control, in control, pleased, displeased), and cultural and family context is important information in forming the case conceptualization.

The interviewer needs to know about the student's physical well-being and ask questions to probe for any signs or symptoms of imminently dangerous medical complications. Asking the student to get a medical evaluation is also necessary as it is beyond the realm of a school psychologist, school mental health professional, or teacher to determine whether or not a student's health is in jeopardy. However, certain signs and symptoms could require a more urgent evaluation than others. Questions should include a brief inquiry assessing the presence or absence of each of the following: chest pain or pressure, light-headedness or fainting, dizziness, blood in stool or vomit, any medical conditions that might be affected by the eating problems (e.g., diabetes, appropriate use of insulin), abdominal pain, irregular or scanty menses, sleep apnea, and dental problems (particularly with bulimics who vomit). An affirmative to any of these indicates that the eating disorder is likely to be having an adverse effect on the person's health, particularly if the symptoms were not there prior to the eating disorder's commencement, and if they abate as the symptoms wane. Even if the student reports that she feels completely fine and healthy, a medical exam should be considered by the student and family. The interviewer can be helpful by exploring the student's comfort with her current primary care physician, encouraging her to change doctors if she does not feel comfortable enough with the current one to talk openly about these issues.

Additionally, an assessment of mental health issues often associated with eating disorders is needed. These include mood disorders, problems with impulsivity, self-harming urges or activities (e.g., cutting oneself), obsessive-compulsive disorder, anxiety disorders, and other addictions (e.g., drug and alcohol).

Although families may not be as involved at a school setting as in an outpatient therapy setting, the shock of discovering that one's adolescent has an eating disorder typically warrants some level of family involvement and school support. In most cases, if a school mental health professional discovers that a student has an eating disorder, parents will need to be informed because eating disorders can be of serious danger. It is a judgment call on the part of the school mental health professional, depending on the severity of the symptoms, as to whether he or she informs the parents. In many cases, unless there is imminent danger, it is best for the school mental health professional to broach the topic of informing the parents collaboratively with the student, so that the adolescent feels prepared for this to be shared, and feels supported when the parents react with great upset, as is a normal reaction when most parents find out that their child has an eating disorder. The school mental health professional can serve as a liaison in that process, helping the student to decide whether she would like to tell her parents or have the school mental health professional call them, deciding how best to explain it and how much detail to share, and setting up a meeting with one or both parents along with the student as a means of facilitating a positive, informative, and supportive exchange.

The school mental health professional should make every attempt to have the parents, possibly the siblings if clinically indicated, come in for a family meeting, once the student and school mental health professional have discussed a plan for this and the student feels prepared for it. The disclosure of the eating disorder could happen in many ways, based on clinical appropriateness: The student could tell the parents if she feels comfortable to do that, the school mental health professional could tell the parents over the phone, or the school mental health professional could call the parents in for a family conference and tell them in person, if there is some concern about how they might react to the news. Once in the family meeting, the school mental health professional needs to assess and collect information about the following issues.

- The quality of the relationships within the family as well as the overall atmosphere and communication styles.
- The family members' thoughts and feelings about the eating disorder, their concerns for the student, for the other children, and for themselves.
- A family history of eating disorders or disordered eating and exercising and details of eating patterns and dieting patterns of family members, especially parents.
- Strengths within the family and other support systems in place to help with overcoming the presenting difficulties.
- Situations in the family that may be sustaining the eating disorder.

Measures

Standardized questionnaires also can be used to gather additional data that will facilitate treatment. There are very few measures for use with children and adolescents and those that are available are mainly adaptations of adult measures. The following is a description of some of the available instruments.

- *Children's Eating Attitudes Test* (ChEAT; Maloney et al., 1988) is a 26-item self-report questionnaire adaptation of the Eat Attitudes Test (Garner & Garfinkle, 1979) that can be used as a screening instrument to help in identifying children at risk. It addresses perceived body image, obsessions and preoccupations with food, and dieting practices. The test can be used with 8- to 13-year-olds and takes about 30 minutes to complete. It is a modified version of the adult version known as the EAT.
- *Kids Eating Disorders Survey* (KEDS; Childress et al., 1992) is a 14-question survey using yes, no, and don't know forms of responses in a simplified format for children.
- *The Child Eating Disorder Examination* (Bryant-Waugh et al., 1996) is a children's version of the EDE (Fairburn & Cooper, 1993). This assessment is a semistructured interview for use with children from 7 to 14 years of age that offers severity ratings for behavior and attitudes of eating disorders. The four scales included are Restraint, Eating Concerns, Shape Concern, and Weight Concern. It is used to assist in diagnosis and monitor treatment progress. *The Eating Disorder Examination* (Fairburn & Cooper, 1993) is considered the "gold standard" assessment tool to use with older adolescents and adults.

Some adult instruments that also can be used with older adolescents include:

- *Eating Disorder Inventory–2* (EDI-2; Garner, 1991) is a 91-item self-report questionnaire that is used to assess psychological and behavioral traits of Anorexia Nervosa and Bulimia Nervosa. The 11 subscales look at the following aspects: (1) drive for thinness; (2) bulimia; (3) body dissatisfaction; (4) ineffectiveness; (5) perfectionism; (6) interpersonal distrust; (7) interceptive awareness; (8) maturity fears; (9) asceticism; (10) impulse regulation; and (11) social insecurity (Garner, Olmsted, & Polivy, 1983). It can be used for screening purposes and to measure treatment effectiveness and symptom severity.
- *The Eat Attitudes Test* (Garner & Garfinkle, 1979) is a self-report questionnaire that has 40 questions and was developed to assess attitudes and behaviors associated with Anorexia Nervosa and Bulimia Nervosa.
- *The Body Shape Questionnaire* (BSQ; Cooper, Taylor, Cooper, & Fairburn, 1987) is a 34-item test used to assess body weight and body shape concerns in those with eating disorders.

CONCEPTUALIZATION FOR TREATMENT

Once the data have been gathered, a case conceptualization leading naturally to a course of treatment can be developed. The interview and assessment measures serve the various purposes of gleaning the relevant information, hearing the student's story in context, and helping her to develop a sense of empowerment, inspiring her to join the clinician as together they move forward with a plan to aid in her recovery process.

Collecting the information and hearing her story in context helps the school mental health professional understand the unique way that the eating problems developed and have worked for the student up until this point. As the interviewer listens to her story, the information gathered is broken down to answer the following questions. In some cases, these questions need not be asked directly, as the student who is expressing her story may naturally answer them. At other times, if the interviewer notices a gap in understanding, it may be helpful to ask these directly, or probe more specifically with related questions. Ultimately, in order to conceptualize and individualize the treatment to meet the student's unique needs, the interviewer needs to know the answers to the following questions (see Table 15.1).

Once the interviewer has gathered all the necessary information, he or she can weave together a conceptualization of both how the eating disorder started and what maintains it, to create an individualized treatment plan addressing all relevant aspects of the disorder.

Table 15.1 Case Conceptualization Questions for Eating Disorders

Functional Analysis Questions	Thought and Belief Questions
When and how did the symptoms develop?	What underlying core beliefs about self are evident?
What maintains or reinforces the symptoms?	
What needs are the symptoms meeting?	What thought processes relevant to the eating behaviors or body image appear to be extreme, distorted, or unusual?
Rerational Questions	**Context of Eating Disorders (Family and School)**
What relational barriers does she face in her social environment, school, and/or family?	What family of origin cultural norms around food contribute to the development of or maintain the eating disorder symptoms?
In what ways has she submerged her authenticity in order to stay in a relationship (albeit with a false front), or to protect herself from further rejection?	How does the culture within the school, including such aspects as the student's participation in given activities, the influence of other students, teachers, peer pressures, or being teased, contribute to the development and/or maintenance of the eating disorder symptoms?
How do the symptoms help her maintain these stances?	
Stage of Change Questions	
What is her willingness to change?	
Which aspects of the symptoms does she like?	
Which aspects of the symptoms does she not like?	

COGNITIVE-BEHAVIORAL INTERVENTION

The role of the CBT school mental health professional is to help the students understand that their interpretation of events, their schemas, and core beliefs shape their experience, and that carefully examining their thought processes and assumed beliefs is an excellent entry point for creating change. Thus, in gathering the history, the CBT school mental health professional listens for assumptions and distorted or extreme statements, to help the students recognize how these possibly incorrect beliefs ultimately create their reality. The CBT school mental health professional approaches distorted or extreme beliefs on two fronts: (1) directly challenging the veracity of the belief, helping the student realize what effect it has on her mood and self-worth to repeat such a belief to herself, and (2) helping the student recognize the core belief that is rooted beneath the distortion by using various techniques such as the "downward arrow" approach. In the latter example, the CBT school mental health professional can ask of the student, "What does it mean about you if that belief were true?" In this way, the school mental health professional begins to address the themes that affect such issues as self-concept, self-esteem, body image, empowerment in social context, and self-efficacy. So-called distorted ways of thinking often present a kernel of truth. The CBT school mental health professional must help the student to both understand the true aspects of the thinking from the distortion, and develop skills to make change if the true aspect is no longer adaptive. For example, if it is true that the student wields a certain power in her family or social world because she is extremely thin and attains both admiration and concern, she must find a healthier way to have that power. Or, if bingeing offers her a certain comfort or distance from people, she must find a healthier and more effective way to give herself comfort or needed boundaries from people. Making these changes is much easier said than done. The beginning of the process for the student is recognizing how the symptoms are working for her, and how the distortions can at times be incorrect and harmful. In the context of a very supportive relationship with the school mental health professional, the student is likely to begin to make these connections, and may be willing to experiment with making changes that will ultimately mean less reliance on the eating disordered symptoms and more on new behaviors that will ultimately be more effective and healthier.

CASE EXAMPLE

Chrissie is a 14-year-old girl who was encouraged to talk with the school mental health professional when someone overheard her throwing up in the bathroom. Reluctantly, she came to an appointment with the school mental health professional. Although she was afraid to talk with someone about her problems with eating and body image, and was feeling ashamed of the fact that she makes herself vomit, she also was secretly relieved that maybe someone could help her. She attended the appointment.

Someone had called the school mental health professional about this, so she knew about Chrissie's vomiting, and, wanting to build rapport, she decided to make an extra effort to be extremely supportive of Chrissie. She told her that it was great that Chrissie decided to attend the appointment.

The school mental health professional started asking some questions about how long Chrissie had been throwing up and how she felt about coming in today to talk about it. Chrissie responded by saying, "It's not a big deal, I don't do it that much." She had her arms crossed and sat low in her seat, as the school mental health professional sat forward and tried to engage her with more questions. "Well, something made you come in, and I'm really glad you did. What were you hoping might happen here today?" "I don't know," said Chrissie. Chrissie was ambivalent. She had a lot to say but it was a real risk to finally share openly about this shameful secret, these behaviors that she felt were disgusting and embarrassing, that the school mental health professional was so directly asking about. As the school mental health professional kept trying to engage her with more questions, at first she gave short answers, one or a few words, yes or no answers, to try to hold ground and not share too much. The school mental health professional remained calm and patient, and validated Chrissie by saying, "I know it can be very hard to talk about these things with someone new. Is there anything I can do to make your more comfortable?"

Tears welled up in Chrissie's eyes against her will. She tried to fight them, looking away from the school mental health professional. The school mental health professional again affirmed, "I know it's hard, I give you a lot of credit for trying to get help," in a gentle voice. Finally, Chrissie began to sob and started to share more openly about her eating disorder. "I have to throw up if I eat too much, I feel like I'm fat and I don't want to be fat. I've tried to stop it and I know I shouldn't do it but I can't stop."

Chrissie explained that she had been doing this for a few years and that this is the first time she's told anyone about it. Going back to how it all started, Chrissie explained that she had gotten many messages that she needed to be thin to be perceived as attractive. Her mother was always on a diet and always complaining that she needed to lose "5 pounds." Once, Chrissie remembers her dad saying she was getting "pudgy" and she was called "fatty" on the playground when she was in 4th grade by a boy she liked. She had even overheard her teacher and coach saying to another girl that the girl needed to watch her weight. Even though it wasn't said to her, she felt badly for that girl, and would never want to be in a position where her coach would say that about her. There were many other examples of these kinds of messages that she needed to control her weight, and as Chrissie spoke, the memories flowed one after another. So finally, about 2 years ago, she remembered eating an ice cream sundae and feeling "disgusting" afterward. She felt so awful, fat, and undeserving that she thought she'd try to throw up, to get rid of the dreaded calories. She had heard about this as a diet tip from other girls, and was surprised that she was able to throw up fairly easily after sticking her finger into her throat. What a relief she felt, knowing she could eat and get rid of the calories.

Eventually, over time, it evolved into her current pattern. Whereas it had started as an occasional activity that she believed helped her to control her weight, as she gradually used the technique more and more she one day found that she no longer had control over the behavior. Now, the behavior had control over her life, and in some ways her life revolved around her eating and negative feelings about herself and her body. She felt that about 95% of time she was thinking about wanting to lose weight, how "fat I feel," finding ways to cover up her secret, planning about how to get the food for her afternoon binge, and trying to hide everything from her parents. It was after school that she normally binged because no one was usually home and she could have the privacy to eat everything she wanted and then vomit. It had gone from a simple one-time discovery to an almost daily routine. And, she still wanted to lose more weight and felt "out of control" with her eating. The school mental health professional's observation was that she appeared to be an average-sized 14-year-old.

She was a popular kid but, recently, more withdrawn, feeling that the pressure to do well in school, be thin and attractive, to be the poised, happy, upbeat together person that everyone thought she was, was starting to make her feel like she just wanted to be left alone. In a sense, when she was alone, she could be more true to her feelings, which were that she did not feel good enough, had much self-doubt, and felt undeserving of positive attention from anyone. So when she was alone at home, it was a respite from the façade; through the bingeing she was giving something to herself she never got—whatever it was that she truly wanted, at least for that moment, and then she had to dutifully give it up afterward. The process was satisfying in the moment; it felt like a reward and a punishment all in one.

The change in personality and behaviors had begun to be noticed by others. Her friends wondered why she didn't want to "hang out" after school, and she felt estranged and distant from her parents, feeling like they had no idea who she was anymore. When she was overheard throwing up in the bathroom, a friend confronted her and said she was worried about her because she seemed different now, like "you don't care about us anymore."

As the school mental health professional listened to Chrissie's story unfold, she listened carefully for negative core beliefs and distortions in thinking. She noticed that Chrissie felt undeserving of positive attention, and heard Chrissie say "If I go back to eating normally, I will become obese because I ruined my metabolism." The school mental health professional was careful to notice possible distortions and extreme statements, but challenged them without necessarily saying they were "wrong" per se. For example, she asked Chrissie, "Why do you feel that you don't deserve for people to like you?" Chrissie said, "Because I'm a liar, I'm disgusting." "What does that mean about you, that you've lied about your eating?" "I'm a bad person for lying." "Did you know that most people do lie about their eating disorder before they feel ready to be honest about it?" Thus, in normalizing her behavior, she helped challenge Chrissie's core belief that she was a bad person, rather than trying to tell Chrissie that she is not a bad person. Although the intervention did not automatically make Chrissie feel good about herself, it opened the door to Chrissie recognizing that she had come to label herself as a bad person, when in fact, she is suffering from a very challenging problem.

Similarly, when Chrissie said, "If I gain 5 more pounds I will hate myself even more," the school mental health professional realized that while this seemed extreme, it may have been true for Chrissie. This may not be a distortion in that it may be true, but the question is, "What does gaining the 5 pounds mean about her?" The school mental health professional asked her to explore that. Chrissie answered, "I would be out of control, weak, ugly." Gradually, it became clearer that Chrissie was struggling with self-doubt and feeling insecure and not attractive and that the feelings were probably there, underlying or to some extent, independent of her eating disorder. A part of healing from her eating disorder would be to address these issues, not just work on changing her eating patterns.

The school mental health professional realized that the severity of the symptoms and complexity of the issues would require the building of a multidisciplinary team. She had gathered enough information to develop a working conceptualization. Chrissie's eating was severely impaired and she needed a strong intervention to stop this pattern that she could not stop on her own. She recognized that there were distortions in her thinking and core beliefs questioning her worth as a person. The reinforcer for her eating behavior is that it satisfied both the need to give to herself (the food she wanted, the pleasure of eating) and punish herself (the vomiting process was painful, the shame she felt afterward felt awful, but deserved), and the whole pattern was helping her to avoid dealing directly with issues of low self-esteem, disconnection from parents, and perfectionism about schoolwork. The school mental health professional communicated to Chrissie that the solution would be multifaceted. A medical doctor would need to assess her physical health, as these behaviors and the frequency with which she engaged in them could be quite harmful. She helped Chrissie prepare to tell her medical doctor. A nutritionist would be needed to help Chrissie develop a step-by-step plan to normalize her eating, introducing foods she'd considered "bad," and practicing eating more frequently to break the pattern of starving and bingeing. Family involvement would probably be helpful, and so perhaps a family mental health professional could be involved, but they would start with a family meeting with the school mental health professional, Chrissie and her parents. In sum, together, they developed a plan of action to ensure her medical safety, intervene with the behavior and symptoms around use of food as a coping strategy, and help her develop new ways to cope with feelings of self-doubt and questioning of her self-worth, so she could return to full engagement into her school life. Chrissie committed to coming in weekly to talk with the school mental health professional about these things, and felt that the school mental health professional would be a support and her ally in helping her get better on all of these levels.

IMPLICATION AND APPLICATIONS IN THE SCHOOL SETTING

When a student develops an eating disorder, it affects his or her learning, the total school experience, and the student's overall developmental process. Chrissie, for example, became more isolated and withdrawn, as the eating disorder took up so much of her thought and time. Although students with eating disorders may appear to "have it all together," inside they often feel unworthy, self-critical, unlovable, and undeserving, an inner experience that no one would expect of them. In some cases it could affect their learning and concentration—even if they are doing well in school, they might have to work harder as they are very distracted by either the nutritional deficits they are experiencing or the degree of obsessional thinking involved with their eating behaviors. Medical consequences that could occur include:

- Cardiovascular—(heart) arrhythmias (a fast, slow, or irregular heartbeat), bradycardia (slow heartbeat), hypotension (low blood pressure)
- Hematological (blood)
- Gastrointestinal (stomach and intestines)
- Renal (kidney)
- Endocrine (hormones)
- Skeletal (bones)

Although some of the problems cannot be identified without medical tests, obvious symptoms and complaints could include tiredness, chest pain, stomach pain, and light-headedness. By contrast, in many cases a student may feel fine and have no awareness that her body is being harmed by her behaviors. She will report that she feels "fine" or even "better than ever." A positive self-report is not necessarily reflective of her true health status.

There is a plethora of causal factors related to the development of eating disorders, including the experiences one has in school. The school environment can produce pressures that contribute to the development and maintenance of the disorder for some youngsters. In the development of the disorder, peer experiences such as bullying, relational violence, being teased, and cliques all can create unbearable degrees of stress for teenagers. Being excluded at an age where peer acceptance is so important is excruciatingly painful. If the student is among the popular, she may feel the pressure to keep up a façade of perfection, as everyone expects of her, or feel guilty and undeserving of the attention. An outside observer cannot accurately evaluate how she perceives her school life. Academic pressure and competition is another stressor that can impact functioning in an adolescent. The need for superior grades and class rank status can become so important that the striving students are unable to maintain a balance that embraces the emotional and social aspects of life.

Students also are greatly affected by the attitudes toward food, body shape, and weight of teachers, coaches, and school staff, as well as the general norms of the school. Casual statements between teachers about their own dieting behavior or a coach who tells a student to lose weight can have a big impact, leading a student to initiate a diet. As in the case of Chrissie, once a student has a belief that she must control her weight, what starts off as a diet, or a one-time attempt to vomit after eating, can blossom into a full-blown eating disorder if other conditions are present. Thus, although school personnel most certainly have their own issues or biases about food and weight, and need not be perfect human beings with no problems of their own, it is important for them to be aware that a small comment can have a powerfully negative effect on a student who may already be vulnerable to external and outside influences. School personnel can be educated to realize that if they have their own issues about food, body, and weight, they can be mindful to limit their expression of these issues in public forums so as not to be poor role models to students who may struggle with these issues themselves.

By contrast, school personnel can be equally instrumental in facilitating recovery and helping to prevent eating disorders. School personnel who help students feel good about themselves, facilitate problem solving, and promote positive peer relationships help create an environment that lends itself to positive mental health status for students. To offset the larger culture where women's looks and sexuality are dispro-portionately overvalued compared to their intelligence, interests, and talents, teachers can be mindful to try to bring out and highlight students' strengths as people. Encouragement and emphasis on students being more than their looks or their pop-ularity can help create an environment that reinforces good character over more shallow aspects of humanity, such as physical beauty and money. It is this latter emphasis in American culture that needs to be offset by thoughtful teachers, parents, and adults who care to help students mature into healthy, whole human beings with positive self-images.

Another role of the school in the recovery process for a student with an eating disorder is to remain supportive and connected to the adolescent and become an active part of the intervention process. Too often, once an eating disorder is identified, a student is referred for therapy and no other services are designed or available within the school setting. Treatment often requires a team approach in which the school plays an integral part. One direct service that could be made available is school-based CBT oriented counseling. CBT helps students examine and reevaluate dysfunctional thoughts that impact behaviors and feelings, focusing on the present and encouraging active and collaborative ways to solve problems. Recognizing that students will normally have some dysfunctional thoughts that they have learned from those around them, or that may stem back to earlier times, school mental health professionals can enlighten students about the powerful connection between thoughts and feelings, helping them see that they can ultimately feel better when they chal-lenge certain thought patterns, and solve problems in creative ways. CBT is empow-ering in that it helps students recognize things they can do, from working on changing their patterns of thought and self-care, to increasing their interpersonal strengths, to solving social problems with peers and families—they have the power to make change in the current day. From dealing with pressures imparted by peers and parents, to the self-imposed pressure of wanting to succeed, dysfunctional beliefs such as "I'm not worth it" or " I can't do it" will fuel a negative cycle that will hinder success. CBT techniques can help break that pattern in a relatively time-limited, efficient manner.

Prevention can be of the utmost help when facing a problem as widespread as eating disorders. A meta-analysis from 1985–2002 found that school-based eating disorders prevention programs do not have a harmful effect and can even have a positive impact in helping these adolescents (Grave, 2003). The common apprehension that talking about something will make it worse is not supported by data; hence, it is a distorted and dysfunctional systemic belief. To the contrary, talking about and providing education about social problems will at worst do no harm, and it may offer some assistance to those who may be in the nascent stages of an eating disorder. Proper education and awareness could help a student seek treatment earlier on, or perhaps empower peers and teachers to deal with students who display the signs and symptoms of an eating disorder. Further research is needed to explore the best ways for prevention programs to positively impact the prevalence of eating disorders. However, the importance of attending to issues of eating disorders is emphasized and supported by the literature indicating that early detection and response intervention can reduce the severity of the eating disorder symptoms, as well as the medical and psychological consequences (http://www.lpch.org/diseaseHealthInfo/HealthLibrary/mentalhealth/anorexia.html).

CONCLUSIONS

Eating disorders are a pervasive problem for young female adolescents who are often faced with much change and are very vulnerable to the pressures and influence of their world. The medical and psychological consequences of an eating disorder affect a youngster's physical, emotional, socials, and academic development and functioning. Given that education plays a dominant role in the lives of youth, it is a natural entry point for identifying treatment needs and developing prevention programs to help curb this destructive behavior. Good treatment relies on a well-thought-out conceptualization for each individual and is grounded in the adolescent's developmental level, specific core beliefs, thought patterns, and subsequent behaviors. Although identification is the crucial first step, school personnel must take further action to implement strategies for treatment on individual, school, and system levels. Early recognition and treatment of eating disorders will help avoid the long-term physical and emotional sequelae of chronic eating-disordered adults.

REFERENCES

American Psychiatric Association (2000). *Diagnostic and statistical manual of mental disorders* (4th ed., text revision). Washington, DC: Author.

Attie, I., & Brooks-Gunn, J. (1989). Development of eating problems in adolescent girls: A longitudinal study. *Developmental Psychology, 25,* 70–79.

Boes, S. R., Ng, V., & Davison, T. (2004). Unmasking eating disorders in the schools. *Professional School Counseling, 7,* 376–378.

Brown, L. M., & Gilligan, C. (1992). *Meeting at the crossroads: Women's psychology and girls' development.* New York: Ballantine.

Brownell, K. D., & Fairburn, C. G. (Eds.). (1995). *Eating disorders and obesity.* New York: Guilford.

Bryant-Waugh, R., Cooper, P., Taylor, C., & Lask, B. (1996). The use of the eating disorder examination with children: A pilot study. *International Journal of Eating Disorders, 19,* 391–398.

Childress, A., Jarrell, M., & Brewerton, T. (April, 1992). *The kid's eating disorder survey (KEDS): Internal consistency, component analysis, and test-retest reliability.* Paper presented at the 5th International Conference on Eating Disorders, New York.

Cooper, P., Taylor, M., Cooper, Z., & Fairburn, C. (1987). The development and validation of the body shape questionnaire. *International Journal of Eating Disorders, 6,* 485–494.

Costin, C. (1996). *The eating disorder sourcebook.* Los Angeles: Lowell House.

Fairburn, C., & Cooper, Z. (1993). The eating disorder examination (12th ed.). In C. G. Fairburn & G. T. Wilson (Eds.), *Binge eating: Nature, assessment and treatment* (pp. 317–360). New York: Guildford Press.

Fairburn, C. G., & Walsh, B. T. (2002). Atypical eating disorders. In C. G. Fairburn & K. D. Brownell (Eds.), *Eating disorders and obesity: A comprehensive handbook* (p. 86). New York: Guilford.

Fallon, P., Katzman, M. A., & Wooley, S. C. (Eds.). (1994). *Feminist perspectives of eating disorders.* New York: Guilford.

Garner, D. (1991). *Eating disorders inventory-2: Professional manual.* Odessa, FL: Psychological Assessment Resources.

Garner, D., & Garfinkle, P. (1979). The eating attitudes test: An index of symptoms of anorexia nervosa. *Psychological Medicine, 9,* 273–279.

Garner, D., Olmsted, M., & Polivy, J. (1983). Development and validation of a multi-dimensional eating disorder inventory for anorexia nervosa and bulimia. *International Journal of Eating Disorders, 2,* 15–34.

Graber, J. A., Brooks-Dunn, J., Paikoff, R. L., & Warren, M. P. (1994). Prediction of eating problems: An 8-year study of adolescent girls. *Developmental Psychology, 30,* 823–834.

Grave, R. D. (2003). School-based prevention programs for eating disorders. *Disease Management and Health Outcomes, 11,* 579–592.

Hsu, L. K. (1996). Epidemiology of eating disorders. *Psychiatric Clinics of North America, 19,* 681–697.

Kohn, M., & Golden, N. H. (2001). Eating disorders in children and adolescents. *Pediatric Drugs, 3,* 91–99.

Kreipe, R. E., & Birndorf, S. A. (2000) Eating disorders in adolescents and young adults. *The Medical Clinics of North America, 84,* 1027–49.

Lask, B., & Bryant-Waugh, R. (Eds.). (2000). *Anorexia nervosa and related eating disorders in children and adolescents.* Hove, UK : Psychology Press.

Lewinson, P. M., Hops, H., & Roberts, R. E. (1993). Adolescent psychopathology: I. prevalence and incidence of depression and other DSM-II-R disorders in high school students. *Journal of Abnormal Psychology, 102,* 133–144.

Maloney, M., McGuire, J., & Daniels, S. (1988). Reliability testing of a children's version of the eating attitude test. *Journal of the American Academy of Child and Adolescent Psychiatry, 28,* 541–543.

Massey-Stokes, M. S. (2000). Prevention of disordered eating among adolescents. *The Clearing House, 335*–340.

Mishne, J. M. (1986). *Clinical work with adolescents.* New York: Free Press.

Pipher, M. (1994). *Reviving Ophelia: Saving the selves of adolescent girls.* New York: Ballantine.

Steiner-Adair, C. (1991). When the body speaks: Girls, eating disorders and psychotherapy. In C. Gilligan, A. G. Rogers, & D. L. Tolman (Eds.), *Women, girls and psychotherapy* (pp. 253–266). New York: Harrington Park.

Striegel-Moore, R. H., & Smolak, L. (Eds.). (2002). *Eating Disorders: Innovative Directions in Research and Practice.* Washington, DC: American Psychological Association.

Sullivan, M. (Executive Producer). (1998). *FAT [Television broadcast].* Boston, MA: Public Broadcasting Service.

Surrey, J. L. (1991). Eating patterns as a reflection of women's development. In J. V. Jordan, A. G. Kaplan, J. B. Miller, I. P. Stiver, & J. L. Surrey (Eds.), *Women's growth in connection: Writings from the Stone Center* (pp. 237–250). New York: Guilford.

16

Substance Abuse Prevention: School-Based Cognitive-Behavioral Approaches

SUSAN G. FORMAN

The prevention of substance abuse among children and adolescents has been a concern of educators for several decades. Prevalence rates of substance abuse among youth have been tracked consistently by the federal government, because of potential negative effects on health, as well as academic, social, and emotional development. *Monitoring the Future* is an annual study, initiated in 1975, funded by the National Institute on Drug Abuse, comprised of surveys of nationally representative samples of students in secondary schools throughout the United States (Johnston, O'Malley, & Bachman, 2003). This survey studies the extent of substance use for students in the 8th, 10th, and 12th grades, as well as attitudinal indicators including perceived risk of harm in taking a drug, disapproval of others who take drugs, and perceived availability of drugs.

The 2003 data indicated that 54% of 12th graders have tried cigarettes, 77% have tried alcohol, 46% have tried marijuana, and 53% have tried other illicit drugs. Vicodin was the second most used drug reported by 12th graders after marijuana.

Of more concern than lifetime use is substance use that is more frequent or that involves large quantities. Over 8% of high school seniors reported smoking at least a half a pack of cigarettes per day, and 16% reported that they are daily cigarette smokers. Alcohol use within the past 30 days was reported by 47.5% of the seniors. Alcohol use to the point of inebriation was reported by 21% of 8th graders, 44% of 10th graders, and 62% of 12th graders. Six percent of high school seniors reported that they had been daily marijuana smokers at some time for at least a month before the survey.

In the 2003 survey, several attitudinal changes were found. There was an increase in perceived risk for regular marijuana use in 8th, 10th, and 12th graders, and a decline in the perceived availability of marijuana. In addition, the degree of risk associated with use of ecstasy rose for all grades, as did disapproval of ecstasy use. Unfortunately, the perceived risk of inhalant use declined among 8th and 10th graders.

Monitoring the Future also provides estimates of age of initiation for various drugs. Based on retrospective responses from 8th, 10th, and 12th graders, it is estimated that by the end of 6th grade between 15% and 20% of students have had their first cigarette, between 7% and 23% have had their first alcoholic beverage, and between 3% and 6% have tried marijuana. Thus, some children are abusing drugs by age 12, and it is likely that some begin earlier. This is significant because early initiation of substance use is associated with later greater drug involvement. However, many youth experiment with drugs and do not repeat the experience. There is substantial discussion in the literature about how to distinguish use from abuse. In general, there is agreement that any regular use of a psychoactive drug by a child is abuse. For adolescents, frequency, quantity, and negative consequences such as health problems, injuries, arrests, and school discipline or academic problems are typically considered in determining abuse.

LITERATURE REVIEW

Substance abuse in youth is usually accompanied by one or more predictable developmental characteristics, personality variables, or stressful life events or environmental conditions. These are called risk factors. A risk factor is defined as any characteristic or condition that, if present in an individual, increases the probability of substance abuse. Research supports a multiple risk factor model; no single risk factor has been found to be related to adolescent substance abuse. Instead, exposure to a larger number of risk factors has been associated with a greater likelihood of substance abuse.

Protective factors are conditions that have been found to prevent, limit, or reduce substance abuse. In the presence of existing risk factors, a protective factor may counter, buffer, or neutralize risk for substance abuse. There may be a cumulative effect for protective factors so that the greater number of protective factors an individual has, the greater the reduction in risk for developing substance use problems (Swadi, 1999).

Risk and protective factors can be viewed in terms of five domains: individual, family, peer, school, and community. Different risk and protective factors become evident at different stages of childhood and adolescence, and the presence of one risk or protective factor can influence the later emergence of another. This is called a developmental risk trajectory or path. For example, aggressive behavior can emerge early in children. Once the child enters school, aggressive behavior can lead to academic failure and rejection by peers, which may in turn lead to school dropout and association with peers who abuse drugs.

Risk factors at the individual level include difficult temperament in early childhood, defined as slow adaptability, low sociability, high emotional reactivity, and low soothability (Lerner & Vicary, 1984). Negative mood, low self-esteem, rebelliousness/impulsivity, aggression, high need for social approval, and low asser-tiveness are also individual psychological risk factors (Swadi, 1999). In addition, high sensation seeking and low harm avoidance are psychological predispositions that have been linked to substance abuse (Cloninger, Sigvardsson, & Bohman, 1988). Sensation seeking is defined as a predisposition toward exploratory behavior and novel experiences, and the willingness to take risks to engage in these behaviors. Harm avoidance refers to a predisposition to react intensely to aversive stimuli. Psychological disorders, including conduct disorder, attention-deficithyperactivity disorder, and depression, also have been identified as risk factors for substance abuse (Swadi, 1999). Behavioral risk factors include aggressive and antisocial behavior in early childhood, delinquency and other illegal behaviors during adolescence, and disregard for conventional social values (White, Metzger, Nagin, & Stouthamer-Loeber, 2004). Also, early initiation of substance use is predictive of later substance abuse. With regard to genetic-biological factors, the biological children of alcoholics are three to four times more likely to develop alcohol problems than children of nonalcoholic parents, regardless of who raised them (Shuckit, 1984). Protective individual personality factors include high self-acceptance or esteem, self-efficacy, high religiosity, harm avoidance, and commitment to societal norms and conventional values (De Wit, Silverman, Goodstadt, & Stoduto, 1995).

The role of life events and experiences as risk factors for substance abuse also has been examined by researchers. Adolescents who abuse substances report expe-riencing a greater number of negative life events and use alcohol or illicit substances to deal with problems, negative feelings, and stressful situations. Thus, for some adolescents, substance use may reflect a maladaptive coping response to stress. Studies have found higher prevalence rates for bereavement, unwanted and teenage pregnancy, and sexual victimization in childhood or adolescence among adolescent substance users relative to nonusers (Swadi, 1999).

Family risk factors include favorable or permissive parental attitudes toward substance use and actual parental substance use. Even if an adolescent is not aware of a parent's substance use, there may still be increased risk if that substance use negatively affects parenting style and the family environment. High family conflict, parental discord or divorce, poor family communication, low levels of parental support or control, low parental monitoring, inconsistent parental discipline, and lack of family closeness are risk factors for adolescent substance abuse (Bry, 1983). Family protective factors include strong family relationships characterized by non-conflictual and affectionate parent-child relationships, family involvement and attachment, parental monitoring, clear and consistent standards and expectations, and nonusing parental (or other appropriate adult) role models (Bry, 1996). Risk is also lowered when parents help their children develop long-term goals and educate them about the negative physical and psychological effects, as well as parentally imposed consequences, of substance use (Brook, Whiteman, & Gordon, 1982). A family environment that encourages clear communication, successful problem solv-ing, and effective discipline may prevent or delay the initiation of substance use.

During adolescence, peer influences are especially important and pressure to conform is intensified, giving the peer group an especially influential role on ado-lescent substance use behavior. Adolescents with friends who drink or use substances are more likely to be substance users themselves (Weaver, Cheong, MacKinnon, & Pentz, 2004). Peer influence sometimes occurs in direct forms of pressure or coercion to use but also often occurs indirectly through an adolescent's desire to fit in, be accepted, or conform to perceived social norms. Peer rejection and peer deviance also have been found to be risk factors for adolescent substance abuse (Brook, Whiteman, & Gordon, 1983). Prosocial bonding and prosocial socialization have been identified as protective factors. Adolescents who associate with a non-substance-using peer group are less likely to use substances themselves (De Wit et al., 1995).

Adolescents spend the majority of their time in school, and poor school adjustment is also an important risk factor. Poor academic performance, low educational aspirations, and dropping out of school are precursors of substance abuse (White et al., 2004). Several school-related variables have been identified as protective factors. Academic achievement and strong attachment or commitment to school lowers the probability of substance abuse (Newcome & Felix-Ortiz, 1992). A supportive learning environment and low conflict with teachers and peers contribute to positive school experiences, which can lead to the development of commitment to school and education. Involvement in academic and extracurricular activities, as well as religious activities, has been found to be positive alternatives to substance use.

Community environmental factors that have been found to increase risk for substance abuse include laws and norms that reflect favorable attitudes toward substance use and availability, economically deprived neighborhoods, and neighborhoods or communities where illicit substance use is widespread. The perception of social norms that disapprove of substance use has been identified as a protective factor (Hawkins, Catalano, & Miller, 1992).

Researchers have concluded that, to be effective, substance abuse prevention programs should target risk factors that can be modified and strengthen protective factors. It is also generally thought that early intervention with risk factors can reverse risks and change a developmental trajectory. The transition from childhood to adolescence has been found to be a developmental period during which protective factors may be especially influential (Scheier, Newcomb, & Skager, 1994). Prevention programs that combine targeting different levels of the social system for children and youth, such as family, school, and community, can be more effective than a program with a single target. However, school-based programs have been the primary approach for reaching children and youth because they allow for universal access.

ASSESSMENT ISSUES

Planning a school-based substance abuse prevention program should begin with an assessment of substance abuse and other child and adolescent problems and risk factors in the school or community. Assessment results can be used to determine the nature and extent of the problem, and guide selection of the most relevant prevention program, as well as raise awareness of the issue and develop commitment to implementing a substance abuse prevention program. An assessment of the school's readiness to implement the program is also important, as effective substance abuse prevention program implementation is not an individual endeavor but one that requires schoolwide commitment and effort.

A variety of public access archival data can be used to provide information about the nature and extent of substance use and related problems in a particular community or school. For example, the school or school district, and the local health department, law enforcement agency, hospital emergency room, and substance abuse treatment facilities have information on school disciplinary incidents, school suspensions, school absenteeism and truancy, school dropout rates, drug abuse arrests, juvenile delinquency, drug-related emergency room admissions, and relevant socioeconomic status and other demographic data that can be examined and analyzed. Large national surveys, such as *Monitoring the Future* (reported by the National Institute on Drug Abuse), mentioned earlier, as well as the National Survey of Drug Use and Health (reported by the Substance Abuse and Mental Health Services Administration), can help comparison of local situations to a national context. These studies also make their data collection instruments available for local adaptation. In addition, qualitative methods such as focus groups of students, parents, and teachers can help planners gain a greater understanding of the nature of the local problem.

In assessing a school's readiness to implement a substance abuse prevention program, it is essential to involve key stakeholders in the decision-making process regarding whether a school-based substance abuse prevention program should be implemented and which program best meets the needs of the school and community. Key stakeholders should include administrators, teachers, other professional staff, parents, and students. Potential programs should be considered for the extent to which they fit the needs of the school population, supplement or coordinate well with existing programs, and fit with the goals and philosophy of the school. In addition, it is essential that staff (with sufficient expertise), training, space, time, equipment, and other financial resources needed for the program will be available. The individuals who are implementing the intervention (typically special services staff or teachers) need to understand the theoretical basis of the program, have sufficient skills to carry it out, and also believe that the program is an effective way to prevent substance abuse and that they can implement it effectively.

Substance abuse prevention researchers have recognized that in addition to assessing student and community variables as a means of choosing an appropriate program and evaluating its success, it is essential to assess the manner in which prevention programs are implemented and to monitor program quality on an ongoing basis. This means monitoring (typically through observations and questionnaires) whether implementation of particular activities and methods is consistent with the way the program is written (adherence), whether program delivery is complete in terms of number, duration, and intensity of sessions, or the amount of program content received by participants (dose), the effectiveness with which program content is delivered (quality), and the extent to which program participants are engaged in and involved in the program (participant responsiveness; Dusenbury, Brannigan, Falco, & Hansen, 2003). This data can provide information about whether program implementation is adequate and if changes in program implementation should be made in order to increase program effectiveness.

COGNITIVE-BEHAVIORAL CONCEPTUALIZATION OF SUBSTANCE ABUSE PREVENTION

The cognitive-behavioral approach to substance abuse prevention in youth focuses on the development of coping skills that can buffer risk factors and serve as protective factors for substance abuse. These skills include self-management skills, decision-making skills, problem-solving skills, communication skills, assertiveness skills, anxiety management skills, and anger management skills. Cognitive distortion and cognitive deficiency (Kendall & MacDonald, 1993) are both considered as important in initiation and development of substance abuse. Cognitive distortion occurs when children and adolescents process information in a distorted fashion or misinterpret reality, such as when they erroneously think almost all of their peers use drugs. Cognitive deficiency exists when their cognitive processing ability is deficient and their actions do not benefit from appropriate forethought, such as social cognitive deficits that result in students getting into fights with peers in school. The main goal of cognitive-behavioral approaches to substance abuse prevention is to help children and youth learn and practice new, effective ways of thinking and behaving about a variety of life experiences that will yield positive outcomes for them, and thus prevent substance use.

Recent literature on substance abuse prevention has emphasized the importance of using evidence-based approaches, or approaches that, through research, have been found to be effective. Reviews of the substance abuse prevention literature reveal that evidence-based programs for substance abuse prevention use a cognitive-behavioral approach or have cognitive-behavioral components in which thoughts or thought processes are targeted for change in order to change behavior. Federal government agencies including the National Institute on Drug Abuse and the Substance Abuse and Mental Health Services Administration, as well as authors reviewing the research literature through meta-analyses, have identified these evidence-based cognitive-behavioral substance abuse prevention programs (Tobler & Stratton, 1997; National Institute on Drug Abuse, 2003; Substance Abuse and Mental Health Services Administration, 2004).

COGNITIVE-BEHAVIORAL STRATEGIES FOR SUBSTANCE ABUSE PREVENTION

Effective substance abuse prevention programs have been found to use interactive, skills training methods (a hallmark of cognitive-behavioral interventions) as opposed to didactic lecture methods. These programs have sought to change behaviors by teaching skills and competencies rather than by changing knowledge and attitudes as a result of lectures (Tobler & Stratton, 1997). Several cognitive-behavioral strategies are found across many of the substance abuse prevention programs that have been identified as evidence-based.

Self-management training teaches children and adolescents to use behavior modification techniques to achieve their goals and address their behavioral or emotional problems. This type of training includes teaching individuals to engage in self-observation, self-evaluation, and self-consequation. Through self-observation or self-monitoring, individuals monitor and record instances of their own specific behaviors. Self-evaluation occurs after self-monitoring when an individual evaluates his or her behavior against a goal that he or she has set. Self-consequation involves administering a reward to oneself contingent upon performance of a specific behavior.

Decision making and social problem-solving training typically encourages the child or adolescent to generate and evaluate several alternative solutions to any problem situation. A systematic means of dealing with social problem situations is taught through a structured sequence of cognitive activity. Decision making and problem solving is presented as a sequence in which the problem is described, goals for the situation are identified, alternative solutions are generated, each alternative is evaluated in terms of achieving the goal, the best alternative is identified and acted upon, and the outcomes of that action are evaluated. This sequence is used to help the child or adolescent deal with a variety of problem situations including social problems involving interaction with peers.

Various forms of social skills training have also been included in substance abuse prevention programs as a means of improving individuals' social competency and their potential to develop positive and fulfilling relationships with others. Social skills training typically focuses on teaching skills that are lacking in the individual's interpersonal repertoire and that will reduce peer-related problems. The training usually includes modeling, coaching, or contingent use of reinforcers. When modeling is used, the individual learns through observations of social behaviors of others. When coaching is used, the individual is presented with a series of instructions for appropriate behavior and then rehearses the specified behaviors with a coach who provides verbal feedback. Reinforcers are used contingently to reward the successful execution of the new social behavior. Many social skills training programs use a training sequence that includes (1) provision of instructions, (2) exposure to a model, (3) rehearsal of the behavior, (4) performance feedback, and (5) real-life practice.

Assertiveness training is a specific type of social skills training that focuses on teaching the individual to act in his or her own best interest without undue anxiety. Assertive behavior is viewed as being the midpoint of a continuum of behavioral styles ranging from passive behavior to aggressive. Assertive individuals are defined as those who stand up for their rights and who express their thoughts in direct and appropriate ways, and do not violate the rights of others. Training methods include didactic instruction, modeling, shaping, and behavioral rehearsal.

Anxiety management training in substance abuse prevention programs has typically included relaxation training. Relaxation training aims to help individuals control their physiological responses in potentially stressful situations or reduce their anxiety or other types of physiological overarousal once it occurs. In the school setting, the most often used methods are deep muscle relaxation, imagery-based procedures, or deep breathing. Deep muscle relaxation training involves a series of tension-release cycles performed on various muscle groups in which the individual is directed to (1) tense the muscle, (2) hold the tension for a few seconds while focusing on the tense feelings, (3) relax the muscle, and (4) notice the difference between the feelings of tension and relaxation and focus on the pleasant feelings of relaxation. Imagery procedures have children imagine various real-world images (such as being a turtle and withdrawing into their shell, or lying on a beach) to achieve relaxation. Deep breathing calls for the individual to take a deep breath, hold it, and then exhale slowly as a means of relaxing.

Anger management training incorporates many of the procedures described here as a means of preventing antisocial behavior. Participants in anger management training learn about the physiological processes associated with anger and how they can serve as signals that one is angry. They are also introduced to the concept of "self-talk" as a means of controlling anger, as well as relaxation and social problem-solving methods.

APPLICATIONS TO THE SCHOOL SETTING

Effective school-based substance abuse prevention programs focus on improving student's peer relationships, self-control, coping skills, social behaviors, and drug refusal skills. They also frequently include an education component about the prevalence of substance use. Substance abuse prevention programs can be implemented as early as preschool to address risk factors such as aggressive behavior, poor social skills, and academic difficulties (Webster-Stratton, Reid, & Hammond, 2001). Prevention programs for elementary school children can address self-control, emotional awareness, communication, social problem solving, and academic support (Ialongo, Podusksa, Werthamer, & Kellam, 2001). Prevention programs for middle and high school students can address study habits and academic support, communication, peer relationships, self-efficacy and assertiveness, drug resistance skills, reinforcement of antidrug attitudes, and strengthening of personal commitment against drug abuse (Botvin, Baker, Dusenbury, Botvin, & Diaz, 1995). It is important that programs address risks specific to the target student population with attention to age, gender, and ethnicity of the participants. Effective programs have been found to be long term with booster sessions, and the effects of middle school programs have been found to diminish without high school follow-up programs (Scheier, Botvin, Diaz, & Griffin, 1999).

Substance abuse prevention programs are categorized into three levels or types based on the population for which the program is designed. Universal programs are for the general population. These programs are delivered universally to general populations of students such as a whole school grade or classroom. Selective prevention programs are provided for at-risk children and adolescents. This would include, for example, programs for children of alcoholics or drug abusers and children in poverty. Indicated prevention programs are for students who are exhibiting specific risk behaviors for substance use such as aggressive behavior or poor school achievement, or who have begun to experiment with drugs.

Reviews of the literature on universal substance abuse prevention programs have found consistently positive effects for programs that use social influences and life skills approaches (Kumpfer, 1998). Social influences approaches focus on social resistance skills training, psychological inoculation against advertising, and normative education. Personal and social skills training approaches focus on teaching generic personal self-management and social skills. In general, less is known about the effectiveness of selective and indicated prevention programs because of the popularity of school-based universal substance abuse prevention programs.

PROGRAM EXAMPLES

Life Skills Training, developed by Gilbert Botvin, is a school-based universal prevention program that has repeatedly shown positive effects. *Life Skills Training* views substance use as a socially learned behavior that may serve a number of purposes such as coping with anxiety or failure, or reacting to the appeals of peers. The program teaches general personal and social coping skills as well as skills and knowledge specifically related to substance use. The program is designed for middle school or junior high school students. The program extends over three years, consisting of fifteen 45-minute sessions the first year (6th or 7th grade), 10 booster sessions in year 2, and five booster sessions in year 3. The sessions may be conducted consecutively every day, or two to three times per week, or once a week.

Life Skills Training is designed to be carried out by classroom teachers, health or mental health professionals, or peer leaders. Implementation of the program requires a teacher's manual, a student guide, and an audiocassette tape for relaxation exercises. Teacher training is highly recommended, although not required. There are three major components of Life Skills Training: drug resistance skills, personal self-management skills, and social skills.

The drug resistance skills component provides information about the prevalence and effects of tobacco, alcohol, and marijuana use, and teaches resistance skills for dealing with peers and the media. Myths and realities of smoking, alcohol, and other drug use are addressed, and students learn about the role advertising and the media play in promoting substance use.

Improvement of self-image through a self-improvement plan is addressed in the personal self-management skills component. In this segment of the training, students conduct a behavioral self-management project. In addition, decision-making skills and problem-solving skills are addressed in this component. Students learn steps and principles for effective decision making and practice through role-play. The role of group pressure in decision making is discussed. Also in this component, students learn how to cope with anxiety through use of imagery, breathing, and muscle relaxation. A session on coping with anger teaches students about the antecedents and physiological concomitants of anger, as well as cognitive techniques for controlling anger.

Nonverbal and verbal communication skills, including guidelines for avoiding misunderstandings, skills to initiate, maintain, and end conversations, and skills needed to handle social requests are addressed in the social skills component. Students learn about how to overcome shyness and how to initiate and respond in dating situations. This component also includes training in verbal and nonverbal assertiveness skills that can be used to resist peer pressure to smoke, drink, or use drugs. Finally, students learn about how to resolve conflicts by controlling anger and building consensus around a problem solution.

Life Skills Training has been evaluated in numerous studies and has been found to reduce the prevalence of tobacco, alcohol, and illicit drug use relative to controls by 50 to 87% (NIDA, 2003). Initial evaluation studies that focused on prevention of cigarette smoking (Botvin & Eng, 1982; Botvin, Eng, & Williams, 1980; Botvin, Renick, & Baker, 1983) indicated that after Life Skills Training conducted by either project staff, peer leaders, or teachers, middle and high school students had lower rates of smoking onset and made more positive changes on cognitive, attitudinal, affective, and social measures than did no-treatment control-group students. These changes were maintained at 1-year follow-up. Effects on alcohol and marijuana use were explored in a study of over 1,300 7th-grade, white, middle-class students from suburban New York City schools. Significant treatment effects were found for substance use, substance knowledge, substance attitudes, locus of control, and influenceability (Botvin, Baker, Renick, Filazolla, & Botvin, 1984). In a subsequent study (Botvin, Baker, Dusenbury, Tortu, & Botvin, 1990) of over 4,400 students in 56 schools in New York State, significant effects were found for cigarette smoking, marijuana use, immoderate alcohol use, normative expectations and knowledge concerning substance use, interpersonal skills, and communication skills. A 6-year follow-up study with 3,600 students in 56 schools found that weekly use of polydrugs (tobacco, alcohol, and an illegal drug) was 66% lower than in control schools and that any use of tobacco, alcohol, or marijuana was 44% lower than in control schools (Botvin et al., 1995).

Life Skills Training has also been evaluated for use with black and Hispanic youth (Botvin, Batson, Witts-Vitalle, Bess, Baker, & Dusenbury, 1989; Botvin, Dusenbury, Baker, James-Ortiz, Botvin, & Kerner, 1992: Botvin, Epstein, Baker, Diaz, & Williams, 1997) and has found to be effective. In a study with 3,600 predominantly minority disadvantaged students in 29 New York City schools, those who received the program reported less smoking, drinking, drunkenness, inhalant use, and polydrug use than controls. In addition, *Life Skills Training* has been found to reduce binge drinking in minority, inner-city, middle school students (Botvin, Griffin, Diaz, & Ifill-Williams, 2001).

Promoting Alternative Thinking Strategies (PATHS), developed by Mark Greenberg and Carol Kusche, is a school-based universal prevention program for elementary school students. This program also repeatedly has shown positive results in controlled outcome studies. *PATHS* teaches children skills for making choices against using substances and aggression to cope with everyday difficulties. The program aims to help students increase self-control, choose effective conflict resolution strategies, reject aggressive responses to frustrating situations, and improve problem-solving skills.

Program materials include more than 100 interactive lessons designed to be integrated into classroom activity continually from kindergarten through 6th grade, with the goal of moving children along a continuum of emotional competency over the elementary school years (Greenberg & Kusche, 1998b). There is a different curriculum manual for each grade level. The program is designed to be administered by classroom teachers, other educators, or youth leaders.

The *PATHS* curriculum covers five areas of social and emotional development: self-control, emotional understanding, self-esteem, peer relations, and interpersonal problem-solving skills. Through this curriculum, children are taught how to attend to emotional cues, how to think about and discuss their feelings, and how to identify problem situations. They are also introduced to the "Turtle Technique" for increasing self-control and decreasing impulsive behaviors. Children are also taught about reflective thinking, how to understand the differences between feelings and behaviors, differences in the points of view of self and others, and to understand how one's feelings and behaviors can affect others. In addition, instruction and practice in the steps of social problem solving are provided.

The effects of *PATHS* have been evaluated in four controlled trials with 1- or 2-year follow-ups. Conduct problems and academic achievement were each affected in a positive direction. Teacher reports of student aggressive behavior were reduced by 32%. The number of conduct problems also was reduced significantly. In addition to 20% increases in student scores on cognitive skills tests, as compared with matched students who did not receive *PATHS*, students exhibited greater self-control, ability to tolerate frustration, and more use of effective conflict resolution strategies (Greenberg & Kusche, 1998a; Greenberg, Kusche, Cook, & Quamma, 1995).

There is some evidence for the effectiveness of *Life Skills Training* and *PATHS* as selective prevention programs. In a randomized, controlled study with youth from 29 inner-city middle schools, students were identified as at high risk for substance use initiation based on exposure to substance-using peers and poor academic performance in school. Less smoking, drinking, inhalant use, and polydrug use was found for high risk youth who participated in *Life Skills Training* compared to controls at 1-year follow-up (Griffin, Botvin, Nichols, & Doyle, 2003).

Project Towards No Drug Abuse is an indicated program for high school students. The program is based on a motivation-skills-decision-making model that views drug use as related to motivation variables including attitudes, beliefs, and desires regarding drug use; general social and self-control skills; and cognitive processing skills for making rational decisions. The program goal is to correct deficits in these areas.

The program consists of twelve 40-minute interactive sessions that address motivation, social skills, and decision making regarding the use of cigarettes, alcohol, marijuana, hard drugs, and violent behavior. Topics include active listening; stereotyping; myths and denials associated with drug use; negative consequences of drug abuse; methods for coping with stress; the value of health; self-control methods; assertiveness; the links between positive and negative thinking and behavior; attitudes about substance use; and decision-making skills and commitment.

In three experimental field trials, over 2,400 high school students from 42 schools in southern California participated in the program. Two of the field trials involved students from continuation high schools (schools that serve youth who have problems such as attendance, academic achievement, or drug use that prevents them from attending a traditional public high school). Reductions in the use of cigarettes, alcohol, marijuana, hard drugs, weapon carrying, and victimization were found at one-year follow-up. The program was administered by project staff health educators and was found to be effective in both regular and alternative high schools (Sussman, Dent, & Stacy, 2002).

SUMMARY AND CONCLUSIONS

Several decades of research have indicated that cognitive-behavioral school-based prevention programs can have a positive impact on the prevalence of substance abuse among youth. These programs focus on building protective factors and reducing risk factors by developing intra- and interpersonal coping skills through a skills training approach.

The programs can be implemented as early as the beginning of elementary school. They are highly structured and use modeling and coaching, direct practice of cognitive and behavioral skills, as well as feedback. The programs have structured training for implementers and materials that can be easily accessed. The content of effective programs includes both information and skills development; drug information alone has been found to be ineffective. With regard to program delivery, use of interactive methods and use of booster sessions are also important to program effectiveness.

Unfortunately, some of the most widely used substance abuse prevention programs in schools are not evidence-based. This has several negative effects. First and most important, students are being shortchanged. Substance use that may have been prevented through use of evidence-based programs is initiated and escalates in large numbers of children and adolescents each year, with concomitant negative effects on their health, emotional, social, and academic development. Second, precious time during the school day is wasted. There are a vast number of concepts, methods, and facts in a variety of academic and related areas that must be addressed through schooling in order to develop healthy and productive individuals; more than can be incorporated during the time typically allotted for schooling. The use of school time to implement ineffective programs results in the waste of an essential educational resource. In addition, all programs have financial requirements, in terms of materials and staff time. Implementation of programs that are not evidence-based results in waste of public funds. Finally, implementation of programs that are not evidence-based bodes poorly for the future of all substance abuse prevention efforts. The effectiveness of all types of school-based programs is being examined by a variety of governmental agencies and various school constituencies more frequently. It has become essential for school-based programs to show positive results; and with time, the lack of effectiveness of programs without an evidence base may dampen enthusiasm for any prevention effort. With time and financial resources in short supply in educational settings, and with the potential negative effects of failed prevention efforts on students, it is important that only evidence-based programs be implemented. Programs that use cognitive-behavioral strategies can provide an effective, evidence-based approach to substance abuse prevention.

REFERENCES

Botvin, G. J., Baker, E., Dusenbury, L., Tortu, S., & Botvin, E. M. (1990). Preventing adolescent drug abuse through a multimodal cognitive-behavioral approach: Results of a three-year study. *Journal of Consulting and Clinical Psychology, 58,* 437–446.

Botvin, G. J., Baker, E., Dusenbury, L., Botvin, E. M., & Diaz, T. (1995). Long-term follow-up results of a randomized drug abuse prevention trial in a white middle-class population. *Journal of the American Medical Association, 273*(14), 1106–1112.

Botvin, G. J., Baker, E., Renick, N., Filazzola, A. D., & Botvin, E. M. (1984). A cognitive-behavioral approach to substance abuse prevention. *Addictive Behaviors, 9,* 137–147.

Botvin, G. J., Batson, H., Witts-Vitale, S., Bess, V., Baker, E., & Dusenbury, L. (1989). A psychosocial approach to smoking prevention for urban black youth. *Public Health Reports,* 104, 573–582.

Botvin, G. J., Dusenbury, L., Baker, E., James-Ortiz, S., Botvin, E. M., & Kerner, J. (1992). Smoking prevention among urban minority youth. Assessing Effects on Outcome and Mediating Variables. Health Psychology, 11(5), 290–299.

Botvin, G. J., & Eng, A. (1982). The efficacy of a multicomponent approach to the prevention of cigarette smoking. *Preventive Medicine,* 11, 199–211.

Botvin, G. J., Eng, A., & Williams, C. L. (1980). Preventing the onset of cigarette smoking through life skills training. *Preventive Medicine,* 9, 135–143.

Botvin, G. J., Epstein, J. A., Baker, E., Diaz, T., & Williams, M.I. (1997). School-based drug abuse prevention with inner city minority youth. The etiology and prevention of drug abuse among minority youth. *Journal of Child and Adolescent Substance Abuse,* 6, 5–20

Botvin, G. J., Griffin, K. W., Diaz, T., & Ifill-Williams, M. (2001). Drug abuse prevention among minority adolescents: Posttest and one-year follow-up of a school-based preventive intervention. *Prevention Science,* 2(1), 1–13.

Botvin, G. J., Renick, N. L., & Baker, E. (1983). The effects of scheduling format and booster sessions on a broad-spectrum psychosocial smoking prevention program. *Journal of Behavioral Medicine,* 6, 359–379.

Brook, J., Whiteman, M., & Gordon, A. (1982). Qualitative and quantitative aspects of adolescent drug use: Interplay of personality, family, and peer correlates. *Psychological Reports, 51,* 1151–1163.

Brook, J., Whiteman, M., & Gordon, A. (1983). Stages of drug use in adolescence: Personality, peer, and family correlates. *Developmental Psychology, 19,* 269–277.

Bry, B. H. (1983). Empirical foundations of family-based approaches to adolescent substance abuse. In T. J. Glynn, C. G. Leukefeld, & J. Ludford (Eds.), *Preventing adolescent drug abuse: Intervention strategies* (Research Monograph No. 47, pp. 154–171). Rockville, MD: National Institute on Drug Abuse.

Bry, B. H. (1996). Psychological approaches to prevention. In W. K. Bickel & R. J. DeGrandpre (Eds.), *Drug policy and human nature: Psychological perspectives on the prevention, management, and treatment of illicit drug use* (pp. 55–76). New York: Plenum Publishing.

Cloniger, C., Sigvardsson, S., & Bohman, M. (1988). Childhood personality predicts alcohol use in young adults. *Alcoholism, 12,* 494–505.

DeWit, D. J., Silverman, G., Goodstadt, M., & Stoduto, G. (1995). The construction of risk and protective factor indices for adolescent alcohol and other drug use. *The Journal of Drug Issues, 25,* 837–863.

Dusenbery, L., Brannigan, R., Falco, M., & Hansen, W. B. (2003). A review of research on fidelity of implementation: Implications for drug abuse prevention in school settings. *Health Education Research, 18,* 237–256.

Greenberg, M. T., & Kusche, C. A. (1998a). Preventive interventions for school-aged deaf children: The PATHS curriculum. *Journal of Deaf Studies & Deaf Education, 3*(1), 49–63.

Greenberg, M. T., & Kusche, C. A. (1998b). Promoting Alternative Thinking Strategies. In *Blueprint for violence prevention* (Book 10). Institute of Behavioral Sciences, University of Colorado, Boulder, CO.

Greenberg, M. T., Kusche, C. A., Cook, E. T., & Quamma, J. P. (1995). Promoting emotional competence in school-aged children: The effects of the PATHS curriculum. *Developmental Research and Psychopathology, 7,* 117–136.

Griffin, K. W., Botvin, G. J., Nichols, T. R., & Coyle, M. M. (2003). Effectiveness of a universal drug abuse prevention approach for youth at high risk for substance use initiation. *Preventive Medicine, 36*(1), 1–7.

Hawkins, J. D., Catalano, R. F., & Miller, J. Y. (1992). Risk and protective factors for alcohol and other drug problems in adolescence and early adulthood: Implications for substance abuse prevention. *Psychological Bulletin, 112,* 64–105.

Ialongo, N., Poduska, J., Werthamer, L., & Kellam, S. (2001). The distal impact of two first-grade preventive interventions on conduct problems and disorder in early adolescence. *Journal of Emotional and Behavioral Disorders, 9,* 146–160.

Johnston, L. D., O'Malley, P. M., & Bachman, J. G. (2003). *Monitoring the Future national survey results on drug use, 1975–2002. Volume 1: Secondary school students* (No. NIH Publication No. 03–5375). Bethesda, MD: National Institute on Drug Abuse.

Kendall, P. C., & MacDonald, J. P. (1993). Cognition in the psychopathology of youth and implications for treatment. In K. S. Dobson & P. C. Kendall (Eds.), *Psychopathology and Cognition.* New York: Academic Press.

Kumpfer, K. L. (1998). Identification of drug abuse prevention programs: Literature Review. Retrieved May 14, 2004, from http://www.NIDA.gov

Lerner, J., & Vicary, J. (1984). Difficult temperament and drug use: Analysis from the New York Longitudinal study. *Journal of Drug Education, 14,* 1–7.

National Institute on Drug Abuse (2003). *Preventing drug abuse among children and adolescents: A research-based guide.* Bethesda, MD: National Institutes of Health Publication No. 04–4212(A).

Newcomb, M. D., & Felix-Ortiz, M. (1992). Multiple protective and risk factors for drug use and abuse: Cross-sectional and prospective findings. *Journal of Personality and Social Psychology, 63,* 280–296.

Scheier, L., Botvin, G., Diaz, T., & Griffin, K. (1999). Social skills, competence, and drug refusal efficacy as predictors of adolescent alcohol use. *Journal of Drug Education, 29*(3), 251–278.

Scheier, L., Newcomb, M. D., & Skager, R. (1994). Risk, protection, and vulnerability to adolescent drug use: Latent-variable models of three age groups. *Journal of Drug Education, 24,* 49–82.

Schuckit, M. (1984). Subjective responses to alcohol in sons of alcoholics and control subjects. *Archives of General Psychiatry, 41,* 879–884.

Substance Abuse and Mental Health Services Administration. (2002). SAMHSA Model Programs. Retrieved May 6, 2004, from http://modelprograms.samhsa.gov

Sussman, S., Dent, C. W., & Stacy, A. W. (2002). Project Toward No Drug Abuse: A review of the findings and future directions. *American Journal of Health Behavior* 26(5), 354–365.

Swadi, H. (1999). Individual risk factors for adolescent substance use. *Drug and Alcohol Dependence, 55,* 209–224.

Tobler, N. S., & Stratton, H. (1997). Effectiveness of school-based prevention programs: A meta-analysis of the research. *Journal of Primary Prevention, 18*(1), 71–128.

Weaver, S., Cheong, J., MacKinnon, D., & Pentz, M. A. (2004, May). *Ethnic differences in alcohol use and peer norms: Investigation of latent growth models.* Paper presented at the annual meeting of the Society for Prevention Research, Quebec City.

Webster-Stratton, C., Reid, J., & Hammond, M. (2001). Preventing conduct problems, promoting social competence. A parent and teacher training partnership in Head Start. *Journal of Clinical Child Psychology, 30,* 282–302.

White, H. R., Metzger, L., Nagin, D., & Stouthamer-Loeber, M. (2004, May). *Racial differences in the developmental predictors of cigarette smoking: Implications for prevention.* Paper presented at the annual meeting of the Society for Prevention Research, Quebec City.

17

Sexual Minority Youth: School-Based Issues and Interventions

ERICA M. WEILER

Within days of the start of his junior year, second period becomes a difficult place to be. Everyday, kids insult his personal appearance. They talk with lisps and mimic his voice. They take one of his diaries. Someone wrote "fag" on his notebook. People start calling him names: "fairy," "queen," "queer," "spermicide," "faggot." His second period teacher witnesses the harassment but remains silent. Someone threatens, "We're going to kill you. Die." In mid-September, three cars full of people from his second period class show up outside his home. They sit there and shout, "Come out; we know you're in there." The student tells the principal what happened. The harassment at school continues. It gets physical. People follow him, chase him and brush up against him. They spit on him or at him.

He cuts the class. He is disciplined for cutting class. He can't pay attention there anyway, so he asks his counselor and the principal to allow him to drop the class. He is told that letting him drop the class would violate school rules ... that it can't be done. He is told that if he doesn't go to his second period class, he will be withdrawn from school. Sometimes he skips whole days of school, to avoid second period. Three weeks into the school year, he is withdrawn (expelled).

By the time he calls the Safe Schools Project to report the sequence of events, it has been over a year. A difficult year. A year in which he became so confused, lonely and depressed (watching television eleven hours a day and sleeping the rest of the time) that he attempted suicide. He was afraid to leave the house to find work, but he felt he couldn't tell his parents about the harassment. Now he is homeless. He says, "[Those three weeks] ruined my life. I was the smartest kid in the school and then I left" (Safe Schools Coalition of Washington State, 1999, p. 51).

This story was reported to the Safe Schools Project of Washington State. This project examined the phenomenon of antigay harassment and violence in schools from grades kindergarten through 12 over a 5-year period. School climate studies have been useful in studying issues faced by sexual minority youth and highlight the need for school-based intervention. It is essential that schools teach students to live in a democratic society and affirm diversity. This chapter will discuss stressors faced by sexual minority youth and cognitive-behavioral interventions that have been effective in improving school climate and individual functioning.

Throughout this chapter, the term *sexual minority youth* will be used to define youth who are not members of the heterosexual majority. This includes gay, lesbian, and bisexual youth. Transgendered, questioning, and gender atypical youth are not discussed in this chapter because of the lack of empirical research with these populations.

RIGHTS OF EQUAL ACCESS TO EDUCATION AND PROTECTION UNDER THE LAW

For many sexual minority youth, schools are unsafe and survival, not education, is the priority. Schools have a legal, ethical, and moral obligation to provide equal access to education and equal protection under the law for all students. Yet many schools fail either to provide adequate safeguards or to promote factual awareness about the nature of sexual orientation in human development. This neglect helps to fuel levels of prejudice, harassment, and discrimination that not only deny sexual minority and gender nonconforming youth basic rights, such as a free and appropriate public education, but also can inflict lifelong harm. An estimated 4.5 to 9% of students identify themselves as sexual minorities currently or may do so at a later point in their development (Seattle Public Schools, 1996). However, many professionals lack training about sexual minority youth and express feelings of inadequacy when working with this population. In a survey of 1,000 high school–based professionals, few received training to prepare them to provide services for sexual minority youth, and of those who did, few found it adequate (Porter, 2001). More than four out of five agreed that a lack of training, knowledge, skills, and materials, along with negative staff attitudes and students' fear of disclosure, are barriers to providing services for sexual minority youth in schools. Some professionals are uncomfortable addressing issues of sexuality in school or dealing with the potential controversy created by doing so. Many schools fail to recognize sexual minority youth, assume that heterosexuality is the norm, and do not address stressors that impact their safety and education. These practices have a negative impact on students and significant legal and financial implications for school districts.

ETHICAL STANDARDS FOR PSYCHOLOGISTS

In 1975, the American Psychological Association (APA) passed a resolution that homosexuality be removed from the official list of mental disorders and urged all mental health professionals to remove the stigma of mental illness associated with homosexuality. However, a survey completed by the APA's Committee on Lesbian and Gay Concerns revealed that high levels of bias among psychologists remain (Garnets, Hancock, Cochran, Goodchilds, & Peplau, 1991). Of the 2,544 psychologists surveyed, 58% were aware of negative practice and they varied widely in their adherence to unbiased practice. Biases included assuming that the client is heterosexual, believing that problems are a result of sexual orientation, making errors about sexual orientation such as assuming that it is an issue when it is not or ignoring it, belittling homosexuality, and not valuing the importance of same-sex relationships.

The codes of ethics of the APA (2002, p. 1063) and the National Association of School Psychologists (NASP, 2000, p. 17) require psychologists to respect all individuals, be sensitive to differences, and not engage in or condone practices that discriminate against sexual minority youth. Psychologists have a critical role in providing leadership to ensure a safe educational environment for all youth, including sexual minority youth. In order to provide equal access to education, interventions at both the school and individual levels are critical.

IDENTITY DEVELOPMENT

Adolescence can be a stressful period for any youth because of the tremendous physical, psychological, and cognitive changes that occur. Discovering one's sexual identity is an important and sometimes confusing part of development. Sexual minority youth can begin to feel different from their peers as early as kindergarten, although there is no sexual connotation to these feelings. By the time they reach middle school, most sexual minority youth realize that they are physically and emotionally attracted to their gender. This awareness may not yet be a fully formed sexual identity but an array of feelings accompanied by uncertainty about self-concept. Full assumption of one's sexual identity usually occurs around the age of 15 or 16 years; however, this varies by individual (Lasser & Tharinger, 1997). Sexual orientation is not automatically determined by sexual behavior. For example, many youth who recognize that they are gay or lesbian may not engage in sex. Likewise, heterosexual or questioning youth may have sex with a same gender person, yet they may not become a sexual minority adult. Once youth have consolidated their identity as a sexual minority, they are then faced with the decision of "coming out" or disclosing their sexual orientation to others, which for some can be an extremely lonely and difficult process.

Although sexual minority youth face the same social and developmental challenges as their heterosexual peers, they must also cope with stigmatization as a sexual minority and the burdens of social isolation, self-doubt, and fear (D'Augelli & Patterson, 1995; Savin-Williams & Cohen, 1996). The importance of peer relationships, role models, and social support during adolescence makes the issues of sexuality even more stressful for sexual minority youth (Safren, Hollander, Hart, & Heimberg, 2001). Sexual minority youth of color face additional challenges in consolidating their sexual, racial, and ethnic identities due to their exposure to multiple stressors and oppressions, access to fewer support systems, and tendency to be less visible. They are minorities within a minority because both their ethnic/racial and sexual identities are devalued and discriminated against. Although sexual minority youth of color tend to not identify themselves as sexual minorities, this does not indicate confusion regarding their sexual orientation.

Adolescents need acceptance and support from peers and significant adults. Yet, sexual minority youth often are denied such support because they are afraid of divulging their identity and of being misunderstood or rejected by their family, friends, and teachers. The instinct for many is to hide their identity, which deepens their sense of confusion, isolation, and self-doubt. Youth who do come out face the very real risk of violence, harassment, prejudice, discrimination, and stigmatization. Stressors related to either hiding or revealing one's sexual orientation place sexual minority youth at higher risk for mental health, physical, and educational problems.

PSYCHOSOCIAL STRESSORS

According to Safren and colleagues (2001), four significant stressors exist for sexual minority youth, which include: (1) overt acts of abuse, harassment, and violence; (2) development of one's identity as a sexual minority person and related internalized homophobia; (3) disclosure of sexual orientation to others and related lack of adult social support; and (4) development of platonic and romantic relationships with other lesbian, gay male, and bisexual peers. Sexual minority youth experience chronic stress due to verbal and physical abuse from both peers and adults (Savin-Williams, 1994). Although many youth are able to cope with chronic stressors, according to Savin-Williams, a number of studies indicate that significant numbers of sexual minority youth are verbally and physically assaulted, abused, robbed, or raped. These incidents place sexual minority youth at risk for adjustment difficulties and self-destructive behavior. For example, studies have found that 23% to 42% of sexual minority youth have attempted suicide at least once in their lifetime (D'Augelli & Hershberger, 1993; Rotheram-Borus, Hunter, & Rosario, 1994; Safren & Heimberger, 1999). These rates are significantly higher than reported rates of 7% or 8% in national studies of youth suicide (Centers for Disease Control, 1992, & Kann et al., 1998, respectively). Studies among sexual minority adults have found that adults may experience excess risk for some mental health disorders as compared with heterosexual individuals (Cochran, Sullivan, & Mays, 2003). Gay and bisexual men evidenced higher prevalence of depression, panic attacks, and psychological distress than heterosexual men. Lesbian and bisexual women showed greater prevalence of generalized anxiety disorder than heterosexual women.

As discussed earlier, identity development may be challenging for sexual minority youth. If sexual minority youth lack adequate coping skills, these stressors may place them at severe risk for maladaptive and self-destructive behaviors (Safren et al., 2001). It is important to assess whether their difficulties are the result of internal stressors related to difficulties with identity development, internalized homophobia, or external stressors. Internalized homophobia may have a significant impact on the presenting problem. Although there is an increase in positive portrayals of sexual minorities in the media, stigmatization of sexual minorities remains high, which can have a profound influence on an individual's self-concept. According to Safren et al. (2001), "from a cognitive perspective exposure to negative attitudes about same-sex sexual attractions can lead to the development of negative core beliefs about the self. These types of beliefs are theoretically linked to the development of psychological dysfunction and are often the ultimate targets of cognitive approaches to case conceptualization and treatment (e.g. Beck, Freeman & Associates, 1990; Persons, 1989)" (p. 18).

Sexual minority youth must make decisions about coming out to themselves and others, often without support or help from others (D'Augelli & Hershberger, 1993). Because sexual minority adults who work with adolescents may fear discrimination for coming out, sexual minority youth may have limited access to role models and support. Youth who are members of ethnic and racial minority groups obtain support and role modeling from their families for their minority status. However, sexual minority youth usually grow up in heterosexual families, which may not be supportive. Child and adolescent research suggests that a significant protective factor for youth who face chronic stress is the availability of adequate social support (Licitra-Klecker & Waas, 1993). Sexual minority youth may not only be rejected by their families, but frequently become homeless due to conflicts related to their sexual orientation (Savin-Williams, 1994). Because homeless sexual minority youth have few marketable skills, some resort to prostitution to support themselves, which greatly increases the risk of HIV infection and drug abuse.

Safren et al. (2001) also examined the stressors of developing relationships with sexual minority peers. In order to develop these relationships, youth must identify other sexual minority youth and seek available community resources. However, for many youth identifying themselves to others and taking the risk to find other sexual minority youth may be a daunting task. Dating also may be more difficult for sexual minority youth because of an intolerant environment, which may result in further harassment and abuse.

SCHOOL CLIMATE

School climate is a significant determinant of whether an environment is healthy and conducive to learning. The Gay, Lesbian, and Straight Educators Network (GLSEN) has provided extremely useful data regarding school experiences for sexual minority youth. In 1999, GLSEN conducted a study that examined 42 of the largest school districts in the country and found that almost half received a failing grade in climate for sexual minority youth. For further information regarding school policies at the statewide level, refer to GLSEN's *State of the States Report* (2004). This report summarized state laws that affect school environments and school safety for all students, especially sexual minority youth, and found that 42 states received failing grades.

Since 1999, GLSEN has administered the *National School Climate Survey*, which is the only national survey to examine the experiences of lesbian, gay, bisexual, and transgendered (LGBT) youth in America's high schools. The 2003 survey demonstrated that hostile school climates have a "direct and measurable link to LGBT students' ability to learn, their sense of belonging in school, their academic performance and their educational aspirations" (GLSEN, 2003, p. 1). The survey found that 84% of LGBT youth experienced verbal, physical, or sexual harassment and/or assault at school, which is significantly higher than for heterosexual youth. More than 39% reported being physically harassed due to their sexual orientation (GLSEN, 2003). Specific acts of school violence included LGBT youth being urinated or ejaculated on, attacked with weapons, receiving death threats, having their clothes pulled off, and being gang raped. Typically, the ratio of perpetrators to victims was at least 2.5 to 1 (Safe Schools of Coalition of Washington, 1999).

Whereas almost 92% of LGBT students reported hearing homophobic remarks frequently or often in school, almost 83% indicated that faculty or staff never intervened or intervened only some of the time when present and homophobic remarks were made (GLSEN, 2003). Overall, more than 64% of LGBT students reported feeling unsafe in school because of their sexual orientation. Consequently, more than 28% of LGBT students reported missing at least one entire day of school in the past month because they felt unsafe. This rate was higher for LGBT youth of color (35.1%) who reported feeling unsafe at school for a variety of reasons. They were three times more likely than their heterosexual peers to miss school because they feel unsafe (Massachusetts Department of Education, 2003).

Because school survival is a priority, many sexual minority youth experience academic and learning problems. Students who reported frequent harassment due to their sexual orientation had GPAs that were more than 10% lower than those who did not (GLSEN, 2003). LGBT students who experienced frequent verbal harassment were less likely to plan to go to college (13.4% versus 6.7%). Because of harassment, sexual minority youth also drop out of school at a rate about three times the national average (U.S. Department of Health and Human Services, 1989).

Many schools omit sexual orientation from antibullying programs or schoolwide codes of conduct. Others fail to enforce existing codes. Although support from school personnel is essential for LGBT students, more than 37% reported that they do not feel comfortable discussing LGBT issues with their teachers (GLSEN, 2003). However, when supportive faculty or resources for sexual minority youth such as a Gay-Straight Alliance and policies protecting them from violence and harassment were provided, sexual minority youth performed better in school and were more likely to attend college.

RESEARCH-BASED TREATMENTS FOR SEXUAL MINORITY YOUTH

Much of the existing research on sexual minority youth is guided by developmental theory. There is a lack of research regarding behavior and cognitive-behavior therapy with this population. Until the early 1970s, behavior therapy's primary involvement with homosexuality was with sexual reorientation therapy, which is based on a model of pathology and is inherently ineffective and harmful. Since that time, behavior therapy did not replace its clinical and research publications with an acceptable approach to gay persons (Campos, Bernstein, Davison, Adams, & Arias, 1996) and has generally neglected underserved populations, including sexual minority youth. The majority of studies assume that the sample is completely heterosexual and fail to identify sexual orientation (Hart, 2001). Therefore, it is unknown whether and to what degree cognitive-behavior therapy is generalizable to sexual minority youth.

However, some researchers report that there is no reason to believe that cognitive-behavior therapy would be less effective in treating the presenting symptoms of sexual minority youth (Safren et al., 2001). Although principles of cognitive-behavioral therapy may be applied to sexual minority youth, they must be tailored to the unique issues of this population.

ASSESSMENT OF SCHOOL CLIMATE

As discussed earlier, a healthy school climate is critical to ensure that all students have equal access to learning. However, many schools fail to provide safe environments and improvements in school climate are indicated. In order to improve school climate, first it is necessary to assess the climate and then determine what kinds of interventions are needed. GLSEN developed a useful survey called *Local School Climate Survey: School Based Version* (2000), and there is also a community-based version. The survey asks students questions about the school climate toward LGBT people as well as their experiences with racist and sexist discrimination and harassment. It includes questions such as the frequency that homophobic remarks are made by students or staff, where homophobic remarks occur at school, and whether staff or students intervene. The strengths of this survey are that it is useful to determine and prioritize intervention strategies and to assess the efficacy of these strategies. However, since this survey emphasizes experiences with verbal harassment, the weakness of this survey is that it does not examine frequencies of physical harassment, assault, and abuse or the outcomes of these experiences.

SCHOOL-BASED MENTAL HEALTH SERVICES

The use of school-based interventions is necessary in order to meet the needs of sexual minority youth. At the school level, cognitive and educational interventions may be effective in changing the cognitive mind-set of students and staff from prejudice or fear of sexual minorities to understanding, acceptance, and, ultimately, an affirmation of diversity. As with prejudice in general, prejudice toward sexual minorities is often based on fear, a lack of knowledge, and generalization or the failure to know or have had a positive experience with a sexual minority person. Furthermore, sexual minority youth may be viewed as highly dissimilar to the heterosexual population; however, as with other minority groups, there is more diversity within the sexual minority population than difference from the heterosexual population. Education, training, school policies, and exposure to healthy role models are critical to begin improving the cognitive mindset of students and staff toward sexual minorities.

Ultimately, school-based interventions not only have a positive impact on the overall climate, but they are also likely to decrease school stressors and the resultant negative impact on sexual minority youth. As school climate improves and stressors decrease, there will also be a decreased need for school-based mental health services. However, sexual minority youth may require school-based mental health services when their problems interfere with their ability to benefit from a free and appropriate public education or if they have a disability. This may include issues such as clinical depression, anxiety, and posttraumatic stress disorder. The disability must interfere with their education and school-based mental health services are typically offered on a short-term basis. Students who present with coming-out issues generally are not eligible for school-based mental health services under the Individuals with Disabilities Education Act (IDEA) unless the resultant anxiety or stressors interfere with their ability to benefit from their education. However, with appropriate consent, these students could be seen at school for supportive mental health services around their issues of coming out. When the intensity of the needs is outside of the school's capacity to provide services, referrals to affirmative agencies and community resources for sexual minority youth are indicated.

COGNITIVE-BEHAVIORAL CASE CONCEPTUALIZATION

Sexual minority youth are at-risk for a broad range of clinical issues because of stressors related to their sexual orientation. Although there is an absence of research regarding the efficacy of cognitive-behavioral therapy with sexual minority youth, it may be a useful treatment modality. Aspects of sexual orientation may have a significant role in the case conceptualization and treatment planning processes (Purcell, Campos, & Perilla, 1996) and must be included. However, many clinicians fail to recognize the importance of the role of sexual orientation and the clinical issues related to sexual orientation even when these issues are highly relevant. Conversely, psychologists may overemphasize the role of sexual orientation, even when it is not related to the clients' problems (Safren & Rogers, 2001).

In order to provide mental health services that are free from bias, it is critical for psychologists to be comfortable with issues related to sexuality and sexual orientation. They must examine their own assumptions and beliefs about sexual minority youth. A conditioned negative response to sexual minority youth will likely lead to changes in the clinician's behavior. This may include avoiding issues related to sexuality, assuming heterosexuality, or making subtle changes in his or her behavior that would affect the therapeutic relationship and treatment outcome (Safren & Rogers, 2001). In order to provide affirmative care for sexual minority youth, clinicians must be comfortable with sexuality and sexual orientations. It is critical to use a nonpathological model that uses gender-neutral and inclusive language. The psychologist must have accurate knowledge about this population, be empathetic, and offer nonbiased or nonjudgmental advice.

As discussed earlier, it is essential to assess how sexual orientation fits into the conceptualization of the presenting problem (Safren & Rogers, 2001). The relationship between the two may be evident in the case of youth who presents with school avoidance following harassment or violence at school or may be less obvious in the case of a youth who presents with anxiety and no overt stressors. In order to assist in identifying the relative role of sexual orientation and the presenting problem, it is helpful to ask youth their thoughts about the connection between the two. This may be a useful opportunity to examine and address any negative beliefs or thought patterns related to their sexual orientation (Safren & Rogers, 2001). It is important to revisit the relationship between their sexual orientation and the presenting problem throughout the course of treatment.

It is useful to recognize the effect of "societal norms in the development and maintenance of negative thoughts or beliefs about same-sex attractions" (Safren & Rogers, 2001, pp. 630–631). There are many psychosocial stressors for sexual minority youth not only in the schools, but within society at large. Discrimination is endorsed by many states and at the federal level. For example, there is discrimination in employment, housing, the military, Boy Scouts, social security, and the absence of the civil right to marry and to obtain the benefits of marriage. These ongoing stressors "can reinforce negative thoughts and beliefs about one's same-sex sexual orientation" and have a "significant influence on one's mood" (Safren & Rogers, 2001, p. 631). According to Safren and Rogers (2001), "an important part of case formulation is help patients identify automatic thoughts about their sexual identity, utilize techniques such as behavioral experiments and cognitive restructuring to test this type of thinking, and develop realistic and effective coping responses" (p. 631).

Because isolation is a common concern for sexual minority youth, an important aspect of cognitive-behavioral therapy is to help youth to identify positive environments where they can meet others who have gone through a similar experience. This may include participation in a Gay-Straight Alliance (GSA), social groups, or community activities.

GUIDELINES FOR AFFIRMATIVE PSYCHOTHERAPY

In 2000, the American Psychological Association published *Guidelines for Psychotherapy with Lesbian, Gay and Bisexual Clients.* The goals of these guidelines are to "provide practitioners with (a) a frame of reference for the treatment of lesbian, gay, and bisexual clients and (b) basic information and references in the areas of assessment, intervention, identity, relationships and the education and training of psychologists" (APA, 2000, p. 1440). These guidelines build on the ethical code and are useful in guiding service delivery. There are four sections of the guidelines including (a) attitudes toward homosexuality and bisexuality, (b) relationships and families, (c) issues of diversity, and (d) education.

SCHOOL-BASED INTERVENTIONS

Schools need to provide environments where diversity is respected and affirmed, to teach youth to live in a democratic society, and to ensure the safety and rights of all youth. An affirmative environment is more likely when personnel are knowledgeable about protective factors and the needs of sexual minority youth, provide support and understanding, and become advocates and allies. School climate will improve for sexual minority youth when school-based supports and resources are utilized. A highly successful program is Project 10, which was founded by Dr. Virginia Uribe in 1984 at Fairfax High School in the Los Angeles Unified School District. Project

10 is the nation's first public school program dedicated to providing on-site educational support services to gay, lesbian, bisexual, transgender, and questioning youth (Uribe & Harbeck, 1991). The focus of the program is dropout prevention with emphases in education, reduction in verbal and physical abuse, suicide prevention, and accurate AIDS information.

Antigay epithets and aggression occur frequently in schools and create a negative climate. Failure to intervene reinforces the message that hate speech and violence are permitted. A schoolwide policy of zero tolerance for antigay harassment, hate epithets, and slurs must be developed either separately or incorporated into an overall school safety effort. The policy should apply to students and staff and include incidents from name-calling and property damage to physical and sexual assault. Most important, the policy must be consistently enforced by all staff.

In addition to preventing antigay behavior, it is important to represent and celebrate diversity throughout the school. Accurate information regarding sexual identity development, sexuality minority issues, and famous sexuality minority individuals must be infused into the curriculum. There are many examples in history, literature, and science, such as Alice Walker, Walt Whitman, Henry David Thoreau, Richard the Lion-Hearted, Alexander the Great, and Margaret Mead, as well as in politics and current events. Setting a positive environment also includes displaying posters about sexual minority youth, literature by sexual minorities, and providing library resources. The use of gender-neutral and inclusive language indicates that sexual orientation is not assumed.

Identify at least one trained staff member to serve as a resource to students. In many cases, this would be the school psychologist, school counselor, or school social worker. However, a teacher or other staff member may be a more effective resource, as this is more likely to normalize sexual orientation. Staff should be trained in issues affecting sexual minority youth, effective strategies for working with students, best practices in implementing antibias programs, and available community resources. The National Association of School Psychologists and GLSEN are among a number of organizations that offer training to educators. Students should know which personnel they can turn to; hanging rainbow posters or "safe zone" stickers on doors are good ways to help identify where staff are located. Another effective way to improve school climate is to establish a school-based GSA, which provides support and companionship, improves self-esteem, and promotes positive school change.

Creating a nondiscrimination school policy for sexual minority students and staff extends additional protections. Including staff in this policy demonstrates to youth that their role models will not be discriminated against. This not only creates equality but also may increase the likelihood of staff being "out" and willing to serve as resources. Extracurricular activities such as after-school clubs, sports teams, and social events need to be explicitly open to all students. Proms and other "couple" events can be particularly uncomfortable for sexual minority youth. Sexuality minority students at some schools prefer to organize their own dances, but this should be a student choice and not in lieu of being welcomed at the main prom.

School should provide ongoing in-services, antibias training, and education regarding the legal responsibility to protect and treat all youth respectfully. Such training should provide a protocol for responding to students who reach out for help and include teachers, bus drivers, and other educational support staff, coaches, and after-school personnel. Guest speakers who are willing to share their school experiences such as a sexuality minority graduate from the school or representative from Parents and Friends of Lesbians and Gays (PFLAG), which is a national organization with local chapters, are also very effective at raising awareness.

There has been a recent increase in efforts to promote "reparative therapy" and "transformation ministry" in schools. Both movements view homosexuality as pathological and attempt to eliminate individuals' sexual desire for people of the same gender, using psychotherapy or religious ministry, respectively. These approaches contradict science and research, have no support among health or mental health professional organizations, and have the potential to do serious harm.

Issues of sexuality can raise strong emotions. Be sure to engage students, staff, and parents in developing codes of conduct and diversity programming. Understand cultural viewpoints within the community. It is important to know the facts about sexual orientation and communicate them to all groups. Consult with clinicians in other schools who have successfully created safe and supportive school cultures for sexual minority youth.

COMMUNITY RESOURCES

When sexual minority youth do not meet the criteria for school-based mental health services but would benefit from intervention, it is important to refer them to outside agencies. The nearest sexual minority community center will likely have useful resources. Referring youth to healthy peer support groups is also beneficial in order help them to develop contacts within the gay community. If families are in need of support, PFLAG may be valuable. Other resources that may be supportive for sexual minority youth include books, Internet groups such as The National Coalition for GLBT Youth, and pen pal services.

Clearly, it is necessary to provide resources and support to students in crisis. Again, local community centers may be useful in offering resources. There are also several national hotlines such as The Trevor Helpline (1-800-850-8078), which is a 24-hour, national suicide hotline for gay and questioning youth; the Covenant House (1-800-999-9999), a 24-hour, national hotline that provides crisis intervention and referrals to young people under 21 and their families; and the National Runaway Switchboard (1-800-621-4000), a 24-hour hotline that offers crisis intervention, family mediation, suicide counseling, and referrals for housing, medical services, and counseling. The National Runaway Switchboard will deliver messages and provide runaways with free bus tickets home.

LEGAL REQUIREMENTS OF SCHOOLS

When schools do not address stressors that impact the safety and education of sexual minority youth, they may be held legally and financially liable. According to the Equal Protection clause of the 14th Amendment of the U.S. Constitution, students are entitled to equal protection under the law. Any educational program or activity that receives federal financial assistance cannot discriminate on the basis of sex or choose which students will be safe. Failure to protect students equally can result in civil lawsuits and administrative intervention by the U.S. Department of Education. This right of equal protection was used in the landmark case of Jamie Nabozny (*Nabozny v. Podlesny,* 1996). Jamie Nabozny was beaten to the point of requiring surgery, urinated on, called antigay epithets, and made to suffer repeated assaults at school. The abuse had a significant impact on Jamie's mental health and he dropped out of school. In spite of frequent meetings with school officials, intervention of Jamie's parents, and identification of his attackers, the school took no meaningful disciplinary action against the perpetrators. The three administrators were found guilty of discrimination because they failed to protect Jamie but responded to harassment directed at others. They were held personally liable for a settlement of nearly $1 million. The legal mandate of equality applies to all decisions that a public school official might make that would treat sexual minority youth differently.

Title IX is a nondiscrimination statute that prohibits sex discrimination in schools. The statute mandates that no individual be discriminated against on the basis of sex in any educational program or activity that receives federal financial assistance. Title IX was originally intended to protect individuals from sex discrimination; however, it has been used to financially compensate victims of sexual harassment in school settings. Title IX does not prohibit discrimination on the basis of sexual orientation, though sexual harassment directed at gay or lesbian students may constitute sexual harassment prohibited by Title IX.

The Equal Access Act, a federal law that was passed in 1984, requires public secondary schools to recognize gay-related groups when the school receives federal assistance and has a limited open forum. A limited open forum provides access to one or more noncurricular student groups to meet on school premises during non-instructional time. A noncurricular student group is any group that does not directly relate to the body of courses offered by the school. If the Equal Access Act applies, a school must provide a gay-related group with access to the school equal to the access provided to other student groups. GSAs can play an important role in ending homophobia and decreasing isolation. Efforts by school districts to deny GSAs have not been successful.

CASE EXAMPLE OF A SCHOOL CLIMATE INTERVENTION

"Sondra" is a 17-year-old, 11th-grade black bisexual female student. She attends an ethnically and culturally diverse public school in the suburbs of a medium-sized city on the East Coast. Sondra has attended the same public school since kindergarten. She is an honor roll student and a strong leader in the school and community. Sondra is a talented artist, popular, and generally well respected by her peers. Beginning at about 12 years of age, Sondra began to realize that she was emotionally and physically attracted to both male and female students. Although Sondra was initially confused by her attractions, as she became older, she began to consolidate her identity as a bisexual female and felt pressured to make difficult decisions about dating. Although Sondra dated a female student briefly in the 10th grade, most of her relationships were with male students. Sondra recently broke up with a 12th-grade black male student who was a popular athlete at the school. Following the breakup, Sondra began spending more time with a Caucasian female student named "Jackie," who was out as a lesbian at the school. Rumors began to spread quickly that they were dating and that Sondra was also a lesbian. Sondra's parents became aware of these rumors and attempted to limit Sondra's contact with Jackie. Although Sondra and Jackie were not dating, Sondra found comfort in this friendship and she felt safe discussing issues related to her sexual orientation. Following the breakup with Sondra's boyfriend, the harassment began to intensify. Sondra was called "dyke" and antigay slurs frequently at school, especially by friends of her former boyfriend. In addition to stressors at school, Sondra's primary concern was her fears of coming out as bisexual, particularly to her family. Sondra's family was very involved in a conservative church community and she felt conflicts between her upbringing and her sexual orientation. With the exception of Jackie and Sondra's first girlfriend, she did not know any other sexual minority youth, knew no sexual minority youth of color, and felt isolated from her friends from childhood.

Sondra was referred to the school psychologist following an incident of harassment at school. Parental permission was obtained in order to discuss the harassment at school with Sondra. Sondra's parents reported being upset about the harassment at school and expressed support of their daughter, although they felt certain that she is "not that way." Sondra shared the information described here with the psychologist. She was tearful, reported feeling upset about the harassment and distressed about possible family conflicts or rejection if she discloses her sexual orientation. Sondra indicated that she felt isolated from childhood friends and uncomfortable discussing her sexual orientation with them.

In order to address the school climate issues, the following plan was developed. The psychologist solicited the assistance of the school principal in order to address the incidents of harassment with the students. Students who have been harassing Sondra were provided with discipline, education regarding diversity, expectations regarding their conduct, and information about consequences for retaliation based on the report. The former boyfriend was provided with additional intervention, as he reported feeling embarrassed about being "dumped for a lesbian" and encouraged the harassment. The school had a schoolwide policy of zero tolerance for antigay harassment, hate epithets, and slurs, which was enforced with the students. Students at the school also were provided with education regarding sexuality and sexual orientations in their health and wellness courses. School staff had been provided with ongoing antibias training, and education regarding the legal responsibility to protect and treat all youth respectfully and the need to consistently report incidents of harassment.

Although Sondra expressed stress regarding her harassment and family issues, it did not limit her ability to benefit from her education at the school. She was not referred for ongoing school-based mental health services, and instead, Sondra was referred for other supports at the school and in the community. Because of Sondra's fears of her disclosure of her sexual orientation to her family and her feelings of isolation, she was referred to the Gay-Straight Alliance and a local support group for sexual minority youth. The goals of these groups were for Sondra to obtain advice, support, and guidance. She also was referred to supportive local community church leaders in order to assist her to cope with her religious conflicts regarding her sexual orientation and to assist her to consolidate her identities. Sondra was given resources for sexual minority youth of color such as books and Internet groups (e.g., The National Coalition for GLBT Youth) and pen pal services. These sources of support were valuable to her until she was comfortable accessing school and community resources. Sondra was provided with supportive information for her family from PFLAG, if needed in the future.

CASE EXAMPLE OF COGNITIVE-BEHAVIORAL TECHNIQUES AND SCHOOL CLIMATE INTERVENTION

Jamie is a 15-year-old 9th-grade Caucasian gay male student. He attends a relatively homogenous public school in a small rural town in the Midwest. Jamie has attended the same public school since the 6th grade. Jamie has typically been an average student with interests in interior and fashion design. He is a shy and withdrawn young man who has few close friends at school.

Jamie reported feeling different from his male peers for as long as he could remember. As a young child, he did not recognize these differences to be sexual; rather, he was not interested in gender-typical activities such as football and basketball, which resulted in him feeling different. Because of Jamie's interests and sensitive nature, he was frequently called names such as "sissy" and "fag" by his peers. The harassment began to intensify, especially in middle school. During this time, Jamie became increasingly aware of his emotional and physical attractions to male students. In high school, Jamie had a few same-sex experiences in the community. He wanted to be involved in a relationship; however, he knew few male peers his age and was worried about confirming his sexuality to others through a relationship. At school, the harassment escalated into incidents of verbal and physical abuse. Jamie considered seeking support at a local gay community center, although he feared that he would be discovered at the center by other students. He was embarrassed to disclose the abuse to school officials and feared that his family would find out about his sexual orientation. As Jamie's stressors and feelings of isolation increased, he became overwhelmed. He experienced feelings of depression and intermittent suicidality. Jamie began to avoid previously enjoyed activities and experienced anxiety at school and in social situations. In order to avoid his peers, Jamie eventually began to skip classes and then days of school. His grades began to drop dramatically.

Jamie was referred to the school psychologist at his parent's request because of their concerns regarding a decline in Jamie's functioning and his lack of school attendance and performance. During the session with the psychologist, Jamie was initially hesitant to share his story as he feared retribution from his peers. Although Jamie also feared rejection from his parents because of his sexual orientation, he requested the psychologist's support in disclosing this information to his parents. Jamie felt that withholding the information was a source of considerable stress and that he could not keep the information from them any longer.

During the initial assessment of Jamie, the psychologist assessed the nature and extent of Jamie's depression, suicidality, and social anxiety. The psychologist examined the role of Jamie's sexual orientation and his presenting symptoms. Jamie reported feeling depressed because he "wasn't like anyone at school and that his family would not accept him." Although Jamie did not wish to die, he felt that he would be better off dead than continue to be faced with the school stressors. The psychologist examined Jamie's negative thought patterns about his sexuality. Jamie believed that he would "never be a happy person because the gay people that he knew did not seem happy" and he felt that they were not treated well in his conservative community. If Jamie were to be seen for ongoing mental health services at school, it would be important to continue to examine his automatic thoughts about his sexual identity, use cognitive restructuring, and help him to develop effective coping responses.

Following the assessment, Jamie's parents were notified regarding Jamie's presenting symptoms and were requested to take him for further clinical assessment as his safety was of concern. Although they were surprised at Jamie's disclosure of his sexual orientation, they were supportive of him and were genuinely concerned about him and about the harassment and abuse at school. They agreed to bring him to a local hospital in order to assess his safety for a determination whether hospitalization was necessary. Jamie's family was also given information regarding local resources of sexual minority youth and contact information for PFLAG following the resolution of the crisis.

In order to address the significant issues regarding the climate in Jamie's school, a similar plan was developed as described in Sondra's case. However, because of the seriousness of the abuse several students were suspended and a mandatory assembly with follow-up education in the classrooms occurred. School staff also were provided with antibias training and education regarding sexual minority youth and the need to consistently report incidents of harassment. Previously, the school district was reluctant to include sexual orientation in the schoolwide policy; however, the psychologist was successful in advocating for its inclusion. Several students expressed interest in forming a Gay-Straight Alliance and the administration was supportive of their request.

SUMMARY

Schools have a legal, ethical, and moral obligation to provide equal access to education and equal protection under the law for all students. For many sexual minority youth, schools are unsafe and survival, not education, is the priority. Therefore, many sexual minority youth experience academic and learning problems. Research regarding school climate has revealed that school-based interventions are desperately needed in many schools and can be effective when implemented successfully. Yet many professionals lack training about sexual minority youth and feel inadequate when working with this population. Education and training for staff are critical in order to better meet the needs of this population.

Sexual minority youth are faced with stressors through overt acts of abuse, harassment and violence, development of their identity as a sexual minority person and related internalized homophobia, disclosure of sexual orientation to others and related lack of adult social support, and development of platonic and romantic relationships with other lesbian, gay male, and bisexual peers (Safren et al., 2001). These psychosocial stressors place sexual minority youth at-risk for adjustment difficulties and self-destructive behavior.

Although there is a lack of research regarding cognitive-behavior therapy with sexual minority youth, there is no reason to believe that cognitive-behavior therapy would be less effective in treating sexual minority youth (Safren et al., 2001). However, it must be tailored to the unique issues of this population. When providing mental health services for sexual minority youth, it is important to help youth "identify automatic thoughts about their sexual identity, utilize techniques such as behavioral experiments and cognitive restructuring to test this type of thinking, and develop realistic and effective coping responses" (Safren & Rogers, 2001, p. 631).

The use of school-based interventions is necessary in order to meet the needs of sexual minority youth. Cognitive and educational interventions may be effective in changing the cognitive mindset of students and staff from prejudice or fear of sexual minorities to understanding, acceptance, and, ultimately, an affirmation of diversity. School-based interventions not only have a positive impact on the overall climate but also are likely to decrease school stressors, the resultant negative impact on sexual minority youth, and the need for school-based mental health services. An affirmative environment is more likely when personnel are knowledgeable about protective factors and the needs of sexual minority youth, provide support and understanding, and become advocates and allies. Creating safe and affirmative schools for all students, including sexual minorities, is essential to increase equal access to education. School-based clinicians have an essential role in improving the physical, social, and psychological functioning of sexual minority youth through their support and advocacy.

REFERENCES

American Psychological Association. (2000). *Guidelines for psychotherapy with lesbian, gay and bisexual clients.* Washington, DC: Author.

American Psychological Association. (2002). Ethical principles of psychologists and code of conduct. *American Psychologist, 57,* 1060–1073.

Beck, A. T, Freeman, A., & Associates. (1990). *Cognitive therapy of personality disorders.* New York: Guilford Press.

Campos, P., Bernstein, G., Davison, G., Adams, H., and Arias, I. (1996). Behavior therapy and homosexuality in the 1990's. *The Behavior Therapist, 19(8),* 113–125.

Centers for Disease Control. (1992). Behaviors related to unintentional and intentional injuries among high school students—United States. *Morbidity and Mortality Weekly Report, 41,* 760–772.

Cochran, S. D., Sullivan, J. G., & Mays, V. M. (2003). Prevalance of mental disorders, psychological distress and mental health services use among lesbian, gay, and bisexual adults in the United States. *Journal of Consulting and Clinical Psychology, 71,* 53–61.

D'Augelli, A. R., & Hershberger, S. L. (1993). Lesbian, gay, and bisexual youth in community settings: Personal challenges and mental health problems. *American Journal of Community Psychology, 21,* 421–448.

D'Augelli, A. R., & Patterson, C. J. (1995). *Lesbian, gay and bisexual identities over the lifespan* (pp. 165–189). New York: Oxford University Press.

Garnets, L., Hancock, K., Cochran, S., Goodchilds, J., & Peplau, L. (1991). Issues in psychotherapy with lesbian and gay men: A survey of psychologists. *American Psychologist, 46,* 964–972.

Gay, Lesbian, and Straight Education Network (2003 and 1999). *National School Climate Survey.* New York: Author.

Gay, Lesbian, and Straight Education Network (2000). *Local School Climate Survey: School Based Version.* New York: Author.

Gay, Lesbian, and Straight Education Network (2004). *State of the States Report.* New York: Author.

Hart, T. (2001, Winter). Lack of training in behavior therapy and research regarding lesbian, gay, bisexual, and transgendered individuals. *The Behavior Therapist,* 217–218.

Kann, L., Kinchen, S. A., Williams, B. I., Ross, J. G., Lowry, R., Hill, C. V., Grunbaum, J., Blumson, P. S., Collins, J. L., & Kolbe, L. J. (1998). *Youth risk behavior surveillance. 1997.* Surveillance and Evaluation Research Branch, Division of Adolescent and School Health. Atlanta, GA: Centers for Disease Control and Prevention.

Lasser, J., & Tharinger, D. (1997). Sexual Minority Youth. In G. G. Bear, K. M. Minke, & A. Thomas (Eds.), *Children's needs II: Development, problems and alternatives* (pp. 769–780). Bethesda, MD: National Association of School Psychologists.

Licitra-Klecker, D. M., & Waas, G. A. (1993). Perceived social support among high-stress adolescents: The role of peers and family. *Journal of Adolescent Research, 8,* 381–402.

Massachusetts Department of Education. (2003). *Massachusetts Youth Risk Behavior Survey.* Malden, MA: Author

Nabozny v. Podlesny, 92 F. 3d 446 (7th Cir. 1996)

National Association of School Psychologists. (2000). *Professional conduct manual: Principles for professional ethics.* Bethesda, MD: Author.

Persons, J. B. (1989). *Cognitive therapy: A case conceptualization approach.* New York: Norton.

Porter, J. D. (2001). *Healthy lesbian, gay and bisexual students project.* Retrieved November 14, 2004, from http://www.apa.org/ed/hlgb.html

Purcell, D., Campos, P., & Perilla, J. (1996). Therapy with lesbian and gay men: A cognitive-behavioral perspective. *Cognitive and Behavioral Practice, 2,* 391–415.

Rotheram-Borus, M. J., Hunter, J., & Rosario, M. (1994). Suicidal behavior and gay related stress among gay and bisexual male adolescents. *Journal of Adolescent Research, 9,* 498–508.

Safe Schools Coalition of Washington State. (1999, January). Understanding anti-gay harassment and violence in schools. *A report on the five year anti-violence research project of the safe schools coalition of Washington State.* Washington: Author.

Safren, S., & Heimberger, R. (1999). Depression, hopelessness, suicidality and related factors in sexual minority and heterosexual adolescents. *Journal of Consulting and Clinical Psychology, 67,* 859–886.

Safren, S., Hollander, G., Hart, T., & Heimberg, R. (2001). Cognitive-behavior therapy with lesbian, gay and bisexual youth. *Cognitive and Behavioral Practice, 8,* 215–223.

Safren, S., & Rogers, T. (2001). Cognitive-behavior therapy with gay, lesbian, and bisexual clients. *Psychotherapy in Practice, 57*(5), 629–643.

Savin-Williams, R. C. (1994). Verbal and physical abuse as stressors in the lives of lesbian, gay male, and bisexual youths: Associations with school problems, running away, substance use, prostitution, and suicide. *Journal of Consulting and Clinical Psychology, 62,* 261–269.

Savin-Williams, R. C., & Cohen, K. M. (1996). *The lives of lesbians, gays and bisexuals: Children to adults.* New York: Harcourt Brace.

Seattle Public Schools. (1996). *1995 Teen Health Risk Survey.* Seattle, WA: Author.

Uribe, V., & Harbeck, K. (1991). Addressing the needs of lesbian, gay, and bisexual youth: The origins of PROJECT 10 and school-based intervention. *Journal of Homosexuality, 22*(3/4), 9–28.

U.S. Department of Health and Human Services. (1989). *Prevention '89/90: Federal programs and progress.* Washington, DC: U.S. Government Printing Office.

18

Interventions for Health Problems: A Multisystemic Cognitive-Behavioral Approach

THOMAS J. POWER & BRANLYN E. WERBA

Chronic health problems are highly prevalent among children and adolescents. For example, common pediatric conditions, such as asthma, obesity, and recurrent abdominal pain each occur in an estimated 5% to 12% of the population (Centers for Disease Control, 1995; McGrath, 1990; Troiano & Flegal, 1998). Furthermore, the prevalence of chronic health conditions has doubled over the past 30 years, which may be due to improvements in early diagnosis and treatment and the survival of low birth weight infants as well as to an increase in environmental toxins and the emergence of diseases such as AIDS and prenatal drug exposure (Brown, 2004).

IMPACT OF ILLNESS ON EDUCATIONAL FUNCTIONING

Chronic medical conditions can have an effect on child development in virtually every domain of functioning, including school, family, and peer group. The following are factors that may contribute to the adjustment of a child with a chronic illness in school.

Central Nervous System Involvement

Medical conditions involving the central nervous system (CNS) generally have the greatest effect on academic performance. These illnesses, which might include brain injury, brain tumor, or strokes associated with sickle cell disease, often have a direct impact on brain structure and function, which may result in deficits in one or more neuropsychological processes involved in learning. Furthermore, children with CNS involvement typically are at high risk for social impairments, related to neurologically based impairments in social perception and executive functioning (Nassau & Drotar, 1997).

Change in Physical Appearance

Alterations in physical appearance resulting from a medical condition can have an effect on a child's peer relationships. Child self-perceptions of unattractiveness have been shown to be related to social anxiety and withdrawal, which may contribute to peer relationship problems (Spirito, DeLawyer, & Stark, 1991). Also, research has demonstrated that peers initiate social contact less frequently with children who have alterations in physical appearance caused by craniofacial conditions than with children who do not have a medical condition (Pope & Ward, 1997).

Absenteeism

Children with chronic illnesses generally are absent from school more frequently than their peers (e.g., see Annett, 2004; Walker & Johnson, 2004). School absence may reduce opportunities for instruction and social engagement, which may contribute to academic underachievement or peer relationship difficulties. Also, absence from school may disrupt student involvement in academic and social activities, which may lead to a sense of isolation in the school environment and a loss of self-efficacy in coping with challenging situations.

Pain

Children with a wide range of medical conditions, including juvenile rheumatoid arthritis, sickle cell disease, gastrointestinal disorders, and musculoskeletal syndromes, experience pain that can lead to impairments in daily functioning. Pain may contribute to emotional distress, which may become exacerbated during periods of separation from the family (e.g., abdominal pain related to separation anxiety; Walker & Johnson, 2004) or periods of increased physical activity (e.g., musculoskeletal pain associated with exercise; Sherry, 2000). Also, pain may contribute to problems sustaining attention during challenging academic assignments.

Traumatic Stress

Medical conditions, particularly those with a sudden onset that are life-threatening and involve repeated experiences that are frightening (serious injury, cancer), can be traumatizing to children and their families. Most children adjust well psychologically after a traumatizing series of medical events, but about 20% develop symptoms of acute or posttraumatic stress disorder (PTSD; Winston, Kassam-Adams, & Vivarelli-O'Neill, 2002). Also, the parents of children who experience a medical trauma are more likely to show signs of PTSD than the children themselves (Kazak et al., 1997). Symptoms of PTSD may contribute to emotional distress in school and may interfere with a child's ability to consistently pay attention and learn.

CONTEXT OF COGNITIVE-BEHAVIORAL APPROACHES

The school adjustment of a child with a health condition depends on numerous factors, including variables pertaining to the school, such as the nature of the teacher-child relationship, the quality of instruction provided, and opportunities to engage in meaningful, cooperative relationships with peers. Consistent with a developmental ecological model, adjustment within the school system also is influenced by factors in other systems of a child's life (e.g., family, health system, community) as well as connections between systems (e.g., school-family relationship, school-health system relationship; Bronfenbrenner, 1979). For example, strong attachment to one or more caregivers is important for child development and success in school, as it has been shown to have an influence on a child's motivation to succeed academically, ability to self-regulate emotions, and ability to engage in successful relationships with peers and adults outside the family (Cicchetti, Toth, & Lynch, 1995). In addition, the quality of the family-school relationship can have an effect on the teacher-child relationship, which in turn influences adjustment in school (Pianta, 1999). In this chapter, we present cognitive-behavioral approaches to intervention for children with health problems within the broader context of an ecological model that posits that child development occurs within the context of systems and interconnections among systems.

RESEARCH REVIEW: PAIN AND NONADHERENCE

Given that numerous intervention approaches have been developed for the wide range of health conditions that affect children (e.g., see the edited texts by Brown, 2004; Roberts, 2003), we limit the focus of this chapter to two targets for intervention: pain and nonadherence to treatment. These targets were selected because they are highly prevalent issues that cut across a wide range of pediatric conditions. Also, established or promising cognitive-behavioral interventions have been developed to address issues of pain and nonadherence. Furthermore, school professionals, parents, and health providers can play critical roles in developing, implementing, and evaluating interventions related to these issues.

Pain

Pain can be defined as "an unpleasant sensory and emotional experience associated with actual or potential tissue damage, or described in terms of such damage" (Merskey & Bogduk, 1994, as cited in Dahlquist & Switkin, 2003). This definition recognizes that pain perception is a function of both biological and emotional processes, and it rejects a differentiation of pain as either organically based or psychologically based (Dahlquist & Switkin, 2003).

Pain complaints are the most common reason for seeking medical care (Covington, 2000) and can greatly impact a child's everyday functioning in school (Palermo, 2000). Common examples of pain among children are migraine headaches, stomachaches, and musculoskeletal pain, and these symptoms are often associated with functional impairments. In particular, recurrent abdominal pain

(RAP) often results in noteworthy functional impairment, including a decrease in school attendance (Wasserman, Whitington, & Rivara, 1988), academic productivity (Kolbe, Collins, & Cortese, 1997), and participation in physical activities (Walker & Greene, 1991).

Recurrent abdominal pain consists of episodes that wax and wane and occur for three or more times over a 3-month period, and is severe enough to impair functioning (Robins, Smith, Glutting, & Bishop, 2005). Although it is not a formal medical or psychological diagnosis, RAP is understood by experts to be a complex interaction of physical pain sensation and psychological responses to pain, as well as the ecological context in which these interactions occur (Robins et al., 2005; Frazer & Rappaport, 1999).

In addition to illness-related factors, individual and family factors such as coping skills, psychological distress, and cultural background may impact the functioning of children with pain. For example, certain coping responses, such as using problem-solving strategies and distraction techniques, may lessen a child's perception of pain and resulting functional disability. Conversely, a pattern of parental encouragement of the "sick role," by providing reinforcement for pain behaviors (e.g., allowing the child to avoid unpleasant activities, providing attention contingent on complaints of pain) has been found to be greater for children with RAP than well children (Walker, Garber, & Green, 1993).

Nonadherence

Adherence is commonly defined as "the extent to which a person's behavior, in terms of medications, following diets, or executing lifestyle changes, coincides with medical or health advice" (Haynes, 1979, pp 2–3). Nonadherence can pose serious health risks, including exacerbation of symptoms, medical complications, and greater likelihood of mortality (Lamanek, Kamps, & Chung, 2001). In addition, nonadherence is associated with increased health care utilization and school absences.

Adherence can be conceptualized as a process that fluctuates from initial diagnosis through the course of intervention (Lamanek et al., 2001). Multiple factors are associated with adherence to pediatric medical regimens, and have been described as falling into four major areas (LaGreca & Bearman, 2003). First, developmental variables, such as level of cognitive, motor, social, and emotional functioning, have been consistently linked to adherence. For example, adolescents usually have more difficulties being adherent than young children, especially with regimens that may result in changes in appearance, interfere with social interactions, or require major lifestyle changes. Second, characteristics of the child and family, particularly knowledge of disease management, problem-solving skills, positive psychosocial adaptation, and family support have been associated with better treatment adherence. Third, aspects of health care systems, such as trusting doctor-patient relationships and clear communication about disease management, are associated with adherence. Finally, aspects of the disease itself and its management, such as more chronic and complex regimens, are associated with poorer adherence.

Asthma affects approximately 12% of children in the United States (Dey, Schiller, & Tai, 2004), making it one of the most common chronic illness of childhood. This lung disease involves intermittent and variable periods of airway obstruction, which are often triggered by airborne irritants, such as cigarette smoke or other allergens. It is the leading cause of hospitalizations, emergency department visits, and restrictions of activities for children and adolescents, and is the leading cause of school absenteeism, with approximately 10 million school days missed per year because of its symptoms (Taylor & Newacheck, 1992).

Predictors of poor asthma adherence include low household income and minority status (Apter, Reisine, Affleck, Barrows, & ZuWallack, 1998; Bender et al., 2000), higher rates of parental criticism toward children (Wamboldt, Wambolt, Gavin, Roesler, & Brugman, 1995), and family dysfunction (Bender, Milgrom, Rand, & Ackerson, 1998). Unlike other pediatric illnesses, there have been mixed findings with regards to whether child knowledge and reasoning about asthma relates to adherence. These results suggest that intervention approaches to improve asthma adherence should not rely on educational approaches directed at the child alone (McQuaid & Walders, 2003).

Asthma management has shifted from episodic treatment to ongoing, preventative care. Adherence to asthma regimen often includes daily medication use, identification and avoidance of triggers, and management of exacerbations (Klinnert, McQuaid, & Gavin, 1997). Therefore, nurses and teachers can be involved in all of aspects of asthma management and prevention of exacerbations. It is vital that the family, medical team, and school team work together to promote optimal adherence.

METHODS OF ASSESSMENT

Several models of assessment have been developed to assist in intervention development and outcome evaluation for children with health concerns (see Power, DuPaul, Shapiro, & Kazak, 2003). The following is a description of these models. Table 18.1 provides examples of measures for assessing each model, with a particular focus on measures useful in the assessment of adherence and pain. For a further description of measures that may be useful in assessing health-related behaviors, see Naar-King, Ellis, and Frey (2004).

Dimensional Assessment

The dimensional approach provides an assessment of functioning related to one or more domains or factors along a continuum with no clear demarcation of the boundary between functional and dysfunctional, normal or abnormal. This approach typically provides an assessment of the severity of functioning related to a particular dimension by comparing the child's level of functioning to that of children of the same age range and gender (Achenbach & McConaughy, 1996). For example, measures have been developed to assess the degree of child and family adherence to medical regimens and the severity of a child's experience of pain.

Table 18.1 Examples of Measures Associated with Dimensional, Cognitive, Functional, and Ecological Models of Assessment

Measure	Method	Purpose
Dimensional Assessment		
Daily phone diary (Quittner & Opipari, 1994)	Interview of parents and/or youth	Assessment of adherence
Medication Electronic Monitoring System*	Electronic recording of bottle opening	Assessment of adherence
Pediatric Pain Questionnaire (Varni, Thompson, & Hanson, 1987)	Youth self-report and parent report scale	Assessment of pain location, intensity, and history
Cognitive Assessment		
Pediatric Pain Coping Inventory (Varni et al., 1996)	Child self-report and parent report scale	Assessment of pain coping strategies
Parent Health Locus of Control (DeVellis et al., 1993)	Parent self-report	Assessment of parental beliefs about their child's health
Asthma Self-Efficacy Scale (Bursh, Schwankovsky, Gilbert, & Zeiger, 1999)	Child self-report and parent report scale	Assessment of self-efficacy in managing asthma
Functional Assessment		
Descriptive and experimental analysis of behavior (Nelson, Roberts, & Smith, 1998)	Parent and child interviews, direct observation, experimental manipulation	Assessment of the function of health-related behaviors
Ecological Assessment		
Family Responsibility Questionnaire (Anderson, Auslander, Jung, Miller, & Santiago, 1990)	Child self-report and parent report scale	Assessment of family member roles in managing illness
Parenting Stress Index (Abidin, 1995)	Parent report scale	Assessment of factors contributing to parenting stress
Student-Teacher Relationship Scale (Pianta, 2002)	Teacher self-report scale	Assessment of teacher-child relationship

*Available from APREX, 1430 O'Brien Drive, Suite F, Menlo Park, CA 94025-1486, http://www.aprex.com.

Cognitive Assessment

The cognitive approach assesses beliefs that may promote adaptive coping with illness or that may contribute to nonadaptive coping. Two constructs that have been commonly investigated in examining the relationship between cognitions and behavior are health locus of control and self-efficacy. Health locus of control refers to the belief that persons can take specific actions to improve their own or their children's health status, regardless of beliefs about their ability to be successful in implementing health-promoting behaviors (Rotter, 1990; Wallston, 1992). Self-efficacy refers to a belief in one's ability to be successful in implementing health promoting behaviors for oneself or one's child (Bandura, 1977; Sarafino, 1994).

Functional Assessment

The functional approach involves the use of procedures that examine environmental events that trigger and maintain health-related behaviors. This approach includes methods for assessing antecedent events that set the occasion for behaviors to occur, as well as contingencies that increase or decrease the likelihood that behaviors will reoccur. Functional assessment may include procedures for conducting a descriptive analysis (e.g., interviews and observations of behavior) as well as strategies used in experimental analysis (e.g., systematic manipulation of environmental events to examine the relationship between these events and targeted behaviors). Functional assessment is useful in identifying hypothesized functions of behavior (e.g., task avoidance, peer or adult attention, tangible reinforcement, automatic reinforcement) that are helpful in intervention planning (Power et al., 2003).

Ecological Assessment

The ecological approach involves an assessment of the contexts in which children function, with a particular emphasis on the relationships among individuals within systems (e.g., parent-child, teacher-child, peer-child). Ecological assessment includes an examination of interconnections among systems (e.g., family-school, family-health system, school-health system). Furthermore, ecological approaches ought to involve understanding of cultural, political, and economic factors (e.g., family religious beliefs, educational law, health reimbursement policies) that can have an effect on systems in which children develop (Power, in press).

CONCEPTUALIZATION OF INTERVENTION

A useful framework for conceptualizing clinical cases is an integration of ecological and cognitive-behavioral perspectives, an approach that we refer to as the Multi-systemic Cognitive-Behavioral Intervention Model (MCBIM), derived from models described by Sheridan, Kratochwill, and Bergan (1996); Kazak, Rourke, and Crump (2003), and Power et al. (2003). This model stresses the importance of promoting resilience and reducing risk as children develop within systems, and facilitating the formation of partnerships across systems. This approach also stresses the importance of shaping child and family beliefs about illness so that they lead to health-promoting behaviors and reduce health-compromising behaviors. An underlying assumption of this model is that cognitive-behavioral interventions are likely to be optimally effective if they are developed, implemented, and evaluated by professionals and family members through collaborative partnerships. The following is a brief description of the steps involved in this model. An illustration of the model is depicted in Figure 18.1.

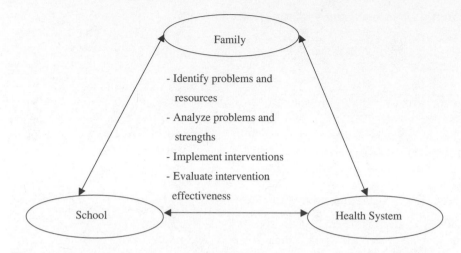

Figure 18.1 The Multisystemic Cognitive-Behavioral Intervention Model (MCBIM). The steps of problem solving and capacity building are addressed in the context of strengthening systems and connections between systems.

Step 1: Understand and Strengthen Systems

A child's ability to cope with illness is strongly influenced by dynamics within systems. The onset of an illness can disturb relationships within systems, and it is important to understand how systems become reorganized during the course of a medical condition. Also, it is helpful to identify contextual variables that promote effective coping as well as factors contributing to dysfunction. This information can be highly useful in designing strategies to strengthen relationships within systems.

Step 2: Understand and Strengthen System Interconnections

Collaborative relationships between systems can help to promote successful adaptation in each of the systems. For children with health conditions, it is important to understand how the family, school, and health systems are interconnected. This information can be helpful to practitioners in formulating strategies to strengthen connections between these systems.

Step 3: Identify Child Problems and Resources to Solve Problems

Once partnerships have been established across systems, professionals and family members are in a position to work together to solve problems and build assets. In this phase, family members, school professionals, and health professionals collaborate to identify key problems to be targeted for change. At the same time, it is critical for them to identify assets existing within and across systems and to use these resources to facilitate the process of problem solving.

Step 4: Analyze Problems and Strengths

This phase involves the assessment of cognitive and environmental factors across systems that promote healthy and unhealthy patterns of behavior. The cognitive and functional methods of assessment described in the previous section are particularly helpful during this phase. The cognitive approach can uncover health beliefs associated with health-promoting and health-compromising behaviors. The functional approach can identify environmental events that trigger and maintain adaptive and non-adaptive behaviors. Information derived through these assessment approaches is highly useful in designing cognitive-behavioral interventions for the key targets identified in step 3.

Step 5: Implementing Interventions

Effective intervention requires the specification of roles and responsibilities for each participant in the process, including the child and parents, school professionals, and health professionals. These assignments are negotiated through collaborative relationships among these individuals. Furthermore, treatment is likely to be successful if intervention agents communicate on an ongoing basis to identify and strengthen factors that promote adherence and to identify and resolve barriers to implementation.

Step 6: Evaluating Intervention Effectiveness

Evaluation of intervention effectiveness is conceptualized as a formative and summative process. Ongoing formative evaluation or progress monitoring is conducted to determine the need for adjustments during the course of intervention. Summative evaluation after a designated period is useful in determining whether the goals of the intervention have been fulfilled and whether an additional or modified course of treatment is indicated.

COGNITIVE-BEHAVIORAL INTERVENTION STRATEGIES

Cognitive-behavioral interventions for children with health conditions and their families represent a range of approaches including those that focus primarily on cognitive factors, those directly targeting behavior, and those involving a combination of cognitive and behavioral components. The focus of cognitively oriented components is on changing the way one thinks about an illness or its management. These thoughts or beliefs can be conceptualized as important antecedents to either adaptive or maladaptive behaviors. The focus of behaviorally-oriented components is on changing the situation or environment that influences healthy or unhealthy behaviors. Antecedent-based behavioral interventions are designed to change environmental conditions that set the occasion for behaviors to occur. Reinforcement-based behavioral approaches aim to increase healthy behaviors by changing the consequences or contingencies for healthy and unhealthy behaviors. We will discuss specific ways in which these cognitive-behavioral approaches have been adapted for children with chronic pain and nonadherence, with special attention to strategies that can be adapted for use in educational settings.

Interventions for Chronic Pain

Cognitive-behavioral pain management interventions typically combine the strategies or components described below into a comprehensive treatment package (Dahlquist & Switkin, 2003). For example, Sanders and colleagues designed and evaluated a family intervention for RAP that included education about the rationale for pain management, self-management strategies for children, and contingency management for parents (Sanders et al., 1989; Sanders, Shepherd, Cleghorn, & Woolford, 1994). In one study, children who participated in the intervention improved more quickly and had less reported pain at a 3-month follow-up than children in the wait-list control group (Sanders et al., 1989). In a second study, children in the treatment group had a lower rate of pain relapse than children who received only reassurance and general advice from their primary care doctor (Sanders et al., 1994). Although these studies did not differentiate the relative value of each of the components, they provided initial evidence for the effectiveness of cognitive-behavioral strategies in general (Dahlquist & Switkin, 2003).

Child Self-Statements. Children can be empowered to help manage their own experience of pain. Children's beliefs about pain and their ability to manage it can influence the subjective experience of pain and negative emotions that can accompany it. One strategy is to teach children to repeat to themselves encouraging self-statements (e.g., "It will get better soon") when they are experiencing pain (Gil et al., 2001; Sanders et al., 1989, 1994).

Relaxation and Distraction. Children can learn relaxation strategies to distract themselves from experiencing pain or reduce subjective pain intensity. One commonly used relaxation strategy is progressive muscle relaxation (PMR). PMR involves teaching children to tense and relax groups of muscles. As a child becomes more skilled at relaxing through practice at home, he or she may learn to relax by using fewer muscle groups or even relax the body at once using a cue word (Dahlquist & Switkin, 2004). Other common ways of teaching relaxation are having the child use imagery (i.e., the child imagines him-or herself in a different, more pleasant situation) and encouraging the child to engage in deep, repetitive, diaphragmatic breathing. In many cases, it is important for parents and teachers to prompt children to use these strategies.

Child Self-Reinforcement. Children can be taught to reinforce themselves for using pain coping strategies or minimizing their experience of pain. It is worth mentioning that the reduction of perceived pain is intrinsically self-reinforcing and can result in the increased use of effective coping strategies. Other forms of self-reinforcement also have been used in pain interventions. For example, children can practice reinforcing themselves by making positive self-statements (Sanders et al., 1994).

Contingency Management for Parents. For children with chronic pain, there are many possible sources of reinforcement and punishment for pain behaviors, including the social responses of friends, family, health care providers, and educators. Reinforcement-based approaches to pain management involve changing the consequences or contingencies for pain behaviors and pain coping strategies (Jensen, Nielson, & Kerns, 2003). Pain behaviors are defined as the actual manifestation of pain symptoms, such as lying down, grimacing, or verbal complaints (Dahlquist & Switkin, 2004).

One strategy for children with chronic pain is for adults to minimize any secondary gain (i.e., positive consequences of the illness), which could be reinforcing continuing displays of pain. For example, parents and teachers may unintentionally encourage pain-related behaviors or the "sick role" by giving special attention or allowing the child to avoid unwanted activities, such as attending school. Parents and teachers can instead reward adaptive coping behaviors, such as practicing relaxation strategies or distraction rather than sitting in the nurse's office or going home. In addition, they can choose to not give children excessive attention for pain behaviors, and not allow children to escape from unwanted activities because of their pain.

Interventions for Nonadherence

Similar to interventions for pain, interventions to improve adherence often include a variety of cognitive-behavioral components. For example, Baum and Creer (1986) found that the combination of self-monitoring, reinforcement, and education improved asthma management. Specifically, these children were more likely to avoid the triggers for an asthma attack, seek immediate adult attention at the start of an attack, and use a greater number of preventive strategies than children who used self-monitoring alone. Below is a description of some common treatment components for improving adherence to treatment regimens, with a particular focus on the management of asthma.

Environmental Modifications. For children with asthma, exposure to known environmental substances can serve as antecedents for asthma attacks. Reducing exposure to triggers such as animals, tobacco smoke, and other airborne allergens is an important component of a comprehensive plan. The National Asthma Education and Prevention Program's Resolution on Asthma Management at School (2004) specifically mandates a smoke-free environment for all school activities as key to asthma attack prevention.

Modeling. Specific knowledge about a disease and its management are necessary for adherence, but actual observation and practice of skills may be needed to successfully execute complex regimens. For example, if adolescents with newly diagnosed Type 1 Diabetes are not given adequate opportunities to observe procedures for injection and practice these skills, they may continue to rely on their parents for injections, or give injections incorrectly (e.g., use the same injection site repeatedly).

Self-Monitoring. Self-monitoring alone has generally shown limited utility for improving disease management for children with complex medical regimens (La Greca & Bearman, 2003). However, one study of children with asthma found that the self-monitoring of pulmonary function by using peak-flow meter readings increased children's overall adherence to asthma medication (Baum & Creer, 1986), but not more general asthma management skills.

Organizational. Organizational strategies involve modifying the context in which nonadherence occurs by changing clinic and regimen characteristics. For example, regimens may be able to be safely simplified, which could lead to improved adherence. Also, making medical appointments more accessible and convenient can increase rates of adherence. The most commonly studied organizational strategies for children with asthma involve expanding physician supervision and tailoring the medication regimen to child preferences (Lemanek et al., 2001). An organizational intervention that could be applied to the school setting is scheduling unobtrusive times for a child to go to the nurse's office to take preventive asthma medications.

Visual Cues. Calendars, signs in key locations, or phone calls can assist children in adhering to medical regimens. For example, placing medications by the bathroom mirror may cue an adolescent to take them in the morning and evening. In the school setting, it might be useful to provide the child with a daily written schedule and include time for the child to get medication from the nurse.

Reinforcement-Based Procedures. A variety of reinforcement-based procedures have been shown to be successful in improving adherence (La Greca & Bearman, 2003). For example, providing reinforcers, such as material items (e.g., stickers), special privileges (e.g., leading the class in line), or verbal praise, contingent on adherent behavior, generally is an effective component to treatment. Contracting, which involves an agreement between an adult and child specifying the reinforcers that will be provided if particular behaviors are performed, has been shown to be useful in improving adherence to interventions for asthma (e.g., see da Costa, Rapoff, Lemanek, & Goldstein, 1997).

APPLICATIONS OF MCBIM FOR SCHOOL CONCERNS

The proposed intervention model (MCBIM) is based on models that have been developed for health professionals and families (Kazak et al., 2003) as well as school professionals and families (Sheridan et al., 1996). A unique focus of MCBIM is that it highlights the importance of partnership between health and school professionals, which is underdeveloped in most communities (Power et al., 2003). The following is a description of some strengths and challenges associated with the application of this model for children with school concerns.

Strengths of MCBIM

1. The model is firmly grounded in developmental psychology, ecological-systems theory, cognitive-behavioral theory, and applied behavior analysis.
2. The model emphasizes the importance of using evidence-based methods of assessment and intervention.

3. The model highlights the importance of intervention and prevention, and balances the use of a strength-based and deficit-based approach.
4. A multi-informant, multimethod approach to assessment is strongly recommended.
5. A multimodal, multiagent approach to intervention is strongly recommended.
6. Data-based methods of intervention planning and evaluation are strongly recommended.
7. The emphasis on using partnership-based approaches enhances the likelihood that intervention strategies will be socially valid and culturally sensitive.

Challenges of MCBIM

1. The model requires forming partnerships across the health and educational systems, which can be highly challenging because of differences in culture, language, and training between health and school professionals, as well as time constraints (for a further discussion of strategies to address this issue, see DuPaul & Carlson, 2005).
2. The model requires the formation of partnerships between families and schools. Some parents and teachers are not ready for close collaboration to address children's health and education needs (for a further discussion of strategies to address this issue, see Sheridan et al., 1996, and Power et al., 2003).
3. Effective use of this model requires a high level of training in theory, scientific method, and practice (for a further discussion of the training needs of professionals, see Power, Shapiro, & DuPaul, 2003).
4. The application of this model can be time-consuming, labor intensive, and relatively expensive. For this reason, it is recommended that practitioners modify and streamline the process so that it is more feasible to apply.

CASE EXAMPLE: A CHILD WITH ASTHMA

Brandon is a 13-year-old African-American boy who was diagnosed with asthma at age 2, when he presented to the Emergency Department (ED) with coughing and wheezing. Over the years, he has been to the ED numerous times and has required acute hospitalization on three occasions. His current regimen, as prescribed by his family doctor in primary care, includes a combination of fluticasone propionate and salmeterol, a long-lasting corticosteroid and bronchodilator to prevent symptoms from emerging (two inhalations twice a day), and albuterol, a short-acting bronchodilator for the treatment of acute attacks (taken as needed).

Brandon lives with his mother and his 10-year-old sister. His parents were divorced last year, at which time his mother noted that Brandon started to become less willing to take his medication. Brandon's mother is a cigarette smoker and smokes in the home. Brandon generally performs well in school (B average), and no significant behavior problems were noted.

The primary care doctor conferred with the psychologist consulting with his practice when Brandon's mother expressed concerns about his nonadherence. The mother and Brandon often forget about his morning medication dose, and they get in arguments when she reminds him about his evening dose. Furthermore, Brandon has been having more asthma attacks in school, which is creating problems for the mother at work. She frequently has to leave work early, or miss work altogether.

Step 1: Understand and Strengthen Systems

The psychologist was able to meet with the family during a primary care visit. An assessment was conducted to determine the severity of Brandon's symptoms, factors that contributed to his asthma symptoms, Brandon's beliefs about taking medication, and family and school factors contributing to nonadherence. Brandon and his mother agreed that he visits the school nurse about twice per week because of asthma attacks. About twice a month his symptoms are so significant that the nurse calls the mother to pick him up from school. During a private interview with Brandon, he admitted that he often fails to take his medicine and gets annoyed when his mother nags him about it. He does not understand why he has to take medicine twice a day if he has not been wheezing that day. Moreover, Brandon stated that he feels embarrassed going to the nurse so often. Brandon indicated that the albuterol seems to help, but he often feels nervous when he takes it, and doesn't want his peers to know about his condition.

The psychologist obtained permission to talk with Brandon's teachers and school nurse to obtain further information about his behavior and asthma management at school. The nurse confirmed that Brandon comes to her office on a frequent basis and typically demonstrates serious symptoms. The nurse expressed frustration with the mother for not having better control of the situation. The teachers (Brandon has five) had little understanding of his health problems and indicated that frequent absences were beginning to affect his grades. The nurse and teachers expressed willingness to work with the psychologist and family to develop an intervention plan.

Step 2: Understand and Strengthen System Connections

The psychologist contacted Brandon's mother and proposed the idea of a joint family-school meeting. Brandon's mother agreed reluctantly and expressed concern about her relationship with the school nurse. The psychologist invited Brandon's primary care physician to attend, although he was not able to do so. However, the doctor prepared a brief report detailing the recommended medical regimen. At the family-school meeting, which Brandon attended, the psychologist facilitated relationship building between the school professionals and family. Everyone joined together in expressing their commitment to do whatever they could to assist Brandon with asthma management. The psychologist outlined some factors that complicated the situation and gave participants a brief opportunity to describe barriers to adherence.

Step 3: Identify Child Problems and Resources to Solve Problems

The school staff and mother agreed that Brandon's failure to take the long-acting medication at least once per day and his reluctance to use albuterol at the initial signs of an attack were significant problems. The team identified multiple strengths to help Brandon with asthma management, including his mother's strong commitment to her son, his ability to make friends, a knowledgeable nurse, and teachers who were invested in Brandon's learning and healthy development.

Step 4: Analyze Problems and Strengths

Next, the team identified several factors contributing to nonadherence. First, it was clear that Brandon did not understand the importance of his preventive medication, and the team took time to talk with Brandon about this. Second, Brandon and his mother were in a rush in the morning, and both of them often forgot about his morning medication dose. Third, Brandon's nonadherence with the evening dose appeared related to his annoyance about his mother nagging him and "treating him like a baby." Finally, a main barrier to use of his inhaler in school was Brandon's belief that his friends would have negative reactions to knowing that he had a "disease."

Step 5: Implementing Interventions

To help Brandon remember to take his morning dose, the nurse suggested that he take the medicine at school when he first arrives. To reduce Brandon's concern about "looking bad" in front of his friends, the teacher of his first-period class agreed to put him in charge of bringing the attendance role to the office each morning, so that the other students would not know he was getting his medication at that time. While at the nurse's office, Brandon would be given the opportunity to self-monitor peak respiratory air flow and to record this on a tracking chart. The nurse, mother, and Brandon agreed that the nurse would e-mail the mother each day to let her know if Brandon took his medication.

To help encourage Brandon to take his evening dose, the mother agreed to remind him to take the medicine on two occasions only. The mother established a contract with him, whereby he could earn additional time with his friends on the weekend (by inviting them to his home) each time he ingested his morning dose. Taking the morning dose of medication was also factored into a behavioral contract, whereby greater adherence resulted in the privilege of having friends over to his house. (At a separate meeting with Brandon and the psychologist, the mother admitted that the smell of cigarette smoke may be aggravating Brandon's condition, and she agreed to discontinue smoking in the home.)

To help Brandon change some of his beliefs about his friends' perception of asthma, the nurse normalized having asthma by informing him that at least 25 other students at his school used inhalers. His teachers suggested that it was better for Brandon to go to the bathroom to use his inhaler, than wait until he had to go to the nurse. In addition, Brandon agreed to several more sessions with the psychologist to talk about helpful ways to cope with his asthma in school.

Step 6: Evaluating Intervention Effectiveness

The same group met 2 weeks later. The nurse indicated that Brandon took his morning dose of medicine on 8 of 9 days. Brandon reported that he was breathing better, and he shared a graph depicting daily recordings of peak air flow. Brandon was proud to report that he missed his evening dose of medication on only one occasion, and his mother reported that he seemed to enjoy spending more time with his friends on the weekend. The mother also indicated that the doctor was pleased about the improved peak flow recordings, and that she was happy to be taking less time off work.

Since the initial meeting, Brandon did have one asthma attack, which he admitted was caused by feeling embarrassed to leave the classroom to use his inhaler. Although this was an improvement, there was still a need to develop coping strategies for him at school. The mother indicated that it was not convenient for her to take him to meetings with the psychologist on a weekly basis. The team thought it would be easier for Brandon to receive counseling if the service could be provided in school. It was arranged for the psychologist to confer with the guidance counselor about recommended strategies to incorporate into counseling. The team agreed to meet again within a month to continue reviewing Brandon's progress.

CONCLUSIONS

Chronic health problems can have pervasive effects on children's functioning in school, including academic achievement, peer relationships, and emotional functioning. The adjustment of children with health problems in school is strongly influenced by the nature of the school environment (e.g., type of instruction provided, quality of teacher-child relationship) as well as connections between the school and other critical systems in a child's life, such as school and home, school and health system. Cognitive-behavioral approaches have been developed to address the needs of children with a broad range of health disorders. The success of cognitive-behavioral strategies depends in large measure upon concurrent efforts to change systems and intersystemic connections so that they foster the implementation of these strategies. In this chapter, we presented a model that integrates a systems/ecological framework to intervention with an approach that focuses on cognitive-behavioral variables. This model, which we refer to as the Multisystemic Cognitive-Behavioral Intervention Model (MCBIM), focuses on creating a context for cognitive-behavioral interventions. This context allows individual techniques, such as a modeling, relaxation, self-monitoring, self-reinforcement, and contingency contracting, to be optimally effective. Although the focus of this chapter was on pain management and the promotion of adherence to medical regimens, MCBIM can be applied to other cross-cutting issues in pediatric health care, including school reentry, medication management, and the reduction of traumatic stress.

REFERENCES

Abidin, R. R. (1995). *Parenting Stress Index*. Lutz., FL: Psychological Assessment Resources, Inc.

Achenbach, T. M., & McConaughy, S. H. (1996). Relations between DSM-IV and empirically-based assessment. *School Psychology Review, 25*, 329–341.

Anderson, B. J., Auslander, W. F., Jung, J., Miller, J. P., & Santiago, J. V. (1990). Assessing family sharing of diabetes responsibility. *Journal of Pediatric Psychology, 15*, 477–492.

Annett, R. D. (2004). Asthma. In R. T. Brown (Eds.), *Handbook of pediatric psychology in school settings* (pp. 149–168). Mahwah, NJ: Lawrence Erlbaum Associates.

Apter, A. J., Reisine, S. T., Affleck, G., Barrows, E., & ZuWallack, R. L. (1998). Adherence with twice-daily dosing of inhaled steroids: Socioeconomic and health-belief differences. *American Journal of Respiratory and Critical Care Medicine, 157*, 1810–1817.

Bandura, A. (1977). Self-efficacy: Toward a unifying theory of behavioral change. *Psychological Review, 84*, 191–215

Baum, D., & Creer, T. L. (1986). Medication compliance in children with asthma. *Journal of Asthma, 23*, 49–59.

Bender, B., Milgrom, H., Rand, C., & Ackerson, L. (1998). Psychological factors associated with medication nonadherence in asthmatic children. *Journal of Asthma, 35*, 347–353.

Bender, B. G., Wamboldt, F. S., O'Connor, S. L., Rand, C., Szefler, S., & Milgrom, H. (2000). Measurement of children's asthma medication adherence by self-report, mother report, canister weight, and doser ct. *Annals of Allergy, Asthma, and Immunology, 85*, 416–421.

Bronfenbrenner, U. (1979). *The ecology of human development*. Cambridge, MA: Harvard University Press.

Brown, R. T. (2004). Introduction: Changes in the provision of health care to children and adolescents. In R. T. Brown (Ed.), *Handbook of pediatric psychology in school settings* (pp. 1–19). Mahwah, NJ: Lawrence Erlbaum.

Bursch, B., Schwankovsky, L., Gilbert, J., & Zeiger, R. (1999). Construction and validation of four childhood asthma self-management scales: Parent barriers, child and parent self-efficacy, and parent belief in treatment efficacy. *Journal of Asthma, 36*, 115–128.

Centers for Disease Control and Prevention. (1995). *Vital and Health Statistics, Current Estimates from the National Health Interview Survey, 1994* (DHHS Publication No. PHS 96–1521). Washington, DC: U.S. Government Printing Office.

Cicchetti, D., Toth, S. L., & Lynch, M. (1995). Bowlby's dream comes full circle: The application of attachment theory to risk and psychopathology. In T. H. Ollendick & R. J. Prinz (Eds.), *Advances in clinical child psychology* (Vol. 17; pp. 1–75). New York: Plenum Press.

Covington, E. C. (2000). The biological basis of pain. *International Review of Psychiatry, 12*, 128–147.

da Costa, I. G., Rapoff, M. A., Lemanek, K., & Goldstein, G. L. (1997). Improving adherence to medication regimens for children with asthma and its effect on clinical outcome. *Journal of Applied Behavior Analysis, 30*, 687–691.

Dahlquist, L. M., & Switkin, M. C. (2003). Chronic and recurrent pain. In M. Roberts (Ed.), *Handbook of pediatric psychology* (3rd ed., pp. 198–215). New York: Guilford.

DeVellis, R. F., DeVellis, B. M., Blanchard, L. W., Klotz, M. L., Luchok, K., & Voyce, C. (1993). Development and validation of Parent Health Locus of Control Scales. *Health Education Quarterly, 20*, 211–225.

Dey, A. N., Schiller, J. S., & Tai, D. A. (2004). Summary Health Statistics for U.S. Children: National Health Interview Survey, 2002, National Center for Health Statistics. *Vital Health Stat, 10* (221). Retrieved November 4, 2004, from http://www.cdc.gov/nchs/data/series/sr_10/sr10_221.pdf

DuPaul, G. J., & Carlson, J. S. (2005). Child psychopharmacology: How school psychologists can contribute to effective outcomes. *School Psychology Quarterly, 20,* 206–221.

Frazer, C. H., & Rappaport, L. A. (1999). Recurrent pains. In M. D., Levine, W. B., Carey, & A. C. Crocker, (Eds.), *Developmental-Behavioral Pediatrics.* 3rd Ed. Philadelphia: W.B. Saunders.

Gil, K. M., Anthony, K. K., Carson, J. W., Redding-Lallinger, R., Daeschner, C. W., & Ware, R. E. (2001). Daily coping practice predicts treatment effects in children with sickle cell disease. *Journal of Pediatric Psychology, 26,* 163–173.

Haynes, R. B. (1979). Introduction. In R. B. Haynes, D. W. Taylor, & D. L. Sackett (Eds.), *Compliance with health care* (pp. 1–7). Baltimore: Johns Hopkins University Press.

Jensen, M. P., Nielson, W. R., & Kerns, R. D. (2003). Toward the development of a motivational model of pain self-management. *The Journal of Pain, 4,* 477–492.

Kazak, A., Barakat, L., Meeske, K., Christakis, D., Meadows, A., Casey, R., Penati, B., & Stuber, M. (1997). Posttraumatic stress, family functioning, and social support in survivors of childhood leukemia and their mothers and fathers. *Journal of Consulting and Clinical Psychology, 65,* 120–129.

Kazak, A. E., Rourke, M. T., & Crump, T. A. (2003). Families and other systems in pediatric psychology. In M. Roberts (Ed.), *Handbook of pediatric psychology* (3rd ed., pp. 159–175). New York: Guilford.

Klinnert, M. D., McQuaid, E. L., & Gavin, L. A. (1997). Assessing the family asthma management system. *Journal of Asthma, 34,* 77–88.

Kolbe, L. L., Collins, J., & Cortese, P. (1997). Building the capacity of schools to improve the health of the nation. *American Psychologist, 52,* 256–265.

La Greca, A. M., & Bearman, K. J. (2003). Adherence to pediatric treatment regimens. In M. Roberts (Ed.), *Handbook of pediatric psychology* (3rd ed., pp. 119–140). New York: Guilford.

Lamanek, K. L., Kamps, J., & Chung, N. B. (2001). Empirically supported treatments in pediatric psychology: Regimen adherence. *Journal of Pediatric Psychology, 26,* 253–275.

McGrath, P. A. (1990). *Pain in children: Nature, assessment, and treatment.* New York: Guilford Press.

McQuaid, E. L., & Walders, N. (2003). Pediatric Asthma. In M. Roberts (Ed.), *Handbook of pediatric psychology* (3rd ed., pp. 269–285). New York: Guilford.

Merskey, H., & Bogduk, N. (Eds.). (1994). Classification of chronic pain, Second Edition, IASP Task Force on Taxonomy (pp. 209–213). Retrieved November 4, 2004, from http://www.iasp-pain.org/terms-p.html#Pain

Naar-King, S., Ellis, D. A., & Frey, M. A. (Eds.) (2004). *Assessing children's well-being: A handbook of measures.* Mahwah, NJ: Lawrence Erlbaum.

Nassau, J. H., & Drotar, D. (1997). Social competence among children with central nervous system-related chronic health conditions: A review. *Journal of Pediatric Psychology, 22,* 71–93.

National Asthma Education and Prevention Program (2004). Resolution on Asthma Management at School. Retrieved November 4, 2004, from http://www.nhlbi.nih.gov/health/public/lung/asthma/resolut.pdf

Nelson, J. R., Roberts, M. L., & Smith, D. J. (1998). *Conducting functional behavioral assessments: A practical guide.* Longmont, CO: Sopris West.

Palermo, T. M. (2000). Impact of recurrent and chronic pain on child and family daily functioning: A critical review of the literature. *Developmental and Behavioral Pediatrics, 21,* 58–69.

Pianta, R. C. (1999). *Enhancing relationships between children and teachers.* Washington, DC: American Psychological Association.

Pianta, R. C. (2001). *Student-Teacher Relationship Scale.* Lutz, FL: Psychological Assessment Resources, Inc.

Pope, A., & Ward, J. (1997). Factors associated with peer social competence in preadolescents with craniofacial anomalies. *Journal of Pediatric Psychology, 22,* 455–469.

Power, T. (in press). Collaborative practices for managing children's health needs. In L. Phelps (Ed.), *Chronic health-related disorders in children: Collaborative medical and psychoeducational interventions.* Washington, DC: American Psychological Association.

Power, T. J., DuPaul, G. J., Shapiro, E. S., & Kazak, A. E. (2003). *Promoting children's health: Integrating school, family, and community.* New York: Guilford Press.

Power, T. J., Shapiro, E. S., & DuPaul, G. J. (2003). Preparing psychologists to link systems of care in managing and preventing children's health problems. *Journal of Pediatric Psychology, 28,* 147–156.

Quittner, A. L., & Opipari, L. C. (1994). Differential treatment of siblings: Interviews and diary analyses comparing two family contexts. *Child Development, 65,* 800–814.

Roberts, M. (Ed.). (2003). *Handbook of Pediatric Psychology* (3rd ed.). New York: Guilford.

Robins, P. M., Smith, S. M., Glutting, J. J., & Bishop, C. (2005). A randomized controlled trial of a cognitive-behavioral family intervention for pediatric recurrent abdominal pain. *Journal of Pediatric Psychology, 30,* 397–408.

Rotter, J. B. (1990). Internal versus external control of reinforcement: A case history of a variable. *American Psychologist, 45,* 489–493.

Sanders, M. R., Rebgetz, M., Morrison, M., Bor, W., Gordon, A., Dadds, M., & Shepherd, R. W. (1989). Cognitive-behavioral treatment of recurrent nonspecific abdominal pain in children: An analysis of generalization, maintenance, and side effects. *Journal of Consulting and Clinical Psychology, 57,* 294–300.

Sanders, M. R., Shepherd, R. W., Cleghorn, G., & Woolford, H. (1994). The treatment of recurrent abdominal pain in children: A controlled comparison of cognitive-behavioral family intervention and standard pediatric care. *Journal of Consulting and Clinical Psychology, 62,* 306–314.

Sarafino, E. P. (1994). *Health Psychology: Biopsychosocial Interactions* (2nd ed.). New York: John Wiley & Sons, Inc.

Sheridan, S. M., Kratochwill, T. R., & Bergan, J. R. (1996). *Conjoint behavioral consultation: A procedural manual.* New York: Plenum.

Sherry, D. D. (2000). An overview of amplified musculoskeletal pain syndromes. *The Journal of Rheumatology, 27,* 44–48.

Spirito, A., DeLawyer, D. D., & Stark, L. J. (1991). Peer relations and social adjustment of chronically ill children and adolescents. *Clinical Psychology Review, 11,* 539–564.

Taylor, W. R., & Newacheck, P. W. (1992). The impact of childhood asthma on health. *Pediatrics, 90,* 657–662.

Troiano, R. P., & Flegal, K. M. (1998). Overweight children and adolescents: Description, epidemiology, and demographics. *Pediatrics, 101,* 497S–504S.

Varni, J., Thompson, K., & Hanson, V. (1987). The Vami-Thompson Pediatric Pain Questionnaire. I. Chronic musculoskeletal pain in juvenile rheumatoid arthritis. *Pain, 28,* 27–38.

Varni, J., Waldron, S., Gragg, R. A., Rapoff, M. A., Bernstein, B. H., Lindsley, C. B., & Newcomb, M. D. (1996). Development of the Waldron-Varni Pediatric Pain Coping Inventory. *Pain, 67,* 141–150.

Walker, L. A., Garber, J., & Greene, J. W. (1993). Psychosocial correlates of recurrent childhood pain: A comparison of pediatric patients with recurrent abdominal pain, organic illness, and psychiatric disorders. *Journal of Abnormal Psychology, 102,* 248–258.

Walker, L. A., & Greene, J. W. (1991). The functional disability inventory: Measuring a neglected dimension of child health status. *Journal of Pediatric Psychology, 16,* 39–58.

Walker, L. S., & Johnson, W. S. (2004). Recurrent abdominal pain and functional gastrointestinal disorders in the school setting. In R. T. Brown (Eds.), *Handbook of pediatric psychology in school settings* (pp. 299–312.). Mahwah, NJ: Lawrence Erlbaum Associates.

Wallston, K. A. (1992). Hocus-Pocus, the focus isn't strictly on locus: Rotter's social learning theory modified for health. *Cognitive Therapy and Research, 16,* 183–199.

Wamboldt, F. S., Wamboldt, M. Z., Gavin, L. A., Roesler, T. A., & Brugman, S. M. (1995). Parental criticism and treatment outcome in adolescents hospitalized for severe, chronic asthma. *Journal of Psychosomatic Research, 39,* 985–1005.

Wasserman, A. L., Whitington, P. F., & Rivara, F. P. (1988). Psychogenic basis for abdominal pain in children and adolescents. *Journal of the American Academy of Child and Adolescent Psychiatry, 27,* 179–184.

Winston, F., Kassam-Adams, N., & Vivarelli-O'Neill, C. (2002). Acute stress disorder symptoms in children and their parents after pediatric traffic injury. *Pediatrics, 109*(6), e90.

Part III

APPLICATION OF CBT INTERVENTIONS WITH SYSTEMS

19

Parent Consultation: A Cognitive-Behavioral Perspective

RAY W. CHRISTNER, JESSICA L. STEWART & LORI LENNON

In today's fast-paced, rapidly changing society, families face a variety of increasingly prevalent and complex problems such as divorce, abuse, terminal illness, financial strain, juvenile crime, teenage pregnancy, and substance abuse. The role of family, and specifically parents, in development is crucial, as children and adolescents tend to develop their values, beliefs, and behavior patterns within their family system. Moreover, parents are essential in ameliorating learning, behavior, and emotional problems experienced by youth. School professionals, now more than ever, are beginning to recognize that it is imperative to develop an awareness of the issues affecting the families of the students they serve. Viewing students' problems within the context of their family system allows for a better understanding of the needs of those students and how best to effectively provide the services necessary. Mullis and Edwards (2001) poignantly note that by increasing one's understanding of the family system, school professionals can more effectively assist and support parents through consultation, while consequently improving the likelihood that the family will support and adopt positive changes.

Educational research suggests that a positive relationship exists between parent involvement in children's education and improved student achievement, school attendance, study habits, reduction in discipline problems, and positive attitude toward school (Epstein, 1987; Henderson, 1987; Henderson & Berla, 1994). Christenson and Sheridan (2001) similarly demonstrate that congruence between home and school in relation to learning and development relates to better outcomes for children. Furthermore, Epstein (1991) proposes that most parents want to know how to help their children at home and how to stay involved in their education. Yet, although research supports parent involvement as a key component to improving the likelihood that interventions will be maximally effective, school professionals have not historically engaged this potentially valuable resource in effecting positive change for students (Sheridan, Kratochwill, & Bergan, 1996).

In order for schools to work productively with parents, it is necessary for school professionals to have extensive knowledge in providing parent consultation services. This knowledge base should include interventions that both aid in problem solving and further enhance the skills of parents—two aims that, together, increase the likelihood of continued success following the termination of the consultation process. Parent consultation from a cognitive-behavioral perspective provides the structure and empirically supported strategies that facilitate parent involvement and a close working relationship between parents and school professionals. Good consultation improves the likelihood that all involved will support attempts at positive change and promote the use of effective interventions for the benefit of students. This chapter will offer information about parent consultation in general, but then move toward describing a model of parent consultation that integrates the basics tenets of cognitive-behavior therapy (CBT) to enhance its effectiveness. For simplicity, we use the word *parent* throughout this chapter. However, it should be noted *parent* can be interchangeable with adult(s) who are serving as guardian to a student.

PARENT CONSULTATION, PARENT EDUCATION, AND FAMILY THERAPY

Parent consultation, parent education, and family therapy share unifying characteristics that are often interchangeably described within the literature. However, there are important delineations among the three that are worth distinguishing. Whereas parent consultation and family therapy often explore parenting influences, family dynamics, and home conditions as they relate to a child's learning and behavior at school, parent education focuses on teaching parents about child development, communication, behavior management, and other aspects of family life (Sheridan et al., 1996). Parent education, like parent consultation, is an indirect service, although it differs in that it primarily involves teaching parents a specific set of skills as outlined in a set curriculum, following a predetermined timetable, and typically depending on a group format of lectures and discussions to impart information (Sheridan et al., 1996; Brown, Pryzwansky, & Shulte, 2001). In addition, parent education is likely less focused on collaborative efforts to identify problems and solutions, and more focused on skill building based on information imparted by professionals. Traditionally, parent-training programs are based on one of three approaches: Humanistic (relationship building strategies), Adlerian (developing an understanding of their children's thought processes and motivation for behaviors), and Behavioral (shaping and reinforcement of desired behaviors; Sheridan et al., 1996).

Parent education is further differentiated from family therapy and parent consultation, in that the latter models both assume that the interpersonal relationship is essential to a successful outcome (Brown et al., 2001). Family therapy often explores specific problematic issues with members of the family, for the purpose of finding resolution to those issues as they negatively influence a child's learning and behavior at school. In contrast to parent consultation and parent education, family therapy is a direct service to the family unit, where the members participate simultaneously with the therapist to work out the problem. Additionally, family therapy tends to be a lengthier intervention and often addresses marital difficulties or pathological behaviors of parents or other family members that may be a significant source of the problem.

Parent consultation, similar to other areas of consultation, is an indirect intervention, primarily directed toward helping the parent (consultee) help the child (client). A chief objective of parent consultation is to improve the parents' ability to facilitate the development of their children, with a related objective to improve the education and psychological functioning of the child (Brown et al., 2001). By consequence of improved problem-solving abilities and enhanced communication, the entire family system is likely to further benefit from parent consultation. Parent consultation follows a process that is determined collaboratively with the consultant and the parent (Brown et al.).

LITERATURE REVIEW ON CURRENT MODELS OF CONSULTATION

Current consultative practices are based on a number of theoretical models of consultation that have been applied throughout several decades in the fields of psychology and education. Although there is a general understanding of consultation as a joint effort at problem solving involving indirect assistance to a third party, each model presents a distinct theoretical framework. The models further differ in conceptualization of the consultative relationship, nature of the problem, goals, methods of intervention, and criteria used to evaluate efficacy of the consultation. Six of the most common theories of consultation are reviewed.

Mental Health Consultation

Gerald Caplan's (1970) *The Theory and Practice of Mental Health Consultation* serves as the foundation of consultation as a service delivery model, and it is based on an intrapsychic and environmental model of behavioral change. Caplan's model was developed as a preventative approach to dealing with mental illness. The emphasis is on a collaborative, nonhierarchical relationship between the consultant and the consultee, whereby both assume responsibility for the outcomes formulated in consultation in reference to a current work problem. A goal of mental health consultation is to equip the consultee with preventative techniques to effectively deal with similar problems in the future.

Caplan (1970) categorized mental health consultation into four categories. In the first, client-centered consultation, the consultant aims to highlight the difficulties exhibited by the client and to communicate recommendations by which the consultee can intervene to resolve and manage the difficulties. Second, in consultee-centered consultation, the focus is on educating the consultee by helping to remedy shortcomings and remove intrapsychic barriers (e.g., consultee's lack of knowledge, skill, self-confidence, or professional objectivity) to the consultee's ability to work with the client. The third category, program-centered administrative consultation, is systems-centered and involves consultative suggestions to improve an existing program or development of a new program. As in the second category, the fourth, consultee-centered administrative consultation, focuses on recognizing and remedying the shortcomings of consultees (such as group difficulties, poor leadership, authority problems, communication blocks, etc.) that interfere with their tasks of program development and organization.

Meyers and colleagues have expanded and modified Caplan's model of mental health consultation to make it applicable to school settings (Meyers, 1981; Meyers & Kundert, 1988; Meyers, Parsons, & Martin, 1979). For example, Meyers et al. (1979) define three levels of service that are provided to the student by the consultant. Level I focuses on the child, whereby the consultant might work with a teacher to develop strategies for dealing with a specific student problem. Level II places an emphasis on the teacher, such that the focus might center on instructional strategies. Finally, the focus of Level III is on the system, perhaps exemplified through the development of trainings for the entire faculty to improve instructional techniques. Meyers and Kundert (1988) further outline the role of school-based mental health consultation in primary prevention and propose that prevention may be most effective when the focus is on supporting teachers and students by working to modify school routines or procedures.

Behavioral Consultation

Behavioral consultation is a problem-solving approach between the consultant and consultee, involving indirect services to a client, grounded in the empirical tradition of behaviorism. Theoretically, behavioral consultation is based on the notion that all behaviors are learned and that the establishment, maintenance, and change of behavior can be explained through a functional assessment of the interactions of the individual, his or her behavior, and the environment (Zins, Kratochwill, & Elliot, 1993). The primary goal of behavioral consultation is to produce change in client behavior (Kratochwill & Bergan, 1990).

There are four fundamental steps in the behavioral consultation process as defined by Bergan and Kratochwill (1990). The first is problem identification in which the consultant interviews the consultee in order to elicit an operational definition of the problem that the child is experiencing. The process of problem identification not only helps to clearly describe the problem but also can enhance the consultee's understanding of the problem and establish a point of reference for monitoring behavior change (Zins et al., 1993). The second step is problem analysis, whereby the consultant and consultee identify variables that might contribute to the problem, generate hypotheses in reference to the antecedents and consequences of the behavior, and develop a treatment plan to resolve the problem. The third step involves implementing the treatment and monitoring progress through ongoing data collection. The fourth step is to evaluate the program through a treatment evaluation interview in which the consultant and consultee determine if the problem solution was achieved or if program refinement or reconceptualization of the intervention is needed.

Conjoint Behavioral Consultation

An expansion of behavioral consultation, conjoint behavioral consultation, promotes a collaborative problem-solving relationship between parents and professionals to address the academic, social, or behavioral needs of the child (Sheridan, Kratochwill, & Bergan, 1996). The interconnections between the reciprocal interacting systems (of home, school, and support systems) are considered critically important to conjoint behavioral consultation. This model of consultation assumes an ecological-behavioral perspective, a cooperative interactive home-school relationship, and a shared implication in the problem and resolution. The four stages involved in conjoint behavioral consultation mirror those of behavioral consultation while expanding the process to include parents, teachers, and other significant individuals. Conjoint behavioral consultation relies on the pooling of information and sharing of resources to obtain a clear conceptualization of the problem and increase the range of solutions (Sheridan et al., 1996).

Problem-Solving Consultation

Problem-solving consultation, as it relates to school, aims to provide solutions to change a child's behavioral, academic, or social problem and to facilitate the consultee's independent productive thinking and development of skills to enable efficacy in future problem solving (Kratochwill, Elliott, & Callan-Stoiber, 2002). Problem-solving consultation as originally described by D'Zurilla and Goldfried (1971) holds that problem-solving outcomes are determined largely by two, partially independent processes: (1) problem orientation: the motivational part of the problem-solving process, and (2) problem-solving proper: the process involved in the application of problem-solving skills, which are necessary for effective problem-solving execution.

Variables involved in problem orientation, which contribute to positive or negative emotions and problem-solving approach tendencies, include: (a) perception of the problem (recognizing and labeling the problem), (b) problem attribution (a person's causal beliefs concerning the problem), (c) problem appraisal (a person's appraisal or evaluation of the significance of a problem for personal well-being), (d) perceived control (problem-solving self-efficacy and outcome expectancies), and (e) time/effort commitment (D'Zurilla & Nezu, 1999). The problem-solving steps involved are as follows: (1) *problem definition and formulation*, to gather information, clarify the nature of the problem, and set goals; (2) *generation of alternative solutions*, to make many solutions available in order to maximize the likelihood that the "best" solution is among those generated; (3) *decision making*, to select the "best" to implement; and (4) *solution implementation and verification*, where the solution outcome and effectiveness is assessed (D'Zurilla & Nezu, 1999). Methods employed through problem-solving consultation are direct didactic methods, Socratic questioning, coaching, modeling, rehearsal, performance feedback, positive reinforcement, and shaping.

Family Systems Consultation

An extension of behavioral consultation, family systems consultation, considers the family system as the client, as described by Bergan and Duley (1981). A family systems perspective is assumed in describing difficulties in family functioning that stem from the behavioral expressions of the "dysfunctional member," while recognizing that the behaviors of each member are interdependent so that changing the behaviors of one member will inevitably effect the others (Mullis & Edwards, 2001). More recently, Carlson, Hickman, and Horton's (1992) model of family therapy is grounded in the principles of brief psychotherapy and promotes solution-oriented family-school consultation. This model focuses on solution identification among the consultant, client, teachers, and family and includes several phases involving explaining the solution-oriented approach, joining, negotiating a solvable complaint, establishing a solution goal, agreeing on the smallest change, eliciting multiple solutions, clarifying individual responsibilities, follow-up, and evaluation. Similarly, stages of family consultation presented by Brown, Pryzwansky, and Schulte (2001) are consistent with behavioral consultation and include structuring and relationship building, problem identification, goal setting, explaining psychological principles, intervention strategy selection, and evaluation/follow-up.

RATIONALE FOR A CBT FRAMEWORK OF PARENT CONSULTATION

Common Flaws in Parent Consultation

Consultation research suggests that problem solving, interpersonal, and interviewing skills all help to maximize one's effectiveness as a consultant (Fine, 1990). However, even a facilitative collaborator, equipped with these necessary skills, can encounter difficulties in the consultative process. A common flaw in current parent consultation process is a tendency to focus on the problem or diagnosis rather than on the solution. Although problem identification is a fundamental initial step, it is important not to over-focus on the problem or diagnosis throughout the consultative process. Whereas a diagnosis often implies a long-term, unchangeable issue, parent consultation that emphasizes a solution-oriented approach and ongoing reconceptualization of the problem enhances a parent's problem-solving skills and perception of control in effecting positive change.

A second common error in the parent consultative process occurs when the consultant ignores the individual factors a parent brings to consultation, namely individual circumstances and personal frames of reference. Family-specific factors such as parental education, socioeconomic status, cultural background, dominant language, and minority status can have an effect on parental participation in the collaborative consultation process (Elizalde-Utnick, 2002). Furthermore, parent perception is a key factor when providing consultative services. In order for parents to perceive a sense of control over the problem situation, they must first assume personal responsibility for change. It is, therefore, important for the consultant to assess the parent's motivation and capability to effect change and then customize the consultative process to their level. A cognitive-behavioral framework facilitates this assessment and management of parent factors by suggesting that the consultant identify parent belief systems and continually remain cognizant of the "meaning" the parent attaches to his or her perceptions (expressed via schema, automatic thoughts, etc.).

A third flawed trend in parent consultation is the overreliance on the consultant's expertise and underreliance on the competencies of the parent. Although the parents may view the consultant as an expert in the area of cognitions and behavior, the parents' expertise relates to their familiarity with the situation and the student, as well as their thoughts, feelings, and behaviors related to the issue at hand. In order for parents to participate actively in the collaborative partnership and problem-solving process, and to assume shared ownership of the situation and resolution of it, it is critical for the consultant to acknowledge the parent's competencies and communicate this appreciation to the parent.

Finally, minimizing the importance of the collaborative relationship is another flaw commonly seen in consultative practices. Establishing rapport and initiating a working relationship with parents lays the groundwork for all future problem-solving efforts (Sheridan, 1993). Issues of trust, genuineness, and openness are regarded as important qualities for both consultant and consultees (Kratochwill et al., 2002). Similarly, as indicated by Horton and Brown (1990), a consultee's perceptions of the consultant and the consultation process is highly influenced by the consultant's interpersonal-and relationship-building skills.

Application of CBT Concepts to Consultation

Cognitive-behavioral consultative approaches are conceptually rooted in the principles of Bandura's (1977) social learning theory in examining the environmental determinants of behavior. Specifically, Bandura's concept of modeling has had a major influence on CBT with children and their parents (Lochman, Whidby, & FitzGerald, 2000). Bandura (1977) proposed that much of childhood behavior is learned through modeling, by which children observe how other people, such as parents and siblings, behave, note the consequences, and begin to imitate the behavior they have observed. Certain characteristics of models, such as how highly they are esteemed and the consequences that result from their performed behaviors, are influential factors in the model's effectiveness (Bandura, 1977). Additionally, Bandura's concept of reciprocal determinism describes behavior as an evolving, dynamic phenomenon, the components of which are reciprocally determined by each other based on the interaction between a person's environment, personal dispositional characteristics, and situational behavior (Friedberg & McClure, 2002). Conceptually, as based on the reciprocal determinism construct, CBT principles relate psychological difficulties to five mutually influential interrelated elements: an individual's physiology, emotional functioning, behavior, cognition, and interpersonal/environmental context (Beck, 1995).

A cognitive-behavioral framework recognizes that cognitions, behaviors, emotions, and physiological symptoms occur in an interpersonal/environmental context (Beck, 1995). Thus, when consulting with parents, it is essential for the consultant to consider this context as well as relevant parent factors. Considering context in conceptualizing the situation affords the consultant the ability to intervene directly with parents, helping them understand how their perception of events influences their emotions and behavior. Using CBT techniques within the context of the consultative process, the consultant and parent can collaboratively explore how the parent's thoughts, behaviors, feelings, and physiological reactions influence the problematic situations.

In conducting consultation with parents, the consultant collaboratively works with the parents to explore their schemas, automatic thoughts, and cognitive distortions as they relate to the problematic situation. Schemas refer to the core beliefs (absolute truths) that are developed in childhood about oneself, other people, and the world (Beck, 1995). For example, a parent's personal schema might be, "I'm incompetent." Although typically unrealized on a surface level, core beliefs can highly influence a parent's perception of a problematic situation, which in turn will impact how he or she thinks, feels, and behaves in that situation. Within a problematic situation, a parent's schema is expressed by situation-specific, brief, rapid, evaluative, automatic thoughts (Beck, 1995). A primary focus of parent consultation is to investigate automatic thoughts (e.g., "I will never be able to get my child to complete his homework.") and how these thoughts, in turn, influence emotions and behavior (e.g., feeling sad and angry, then starting to cry and yell at the child).

People tend to make consistent errors in their thinking (Beck, 1995), thus, in parent consultation, a parent's pattern of cognitive distortions, or systematic errors in his or her reasoning, can be detected through exploration of his or her automatic thoughts. As outlined by Beck (1995), cognitive distortions, or typical mistakes in thinking, take on various forms, two examples of which include *All or nothing thinking*, where a parent views a situation in only two categories, such as "If I'm not a total success as a parent, I'm a failure," and *Catastrophizing*, where a parent predicts the future negatively without considering more likely outcomes, such as "If I can't get Chris to do his homework, he will never go to college." In consulting with parents, the consultant will help teach the parent to recognize, evaluate, and modify his or her dysfunctional thinking. See Table 19.1 for selected examples of cognitive distortions seen in parent consultation.

Parent consultation, as viewed within a CBT framework, is a structured, short-term form of consultation directed toward solving parent-child problems and modifying dysfunctional thinking and behavior. Within a structured format, the consultant works collaboratively with the parent to form a conceptualization of the problematic situation and explore a variety of ways to produce change in the parent's thinking and belief system in order to bring about enduring change in emotion and behavior. The application of the CBT framework to the provision of consultative services is outlined below in a cognitive-behavior-based model of consultation (Christner & Stewart-Allen, 2004), that is applicable to a variety of settings and populations, but is outlined here as it can be applied to parent consultation within a school setting.

COGNITIVE-BEHAVIORAL MODEL OF CONSULTATION

Christner and Stewart-Allen (2004) incorporated the basic tenets and principles of cognitive-behavioral theory and practice into a brief, structured, effective delivery of knowledge and skills through consultation. Although this cognitive-behavioral model shares some components in common with other consultation theories, it is unique in that it offers important concepts and techniques grounded in CBT theory. Consultation

Table 19.1 Common Cognitive Distortions Encountered in Parent Consultation

Common Cognitive Distortions Encountered in Parent Consultation
1. Dichotomous thinking—The parent views situation in only two categories rather than on a continuum. The world is either black or white with no shades of gray. For example, "My child is either a good student or a failure."
2. Overgeneralization—The parent sees a current event as being characteristic of life in general, instead of one situation among many. For example, "Because Johnny failed his science test, he will never be able to graduate or make it in college."
3. Mind reading—The parent believes he or she knows what others are thinking about him or her without any evidence. For example, "I just know that Mr. P. thinks I am a good parent."
4. Emotional reasoning—The parent assumes that his or her feelings or emotional reactions reflect the true situation. For example, "I feel inadequate at those school meetings, so others must think I am inadequate as well."
5. Disqualifying the positive—The parent discounts positive experiences that conflict with his or her negative views. For example, "The school staff was only nice to me in the last meeting because their supervisor was there and because they wanted me to put my child in special education."
6. Catastrophizing—The parent predicts that future situations will be negative and treats them as intolerable catastrophes. For example, "I better not attend that meeting because I might look stupid in front of the team members, and that would be awful."
7. Personalization—The parent assumes that he or she is the cause of negative circumstances. For example, "My child's teacher is expecting so much from my child, so I must not have done a good job teaching him to behave and follow rules."
8. Should statements—The parent uses *should* or *must* to describe how his or her child or others are to behave or act. For example, "My child is gifted. She must always get As and she shouldn't make mistakes."
9. Comparing—The parent compares his or her child's performance to others. Oftentimes, the comparison is made to higher performing or older students. For example, "Compared to my older children, Sarah's work looks like a kindergartener did it."
10. Labeling—The parent attaches a global label to describe him- or herself, his or her child, or others, rather than looking at behaviors and actions. For example, "Alex is a bad student" rather than "Alex really did poorly on that test."

based on a systematic, theoretically driven model allows for appropriate conceptualization of information, anticipation of obstacles, and determination of a structured intervention approach; whereas an unsystematic consultation lacks direction and attempts to problem-solve haphazardly (Brack & Brack, 1996). A well-developed theoretical model allows for the definition of process and content, while also guiding the consultant in efficiently facilitating change through these elements (Brack & Brack). In addition, a cognitive-behavioral model of consultation avoids many of the common errors in delivery of consultation services described above. Although we present this model here as a stand-alone approach to consultation, practitioners can use its principles and strategies to enhance the aforementioned consultation models as well. Christner and Stewart-Allen's model involves four multistep phases aimed to guide professionals through the consultation process—from developing an effective working relationship and educating parents about the process of consultation to generating, implementing, and evaluating solutions and their effectiveness, including many of the components of CBT outlined earlier. Although this model is presented in a linear fashion, it is important to note that the phases can be viewed as multidirectional in that consultants may need to move back and forth between the phases and steps, particularly when involved in cases that are more challenging. It is necessary, however, for consultants practicing this model to progress through each phase before the next, so as to effectively build and maintain the working relationship and ensure a thorough understanding of the issues that may be affecting the parents and child. Figure 19.1 offers a summary of phases and stages and highlights the interaction between them.

Phase One: Initiation

As in the case of most professional service deliveries, change is most successful when a positive working relationship exists. In the case of effective parent consultation, and essential to the proposed model, the most important first (and ongoing) consideration is the collaborative relationship, or working alliance, between the consultant and the consultee(s). When consulting with parents in the school setting, this is especially important as the issues that require intervention are intimate in nature, relating to their children and their family. The relationship the consultant develops must be one of trust, compassion, and equality, as, although the consultant may be the expert on behavioral, social, and emotional factors at work, the parents are the experts on their children. This collaborative relationship must be monitored throughout the consultation process for progression and potential threats to its stability.

In addition to facilitating the ongoing collaborative alliance with parents, the cognitive-behavioral consultant will also utilize agenda setting to maintain focus during consultation times from the outset and provide parents with an understanding of the steps ahead. Agenda setting sets the stage for what will happen in the consultation session and determine how the time will be allocated. Setting the agenda early in the session allows for the consultation time to be used efficiently. Furthermore, from our experiences, having an agenda of "what will happen" eliminates the "unknown process" for the parents, which ultimately lessens their anxiety and defensiveness and increases their sense of involvement in the process. The agenda set in consultation is not much different from that seen in traditional cognitive-behavior therapy. We suggest that the following elements be included when consulting with parents: review how things are going at the present time, obtain an update since the referral, discuss specific problems to work on, offer some education about the

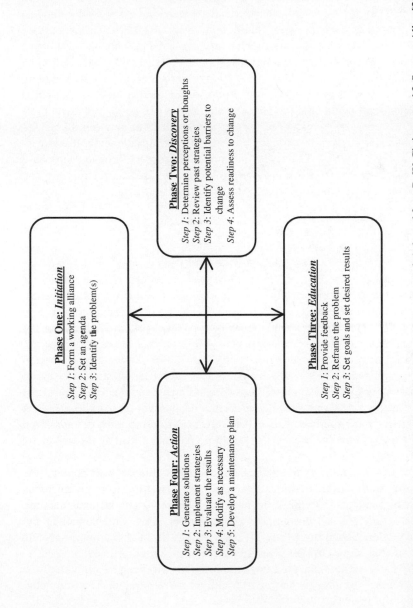

Figure 19.1 Cognitive-behavioral model of consultation: a four-phase approach (adapted from R. W. Christner and J. Stewart-Allen [2004])

problem, collaboratively consider strategies to help the situation, elicit feedback, and provide "between-session work."

The final stage in the initiation phase is the identification of problem(s) to be addressed. Each of these should be reviewed to ensure the consultant's understanding is accurate and that the problems are specifically defined. As noted by Murphy and Christner (Chapter 3 of this book), it is important to have a comprehensive problem list that looks at issues across domains. This will allow the consultant to work with the parents to help identify "themes" within the current difficulties experienced by the child.

Phase Two: Discovery

Following the initiation of a positive, collaborative working alliance and specific identification of the problems to be addressed, additional information must be obtained related to the factors that have created and maintained those problems. Following CBT theory, this consultation model relies on the identification of parents' perceptions of problems, contributory factors, their roles in relation to the problems, and barriers to change. The CBT model assumes a connection between a given situation, an individual's belief system (through which he or she interprets given situations), the individual's thoughts about the event, the resulting emotions, and the accompanying behaviors. In parent consultation, this connection is a key factor, as the parents' perceptions can have a notable impact on their acceptance of interventions and the overall outcome of the consultation. For instance, consider the example of a mother whose child was referred for having behavioral difficulties at home and in school. The mother held the belief, "If you are too strict with your kids they will not love you." Because of this belief, she did not set limits at home and did not reinforce behavior plans set forth at school. The mother and child underwent many interventions; however, all were unsuccessful because they did not consider the importance of the mother's thoughts in the maintenance of the child's behaviors. Thus, it is essential for the consultant to explore the parents' thoughts and how these thoughts influence interventions, as well as the overall success of the consultation.

It is also important for consultants to review what strategies the parents have attempted to resolve the problem in the past. When consultants suggest strategies that have been attempted and failed in the past, there will be a greater likelihood that they will fail again. In turn, parents may perceive the consultant as less credible, as he or she "had the same ideas as everyone else." For example, if you recommend an intervention such as *1–2–3 Magic* (Phelan, 2003) that has been attempted by the parents in the past and perceived as failing, even though the parents may have not implemented it correctly, they will likely be more resistant to attempting it again unless the consultant can provide a rationale for reattempting the strategy.

In addition to past interventions tried, the consultant must further explore other factors that may impede change and adherence, essentially asking, "What are the potential roadblocks that would inhibit follow-through with strategies developed during the consultation process?" Meichenbaum and Turke (1987) noted that anticipating potential problems could help increase treatment adherence. These roadblocks may be logistical factors such as time or resources, or those that are more personal such as procrastination or lack of follow-through. Although a number of these factors may be attributed to the parents, impediments to change could also involve other areas such as child-specific, school-specific, or teacher-specific barriers. Not only is it important to identify potential barriers, but it is essential for the consultant to directly discuss them with the parents and what could be done to overcome these factors as they arise.

The final area reviewed in the discovery phase is the identification of parents' motivation for change and readiness to engage in a potentially difficult, complex process to implement that change and resolve the presenting problem. As the consultation process involves a collaborative effort between at least two people, it is important that all members of the working alliance be motivated to progress to the point of successful change together. Otherwise, the consultant's efforts to facilitate the process of change will be met with resistance and frustration and, ultimately, a lack of success. An awareness of the parents' motivation and readiness to participate actively and follow-through with agreed upon interventions affords the consultant the ability to meet the parents where they are and, if necessary, assist in moving them through the stages of change to the point of effective service delivery and outcome. The concept of readiness to change is often cited in the substance abuse and health care literature (Prochaska et al., 1994), yet there is no known research on its use within a school setting or in parent consultation. Freeman and Dolan (2001) provided a reconceptualization of the original stages of change (Prochaska, DiClemente, & Norcross, 1992), in which they identified 10 stages, including (1) noncontemplation, (2) anticontemplation, (3) precontemplation, (4) contemplation, (5) action planning, (6) action, (7) lapse activation, (8) relapse, (9) redirection, and (10) maintenance. For a thorough review of the revised stages of change, see Freeman and Dolan (2001).

Phase Three: Education

Once information regarding all aspects of the identified problem has been obtained, the consultant must formulate an accurate conceptualization of the problem. This should include the precipitating and facilitating factors, consequences of the problem, the people involved and their roles in perpetuating or minimizing the problem, obstacles to resolving the problem, consequence of resolution (both positive and negative), and available resources and limitations. This "case conceptualization" must then be shared with the parent, simplifying the problem and restating it to include details and overall impressions. It is at this point that the individual problems become less important and the "underlying issues" become the focus of intervention. In providing feedback to parents, it is at times necessary for the consultant to reframe the issues in a manner that promotes change and minimizes blame. For instance, in consulting with a parent regarding behavior problems at home, the consultant formulates the conceptualization that the child's behaviors are the result of a need for attention. Instead of framing the problem to the parents as, "You need to pay more attention to Chuck," the consultant can use more productive wording such as, "It seems that Chuck wants to have a good relationship with you, and his behaviors are his way of interacting with you. Let's begin thinking of ways to change the interactions to something more positive for both of you."

Once feedback has been given and the consultant and parent share an understanding of the problem, components of the problem, and an impression of a desired resolution, they collaboratively set goals that are more specific. This step in the process requires more than a listing of goals. Collaboratively, the consultant and parent must determine the desired outcomes and identify goals to procure that end. In order to identify what specific interventions to pursue and be able to determine when the desired goals have been met, both the parent and consultant must have an understanding of how the situation will be different after successful intervention.

Phase Four: Action

The final phase involves maintaining the collaborative relationship while putting the conceptualization into effect to generate potential solutions, implement strategies to reach desired goals, evaluate the effectiveness of the derived plan, and develop a plan to maintain the benefits and positive results obtained. In generating solutions to the problem, the consultant relies on intervention strategies within CBT to correct skill deficits that may facilitate the problem (such as problem-solving skills, communication or coping skills, etc.), teach and implement self-monitoring strategies, address misperceptions, and correct distorted thinking and detrimental behaviors. It is not within the scope of this chapter to provide a complete overview of cognitive and behavioral interventions, and, thus, readers are encourage to consult other CBT texts for a review of specific strategies (see Freeman, Pretzer, Fleming, & Simon, 2004; McMullin, 2000). Once solutions or strategies are collaboratively identified and agreed upon as realistic and feasible, they are implemented while continuing to monitor cognitions and consequent negative behaviors and emotions. Behavioral strategies, such as role-playing and practice, self-talk, contingency contracts, and behavioral experiments, are beneficial to help parents practice certain strategies and skills before they attempt interventions independently. This assists in making the parents more comfortable while ensuring they understand what they are to do.

An essential step within the action phase relates to what happens after the identification and implementation of solutions. Consistent with other programs within educational settings, it is important to document and assess progress. Through progress monitoring, the consultant and parents can determine if the designated goals were met, while understanding that if the desired results were not obtained the consultant and parents must return to an early phase in the consultation process, make adjustments as necessary, and again regenerate solutions and implement them. Once successful strategies are in place, the final step of the cognitive-behavioral consultation process is the development of a maintenance plan that includes anticipating regression and future obstacles to success.

IMPLICATION TO SCHOOL SETTINGS

As consultation is provided within the school setting to teachers, parents, administrators, and students, cognitive-behavioral consultation can be used to improve single student issues, to change systemic issues, and to enhance teacher effectiveness. In terms of specific use when consulting with parents, this model may be used to improve parents' skill levels and to help parents address the specific needs of their children. Despite a variety of potential applications, the provision of consultation services requires an appropriate degree of direction, guidance, and intervention that depends on the presenting problems, setting, and needs of the identified client. Therefore, it is necessary to differentiate levels and degrees of consultation including (1) *single case level*—a consultation occurring one or more times regarding a specific case, (2) *consultee level*—an ongoing consultation directed to assist consultees in promoting change within themselves or their provision of services, and (3) *systemic level*—an ongoing consultation directed toward organizational change. Within the school setting and in consultation with parents, a single case level consultation would be, for example, one in which a professional provides assessment and services to parents to address a specific concern for an individual child. The consultee level of service is appropriate when parents request the services of the service provider (i.e., school psychologist, counselor, social worker) for an ongoing period of time to identify areas in which they may need to develop skills or competencies to directly implement or facilitate change to benefit their child. Finally, the systemic level consultation relates to the services provided directly to the family regarding its functioning and ways to improve the overall system for desired change.

CASE STUDY

Eric is a 10-year-old Caucasian boy who was experiencing a number of academic and behavioral difficulties at school. His grades were marginal, ranging from Bs to Ds. His behaviors were disruptive, as he tended to call out in class, play with items in his desk, and on occasion leave the room. Eric was referred to the Child Study Team (CST) to assist in developing interventions to help him become successful at school. The CST invited Eric's parents, Mr. and Mrs. Jones, to meetings; however, despite the invitation and confirmation of coming, Mr. and Mrs. Jones never attended. Eric began to show progress at school through the implementation of a positive behavior support plan and tutoring services. However, there continued to be concern with his lack of homework completion and the regression in his behaviors following weekend or holiday breaks. It was imperative to involve Eric's parents in the process, though they appeared "resistant" to attending school meetings.

Following the second meeting, which Mr. and Mrs. Jones did not attend, the school psychologist volunteered to make contact with Mr. and Mrs. Jones to review the information discussed during the CST meeting. This telephone call served as the beginning of the *Initiation* phase of the consultative process. The school psychologist provided information about the meeting, but also began forming a working, collaborative relationship with Mr. and Mrs. Jones. He did not question their absence from past meetings nor did he actually address the issues of concern.

Simply, the school psychologist indicated what was discussed at the meeting and reinforced the fact that progress was being seen. Toward the end of this conversation, the school psychologist asked if it would be possible to meet face-to-face with Mr. and Mrs. Jones and questioned them regarding a good time and place to meet. Mr. and Mrs. Jones seemed hesitant to come to the school, so they agreed to meet at Mr. and Mrs. Jones's home.

At the first meeting, Mr. and Mrs. Jones seemed very apprehensive, though they expressed their appreciation for the school psychologist's flexibility in meeting at their home. To enhance the working relationship with the parents, the school psychologist started by reiterating Eric's progress and asking the parents for their assistance in making Eric even more successful. Mr. and Mrs. Jones expressed that they were very concerned about Eric, but did not know "how to help." The school psychologist took this opportunity to set the agenda, which is illustrated in the following dialogue:

School Psychologist (SP): "Well, the purpose of this meeting is to talk about ways that we [the school and parents] can work together to help Eric. I would also be willing to answer any questions you may have to help with what you are doing with Eric. Since we only have about an hour, let's plan out what we are going to discuss this afternoon. I would like to start by getting an update from you on how you see things going with Eric and concerns you may have. We can then discuss the things you have tried before and determine what has worked and what has not. Then together we can develop some goals for working with Eric and figure out some strategies that may help him. We'll end by deciding how we can keep track of Eric's progress to be sure what we are doing is working. Are there any things you want add to the plan or be sure we talk about today?"

Parent (P): I would like to talk with you about getting Eric to listen to us. We want him to do well, but he doesn't listen. We tell him to do his homework. He just doesn't do it.

SP: Okay. So, we will be sure that we talk about homework and ways to get Eric to follow-through. Anything else?

P: [tentatively] Is it okay to talk with you about the school?

SP: What specifically would you like to talk about?

P: I am afraid the school thinks we don't care about what happens or that we are not good parents. We do try to help Eric, but nothing works for us at home.

SP: Let's be sure that we set some time aside to talk about this concern then.

After setting the agenda, the consultation process moved to problem identification. The school psychologist again talked about Eric's progress, while expressing continued concern with Eric not finishing homework and with him having problems each Monday. He then followed by stating, "Those are the main concerns at school, are there any other issues you can think of?" Mr. and Mrs. Jones indicated their agreement, but further disclosed that they believe that Eric's problems on Monday are the result of him staying up late (until 2:00 to 3:00 A.M.) on Friday and Saturday night. "He stays up late, and then gets out of sorts when he is tired." Mr. Jones was quiet for the most part, but then expressed his frustration and concern that he is doing something wrong. He also restated that he fears the schools is "blaming" him and Mrs. Jones. The school psychologist used this time to move into the *Discovery* phase by assessing perceptions and thoughts.

SP: I know that over the last few years Eric has had some difficulties and the school has called you a number of times. When you get these calls, what goes through your head?

P: Here we go again!

SP: Here we go again. When you say that to yourself, what does it mean?

P: Hummm. I guess it means Eric's still not straightening out, and that we must not be doing something right.

SP: What about the phone call makes you think that?

P: I was never good with school stuff. Neither was Nancy [Mrs. Jones]. We just don't know what we're doing when it comes to helping him with school.

SP: So what does that mean about you?

P: It means we're bad parents, or at least we think his teachers think that.

Using this knowledge, the school psychologist was able to discuss how important it is that Mr. and Mrs. Jones are a part of the school process, and how the school could work with them to help Eric. In reviewing past strategies, Mr. and Mrs. Jones reported only using a few approaches, primarily grounding him to his room or removing his video games, both of which were ineffective. They reported the primary "barriers" for them include their own lack of follow-through, their anxiety about the school thinking they are "bad parents," and having time to make the meetings at school. Mr. and Mrs. Jones were in the *Action Planning* stage of readiness, as they were willing to plan for change in their behavior to help their son.

When providing feedback to Mr. and Mrs. Jones, it was important to continue focusing on the positive and to help them feel "hopeful" for a positive outcome, and not to assign blame or highlight the problematic behaviors of the parents directly. Feedback to the parents involved facilitating their understanding of Eric's role in playing his parents against the school, as he noticed the two "sides" were not working together. Furthermore, the school psychologist emphasized that, based on Eric's progress at school, he seems to respond well to, and need, consistent structure. Collaboratively, the school psychologist worked with Mr. and Mrs. Jones on setting goals to assist Eric. The three goals identified included (1) Eric will complete homework assignments 85% of the time each week; (2) Eric will be in bed by 10:00 P.M. each night, even on weekends; (3) Mr. and Mrs. Jones will keep consistent contact with the school team and attend school meetings. It was clear that Mr. and Mrs. Jones desired the same results as the school psychologist and Eric's teachers—to see a more consistent and adequate effort from Eric that would ensure his academic success and greater compliance in following the rules his parents set at home.

To address the homework and bedtime issues, the school psychologist assisted Mr. and Mrs. Jones in developing a positive behavior support plan using a daily reinforcement system (e.g., Eric can play his video game for 30 minutes each night following the completion of his homework), a weekly reinforcement (e.g., if Eric turns in 85% or more of his homework, he will be allowed to stay up 30 minutes later on Friday and Saturday nights), and long-term reinforcement (e.g., every 4 weeks that Eric meets his goal, he will be able to select, from a list of options, a weekend activity to do with his parents). Additionally, consultation was provided to Mr. and Mrs. Jones about setting up a study environment and homework schedule. To address the collaboration between home and school, Mr. and Mrs. Jones agreed to attend school meetings; however, they noted concern that they will "back out" if they begin feeling "intimidated." To lessen their apprehension, the school psychologist agreed to meet with Mr. and Mrs. Jones and Eric's teacher at school, separate from the CST meeting, until Mr. and Mrs. Jones began feeling more comfortable with attending the CST meetings. Also, the school psychologist arranged to contact the parents by phone prior to the meetings to discuss the meeting agenda and help them feel more "in the loop."

The strategies were implemented and monitored over 6 weeks. The school psychologist contacted Mr. and Mrs. Jones each week by telephone to discuss any problems they were having with implementing the behavior plan on their end. There were no concerns over the first 2 weeks, though the parents reported having a hard time getting Eric to bed on the weekends at around week 3. Mr. and Mrs. Jones came into the school that week to meet with the school psychologist to discuss options of adding a consequence when Eric did not follow through with the weekend routine. During this meeting, it was necessary to return to the *Discovery* phase, as Mrs. Jones reported that she did not like "disciplining Eric for staying up late" because she "hated it" when her mother did the same thing to her. It was necessary to discuss and process Mrs. Jones's thoughts and beliefs around this issue. If not, it was likely that her beliefs would serve as a "roadblock" for future progress. After the meeting, Mrs. Jones agreed to attempt the suggestions generated for the next four weeks and to evaluate if they made a difference.

Eric's homework completion was documented at school over the 6 weeks, and Mr. and Mrs. Jones collected information on the homework routine and bedtime issues. Before the next CST meeting, all information was given to the school psychologist and graphs were made to illustrate the progress obtained. The school psychologist contacted Mr. and Mrs. Jones the day before the meeting to discuss the agenda. They reported that they were comfortable attending the meeting and deferring the option to meet with the school psychologist and teacher separately. The day of the meeting, the school psychologist again called Mr. and Mrs. Jones to reinforce the job they did and to remind them of the meeting. Mr. and Mrs. Jones attended the meeting, although they were noticeably nervous. Progress was noted in all areas, and a maintenance plan was discussed. Eric's teacher agreed to continue e-mailing progress notes home at the end of the week to monitor his homework completion. The school psychologist would remain a contact person for the parents, and they would communicate on a biweekly basis, with plans on moving to monthly communications after 1 month.

CONCLUSION

Given the importance and influence of parents on the development and functioning of children, any attempts to address the needs of those children must involve the parents. Whether a one-time, single-case situation or an ongoing consultative relationship, consultants in the school setting working specifically with parents must consider what those parents bring to the situation. This includes potential negative contributing factors and resistance, to their individual competencies as well as expert knowledge of their child. In addition, it is imperative that consultants begin understanding and using parents' perceptions of the problem, their child, themselves, and the school system, as well as their emotional and behavioral reactions to those perceptions, as a means to facilitate effective interventions. Working closely with parents will allow a consultant to identify these perceptions, emotions, and behaviors for the sake of addressing them in the provision of services.

This emphasis on the consultation process as one of a collaborative effort stems from the emphasis placed on the working relationship, or alliance, found in cognitive-behavior therapy (CBT). The cognitive-behavioral consultation model presented here offers consultants a framework with which to deliver services rooted in empirically supported theory, intervention, and outcome, from the initiation of the relationship to the maintenance of positive change. Its aim is to provide a rationale and structure to the process that affords consultants the ability to identify the dysfunctional or distorted beliefs of parents that may contribute to the problems experienced by students. Furthermore, the consultant can use this information to develop a conceptualization of those factors in order to facilitate the collaborative identification and implementation of effective interventions to achieve a desired outcome for the ultimate benefit of improved student functioning.

REFERENCES

Bandura, A. (1977). *Social learning theory.* Englewood Cliffs, NJ: Prentice Hall.

Beck, J. S. (1995). *Cognitive therapy: Basics and beyond.* New York: Guilford Press.

Bergan, J. R., & Duley, S. (1981). Behavioral consultation with families. In R. W. Henderson (Ed.), *Parent-child interactions: Theory, research, and prospects* (pp. 265–291). New York: Academic Press.

Bergan, J. R., & Kratochwill, T. R. (1990). *Behavioral consultation and therapy.* New York: Plenum Press.

Brack, C. J., & Brack, G. (1996) Mental health consultation: In defense of merging theory and practice. *Journal of Mental Health Counseling, 18,* 347–358.

Brown, D., Pryzwansky, W. B., & Schulte, A. C. (2001). *Psychological consultation: Introduction to theory and practice* (5th ed.). Boston: Allyn & Bacon.

Caplan, G. (1970). *The theory and practice of mental health consultation.* New York: Basic Books.

Carlson, C. I., Hickman, J., & Horton, C. B. (1992). From blame to solutions: Solution-oriented family-school consultation. In S. L. Christenson & J. C. Conoley (Eds.), *Home-school collaboration: Enhancing children's academic and social competence* (pp. 193–213). Silver Spring, MD: National Association of School Psychologists.

Christenson, S. L., & Sheridan, S. M. (2001). *Schools and families: Creating essential connections for learning.* New York: Guilford Press.

Christner, R. W., & Stewart-Allen, J. (2004, October). *Parent consultation: Applying cognitive-behavioral skills.* Workshop presented at the 2004 Pennsylvania Psychological Association Ethics and Continuing Education Conference, Exton, PA.

D'Zurilla, T. J., & Goldfried, M. R. (1971). Problem solving and behavioral modification. *Journal of Abnormal Psychology, 78,* 107–126.

D'Zurilla, T. J., & Nezu, A. M. (1999). *Problem-solving therapy: A social competence approach to clinical intervention.* New York: Springer.

Elizalde-Utnick, G. (2002). Best practices in building partnerships with families. In A. T. Thomas & J. Grimes (Eds.), *Best practices in school psychology-IV* (pp. 413–429). Washington, DC: National Association of School Psychologists.

Epstein, J. (1991). Effects on student achievement of teachers' practices of parent involvement. In S. Silver (Ed.), *Advances in reading/language research: Vol. 5. Literacy through family, community, and school interaction* (pp. 261–276). Greenwich, CT: JAI.

Epstein, J. L. (1987). What principals should know about parent involvement. *Principal, 6–9.*

Fine, M. J. (1990). Facilitation home-school relationships: A family-oriented approach to collaborative consultation. *Journal of educational and psychological consultation, 1,* 169–187.

Freeman, A., & Dolan, M. (2001). Revisiting Prochaska and DiClemente's stages of change theory: An expansion and specification to aid in treatment planning and outcome evaluation. *Cognitive and Behavioral Practice, 8,* 224–234.

Freeman, A., Pretzer, J., Fleming, B., & Simon, K. M. (2004). *Clinical applications of cognitive therapy* (2nd ed.). New York: Kluwer Academic/Plenum Publishing.

Friedberg, R. D., & McClure, J. M. (2002). *Clinical practice of cognitive therapy with children and adolescents: The nuts and bolts.* New York: Guildford Press.

Henderson, A. T. (1987). *The evidence continues to grow: Parent involvement improves student achievement.* Columbia, MD: National Committee for Citizens in Education.

Henderson, A., & Berla, N. (Eds.). (1994). *A new generation of evidence: The family is critical to student achievement.* Washington, DC, National Committee for Citizens in Education.

Horton, E., & Brown, D. (1990). The importance of interpersonal skills in consultee-centered consultation: A review. *Journal of counseling and development, 68,* 423–426.

Kratochwill, T. R., & Bergan, J. R. (1990). *Behavioral consultation in applied settings: An individual guide.* New York: Plenum Press.

Kratochwill, T. R., Elliott, S. N., & Callan-Stoiber, K. (2002). Best practices in school-based problem-solving consultation. In A. T. Thomas & J. Grimes (Eds.), *Best practices in school psychology-IV* (pp. 583–608). Washington, DC: National Association of School Psychologists.

Lochman, J. E., Whidby, J. M., & FitzGerald, D. P. (2000). Cognitive-behavioral assessment and treatment with aggressive children. In P. C. Kendall (Ed.), *Child & adolescent therapy: Cognitive-behavioral procedures* (p. 31–87). New York: Guilford Press.

McMullin, R. E. (2000). *The new handbook of cognitive therapy techniques.* New York: W. W. Norton & Company.

Meichenbaum, D., & Turk, D. C. (1987). *Facilitating treatment adherence: A practitioner's guidebook.* New York: Plenum Press.

Meyers, J. (1981). Mental health consultation. In J. C. Conoley (ed.), *Consultation in school* (pp. 35–58). New York: Academy Press.

Meyers, J., & Kundert, D. (1988). Implementing process assessment. In J. L. Graden, J. E. Zins, & M. J. Curtis (Eds.), *Alternative educational delivery systems: Enhancing instructional options for all students.* Washington, DC: National Association of School Psychologists.

Meyers, J., Parsons, R. D., & Martin, R. (1979). *Mental health consultation in the schools.* San Francisco: Jossey-Bass.

Mullis, F., & Edwards, D. (2001). Consulting with parents: Applying family systems concepts and techniques. *Professional School Counseling, 5*(2), 116–123.

Phelan, T. W. (2003). *1–2–3 magic: Effective discipline for children 2–12* (3rd ed.). Glen Ellyn, IL : ParentMagic, Inc.

Prochaska, J. O., DiClemente, C. C., & Norcross, J. C. (1992). In search of how people change: Applications to addictive behaviors. *American Psychologist, 47,* 1102–1114.

Prochaska, J. O., Velicer, W. F., Rossi, J. S., Goldstein, M. G., Marcus, B. H., Rakowski, W., et al. (1994). Stages of change and decisional balance for twelve problem behaviors. *Health Psychology, 13*(1), 39–46.

Sheridan, S. M. (1993). Models for working with parents. In J. E. Zins, T. R. Kratochwill, & S. N. Elliot, (Eds.), *Handbook of consultation services for children: Application in educational and clinical settings* (p. 110–133). San Francisco: Jossey-Bass.

Sheridan, S. M., Kratochwill, T. R., & Bergan, J. R. (1996). *Conjoint behavioral consultation: A procedural manual.* New York: Plenum Press.

Zins, J. E., Kratochwill, T. R., & Elliot, S. N. (1993). *Handbook of consultation services for children: Applications in educational and clinical settings.* San Francisco: Jossey-Bass.

20

Working with Family Systems from a Cognitive-Behavioral Perspective in Educational Settings

STUART B. BADNER & JILL K. CAREY-MELTON

An often misrepresented and misunderstood, yet most important, member of multidisciplinary teams in educational settings is that of the child's family. Even though parental involvement with children's schooling has often been associated with better attendance, higher achievement test scores, and stronger cognitive skills, family members in many educational settings are still viewed as part of the child's problem, and not necessarily as part of the solution. In fact, enlisting the aid of family members is a central component to understanding and effecting desired change, and with proper guidance and support, most would respond well to cognitive-behavioral interventions and management of their child's presenting problems. When education systems are able to shift their views of families to that of being central resources in the resolution of their children's problems, family members will have an opportunity to better understand and become responsible partners in the remediation of problem behaviors. It also positions families to be perceived as an enhancement and not a burden to a system that is often overtaxed in its own right.

However, as schools still tend to function around a two-generational traditional family model, they run the risk of being viewed as insensitive to parents' working hours, financial constraints, and child-rearing responsibilities, as families' compositions and roles are shifting. Contemporary, nontraditional families are becoming the norm and include, but are not limited to, single-parent mothers or fathers, grandparents raising grandchildren, foster parents, adoptive parents, biracial parents,

parents who conceive through in vitro fertilization or surrogacy, and sexual minority parents. Census data further reveals that schools often lack sufficient resources aimed at students that are not from two parent traditional households, and less than a quarter of U.S. households with children under the age of 18 years are households of married couples. Single-parent-run households are on the rise and they are struggling more financially than two-parent-run households (Trotter, 2001). The impact on children is significant, not just in terms of their ability to further their education, but in their ability to complete high school because of enormous financial burdens, especially in areas where schools are significantly lacking necessary resources. For example, 62% of African-American homes are single-parent families, where more than one low-paying job is often held because of economic hardships (Ricciuti, 2004). In practice, circumstances such as these often make it difficult for parents from single-parent households to attend school meetings during school hours, and until schools make it a point to accommodate their needs, schools run the risk of inadvertently fostering an inherent lack of trust and resultant hostility toward their perceived lack of cultural sensitivity.

As a result, schools need to equip themselves with available resources for nontraditional families, including various and diverse counseling options, tutoring services, and health care options, keeping financial considerations and time constraints in mind. It is our job as educators to provide guidance relevant to the individual needs of the families we work with and gain their trust by informing them of services that could be of help to them and their children. For example, according to the No Child Left Behind Act (U.S. Department of Education, 2002), impoverished families in disadvantaged and unsafe neighborhoods are to be given more choices for their children if schools are not meeting state standards. However, the same families that could benefit from increased choices of supplemental services, including tutoring programs, after-school programs, and summer school programs, often do not know what is available to them unless they are made aware. As we move closer toward a "community schools" model, schools more than ever need to become acutely aware of the depth and diversity of the families they work with. Educators are being required to expand their skill levels as well as their resource banks, and are viewed as the bridge or liaison for families' accessibility to community resources. However, schools are also being asked to take a more proactive role in the coordination of services for children and their families, and are beginning to feel the pressure to change and provide what used to be known as "home" responsibilities. For example, many schools are offering courses on healthy parenting practices, as unhealthy parenting styles have long been associated with compromised development of the children they serve.

Vast economic and demographic changes have also resulted in increased economic hardship and stress for many families, as well as an accompanying pressure on schools to increase our nation's competitiveness in a global economy, as evidenced by recent No Child Left Behind federal legislation. However, even though education systems may see the value of promoting responsible partnerships with families, teacher-training programs have typically offered little direct training in forming parent-teacher relationships, and traditionally public schools have not endorsed strong emphasis on family involvement and support. As a result, educational staff of the 21st century, including school psychologists, social workers, learning consultants, guidance counselors, teachers, related services personnel, nurses, para-professionals, support staff, administrators, and so on, are charged with the respon-sibility of knowing how to work competently with all children and families regardless of their race, culture, disability, and religious or sexual orientation, with limited preparation. Educators are responsible now more than ever to put into practice skills necessary to effectively implement culturally sensitive and competent interventions with those they serve.

CULTURAL COMPETENCE

Becoming more aware and accepting of differences is an absolute necessity in today's schools as educators attempt to reach and help children and their families develop good coping skills not only to deal with crises and disasters but also with general concerns regarding daily living. In becoming more culturally competent, educators must first respect the differences in family structure, as well as the dynamics that exist within families, and be respectful and mindful of those differ-ences. Educators must be able to reach beyond their comfort level and be willing to interact with those different than themselves while being open minded to learning about new cultures, religious affiliations, parenting styles, and traditions of the families they are servicing if different from their own. It is then that they can become more connected to others, void of myths that effect their interactions, and accepting of differences that vary from their way of thinking, while increasingly becoming more comfortable with various groups of people. During this self-exploration and educational process, it is imperative that educators constantly check their own biases to ensure they are approaching each family in a nonjudgmental way and that personal beliefs do not interfere with optimal delivery of service. An "authentic connection" is paramount in establishing trustworthy relationships. Being falsely comfortable is noticeable and causes disconnect, which can ultimately lead to inadequate parental involvement.

In working effectively with families, our primary goal as educators is to make certain to establish strong and reciprocal connections with them. In this regard, it is essential for educators to become aware of and overcome any cultural disconnect that may exist, and always advocate for what is best for the individual needs of families, not necessarily what is convenient for them. It is only then that families will view our actions as genuine. Dialoguing and recognizing what causes disconnect with others is a step toward understanding underlying thoughts, feelings, and actions toward those different from ourselves. Growing "ourselves" through the relationships we have with others, helps to establish a reconnection, by making ourselves acces-sible to the experience of challenge while expanding our ability to be empathetic to another's situation (Jordan, Walker, & Hartling, 2004).

Best practice suggests that it is our job as educators to understand how we are influenced by the environment in which we socialize and realize how our thoughts affect our behavior in our daily interactions (Thomas & Grimes, 2002). The families we work with need us to be relationally competent and not accepting of our school cultures as is, which are often filled with conflict and reflects the problems of our society at large. Since the 1954 *Brown vs. Board of Education of Topeka* ruling, whose mission was to end racial segregation and make certain that public schools had adequate resources for all children regardless of their race, ethnicity, or socio-economic status, schools have made some progress; however, many have since begun to backslide (NEA Today, 2004). As a result, many of the families of children where there is high poverty and high need are left disheartened with the education, health, and welfare their children receive and are therefore angry with school personnel before they even meet with them. Consequently, many families, especially families in inner-city schools in many school districts, continue to look toward vouchers and charter schools as a way of rescuing their children from failed school personnel–parent relationships and feeling a lack of concern for their individual child's needs (Sarason, 1996).

We must practice putting our fears and personal beliefs aside when dealing with diverse and complex families and respect the choices of others. We must be willing to seek peer guidance when dealing with families different from what we are accustomed to, consulting with those who may have a better understanding of the ethnicity or identity of the family we are working with, in order to gain a better understanding of their belief systems. Establishing connections not only increases parental involvement and participation but also improves our own capacity as educators for dealing with a variety of family structures, and ultimately results in gaining parents' trust. However, understanding is only one part of acceptance. Educators must be willing to challenge their own beliefs and values every day, and make certain that their thoughts, feelings, and actions are in alignment. As subtle as the educator's behavior may be, whether it is a lack of eye contact, fast-talking speech, elaborate vocabulary, or unfamiliar educational jargon, minority groups in particular are attuned to picking up on negative feelings or prejudices directed toward them because of a cultural mistrust of races different than their own (Dovidio & Gaertner,1998). Educators must remain cognizant of the hidden signals that can be given off that could potentially cause a disconnection when forming relationships. Cultural mistrust causes a disconnect between relationships within a variety of settings caused by a fear of being mistreated, feelings of discomfort, and a fear of not being understood (Alston & Bell,1996), with the end result being a reluctance for families to become fully involved in the educational process.

The roles of educators are changing and there is an increased expectation for educators to know how to deal with a variety of challenges that children bring with them to school, whether it be an urban, suburban, or rural setting. Children are frequently presenting in schools without their basic needs of food and safety being met, leaving them at risk for the development of mental health issues. School personnel need to be able to recognize the signs of when a child is presenting in distress and understand that chronic absenteeism and a lack of work completion could be signals of a much larger issue at hand. For example, although incidents of child sexual abuse and physical abuse are on the rise, feelings of shame on the child's part may prevent the child from reporting it. Therefore, it is our responsibility to look for the signs and refer out immediately to the proper child protection service authority when we suspect that abuse may be occurring.

FAMILY SYSTEMS IN EDUCATIONAL SETTINGS: A "FAMILY FIRST" APPROACH

As educators, it is our job to advocate for the families we work with whenever possible and involve community agencies and organizations whenever necessary to help families deal with life stressors and improve their coping skills. However, in all cultures, although the family imprints its members with selfhood, every individual's sense of identity is influenced by a sense of belonging to different groups (Minuchin, 1999). The family is an open system in transformation; it constantly receives and sends inputs to and from the extrafamilial, and it adapts to the different demands of the developmental stages it faces. Although the family is the matrix of its members' psychosocial development, it must also accommodate to society and ensure some continuity to its culture. According to Minuchin, this interdependence of societal function is the source of attack on the family.

Systems theory has guiding principles that apply to all kinds of systems including business and industry, community organizations, schools, and families. These principles are helpful in understanding how families function and how families and communities interact (Connard & Novick, 1996). Some principles of systems theory relevant to working with families in educational settings are:

- *Interdependence.* The system maintains itself and one part of the system cannot be understood in isolation from the other parts (Connard & Novick, 1996). According to Minuchin (1999), it offers resistance to change beyond a certain range, and maintains preferred patterns as long as possible. Children cannot be understood outside the context of their families, and a family is more than the sum of its parts. Each individual belongs to different subsystems formed by generation, by gender, by interest, and by function (e.g., spousal, parental, sibling), in which the individual has different levels of power and learns different skills.
- *Circularity.* Family systems are constantly evolving, and every member of the system influences every other member in a circular chain of influence. Every action is also a reaction (Walsh, 1984).
- *Adaptation.* Families are subject to inner pressures coming from developmental changes in their own members, as well as outer pressures coming from the demands of social institutions that impact them (Minuchin, 1999). Responding to these demands requires accommodations of all family members, and the two-way patterns of interaction within the child's family and between the family and its social environment are subject to both internal and external driving forces.

By understanding and appreciating the dynamic interaction between self and system, in addition to the individual needs and cultures of the families educators work with, systems theory allows educators the opportunity to better join with families when problems arise.

Systems theory teaches us to appreciate the unique concerns families represent, to determine what strengths the family already has, and to recognize the two-way exchange that occurs between families and environments. Individuals and families are seen as constantly evolving, and stress, coping, and adaptation are accepted as normal developmental processes. By putting families first, it sets the foundation for delivering cognitive-behavioral interventions from a strength-based perspective in educational settings. Key components to a "Family First" approach involve:

- *Celebrating differences.* Differences are enriching in nature and accepted as the norm. Families are appreciated for their ability to communicate unique perspectives.
- *Viewing families as responsible partners.* Families are supported and embraced as integral members of multidisciplinary teams. They are viewed as the "experts" when it comes to their child, and as someone educators can learn from. Child development is enhanced through fostering helping and partnering relationships.
- *Building bridges and linking families with community partners.* Families gain information, resources and support through their connections to local as well as extended network community providers.

Although systems theory gives us a framework for better understanding how families work within their respective communities, working with families in school settings provides a somewhat different set of challenges for educators. The same two-way exchange that occurs between families and environments occurs with educators as well, and, as a result, an extra layer is added to the circularity and adaptation of the newly formed system. Just as it is important for educators to understand and appreciate the scope of values and beliefs of the families they work with, it is essential for educators to understand and appreciate their own role as well as the dynamics of the system that employs them. Although it is the school district's job to establish and implement a core set of values and beliefs for each and every elementary, middle, and high school within the district, in practice, it is likely that each school will develop its own variation of the same theme, developed from the values, beliefs, and habitual practices of the individuals that work in their respective environments. Even though two school buildings may have been built from identical blueprints and commissioned at the same time, their climates may be vastly different and quite noticeable as one walks down the halls.

A competent system requires several significant shifts: from unconnected thinking to systems thinking, from an environment of isolation to one of collegiality, from perceived reality to information-driven reality, and from individual autonomy to collective autonomy and collective accountability (Zmuda, Kunklis, & Kline, 2004). Whereas successful family functioning is often dependent on the goodness of fit or compatibility between family members and the network of social systems with which they are involved, family distress may be generated by both internal and external stressors, ranging from natural developmental processes (e.g., adolescence), as well as strain associated with coping with an illness, to inadequate housing, health care, and educational concerns. Likewise, educator distress may be generated by internal and external stressors as well, stemming from personal issues and biases, demanding workloads, policies and procedures, and administrative concerns. To no surprise, people do make the difference, and in order to work effectively with the families we serve, educators must also fully appreciate and understand the individual differences celebrated in their own work environments, and ultimately the dynamic interaction of internal and external forces driving both families and educators, or in other words, two selves within and between two systems (see Figure 20.1).

It is at the merge points between systems that educators can effect change; however, educators need to be especially careful and remember they are attempting to broker agreement with two distinct entities, often with competing agendas. Educators must not only find a way to reach and immerse themselves within the family system they are working with but also must maintain a strong connection to the school system they are obligated to at the same time. In addition, educators need to be cognizant of any preconceived notions that families may already have about the school, as they may become indirectly cast in the same light, deserved or not, in the families' eyes (see Figure 20.2).

Dissonance created along any lines, whether attributed directly to family and educator interactions, and educator and school interactions, or indirectly attributed to family and school interactions, not only can impact the quality of

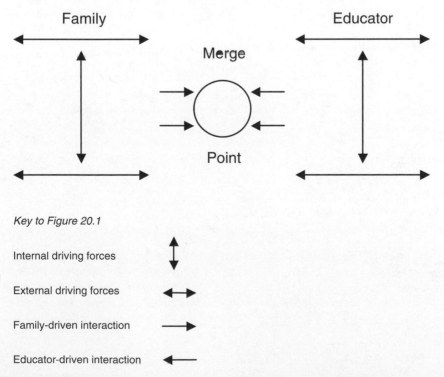

Figure 20.1 The dynamic interaction of two selves within and between two systems.

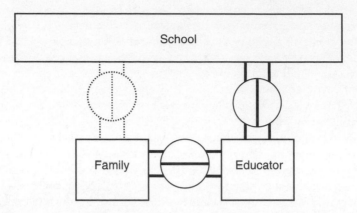

Figure 20.2 Family and school-based interactions exemplifying open connections at merge points between family and school, family and educator, and educator with school, when brokering change.

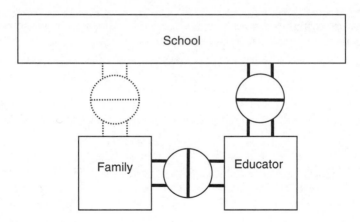

Figure 20.3 Family and school-based interactions exemplifying closed connections at merge points between family and school, family and educator, and educator with school, when brokering change.

the interaction, but seriously compromise the outcome of the interaction as well (see Figure 20.3).

USE OF "SOFT SKILLS"

So what are the common threads that can help educators navigate and effect change when attempting to connect and remain connected with families and their own institutions at merge points? Nathan and Radcliffe (1994) interviewed 1,823 educators in 29 states. More than half of the educators ranked the following skills as important when working with families:

- Conducting effective conferences.
- Working with parents when the student has a problem.
- Communicating with parents about student progress.
- Helping parents understand class goals, strategies, and methods of assessment.

Recent educational reform by the U.S. Department of Education (1994), such as *GOALS 2000*, stresses parental participation in children's schooling as a primary goal. Many other educational reforms and policies—from site-based management to family support initiatives—emphasize building relationships among families, schools, and communities to promote children's academic success. The priority of family involvement grows out of convincing evidence of the strong contributions that families make to student achievement and school quality.

Working alliances are critical to the success of any worthwhile endeavor and are certainly central tenets to cognitive-behavioral family interventions, particularly in educational settings. Although it is true that educators are faced with the need to learn about different cultures and be sensitive to the complex needs of children and their families in today's ever-changing society, there are some basic universal needs that impact individuals young and old alike, regardless of their similarities or differences: a need to feel listened to, understood, and to be treated with respect. These basic needs are ever-present, constantly challenged with each and every situation that arises, dependent on the quality of the interaction, and typically magnify in direct relation to the level of concern about what is at stake. The ability to communicate understanding and respect are foundational "soft skills" that need to remain in the forefront when working with families, regardless of the complexity of the situation that educators are presented with. Soft skills are critical for those of us who work in school systems to possess; however, they are rarely taught and unfortunately often assumed to be present. Although "hard skills" equate more to the technical skills a job requires, soft skills are those interpersonal skills that are not typically found on resumes; however, they are the cornerstone to developing effective and satisfactory relationships, particularly in educational settings.

Although soft skills have typically been associated with business and industry, their utility is fundamental and can be applied to any setting that involves working successfully with people. Soft skills are best defined as those basic nontechnical skills, attributes, and traits that workers need to possess in promoting successful outcomes with their clients and coworkers. In fact, these skills are so basic that the United States Department of Labor (1990) appointed a commission to study the "know how" that workers needed to perform their job well. This commission, called SCANS (Secretary's Commission on Achieving Necessary Skills), identified specific competencies and foundation skills that everyone needs in order to succeed in the workforce, and life, including the ability to

- work well and cooperatively with men and women, and people from a variety of ethnic, social, or educational backgrounds
- work toward an agreement that may involve exchanging specific resources or resolving divergent interests
- work and communicate with clients and customers to satisfy their expectations

- help others learn needed knowledge and skills
- understand how social, organizational, and technological systems work and how to operate effectively within them

Soft skills are not just to be reserved for the families with whom we work, as they are a mindset that can help educators increase ongoing and collaborative efforts with all team members. With frequent application, they can become an integral part of a school's culture, and as it is not uncommon for several team members to be working together with a given family, it is critical for all team members to be perceived in the same light and to be delivering the same message. Regardless of the diversity or number of educators involved in working with a given family, even though educators may be perceived as being separate and distinct bodies, it is essential for them to be heard as one voice.

We are only at our best in the right environment, and although relationships are the foundation of a good, personalized school, one cannot build relationships without first cultivating a culture of trust and respect. Caring and conviviality are seen as "friends of change" in which the quality of acceptance, geniality, and good-naturedness helps create a culture where people are known and valued for who they are, not just for the work they do (Littky, 2004). It is through the ongoing practice of soft skills that educators cannot only help achieve and maintain group consensus and cohesiveness but also can establish a precedent for future interventions.

ASSESSMENT TOOLS

When it comes to recordkeeping, schools are legendary for generating a wealth of data, and when working with families from a cognitive-behavioral perspective, it is often very useful to display data through visual and concrete methodologies to help work toward fostering understanding and problem resolution. By knowing where to look and adapting already existing information into a more family-friendly format, educators can help provide families with a wide range of ongoing and periodically collected empirically based data determined by level of need and involvement, including ongoing teacher/counselor-driven assessments (e.g., report cards, academic probes, cognitive-behavioral support plans); group-administered standardized measures used for monitoring compliance with federal/state initiatives and progress within the district curriculum (e.g., curriculum-based assessments [CBA], norm-referenced tests, criterion-referenced tests, and competency-based assessments); and available administrative outcomes (e.g., attendance records, discipline reports, character education, and anti-bullying program progress reports) (Figure 20.4).

For children that are identified at risk or in need of receiving special education, additional standardized and descriptive data can be found from a review of Prereferral Support Team interventions (e.g., developed from established baselines of targeted areas of academic and/or behavioral concern); Related Services evaluation and assessment reports and curriculum based measures (e.g., results generated from teacher/ program-generated curriculum based measures [CBM], psychological evaluations,

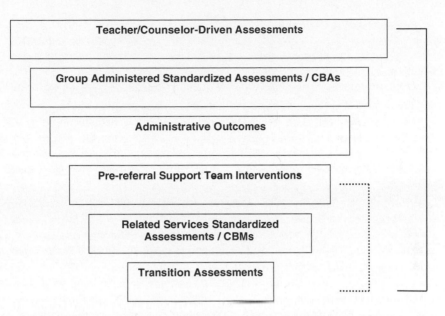

Figure 20.4 Areas to look for empirically based data determined by level of need and involvement in educational settings.

speech and language evaluations, occupational therapy evaluations, physical therapy evaluations, vision and hearing evaluations, and physician reports); and individually tailored Transition assessments (e.g., student, parent, and teacher interviews; portfolios; work adjustment inventories; quality of life assessments; interest inventories; learning and working styles inventories; work samples; and situational assessments provided by job coaches).

Targeted and easy to understand empirically based data can help shift a family member's cognitions and behaviors to clarify and better understand the full scope of how his or her child is performing in the school environment. For example, the *Dynamic Indicators of Basic Early Literacy Skills* (DIBELS) are a set of standardized and individually administered fluency measures designed to regularly monitor the development of prereading and early reading skills in grades kindergarten through 3 (Good & Kaminski, 2002). Each measure (e.g., Initial Sounds Fluency, Phonemic Segmentation Fluency, Nonsense Word Fluency, and Oral Reading Fluency) has been found to be a reliable and valid indicator of early literacy development and predictive of later reading proficiency.

The results can be used to evaluate individual student development, provide grade-level feedback toward validated instructional objectives, and aid in the early identification of students who are not progressing as expected. Testing takes less then 10 minutes per child and DIBELS data is typically collected on a quarterly basis. The DIBELS Data System provides reports to evaluate the effectiveness of reading programs at classroom, school, and district levels, in two formats: Web reports for viewing online, and PDF reports (Adobe's Portable Document Format) for downloading and printing in the form of histograms, box plots, cross-year box plots, class list reports, scatter plots, district norms, class, school, and district progress summary reports, individual student profiles, demographics, and summary of core program effectiveness reports. Raw scores and percentiles are reported to indicate individual children's performance in relation to big idea goals and in relation to all children in the same grade within the school. In addition, instructional recommendations based on a summary of student performance are provided. Most DIBELS measures have additional progress monitoring capabilities, which allows for schools to regularly monitor student progress (e.g., weekly, bimonthly, and regular benchmark intervals) and provide timely feedback to teachers and parents about how students are responding to given interventions through easy-to-understand graphic displays.

Administrative data and outcomes are often overlooked sources of valuable information when crafting cognitive-behavioral interventions in educational settings. Consider the following case.

Eric presented as a very large and outspoken 17-year-old Caucasian male student who was attempting to return to his regular Emotional Support classroom from an alternative placement outside of his home school district. In addition to his history of disruptive and threatening behaviors, which is what prompted his alternative placement, Eric presented with a significant history of somatization, learning disabilities, and attendance problems. Eric routinely complained about experiencing debilitating headaches, which prevented him from going to school; however, exhaustive medical testing showed no evidence of any pathology. Eric's parents divorced in his early teens and remarried different partners. Eric elected to live with his father, although he eventually moved in with his mother because of his father's inability to manage his difficult behaviors at home and in school. Eric's relationship with his mother was a generally reverent one; however, she tended not to place many restrictions, if any, on his behavior. Although his stepfather had a history of being a disciplinarian, he was careful not to interfere in the decisions made between Eric and his mother. Eric knew how to use his large size and booming voice in an intimidating manner, and was skilled at engaging adults into a frustrating process of circular reasoning, avoiding the issue at hand. Although Eric was making some gains academically and behaviorally, his placement was failing because of his nonattendance, and it was preventing him from returning to his district placement, which is what he desired. Any attempts at reasoning with Eric about his nonattendance were met with a barrage of justifications and rationalizations for his behavior, blaming others for his misfortunes, and storming out of meetings. Eric believed himself to be a victim of circumstance, which was indirectly reinforced by his mother's own feelings of helplessness and inertia. In an attempt to work with Eric's beliefs about his situation and help him achieve his stated goal of returning to his district placement, the multidisciplinary team decided to let his attendance record do the talking and avoided entering into lengthy and nonproductive discussions with him. They produced a series of easy to read graphs and charts detailing his attendance and nonattendance history, and they established a fairly reasonable and attainable threshold of attendance needed to return to his desired placement. The graphs and charts were displayed in the meeting room and all participants were given copies, including Eric and his parents. The attendance graphs became an anchor and a reference point for the team, which now included Eric and his parents to help them "see" his actual performance and established goals. The meeting was focused and productive, and Eric was eventually able to comprehend through the graphic display that what was being asked of him was not unreasonable and actually well within his reach of accomplishing.

BELIEF SYSTEMS AND SCHEMAS

When working with families from a cognitive-behavioral perspective, the context of one's environment is most instrumental in shaping who that person is. In order to help conceptualize a family's presenting problem, educators must first understand the belief system that underlies and defines the actions of the family. Belief systems are based on a family's morals and values and are the rules that guide them in their relationships with others. As educators, we encourage the use of timeout, medication, and mental health services to control fidgetiness and restlessness in children as a form of behavior management. However, we must understand that many cultures do not see fidgety behavior, loud talking, or movement as problematic. When working with families in educational settings, it is critical for educators to appreciate both the strengths and needs of the families they are working with, as well as the scope of the problems they may be asked to modify. Educators must find the time to get to know the family they are working with and an effort must be made to fully understand the family's perspective about the presenting problem; if not, then not only is much valuable and precious time wasted, but much larger problems can potentially result as well. A resultant family's lack of follow-through on recommendations then should not be interpreted as reluctance to change but, rather, the conceptualization of the problem was unclear or not agreed on.

Educators walk a fine line and cannot afford to disregard the importance of belief systems, otherwise known as schemas, in building a family's trust in them. These schemas form a framework of how families perceive recommendations (Freeman & Dattilio, 1992). Educators must not only empathize with families about what they are asking them to do and verbalize their awareness about how difficult the tasks may be, but also at the same time increase skill sets and strategically educate parents about current research on best practices of raising children, while working together toward a plan of change. Educators must be able to show families that they do understand and appreciate the importance of the family's religion, the discipline practices used, their customs and ways of living, and, in certain cultures, the importance of extended family involvement. They must also take into account how these practices may be impacted and potentially conflict with outside influences.

For example, many cultures involve extended family members in child rearing, as seen in African-American and Hispanic communities. Educators must be aware of the strong matriarchal presence in the African-American community and the powerful patriarchal presence in the Hispanic community. Educators must keep in mind the strong Christian beliefs of both African Americans and Hispanics and the belief in the "power of prayer" in healing both physical and mental ailments. African Americans also have a strong belief in turning toward pastoral counseling over psychotherapy and in holistic measures and natural remedies over prescription medication, because of a fear of Western medicine. As educators, we must understand that reasons for the fear and mistrust that exist among African Americans toward physicians and mental health providers are real and in a large part caused by a history of medical mistreatment in which African Americans were used as test cases and denied medical treatment that could heal (Whaley, 2001; Jones,1993).

Educators must understand the mistrust that African-American parents have toward schools is ever present and directly related to the mistreatment that African-American males have experienced and currently encounter in society as a whole. African-American parents often lack trust in authority figures because of an overriding belief that their male children are being targeted and subjected to unfair discipline practices in schools, and are being overrepresented in special education populations. In fact, in a report to Congress on the implementation of the Individuals with Disabilities Education Act (IDEA), the U.S. Department of Education (1997) indicated that African-American and Hispanic children are more likely to be over identified as Learning Disabled, Mentally Retarded, or Emotionally Disturbed (Zhang & Katsyannis, 2003). Furthermore, students who were identified as Emotionally Disturbed were more likely to drop out of school, had more difficulty securing gainful employment, and were more likely to be found in correctional institutions. When developing cognitive-behavioral interventions in school settings, educators need to realize how deeply African-American parents often feel that their children's futures are being negatively influenced by racially oppressive attitudes, behaviors, and beliefs (Townsend, 2000), which in turn contributes to unfavorable educational outcomes for their children and ultimately their ability to trust. Educators must be able to anticipate and embrace any resistance that arises and work from a neutral and unbiased position, while helping all families regardless of their culture reach beyond their circumstances and achieve their goals. Consider the following case.

Shante is an 11-year-old African-American female student who recently transferred into a semirural 5th-grade General Education classroom from an urban inner-city setting. It did not take long for Shante's teacher to recognize significant gaps in her learning, particularly in Language Arts, and a referral to the school's prereferral support team was generated. On contacting Shante's mother, both the mother and maternal grandmother who lived with them wanted nothing to do with any sort of testing and made it clear over the telephone that they had no intention to pursue special education programming for Shante. They did, however, reluctantly agree to meet with the prereferral support team to further discuss concerns regarding Shante's performance. On meeting with Shante's mother and grandmother, it was again made clear that they were "going to fix" Shante and would find the money somehow to hire tutors for her. They did not want Shante to have any labels attached to her, and maintained that her learning gaps were present because her previous school "didn't teach her right." The team listened intently to what Shante's mother and grandmother had to say and assured them that the team would exhaust all of their resources within the General Education curriculum to help Shante, before taking any further steps. The team established a plan designed to introduce concepts to Shante that she may not have learned or been taught previously, and monitor progress through ongoing curriculum-based, competency-based, and teacher-generated assessments. Additional meetings with Shante's mother and grandmother were scheduled over the next three months to review progress made, with the focus being on working together to fill in the gaps, providing ongoing education and praise for their efforts, and validating any concerns as they arose. Rather than rush into testing, which was the teacher's immediate reaction after witnessing Shante's learning gaps, the team decided to adopt a "let's take our time" attitude, which not only allowed them the opportunity to collect much needed data on Shante, but gave them an opening to develop a working relationship with Shante's mother and grandmother, in the event that formal testing would become a necessity.

Without an established working knowledge of the family, rapport will be seriously compromised and educators run the risk of being seen as unhelpful school personnel. It is critical for educators to get to know the families they work with on a more personal level, and it is important that we talk to and with our families, not at them. It is important to present ourselves as real and genuine, regardless of our professional titles, and be willing to reach out and help families meet their basic needs. We must be willing to share our resources with families even if it means to volunteer to make phone calls for them if that will help reduce their struggle in navigating the system. It is the little things that make the difference, and it is then that families will listen to suggestions based on a relevant and clear conceptualization of the presenting problem and mutually agreed-on goals for change.

STRATEGIC AND TECHNICAL INTERVENTIONS

As educators, we have to be open to and prepare ourselves for increasingly complicated referral issues and questions that may arise. We are confronted more than ever with complex school-based, home-based, and institution-based issues such as suicide, age-inappropriate sexual behavior and sexual abuse, school phobia as a result of bullying and victimization, domestic violence, and physical abuse and neglect. It is critical for educators to be on the forefront of instituting antibullying policies and educating others about signs in children of deeper emotional issues.

However, educators also need to have a working and current knowledge about available resources in the community and know the proper time to refer out when a presenting problem is beyond their scope of expertise. Not knowing what is available or not knowing what to do is not an acceptable answer, and it is incumbent on educators to seek out alternative programs and treatments for families, while at the same time not abandoning them in mid-stream. Educators need to turn to each other and be open to utilizing other personnel to promote collaboration with families, including people of related ethnicities and gender to help families feel more comfortable and better understood. Consider the following case.

Jin is a 9-year-old female of Korean descent who was placed in a full-time Learning Support class in 2nd grade; however, some question was raised by her parents regarding the type and extent of her disability. Both Korean and English are spoken in her home, although the preferred language is Korean. They expressed concern over whether Jin understood what was being asked of her during her initial evaluation because English was her second language, and wondered if she did not perform at a level at which she was capable. The school agreed to a reevaluation for her, and even though her ESL teacher assured Jin's parents and school administrators that Jin was proficient in English, the district still decided to hire an interpreter to be present during testing. As it turned out, Jin did not have any difficulty understanding the directions or what was being asked of her during the reevaluation. However, the interpreter remained present to reassure Jin's parents that her performance was based entirely on whatever effort she put forth. The interpreter also attended a series of lengthy meetings with Jin's parents in order to review biopsychosocial history and behavior scales. In the end, Jin's learning disabilities were substantiated and it was recommended that she remain in her current placement. By respecting their concerns and spending time to get to know Jin's family better, with the interpreter's help, both school and family not only developed a clearer and unbiased understanding regarding Jin's needs, but helped turn around a once adversarial situation to one of trust and compassion.

CASE EXAMPLE: PETER

Peter is an 11-year-old Caucasian male 6th grader who is diagnosed with Attention-Deficit/Hyperactivity Disorder (ADHD), Hyperactive Type, but is unmedicated. He was referred to the school's prereferral support team because of failing grades and depressive symptomology. A meeting was requested by the school with Peter's mother to share the mounting accumulation of teacher concerns. However, Peter's mother was very difficult to reach by phone and, although she received reminder calls the day before each appointment, she missed three scheduled meetings before eventually coming in. After a substantial amount of team patience and persistence, Peter's mother finally arrived at the fourth scheduled meeting, but only after a staff member volunteered to pick her up at her home and she was able to select the day and time of the meeting. Additional time and coverage was secured ahead due to the complexity of the case. At the meeting, Peter's mother revealed that she had been avoiding the school meeting because of fear that she would be judged for being a single mother. She also indicated that she disliked large meetings and her past experience in meetings with the school included everyone at the table speaking negatively to her about her son. Peter's mother further revealed that Peter was the result of an unplanned teenage pregnancy and that she was struggling with parenting him. She was forthcoming in indicating that she had her own history of ADHD diagnosis, was struggling financially and emotionally, and has to work more than one job, including night work. With the team's support and encouragement, Peter's mother was able to articulate her own negative memories of being classified as Learning Disabled and how she felt segregated from her peers. The prereferral support team validated her concerns and reassured her that the least restrictive program would be tried with Peter first if he became eligible to receive services. The members present were all in accord and spoke about the helpful interventions they were currently doing with Peter. They stayed away from discussing special education services, and instead described how they had been providing for Peter's basic needs in the morning, including breakfast in the cafeteria as he complained of being hungry, even though the school does not have a breakfast program. The team shared how they provided Peter with additional out-of-pocket school supplies to assist him with his organizational skills, including notebooks and folders.

Peter's mother expressed her gratitude for the generosity the school had shown. She was further provided with and guided through the process of accessing free health insurance for Peter and was given information on how to seek sliding scale counseling services as well. After Peter's mother seemed comfortable in the company of those present, data gathered on Peter's academic and emotional needs was presented visually to help Peter's mother understand the need for further intervention. Visual data included work samples, teacher testing, stories written by Peter indicating depression, and discipline reports.

The meeting was lengthy, as the team was careful not to appear pushy with Peter's mother. Toward the end of the meeting Peter's mother became more receptive to hearing the team's suggestions, but it was only after the team had taken its time to establish a relationship with her, address her fears, and demonstrate empathy for her and her son's needs. The long-awaited meeting with Peter's mother was pivotal and productive. Peter eventually did qualify for specially designed instruction, however, and spends more than 80% of his day in the general education classroom. Supplementary help is provided to assist with task completion and a cognitive-behavioral support plan is used to help Peter process his thoughts, feelings, and behavior when situations of conflict arise. Peter's mother is now easy to reach by phone, is an active participant in Peter's meetings, and is open to school suggestions for additional intervention strategies. She comes to the school now on her own accord to meet with various school personnel, and she is frequently praised for her efforts in helping Peter at home with organization and focusing, in spite of her own long workday.

CASE EXAMPLE: JENNIFER

Jennifer is a 7-year-old Caucasian female student who was transitioning into 1st grade from a half-day kindergarten. Jennifer lives in a trailer park with her mother and two older half-siblings who are already receiving Special Education services. Concerns were initially raised by Jennifer's kindergarten teacher regarding her fine motor skills and visual-motor coordination; however, when the prereferral support team first approached Jennifer's mother about conducting an Occupational Therapy evaluation, they were met with the following angry and pointed response: "There is no way you are putting my child in Special Ed." The team agreed to monitor Jennifer's progress and planned to reconvene in 1st grade.

As a result of her visual perceptual difficulties, Jennifer began having difficulty in 1st grade with sight words in addition to her problems with cutting and writing. The prereferral support team again approached Jennifer's mother and encouraged her to voice her concerns. Jennifer was her last child from a different father and she was having difficulty accepting that her normally developing child was also having learning problems. The team agreed to work with Jennifer to help remediate her emerging academic concerns within the General Education setting. Through various probes and DIBELS assessments, it became apparent that Jennifer was more of an auditory learner, and that Phonemic Awareness was an area of strength for her. In addition to reading support, Jennifer received ongoing assistance from the prereferral support team teacher and worked with a computer-generated, phonics-based reading program for 3 days a week.

The team worked with Jennifer for over a year. During that time, they sent home numerous charts and graphs displaying progress made and continued to be a sounding board for her mother. Although some progress was made, gaps in her learning became increasingly obvious. Once Jennifer's mother was able to actually see the gaps through ongoing and clear visual displays of where her daughter was struggling, Jennifer's mother finally agreed to an Occupational Therapy evaluation, and asked the team to consider more formal psychoeducational testing as well. It was essential for the team to look beyond the mother's initial angry comment to have any chance at getting the proper help for Jennifer.

SUMMARY

More than ever, educators are interacting with nontraditional family systems in which complex issues are present. It is important for educators to keep the following things in mind when working with families in educational settings:

- Know how and when to "slow down" or "speed up" the process. Be certain to make the time to get to know each family member, as well as what other developmental and environmental stressors they are facing or coping with (e.g., financial burdens, history with the school and community, other family stressors, lack of availability caused by job demands).
- Make data more visual and accessible through charts and graphs, and decrease confusing jargon, to help parents and other professionals become more engaged.
- Include multiple sources of information and assessment tools to increase parents' confidence in the idea that their child's issues are fully known and understood.
- Establish an approachable position that promotes growth and sensitivity to the needs of all involved, one that is culturally competent, current, and positive in scope.
- Be willing to be creative and think "outside the box"; however, at the same time be respectful of how potentially threatening new ideas can be to both family members and school personnel, no matter how small.
- Recognize how cultures are different in various schools, even within the same district.
- Make certain to establish "buy in" from all group members at all levels (e.g., initiating an anti-bullying campaign districtwide, settling a dispute between two students, etc.) before implementing any change.
- Incorporate "can-do" environmental interventions whenever possible. Work from a position of creativity and availability, emphasizing what you have, not what you don't have (e.g., flex time for staff to accommodate parents who need evening appointments).

- Have a clear understanding about how other systems and potential referral sources work before attempting to initiate strategic interventions with families.

Educators must be sensitive to and be able to work with culturally diverse families from a position of acceptance and be able to recognize the unlimited power of their belief system. They also need to remain keenly aware of the dynamic and fluid interactions that occur within and between families and school systems, and of how to apply "soft skills" to promote the development of working relationships that are genuine and productive between the two systems. These relationships serve as the foundation from which to develop cognitive-behavioral interventions that are sensitive to what both families and schools are able to accept and appreciate.

REFERENCES

Alston, R. J., & Bell, T. J. (1996). Cultural mistrust and the rehabilitation enigma for African Americans. *Journal of Rehabilitation, 62*(2), 16–20.

Connard C., & Novick, R. (1996). *The ecology of the family: A background paper for a family-centered approach to education and social service delivery.* Portland, OR: Northwest Regional Educational Laboratory.

Dovidio, J. F., & Gaertner, S. L. (1998). On the nature of contemporary prejudice: The causes, consequences, and challenges of aversive racism. In J. L. Eberhardt & S. T. Fiske (Eds.), *Confronting racism: The problem and the response* (pp. 3–32). Thousand Oaks, CA: Sage.

Freeman, A., & Dattilio, F. M. (1992). *Comprehensive Casebook of cognitive therapy.* New York: Plenum Press.

Good, R. H., & Kaminski, R. A. (2002). *Dynamic indicators of basic early literacy skills* (6th ed.). Eugene, OR: Institute for the Development of Achievement.

Jones, J. H. (1993). *Bad blood: The Tuskegee syphilis experiment.* New York: The Press.

Jordan, J. V., Walker, M., & Hartling, L. M. (2004). *The complexity of connection. Race, self, society relational challenges in a culture of disconnection.* New York: Guilford Press.

Littky, D. (2004). *The big picture: Education is everyone's business.* Alexandria, VA: Association for Supervision and Curriculum Development.

Minuchin, S. (1999). *Families and family therapy.* Cambridge, MA: Harvard University Press.

Nathan, J., & Radcliffe, B. (1994). *It's apparent: We can and should have more parent/educator partnerships.* Minneapolis: University of Minnesota, Humphrey Institute of Public Affairs, Center for School Change.

NEA Today. (2004 May). *Brown vs. Board of Education. NEA Today, 22*(8), 22–28.

Ricciuti, H. N. (2004). Single parenthood, achievement, and problem behavior in white, black, and Hispanic children. *The Journal of Educational Research, 97*(4), 196–207.

Sarason, S. (1996). *Revisiting the culture of the school and the problem of change.* New York. Teachers College Press.

Thomas, A., & Grimes, J. (2002). *Best practices in school psychology* (4th ed.). Bethesda, MD: The National Association of School Psychologists.

Townsend, B. (2000). The disproportionate discipline of African American learners: Reducing school suspensions and expulsions. *Exceptional Children, 66*(3), 381–391.

Trotter (2001). Census shows the changing face of U.S. households. *Education Week, 20*(37), 5,1.

U.S. Department of Education. (1997). *Nineteenth annual report to Congress on the implementation of the Individuals with Disabilities Education Act.* Washington, DC: Author.

U.S. Department of Education. (2002). *No Child Left Behind Act.* Retrieved August 8, 2004, from http://www.ed.gov/nclb/landing.jhtml.

U.S. Department of Education. (1994). *Goals 2000.* Washington, DC: Author.

U.S. Department of Labor. (1990). *The secretary's commission on achieving necessary skills.* Washington, D.C.: Author.

Walsh, F. (1984). *Normal family processes.* New York: Guilford Press.

Whaley, A. L. (2001). Cultural mistrust and mental health services for African Americans: A review and meta-analysis. *Counseling Psychologist, 29*(4), 513–531.

Zhang, D., & Katsyannis, A. (2002). Minority representation in special education: A persistent challenge. *Remedial and Special Education, 23*(3), 180–188.

Zmuda, A., Kunklis, R., & Kline, E. (2004). *Transforming schools: Creating a culture of continuous improvement.* Alexandria, VA: Association for Supervision and Curriculum Development.

21

Cognitive-Behavioral Strategies for School Behavioral Consultation

BARBARA BOLE WILLIAMS, DIANE L. SMALLWOOD & TERRY M. MOLONY

School mental health practitioners typically spend a large portion of their working day engaged in activities that involve one of three traditional roles: *assessment*, *counseling*, and *consultation*. This chapter will explore the latter topic of school consultation, including a definition, its goals, discussion of various models, and offer an explanation and case example of school consultation based on cognitive-behavioral principles. Two specific components addressed in this chapter include (a) the consulting school mental health practitioner utilizes cognitive-behavioral therapy (CBT) strategies to work with the teacher or parent to address the student's problem, and (b) the consulting school mental health practitioner teaches CBT strategies to the teacher and/or parent to use directly with the student.

The goals for school consultation are to build the teachers' and parents' capabilities by *giving away the skills of the professional*, with the ultimate goal of the teachers, parents, and students effectively handling problems independently. As a parallel to Beck's (1995) goal of cognitive therapy, the goal for CBT-based consultation is to both facilitate the development of the consultee's effective problem-solving strategies, and to teach the consultee to become his or her own consultant, not to become dependent upon the school mental health consultant to solve all the problems. Ultimately, by effectively dealing with the student's problem, the outcome will be to improve his or her social/emotional functioning, which will lead directly to improved student academic achievement and more positive school adjustment.

Applying a cognitive-behavioral model of school consultation has multiple benefits to the consultee, client, and consultant by allowing an opportunity to address both individual and systemic issues. First, on an individual issues level, this process will help teachers become more resilient and feel a greater sense of self-efficacy, and students will have a greater likelihood of achieving improved academic functioning and healthier school adjustment. On a systemic level, improved academic and behavioral functioning offer the benefit of providing preventive services that will contribute to a safer and healthier school environment. Finally, from a supply-demand perspective, providing consultative services within the school will help to address the issue of high ratio of school mental health practitioners to students, by offering indirect intervention, when individual direct services may not be available to all children. In most situations, school mental health practitioners may have a greater likelihood of positively influencing the lives of students when they provide an indirect, consultative service to teachers and parents. Gutkin and Conoley (1990) first referred to this as the paradox of school psychology: "To serve children effectively, school psychologists must... concentrate their attention and professional expertise on adults" (p. 212).

THEORETICAL BACKGROUND AND REVIEW OF THE LITERATURE

Discussions of mental health services in schools typically include attention to consultation as a form of indirect service delivery. Although specific approaches vary, most studies of professional practices report that consultation is one of the job responsibilities for school psychologists (Reschly & Wilson, 1995; Curtis, Hunley, & Grier, 2002), school counselors (Borders & Drury, 1992), and school social workers (Dupper, 2003). Based on the number of children and youth who require some form of mental health support, which has been estimated to be at least 10% of the total student population (NIMH, 2000), efficient approaches to consultation are needed.

For the purposes of this chapter, the definition of consultation provided by Zins and Erchul (2002) will be utilized. According to these authors, "school consultation is defined as a *method of providing preventively oriented psychological and educational services in which consultants and consultees form cooperative partnerships and engage in a reciprocal, systematic problem-solving process guided by ecobehavioral principles. The goal is to enhance and empower consultee systems, thereby promoting students' well-being and performance*" (p. 626). The consultation model has been utilized effectively at multiple levels (i.e., individual, group, and organizational) to address both academic and behavioral factors that impact student learning. Before discussing the use of cognitive-behavioral principles in school consultation, it is first necessary to understand various models of consultation in general. Table 21.1 provides a framework for organizing this background discussion.

Consultation Models

Most discussions of consultation identify three major types of consultation models: behavioral consultation, mental health consultation, and organizational consultation. The process of consultation is generally considered to have its roots in the mental health consultation model developed by Gerald Caplan (1970) to address widespread emotional needs of displaced persons following World War II. As an indirect service, consultation enables a highly skilled mental health practitioner to assist a number

Table 21.1 A Review of Various Models of Consultation

Consultation Model	Theoretical Framework	Focus
Mental health	Psychodynamic	Primary focus on consultee (relationship between consultee and client)
Behavioral	Social-learning theory	Primary focus on client behavior (data-based analysis of problem situation)
Organizational development	Systems theory	Primary focus at program or organizational level

of individuals who have direct service responsibilities related to the well being of large client populations. In school settings, consultation services typically are provided by mental health professionals (e.g., school psychologists, school counselors, or school social workers) to assist teachers in their work with individual students or groups of students.

Mental health consultation is based on a psychodynamic model of change, in which it is assumed that difficulties experienced by the consultee in working with the client have a significant impact on client outcomes. Within this framework, the focus of the consultation process is on consultee issues, with the consultant helping the consultee to explore his or her own interpretations of the problem situation (Meyers, Parsons, & Martin, 1979). One of the hallmarks of the mental health consultation model is its emphasis on the collaborative relationship between consultant and consultee, as a vehicle for changing the consultee's attitudes and beliefs in order to accomplish positive changes in student behavior (Alpert, 1976). When using a traditional psychodynamic approach to mental health consultation, the consultant typically would focus a substantial amount of attention on entry issues and on establishing the relationship with the consultee as a means to change.

Behavioral approaches to consultation are rooted in social learning theory, and emphasis is placed on analyzing the impact of antecedents and consequences on both client and consultee behavior. Moreover, contextual factors are considered a critical influence on behavior, resulting from the reciprocal relationship between persons and their environment (Bergan & Kratochwill, 1990; Brown, Pryzwansky, & Schulte, 2001; Bandura, 1978). Consistent with other behaviorally oriented interventions, behavioral consultation utilizes a systematic problem-solving model, with clearly defined stages of problem identification, problem analysis, plan implementation, and problem evaluation (Bergan & Kratochwill, 1990). Conjoint behavioral consultation (Sheridan, Kratochwill, & Bergan, 1996), an adaptation of traditional behavioral consultation, promotes a collaborative relationship between parents and school professionals. The stages of conjoint behavioral consultation are essentially identical to those of traditional behavioral consultation, but the consultant works jointly with a teacher and parent to resolve a student's school difficulties.

Organizational development consultation uses principles derived from systems theory to address the need for change in communication patterns and other socio-ecological factors in order to increase the efficiency and effectiveness of an organizational system (Brown, Pryzwanksy, & Schulte, 2001). Many of the techniques used by organizational consultants focus on group dynamics, which are grounded in social-psychological principles (Meyers & Yelich, 1989).

Cognitive, Behavioral, and Environmental Influences in Consultation

Regardless of the consultation model that is employed, attention to cognitive, behavioral, and environmental factors can facilitate exploration of problem situations and development of workable plans for resolving school-based problems. It should be noted that these factors are relevant to understanding student performance and behavior as well as developing an effective working relationship with a consultee.

Social Cognition. Research in the area of social cognition can provide school-based consultants with a theoretical framework for understanding many of the cognitive factors that influence the consultative process. Specific topics that will be addressed as part of this discussion include attribution theory, cognitive dissonance, self-efficacy, reactance, and social power.

Attribution theory can be defined as a "set of ideas coming out of research in social psychology which attempts to describe how persons explain their own behavior and the behavior of others in their social environment" (Martin, 1983, p. 35). As cognitive processes, attributions stem from an individual's innate desire to predict and control one's environment, as well as to understand cause-and-effect relationships (Brehm, 1976). Attributions usually are classified according to three dimensions: internality (i.e., whether the cause of an event is attributed to the individual or to external factors), stability (i.e., the degree to which causal factors change over time or remain the same), and intentionality (i.e., the degree to which an individual has voluntary control over a causal factor). Clearly, the nature of the causal attributions that a teacher makes about a student's problem behaviors (as well as the causal attributions that a consultant makes about a consultee's behavior) will influence the problem-solving process (Martin, 1983). In addition, the "fundamental attribution error," or the tendency for people to attribute others' behavior to stable, internal, and intentional factors (i.e., personality traits) and their own behavior to unstable, external, and unintentional factors (i.e., situational events), can have all of the parties within a consultation process working at cross purposes with each other.

Applications of cognitive dissonance theory to consultation have been described by Hughes (1983) and by Meyers and Yelich (1989). Although explanations of dissonance theory can be somewhat complex, the basic effect of cognitive dissonance is such that when personal behavior is dissonant with one's belief system, the theory would predict that the individual would change his or her belief system in order to be consistent with the behavior (Festinger, 1957). When consultants attempt to influence consultees to implement interventions that are inconsistent with the consultees' belief system (i.e., asking a teacher who perceives extrinsic rewards as inappropriate "bribery" to institute a reinforcement system using stickers as rewards for prosocial behavior), dissonance may be activated. According to Hughes (1983), this arousal of cognitive dissonance can have a beneficial effect in consultation, as teachers who are persuaded to try a new strategy that conflicts with their preexisting attitudes are likely to reduce dissonance with attitudinal changes that can support and maintain new behaviors.

Self-efficacy (Bandura, 1982) is an important variable in consultation with regard to plan implementation and problem resolution (Hawryluk & Smallwood, 1986). When consultees lack a self-expectation of competence related to implementation of a new strategy, they are unlikely to perform the needed skills successfully. For this reason, it is important for consultants to consider potential sources of self-efficacy expectations, such as vicarious experiences (modeling), verbal persuasion, performance accomplishments, and emotional or physiological arousal (Bandura, 1977).

The need for consultees to perceive consultation as a voluntary and collaborative process is emphasized in discussions regarding the applications of psychological reactance to consultation (Hughes & Falk, 1981; Meyers & Yelich, 1989). Reactance theory predicts that when individuals perceive a loss of freedom to personal autonomy, they will act in a way to regain their sense of freedom (Brehnm, 1976). Examples of reactance include the increased desirability of a forbidden object (e.g., a toddler who is not allowed to play with a specific toy) or the refusal to conform to rules that are perceived to be unfairly restrictive (e.g., a teenager who stays out past curfew). Within the consultation relationship, reactance can be activated when a consultant attempts to influence the attitudes or behavior of the consultee. Hughes and Falk (1981) noted that the likelihood of reactance could be reduced in consultation when the consultant maintains a strong emphasis on the collaborative nature of the process.

A final cognitive factor that can influence consultation outcomes is treatment acceptability, which refers to perceptions of consultees related to intervention procedures (Sheridan, Kratochwill, & Bergan, 1996).

Intervention plans that are perceived by consultees as being easy to implement and consistent with personal orientation or philosophy are more likely to be accepted and utilized by teachers, compared with interventions that are viewed as requiring a substantial amount of time or effort. In addition, consultees are more likely to view any intervention more favorably if the problem situation is judged high in severity (Witt, Martens, & Elliott, 1984; Witt & Elliott, 1985).

Behavioral Factors. Behavioral variables play a central role in the consultation process, from the perspective of student performance as well as adult behavior. Within the behavioral consultation model, a substantial amount of attention typically is given to analyzing antecedent and consequent conditions that are associated with target behaviors (Brown, Pryzwansky, & Schulte, 2001). Several aspects of behavior are relevant to problem clarification and plan development in school-based consultation, including parameters that define target or terminal behaviors (i.e., frequency, intensity, duration, latency, etc.), as well as the nature of the problem behavior (i.e., internalizing vs. externalizing, behavioral excesses vs. behavioral deficits, etc.).

Consultee behavior is equally important to student behavior within the consultation model. Although it is not the primary focus of the problem clarification interview, it is helpful for consultants to make a systematic effort to obtain information about teachers' classroom behaviors and strategies that have been previously attempted. This can be accomplished through direct observations and interview, as well with structured questionnaires that explore characteristics of the instructional program.

A final consideration with regard to the behavioral factors influencing consultation is determination of whether the presenting concern represents a "skills problem" or a "conditions problem." Skills problems are those manifested by a deficit in the behavioral, academic, or social skills required to meet task demands. Conditions problems are identified when the individual has the requisite skills but fails to utilize appropriate behaviors under specified conditions. This is a critical determination in the problem identification stage, because much time could be wasted with unnecessary skill training to address a problem behavior that could be easily addressed through contingency management approaches (i.e., modification of environmental events). The reverse is equally true, that attempts to modify environmental conditions will meet with little or no success if the underlying problem is a skill deficit on the part of either the student or the teacher.

Environmental Conditions. Gaining an in-depth understanding of the context in which a school-based problem occurs is an important aspect of the problem-solving process. Based on the principle of reciprocal determinism (Bandura, 1978), problem behaviors can be viewed as occurring within a specific situational context. Thus, one of the tasks within the problem clarification phase of consultation must be an assessment of environmental variables that negatively influence behavior or could potentially support more adaptive behavior (Brown, Pryzwansky, & Schulte, 2001; Bergan & Kratochwill, 1990).

Contextual factors that warrant attention within the consultation process include classroom climate, scheduling, physical facilities, and interpersonal relationships, as well as instructional strategies and materials. An accurate analysis of the physical and social environment in which a learning or behavioral problem occurs is a critical component of the consultative problem-solving process.

Several researchers have emphasized the importance of relationships between students and teachers as a critical factor that contributes to educational success (Pianta, 1999; Chaskin & Rauner, 1995). Longitudinal studies that have examined factors associated with resiliency in students from high-risk environments have consistently cited the effects of a bond with a caring and nurturing adult, often a teacher, as a critical ingredient leading to life success (Werner & Smith, 1992; Laursen & Birmingham, 2003).

Doll and her associates (Doll, Zucker, & Brehm, 2004; Doll, Siemers, & Brey, 2003) have identified six characteristics that contribute to the establishment of healthy classroom contexts that are likely to promote student success: academic efficacy, behavioral self-control, academic self-determination, effective teacher-student relationships, effective peer relationships, and effective home-school relationships. Attention to each of these contextual factors as part of the problem-solving process in consultation could add to the successful resolution of learning and behavioral problems.

Academic efficacy (Doll, Zucker, & Brehm, 2004) is derived from the more global construct of self-efficacy described by Bandura (1977, 1982). Simply stated, academic efficacy consists of a set of beliefs that students hold about their individual learning abilities. It should be noted that efficacy beliefs are specific to each subject area, and may be quite dissimilar within individuals with regard to different forms of academic content (Smith & Fouad, 1999; Doll, Zucker, & Brehm, 2004). Within a consultative framework, a variety of cognitive-behavioral strategies can be utilized to enhance students' academic efficacy. For example, attribution retraining, cognitive restructuring, and peer coping models all can be used successfully to increase the likelihood that students will expect to be successful with academic demands.

Classroom environments in which students demonstrate appropriate amounts of behavioral self-control are more conducive to learning and demonstrate greater learning outcomes (McDermott, Mordell, & Stoltzfus, 2001). As Doll, Zucker, and Brehm (2004) point out, behavioral self-control is established through expectations for the classroom behavior that are jointly identified by students and teachers. Having a set of explicit prosocial rules for the classroom creates a tone that is cooperative and positive within a classroom. When appropriate, school-based consultants also can work with classroom teachers to set up group-oriented and individual interventions to address self-control issues and to help with classroom management. Cognitive-behavioral strategies, such as self-monitoring and self-instruction training (Meichenbaum & Goodman, 1971; Kendall & Braswell, 1985; Braswell & Bloomquist, 1991) can promote successful self-regulation in students and help to create classroom environments that support academic learning. In addition, students can receive instruction either individually or in groups in using CBT strategies for anger control (Feindler & Ecton, 1986), so that personal or interpersonal difficulties can have a reduced impact on the classroom environment.

Academic self-determination is the ability to take responsibility for one's own learning. This means that students have personal learning and can recognize factors that might interfere with their ability to achieve those goals (Doll, Zucker, & Brehm, 2004). In addition to classroom practices that support student autonomy, such as allowing students to set their own pace for assignments or to select topics that are of interest for self-directed study (Ryan, Connell, & Deci, 1985), consultants can assist teachers in applying cognitive-behavioral principles that will support students in becoming self-sufficient learners. A social problem-solving curriculum (Weissberg & Gesten, 1982; Elias & Clabby, 1992) can be utilized at the classroom level to teach students to engage in means-end thinking (i.e., identifying a goal and the interim steps that are required to reach the goal) as well as alternative thinking (i.e., generating alternative solutions) and consequential thinking (i.e., predicting consequences for specific behavioral choices). Once students have mastered these cognitive skills, they can apply the set of skills within both social and academic settings.

The relationship factors (student-teacher, peer groups, and home-school) identified by Doll, Zucker, and Brehm (2004) as contributors to healthy learning contexts all can be influenced by a cognitive-behavioral orientation in the classroom. The role of the consultant in this regard is to help teachers, students, and parents to recognize how their personal thought patterns (i.e., expectations, beliefs, perceptions) play a role in their satisfaction with relationships with others. Learning to recognize the role of one's own self-talk in creating or maintaining a challenging interpersonal situation can help to resolve problems and thereby strengthen relationships.

As a summary to this section, it should be emphasized that school-based consultants can utilize CBT theories and techniques to address multiple aspects of the consultation process. Throughout all of the stages of consultation, CBT strategies can help consultants and consultees to understand problem situations, plan appropriate interventions, and evaluate outcomes. In addition, a cognitive-behavioral orientation will ensure that attention is given throughout the consultation process to the complex interaction of cognitive, behavioral, and contextual factors that are inherent in problems of learning.

SPECIFIC ASSESSMENT TOOLS AND TECHNIQUES

According to Bergen and Kratochwill (1990), behavioral consultation traditionally occurs in four stages: (1) problem identification, (2) problem analysis, (3) plan implementation, and (4) problem evaluation. Verbal interaction between consultant and consultee via a series of structured interview questions is one of Bergen and Kratochwill's unique contributions in their model of consultation. This model serves as the basis for applying cognitive-behavioral strategies to consultation intervention planning.

In cognitive-behavioral school consultation, an important first step in the problem identification stage is for the consultant and consultee to define the client's problem and identify the target behavior(s). To accomplish this, assessment of the problem both on an initial and ongoing basis is required. Initially, functionally assessing the client's problem in order to identify the target behavior(s) is best accomplished through a combination of interviews and observations, review of anecdotal information, administration of formal and informal rating scales, and analysis of cognitive-behavioral measures. Critical to using CBT consultative strategies is developing target behaviors. Once the client's problems are identified, the process of understanding how the teacher or parent view the student's problem is the next important step. Questions to ask include, what meaning does the teacher or parent give to the student's behavior, and what does he or she attribute the cause of the problem to be?

CBT consultation uses these attributions of the individual to conceptualize the problem. The attribution of the child, teacher, or parent is explored in order to develop a clear understanding of the individual's explanatory style, or how the individual explains the interaction or event. The techniques of CBT are then used to help the individual shift to more functional attributions that better facilitate problem solving and offer possible solutions to experiment. Seligman's (1995) work with learned optimism suggests that people can learn to change their attribution styles if they recognize their explanatory style and determine its effectiveness in achieving a desired goal.

Following the problem identification stage, the consultant and the consultee begin to select appropriate interventions to address both the student's problem and the attributional style of the teacher and/or parent. Working with the adults, the consultant teaches CBT strategies to the teacher or parent in order to help dispute his or her dysfunctional thoughts. Once these strategies and techniques are understood by the teacher or parent, he or she can begin to implement similar strategies with the student as part of the intervention implementation stage of the model. As a final step, it is important to determine if the intervention has been effective in addressing or ameliorating the client's problems, that is, the evaluation stage. Using the data collected in the problem identification stage, the consultant and consultee compare the later functional assessment data to the original to determine if the problem behaviors have improved. Figure 21.1 depicts the stages of the CBT model of school consultation.

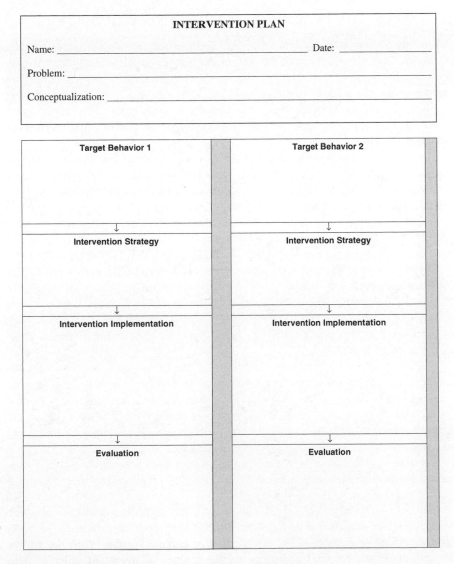

Figure 21.1 Stages of CBT model of school consultation

Conceptualization of the Problem

A cognitive-behavioral approach to conceptualizing a problem is based on the understanding of schema, automatic thoughts, and cognitive distortions (Beck, 1967, 1976). *Schemas* are the basic *rules of life* or *core beliefs* derived from one's personal, family, cultural, gender-related, age-related, and religious experiences. Freeman and Dattilio (2000) describe schemas as the hypothesized structures that guide and organize the processing of information and the understanding of life experiences. Insight into an individual's schema comes from analysis of a person's *automatic thoughts* (assumptions about self, world, experience, and future) and an understanding of the *cognitive distortions* (systematic errors in reasoning) he or she uses in interpreting the world. Beck (1967, 1976) writes that schema is the cognitive substrate that generates various cognitive distortions. When automatic thoughts become dysfunctional, they contribute to maladaptive behavior.

Underlying a cognitive-behavioral model of consultation is a psychoeducational approach to changing behaviors. It is a skill-building model that focuses on teaching coping strategies when a skill deficit is evident. A CBT approach requires active participation from consultees and clients.

Students, teachers, and parents that participate in a CBT approach will develop better coping skills, that is, they will gain skills to cope more effectively with their own thoughts and behaviors that may be dysfunctional. By using assessment tools to conceptualize the problem, we are able to look at an individual's automatic thoughts, underlying assumptions, and cognitive distortions. These assessment tools will include information from parent and teacher interviews, observations, self-reports, and rating scales. The goals of assessment are twofold: (a) to identify and conceptualize the problems that are interfering with the consultee's ability to be successful, and (b) to understand the underlying bases of the complaints so that they could be recognized as core to a specific environmental, contextual, cognitive, or behavioral problem. Cognitive change is prerequisite to behavioral and emotional improvement. Thus, once a clear picture of the presenting problem is conceptualized, the school mental health practitioner can continue to work with the teacher and parent within a school consultation relationship to plan, implement, and evaluate interventions.

The interventions that can be implemented are based on the varied techniques of CBT, which can be focused on changing cognitions or changing behaviors. Once the teacher or parent learns the skills of CBT, the techniques can be practiced regularly and modeled for children to learn. The ultimate goal of CBT is for the client to be his or her own therapist, in much the same way as the goal of the consultant is to give away the skills of consultation.

Techniques within the CBT Model

The school mental health practitioner can formally or informally teach parents and teachers about the CBT model either on an individual basis or through workshops or evening programs. It is essential for teachers and parents to understand the vocabulary and structure of CBT, including the cognitive model, the problem-solving orientation of CBT, and the emphasis on homework. Understanding the cognitive model requires the individual to clarify expectations and to evaluate beliefs and the level of willingness to change. Using CBT is based on the realization that distorted thinking can influence an individual's moods and behaviors. Discussing CBT with teachers and parents can sometimes be a delicate situation when the focus is specifically on a child as the identified client. There may be a resistance to the fact that negative interactions with the child may be caused by a pattern of thinking demonstrated by the adult, which interferes with a problem-solving orientation (i.e., internal, stable, and pervasive). Honest conversations are necessary to discuss these concerns. Often the teacher will be willing to attempt the CBT model because of a desire to help the student and an acknowledgment of dissatisfaction with the interactions that take place with the child.

The teacher's expectations also must be explored. Does he or she expect the school mental health practitioner to solve the problem? CBT is based on collaborative empiricism and the teacher needs to understand and be agreeable to active participation in the joined effort. This implies that the teacher must also be willing to change through the process. This change occurs through the learning and practice of the techniques of CBT. For a review of CBT techniques and strategies, see *Cognitive Therapy Techniques a Practitioner's Guide* (Leahy, 2003) and *Clinical Applications of Cognitive Therapy* (Freeman, Pretzer, Fleming, & Simon, 2004).

Implications and Applications to the School Setting

A cognitive-behavioral model of consultation can play an important role in addressing the needs of teachers, parents, and students within a school setting. As a psychoeducational approach to consultation that teaches skills and helps develop coping strategies, its application can address the dysfunctional thinking that results when teachers and parents encounter problems or concerns with their students and their children.

Consider the role of the school mental health practitioner as a member of building-based problem-solving teams. As a member of a problem-solving team, a teacher typically requests assistance from his or her colleagues because of problems a student is experiencing in academic, behavioral, social, or emotional areas. This is an ideal opportunity for the school mental health practitioner trained in the cognitive-behavioral model of consultation to intervene to address the teacher or parent concerns. By intervening early, the school mental health practitioner can address the issues raised by the teacher or parent before the problems become more severe.

When the school mental health practitioner serves in the role of the consultant, such as a being a member of the building-based problem solving team, he or she is able to accomplish the two components of the CBT model of consultation: (a) utilize CBT strategies to work with teachers and/or parents to address the student's problem, and (b) teach CBT strategies to the teacher or parent to use directly with the student.

Furthermore, consider Osher, Dwyer, and Jackson's (2004) description of a three-tiered model of intervention composed of the universal, selected, and indicated levels. Teachers and parents trained in CBT strategies through a cognitive-behavioral model of consultation are better equipped to participate in the services and programs delivered to children at each level. At the universal level, interventions are provided to all students as part of the school curriculum to build a schoolwide foundation of positive discipline, academic success, and mental and emotional wellness for all children. When, as a result of a consultation with a school mental health professional, a teacher learns and uses CBT strategies to deal with a student who was a client, the teacher or parent can then incorporate these skills into his or her repertoire of teaching or parenting, and this will enhance his or her effectiveness with other children. At the selected level, interventions are designed to eliminate or address risk factors and build or strengthen protective factors for students at risk for more severe academic or behavioral problems. Finally, at the indicated level, intensive interventions are designed to provide comprehensive child- and family-focused services for students to support the intense levels of need.

By definition, consultation is an indirect service offered to teachers and parents by a school mental health practitioner. Because the coping skills, strategies, and new CBT techniques that teachers and parents learn when they participate in a cognitive-behavioral consultation have the potential to reach many children with whom the teacher and parent come in contact, a cognitive-behavioral approach to school consultation can provide early intervention. Adopting this approach can improve the overall wellness of children in terms of improved mental health and improved academic achievement. If problems are caught early and ameliorated, the numbers of children requiring more intense services should be reduced. Strategies taught through a cognitive-behavioral approach to consultation can be effective in reducing the problems when working with children with attentional, anxiety, and depressive-based difficulties. Ultimately, if problems are addressed early, the net effort will be to reduce the number of students requiring individualized services through special education programs.

A case study is provided to illustrate how the CBT model of consultation can be used in schools. This first case study illustrates how a teacher, under the guidance of the school mental health practitioner, can use the principles of CBT to help a specific child in the classroom.

CASE STUDY: DEALING WITH THE ANXIOUS CHILD

Identifying Information

Mrs. T., an experienced 3rd-grade teacher, consults with the school mental health practitioner regarding Joey, a 3rd grader who appears anxious in school. Joey is a 9-year-old boy who had been retained in 1st grade because of poor academic progress. He hardly spoke during both kindergarten and 1st grade. He was referred for a Speech and Language evaluation in 1st grade, and he has received ongoing speech and language services focused on articulation and phonemic awareness. The Speech and Language therapist has ruled out language issues as the sole reason for his consistent failure to speak in school. The school staff had recommended outside counseling to the parents, who have not pursued this option. Joey is currently on no medication. Joey receives additional help in school in reading because a mild reading problem was identified. He generally earns Cs on his report card.

Joey lives with both parents and is the middle child of three boys. His father is a police officer in the community and his mother works as a librarian in a college library. Joey's older brother Tom, age 12, demonstrated some behavioral difficulties in elementary school including impulsive behaviors and physical aggression when he became frustrated. His younger brother Mike, age 5, is currently in kindergarten; no academic or behavior problems have been identified.

Mrs. H., Joey's mother, indicates that at home Joey does not demonstrate any signs of anxiety. He talks a great deal and rarely cries, except in relation to school, and he fights with his brothers "like normal children." However, she indicates that almost every day, he cries and begs her to allow him to miss school. As a result, he often arrives to school late because it is difficult to get him in to school.

Mrs. H. stated that no one in the family is diagnosed with any emotional disorders; however, she describes herself as very anxious. She feels that she does not have control over her sons and is very busy and tired at the end of the day. She indicates that her husband is the disciplinarian in the family. Although she is not forthcoming about family problems, she suggests that she and her husband sometimes disagree about child rearing, but she always gives in to him because he is more forceful and she is too exhausted to argue.

Presenting Concerns: Problem Identification

At the initial consultation with school mental health practitioner, Mrs. T. describes Joey as appearing anxious in the classroom. He often does not participate in class and speaks in a very quiet voice. He cries or appears to be on the verge of tears on a daily basis. He frequently asks to go to the nurse's office, complaining of stomachaches and headaches. The nurse usually gives him a drink of water and tells him to return to the classroom. These somatic complaints occur on a regular basis but especially on days that he is required to take tests. He rarely completes his work and spends a great deal of the day simply looking down at his books or papers without doing any tasks. He makes minimal eye contact. He appears to have one friend in class, but at recess he usually stands off by himself. He complains of gym class, stating that it makes him feel sick.

The school mental health practitioner met with Joey to ascertain his present level of discomfort. In the one-on-one setting, Joey confides that he does not feel comfortable in school. He misses his mother and is worried when he is not with her. He does not like to answer questions in class, even if he knows the correct answer. He tries to talk in a loud voice but is unable to do so in school. However, at home he talks and interacts freely with his family.

Joey's Automatic Thoughts

During the interview with Joey, the school mental health practitioner helps Joey to conceptualize the problem in terms of identifying his automatic thoughts that are contributing to his anxiety. These thoughts include, "I'm afraid to say the answer." "The other kids will laugh at me if I'm wrong." "Whenever I try to talk, my voice comes out real low." "I wish I were home with my mother." "I always feel so sick." "I'm afraid."

Joey admits to the school mental health practitioner that he does not like the way he feels; therefore, he agrees to work with her and the teacher. The three of them met to develop a plan of action. The school mental health practitioner modeled for the teacher how to help Joey discover his attributional style. They decided to focus on helping him to concentrate on relieving his physical symptoms of anxiety and on his negative cognitions. The school mental health practitioner also modeled the decatastrophizing technique, which the teacher will later use in the classroom.

Joey's Attributional Style

Joey's automatic thoughts were generally permanent (I always feel so sick), global (Whenever I talk, my voice comes out real low), and internal (I'm afraid). This style of attribution increased Joey's feelings of anxiety and made him feel that he has little influence on making changes in his life. These attributions are related to his core beliefs that he is helpless, powerless, weak, and vulnerable. With the teacher's awareness of this attributional style, she can model a different style: temporary (Right now I feel sick. I'm going to do something about it), specific (When I'm at home, my voice is loud. Maybe I could figure out how to make it loud in school), and external (I feel afraid right now, but if I try, I can learn to be brave). With this information in mind, the teacher has a more accurate conceptualization of the problems that Joey is experiencing and will be able to reinforce and shape behaviors to improve his functioning in the classroom.

USING CBT STRATEGIES

Relaxation Training

The school mental health practitioner will visit the classroom to teach the teacher and the whole class about the physical sensations of anxiety and tension and how to stop the cycle of stress using relaxation breathing and other techniques. The teacher will reinforce this activity for the whole class and specifically for Joey throughout each day. Joey will use the feeling thermometer at least three times a day to measure his level of anxiety and share the information with the teacher. As Joey learns how to control his level of physical stress, the teacher will provide positive reinforcements, initially for trying the techniques, even if he is not successful, and fading the reinforcement as mastery of the skill is achieved.

Replacement Imagery

Under the direction of the school mental health practitioner, the teacher will utilize guided imagery where the children can visualize themselves feeling powerful as they succeed at a goal. At check-in sessions each day, the teacher can suggest some replacement images for Joey to use during his school day, such as imagining himself raising his hand and giving the correct answer or playing at recess with friends. He can visualize scenes where he successfully copes with the dilemma.

Questioning the Evidence

When Joey says that no one likes him, the teacher and the school mental health practitioner can help him to question the evidence. What evidence supports or disputes the idea that no one likes him? Does anyone ever ask him to play? If so, how does he respond? Does he ever ask anyone else to play? Perspective taking could be implemented and Joey could be asked to pretend that he is someone else watching a boy like himself. Does he think it looks like the boy wants to play with anyone? What makes someone look like a good playmate? Is it possible that other children think he does not want to play since he never plays at recess? Does he need or want help figuring out how to ask someone to play?

Decatastrophizing

When Joey states his automatic thought, "I'm scared. If I give the wrong answer, everyone will laugh at me," the technique of decatastrophizing can be used.

Teacher: Joey if you give a wrong answer, what's the worst thing that can happen?

Joey: Everybody will laugh at me.

T: How likely do you think it is that everyone will laugh at you?

J: I don't know. They might laugh.

T: They definitely will laugh or they might laugh?

J: They might.

T: Did they ever laugh before when you gave a wrong answer?

J: No. But they might.

T: I remember a time during the year, when you gave the wrong answer, and everybody didn't laugh at you. Do you remember that time?

J: They didn't but I was afraid they would.

T: How about math yesterday. I think a couple of children gave the wrong answer in math. That was a hard lesson. But I don't remember anyone laughing at them. Do you?

J: Not really.

T: Do you think the kids will laugh at you but they won't laugh at each other?

J: Not really.

T: So they haven't ever laughed at you for giving a wrong answer?

J: No I guess not. But when I get afraid, I get nervous and I can't talk loud.

T: Well if you keep telling yourself in your mind that the other children are going to laugh at you, I can see why you get afraid. But since they haven't laughed at you before maybe you can tell yourself something different. For instance, what happened yesterday when it was your turn to answer for your team?

J: I gave the right answer.

T: And what did your team do?

J (smiles): They cheered.

T: How did that feel?

J: Good.

T: Maybe instead of thinking about them laughing at you, you can think of them cheering. Especially since they never did laugh at you, but they actually have cheered for you.

J: Yeah maybe.

T: You know a lot of children tell me they're afraid to give wrong answers. Maybe we should cheer for each other, not just for getting the answer right, but also for trying, or for being brave. Maybe if we try more cheering, it will help a lot of children.

J: Yeah maybe. Just please don't call on me if I don't have my hand raised. Please.

T: Why not?

J: Because if I don't have my hand raised, I don't know the answer.

T: Well, how about I won't call on you if you don't have your hand raised for starters, but you still have to raise your hand during each lesson. I know you know the answers often.

J: Okay. I'll try. Especially if we do the cheering thing.

T: Great!

Positive Self-Talk

As Joey becomes more aware of his negative thinking, he and the teacher could reframe the statements to facilitate management of his anxiety. Joey could think, "I'm calm and relaxed." "I'm in control." "I know the answer." "My teacher cares about me." "I feel comfortable in my class." "I have friends in my class." At the first signs of anxiety, he can employ his relaxation techniques and his positive self-talk.

Cognitive Rehearsal/Role-Play

Joey can rehearse or practice scenes that would be difficult for him to perform in vivo. He can rehearse what he needs to say to someone when he wants to invite him to play. He and the teacher can agree on which questions she will ask him the next day in class so that he can practice the answers at home.

Conclusion

Throughout the consultation process, the school mental health practitioner teaches the techniques of CBT for the teacher to use in the classroom. The teacher models the techniques for the whole class, in addition to teaching them directly to Joey. As Joey feels the support of his teacher and classmates, the environment of the classroom will feel more comfortable for him. He will engage in fewer negative thoughts and therefore will no longer need to engage in avoidance behavior such as going to the nurse as often. He also will have strategies available to him to deal with the stresses he experiences. For the evaluation phase, Joey's progress can be monitored by the number of visits to the nurse, the number of times he cries, and the number of times he answers questions in class.

SUMMARY

This case study provides an example of how a cognitive-behavioral model of school consultation can be applied when school mental health professionals consult with teachers and parents. In this example, the school mental health practitioner works with a teacher to address the issues that an anxious student is experiencing. It further illustrates how school mental health practitioners *give away their CBT skills* with the ultimate goal of teachers, parents, and students learning to handle their problems independently.

REFERENCES

Alpert, J. (1976). Conceptual bases of mental health consultation in the schools. *Professional Psychology, 7,* 619–626.

Bandura, A. (1977). Self-efficacy: Toward a unifying theory of behavioral change. *Psychological Review, 84,* 191–215.

Bandura, A. (1978). The self system in reciprocal determinism. *American Psychologist, 33,* 344–358.

Bandura, A. (1982). Self-efficacy mechanism in human agency. *American Psychologist, 37,* 122–147.

Beck, A. T. (1967). *Depression: Clinical, experimental, and theoretical aspects.* New York: Hoeber.

Beck, A. T. (1976). *Cognitive therapy and emotional disorders.* New York: International Universities Press.

Bergen, J. R., & Kratochwill, T. R. (1990). *Behavioral consultation and therapy.* New York: Plenum.

Borders, L., & Drury, S. M. (1992). Comprehensive school counseling programs: A review for policymakers and practitioners. *Journal of Counseling and Development, 70*(4), 487–498.

Braswell, L., & Bloomquist, M. L. (1991). *Cognitive-behavioral therapy with ADHD children: Child, family, and school interventions.* New York: Guilford Press.

Brehm, S. S. (1976). *The application of social psychology to clinical practice.* New York: Halstead.

Brown, D., Pryzwansky, W. B., & Schulte, A. C. (2001). *Psychological consultation: Introduction to theory and practice.* Boston: Allyn & Bacon.

Caplan, G. (1970). *The theory and practice of mental health consultation.* New York: Basic Books.

Chaskin, R. J., & Rauner, D. M. (1995). Youth and caring. *Phi Delta Kappan, 76,* 667–679.

Curtis, M. J., Hunley, S. A., & Grier, J. C. (2002). Relationships among the professional practices and demographic characteristics of school psychologists. *School Psychology Review, 31*(1), 30–42.

Doll, B., Siemers, E. E., & Brey, K. (2003, August). *ClassMaps consultation: An ecological measurement of successful classroom contexts.* Annual convention of the American Psychological Association, Toronto, Ontario.

Doll, B., Zucker, S., & Brehm, K. (2004). *Resilient classrooms: Creating healthy environments for learning.* New York: Guilford Press.

Dupper, D. (2003). *School social work: Skills and interventions for effective practice.* Hoboken, NJ: John Wiley & Sons.

Elias, M. J., & Clabby, J. F. (1992). *Building social problem solving skills: Guidelines from a school-based program.* San Francisco: Jossey-Bass.

Feindler, E. L., & Ecton, R. B. (1986). *Adolescent anger control: Cognitive-behavioral techniques.* New York: Pergamon Press.

Festinger, L. (1957). *A theory of cognitive dissonance.* Evanston, IL: Row Peterson.

Freeman, A., & Dattilio, F. M. (2000). Introduction Part I: Treatment of clinical problems. *Cognitive-behavioral strategies in crisis intervention* (2nd Ed., pp. 1–23). New York: Guilford Press.

Freeman, A., Pretzer, J., Fleming, B., & Simon, K. M. (2004). *Clinical applications of cognitive therapy* (2nd ed.). New York: Kluwer Academic/Plenum Publishers.

Gutkin, T. B., & Conoley, J. C. (1990). Reconceptualizing school psychology from a service delivery perspective: Implications for practice, training, and research. *Journal of School Psychology, 28,* 203–223.

Hawryluk, M., & Smallwood, D. L. (1986). Assessing and addressing consultee variables in school-based behavioral consultation. *School Psychology Review, 15*(4), 519–528.

Hughes, J. N. (1983). The application of cognitive dissonance theory to consultation. *Journal of School Psychology, 21,* 349–357.

Hughes, J. N., & Falk, R. S. (1981). Resistance, reactance, and consultation. *Journal of School Psychology, 19,* 134–142.

Kendall, P. C., & Braswell, L. (1985). *Cognitive-behavioral therapy for impulsive children.* New York: Guilford Press.

Laursen, E. K., & Birmingham, S. M. (2003). Caring relationships as a protective factor for at-risk youth: An ethnographic study. *Families in Society, 84*(2), 240–246.

Leahy, R. L. (2003). *Cognitive therapy techniques a practitioner's guide.* New York: Guilford Press.

Martin, R. P. (1983). Consultant, consultee, and client explanations of each others' behavior in consultation. *School Psychology Review, 12*(1), 35–41.

McDermott, P. A., Mordell, M., & Stoltzfus, J. (2001). The organization of student performance in American schools: Discipline, motivation, verbal learning, and nonverbal learning. *Journal of Educational Psychology, 93*(1), 65–76.

Meichenbaum, D., & Goodman, J. (1971). Training impulsive children to talk to themselves: A means of developing self-control. *Journal of Abnormal Psychology, 77,* 115–126.

Meyers, J., Parsons, R. D., & Martin, R. (1979). *Mental health consultation in the schools.* San Francisco: Jossey-Bass.

Meyers, J., & Yelich, G. (1989). Cognitive-behavioral approaches in psychoeducational consultation. In J. N. Hughes & R. J. Hall (Eds.), *Cognitive-behavioral psychology in the schools: A comprehensive handbook* (pp. 501–535). New York: Guilford Press.

National Institute of Mental Health. (2000). *Treatment of children with mental disorders* [Brochure]. Bethesda, MD: National Institute of Mental Health, National Institutes of Health, U.S. Department of Health and Human Services.

Osher, D., Dwyer, K., & Jackson, S. (2003). *Safe, supportive, and successful schools step by step.* Longmont, CO: Sopris West.

Pianta, R. C. (1999). *Enhancing relationships between children and teachers.* Washington, DC: American Psychological Association.

Reschly, D. J., & Wilson, M. S. (1995). School psychology practitioners and faculty: 1986 to 1991–92: Trends in demographics, roles, satisfaction, and system reform. *School Psychology Review, 24,* 62–80.

Ryan, R. M., Connell, J. P., & Deci, E. L. (1985). A motivational analysis of self-determination and self-regulation in education. In C. Ames & R. Ames (Eds.), *Research on motivation in education* (Vol. 2, pp. 13–51). San Diego, CA: Academic Press.

Seligman, M. (1995). *The optimistic child.* Boston: Houghton Mifflin.

Sheridan, S. M., Kratochwill, T. R., & Bergan, J. R. (1996). *Conjoint behavioral consultation: A procedural manual.* New York: Kluwer Academic/Plenum Publishers.

Smith, P. L., & Fouad, N. A. (1999). Subject-matter specificity of self-efficacy, outcome expectancies, interests, and goals: Implications for the social-cognitive model. *Journal of Counseling Psychology, 46*(4), 461–471.

Weissberg, R. P., & Gesten, E. L. (1982). Considerations for developing effective school-based social problem-solving (SPS) training programs. *School Psychology Review, 11*(1), 56–63.

Werner, E. E., & Smith, R. S. *Overcoming the odds: High-risk children from birth to adulthood.* Ithaca, NY: Cornell University Press.

Witt, J. C., & Elliott, S. N. (1985). Acceptability of classroom intervention strategies. In T. R. Kratochwill (Ed.), *Advances in school psychology* (Vol. 4, pp. 251–288). Hillsdale, NJ: Lawrence Erlbaum.

Witt, J. C., Martens, B. K., & Elliott, S. N. (1984). Factors affecting teachers' judgments of the acceptability of behavioral interventions: Time involvement, behavior problem severity, and type of intervention. *Behavior Therapy, 15,* 204–209.

Zins, J. E., & Erchul, W. P. (2002). Best practices in school consultation. In A. Thomas & J. Grimes (Eds.), *Best practices in school psychology IV* (pp. 625–642). Bethesda, MD: National Association of School Psychologists.

22

Cognitive-Behavioral Approaches to School Crisis Response

DIANE L. SMALLWOOD, BARBARA BOLE WILLIAMS & DAWN M. McDONALD

It is impossible today to pick up a newspaper or turn on a television set without being exposed to tragic events occurring around the world, including a devastating tsunami in Southeast Asia, a hostage takeover of an elementary school in Chechnya, graphic images of the war in Iraq, mudslides in California, floods along the southern coast, a series of hurricanes in Florida, genocide in Rwanda, and terrorist attacks on the World Trade Center and the Pentagon. The list goes on and on, and with 24-hour news coverage and ready access to the Internet, children and youth are exposed in graphic detail to these and other terrifying events on a daily basis.

School personnel further confront more ordinary, everyday situations that require immediate intervention to solve or defuse problems. The severity and scope of such events vary from minor and involving just one or two students to catastrophic and impacting the entire school community. As Brock and Jimerson (2004) have noted, it is important to differentiate between those events that are potentially traumatic and require crisis intervention and those events that are simply stressful and can be managed with fewer resources.

Traumatic events are those that are beyond our ordinary experience and overwhelm our normal capacity for coping. In its description of posttraumatic stress disorder (PTSD), the *Diagnostic and Statistical Manual of Mental Disorders, Fourth Edition, Text Revision* (*DSM-IV-TR*; American Psychiatric Association, 2000) includes experiencing, witnessing, or learning about an event that involves actual or threatened death or physical injury as examples of "extreme traumatic stressors." As others have noted, such events are not part of the typical school experience (Brock & Jimerson, 2004; Everly & Mitchell, 2000).

For the purposes of this chapter, *crisis* is used to refer to a situation that involves a potentially traumatic event, in which ordinary coping capacities of individuals and groups are overwhelmed or compromised by situational demands. Other characteristics of crisis situations include the presence of events that are extremely negative, uncontrollable, depersonalizing, and/or unpredictable (Brock, 2002a).

Some controversy exists regarding the appropriateness of allocating educational resources to address the social and emotional consequences of crisis events, based on concerns that the focus of the instructional program should not be diverted from the goal of attaining high academic standards. Although the mission of schools is primarily focused on academic learning, it is our firm belief that attention to social and emotional factors within the school setting is not only an appropriate use of resources, but a necessary aspect of the educational program. When the impact of crisis events is acknowledged, and appropriate prevention and intervention services are made available, the school environment is more likely to be conducive to learning and attainment of academic goals.

A number of excellent resources are available to assist educators with comprehensive programs and services related to school-based crisis response (e.g., Brock, Lazarus, & Jimerson, 2002; Klingman & Cohen, 2004; Poland & McCormick, 1999; Pitcher & Poland, 1992). The unique contribution of this chapter is the authors' explicit use of a cognitive-behavioral framework for considering all aspects of school-based crisis prevention, intervention, and response. This chapter presents a cognitive-behavioral model for planning and managing programs and services to address crisis events of all proportions. A brief review of relevant studies will be followed by a discussion of conceptual issues that permit an understanding of trauma from a cognitive-behavioral perspective, as well as specific strategies and techniques that can be utilized within school settings.

SCHOOL CRISIS RESPONSE: REVIEW OF THE LITERATURE

A review of the literature on crisis intervention frequently cites Slaikeu's (1990) definition of a *crisis state* describing it as "a temporary state of upset and disorganization, characterized chiefly by an individual's inability to cope with a particular situation using customary methods of problem solving, and by the potential for a radically positive or negative outcome" (p. 15). Others (Aguilera, 1998; Brock, 2002a; Carlson, 1997) suggest that potentially traumatic crisis events share the characteristics of being (a) extremely negative, (b) uncontrollable, (c) depersonalizing, (d) sudden and unexpected, and (e) having the potential for a large-scale impact.

Brock, Sandoval, and Lewis (2001) categorize crisis events into six classifications, which include (a) severe illness and injury, (b) violent or unexpected death, (c) threatened death or injury, (d) acts of war, (e) natural disasters, and (f) manmade/industrial disasters. How individuals respond to each of these situations is influenced in part by how threatening the event is perceived to be.

The nature of crisis is unexpected, often unpredictable, and overwhelms an individual's ordinary resources for coping. Herman (1993) defines traumatic events as *extraordinary* because they overwhelm our ability to adapt. Young (2002) notes that an individual's adaptive capacities that help him or her deal effectively with daily life events include physical health, cognitive skills, emotional abilities, spiritual connections, education and experience, and community and family support. Human beings also have stressors present in their daily lives including family and work issues, finances, addictions, and previous experiences. To remain emotionally healthy, a balance between these stressors and adaptive capacities needs to be maintained. When trauma strikes, an individual's adaptive capacities can be either injured or destroyed. Thus, the goal of crisis intervention is to build human capacities, while diminishing the stressors triggered by the traumatic events.

School crisis intervention literature emphasizes that the typical models and techniques recommended for use in the schools are directive, time-limited, and goal-oriented procedures (Roberts, 1990) designed to assist individuals and the school as a community to regain equilibrium after a crisis situation. Brock, Sandoval, and Lewis (2001) outline recommendations for developing a comprehensive school crisis preparedness plan. First, the authors distinguish between the terms *crisis response* and *crisis intervention*. Preferring the more inclusive term, the authors endorse *crisis response* to describe their work, stating it refers to the variety of activities required to manage the aftermath of a crisis. By contrast, *crisis intervention* is viewed as denoting more specific services that provide direct psychological first aid and mental health activities delivered to the traumatized individuals. Brock, Sandoval, and Lewis recommend that a comprehensive school crisis response plan include forming a crisis response team, providing training, and developing procedures to follow that are adopted by the school's governing body (i.e., the board of education). A triage approach is recommended in order to provide crisis intervention services to those most in need as soon as possible. The authors provide suggested strategies for school crisis interventions for individual and group psychological first aid. And, finally, school crisis response plans should include debriefing and evaluation components.

School mental health practitioners are also reminded that cultural competence has the potential to enhance their abilities to respond to traumatic events in schools that affect a diverse student body. Young (2002) states that traumatic events are better understood within the social and cultural context in which they occur. What type of event is perceived as traumatic and how individuals interpret and respond to crisis are influenced by their cultural backgrounds.

COGNITIVE-BEHAVIORAL APPROACH TO CRISIS INTERVENTION

Dattillo and Freeman (1994, 2000) write that cognitive-behavioral therapeutic (CBT) approaches focus on an individual's automatic thoughts and schemata. Schemata are defined as an individual's belief system or the hypothesized structures that organize the processing of information and understanding of life experiences. CBT is structured, directive, active, collaborative, time-limited, psychoeducational, and focuses on changing behaviors by teaching coping skills. Dattillo and Freeman believe that these attributes of a cognitive-behavioral approach make it ideal for becoming the basis of short-term crisis intervention strategies and models. Slaikeu (1990) would agree when he writes, "short-term, time-limited therapy is the treatment of choice in crisis situations" (p. 98).

What does a CBT model of crisis intervention look like? Dattilo and Freeman (1994, 2000) outline a five-stage model underlying a cognitive-behavioral approach to crisis intervention. The first stage is for the crisis responder to develop rapport and establish a relationship with the individual exposed to traumatic events. Second, the crisis responder must evaluate the immediate threat for physical danger or injury to the individual in order to determine an immediate course of action. Third, the crisis responder helps the individual assess and mobilize his or her internal strengths and cognitive-behavioral resources. Fourth, the crisis responder and the individual in crisis must collaborate to develop a positive action plan, and secure the individual's commitment to the plan for developing coping strategies. Finally, the two should collaboratively evaluate the effectiveness of the plan of action specifically for developing coping strategies.

CORE BELIEFS REGARDING SCHOOL CRISIS PREVENTION, INTERVENTION, AND RESPONSE

In discussing school crisis response from a cognitive-behavioral perspective, it is appropriate to make explicit the core beliefs that shape our approach to prevention, intervention, and response. First, traumatic events have the most devastating impact at the local level. Studies have shown that proximity to an event is closely related to the severity of trauma that is experienced by individuals and communities (Young, 2002). Consequently, it is our firm belief that responding to crisis events is a local responsibility. Community members, including educators, mental health professionals, law and public safety officials, and social services agencies need to form partnerships to identify and maintain comprehensive local resources that can be accessed without delay during an emergency. Although outside resources are often needed and welcomed, the ultimate task of restoring stability and competence to a traumatized community requires coordinated efforts by local caregivers.

Second, school-based crisis response takes place most appropriately within a multilevel model of prevention and intervention. At the primary prevention, or universal, level, programs and services are targeted to the entire school population, with the goal of establishing social and emotional competence in all members of the community. Strategies and activities that foster resilience and positive skills for coping effectively with life demands are incorporated into the framework of a comprehensive school curriculum. At the secondary prevention level, services are designed for a target group of individuals identified as being at risk for maladaptive reactions to daily stresses and extraordinary life events. The goal at this selective level is to intervene early, to activate social supports, and to develop enhanced coping strategies. The most intensive level of intervention is that of tertiary prevention, which provides assistance for those individuals who are showing fully developed symptoms of behavioral or emotional disorders. At this indicated level, intensive clinical services are needed, which typically requires collaboration between school and community resources. By coordinating programs and services at all three of these levels, schools can address the goals of (a) preventing certain types of crisis situations from occurring, (b) being prepared for unexpected events, (c) responding to tragic events when they do occur, and (d) facilitating a healthy recovery from trauma on both individual and community levels.

In addition to this, Klingman and Cohen (2004) offer 10 assumptions for their model of school-based multisystemic interventions for mass trauma, several of which we believe are particularly applicable to the issues presented in this chapter and will be described in more detail here (see Table 22.1). Their first assumption is that humans are capable of natural recovery from traumatic events, and intervention efforts must be linked to these human capacities. Our experience in responding to school crisis situations has supported this assumption, in that a large majority of children and adults are able to activate preexisting coping abilities relatively quickly to adapt to unexpected and potentially traumatic events. This is one of the reasons for providing initial crisis intervention services within classroom settings, which represent the most basic level of naturally occurring social support systems within the school environment.

A second assumption advanced by Klingman and Cohen (2004) is that preplanning is essential for higher levels of individual and organizational coping. Although no amount of preparation can totally avert the confusion and disorientation that is experienced in disaster situations, having a preestablished protocol to follow can provide a structure that enables the organization to function successfully in the midst of crisis. By definition, traumatic events are disorienting and overwhelming; without a standard set of procedures, agreed on and practiced in advance, school personnel can lose precious time trying to organize an appropriate response to disastrous situations.

Table 22.1 Core Assumptions Associated with a School-Based Multisystemic Prevention Approach to Disaster (Klingman & Cohen, 2004)

Assumption 1:	Humans possess strong mechanisms for natural recovery from potentially traumatic events.
Assumption 2:	Preparation is essential for better coping.
Assumption 3:	Significant adults who cope effectively and regulate their own emotions in stressful situations play a key role in helping children cope and adjust.
Assumption 4:	The school can and should be viewed as a natural support system.
Assumption 5:	Coordinated interventions, enacted simultaneously in more than one relevant system, will have stronger impact that the cumulative effects of separate interventions.
Assumption 6:	Intervention for children and related adults should be offered in the least stigmatizing context of treatment that is available.
Assumption 7:	Prevention comprises the best immediate community response to a potentially traumatic event.
Assumption 8:	Following a disaster, schools can function as sites for both schoolwide preventive initiatives targeting the whole student population and specialized follow-up programs targeting those at risk or showing signs of maladaptive symptomatology.
Assumption 9:	An emphasis on wellness promotion in trauma work is preferable to an emphasis on the reduction of posttraumatic symptomatology.
Assumption 10:	Clinical and preventive approaches should complement one another.

In addition, Klingman and Cohen (2004) emphasize the importance of adults in helping children adapt and cope with difficult situations. When adult caregivers are able to cope effectively and regulate their own emotional reactions, they model similar skills for children in their care. It is essential that adults make an effort to provide safe havens for children during traumatic events, with regard to both psychological and physical safety. The authors note as well that schools can and should be considered natural support systems that serve a vital function in providing a familiar and central meeting place for students, the adults in their lives, and other community members. School personnel, like parents and guardians, can model effective coping strategies, and the availability of supportive peer groups adds yet another dimension to the role that schools play in supporting students in the aftermath of crisis.

CONCEPTUALIZATION OF PSYCHOLOGICAL REACTIONS TO TRAUMA

A cognitive-behavioral orientation is useful in understanding and treating the effects of trauma on individuals and communities from both a theoretical and practical perspective. On a theoretical level, trauma reactions are multifaceted, and involve both mind and body. The physical response typically begins with a sense of shock and disorientation, which may be accompanied by a variety of autonomic responses associated with the "flight or fight" response (e.g., increased heart rate, rapid breathing, increased flow of adrenaline, nausea, etc.). A characteristic pattern of cognitive reactions usually accompanies the physical reaction to trauma, which includes disbelief, denial, and mental confusion. Ordinary thinking patterns are disrupted, impacting memory and learning. From a brain functioning perspective, the limbic system takes over from the cerebral cortex, and the event is experienced primarily through sensory input rather than coherent thought. One of the goals of psychological intervention following trauma is to restore the capacity to construct a cognitive (i.e., language-based) understanding of the event. On a practical level, CBT strategies and techniques are useful and well-researched tools that clinicians can utilize to facilitate this recovery process.

Each year, a significant number of children are exposed to traumatic events that have the potential to dramatically alter the child's view of self and the world. Studies of the general population have estimated that 14 to 43% of children and adolescents will have experienced at least one traumatic event during childhood (Young, Ford, Ruzak, Friedman, & Gusman, 1998). Although the majority of children who respond to a traumatic event with an acute stress reaction will gradually return to premorbid functioning, other children will experience a prolonged and profound reaction to the trauma that manifests itself in a constellation of symptoms known as posttraumatic stress disorder (PTSD).

Posttraumatic Stress Disorder (PTSD) is classified as an anxiety disorder that is developed in response to an extreme, traumatic stressor. The individual must experience, witness, or be confronted with a potentially life-threatening stressor that induces intense fear, helplessness, or horror (American Psychiatric Association,

2000). PTSD is comprised of three interrelated symptom clusters: reexperiencing, numbing, and arousal.

When assessing children for a posttraumatic stress response, it is important to be cognizant that the developmental level of the child plays an important role in the differences in symptom manifestation. Children may express distress over traumatic events in ways that differ from adults. The reexperiencing symptoms may be demonstrated through a child's play behavior. The child also may engage in reenactment of the trauma (American Psychiatric Association, 2000). Children may respond with disorganized, agitated behavior. They may also be unable to verbalize and explain feelings of anxiety and hyperarousal. Many present with somatic complaints and regressive behavior such as bedwetting or separation anxiety. Reexperiencing symptoms may present in the form of nightmares that may or may not be trauma specific. The artwork and play of traumatized children may reveal themes related to the traumatic event.

PTSD and posttraumatic responses have been observed and studied in child and adolescent victims and witnesses of natural disaster, war, violence, kidnapping, motor vehicle accidents, critical illness, and physical and sexual abuse. Although the type and severity of the traumatic stressor is a primary factor in the development of PTSD, it does not account for the fact that some individuals develop a pathological response to a particular stressor while others do not. An individual's proximity to the traumatic incident, the severity of the stressor, and the perception of the degree of threat to the individual's safety are factors that are associated with the development and severity of posttraumatic symptoms. PTSD has often been conceptualized as evolving out of a complex interaction between the individual's risk factors and the factors that promote resilience. McKeever and Huff (2003) outline a detailed diathesis-stress model of PTSD. This is a variation of previous interactional models (Foy, Madvig, Pynoos, & Camilleri, 1996), which contend that the subsequent development of PTSD in an individual is influenced by the interaction of biological and environmental factors. McKeever and Huff (2003) assert that ecological diatheses (risk factors related to the individual's self and environment) and biological diatheses (risk factors related to genetic and biological factors) interact with the severity of the stressor to determine whether an individual will develop PTSD.

Previous psychopathology and previous exposure to trauma have also been cited as factors that may make a child vulnerable to the development of PTSD. Indeed, a recent study examining comorbid behavior disorders in victimized children with and without PTSD revealed that the mean number of traumas reported by the victimized group of children with PTSD was significantly higher than the number of traumas reported by the victimized children who did not meet the criteria for PTSD (Saigh, Yasik, Oberfield, Halamandaris, & McHugh, 2002). This suggests that traumatic stressors may have an additive effect that can diminish or compromise effective coping strategies. School-based clinicians in particular need to be sensitive to the potential impact that cumulative psychological traumas may have on cognitive functioning and academic performance.

Research suggests that traumatic stress may have a significant impact on children because of its capacity to interfere with normal stages of childhood development and potentially alter brain structures during critical periods (Lipshitz, Rasmusson, & Southwick, 1998). Heim, Meinlschmidt, and Numeroff (2003) have reported that stress or emotional trauma during development may permanently shape brain circuits that are involved in the regulation of stress and emotion. Neurotransmitter systems including the catecholaminergic, dopaminergic, and serotonergic systems can conceivably be affected by early trauma (Lipschitz, Rasmusson, & Southwick, 1998) and may underlie memory disturbances such as intrusive memories that are characteristic of PTSD.

More studies are emerging that utilize neuroimaging techniques to investigate potential brain changes in individuals with PTSD. Neuroimaging studies performed on adults with abuse-related PTSD report alterations and atrophy in brain structures, particularly the hippocampus, which is a limbic structure involved in learning and memory (Bremner, Vythilingham, Vermetten, & Southwick, 2003). It is not completely clear whether these brain differences are the result of trauma or if they are neurological anomalies that may contribute to the vulnerability to and persistence of PTSD (Layton & Krikorian, 2002). Beers and De Bellis (2002) report that although the structural changes of the hippocampus are commonly seen in neuroimaging studies of adults with PTSD, children with PTSD have been shown to have smaller cerebral volumes without changes in limbic system structures. Research has shown that prefrontal cortical dysfunction may be associated with PTSD in both adults and children (Beers & DeBellis, 2002). A previous longitudinal study on adults with posttraumatic stress disorder that did not observe changes in hippocampal volume up to 6 months posttrauma (Bonne, Brandes, Gilboa, Gomori, et al., 2001) suggests these types of structural brain changes may only occur in complicated or chronic PTSD. In an investigation examining the neuropsychological functioning of traumatized children, Beers and De Bellis (2002) found that children with PTSD performed more poorly than comparison children on neuropsychological measures of attention and abstract reasoning.

Trauma has the potential of changing children in profound ways by altering their view of themselves and the world around them. Having had basic expectations of safety and security breached, the child may come to see the world as a dangerous and unpredictable place. The child remains hypervigilant, perceiving information in the environment as threatening. The child's view of "the self" may be similarly distorted with a sense of inefficacy and helplessness pervading from and contributing to posttraumatic symptomatology and collateral depression. Studies have demonstrated that PTSD symptomatology in children and adolescents has been associated with an external locus of control that reverts to an internal locus of control as treatment gains are made and PTSD symptoms begin to subside (March, Amaya-Jackson, Murray, & Schulte, 1998). Increasing feelings of self-efficacy and control, while reducing feelings of self-blame, have been associated with decreased symptoms of depression and PTSD. Attribution retraining or cognitive restructuring is a cognitive technique that attempts to challenge traumagenic beliefs, which may help to maintain dysphoria.

STRATEGIC AND TECHNICAL INTERVENTIONS—COGNITIVE, BEHAVIORAL, ENVIRONMENTAL

Although there are some philosophical differences in approach and degree of emphasis, experts agree that there are four distinct and critical phases of crisis management: (1) mitigation and prevention, (2) preparedness, (3) response, and (4) recovery (U.S. Department of Education, 2003). It is our belief that a general cognitive-behavioral theoretical orientation as well as specific cognitive-behavioral techniques can enhance the quality of crisis management in school settings at each of these stages. It should be emphasized that crisis response requires a comprehensive system that integrates emergency services (i.e., fire and rescue workers), medical care as needed, law enforcement and victim assistance, spiritual guidance and support when requested, as well as mental health services in the form of psychological first aid and after-care. This chapter limits its focus to a discussion of the mental health aspects of school crisis response, recognizing that psychological support takes place within the context of a much broader response system.

Mitigation/Prevention

Activities associated with mitigation and prevention focus on reduction or elimination of risk to life and property. Thus, the first stage of crisis planning is giving systematic attention to strategies that can help to prevent crisis events from occurring, or when they do occur, to minimize loss of life or destruction of property. Violence prevention and intervention begin by creating a positive school environment that promotes a sense of respect for all students, sensitivity to diversity among students, and active student and faculty involvement to maintain a safe school community (Brooks, 2002). These values also must be reflected in school policy.

One essential component for promoting a safe school environment is the development of a school crisis prevention and intervention plan. Stephens (1994) defines a safe school plan as a continuing, broad-based, comprehensive, and systematic process to create and maintain a safe, secure, and responsive school climate. Creating a safe physical environment that provides appropriate supervision for students during their daily schedule contributes to a sense of personal safety. Collaboration between school district personnel and local law enforcement officials is important as a means of conducting regular safety reviews of facilities and establishing procedures for risk assessment and emergency management.

Risk assessment is an important component during the mitigation phase, as it requires school personnel to do an assessment of critical aspects of the school environment in order to (a) identify potential hazards (both physical and social/psychological), (b) to decide who might be harmed by each of the hazards and in what way, (c) to evaluate the risks and decide whether additional precautions are necessary, (d) to document findings of the risk assessment, and (e) to establish a system for continuous review and revision of safety plans (Health & Safety Executive, 1999). Within school settings, risk assessment should address a systematic review of the social-emotional-behavioral environment as well as a careful consideration of the physical security of school facilities. Redesign of environmental factors identified through the risk assessment process may help to mitigate the impact of natural disasters or manmade tragedies.

In a subsequent section, more attention is given to a framework for prevention, which incorporates cognitive-behavioral interventions at three different levels of intervention. It is important to note here, however, that a key cognitive component of the mitigation/prevention phase of crisis management is building the expectation among all members of the school community that they can establish practices and procedures that will decrease their vulnerability to certain types of crisis situations. Furthermore, although it is not possible to control external events or to absolutely prevent bad things from happening, school personnel can take charge of preparing for their response to unexpected and tragic circumstances.

Preparation

The preparation stage of crisis planning addresses the need to plan for worst-case scenarios. Preparation involves the development of a comprehensive plan for management of different types of crisis situations, including natural disasters, accidental death or injury, suicide and homicide, industrial accidents, or even terrorist attacks.

When tragedy occurs in a school, the events are recorded in national and international headlines. Remember Columbine High School, Littleton, Colorado, in April 1999, when two adolescents terrorized their school, killing 14 students and 1 teacher and leaving 24 wounded. Or Jonesboro, Arkansas, in March 1998, when two middle school boys, one 13 years old and the other 11, ambushed their schoolmates during a fire drill, killing four girls and one teacher. In such situations, the eyes of the world may be on the school community as it responds to the tragic event, making it much too late to do the initial planning and organizing of a crisis response team.

Best practice recommends that a school crisis team be formed to develop, implement, and monitor the effects of the school safety initiative. Preplanning is critical, including forming the crisis team and investing the resources of time and financial costs to train the team in the fundamentals of crisis responding. The school crisis team can be instrumental in planning prevention activities to help develop resiliency among the students, faculty, staff, and administration. Efforts include engaging in activities to create a safe school by focusing on academic achievement, involving families; developing links to the community; fostering positive relationships among staff, students, and administration; and assuring there are avenues for students to discuss their concerns so problems can be identified and progress can be made to move toward solutions.

In addition, the school crisis team can have input into the process of developing written crisis response procedures. The crisis response teams' written procedures should address three components that outline (a) initiatives to prevent a crisis from occurring, (b) initial arrangements to intervene during a crisis to ensure safety, and (c) methods of responding in the aftermath of a crisis.

In the event of an actual crisis, the school crisis plan should clearly address how the school will deal with parents, police, medical personnel, and the media. Typically, one member of the staff or administration is designated as the spokesperson to inform parents and address questions from the media. It is important that factual information, as it becomes available, be shared with the staff. The crisis response team should have a plan for conducting meetings, typically before and after the scheduled school day. Large-group meetings will need to be held in order to provide guidance to teachers who will be interacting with students during the school day. Decisions will need to be made as to how to deal with curricular issues, and how to provide opportunities for the faculty to talk and ask questions. Plans will need to be made to designate staff members who will be available to supervise students in waiting areas.

Response

The response stage of crisis intervention addresses the steps that are taken during a crisis, including assessment of the situation, notification of appropriate personnel, and actions taken to intervene with the school community. At the response stage, decisions must be made quickly regarding the need for evacuation or lockdown, the need for emergency medical services, and other actions considered necessary to respond to the demands of the situation.

Trained crisis responders typically provide crisis intervention on a face-to-face basis to individuals or small groups. The National Organization of Victims Assistance (NOVA), the American Red Cross, and other organizations train crisis responders to address the cognitive and behavioral variables present within an individual during a crisis. Each individual has critical adaptive capacities that help him or her deal effectively with daily life. These adaptive capacities include physical health, cognitive problem-solving abilities, emotional functioning, spiritual connections, educational experiences, and the amount of community and family support available. Each individual also encounters typical stressors in daily life, including family issues, work dilemmas, finances, addictions, and previous experiences. To maintain the ability to function, an individual needs to maintain a balance between the stressors present within the environment and his or her adaptive capabilities. In trauma, adaptive capacities can become injured or destroyed. Thus, the first step in crisis intervention is to build an individual's adaptive capacities while diminishing the stressors within the situation.

An individual experiences trauma through his or her sensory perceptions including sight, touch, taste, hearing, and smell. Trauma is not typically experienced in words, but in images, sensations, and affective and behavioral states. Victims may experience a "freeze-frame" phenomenon when they are suspended in the moment in time when they first experienced the trauma. They may have an image, a sound, or a sensation embedded in their memory of where they were when they first saw or learned about the tragic event. Victims or survivors typically have a strong desire to stay in the present and their sense of time may be distorted or suspended. The victim's emotional response to trauma may include fear, horror, anger, confusion, or frustration. When possible, it is critical for crisis intervention to occur at this point in time.

The goals of crisis intervention are to defuse the emotional memory so the victim or survivor's cognitive processes can take over. By talking to the crisis responders, the victim is helped to organize his or her experiences into *words* and thus begin to interpret or understand what has happened. The goal of the crisis responder is to help the victim integrate the traumatic events and sensations into words and to tell his or her story. Once language takes over, the victims or survivors are able to begin to derive meaning from the past and be better prepared for the events to come in the future. Through this, individuals are able to process the events both cognitively and emotionally.

Within school settings, a commonly used approach to crisis intervention is based upon principles of psychological debriefing (Mitchell & Everly, 1995; Bisson, McFarlane, & Rose, 2000). At the classroom level, an adult facilitates a group discussion during which the known facts of the incident are reviewed, and students are provided with an opportunity to share reactions and ask questions (Brock, 2002b). Although psychological debriefing has not been empirically validated as a treatment likely to prevent the development of posttraumatic stress disorder in trauma victims, it is a form of psychological first aid viewed by most individuals as helpful and as an appropriate initial intervention (Litz, Gray, Bryant, & Adler, 2002). The reader is referred to Brock (2002b) for further information on classroom debriefing strategies and activities.

The NOVA crisis response protocol (Young, 2002) addresses three primary tasks for assisting victims and survivors of traumatic events. First, in the immediate aftermath of a crisis situation, it is necessary to reestablish a sense of safety and security in individuals who have experienced trauma. When working with young children, this often takes the form of providing reassurance that, even in the possible absence of a parent, someone is there to care for and protect the child from further harm. In addition, efforts made by school personnel to reestablish regular school and classroom routines as quickly as possible following a crisis event also can help to reestablish a sense of normalcy and security for students.

A second task for crisis responders is to address the need of trauma victims for ventilation and validation. Once physical safety has been secured, individuals often need opportunities to "tell their story," and to begin to construct a narrative formulation of what happened as well as their reactions to the event. Because there are multiple kinds of reactions to traumatic situations, it is important for crisis responders to validate diverse and individual thoughts and feelings that are expressed by victims and survivors. Some students will be deeply affected by a specific event and others may be seemingly nonreactive; crisis responders may need to help groups normalize both types of responses.

Third, the NOVA protocol includes an effort to help individuals predict characteristics of a post-trauma future and to prepare for required changes or subsequent events associated with the crisis situation. An example of this within a school setting might be a class discussion of what the group dynamic will be like following a classmate's death, as well as preparing students for a funeral service or possible removal of a deceased student's desk or personal materials.

It should be noted that although community response teams frequently provide on-site assistance to disaster victims and survivors, much of the crisis work done in schools takes place days or even weeks after an event has occurred. Specific activities have to be tailored to the characteristics of the situation and to the needs of the school population. Table 22.2 provides examples of strategies that could be used in school settings to address each of the crisis response tasks identified earlier. The intent is not to prescribe specific actions, as they may not be universally appropriate, but to offer practical suggestions for how these tasks might be accomplished at school and classroom levels.

Recovery

The goals of the recovery stage of school crisis intervention are to resume normal operations and to restore the learning environment as quickly as possible. An important task for mental health practitioners is to assess the needs of various members of the school community and to organize and implement follow-up care at individual, group, and organizational levels.

Once the immediate aftermath of the crisis has passed, there will be those victims or survivors who require postcrisis intervention in the form of longer term counseling or treatment to resolve the lingering effects of trauma. Victims and survivors will

Table 22.2 Examples of Strategies for Addressing Crisis Response Tasks

Safety/Security	Communicate a realistic sense of physical and emotional safety to students; this can be accomplished with simple phrases, such as those used in introducing a NOVA group crisis intervention session (Young, 2002):
	- "I'm sorry this happened to you"
	- "It's not your fault"
	- "You're safe now"
	Provide adult support/supervision for students who are in distress until a parent or other family member is available
	Reestablish school and classroom routines as quickly as possible
	To the maximum extent possible, provide an opportunity for staff members to process their own reactions before they have to address needs of students; adult modeling of a calm and "in control" manner will help students cope with emergency situations
Ventilation/Validation	Provide opportunities for staff and students to participate in psychological debriefing sessions (see Brooks & Siegel, 1996, or Brock, 2002b, for guidelines on conducting debriefing with children and adolescents)
	Encourage verbalization of cognitions related to the traumatic event; this can help to assess the presence of cognitive distortions that might interfere with the student's ability to cope with what has happened (e.g., "It's my fault this happened" or "The world will never be safe again")
Prediction/Preparation	At the high school level, involve students in planning appropriate memorial activities (see suggestions provided by the National Association of School Psychologists, n.d.)
	Utilize stress management techniques in conjunction with discussions about traumatic events; this enables students to gain a sense of control over thoughts and feelings associated with the event (Cohen, 1998)
	Include parents in crisis response activities, in order to increase the likelihood that they will be able to provide positive coping models for their children (Cohen, 1998)

require careful follow-up to determine how well they are coping with the effects of the trauma.

Cognitive-behavioral group therapy with children and adolescents as an intervention to crisis and trauma typically is brief, structured, and utilizes a combination of age-appropriate didactic presentations, games, stories, writing, drawing, and discussion. Students are educated about common reactions to stress and introduced to the cognitive-behavioral model, which emphasizes the link between thoughts and feelings. Cognitive-behavioral group therapy can teach students traumatized by a crisis how to combat anxiety using specific relaxation techniques, how to counter negative thoughts that contribute to undesirable symptoms and behavior, and how to implement effective alternative coping strategies and problem solving.

Recent empirical data have supported the efficacy of a brief cognitive-behavioral group intervention in decreasing symptoms of PTSD, depression, and psychosocial dysfunction (Stein, Jaycox, Kataoka, & Wong, 2003). Stein et al. (2003) investigated the efficacy of a standardized cognitive-behavioral group intervention for middle school students with symptoms of PTSD secondary to exposure to violence and found that students who received the early intervention had significantly lower scores on symptoms of PTSD after 3 months than did the wait-list group of students who did not receive intervention. This study underscores both the importance of early intervention and the efficacy of providing school-based interventions following exposure to violence.

In addition to addressing individual needs, school-based crisis response teams will need to review the impact of the event and to monitor the ongoing needs of the school community. Several specific tasks for the recovery phase of crisis intervention include (a) debriefings with staff and first responders, (b) ensuring that crisis responders and caregivers receive whatever emotional support is needed in the aftermath of the event, (c) planning and implementing curriculum-based activities that address the crisis or its impact on the community, (d) establishing a system for monitoring the long-term or delayed impact of the event, (e) planning ahead for anniversaries of the event, (f) evaluating the effectiveness of the crisis response, and (g) incorporating "lessons learned" into revisions of the school crisis plan.

To evaluate the effectiveness of crisis intervention services, Brock, Sandoval, and Lewis (2001) suggest there are some outcomes that would indicate an effective crisis response. These include (a) crisis being resolved quickly with less time away from a productive learning environment; (b) information revealed during defusing sessions will be less dramatic; (c) there are no follow-up crises; and (d) improved morale among the faculty as a result of an effective intervention.

IMPLICATIONS AND APPLICATIONS TO THE SCHOOL SETTING

As described earlier, school-based crisis response should take place within a multilevel framework of universal prevention for all students, early intervention for those at risk for developing maladaptive responses, and intensive intervention for individuals showing fully developed symptoms of behavioral and emotional disorders. In this section, examples of cognitive-behavioral strategies at each of these levels are discussed, with particular emphasis on aspects that are associated with response to crisis events.

Universal Level of Intervention (Primary Prevention)

Universal (primary) prevention programs in school settings typically aim to prevent the onset of learning or behavioral disorders (Dulmus & Rapp-Paglicci, 2004). Although a number of programs are targeted to prevention of specific problem behaviors, such as substance use (LeCroy & Mann, 2004), school dropout (Doll & Hess, 2004), suicide (McCarter, Sowers, & Dulmus, 2004), or teenage pregnancy (Armistead, Kotchick, & Forehand, 2004), a recent trend has been the establishment of more global prevention efforts that are intended to promote resilience and emotional and physical wellness among the general school population.

Resilience refers to the capacity to thrive despite the presence of risk factors or exposure to stressful conditions (Dulmus & Rapp-Paglicci, 2004). Several protective factors are commonly identified as contributing to resilience, including social competence, positive peer relationships, and the presence of one or more caring adults in the life a child. As the empirical research on resilience has grown, more attention has been given to implementing schoolwide and districtwide programs that target social competence. Such programs usually are designed to teach all students the basic foundation skills needed for effective social behavior: self-awareness, social awareness, self-management, relationship skills, and responsible decision making (CASEL, 2003).

Cognitive-behavioral perspectives are evident in many programs that promote social competence. For example, programs that utilize a basic social problem-solving format (e.g., *I Can Problem Solve*, Shure, 2001; *PATHS*, Kusché & Greenberg, 1994) focus on teaching students to develop and apply a set of cognitive problem-solving skills that includes alternative solution thinking, consequential thinking, and means-end thinking (Weissberg & Gesten, 1982). Such programs usually include an emphasis on recognizing emotional states in oneself and others, self-regulation, empathy, and decision making.

With respect to crisis intervention services, universal activities to address the needs of all students might include classroom sessions for talking about the traumatic event, providing opportunities to defuse emotional reactions, and beginning to activate positive coping strategies (that presumably have been strengthened through other primary prevention programs). The emphasis at this level would be to reestablish a sense of safety and security, and to resume normal school operations as soon as possible after the crisis. Many students will respond to these efforts to promote wellness through the use of normal coping strategies, and will not require additional follow-up services from mental health professionals.

Early Intervention (Secondary Prevention) for Students at Risk

At the level of early intervention, students identified as being in a particular high-risk group or who are beginning to show early warning signs of difficulty in personal adjustment might participate in individual or small-group interventions designed to increase problem-solving and coping strategies. Cognitive-behavioral strategies for anger management and impulse control are often utilized for this purpose.

As part of the crisis response plan, it is important to identify students within this at-risk category, so that additional supports can be organized and implemented. Although some students will be included in the high-risk group by virtue of their preexisting vulnerabilities to stress or difficult life circumstances, others may have a direct connection to victims or survivors of the crisis incident. Crisis teams should consider the effects of proximity to the epicenter of the crisis, the impact of previous losses, and effects of secondary traumatization (i.e., living with someone who has been traumatized), as well as prior levels of coping and social support as factors in determining which students require additional intervention services at times of crisis.

Intensive Intervention (Tertiary Prevention) for Students with Psychological Symptoms

It is a well-known fact that most of our school mental health resources are devoted to a limited number of students who have significant behavioral and emotional needs. Schools that have implemented comprehensive programs of positive behavioral supports at the universal and selective levels have found that the number of students with severe symptoms can be reduced, but there will continue to be a small group of individuals who require more extensive and intensive psychological supports before, during, and following traumatic events. Collaboration between school personnel and community agencies is needed to ensure that these students receive needed treatment services, on either an outpatient or inpatient basis.

CASE EXAMPLE: SUDDEN DEATH OF A STUDENT

On a sunny afternoon in May at a suburban high school, six students, riding in two separate cars, drove off on a busy interstate highway for a fun afternoon of picnicking and swimming. One of the cars never made it to its destination. There was an accident during which one 17-year-old female, Jennifer, driver of the lead car, was killed and another young woman was critically injured. First to arrive on the scene were the occupants of the second car, two female and two male adolescents, who witnessed the accident. By the account of the state police, the accident scene was one of the most brutal and gruesome they had witnessed in recent memory. Jennifer, the deceased, had lost control of her car and crossed the median and was thrown from the car into oncoming traffic. Her body was mangled when she was run over at least three times by oncoming vehicles. Her friends witnessed her death. One of the young men had the presence of mind to remove his shirt to cover her body and suggested the others not view it. The second young woman's body lay motionless on the pavement. Fortunately, several Good Samaritans stopped immediately and the police were called.

What followed that evening was an example of a school community responding to crisis—one child dead, one critically injured, and four other traumatized witnesses. Students and families, after viewing the 6:00 P.M. news or receiving phone calls, spontaneously came to the high school building. Students gathered, wanting to hear information about their friends. The 700-student junior/senior high school is in a typical small, northeastern, suburban community. It is an example of middle-class America; baseball is still the favorite pastime in the spring, and school activities are always well attended by parents and children. Family is important and the school is often the center of the community.

Fortunately, the local high school had a crisis plan and a well-trained crisis response team. As the students arrived at the school building, the doors were open to all those who came. The crisis team was mobilized and the building was staffed. Before the night was over, more than 200 students, parents, and family members had come together in the high school library to receive information about their friends and find comfort in talking to each other.

The four students who witnessed the accident had been taken to the state police barracks and questioned for several hours. They were not permitted to call their parents to let them know they were safe. Only after Jennifer's parents were notified of her death were they permitted to call home. Amazingly, soon after leaving the police barracks, these four students also arrived at our makeshift crisis center.

Working with these four traumatized students, they were able to process the horrifying incident experienced earlier that afternoon. Applying the NOVA model of crisis intervention, these four students told their stories. Using the suggested intervention of saying, "I'm sorry this happened to you," "It's not your fault," and "You're safe now" allowed the students to process the tragic events of the day and share their experiences. As they discussed the day's horrifying events, the goal was to assist them to process their sensory experiences and verbalize their emotions into a story that would allow their cognitive capacities to take over.

Moreover, using Dattlllo and Freeman's cognitive-behavioral therapy model as a basis for short-term crisis intervention, we followed the steps of establishing rapport, evaluating the threat to their physical danger and injury, assessing and mobilizing their internal strengths and cognitive-behavioral resources, developing a positive action plan, securing individual commitment to plan for developing coping strategies, and eventually evaluating the effectiveness of the plan.

Among the four traumatized students, there existed a sense of urgency in their plan to return the next day to that busy highway to leave flowers on the spot where Jennifer had died. Understanding their determination, the event was coordinated with the local police, who in turn networked with the state police to assure their safety. The next morning, all traveled together on a school bus with parents following in their cars, while the state police stopped traffic on this extremely busy interstate highway to allow the students to safely visit the site of the accident.

Preparation for the following day of school was guided by the school district's adopted policy on crisis intervention dealing with the sudden death of a student. First, the faculty was notified via the emergency telephone list and requested to arrive before school for a faculty meeting during which information was shared with teachers and staff members. Factual details on the student's death, and injury to the second student, were discussed with the faculty. In addition, scripts were provided for teachers to use when sharing this information with their students. As provided in the crisis intervention policy, any teacher who desired assistance in talking with their students could request services of a school mental health practitioner or crisis team member. Suggestions were offered on how to share the information with students and specific instructions were detailed on how students needing more assistance were to be referred to the crisis center that would be open during the school day in the high school library. The school crisis response team was able to mobilize and respond appropriately to the emergency situation. Built into the day's schedule was a time at the end of the day when the crisis team members would meet in order to discuss and process the day's events and take time to care for the caregivers.

What had the school crisis team done to prepare for a trauma of this magnitude? Fortunately, sufficient time, energy, and school financial resources had been devoted to formulating a crisis response plan. The crisis team had been trained, and an appropriate crisis response plan had been developed detailing procedures, which was adopted by the Board of Education. In essence, procedures had been outlined in advance of the crisis and the mechanics were in place to activate the crisis team. Efforts to increase problem-solving and coping strategies were planned through universal activities to address the needs of all students, as well as identifying the acute needs of those students who had a direct connection to the victim and survivor of the crisis incident. As a result of the training of the school psychologist, a triage approach was developed to allow those most in need of crisis intervention to be first to receive direct face-to-face services through the crisis response team efforts.

SUMMARY

School personnel are confronted on a daily basis with local, national, and international events that are experienced as traumatic and require the provision of crisis intervention services for students, teachers, and parents. Schools are an appropriate site for crisis response, but it is important that school-based mental health practitioners coordinate their activities with community-based providers. There are four distinct and critical phases of crisis management: (1) mitigation and prevention, (2) preparedness, (3) response, and (4) recovery (U.S. Department of Education, 2003). As noted earlier, it is our belief that a general cognitive-behavioral theoretical orientation as well as specific cognitive-behavioral techniques can enhance the quality of crisis management in school settings at each of these stages.

School crisis response requires a comprehensive system that integrates emergency services (i.e., fire and rescue workers), medical care as needed, law enforcement and victim assistance, spiritual guidance and support when requested, as well as mental health services in the form of psychological first aid and after-care. For maximum effectiveness, school-based crisis response should take place within a multilevel framework of universal prevention for all students, early intervention for those at risk for developing maladaptive responses, and intensive intervention for individuals showing fully developed symptoms of behavioral and emotional disorders. The empirical and theoretical literature on cognitive-behavioral interventions can provide a valuable resource to school personnel for assessing and addressing needs at multiple levels and in preparation for unexpected and potentially traumatic events.

REFERENCES

Aguilera, D. C. (1998). *Crisis intervention: Theory and methodology* (8th ed.). St Louis, MO: Mosby.

American Psychiatric Association. (2000). *Diagnostic and statistical manual of mental disorders* (4th ed., text revision). Washington, DC: Author.

Armistead, L., Kotchick, B. A., & Forehand, R. (2004). Teenage pregnancy, sexually transmitted diseases, and HIV/AIDS. In L. A. Rapp-Paglicci, C. N. Dulmus, & J. S. Wodarski (Eds.), *Handbook of preventive interventions for children and adolescents* (pp. 227–254). Hoboken, NJ: John Wiley & Sons.

Beers, S. R., & DeBellis, M. D. (2002). Neuropsychological function in children with maltreatment-related posttraumatic stress disorder. *American Journal of Psychiatry, 159*(3), 483–487.

Bisson, J. I., McFarlane, A. C., & Rose, S. (2000). Psychological debriefing. In E. B. Foa, T. M. Keane, & M. J. Friedman (Eds.), *Effective treatments for PTSD* (pp. 39–59). New York: Guilford Press.

Bonne, O., Brandes, D., Gilboa, A., & Gomori, J. M. (2001). Longitudinal MRI study of hippocampal volume in trauma survivors with PTSD. *American Journal of Psychiatry, 158*(8), 1248–1252.

Bremner, J., Vythilingam, M., Vermetten, E., & Southwick, S. M. (2003). MRI and PET study of deficits in hippocampal structure and function in women with childhood sexual abuse and posttraumatic stress disorder. *American Journal of Psychiatry, 160*(5), 924–933.

Brock, S. E. (2002a). Crisis theory: A foundation for the comprehensive crisis prevention and intervention team. In S. E. Brock, P. J. Lazarus, & S. R. Jimerson (Eds.), *Best practices in school crisis prevention and intervention* (pp. 5–17). Bethesda, MD: National Association of School Psychologists.

Brock, S. E. (2002b). Group crisis intervention. In S. E. Brock, P. J. Lazarus, & S. R. Jimerson (Eds.), *Best practices in school crisis prevention and intervention* (pp. 385–399). Bethesda, MD: National Association of School Psychologists.

Brock, S. E., & Jimerson, S. R. (2004). Characteristics and consequences of crisis events: A primer for the school psychologist. In E. R. Gerler, Jr. (Ed.), *Handbook of school violence* (pp. 273–284). New York: Haworth Reference Press.

Brock, S. E., Sandoval, J., & Lewis, S. (2001). *Preparing for crises in the schools: A manual for building school crisis response teams* (2nd ed.) New York: John Wiley & Sons.

Brooks, B., & Siegel, P. M. (1996). *The scared child.* New York: John Wiley & Sons.

Brooks, R. B. (2002). Creating nurturing classroom environments: Fostering hope and resilience as an antidote to violence. In S. E. Brock, P. J. Lazarus, & S. R. Jimerson (Eds.), *Best practices in school crisis prevention and intervention* (pp. 67–93). Bethesda, MD: National Association of School Psychologists.

Carlson, E. B. (1997). *Trauma assessments: A clinician's guide.* New York: Guilford Press.

CASEL. (2003). Creating connections for student success: Annual Report. Chicago: Author.

Cohen, J. A. (1998). Summary of the practice parameters for the assessment and treatment of children and adolescents with posttraumatic stress disorder. *Journal of the American Academy of Child and Adolescent Psychiatry, 37*(9), 997–1001.

Dattilio, F. M., & Freeman, A. (Eds.). (1994). *Cognitive-behavioral strategies in crisis intervention.* New York: Guilford Press.

Dattilio, F. M., & Freeman, A. (Eds.). (2000). *Cognitive-behavioral strategies in crisis intervention* (2nd ed.). New York: Guilford Press.

Doll, B., & Hess, R. (2004). School dropout. In L. A. Rapp-Paglicci, C. N. Dulmus, & J. S. Wodarski (Eds.), *Handbook of preventive interventions for children and adolescents* (pp. 359–380). Hoboken, NJ: John Wiley & Sons.

Dulmus, C. N., & Rapp-Paglicci, L. A. (2004). Prevention and resilience. In L. A. Rapp-Paglicci, C. N. Dulmus, & J. S. Wodarski (Eds.), *Handbook of preventive interventions for children and adolescents* (pp. 3–11). Hoboken, NJ: John Wiley & Sons.

Everly, G. S., & Mitchell, J. T. (2000). The debriefing "controversy" and crisis intervention: A review of lexical and substantive issues. *International Journal of Emergency Mental Health, 2,* 211–225.

Foy, D. W., Madvig, D. T., Pynoos, R. S., & Camilleri, A. J. (1996). Etiological factors in the development of posttraumatic stress disorder in children and adolescents. *Journal of School Psychology, 34,* 133–145.

Health and Safety Executive. (1999). *Five steps to risk assessment* [Brochure]. Sudbury, UK: HSE Books.

Heim, C., Meinlschmidt, G., & Numeroff, C. B. (2003). Neurobiology of early life stress. *Psychiatric Annals, 33*(1), 18–30.

Herman, J. (1997). *Trauma and recovery.* New York: Basic Books.

Klingman, A., & Cohen, E. (2004). *School-based multisystem interventions for mass trauma.* New York: Kluwer Academic/Plenum Publishers.

Kusche, C. A., & Greenberg, M. T. (1994). *The PATHS (Promoting Alternative Thinking Strategies) curriculum.* Seattle, WA: Developmental Research and Programs.

Layton, B., & Krikorian, R. (2002). Memory mechanisms in posttraumatic stress disorder. *Journal of Neuropsychiatry and Clinical Neurosciences, 14*(3), 254–262.

LeCroy, C. W., & Mann, J. E. (2004). Substance abuse. In L. A. Rapp-Paglicci, C. N. Dulmus, & J. S. Wodarski (Eds.), *Handbook of preventive interventions for children and adolescents* (pp. 198–226). Hoboken, NJ: John Wiley & Sons.

Lipschitz, D. S., Rasmusson, A. M., & Southwick, S. M. (1998). Childhood posttraumatic stress disorder: A review of neurobiologic sequelae. *Psychiatric Annals, 28*(8), 452–458.

Litz, B. T., Gray, M. J., Bryant, R. A., & Adler, A. B. (2002). Early intervention for trauma: Current status and future directions. *Clinical Psychology: Science and Practice, 9*(2), 112–134.

March, J. S., Amaya-Jackson, L., Murray, M. C., & Schulte, A. (1998). Cognitive-behavioral psychotherapy for children and adolescents with posttraumatic stress disorder after a single incident stressor. *Journal of the Academy of Child and Adolescent Psychiatry, 37*(6), 585–593.

McCarter, A. K., Sowers, K. M., & Dulmus, C. N. (2004). Adolescent suicide prevention. In L. A. Rapp-Paglicci, C. N. Dulmus, & J. S. Wodarski (Eds.), *Handbook of preventive interventions for children and adolescents* (pp. 85–99). Hoboken, NJ: John Wiley & Sons.

McKeever, V. M., & Huff, M. E. (2003). A diathesis-stress model of posttraumatic stress disorder: Ecological, biological, and residual stress pathways. *Review of General Psychology, 7*(3), 237–240.

Mitchell, J. T., & Everly, G. S. (1995). *Critical incident stress debriefing: An operations manual for the prevention of traumatic stress among emergency services and disaster workers.* Ellicot City, MD: Chevron.

National Association of School Psychologists. (n.d.). *Memorials/activities/rituals following traumatic events: Suggestions for schools.* Retrieved January 26, 2005, from www.nasponline.org: http://www.nasponline.org/NEAT/memorials_general.html

Pitcher, G. D., & Poland, S. (1992). *Crisis intervention in the schools.* New York: Guilford Press.

Poland, S., & McCormick, J. S. (1999). *Coping with crisis: A resource guide for schools, parents, and communities.* Longmont, CO: Sopris West.

Roberts, A. R. (1990). An overview of crisis theory and crisis intervention. In A. R. Roberts (Ed.), *Crisis intervention handbook: Assessment, treatment, and research* (pp. 1–15). Belmont, CA: Wadsworth.

Saigh, P. A., Yasik, A. E., Oberfield, R. A., Halamandaris, P. V., & McHugh, M. (2002). An analysis of the internalizing and externalizing behaviors of urban youth and without PTSD. *Journal of Abnormal Psychology, 111*(3), 462–467.

Shure, M. B. (2001). *I can problem solve (ICPS): An interpersonal cognitive problem-solving program.* Champaign, IL: Research Press.

Slaikeu, K. A. (1990). *Crisis intervention: A handbook for practice and research* (2nd ed.) Newton, MA: Allyn & Bacon.

Stein, B. D., Jaycox, L. H., Katoka, S. H., & Wong, M. (2003). A mental health intervention for schoolchildren exposed to violence: A randomized controlled trial. *Journal of the American Medical Association, 290*(5), 603–608.

Stephens, R. D. (1994). Planning for safer and better schools: School violence prevention and intervention strategies. *School Psychology Review, 23*(2), 204–215.

U.S. Department of Education, Office of Safe & Drug Free Schools. (2003). *Practical information on crisis planning: A guide for schools and communities.* Washington, DC: Author.

Weissberg, R. P., & Gesten, E. L. (1982). Considerations for developing effective school-based social problem-solving (SPS) training programs. *School Psychology Review, 11*(1), 56–63.

Young, B. H., Ford, J. D., Ruzek, J. I., Friedman, M. J., & Gusman, F. D. (1998). *Disaster mental health services: A guidebook for clinicians and administrators.* Washington, DC: National Center for Post-Traumatic Stress Disorder.

Young, M. (2002). *The community crisis response team training manual* (3rd ed.) Washington, DC: National Organization for Victim Assistance.

Part IV

SUMMARY

23

The Future of Cognitive-Behavioral Interventions in Schools

DAVID M. POPONI & ROSEMARY B. MENNUTI

Contemplating the future is an enticing exercise. Too often, the general media approaches the topic of the future from the perspectives of utopian visionaries or apocalyptic cynics. As history has disclosed, reality usually remains between these extremes. The process of evolution occurs slowly, whether the subject of study is organic or organizational. This is particularly true of a system as large and complex as public education. The overall functioning of our schools in another decade will probably appear more similar than dissimilar to the present. Despite the hopes (or fears) of many, radical reform is unlikely. Yet, some change is inevitable and must be shaped by mental health practitioners to meet the ever-increasing social and emotional needs of children and families. There is more support now than any time in history to address the unmet mental health needs of children, and schools have emerged as central to this mission. From the vantage point of the present, the greater utilization of cognitive-behavioral approaches in addressing needs in schools has promise as a future trend in education.

RESOURCES, ACCOUNTABILITY, AND EVIDENCE-BASED INTERVENTIONS

Few institutions are as scrutinized and critiqued as public education. This is understandable, and justifiable, because of the quantity and diversity of stakeholders in our educational system. Historically, many changes in the provision of educational services have occurred in response to legislative initiatives and funding considerations. These in turn have been subject to the influence of political pressures, judicial decisions, and public perceptions. Unfortunately, the driving force behind the development of many educational practices has not always been scientific theory or empirically documented research. Although future policies will probably be molded by many of the same forces as the past, it is likely that the results of outcome-based studies will have increased influence.

Faced with the enormity and variety of needs experienced by our schoolchildren, funding issues will remain a serious concern. With tighter budgets, the allocation of assets requires more deliberation and direction. The contrast between immense need and limited resources manifests itself through greater emphasis on accountability. Good intentions are insufficient. Effectiveness requires documentation. This view is repeatedly evident throughout the No Child Left Behind Act of 2001 (PL 107–110). Although the increased emphasis on accountability is laudable, its method of measuring outcomes and attributing blame is worrisome. Academic proficiency does not always equate to a test score. Accountability concerns are also reflected in No Child Left Behind's emphasis upon educational practices that are grounded in scientifically based research. Likewise, greater attention is now directed to the importance of using evidence-based interventions (EBI) to address the mental health needs of children (National Advisory Mental Health Council's Workgroup on Child and Adolescent Mental Health Intervention Development and Deployment, 2001).

In this context, Cognitive-Behavior Therapy (CBT) is a promising option for addressing mental health needs within schools. Among the available psychotherapeutic approaches, CBT is noteworthy as an evidence-based intervention with proven efficacy when applied to a range of disorders. As the expectation emerges for schools to rely on programs that have documented success, cognitive-behavioral interventions are a likely choice for addressing mental health needs of children and families.

As with all EBIs, a distinction exists between rigidly controlled studies of *efficacy* and studies of *effectiveness* that occur in the context of more naturalistic environments, such as schools. Additional study of cognitive-behavioral strategies within school settings is necessary in the future. Walker (2004) identifies three important areas in the continuing development of an applied science: the study of implementation integrity, the study of diffusion and sustainability of interventions, and the study of transportability. Although the efficacy of CBT has been documented with children in research settings, is it transportable to schools? Can CBT techniques that have been initially developed for use with individuals be successfully applied in the group-focused service delivery approach of public education? Despite differences in clients, problems, and practitioners, can the specific conditions be identified that maximize therapeutic effects? There are many potential avenues of inquiry for the future.

Adapting EBIs to practice can be challenging. Those on the front lines of providing services within schools are often skeptical of recommendations that emanate from university and laboratory-based research. Too often, the development of interventions occurs in different contexts from the site of service delivery. The issue of linking research to practice is addressed in *Blueprint for Change: Research on Child and Adolescent Mental Health* (National Advisory Mental Health Council's Workgroup on Child and Adolescent Mental Health Intervention Development and Deployment, 2001). It recommends that "a focus on the endpoint and its context—the final resting place for treatment or service delivery—be folded into the design, development, refinement and implementation of the intervention" (p. 84). Kratochwill and Shernoff (2004) also stress that the development of EBIs is a shared responsibility. In the future, researchers, trainers, and practitioners should be jointly involved in the process.

To address the issue of integrating theory with application, many graduate programs training mental health clinicians promote a scientist-practitioner model. In keeping with this model, the involvement of mental health practitioners in such projects could be substantial. Not only is there a need to implement research-supported methodology, but there should be a commitment by practitioners to monitor the outcomes of their interventions and collect their own data. The stipulations regarding accountability in No Child Left Behind suggest a need for practitioners such as school psychologists to conduct such research (Charvat, 2004). Also supporting additional research by scientist-practitioners is the view of Hoagwood, Hibbs, Brent, and Jensen (1995), who propose that the relationship between efficacy and effectiveness can be conceptualized as bidirectional. Rather than awaiting the conclusions of researchers, new applications of cognitive-behavioral interventions, or other techniques, could be attempted in schools and later refined under more controlled conditions.

The increased need for proficient skills in research and program evaluation should be addressed in the future preparation of practitioners. They will need a deeper understanding of quantitative and qualitative research design than necessary to merely comprehend journal articles. Practitioners should be adept at conducting investigations into their own interventions and measuring outcomes. Training programs will need to expand their focus upon the application of requisite research techniques.

Assuming that the funding of education will remain a challenge, the need for accountability will extend beyond the selection of evidence-based interventions. Cost effectiveness and efficiency will also be major considerations. With its emphasis on short-term, goal-directed practice, cognitive-behavioral strategies make sense as a preferred alternative in the future. Its directive focus on the here-and-now is an efficient means of addressing present problems. Although cognitive-behavioral interventions may be attractive to those whose primary focus is fiscal, it does not sacrifice quality at the expense of the client. The techniques of intervention stress the uniqueness of the individual and the value of the therapeutic relationship. Cognitive-behavioral approaches are an effective, affordable treatment choice that has appeal to practitioners, clients, and administrative overseers alike.

MENTAL HEALTH NEEDS AND A PUBLIC HEALTH MODEL

Evidence exists to indicate that today's school-age children have many unmet mental health needs. It has been estimated that approximately 10% of children meet the diagnostic criteria for a mental disorder with symptoms that relate to an exhibited impairment in functioning (Burns, Costello, Agnold, Tweed, Stangl, & Framer, 1995). Of these children, the majority are not receiving professional help for those needs (Burns et al., 1995). Mental health must be considered as a critical component of children's general health and their ability to learn. Recommended within the *Report of the Surgeon General's Conference on Children's Mental Health: A National Action Agenda* (U.S. Department of Health and Human Services, 2000) are a number of *action steps* for the future. These include recommendations to support the use of scientifically-proven interventions and to promote proactive, cost-effective methods of behavior support at the school level.

An approach to mental health programming that has implications for schools is a public health model of service delivery. Public health models emphasize prevention and early intervention, data-based decision making, and addressing needs at a societal, rather than individual, level (Strein, Hoagwood, & Cohn, 2003). Through the application of evidence-based interventions, they attempt to minimize impact on children's lives by eliminating or reducing potential problems as early as possible. The focus is proactive, rather than reactive. This philosophy is also reflected in the findings of the President's Commission on Excellence in Special Education. Instead of present policies that wait for a child to fail before providing services, the commission recommends a prevention model that uses evidence-based interventions (U.S. Department of Education, 2002).

From a public health perspective, prevention can be viewed as a three-tiered model (Institute of Medicine, 1994). A *universal* preventive measure is applied to the entire population, a *selective* preventive measure is applied to at-risk groups, and an *indicated* preventive measure is targeted at high-risk individuals. Meta-analysis studies by Durlak and Wells (1997, 1998) have examined the outcomes of primary and secondary preventive mental health programs for children and adolescents. With regard to attempts at primary (universal) prevention, programs employing behavioral or CBT forms of intervention were twice as effective as those using nonbehavioral techniques (Durlak & Wells, 1997). When assessing mental health programs that were considered forms of secondary prevention, CBT approaches were significantly more effective in reducing problems than behavior treatments, which, in turn, were more effective than nonbehavioral treatments (Durlak & Wells, 1998). Of note is the fact that 72.9% of the primary prevention programs and 93.4% of the secondary prevention programs studied were school-based.

Public health models of service emphasize prevention and early intervention. As applied to the needs of schoolchildren, they incorporate attention to social and emotional functioning into the promotion of general wellness. For school-based professionals, this approach meshes with an anticipated reduction in their traditional roles. For instance, school psychologists who formerly spent a majority of their time administering tests and serving as gatekeepers for special education may begin devoting more attention to the provision of direct services. The reauthorization of the Individuals with Disabilities Education Act (IDEA) as the Individuals with Disabilities Education Improvement Act of 2004 (H.R. 1350) potentially modifies the roles of the school psychologist. The revised law could reduce existing requirements for test administration by eliminating the need to document an IQ-achievement discrepancy when diagnosing a specific learning disability. Instead of conducting traditional assessments with students who already have a longstanding history of problems, school psychologists may have more time to focus on preventive and early intervention services.

As emphasis shifts and roles change, greater use of cognitive-behavioral strategies for intervention and treatment of students could be in the future of school practitioners. More than half of the children and adolescents who receive mental health services use the education sector as the initial point of entry (Farmer, Burns, Phillips, Angold, & Costello, 2003). The many mental health services already provided by schools could expand. If our nation adopts a future goal of increasing access to mental health services for children, the schools are a logical site. In *Mental Health: A Report of the Surgeon General* (U.S. Department of Health and Human Services, 1999), school is identified as a major setting for identification and treatment. As places familiar to the population, children and parents may view services housed in local schools as more approachable than those at unknown agencies. School locations have been deliberately selected for convenient community access and are widely dispersed across the nation.

Just as schools represent a favorable locale for mental health service delivery, CBT represents a likely choice as the preferred therapeutic approach. With its grounding in empirically supported methods, CBT is appropriate for many types of presenting problems. Despite the fact that knowledge of its techniques is relatively widespread and commonly used, CBT is often not prominent in training programs for school psychologists, school social workers, and guidance counselors and will need to increase. Its use of standardized treatment manuals enhances CBT's adaptability for practice by school-based professionals. When considering personnel shortages in the mental health field, the Surgeon General's report specifically recommends increases in specialists with expertise in CBT (U.S. Department of Health and Human Services, 1999).

OTHER FUTURE APPLICATIONS OF CBT IN SCHOOLS

In addition to traditional applications of CBT that may be transferred to school settings, the future may include the expansion of CBT techniques and theory into new areas. For instance, IDEA mandates the development of Functional Behavioral Assessments (FBA) for students exhibiting severe disciplinary concerns. Typically, FBAs examine the antecedents of problematic behaviors. In doing so, they often highlight the environmental circumstances that increase the likelihood of misconduct. As currently conducted, many FBAs devote minimal attention to the cognitions that precipitate targeted behaviors. If FBAs began to incorporate elements of CBT theory, the identified antecedents may also include those automatic thoughts and cognitive distortions that are influential in the process.

Another example of the potential application of CBT techniques in the future could include assessments for special education eligibility. The most recent reauthorization of IDEA reflects a trend to reduce the traditional emphasis on psychometric tests and other normed measurement instruments. In this context, a case conceptualization model as used in CBT might also provide a useful assessment approach for determining special education eligibility. Case conceptualizations are extensively utilized in CBT to understand how clients view and interact with the world. Particularly when working with students who exhibit emotional and behavioral difficulties, a case conceptualization could identify the need for special services and provide direction for recommending interventions.

THE EXPANDING CBT ORIENTATION OF PERSONNEL

Many states now require certificated school personnel to be involved in ongoing continuing education. The mandate for obtaining specific hours or units of training within a fixed timeframe is similar to the professional development requirements imposed by licensing boards for mental health providers. Because additional training is a necessity, many school psychologists, school social workers, and guidance counselors could choose to learn CBT techniques as a method of meeting their professional development obligations. Many workshops and programs of advanced graduate study are already offered in CBT. The future could include increased numbers of existing school professionals taking advantage of these opportunities.

Within the profession of school psychology, a shortage of available practitioners is anticipated in the future (Curtis, Grier, & Hunley, 2004). Meanwhile, many clinical psychologists are increasingly frustrated by the restrictions imposed by managed health care. Some have turned to school psychology as a new career direction. If additional personnel pursue such a change in the future, they will bring with them their existing repertoire of skills and practices. For many, this includes a CBT orientation. As new graduates of school psychology programs enter the field to replace the disproportionately large number of retirees, they also may bring a CBT orientation. The application of CBT within schools could increase as the practitioners of school psychology expand to include those with clinical psychology backgrounds and recently trained beginners.

CULTURAL CONSIDERATIONS

The demographics of America are changing. The future will include an ongoing transformation in the cultural composition of the school age population. Culturally, ethnically, and linguistically, we are becoming an increasingly diverse nation. Between 1980 and 2000, the minority population of the United States has grown 11 times more rapidly than the white, non-Hispanic population (Hobbs & Stoops, 2002). Schools must adapt to this changing cultural makeup.

The expanding diversity among schoolchildren is not proportionately represented among school personnel. Among the providers of mental health services in schools, this is not likely to change significantly in the near future. Despite increases in the cultural diversity of students, the profession of school psychology is expected to remain predominantly composed of individuals from the majority culture (Curtis, Grier, & Hunley, 2004). Emphasis placed on the recruitment of additional minority practitioners is encouraging, but unlikely to make significant impact in the near future. Therefore, the profession must address the issue through other means. A likely response is an ongoing emphasis on cultural competence. Practitioners must be adept at functioning in cross-cultural situations, particularly in the future. As an intervention approach, CBT is compatible with cultural competence. The collaborative process emanating from a therapeutic relationship, in which client values are understood and accepted, functions well even when diverse cultures are represented. CBT practitioners encourage clients to examine the impact of their beliefs within a cultural context, while respecting, accepting, and appreciating the differences that may exist between them.

CONCLUSION

The future of cognitive-behavioral interventions in schools is expected to be one of slow expansion rather than radical conversion. As funding sources and the public demand greater accountability and results, education and mental health practitioners will expand their use of evidence-based interventions, including CBT. Schools will increasingly be viewed as primary sites of mental health service delivery, and the providers of service will rely on CBT as an important part of their therapeutic repertoire. As a public health perspective exerts greater influence, increased attention will be placed on prevention and early intervention. Instead of a system that delays interventions until problems are manifested, programs will promote social competence and emotional wellness. Of the available psychotherapeutic approaches, CBT offers an incredibly versatile assortment of techniques that can be applied separately, or combined, to treat a variety of presenting problems. Backed by an integrative theory and an ever-growing body of research-supported results, CBT will be an essential method of addressing the mental health needs of schoolchildren in educational settings.

REFERENCES

Burns, B. J., Costello, E. J., Angold, A., Tweed, D., Stangl, D., Farmer, E. M. Z., Erkanli, A. (1995). Children's mental health service use across service sectors. *Health Affairs, 14,* 147–159.

Charvat, J. L. (2004). Strengthening research-policy connections. *NASP* Communiqué, 33. Retrieved January 15, 2005, from http://nasponline.org/publications/ cq332research .html

Curtis, M. J., Grier, J. E. C., & Hunley, S. A. (2004). The changing face of school psychology: Trends in data and projections for the future. *School Psychology Review, 33,* 49–66.

Durlak, J. A., & Wells, A. M. (1997). Primary prevention mental health programs for children and adolescents: A meta-analytic review. *American Journal of Community Psychology, 25,* 115–152.

Durlak, J. A., & Wells, A. M. (1998). Evaluation of indicated preventive intervention (secondary prevention) mental health programs for children and adolescents. *American Journal of Community Psychology, 26,* 775–802.

Farmer, E. M. Z., Burns, B. J., Phillips, S. D., Angold, A., & Costello, E. J. (2003). Pathways into and through mental health services for children and adolescents. *Psychiatric Services, 54,* 60–66.

Hoagwood, K., Hibbs, E., Brent, D., & Jensen, P. (1995). Introduction to the special section: Efficacy and effectiveness in studies of child and adolescent psychotherapy. *Journal of Consulting and Clinical Psychology, 63,* 683–687.

Hobbs, F., & Stoops, N. (2002). Demographic trends in the 20th century. U.S. Census Bureau. Retrieved January 15, 2005, from http://www.census.gov/prod/2002pubs/censr-4.pdf

Individuals with Disabilities Education Act Amendments of 1997, P.L. 105–17 (1997).

Individuals with Disabilities Education Improvement Act of 2004, H.R. 1350 (2004).

Institute of Medicine. (1994). *Reducing risks for mental disorders: Frontiers for preventive intervention research.* Washington, DC: National Academy Press.

Kratochwill, T. R., & Shernoff, E. S. (2004). Evidence-based practice: Promoting evidence-based interventions in school psychology. *School Psychology Review, 33,* 34–48.

National Advisory Mental Health Council's Workgroup on Child and Adolescent Mental Health Intervention Development and Deployment. (2001). *Blueprint for change: Research on child and adolescent mental health.* Washington, DC: U.S. Department of Health and Human Services, Public Health Service, National Institutes of Health, National Institute of Mental Health.

No Child Left Behind Act of 2001, P.L.107–110 (2001).

Strein, W., Hoagwood, K., & Cohn, A. (2003). School psychology: A public health perspective. *Journal of School Psychology, 41,* 23–38.

U.S. Department of Education Office of Special Education and Rehabilitative Services. (2002). *A new era: Revitalizing special education for children and their families.* Washington, DC: U.S. Department of Education.

U.S. Department of Health and Human Services. (1999). *Mental Health: A report of the Surgeon General.* Rockville, MD: U.S. Department of Health and Human Services, Substance Abuse and Mental Health Services Administration, Center for Mental Health Services, National Institutes of Health, National Institute of Mental Health.

U.S. Department of Health and Human Services. (2000). *Report of the Surgeon General's conference on children's mental health: A national action agenda.* Washington, DC: U.S. Department of Health and Human Services.

Walker, H. M. (2004). Commentary: Use of evidence-based interventions in schools: Where we've been, where we are, and where we need to go. *School Psychology Review, 33,* 398–407.

24

Concluding Comments

RAY W. CHRISTNER & ROSEMARY B. MENNUTI

Using a cognitive-behavioral orientation with students in school settings requires practitioners to first and foremost be attentive to the uniqueness of working with youth, which is very different than providing mental health services for adults. Providing help to a child requires us to be mindful of his or her developmental level including levels of thinking, language, memory, social skills, emotional maturity, and motivation if the interventions are to be of value. In addition, we must be cognizant of working within the context of the school environment and embrace the context of family and home.

Particularly with children, we are the most valuable resource in the intervention process. Our relationship and connection with a child allows the work to be done that is needed for growth and change to occur. Children "know" when people are there to help them. They see beyond the jargon and sophistication—they see us for who we are, and, in their knowing and seeing, they risk becoming known. We, therefore, must bring our authentic selves fully prepared with the necessary knowledge of both the child and effective interventions. Through collaborative efforts with the child, our knowledge can be successfully implemented by understanding when to intervene and knowing what strategies to use to facilitate change and promote healing.

We could have selected a myriad of topics for discussion in this book. We chose to combine theory and practice through a comprehensive understanding of the literature, as well as highlighting the application to direct and indirect service delivery for the more common emotional and behavioral challenges of youth. It is our hope that these efforts will serve as a resource to school-based practitioners who have dedicated themselves to facilitating healing and promoting wellness in children and families.

Index